D1597132

Healing Gardens

Wiley Series in Healthcare and Senior Living Design

Elizabeth C. Brawley
Designing for Alzheimer's Disease: Strategies for Creating Better Care Environments

Sara O. Marberry
Healthcare Design

Alfred H. Baucom
Hospitality Design for the Graying Generation: Meeting the Needs of a Growing Market

Joan M. Whaley
Wellness Centers: A Guide for the Design Professional

Clare Cooper Marcus and Marni Barnes
Healing Gardens: Therapeutic Benefits and Design Recommendations

Healing Gardens

Therapeutic Benefits and Design Recommendations

Edited by

Clare Cooper Marcus

Marni Barnes

JOHN WILEY & SONS, INC.

New York • Chichester • Weinheim • Brisbane • Singapore • Toronto

Copyright © 1999 by John Wiley & Sons. All rights reserved.

Published simultaneously in Canada.

This publication is designed to provide accurate and authoritative information in regard to the subject matter covered. It is sold with the understanding that the publisher is not engaged in rendering professional services. If professional advice or other expert assistance is required, the services of a competent professional person should be sought.

Library of Congress Cataloging-in-Publication Data:

Healing gardens : therapeutic benefits and design recommendations /
    edited by Clare Cooper Marcus, Marni Barnes.
        p.   cm. — (Wiley series in healthcare and senior living
    design)
        Includes bibliographical references and index.
        ISBN 0-471-19023-1 (cloth : alk. paper)
        1. Gardening—Therapeutic uses—Research. I. Marcus, Clare Cooper.
        2. Hospitals—Outdoor spaces.
        3. Medical Facilities—Exterior environments.
        4. Nature—Stress reduction—Research
    II. Barnes, Marni. III. Series.
    RM735.7.G37H43 1999
    615.8'515—dc21   98-42154

Printed in the United States of America.

10 9 8 7 6 5 4 3 2 1

Contents

Acknowledgments

Our interest in the topic of design and healthcare was first encouraged by Wayne Ruga, CEO, Center for Health Design, Martinez, CA, who supported us with a grant to study four hospital gardens in the San Francisco region, in 1994. His inspiring Symposia on Healthcare Design have expanded our understanding enormously and allowed us to meet colleagues from all over the world.

We greatly appreciate those colleagues who kindly wrote or contrtibuted to individual case studies of healthcare gardens that they designed, studied, or helped facilitate. These include James Burnette (Chapter 5); David Mitchell, Nathan Perkins (Chapter 6); Deborah LeFrank (Chapter 8); Margarette E. Beckwith, Susan D. Gilster, Robert Hoover, Erna Jacobs, Mary Jane Lovering, Twyla Rusnak, Edward A. Stillinger (Chapter 9); Dr. Derek Kerr, Arezu Movahed, Anne Wood (Chapter 10); Barbara Crisp, Mary Jane Ensberg, Sandra Fawcett, Alain Kinet, Helen Tilley, Joan Varney (Chapter 11).

We are particularly grateful to those who prepared the graphics for this book: Kim Pearson, Deva Designs, Palo Alto, CA, who drew the site plans for the case studies; except those in chapter 6, which were drawn by Curtis Cahoon, School of Design, North Carolina State University, Raleigh, NC.

We are grateful to so many other people who helped make this book possible. First are those — in four countries — who led us to sites, loaned us material, took us on tours, or answered critical questions. These include: Paul Alcock, North Staffordshire Hospital, UK; Paul Allison, Horticultural Therapist, Victoria, Canada; Steve Barnhart, Department of Landscape Architecture, University of Guelph, Guelph, Ontario, Canada; Antonia Bava, Antonia Bava Landscape Architects, San

Francisco, CA; Bill Bergstrom, R.N., Whitby Mental Health Centre, Whitby, Ontario, Canada; Josie Blascoe, Arts Coordinator, West Dorset Hospital, UK; John Boerger, The Design Partnership, San Francisco, CA; Elizabeth Byrne and Deborah Sommer of the College of Environmental Design Library, University of California, Berkeley, CA; Ian Carter, Architect, Vancouver, Canada; Mother Celine, Mother Superior, and Sister Gonzague, Little Sisters of the Poor, Villa Guadalupe, Gallup, NM; Christie Coffin, Architect, Berkeley, CA; Joyce Connolly, Archives Specialist, National Park Service Frederick Law Olmsted National Historic Site; Barbara Crisp, Underwood and Crisp, Architects, Tempe, AZ; Betty Drake, City Planner, Scottsdale, AZ; Mark Epstein, Landscape Architect, Portland, OR; Sal Fatani, Chief, Facility Management Service, and Robert Bartolina, Chief, Projects Section, Jerry L. Pettis Memorial Veterans Medical Center, Loma Linda, CA; Colin Ferguson, General Manager of Hotel Services, Homewood Health Centre, Guelph, Ontario, Canada; Rosemary Glanville, Medical Architecture Research Unit, South Bank University, UK; Charlotte Grant, Landscape Architect, Atlanta, GA; Clarice Guillon, Director Chemainus Health Care Centre, Chemainus, British Columbia, Canada; Jim Hallan, Butler Hospital, Providence, RI; Vince Healy, Landscape Designer, San Francisco; Randy Hester, Department of Landscape Architecture, University of California, Berkeley, CA; Roberta Hursthouse, Garden Play Program, Children's Memorial Hospital, Chicago, IL; Dorothy Julin, John George Psychiatric Pavilion, San Leandro, CA; Anne Kelly, Public Relations, Children's Hospital, Boston, MA; Dr. Derek Kerr, Attending Physician, Laguna Honda Hospice, San Francisco, CA; Richard Klotz, Sub-Acute Treatment for Adolescent Rehabilitation Services (STARS), San Leandro, CA; Life-Quality Directors Amy Anderson, Carol Cahill, Omar Jorge, Pat McKinney, Pat O'Connor, and Isabelle Skaburskis, Hearthstone Alzheimer's Care Treatment, Lexington, MA; Mary Jane Lovering, Vertechs Designs Inc., Toronto, Canada; Chrissie McDonnell, York, UK; Jill McHale, The Retreat, York, UK; David Mitchell, Estate Manager, The Retreat, York, UK; Louise Mozingo, Department of Landscape Architecture, University of California, Berkeley, CA; Michael Oldham, Environs Partnership, Dorchester, UK; Barbara Ostrove, Butler Hospital, Providence, RI; Margaret Ovitt, Landscape Architect, Champaign, IL; Gloria Perkins, John George Psychiatric Pavilion, San Leandro, CA; David Pinder, Manager, Joseph Weld Hospice, Dorchester (UK); Douglas Reed, ASLA, designer of the Therapeutic Garden, Institute for Child and Adolescent Development, Wellesley, MA;

Rhode Island Historical Society reference librarians; Virginia Salamy, Landscape Architect, Bexley, OH; Chris Searle, Bernardo's Spring Hill School, Ripon, UK; Charles Smith, Hospital Architect, Office of Facility Planning, Children's Hospital, Boston, MA; Edward Stillinger, Landscape Architect, Victoria, British Columbia, Canada; Jeanne Stratford, Director, Lucas Gardens School, Canada Bay, New South Wales, Australia; Tib Tussler, Architect, Stone, Marracini, and Patterson, San Francisco, CA; Birgit Urmson, Landscape Architect and filmmaker, Oakland, CA; James Varni, Children's Hospital, San Diego, CA; Stephen Verderber, Department of Architecture, Tulane University, New Orleans, LA; Tijno Voors, Project Director, Blackthorn Garden Project, Maidstone, Kent, UK; and Peter Zucker, STARS, San Leandro, CA.

A second group of people aided us greatly in our travels to look at hospital gardens by providing hospitality, good meals, and transportation. These include: Benjamin Barnes and Pam Thayer, Lincoln, MA; Sherry Bartlett, Putney, VT; Robbie Bean, York, UK; Jane Cooper, London, UK; Paul and Mary Cooper, Metcalfe, Ontario, Canada; Gus and Sue Godliman, Borehamwood, Hertfordshire, UK; Jean and Don Halstead, London, UK; Joyce Murphy, Victoria, British Columbia, Canada; Nina Payne, Enfield, Middlesex, UK; Shelly Sparks, Los Angeles, CA; and Colin Whitston, Stoke-on-Trent, UK.

In addition, we are most grateful to various friends who, upon hearing about this book, shared with us their personal experiences of hospital gardens. These appear, along with quotes from published works, in the minor columns of this book. Also located in the minor columns are quotes from two other sources: informal interviews with staff and residents at Hearthstone at New Horizons, Marlborough, MA, supplied by John Zeisel, and appearing in Chapter 9; and quotes in Chapter 7 from patients, staff and visitors at Children's Hospital, San Diego, from a working paper by Sandra Whitehouse, James Varni, et. al. We appreciate being able to quote from these sources. All these add, we hope, a human dimension to the many issues discussed in the text.

We greatly appreciate the untiring efforts of Kaye Bock, Sue Cole, and Deyan Ivanovic to transform our handwritten text and field notes into today's electronic format.

Finally, we are indebted to Sam Bass Warner, Historian, Cambridge, Massachusetts, who greatly encouraged us in our work, allowed us to draw on his invaluable writing on the history of hospital gardens, and gave us his contact files on hospital gardens in the United Kingdom. The last were especially helpful in expanding our coverage of this topic outside the United States.

NOTE
In each chapter, the photos were taken by the chapter author (or one of the co-authors) unless otherwise noted. In cases where a problem is illustrated, the name of the facility is omitted.

CONTRIBUTORS

Marni Barnes
Landscape Architect, Deva Designs, Palo Alto, California

Clare Cooper Marcus
Professor Emerita, Departments of Architecture and Landscape Architecture, University of California, Berkeley

Terry Hartig
Institute for Housing Research, Uppsala University, Sweden

Deborah L. McBride
Landscape Designer, Berkeley, California

Robin C. Moore
Professor, Department of Landscape Architecture, North Carolina State University, Raleigh, North Carolina

Naomi Alina Sachs
Department of Landscape Architecture, University of California, Berkeley, California

Martha M. Tyson
Landscape Architect, Douglas Hills Associates, Inc., Evanston, Illinois

Roger S. Ulrich
Professor, Center for Health Systems and Design, Texas A&M University, College Station

John Zeisel
President, Hearthstone Alzheimer's Care, Lexington, Massachusetts

Healing Gardens

CHAPTER

1

Introduction: Historical and Cultural Perspective on Healing Gardens

Clare Cooper Marcus,
with Marni Barnes

The idea of a healing garden is both ancient and modern. Long after humans had begun to erect dwellings, local healing places were nearly always found in nature—a healing spring, a sacred grove, a special rock or cave. The earliest hospitals in the Western world were infirmaries in monastic communities where herbs and prayer were the focus of healing and a cloistered garden was an essential part of the environment.

Over the centuries, the connection between healing and nature was gradually superseded by increasingly technical approaches—surgery, medicines, drugs, X-rays. A separation occurred between attention to body and spirit, and increasingly, different parts of the body (eyes, heart, digestive tract, etc.) and different afflictions (cancer, arthritis, etc.) were treated by specialists. The idea that access to nature could assist in healing was all but lost. By the late twentieth century, in many health care settings, "landscaping" came to be seen as merely decoration used to offset the hospital building or per-

"Nature is but another name for health…"
HENRY DAVID THOREAU

1

haps to impress potential customers. Even when a courtyard or roof garden exists, it rarely appears on hospital way-finding maps or signage.

The goal of this book is to stimulate a discussion of the healing qualities of nature and to communicate what is known about successful healing garden design to those professionals responsible for creating and maintaining medical facilities (architects, landscape architects, hospital CEOs, and facility managers) and to those responsible for patient care (doctors, psychologists, medical staff, nurses, and hospital administrators).

This is an appropriate time to do so. Research exists to support the notion of nature as healer. Studies have been conducted that confirm the clearly positive benefits to patients, staff, and visitors of hospital outdoor space. Specifically designated "healing gardens" have begun to appear in hospitals. Certain relatively new categories of medical settings that specialize in the care (rather than cure) of their patients—for example, the hospice and facilities for Alzheimer's patients—have enthusiastically embraced the importance of a garden along with a homelike interior. Books have appeared that urge readers to consider their own gardens as a healing or sanctuary space (Mintner, 1993; McDowell and Clark-McDowell, 1998; Jay, 1998). The organization that accredits 85 percent of U.S. acutecare hospitals now requires that for certain patient groups (pediatrics, long-term care) and those experiencing long stays, the hospital provide "access to the outdoors through appropriate use of hospital grounds, nearby parks and playgrounds, and adjacent countryside" (The Center for Health Design, 1998).

Figure 1-1 Early places of healing and ritual in the West were often set in nature. (Avebury, UK.)

Clearly, ancient knowledge about the restorative power of nature is not completely lost. The time is ripe to present what we currently know from research and what we can learn from best practice in landscape design to promote the reintegration of nature and the healing process.

DEFINITIONS OF "HEALING" AND "GARDEN"

The common usage of the term "healing" is quite broad and generally refers to a beneficial process that promotes overall well-being. Within the healthcare setting however, there are three specific aspects of the healing process that can be identified and that will help to clarify how a garden environment may provide therapeutic benefit. Throughout this book we have used the term "healing" or "therapeutic" to describe one, or a blend, of the following enhancements to well-being. First is achieving a degree of *relief from physical symptoms* or awareness of those symptoms. This relief is a significant factor in the life an individual with an acute illness or trauma from which s/he is recovering, such as a routine postoperative patient. This component of healing also plays an important role in the life of the patient with a chronic illness, for pain management can be a significant part of a treatment process. A second form that healing can take is that of *stress reduction* and increased levels of comfort for an individual dealing with the emotionally and physically trying experiences of a medical setting. Stress reduction may be the most relevant component for visitors and staff, where relaxation and rejuvenation are the goal, in and of themselves. It is also one of the most significant components of well-being for the individual with a chronic or terminal condition, when the quality of his or her life is of paramount concern. Stress reduction becomes the precursor to the third healing concept, that of facilitating an *improvement in the overall sense of well-being* and hopefulness that an individual is experiencing and thereby assisting physical improvement. For patients with chronic conditions, a sense of well-being will often be reflected in an increased level of functioning. For those who are recovering, hopefulness has been proven to be a significant factor in the rate of improvement; to facilitate hope is to enhance health. Any environment can hinder or enhance these components of healing. It is the goal of this book to demonstrate how gardens can be particularly well suited to support and even stimulate these therapeutic processes.

"I don't have any windows in the lab where I work. It's neat to have a place to go outside, to get fresh air; it's really relaxing. I park my car out back there because I get here so early, so I walk by the garden every day and look in on it; it is a nice start to my day. On the way out, I look in, too. It helps to connect me to the outdoors. I enjoy it so much; it's a nice place to meditate, to read, and relax."

(STAFF MEMBER)

"I only went out for a walk and finally concluded to stay out until sundown, for going out, I found, was really going in."

JOHN MUIR

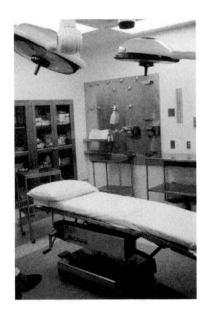

Figure 1-2 By the late twentieth century, the connection between nature and healing was all but lost.

The term "garden" has a long, multicultural history, but for our purposes, we are using it broadly, to encompass any green outdoor space within a healthcare setting that is designed for use. Inside the buildings of a healthcare facility, one is "acted upon"; that is, healing is mediated via surgical interventions, drugs, and monitoring by trained personnel. In the garden, healing occurs as a result of a direct connection between the patient and the physical/natural environment. A garden is a place to just "be in"; it can be therapeutic without the mediation of medical personnel.

Gardens can be healing and restorative via a number of mechanisms. The most obvious is the aesthetics of nature, that is, creating a beautiful verdant place that will be a powerful enticement to go outdoors. Being outdoors in a natural or quasi-natural setting, experiencing sunlight, viewing trees and flowers, listening to the sounds of water or birdsong—the combination of these and other elements that make up a garden can have measurable stress-reducing benefits (see Chapter 2). But the healing effects of a garden will be powerfully enhanced by how it is detailed to support other sought-after activities beyond the basics of being in a plant-filled space. These include design elements that encourage people to socialize, to spend desired time alone, to stroll, to engage in more vigorous exercise, to choose being in the sun or shade, and so on. Without attention to these and other details elaborated throughout this book, a garden will not fulfill its fullest potential as a healing place. It may provide an attractive nature view from inside a facility, and that is certainly important, but it will not motivate people to spend time outside where other experiences besides *viewing* nature can enhance the healing function of the garden. Finally, a garden can be healing for people who are actively engaged in creating and maintaining it.

For the purposes of this book, healing gardens encompass the first two categories discussed above: a space to look out at, and a space for passive or quasi-passive activities such as observing, listening, strolling, sitting, exploring, and so on. While some healthcare facilities do have spaces, programs, and staff where patients can engage in horticultural therapy—active engagement in gardening and plant propagation—this book does not cover this topic (exceptions are to be found in Chapter 7, where two case studies of children's hospital gardens address spaces where horticultural therapy is a component, and in Chapter 6, where one case study describes a gardening program for mental health patients).

Figure 1-3 In a study of the use of hospital gardens, 95 percent of those interviewed reported a positive change of mood after spending time outdoors (From Cooper Marcus and Barnes, 1995).

Stress Reduction and Access to Nature[1]

Three exploratory studies authored by the co-editors of this book inspired them to pursue the task of organizing and contributing to the present volume, and first alerted them to the pervasive desire for access to nature and gardens as a conscious antidote to stress.

These studies posed the simple question: Where do people choose to go when stressed? In one study of the use of outdoor space in hospitals, 95 percent of those interviewed reported a positive change in mood after spending time outside, from feeling depressed, stressed, and anxious to a more calm and balanced outlook. When asked which specific qualities seemed to be helpful in triggering this mood change, more than two-thirds mentioned elements of the plant world (trees, flowers, colors, seasonal change, greenery); these were essentially aspects that attracted the eyes. More than half also mentioned elements that stimulated other senses (auditory, olfactory, tactile); these were features such as birdsong, the sound of water from a fountain, fresh air, fragrances, and so on (see Table 1-1).

---

[1]A model of stress reduction and its relationship to the physical environment with a primary emphasis on scientific research findings is presented in full by Roger Ulrich in Chapter 2 of this book.

TABLE 1-1

Percent of Respondents Who Named These Qualities as Helpful in Attaining a Mood Change in Four Hospital Garden Settings[1]

	Percent
Trees and Plants	69
flowers, colors, greenery, heritage trees, being in nature, seasonal changes	
Features involving auditory, olfactory, or tactile sensations	38
birds/squirrels, wind/fresh air, water, quiet, light/sun, shade, fragrances	
Psychological or social aspects	50
peaceful, escape from work, openness/large, privacy/secret places, oasis, companionship, watching others, knowing it is here	
Visual qualities relating to more than plant materials	26
attractive landscape design, views, variety of elements, textual contrast/quality, differing shapes/sizes	
Practical Features	17
seating, well-maintained, accessibility, vending machines, smoking allowed, pathways	
No answer or "don't know"	8
(Number of respondents: 143)	

[1] Cooper Marcus and Barnes, 1995.

Figure 1-4 When asked to recall a place they had gone to when feeling stressed or upset, 60 percent of a sample of university students reported going outdoors (From Francis and Cooper Marcus, 1992).

Responses suggested that these natural elements were critical because they represented a complete contrast to the experience of being *inside* a hospital; they stimulated the senses, and that seemed to be a precursor to a calming or centering experience.

In another study, conducted a few years earlier, we posed a question to a sample of university students regarding places of emotional healing (Francis and Cooper Marcus, 1992). In this case, we asked them to recall an occasion when they had been feeling particularly stressed, upset, depressed, angry, confused, or grief-stricken, and they had gone to a particular *place* that helped them feel better. Subjects were asked to describe the place, what happened to them there, and which specific elements or place qualities seemed to ameliorate their mood. In this case, subjects were free to recall any past experience. Significantly, there was a marked preference for outdoor settings (71 percent of the sample of 154 students; see Table 1-2).

When asked to describe the actual elements or qualities that seemed to contribute to their change of mood, four broad characteristics stood out (see Table 1-3).

TABLE 1-2

Types of Places Selected by University Students When feeling Stressed

Places	Number		Percent
Natural settings		62	40%
• With water	34		22%
• Without water	28		18%
Designed outdoor settings		47	31%
• Campus, sports facility, yard, etc.	29		19%
• Urban park	18		12%
Enclosed spaces		27	18%
• Own room, home, etc.	25		17%
• Other	2		1%
Urban and built settings (e.g., mall, movie theater, bar, store, church)		18	12%
TOTALS		154	100%

Source: Francis and Cooper Marcus, 1992.

TABLE 1-3

Significant Elements and Qualities of Places Chosen by University Students When Feeling Stressed

Types of Elements or Qualities	*Number of Mentions*	*Percent of Total Sample Who Mentioned*
Natural elements	106	69%
Sensory qualities	97	63%
Evokes safety/comfort	94	61%
Provides privacy/solitude	79	51%
Viewpoint, expansive scale	43	28%
Urban milieu	42	27%
Opportunities for movement	36	23%
Opportunities for exploration/challenge	6	4%

Source: Francis and Cooper Marcus, 1992.

A study by Barnes (1994) used a similar but more in-depth instrument to that used by Francis and Cooper Marcus, and a broader sample. Only one-fourth of the sixty-five participants interviewed were students; the remainder were employed in diverse occupations and were of varying ages. One goal of this research was to test whether the results of the Francis and Cooper Marcus study (1992) were skewed, because the sample in that study was entirely of students in environmental fields (mostly landscape architects), therefore, the emphasis on nature experiences might be biased by the background of those surveyed. This was found not to be the case. Table 1-4 illus-

"I used to work at another hospital without any gardens; it was just a tall, stark building; there was not even a place to go outside. You're there in the hospital and you know you're there. There's no escape. At hospitals like that, the patients' families have to visit them in their rooms; there's noplace else to go; it's got to be depressing and make them feel trapped in their illness. Here, with the gardens and all the outdoor places, it's so much better."

(STAFF MEMBER)

TABLE 1-4

Selection of Natural versus Designed Exterior Sites

	Francis and Cooper Marcus Study	Barnes Study
Natural settings	**57%**	**64%**
• With water	54%	59%
• Without water	46%	41%
Designed outdoor settings	**43%**	**36%**
• Campus, sports facility, yard, etc.	60%	57%
• Urban park	40%	43%

Source: Francis and Cooper Marcus, 1992; Barnes, 1994.

trates that, when asked about places of solace outdoors, approximately the same proportion in each of the two studies chose a natural setting (beach, forest, national park, etc.) and approximately the same chose a designed outdoor space.

It is worthwhile here to cite another exploratory study that supports the preceding findings. In a series of workshops entitled "Spaces Can Heal," 300 participants were asked to recall a time and place when they, or someone close to them, felt helpless, wounded, or in pain, then to visualize "an environment that would be healing for that wounded person." Every environment cited envisaged *nature* (trees, grass, water, sky, rocks, flowers, birds) as a significant healing agent; many incorporated the stimulating yet soothing qualities of "difference within sameness" (moving water, breezes in vegetation, visual scanning); many described vistas viewed from secure locations (Olds, 1985). It is ironic that when asked to *imagine* a healing environment, nearly everyone makes some reference to nature, yet when seeking medical (healing) treatment, we find ourselves in environments virtually devoid of nature or access to it.

Hospital gardens consciously created to be "healing" are few and far between. Of these, only one (as far as we know) has ever been evaluated as to its effects. (Center for Child Health Outcomes, 1998). Designed in bright colors, with many sculptural elements, the garden was attractive to people, but few stayed more than five or ten minutes; 50 percent requested more trees, vegetation, and greenery, a finding consistent with other research on what people value in hospital outdoor space (Cooper Marcus and Barnes, 1995). There seems to be no doubt that those elements that the general public associates with a garden—green, growing things—are exactly what people seek in order to destress outdoors in a medical setting.

Figure 1-5 When 300 people were asked to visualize "an environment that would be healing for a wounded person," every one of them envisaged nature (Olds, 1985).

While the above studies are exploratory and their findings suggestive rather than definitive, it is significant that—given the choice—high proportions of stressed (but not necessarily medically ill) people select natural or designed *outdoor* settings to find solace, and to evoke a calmer and more balanced mood. This sets the stage for us to delve more deeply into the stress-nature-health connection and to look at the cultural and historical aspects of these linkages.

RELIGION, CULTURAL VALUES, AND VENERATION OF THE NATURAL WORLD

In the Judaic, Christian, and Islamic religions, paradise is symbolized by a garden. The expulsion of Adam and Eve from the Garden of Eden is a pivotal belief in Western thought. Buddha was born, attained enlightenment, and died under specific venerated trees. A core component of Buddhist belief is the interconnection of all matter. Nature is not just something around us; we are part of nature and it is part of us. "Whether one accepts religious dogma or views it anthropologically, religion, nature, and spirituality are fundamentally bound" (Carey, 1986, p. 229).

For those people who have no formal religious affiliation, many reside within a culture whose basic values include a close connection to nature. Native American beliefs espouse deep connections with wildlife and the natural world. For Scandinavians and central Europeans, the forest is a setting of profound historic and contemporary importance dating back to pre-Christian pagan beliefs. For the English, access to, and protection of, the countryside is so imbedded in the culture that military recruitment posters for both world wars featured familiar landscape images as "something worth fighting for." In North America and Australia, veneration of the wilderness, the national parks, and natural wonders stems in part from the frontier experience. Whatever our religious or cultural background, the garden, the forest, and wilderness appeal to our senses and spirit. "For the pantheist, monotheist, or existentialist, nature provides a symbolic realm for reflection upon beauty, eternity, timeliness, and the mutability of existence" (Carey, 1980, p. 230).

How did the current amnesia regarding the value of nature in medical environments come about, even within parts of the world where a veneration for the forest, the wilderness, or the countryside is a deeply held cultural value? To answer this question—essential to a full understanding of the philosophy

Figure 1-6 *Many religious beliefs and cultural norms incorporate a strong connection between humans and the natural world. (Painting in a Buddhist temple, Mongolia.)*

"After meditating, I always feel more calm, peaceful, and aware. Everything seems wonderful, beautiful, and filled with life. . . . Just sitting in my garden takes me out of myself and brings me back to my true, essential self. A sense of balance and well being pervades. Nothing in the world changes, but I see and approach everything differently."

VERONICA RAY

of the healing garden—we need to consider in turn the history of hospital design and the varying cultural approaches to medical treatment. History allows us to look at the architectural setting of contemporary medical practice within the perspective of time and change. Cultural attitudes to medical treatment provide some insight as to how medical philosophy shapes the settings in which we receive care. The two are of course inextricably linked: culture shapes values in a particular region; those values influence architectural form—whether of hospitals, schools or other institutions—and those environmental settings in turn reinforce cultural values.

HISTORICAL OVERVIEW OF THE PROVISION OF OUTDOOR SPACE IN MEDICAL SETTINGS[2]

The first flowering of restorative gardens in Europe occurred during the Middle Ages when hospitals and monasteries ministering to the sick, the insane, and the infirm often incorporated an arcaded courtyard where residents could find the degree of shelter, sun, or shade they desired in a human-scale, enclosed setting. St. Bernard (1090–1153) wrote of the intentions at his hospice in Clairvaux, France:

> Within this enclosure many and various trees . . . make a veritable grove. . . . The sick man sits upon the green lawn . . . he is secure, hidden, shaded from the heat of the day . . . ; for the comfort of his pain, all kinds of grass are fragrant in his nostrils. The lovely green of herb and tree nourishes his eyes. . . . The choir of painted birds caresses his ears . . . the earth breathes with fruitfulness, and the invalid himself with eyes, ears, and nostrils, drinks in the delights of colors, songs, and perfumes (quoted in Warner, 1995, p. 8).

Remarkably, this account of the sensory delights of a garden for those who are sick is virtually the same as responses recorded nine hundred years later in interviews with the users of contemporary hospital gardens (Cooper Marcus and Barnes, 1995).

During the fourteenth and fifteenth centuries, a number of trends combined to render a decline in the monastic provision of medical care: periodic plagues, crop failures, and waves of migration into the burgeoning cities overwhelmed the facilities

---

[2]We are very grateful to historian Sam Bass Warner, Jr., who kindly allowed us to read and quote from his unpublished papers (1994 and 1995). The following brief overview owes much to his work, as well as to a major published work by Thompson and Goldin (1975).

Figure 1-7 The monastic cloister garden was one of the earliest outdoor spaces designed for contemplation and healing. A modern-day cloister garden at Santa Sabina Retreat Center, Dominican College, San Rafael, California.

that existed. With the decline of monasticism itself, the significance of the meditative/restorative garden declined, and open spaces attached to hospitals became accidents of local architectural tradition, if they existed at all (Warner, 1994, pp. 7–8). The care of the sick fell upon civic and ecclesiastical authorities, and within the Roman Catholic tradition, one of the primary design incentives was to create long wards where the priest celebrating Mass could be viewed from every bed. The influential Ospedale Maggiore in Milan (1458), for example, was built in a cruciform plan, like a church nave with windows so high that no one could see the formal gardens outside (Thompson and Goldin, 1975, p. 31).

Nevertheless, some hospitals did continue the courtyard tradition. Les Invalides in Paris (1671) incorporated a number of courts planted with rows of trees. The English hospital and prison reformer John Howard (1726–1790) described gardens for patients in hospitals in Marseilles, Pisa, Constantinople, Trieste, Vienna, and Florence. "In all these hospitals he admired the flow of fresh air, the chance for patients to see gardens through their windows and doorways and the opportunity for convalescent patients to walk in the gardens" (Warner, 1994, p. 18).

Recommendations for hospital garden design written by German horticultural theorist Christian Cay Lorenz Hirschfield at the end of the eighteenth century (and quoted in Warner, 1994) uncannily foreshadow the findings of researchers such as Ulrich, who documented in one study the

Figure 1-8 Courtyard at Guy's Hospital, London, founded in 1725.

healing benefits of a view onto vegetation for patients recovering from surgery (Ulrich, 1984).

> A hospital should lie open, not encased by high walls. The garden should be directly connected to the hospital, or even more so, surround it. Because a view from the window into blooming and happy scenes will invigorate the patient, also a nearby garden encourages patients to take a walk…. The plantings, therefore, should wind along dry paths, which offer benches and chair…. A hospital garden should have everything to enjoy nature and to promote a healthy life. It should help forget weakness and worries, and encourage a positive outlook…. The spaces between could have beautiful lawns and colorful flower beds…. Noisy brooks could run through flowery fields, and happy waterfalls could reach your ear through shadowy bushes. Many plants with strengthening aromas could be grouped together. Many singing birds will be attracted by the shade, peace, and freedom. And their songs will rejoice many weak hearts (Hirschfield, quoted in Warner, 1994; p. 30).

In the seventeenth and eighteenth centuries, the dual emergence of scientific medicine and Romanticism fortuitously combined to encourage the reemergence of usable outdoor spaces in hospitals. The notion that infections were spread by noxious vapors spawned designs that paid special attention to hygiene, fresh air, and cross-ventilation. Two- and three-story buildings linked by a continuous colonnade and ventilated with large windows marked the design of the influential Royal Navy Hospital at Plymouth, England. The medieval Hôtel Dieu in

Paris was rebuilt with a series of twenty-four-bed wards joined at their ends by a service corridor, like the teeth of a comb (Warner, 1994, p. 23). These new designs, known as *pavilion hospitals,* incorporated outdoor spaces between the wards. Meanwhile, the rise of Romanticism was prompting a reconsideration of the role of nature in bodily and spiritual restoration. Outdoor spaces began to be viewed again as an intrinsic component of the healing environment.

The influential nurse and public health reformer Florence Nightingale (1820–1910) wrote with enthusiasm of these new hygienic hospital plans, which became the predominant form throughout the nineteenth century:

> Second only to fresh air...I should be inclined to rank light in importance for the sick. Direct sunlight, not only daylight, is necessary for speedy recovery.... I mention from experience, as quite perceptible in promoting recovery, the being able to see out of a window, instead of looking against a dead wall; the bright colors of flowers; the being able to read in bed by the light of the window close to the bed-head. It is generally said the effect is upon the mind. Perhaps so, but it is not less so upon the body on that account (quoted in Warner, 1995, p. 24).

Figure 1-9 Royal Chelsea Hospital, London; seventeenth century hospital designed by Sir Christopher Wren.

Good nursing practice by the end of the nineteenth century and in the first decades of the twentieth century called for wheeling hospital beds out onto sun porches and roofs; indeed, in the treatment of tuberculosis, this fresh air and sunlight regimen was seen as the key to recovery. In the Catholic hospital St. Mary's, in San Francisco, historic photos depict rows of patients in beds on the trellised roof garden. Yet all that is now left of this space is a neglected segment of roof with a few flower boxes, where staff retreat for a quick cigarette break.

The late eighteenth and early nineteenth centuries also saw radical reforms in the treatment of psychiatric patients and in the design of psychiatric hospitals. Psychological nurturance began to replace physical punishment as the core of treatment. New asylums were laid out with peripheral grounds and plantings to protect the patients from curious onlookers; landscape vistas were created to provide therapeutic experiences; and grounds maintenance, gardening, and farming became intrinsic components of the therapeutic regimen (Warner, 1994, pp. 30–37).

The twentieth century has seen one of the most rapid periods of social change in human history. Two world wars had devastating effects on parts of the Western world. Technical innovations in transportation, communication, and information dissemination have created an increasingly fast-moving

Figure 1-10 Radclyffe Infirmary, Oxford. All that is left of formerly extensive grounds for the convalescence of patients is the lawn and decorative pool at the main entrance.

world. Progress is associated with profits and efficiency. In the medical world, understanding of germ theory, rapid advances in medical science, technical advances in high-rise construction and the use of elevators, and increasing demands for efficiency led to the replacement of low-rise pavilion hospitals with multistory medical complexes. As Warner (1994, p. 46) describes this trend:

> In acute care hospitals, the design emphasis shifted towards saving steps for physicians and nurses, and away from attention to the environments the patients experienced. Gardens disappeared, balconies and roofs and solaria were abandoned, and landscaping turned into entrance beautifications, tennis courts for the staff, and parking lots for employees and visitors. These trends which so captured the twentieth century American acute care hospitals spread, after World War II, by the processes of fashion to long-term and chronic care facilities, to the hospitals of the Veterans Administration, to mental hospitals, and to nursing homes. The prestige of the big city teaching hospitals with their gardenless patient environments set the styles for all the others.

In one type of hospital, however—catering to long-term care of chronic illnesses—the garden was not completely lost. The profession of occupational therapy was established in the early decades of this century, extending a practice previously limited to psychiatric patients into the rehabilitation of patients with physical problems. After World War I, garden work entered the arena in rehabilitation hospitals; after World War II, horticultural therapy programs with special-purpose garden facilities began to be provided in hospitals for veterans, the elderly, and the mentally ill. With rising mortality rates from AIDS and cancer, the hospice facility has become more familiar in U.S. cities. These facilities have recognized the therapeutic effect of the garden. In the specialized facilities for seriously ill children and their families, known as Ronald McDonald Houses, a homelike environment and adjacent garden are the norm.

Sadly, however, these examples are the exceptions in the healthcare field. Pressure from insurance companies to minimize hospital stays have largely worked against the provision of actual usable gardens in new or refurbished medical complexes. Ironically, even when suitable garden spaces do exist, inquiries at the information desk are often met with blank stares or an outright "No—we don't have a garden here." Only two acute care hospitals out of more than seventy visited by the co-editors in the United States, Canada, Australia, and England provided any graphic directions to such an amenity, or mentioned it in information handed to new patients. It seems as

Figure 1-11 At a hospice, medical treatment is secondary to nursing and spiritual care, and a garden is often part of the environment. (Gardens at Trinity Hospice, London, UK.)

though the hospital garden in the late twentieth century has become an invisible and ignored amenity, and awareness of its possible restorative benefits has been lost in the world of high-tech machines, high-cost drugs, and increased medical specialization.

Twentieth-Century Literature on Hospital Design and the Significance of Outdoor Space

Reviewing hospital design literature published in the twentieth century, we see further evidence of the unfortunate changes just discussed: a clear diminution in concern for the outdoors in medical environments. One of the most comprehensive accounts of modern hospital design in the early decades of the century is found in Edward Stevens' work (1918). Not only does he include a chapter titled "Landscape Architecture as Applied to Hospitals," but in descriptions and illustrations of many contemporary institutions, he refers frequently to extensive grounds, parklike settings, courtyards for convalescence, outdoor sleeping porches, vistas, sunlight, and fresh air. His book was published during a period when rest and recuperation outdoors were perceived as an essential part of recovery, not only for TB patients in sanatoria, but for patients with all manner of diagnoses, both physical and mental. In describing the pavilion plan of Rudolph Virchow Hospital in Berlin—"...perhaps the most familiar of modern hospitals..."—Stevens writes:

> Owing to the ease with which the patients can be taken from the buildings, the beautifully laid-out grounds and parks,

"Not long ago, operating rooms had windows. It was a boon and a blessing in spite of the occasional fly that managed to strain through the screens and threaten our very sterility... there was the benediction of the sky, the applause, and reproach of thunder... the longevity of the stars to deflate a surgeon's ego. It did not do the patient a disservice to have Heaven looking over his doctor's shoulder. I very much fear that, having bricked up our windows, we have lost more than the breeze; we have severed a celestial connection."

RICHARD SELZER

with their walks and drives, become the ideal place for conva-
lescents. One of the rules of these parks is that on every third
day they are for the sole use of the patients, every third day for
the sole use of the staff, and every third day for the sole use of
the nurses (Stevens, 1918, p. 4).

In researching this book, Stevens visited dozens of hospitals in
Europe and reported:

> Wherever one goes in any of the larger institutions of Europe,
> one will see the convalescent patients walking or being
> wheeled along the shady paths, sitting under special arbors or
> awnings, enjoying the green grass and the flowers, and chat-
> ting with one another. Comfortable benches and easy seats,
> splashing fountains, and simple forms of amusement, all add
> to the pleasure, and shorten the convalescence (*Ibid.*, p. 228).

*Figure 1-12 Courtyards in late twenti-
eth century hospitals are sometimes
poorly maintained, permanently
locked...*

Throughout Stevens' book, reflecting the philosophy of hospital design at the time, it is the comfort and recovery of the
patient that appears to be paramount in how a hospital is sited,
planned, detailed, and landscaped. "It is true in landscape planning as in building planning that the patient must be considered, and the therapeutic and healing benefits of the sun's
direct rays must outweigh the architecture, for... the hospital is
built for the patient and not for the glorification of the architect
or his running mate, the landscape architect" (*Ibid.*, p. 228).

In contrast, more than sixty years later, Anthony Cox and
Philip Groves (1981) present many case examples of healthcare
facilities in an overview of current best practice in the United
Kingdom and the developing world. Whereas Stevens' comprehensive coverage from 1918 included the depiction of landscaped grounds in almost every plan presented (some with
specific portions of the grounds individually named), by 1981,
plans in *Design for Health Care*, and in similar books in other
Western countries, are quite devoid of any information beyond
the walls of the building, as if the hospital hung in white space.
Unlike the early twentieth century hospital, which was often set
in parklike surroundings, the late twentieth century hospital
tends to be one of two models: a tower on a podium or an elongated, low-rise, streetlike "spine" with wards and departments
attached to it. In the first of these modern models, outdoor
space is barely more than peripheral landscaping; in the second, a checkerboard pattern of interior courtyards is often only
marginally developed as usable, therapeutic space.

*Figure 1-13 ...or designed to be looked
down onto from above.*

In an updated version of this book (Cox and Groves, 1990)
only the chapters on psychiatric services and terminal care
refer to the importance of views to and use of attractive garden
spaces. The implication is that only those clearly dealing with

emotional and psychological issues need access to the outdoors. The relative lack of attention to attractive, usable gardens in acute care general hospitals conveys the message that the emotional repose facilitated by a garden is of little importance in healing that is essentially of the physical body.

Until recently only one short book had ever been published specifically on hospital landscape architecture, *Landscape Architecture for New Hospitals*. Authored by landscape architect Bodfan Gruffydd, it was published by King Edward's Hospital Fund, in London, 1967. From the perspective of a 1990s people-based user approach to design, this is a disappointing volume. The book focuses on how to do site analysis (soil, water, topography, etc.), how to position a building on the land, and how to organize the site during construction, all of which is basic knowledge, no different for hospitals than for any other building. Discussion of how outdoor space might be designed for the needs of patients and staff covers a scant three pages out of fifty-four. Illustrations of, for example, an "attractive elevated courtyard" are quite dismal; photographs of supposedly "good examples" depict (without comment) crazy-paving paths that would be very difficult for an infirm person or patient using a wheelchair to negotiate; and numerous backless and armless cold stone or concrete benches are included, seating that is entirely unsuitable for infirm, convalescent, or elderly people. Some of the more attractive garden spaces depicted are, in fact, not in hospital settings, but are parts of lushly planted campuses in the United Kingdom and the United States. It is unfortunate that this report has never been updated or expanded to incorporate more relevant detail on how hospital spaces work (or don't work) for *people*.

The forgotten garden in today's medical arena might be thought of as analogous to the ignored psyche and spirit in the treatment of illness. The value of a garden and the role of the psyche in healing are both difficult to quantify or prove. Just as alternative or complementary medicine is beginning to reexamine the intricacies of the mind-body connection, so also are the design professions beginning to rediscover the therapeutic possibilities of sensitive garden design.

Figure 1-14 In the grounds of West Park Hospital, Toronto, Canada, the ruins of a nineteenth-century farmhouse-sanitarium are a favorite destination for young rehabilitation patients using wheelchairs who like the challenge of getting there on gravel paths, and enjoy spending time in a place that feels a long way from the hospital milieu.

"A peculiar delight suffused the garden outside my window. There had been no real outside before, no daylight, no sun rising and setting, no grass, no trees, no sense of space or life. Like a man parched, I gazed thirstily, yearningly, at the green quadrangle, only realizing how cut off from life I had been in my sterile, windowless, artificial cubicle. No picture sufficed. I had to see it— and since it was physically very difficult for me … I gazed at its reflection in my shaving mirror held aloft."

OLIVER SACKS

CULTURAL DIFFERENCES IN THE PRACTICE OF MEDICINE

How a culture views illness, cure, and healing radically affects medical care and the settings in which it is practiced. In a revealing comparative study of the varieties of treatment in the

United States, England, West Germany, and France, Lynn Payer documents that even among Western cultures with close ties to each other, there are remarkable differences in how illness is viewed and treated.

The French, for example, with a cultural emphasis on the aesthetic and sexual reproduction, perform significantly fewer routine circumcisions, hysterectomies, and mastectomies than are done in the United States. French medicine pays great attention to the "terrain" and constitution of the patient; hence, antibiotics are much less frequently prescribed than in the United States, where disease tends to be seen as the invader. French medical practice favors ways to stimulate the immune system, favors treatments such as rest and stays at France's spas, fringe treatments such as homeopathy and aromatherapy, and makes France the leader in fields such as immunotherapy for cancer (Payer, 1996, p. 62). "If the 'terrain' is more important than the disease, it becomes less important to fight the disease 'aggressively,' and more important to shore up the 'terrain.' While American doctors love to use the word 'aggressive,' the French much prefer 'les médicines douces,' or 'gentle therapies'" (*Ibid.*, p. 65).

The French have the right to five weeks of paid vacation a year; it is commonly accepted that this period of time is necessary for a healthy person to recuperate from a year's work. Not surprisingly, French hospital stays are typically twice as long as those in the United States for the same procedure (Payer, 1996, p. 70). One in every two hundred medical visits in France results in a prescription for a visit to a spa: Aix-Les-Bains for rheumatic complaints, Vichy for liver complaints, Le Mont-Doré for allergies. Almost all these visits are paid for, at least in part, by health insurance. When asked about the Anglo-Saxon disbelief in spas, Dr. Jacques Forestier, a leading proponent, responded: "It certainly shouldn't be said they are behind us; it's simply a position they have taken. Medicine is not yet a very exact science, and there should still be room for many different points of view" (*Ibid.*, p. 73).

German doctors are much more likely than their counterparts in the United States, France, or England to treat many complaints as deficiencies of the heart or poor circulation. Payer argues that this is due to the lingering influences of nineteenth-century Romanticism and a cultural belief that the heart is not just a pump or mechanism (the American view), but an organ that has a life of its own and responds to a variety of stimuli, including the emotions. "Still another legacy of Romanticism to German medicine is the healing powers accorded to nature, whether it be in the form of long walks in

Figure 1-15 The hospital as workplace: Staff spend most of the day under fluorescent lights, with no view to the outdoors.

the forest, mud baths, or herbal medicine" (Payer, 1996, p. 96). Of 8,250 preparations listed in the German pharmacopoeia (the Rote Liste), 1,400 are of herbal base. One-fifth of German doctors practice either homeopathy or anthroposophic medicine, both of which are recognized by the German health system.

The cultural attitude toward medicine in Great Britain is characterized by caution and economy. A British patient is half as likely to have an X ray or surgery of any kind as an American, is prescribed fewer drugs than a French or German patient, and will have one-eighth the number of lab tests as a Canadian patient (Payer, 1996, pp. 102–105). While part of the explanation may lie in the economic efficiencies inherent in a national health system, Payer presents evidence that the system itself grew out of a long-standing medical philosophy of critical questioning and caution regarding treatment. As a nation of empiricists, the British have been the leading proponents of randomized controlled trials in medical research. Britain has been the leader in pain control, geriatric medicine, and the hospice movement—all dedicated to a caring attitude and to quality of life and a lesser belief in medicine's ability to cure.

Figure 1-16 The hospital as workplace: A bridge with a view of a delivery drive is the only place for an outdoor break at an urban hospital.

In addition to empiricism, a strain of Anglo-Saxon Romanticism is also part of the British national culture, rooted in the landscape painters of the eighteenth and nineteenth centuries, the nature poets such as Wordsworth, and exemplified today in almost a national obsession with gardening and with the countryside (being in it, writing about it, defending it). This philosophy partially explains the embracing of complementary treatments involving plants—homeopathy, Bach Flower Remedies, and aromatherapy; nurses trained in the latter are becoming more and more common in National Health Service hospitals. However, it is ironic to note that even in a culture with strong roots in nature and the garden, the idea of the therapeutic value of gardens in hospitals is not well established.

Early Americans were focused on conquering nature, in order to gain a foothold on a new continent. Since those times, American medical practicioners have been much more aggressive than those in Europe. American doctors perform more diagnostic tests than doctors in France, West Germany, and England, perform surgery more often, and prescribe higher doses of drugs.

> The once seemingly limitless lands gave rise to a spirit that anything was possible if only the natural environment, with its extremes of weather, poisonous flora and fauna, and the sometimes unfriendly Native Americans could be conquered. Disease also could be conquered, but only by aggressively ferreting it out diagnostically and just as aggressively treating it, preferably by taking something out rather than adding something to increase the resistance (Payer, 1996, p. 127).

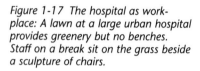

Figure 1-17 The hospital as work-place: A lawn at a large urban hospital provides greenery but no benches. Staff on a break sit on the grass beside a sculpture of chairs.

Benjamin Rush, one of the signers of the Declaration of Independence and a doctor whose influence on medicine lasted for decades, believed that one of the hindrances to the development of medicine had been an undue reliance upon the powers of nature in curing disease, a thesis he blamed on Hippocrates (*Ibid.*, p. 127). A historian of medicine, Martin S. Pernick, writes that Rush promoted his aggressive therapies by arguing that they were heroic, manly, and patriotic. "Americans were tougher than Europeans; American diseases were correspondingly tougher than mild European diseases; to cure Americans would require uniquely powerful doses administered by heroic American physicians" (quoted in Payer, 1996, p. 128).

The can-do attitude in American culture, reflected in American medicine, has resulted in successes in treating many infectious (i.e., curable) diseases and reductions in the rates of heart attack and stroke, but an aggressive approach has proven less successful with chronic (i.e., incurable) conditions. Identical clinical trials interpreted cautiously in England are touted as definitive proof that the treatment works in the United States. Long-term conditions, such as chronic bronchitis and chronic rheumatism, are not well treated in the United States; medical spas, which have evolved elsewhere into successful treatment centers for chronic diseases, do not exist in the United States. Embracing the benefits of nature—in the form of curative waters, herbal treatment, or stress reduction in a garden setting—is antithetical to the cultural demand for action, aggressive measures, and fast results in the treatment of disease. In a culture where many regard the body as an efficient machine in need of occasional checkups (not unlike a car), the subtle, positive effects of spending time in nature are not given much attention and seem dubiously "unscientific" compared with a "race for the cure."

However, the increasing interest in alternative practices suggests widespread dissatisfaction with mainstream medicine. An entire issue of the *Journal of the American Medical Association* (November, 1998) was devoted to the phenomena of alternative medicine, and reported a significant survey conducted by Dr. David M. Eisenberg and colleagues at Beth Israel Deaconess Medical Center in Boston and the Harvard Medical School. This national survey stated that an estimated four in ten Americans used at least one alternative or complementary remedy in 1997. Visits to alternative practitioners between 1991 and 1997 jumped by 41 percent. "Americans are now making more visits to alternative healers than to primary care medical doctors" (*San Francisco Chronicle*, November 11, 1998, p. A1, A15).

Some health insurance schemes now cover certain alternative practices such as acupuncture. While most major hospitals have been reluctant to recognize complementary therapies, some have begun to embrace these practices. Harvard Medical School offers workshops at various locations in the United States on the spiritual component of healing. Vancouver Hospital in Vancouver, BC, recently opened the Tzu Chi Institute for Complementary and Alternative Medicine, housed in its own two-story building, complete with a meditation garden. A few medical schools now offer courses in integrative medicine, the blending of Western and complementary approaches to healing.

The 1990s have also seen a major upswing of interest among the American public in taking care of one's own health. Sales of herbal remedies are booming; exercise and fitness gyms are flourishing; sales of popular literature on self-healing and health promotion are expanding; increasing numbers of consumers are willing to spend more on organic produce. People experiencing stress are well aware that spending time in nature has a healing effect (Francis and Cooper Marcus, 1991; Barnes, 1994)

Part and parcel of this significant paradigm shift is the burgeoning interest in healing or sanctuary gardens in both residential and healthcare settings. A major study using focus groups of patients and families to probe their basic perceptions about health care environments found that "closeness to nature" was one of seven consistent themes that consumers

Figure 1-18 The hospital as workplace: Taking a nap on a bench in a quiet hospital garden. (St. Mary's Hospital, San Francisco)

Figure 1-19 The holistic model of healing considers the whole person. The Blackthorn Medical Centre, Maidstone, Kent, UK, is set in a garden. Patients are treated with a combination of traditional approaches and therapeutic modalities based on the anthroposophical principles of Rudolf Steiner.

"The day before my transfer to Caenwood, the convalescent home in Hampstead, I was taken down to the little garden I had so yearningly gazed at—taken down in a wheelchair, dressed in hospital pajamas. This was a great joy—to be out in the air—for I had not been outside in almost a month. A pure and intense joy, a blessing, to feel the sun on my face and the wind in my hair, to hear birds, to see, touch and fondle living plants. Some essential connection and communion with nature was re-established after the horrible isolation and alienation I had known. Some part of me came alive, when I was taken to the garden, which had been starved, and died, perhaps without my knowing it."

OLIVER SACKS

looked for from the built environment[3] (The Picker Institute, 1998). Hospitals are beginning to reconsider the value of outdoor spaces in and around their buildings as restorative environments not only for patients, but also for the well-being of staff and visitors.

This is a time of great flux in society as a whole, and in the institutions of medicine within it. Boundaries are blurring; the adherence to traditional approaches is being questioned; the embracing of complementary practices by the general public is raising difficult questions for the medical, health insurance, and scientific research communities. It seems a particularly appropriate time to reconsider the therapeutic value of nature and gardens in medical facilities.

ORGANIZATION OF THE BOOK

The intent of this book is to present the most comprehensive account to date of current practice in healing garden design and the latest research on the healing benefits of nature. We have tried to present this material via text and illustrations in such a way that it will be equally interesting and appealing to both the medical and design worlds, for only when these two broad groups of professionals work together will there be advances in the arena of effective therapeutic outdoor space.

In Chapter 2, Roger Ulrich provides a detailed account of up-to-date research on the restorative value of nature, and presents a theory of supportive design. Chapter 3 by Marni Barnes links research to the implementation of design through a review of several design approaches and an introduction to the interpretation and relevance of research to the design process. Chapters 4 through 9 present case studies and design guidelines for gardens in a variety of medical settings, where types of treatments and lengths of patient stay warrant slightly different approaches to therapeutic garden design. Clare Cooper Marcus and Marni Barnes co-author chapters on acute care general hospitals; Naomi Sachs writes on psychiatric hospitals; Robin Moore discusses outdoor needs in children's hospitals; Deborah McBride presents material on nursing homes; John Zeisel and Martha Tyson discuss gardens in Alzheimer's facilities; and Clare Cooper Marcus writes on outdoor spaces in hospices.

---

[3]Regardless of the setting, people also want an environment that facilitates a connection to staff and caregivers; is conducive to a sense of well-being; is convenient and accessible; promotes confidentiality and privacy; is caring of the family; and is considerate of impairments.

Chapter 11, "Getting It Done," recounts the stories of how five healing gardens were promoted, funded, and built. A concluding chapter by Terry Hartig, Marni Barnes, and Clare Cooper Marcus points to needed future research on nature as healer. This discussion includes the necessity for more postoccupancy evaluations of hospital gardens, the importance of using existing research, and the hopeful societal changes that suggest an expanded role for healing gardens in medical treatment and design.

It should be noted that two types of gardens are omitted from this book: outdoor space specifically designed for physical rehabilitation and gardens created for programs in horticultural therapy. Both engage the patient in physical activities outdoors and require professionally trained staff. Though they are very important in certain medical settings, these categories of gardens are omitted because the emphasis here is on the more passive experience of nature as healer.

Chapters 4 through 9 are organized in a similar fashion. First, a definition of the type of outdoor space to be covered is given, followed by a brief history of the provision of that kind of facility and of the significance of outdoor space. This is followed in most chapters by a review of the literature on the design of this type of facility and (if there are any) studies of how outdoor spaces are used. A typology (or list of categories) of outdoor areas currently provided in each kind of facility is presented. A major section of each chapter is composed of a series of case studies of actual gardens, their design, and use.

Figure 1-20 Patient rooms at the Lambeth Community Care Center (London, UK) open onto a terrace and look out over a garden.

Finally, each chapter concludes with a series of design guidelines pertinent to the particular type of medical facility being discussed.

The reader should be aware that the design recommendations presented are performance guidelines rather than prescriptions. They are not intended to "tell the designer what to do," but rather, to provide reminders of recommended qualities and elements. Not all can be applied in every case; the designer will use his or her own judgment as to which recommendations are appropriate, or have highest priority, in the physical and cultural setting in which he or she is working. It should also be noted that these recommendations do not encompass local building regulations, zoning, legal requirements for disabled access, or the specifics of locally appropriate plant materials.

Each of Chapters 4 through 9 of this book covers a different type of medical facility—acute care general hospital, children's hospital, hospice, and so on. In order to avoid a great deal of repetition concerning guidelines that would apply to every setting—for example, the design of a comfortable bench—a "master list" of recommendations appears in the acute care general hospital chapter (Chapter 5); this should be consulted first. There are, in addition, recommendations in every other chapter referring to elements or qualities that should be given high priority for that particular patient population. Inevitably, there is some overlap and repetition between chapters.

CONCLUSION

The time is ripe for a concerted appraisal of outdoor space in medical settings and for a consideration of the elements that might make up a healing garden. Articles on healing gardens began to appear in the popular press and in design magazines in the mid- to late-1990s ("Healing Gardens," 1995; Evans, 1996; "Sanctuary," 1996; Radley, 1997; Thompson, 1998). Several books embracing the area of therapeutic or healing garden design also appeared in the same time period (Mintner, 1993; Tyson, 1998; Gerlach-Spriggs et al., 1998; McDowell and Clark-McDowell, 1998; Jay, 1998). A groundswell of interest seems to be sweeping this ancient idea back into human consciousness. We hope that the contributions in this book will add to the current debate, and that in the twenty-first century, the healing garden will be seen as an essential, intrinsic component of every healthcare setting.

Figure 1-21 With the "greying" of the population in Western societies, nursing homes and retirement communities are home to many older people. Gardens are an intrinsic part of these environments and are enjoyed for exercise, solitary relaxation, and socializing.

REFERENCES

Barnes, M. A. (1994). "A Study of the Process of Emotional Healing in Outdoor Spaces and the Concomitant Landscape Design Implications." Master of Landscape Architecture Thesis, University of California, Berkeley.

Browell, M. (1986). "Hospital Landscape Design." *Landscape Design,* June, pp. 42–44.

Canter, D. and S. Canter (1979). *Designing for Therapeutic Environments: A Review of Research.* Chichester, UK: Wiley

Carey, D. A. (1986). *Hospice Inpatient Environments: Compendium and Guidelines.* New York: Van Nostrand Reinhold.

Center for Child Health Outcomes, Children's Hospital and Health Center, San Diego (1998). "Leichtag Family Healing Garden Postoccupancy Evaluation" (unpublished report).

Coates, G. J. (1996). *Erik Asmussen: Architect.* Byggförlaget. Stockholm, Sweden.

Cooper Marcus, C. (1990). "The Garden as Metaphor." In M. Francis and R. Hester (Eds.). *The Meaning of Gardens.* Cambridge, MA: M.I.T. Press.

Cooper Marcus, C. and M. Barnes. (1995). *Gardens in Health Care Facilities: Uses, Therapeutic Benefits, and Design Considerations.* Martinez, CA: The Center for Health Design.

Cox, A. and P. Groves. (1981). *Design for Health Care.* London: Butterworth Architecture.

———. (1990). *Hospitals and Health Care Facilities: A Design and Development Guide.* London: Butterworth Architecture.

Crisp, B. (1998). *Human Spaces: Life-Enhancing Designs for Healing, Working, and Living.* Gloucester, MA: Rockport Publishers.

Darton, E. (1996). "The Evolution of the Hospital." *Metropolis,* October, pp. 66–72, 91–97.

Evans, L. (1996). "Healing Gardens." *Metropolis,* October, pp. 78, 135–137.

Francis, C. and C. Cooper Marcus. (1992). "Restorative Places: Environment and Emotional Well-Being." In *Proceedings of 24th Environmental Design Research Association Conference.* Boulder, CO: EDRA.

Francis, S. (1997). Presentation at conference on Human-Centered Design for Health Care Buildings. 1st International Conference, August, 28–30, Trondheim, Norway.

Gerlach-Spriggs, N., R. Kaufman, and S. B. Warner (1998). *Restorative Gardens: The Healing Landscape.* New Haven, CT: Yale University Press.

Gruffydd, B. (1967). *Landscape Architecture for New Hospitals.* London: King Edward's Hospital Fund.

"Healing Gardens" (1995). A special issue of *Landscape Architecture,* Vol. 85, No. 1, January.

Jay, R. (1998). *Sacred Gardens: Creating a Space for Meditation and Contemplation.* London: Thorsons.

Lindheim, R. (1995). "New Design Parameters for Healthy Places." Places, Vol. 2, No. 4.

McDowell, C.F. and T. Clark-McDowell (1998). *The Sanctuary Garden.* New York: Simon and Schuster.

Metzner, R. (1993). "The Split Between Spirit and Nature in European Consciousness," *ReVision,* Vol. 15, No. 4, pp. 177–184.

Mintner, S. (1993). *The Healing Garden.* London: Headline Book Publishing.

Olds, A. R. (1985). "Nature as Healer." In J. Weiser and T. Yeomans, *Readings in Psychosynthesis: Theory, Process, and Practice.* Toronto, Ont.: Institute for Studies in Education.

Payer, L. (1996). *Medicine and Culture: Varieties of Treatment in the United States, England, West Germany, and France.* New York: Henry Holt and Co.

Radley, S. (1997). "Health Care Guidance." *Landscape Design,* February, pp. 19–21.

Ray, V. (1998). *Zen Gardening: A Down-to-Earth Philosophy.* New York: Berkley Publishing Group.

Sacks, O. (1994). *A Leg to Stand On.* New York: Harper Perennial.

"Sanctuary". (Summer 1996). *Design Quarterly.* 169.

San Francisco Chronicle, "Alternative Healers Gain Lead On Doctors." Nov. 11, 1998.

Selzer, R. (1974). *Moral Lessons.* New York: Simon and Schuster.

Siegel, B. S. (1980). *Love, Medicine, and Miracles.* New York: Harper and Row.

Stevens, E. F. (1918). *The American Hospital of the Twentieth Century: A Treatise on the Development of Medical Institutions, Both in Europe and in America Since the Beginning of the Present Century.* New York: Architectural Record Publishing Company.

The Center For Health Design (1998). "Strategies for Success: The Enhanced Standards of the Joint Commission on Accreditation of Healthcare Organizations" (working document).

The Picker Institute (1998). *Working Paper: Consumer perceptions of healthcare: An investigation to determine what matters.* Martinez, CA: The Center for Health Design, Inc.

Thompson, J. D. and G. Goldin. (1975). *The Hospital: A Social and Architectural History.* New Haven: Yale University Press.

Thompson, W. (1998). "A Question of Healing." *Landscape Architecture,* Vol. 88, No. 4, pp. 66–73, 89–92.

Tyson, M. (1998). *The Healing Landscape: Therapeutic Outdoor Environments.* New York: McGraw-Hill.

Ulrich, R. (1986). "Human Responses to Vegetation and Landscapes." *Landscape and Urban Planning,* Vol. 13: pp. 29–44.

Warner, S. B. (1994, 1995) "Restorative Gardens: Recovering Some Human Wisdom for Modern Design." (Unpublished papers).

CHAPTER

2

Effects of Gardens on Health Outcomes: Theory and Research

Roger S. Ulrich

The belief that gardens are beneficial for people with illness dates back centuries and has appeared in widely different cultures (e.g., Warner, 1994; Nightingale, 1996, 1860; Ulrich and Parsons, 1992; Horsburgh, 1995, 1997; Burnett, 1997). During the early decades of the twentieth century, however, healthcare designers and administrators understandably became preoccupied with creating environments that would succeed as functionally efficient delivery platforms for important new medical technology and science. The imperative need to accommodate modern technology in healthcare facilities overshadowed traditional beliefs about the importance of including presumed therapeutic features such as gardens. In the decades that followed, the functional emphasis produced environments that were efficient but often sterile and starkly institutional, and are now considered stressful and otherwise unsuited to the emotional or psychological needs of patients, visitors, and staff (Ulrich, 1992b; Malkin, 1992; Horsburgh, 1995).

In recent years a growing awareness has developed internationally among healthcare administrators and designers of the need to create functionally efficient environments that also have patient-centered (Gerteis et al., 1993) or psychologically supportive characteristics that help patients cope with the major stress that accompanies illness (Ulrich, 1992a). Resurgent interest recently in healing gardens represents part of a broader international movement that seeks to improve the quality of healthcare by creating new types of facilities that are cost-effective yet emphasize *supportive* design coupled with patient-centered organizational practices.

GROWING EMPHASIS ON HUMAN-CENTERED HEALTHCARE ENVIRONMENTS

One impetus for the growing attention to facility design has been the recognition by many healthcare providers that psychologically unsupportive facilities are unsatisfactory from the standpoint of marketing and provider image, especially in the highly competitive conditions of managed care and the changing healthcare system. The most important factor motivating awareness of facility design, however, has been mounting scientific evidence that environmental features or characteristics can play a role in improving patient health outcomes. Dozens of published medical and other scientific studies have shown that environmental design can, for instance, reduce patient anxiety, lower blood pressure, lessen pain, and in certain situations may shorten length of hospital stay. (For a survey of scientific studies, see Rubin et al., 1997.) Conversely, research has linked poor design — or psychologically inappropriate physical surroundings — to detrimental effects such as higher anxiety, delirium, increased need for pain medication, elevated blood pressure, and sleeplessness.

A recent report by Johns Hopkins medical researchers identified upwards of seventy published scientific-experimental studies concerned with the effects of healthcare design on medical outcomes (Rubin et al., 1997). The authors observed that this amount of scientific research is small by the standards of medical fields, but there is now enough quality research to justify the conclusion that "there is suggestive evidence that aspects of the designed environment exert significant effects on clinical outcomes for patients" (Ibid., p. 14). It is important to point out that the Johns Hopkins report also reveals that very little research directly relevant to gardens has used the types of experimental-scientific methods that are considered sound and persuasive by the medical community. Rather than addressing gardens, the preponderance of the rigorous scientific research has investigated influences on health outcomes of such environmental characteristics as light, temperature, noise, and music. Although few of these latter studies are directly useful for persons interested in gardens, such investigations of non-garden environmental features nonetheless have been important in gaining credibility for this emerging research area generally, and for achieving broader acceptance within the medical community of the notion that the design of the health-care environment affects helath outcomes. This growing acceptance probably has tended to bolster the credibility of research findings on gardens that for the most part are derived from less scientifically rigorous methods.

CHAPTER OBJECTIVES AND OVERVIEW

Patients, visitors, and staff in healthcare facilities doubtless derive benefits from quite different types of experiences with gardens, including: active experiences such as physical rehabil-itation and horticultural therapy; less physically active modes such as sitting and talking; and physically passive contacts such as looking at a garden through a window. This chapter gives particular emphasis to the effects of passive visual experiences with gardens on stress reduction and other medical outcomes, and devotes less discussion to the influences of active garden contacts. A major objective of this chapter is to selectively sum-marize research and theory relevant to the effects of gardens in healthcare facilities, with emphasis on material relating to medical outcomes. The research discussion concentrates on findings derived from empirical observation structured by a research design, ranging from controlled scientific-experimen-tal studies to semiscientific methods such as post-occupancy evaluation. The nonempirically-based literature on healing gar-dens is largely omitted.

In the next section we define certain terms and concepts that are important throughout the rest of the chapter. Stress is discussed as a widespread problem for patients, a problem that affects many health outcomes. It is emphasized that by foster-ing patients' ability to cope with stress and promoting restora-tion from stress, gardens potentially can improve various health outcomes. The role of stress is central in subsequent sec-tions, which outline a research-grounded theory for under-standing how specific characteristics of gardens affect patients and staff. This theory serves as an organizing framework for later sections, which discuss research findings relating to the potential beneficial influences of gardens in healthcare facili-ties, including restoration from stress and other improved health outcomes. The theory also suggests design strategies or approaches for achieving supportive, successful gardens. The final section summarizes the potential advantages of gardens for patients and healthcare providers, and identifies needs and directions for future research.

KEY CONCEPTS

What Is a "Healing" Garden?

The term "healing garden" is used here in a fairly broad sense to refer to a variety of garden features that have in common a consistent tendency to foster restoration from stress and have other positive influences on patients, visitors, and staff or caregivers. To qualify as a "garden," the feature should contain prominent amounts of real nature content such as green vegetation, flowers, and water. The better known examples of healing gardens are found in healthcare facilities such as hospitals and Alzheimer's facilities. Healing gardens can be either outdoor or indoor spaces, and vary greatly in size—ranging from atriums covering a few square meters to outdoor spaces the size of some urban parks. (For a useful typology of healing gardens see Chapter 4 in this volume, by Cooper Marcus.)

The contention here is that to justify the label "healing," a garden should have therapeutic or beneficial effects on the great majority of its users. Regardless of whether a garden might garner praise in professional design journals as "good" design, the environment will qualify as bad or failed design in healthcare terms if it is found to produce negative reactions. These points imply that use of the term "healing" in the context of healthcare gardens ethically obligates the garden designer to subordinate or align his or her personal tastes to the paramount objective of creating a user-centered, supportive environment. Designers who succeed in creating healing gardens will usually be those who seek input from patients and staff, and assiduously utilize the available research to inform their creativity and design approach.

What Are Health Outcomes?

An important term relevant to healing gardens research and theory is "health outcome," which refers to an indicator or measure of a patient's condition or progress. Health or medical outcomes are numerous and varied. Some are based on subjective or verbal data such as self-reported depression and pain, whereas others are comparatively objective medical indicators such as blood pressure, infection occurrence, intake of certain drugs, level of motor functioning, and length of hospital stay. Different clusters of outcomes are applicable to different types of patients or diagnostic groups. In the case of many surgical patients, for instance, relevant outcomes would include anxiety, self-reported pain, intake of pain drugs, occurrence of minor complications such as nausea, and length of time from surgery to discharge. For persons with chronic or terminal illness, however, recovery measures are much less applicable but such outcomes as perceived quality of life, depression, and ability to function independently become appropriate and important.

Outcome studies have long been of major importance in medicine because they provide the most sound and widely accepted basis for evaluating whether particular treatments are medically effective and cost-efficient. A related point, which cannot be overemphasized, is that outcomes research potentially can indicate the degree to which gardens in healthcare facilities are medically beneficial and cost-effective relative to such alternatives as not having gardens.

In recent years, as managed care has emerged as the predominant healthcare model in the United States, and as healthcare systems in most other countries likewise have faced strong pressures to be more medically—and cost—effective, outcomes research has become more influential than ever in affecting decisions by physicians and healthcare administrators. Outcomes studies increasingly exert a dominant influence on decisions concerning which medical treatments and therapeutic measures will be provided to patients and reimbursed. Importantly, there are clear indications that healthcare providers' decisions regarding the design and budget for facilities are taking into account the potential for certain design strategies and environmental features to positively affect outcomes. In view of these trends there is no question that the future importance of gardens in healthcare facilities will be strongly affected by the extent to which sound and credible research shows that gardens can promote improved health outcomes, foster higher patient/consumer satisfaction with healthcare providers, and be acceptably cost-effective.

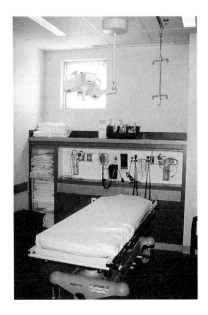

Figure 2-1   An ICU room, with all of the necessary equipment and supplies, is a strange and intimidating environment. Designed for efficiency, no attempt has been made to help people feel more comfortable. (Photo by Clare Cooper Marcus.)

STRESS: A MAJOR PROBLEM IN HEALTHCARE SETTINGS

Stress is a centrally important concept, generally, in understanding the relationship between people's physical well-being and their surroundings (Gatchel et al., 1989), and, more specifically, for explaining why gardens in healthcare facilities should affect medical outcomes (Ulrich, 1986a, 1992a; Parsons, 1991a; Parsons et al., 1994). The fact is only too well-documented that the vast majority of persons with illness experience stress, and that many unfortunately suffer acute stress (e.g., Burish et al., 1987; Van Der Ploeg, 1988; Taylor and Aspinwall, 1993; Ott and Levy, 1994). The importance of stress as a problem in medical contexts implies considerable significance for the finding that restoration from stress appears to be the major benefit motivating persons to use gardens in healthcare facilities (Cooper Marcus and Barnes, 1995).

The term "stress" is used here in a broad sense to refer to a process of responding to events and environmental features that are challenging, demanding, or threatening to well-being. The demanding events and environmental features are called "stressors." Much research has shown that numerous aspects of the experience of hospitalization, as might be expected, engender stress and are appraised by patients as highly unpleasant and aversive. (For survey of research see Gatchel et al., 1989.) Examples of stressful aspects of hospitalization include: fearful things such impending surgery, pain, and unknown diagnostic procedures; loss of control, including loss of privacy; depersonalization through, for instance, bureaucratic processing and uniform structuring of activity, dress, and visiting hours; and disruption caused by hospitalization on social relationships and job activities (Gatchel et al., 1989; Taylor, 1979; Connelly, 1992; Winkel and Holahan, 1985; Baier and Schomaker, 1985). Many of these stressors stem from characteristics of the healthcare provider organization, while others are unavoidable accompaniments of modern medical technology. It should be emphasized that additional major stress, including that produced by loss of control, results from poorly designed healthcare environments that, for instance, are noisy, confusing from the standpoint of way-finding, deny privacy, prevent personal control over television, force bedridden patients to stare directly at glaring ceiling lights, and have rooms arranged so that patients cannot see out of windows (Ulrich, 1992a).

In addition to affecting patients, stress is also a problem for families of patients and visitors, and is pervasive among healthcare staff (Parkes, 1982; Shumaker and Pequegnat, 1989; Ulrich, 1992a, 1992b; Miracle and Hovekamp, 1994). Healthcare occupations such as nursing are known to be stressful because they commonly combine lack of control, overload from demanding responsibilities, stress from rotating shifts, and stressful events such as the death of a patient (e.g., Foxall et al., 1990; Coffey et al., 1988). Further contributing to staff stress are unsupportively designed healthcare facilities that reduce control by, for instance, lacking adequate employee lounges or break areas. When staff experience considerable stress, this can in several ways lower the quality of care and potentially worsen patient health outcomes. Job-related stress is associated with lower job satisfaction, increased absenteeism, and higher turnover rates, all of which detract from the quality of patient care (e.g., Waxman et al.,1984; Ulrich, 1992a).

Patient Stress and Health Outcomes

Stress is centrally important in this chapter because it is both a significant outcome in itself, and it *directly affects many other health outcomes* (e.g., Cohen et al., 1991). These health effects stem from the fact that stress responses include numerous psychological/emotional, physiological, biochemical, and behavioral changes (Gatchel et al., 1989; Evans and Cohen, 1987; Selye, 1956). The *psychological* components include cognitive appraisal of the situation, and widely varying emotional reactions such as fear, anger, and sadness. The *physiological* aspect involves changes in activity levels in different bodily systems as indicated, for example, by increases in blood pressure, skin conductance, and respiration rate. The *neuroendocrine* component involves secretion into the bloodstream of stress hormones, including epinephrine and norepinephrine (also called adrenaline and noradrenaline) and cortisol, a natural steroid. These hormones have many influences, such as stimulating the heart and constricting the blood vessels. Examples of *behavioral* manifestations of stress in patients include sleeplessness, alcohol or drug abuse, angry outbursts, helplessness and passivity, and noncompliance with medical regimens.

As suggested above, stress manifestations such as helplessness and increased blood pressure are themselves health outcomes, but these and other stress aspects have direct effects on additional health-related indicators. For instance, persistently elevated blood pressure from chronic stress heightens susceptibility to developing permanent high blood pressure or hypertension. As another example, stress manifestations such as helplessness, depression, and social withdrawal may be linked with noncompliance or reduced adherence by patients to prescribed medical regimens and advice from doctors. When stressed patients discontinue taking medications, do not adhere to a diet, or miss physician appointments, there are often serious negative health consequences. Additionally, a large body of research has shown that stress manifestations such as arousal of the central nervous system and elevated lev-

Figure 2-2 Nursing stations are busy areas. Often located on a central corridor with fluorescent lighting and no views to the outside, there is little escape from the often charged atmosphere. (Photo by Clare Cooper Marcus.)

els of stress hormones have significant suppressive effects on functioning of the immune system (e.g., Rabin et al., 1989; Calabrese et al., 1987; Kiecolt-Glaser and Glaser, 1991). Reduced immune functioning can worsen recovery outcomes as well as decrease resistance to infection and illness. For a recent review of studies, see Kiecolt-Glaser et al., 1998.

Emotional Manifestations of Patient Stress

It was briefly mentioned above that negatively toned emotions such as fear and sadness are prominent aspects of patient stress. The particular emotions that characterize stress responses, however, can vary widely among different categories of patients and may change over time in a given patient. Very broadly speaking, *anxiety* (fear, tension) is the salient emotion experienced by patients in nonchronic disease categories with shorter hospital stays. These patients commonly also experience some degree of anger and depression, but feelings of anxiety and tension tend to be dominant. This stress category includes large numbers of persons who undergo surgery and suffer moderate to high anxiety, especially during the presurgical phase and the first few days following surgery (e.g., Janis, 1958). Anxiety is a major problem as well for the many patients who must undergo unpleasant diagnostic or treatment procedures such as cardiac catheterization, endoscopic examination, and chemotherapy (e.g., Pederson and Harbaugh, 1995; Peterson, 1991). Anxiety is also a common reaction to the uncertainty of waiting for a potentially serious diagnosis.

By contrast, *depression* is often the most serious emotional manifestation of stress in long-term patients, especially those with chronic and terminal illness. In this regard, depression is a debilitating problem for many patients with such chronic conditions as AIDS, kidney disease requiring dialysis, and heart disease (e.g., Holahan et al., 1995). These comments are, again, very general because anxiety and anger often occur together with depression in these diagnosis groups. It should also be mentioned that patients in nursing homes and other long-term care contexts often suffer from depression and boredom related to social-physical environments that are chronically *understimulating* and hence stressful—rather than overstimulating and stressful.

In sum, the vast majority of patients have in common the problem of stress, but the emotional and other manifestations of their stress responses vary widely as a function of type of diagnosis, length of treatment, and factors such as personality and coping style (e.g., Janis, 1958; Lazarus and Cohen, 1973). This implies that for gardens to have supportive benefits for widely different patient categories, gardens are needed that effectively foster coping and restoration in persons who range from being anxious to depressed, and from overexcited to understimulated. Accordingly, it seems possible that certain garden characteristics that might be found effective for reducing stress in acutely anxious surgery patients, for instance, will not necessarily be as effective for, say, many elderly in nursing homes.

THEORETICAL PERSPECTIVES: WHY GARDENS SHOULD IMPROVE HEALTH OUTCOMES

The foregoing discussion indicates that stress is a centrally important mechanism through which gardens potentially can have significant beneficial effects on health outcomes. There are sound scientific grounds for contending that gardens in healthcare facilities will improve health outcomes to the extent they are effective in fostering restoration and coping with respect to the stress that accompanies illness and hospitalization. Importantly, the concept of stress makes it possible to develop a scientifically grounded theory of supportive garden design that conceptualizes the impacts of environmental features and design approaches in ways that are directly and credibly linked to effects on health outcomes (Ulrich, 1992a). The term "supportive" here refers to gardens with environmental characteristics that facilitate or support stress coping on the part of patients, visitors, and healthcare staff. By having restorative and buffering effects on stress, supportive gardens can foster gains in numerous other patient medical outcomes. Accordingly, supportive gardens in healthcare facilities potentially can be an important complement to the healing effects of drugs and other modern medical technology, and help improve the overall quality of care.

The theory of supportive garden design outlined below has its origins in an earlier conceptual framework oriented mainly to architectural and interior design aspects of healthcare facilities (Ulrich, 1992a, 1992b), but has been modified and updated to pertain directly to gardens. The theory is not intended to be comprehensive or include all factors that conceivably play a role in the effects of gardens on health outcomes. Any conceptual framework for this topic must necessarily be tentative because research and theory on healthcare gardens is only at an embryonic stage of development.

Although theory development is hindered by the shortage of research focusing directly on gardens, this disadvantage is offset partially by the existence of a large amount of high quality research on important related topics, including environments, stress, and health outcomes. The remaining sections draw heavily on pertinent material from this valuable multidisciplinary resource, which is found scattered through such fields as environmental psychology, health psychology, behavioral medicine, and clinical psychology. The discussion in subsequent sections relates this theory and research directly to healthcare gardens, and integrates it with the limited amount of work specifically on gardens. This makes it possible to outline research-grounded elements of a preliminary Theory of Supportive Garden Design.

A THEORY OF SUPPORTIVE GARDENS

As suggested by previous sections, the basic premise underlying the conceptual framework is that the capability of gardens to have healing influences stems in large part from their effectiveness in facilitating stress coping and restoration. The appropriateness of a stress-centered theory is underscored by Cooper Marcus and Barnes' aforementioned finding that restoration from stress was by far the most important benefit reported by persons interviewed in four California healthcare gardens.

On the basis of theory and research in the behavioral sciences and health-related fields, and the limited literature on gardens, it is justified to propose that gardens in healthcare situations are important stress mitigating resources for patients and staff to the extent that they foster:

- Sense of control and access to privacy
- Social support
- Physical movement and exercise
- Access to nature and other positive distractions

The theory further contends that a requisite condition for these four stress-coping resources or mechanisms to be effective is that a garden must convey a sense of security. If the design or locational characteristics of a garden engender feelings of insecurity or even risk, the setting will likely have stressful rather than restorative influences, and many patients, visitors, and staff will avoid the space (Ulrich, 1983; Ulrich et al, 1991b; Schroeder and Anderson, 1984; Nasar et al., 1993). Persons who undergo medical treatment often feel psychologically vulnerable, which has been demonstrated to heighten their sensitivity to insecurity in an environment.

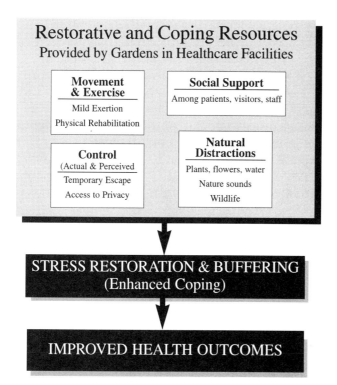

Figure 2-3   Conceptual model: Effects of gardens on health outcomes

In the following sections, each of the four main restorative resources of supportive gardens is defined, and related theory and empirical findings are discussed. As becomes apparent, there is evidence from scientific studies that each of the restorative components or coping resources can reduce stress in patients and improve other health outcomes. As this implies, a key criterion for including a restorative resource in the theoretical framework was the existence of a credible basis in scientific or medical research. The discussion of the fourth resource—natural distractions—will be more extensive because of the centrality of nature to the concept of "garden," and the mounting scientific evidence that passive experiences with nature can effectively reduce stress.

SENSE OF CONTROL

Much research has shown that a sense of control is an important factor affecting a person's ability to cope with stressful events or situations, including stress associated with illness and hospitalization. Control refers to persons' real or perceived ability to determine what they do, to affect their situations, and to determine what others do to them (Gatchel et al., 1989).

Generally, people who feel they have some control over events and situations cope better with stress, experience less stress, and have better health status than people who feel they lack control. Importantly, many studies have found that provision of actual or perceived control over stressors usually alleviates the negative effects of environmental stressors (Evans and Cohen, 1987). On the other hand, uncontrollable environmental conditions (noise or lighting, for example) typically are aversive and stressful (e.g., Glass and Singer, 1972; Evans and Cohen, 1987). Lack of *privacy* is considered here an environmental-social stressor related to lack of control over regulation of personal exposure and access to oneself (Proshansky et al., 1970; Altman, 1975). Stress stemming from lack of control has been shown to have many negative effects, including depression, helplessness, reduced cognitive performance, elevated blood pressure, higher levels of circulating stress hormones, and suppression of immune functioning (e.g., Schulz, 1976; Abramson et al., 1980; Weiss et al., 1990).

For persons who are ill, loss of the sense of control is a major problem that engenders much stress and adversely affects outcomes (Steptoe and Appels, 1989). Many experiences related to illness and injury are stressful in large part because they are uncontrollable—for instance, unavoidable and unpleasant diagnostic procedures, chronic pain, impaired physical capabilities, and demanding adjustments in the workplace (Ulrich, 1992a). Further, much of the stressfulness of hospitalization appears to derive from loss of control (Taylor, 1979; Allshouse, 1993). Examples of the many aspects of hospitalization eroding patients' feelings of control include: lack of information, loss of privacy, loss of control over eating and sleeping times, lack of authority over what to wear, inability to adjust room lighting and temperature, and way-finding difficulties in complex and unfamiliar buildings.

Growing awareness among healthcare providers that lack of control is a serious problem has motivated attempts to modify hospital routines and regulations in ways that enable patients to have more control. As a prominent example, several American and European hospitals have adopted the Planetree healthcare philosophy, which promotes a sense of control, for instance, by permitting patients access to their medical records, making extensive information available through a variety of means, and allowing patients to determine their own wake-up times (Orr, 1992). A number of studies have found that fostering control by providing information and allowing patients to take responsibility for some aspects of their care reduces helplessness and appears to improve other outcomes (e.g., Langer and Rodin, 1976; Keeri-Szanto and Heaman, 1972; Johnson et al., 1985). In the case of healthcare staff, there is evidence that increased control achieved through greater involvement in decision-making improves job satisfaction and reduces turnover (Waxman et al., 1984).

Gardens , Control, and Stress Coping

Against this background, it is justified to propose that one key stress mitigating property of appropriately designed gardens is the capacity to increase feelings of control in patients and other users (Ulrich, 1992a; Grant, 1994). Research support for this contention, however, is only indirect or circumstantial in the sense that it consists mainly of studies on environments other than gardens, and of a few garden studies that have dealt indirectly with control issues. No study has yet used an experimental research design to examine in a direct manner whether by altering certain garden features to increase control it is actually possible to reduce patient stress and thereby improve other outcomes.

Indirect support for the notion that healthcare gardens can benefit persons by providing control comes from a large body of research on nonpatient users of urban parks and wilderness areas. Findings from more than 100 published studies of recreationists in parks and other natural environments have shown

Figure 2-4   Gazing out of a window and daydreaming are two ways to find a temporary escape from the immediate circumstances. Used as a means to gain a level of control over one's situation, these are vehicles for reducing stress. (Planetree Unit at a Hospital in Trondheim, Norway, photo by Marni Barnes.)

that restoration through stress mediation is the most consistently important perceived benefit. (For surveys see Knopf, 1987; Ulrich et al., 1991a.) B. L. Driver and his associates identified a control-related benefit called *temporary escape* that has emerged subsequently in many such studies as being of high importance in restoration (e.g., Driver and Knopf, 1976). Temporary escape might be passive, such as gazing out of a window at a pleasant garden view, or in the mind only, as when daydreaming about a favorite nature area that one could escape to. Additionally, temporary escape includes active coping with stress, as when a person actually goes to a park (Driver and Knopf, 1976). Kaplan and Talbot (1983) use the phrase "being away" in a manner similar to temporary escape, in the context of distancing oneself from day-to-day work demands or from negative situations. Temporary escape appears to be strongly related to control, because persons who "escape" stressors or negative situations probably are achieving either actual or perceived control (Ulrich et al., 1991). It is important to mention here that several studies in nongarden settings have found that provision of either actual or perceived "escape" from aversive conditions mitigates stress responses (e.g., Corah and Boffa, 1970).

A study of a park located adjacent to a sizable residential population found that provision of perceived control, in addition to actual control, appeared to be an important psychological benefit of the park (Ulrich and Addoms, 1981). Many residents derived important benefits associated with frequent on-site or actual use of the park, but low users and even nonusers of the park also appeared to derive substantial psychological benefits from the space. Nonusers reported it was important "just knowing the park is there" and "having it there because I know I can use it if I have to" (Ulrich and Addoms, 1981, p. 60). The findings suggested that mere awareness of the park's presence induced feelings in the residents that they could if necessary avoid or escape, for instance, work stresses, interpersonal conflicts, or the monotony of day-to-day routines. Perhaps perceived control applies as well to gardens in healthcare facilities, and that mere awareness of the nearby presence of a pleasant garden might facilitate stress mitigation to some degree. If so, garden studies limited to on-site users might tend to underestimate the importance of gardens as stress coping resources.

A small amount of research focusing directly on gardens in healthcare facilities has yielded some evidence consistent with the notion that one major way in which such settings reduce stress is by providing control. Cooper Marcus and Barnes

(1995) found that restoration from stress was the most important category of benefits derived by persons studied in four healthcare gardens. The investigators included in their report statements by several respondents that imply that the gardens fostered restoration in part by providing escape (control) from stress. For example, a patient using a garden commented: "It's a good escape from what they put me through. I come out here between appointments…. I feel much calmer, less stressed" (Cooper Marcus and Barnes, 1995, p. 27). A patient in a garden at another hospital said: "I felt really depressed in there [the hospital]; I was getting really teary. You go from having control of your life to less control. Out here you're on your own; there's time to forget about it. You feel relieved from all the medical aspects of your case" (*Ibid.*, p. 35). Cooper Marcus and Barnes further concluded that a major reason why many employees used gardens was to escape from work stress and aversive conditions in the hospital.

Design Considerations for Control

If a garden in a healthcare facility is to foster restoration and coping by providing control, potential users must know the garden exists, be able to find their way to the setting without difficulty, and be able to use the garden in an active and/or passive manner. Accordingly, way-finding and access are very important design and planning considerations for gardens. If patients and visitors know a garden exists in a healthcare facility, but experience difficulty or frustration in trying to find or get access to the setting, such impediments will tend to produce loss of control and engender further stress.

Control-related benefits should be increased by garden designs that facilitate on-site usage by patients, including accessibility and independence for persons in wheelchairs. A given patient will be much more likely to engage in on-site use of a garden that is located close to his/her room and can be traveled to easily (Carpman and Grant, 1993). Generally speaking, on-site usage rates will be higher for gardens situated adjacent to building interior spaces that are used by large numbers of patients, visitors, and/or staff, such as cafeterias or major corridors. Other examples of garden design strategies that should foster control include providing: spaces in gardens that enable users to have privacy, including visual privacy with respect to windows looking on to a garden; variety in types of spaces, making choices possible; and an adequate number of spaces to help prevent crowding that would otherwise erode control advantages of the garden. In the case of staff, and patients in long-term facilities, feelings of control may be enhanced by involving them as participants in designing gardens (Francis, 1989; Hester, 1984; Ware, 1994). Grant (1994) has described a site plan for a healthcare garden that attempts, among other main objectives, to boost control through design characteristics that facilitate way-finding and enable users to regulate privacy, thus preventing loss of control and crowding stress.

SOCIAL SUPPORT

In addition to control benefits, there are strong grounds for proposing that another important salutary property of appropriately designed gardens is the capacity to increase social or emotional support for patients, visitors, and employees (Ulrich, 1992a). Very generally, social support refers to perceived emotional support or caring, and material or physical aid, that a person receives from others (Brannon and Feist, 1997). Specific definitions of social support vary, but most encompass a range of different kinds of supportive social behaviors including, for example: expressing to a sick person that he/she is cared about, loved, or esteemed; encouraging the patient to express beliefs and feelings openly; giving the patient a sense of belonging to a social network or support group; and providing tangible assistance (Wortman, 1984; Edgman-Levitan, 1993). Although certain types of supportive interactions may be more beneficial than others, studies of large groups have found there tends to be a general positive association between the overall number of social ties or contacts people have and their health status.

During the last two decades, a large body of research has shown across a wide range of healthcare and nonhealthcare situations (workplaces, for example) that people who receive higher levels of social support are usually less stressed and have better health status than persons who are more socially isolated (e.g., Cohen and Syme, 1985; Sarason and Sarason, 1985; Schwarzer and Leppin, 1989; Shumaker and Czajkowski, 1994). An indication of the major importance of social support for health is the finding that low social support may be as great a risk factor in mortality as is cigarette smoking (e.g., Berkman and Syme, 1979). Several studies have found that women tend to derive even greater health benefits from social support than men, possibly because women have larger social networks (Schwarzer and Leppin, 1989; Brannon and Feist, 1997).

As is often the case with findings in medical research, the mechanisms or reasons accounting for the association between

Figure 2-5 Two staff members take a few minutes out of their busy day to comment on the garden and offer each other support. (San Francisco General Hospital, CA, photo by Marni Barnes.)

social support and health are not well understood. It appears, however, that social support enhances health through a combination of effects that prominently include reduction of deleterious stress effects, and protection through *buffering* or dampening of stress responses when difficult challenges are experienced (e.g., Cohen, 1988). Importantly, studies in several healthcare contexts have consistently found that higher social support improves, for example, recovery outcomes in heart attack patients, survival length in patients with metastatic cancer, and immune functioning in family care givers of Alzheimer's patients (e.g., Spiegel et al., 1989; Kiecolt-Glaser et al., 1988). In view of the considerable scientific evidence showing social support to be robustly beneficial, many healthcare facilities have instituted programs to provide social support to patients and families (for survey see Edgman-Levitan, 1993). Further, there is a clear trend for hospitals to give greater attention to fostering social support for patients through interior environmental design strategies such as providing comfortable visitor waiting areas having movable seating, and bed sofas or sleep chairs for family members in patient rooms (e.g., Ulrich, 1992a).

Gardens, Social Support, and Improved Outcomes

In light of the strong medical evidence concerning social support, there are convincing grounds for contending that gardens in healthcare facilities mitigate stress and improve other health outcomes to the extent that they foster access to social support for patients, families, and staff. There is a strong possibility that healthcare gardens in fact produce health-related benefits via social support, because research findings indicate that gardens and parks often are important settings for social interaction. As with research on control, however, there is a lack of studies that have used experimental-scientific methods to investigate directly whether social interaction or support produced by healthcare gardens actually improves patient outcomes.

The notion that healthcare gardens foster access to social support receives some circumstantial empirical support from studies of nonpatient users of urban parks and other outdoor nature settings, which show that social interaction is often perceived as an important benefit derived from the spaces (e.g., Driver and Brown, 1986; Tinsley and Kass, 1979; Ulrich and Addoms, 1981). In this regard, several studies of nature settings other than healthcare gardens have found that persons frequently report using the spaces to achieve psychological benefits that appear linked with social or emotional support—for example, "companionship," "being with friends," and "family kinship" (Tinsley and Kass, 1979; Knopf, 1987; Driver and Brown, 1986). Other research has confirmed that on-site usage rates for parks and other urban public spaces can sometimes be very high for activities related to social contact (e.g., Whyte, 1980; Cooper Marcus et al., 1990). This work has also shown that whether or not usage rates for socializing are high depends heavily on such specific design features of the spaces as seating (Cooper Marcus and Francis, 1990). A recent noteworthy study by Kweon and her associates (Kweon et al., 1998) of inner-city adults living in high-rise public housing found that the residents' use of common outdoor nature spaces predicted both the strength of social ties and sense of community. Findings also suggested that the beneficial social integration that older adults derived from spending time in outdoor spaces was higher when the spaces had more trees and grass rather than fewer trees and less grass (Kweon et al., 1998). In addition to such findings for parks and other nongarden nature spaces, there is evidence that urban gardening projects may be especially effective in promoting social interaction and a sense of community, including among residents of inner-city areas where high crime rates and other social problems otherwise reduce local interaction (Lewis, 1996).

A small amount of research focusing on gardens in healthcare facilities has produced evidence implying that these settings can be very important for increasing access to social support for patients, families, and staff. More specifically, the findings suggest that a large proportion of on-site garden users often engage in activities involving social interaction. In their report on four California healthcare gardens, Cooper Marcus and Barnes (1995) found that 73 percent of all users engaged in talking at one time or another. Importantly, 36 percent of the persons they interviewed reported using the garden at least sometimes to visit with a patient. Rates of use for talking/socializing varied considerably, however, among different groups of users. The vast majority of employees reported using the garden for talking, often with other employees, and about two-thirds of visitors likewise indicated they conversed in the garden. By contrast, less than half of the patients reported socializing. It is not clear if the lower rates of socializing by patients reflected a possibly greater need on their part for privacy, or perhaps that many patients were socially isolated in the hospital and did not know other patients and employees (Ibid.).

Singleton (1994) assessed feelings and attitudes toward gardens in two community hospitals in the United Kingdom by conducting open-ended interviews with visitors, patients, and employees. He reported that users valued the gardens both for providing opportunities for social contact and for offering access to privacy. On the basis of case studies of three hospitals, Paine and Francis (1990) suggested that socializing was one of the principal types of activities engaged in by patients, visitors, and staff who used outdoor gardens and other nature spaces. In a more descriptive or anecdotal vein, Cohen and Day (1993) described three Alzheimer's care facilities having gardens or planted courtyards where administrators reported that family members preferred to visit with patients outdoors if weather permitted, rather than use alternative indoor locations.

It is worth digressing briefly to mention that research on social support also is relevant to understanding why horticultural therapy should be effective for reducing stress and improving health outcomes. In this regard, part of the therapeutic benefit of horticultural therapy almost certainly stems from emotionally supportive contacts with a caring and motivated therapist. Horticultural therapy probably provides patients social support as well through interaction with other patients in a therapy program.

To summarize briefly, a small but growing amount of research suggests that gardens can be important and effective for fostering social contact, and that the social contacts occurring in healthcare gardens probably include emotionally supportive interactions of the type known to mitigate stress and improve medical outcomes. Studies are needed, however, to confirm that social contacts in gardens actually are linked to positive health influences. Despite this gap in research, the pattern of evidence indicating that social support improves medical outcomes in other healthcare contexts is so convincing that it seems clearly justified to assume that gardens that foster opportunities for supportive contacts will tend to ameliorate stress and otherwise benefit user health (Ulrich, 1992a).

Design Considerations for Social Support

At a general design level, social or emotional support benefits of gardens will be increased by design and planning that facilitate on-site access by patients, visitors, and staff, and provide settings conducive to social interaction among small groups. Because many hospitals have initiated programs that involve patients and families in social support groups, there may be instances when it is appropriate for the designer to create gardens that accommodate these larger social groups, yet provide the privacy such programs usually require. Also, there may be

ethnic or cultural considerations that sometimes favor designing social spaces for larger groups, including for visitors in
large or extended families. In this regard, King (1995) found
indications of a tradition among Hispanic families in south
Texas of furnishing social support to sick persons by providing
companionship and tangible assistance through large, often
extended families. King used these findings to inform her
design of a long-term care facility for predominantly Hispanic
elderly in San Antonio, and accordingly provided a number of
interior and outdoor spaces suited to larger family groups.

In discussing design considerations for promoting social
support, attention should be called to a recent study by
Barnhart et al. (in press, 1998) of the types of outdoor settings
preferred by patients and staff in a large Canadian psychiatric
hospital. Using an interactive computer survey procedure to
assess responses to visual simulations of outdoor settings, the
investigators found that both patients and employees preferred
natural, spatially *enclosed* settings for active socializing such as
"talking with others." By contrast, patients and staff both preferred natural, spatially *open* settings for more passive and
often private activities such as "sitting and viewing scenery," or
"sitting watching others." Settings dominated by vegetation
and other nature were preferred over built-dominated settings
by both groups across different types of activities (Barnhart et
al., in press, 1998).

Finally, designers should be cautioned to avoid garden
design approaches that strongly promote social interaction to
the point of interfering with access to privacy. Garden settings
that enforce social contacts but deny privacy will often undermine control, be appraised as crowded and aversive, engender
stress, and accordingly be underutilized. In emphasizing the
benefits of social support, it is important not to lose sight of the
fact that providing privacy is likewise a significant function of
gardens. In this regard, it appears that a large percentage of
persons may use gardens in healthcare facilities to seek privacy
or be alone (Cooper Marcus and Barnes, 1995).

Garden designers seeking to promote social support can,
fortunately, take advantage of a large amount of quality environment-behavior research pertinent to creating settings that
foster both social interaction and access to privacy (e.g.,
Altman, 1975). The knowledge gained from these and other
studies has provided part of the underpinning for the useful
design guidelines developed by Cooper Marcus and others for
gardens and other outdoor spaces used by the general public
(e.g., Cooper Marcus and Francis, 1990; Cooper Marcus and
Barnes, 1995; Carpman and Grant, 1993; Carr et al., 1992).

Moreover, several of these studies have focused on patients in healthcare environments (e.g., Osmund, 1957; Sommer and Ross, 1958; Sommer, 1969; Holahan, 1972).

PHYSICAL MOVEMENT AND EXERCISE

Exercise is associated with a spectrum of significant physical health benefits, and clearly is a positive factor in reducing risk for mortality in the general population. Regular physical exercise, for example, is known to be very important for cardiovascular health, and appears to lower risk for certain types of cancer (e.g., Lee et al., 1992). However, the main concern here is with *psychological* or emotional benefits of exercise and related therapeutic effects on stress. As with social support and control, there is substantial scientific evidence that exercise reduces stress, including in patient populations. The research provides a strong foundation for proposing that healthcare gardens that promote exercise should improve psychological well-being and foster gains in other health outcomes.

While physical exercise often produces broad improvements in psychological well-being, several studies have found it to be especially beneficial in reducing depression. Both aerobic and nonaerobic strengthening exercise such as lifting weights are so effective in reducing depression that they are commonly used for helping clinically depressed patients (Greist, 1984). In fact it has been suggested that regular exercise is as effective as any form of psychotherapy in reducing depression (Brannon and Feist, 1997). The potential importance of exercise as a psychologically beneficial intervention in healthcare situations is underscored by the point emphasized earlier that depression is a widespread and serious problem among patients, especially for the elderly and those with chronic illness such as heart disease.

As an example of a study relevant to healthcare situations, Ruuskanen and Parketta (1994) found that higher levels of physical activity were associated with lower depression among elderly in nursing homes. Several investigators have reported that exercise significantly alleviates depression and produces other positive psychological changes in physically impaired older adults, such as patients with chronic obstructive lung disease (for survey of studies, see Emery and Blumenthal, 1991). Although beneficial effects are often greater when exercise is regular or strenuous, even comparatively mild exercise can be associated with significantly reduced depression. For example, a controlled study of moderately depressed elderly found that simply taking a twenty-minute walk three times a week reduced

Figure 2-6   Outdoor spaces at medical facilities can meet a variety of patient needs. Here we can see a woman relaxing and reading the newspaper— a means of psychological escape— while a gentleman is getting his exercise. (Homerton Hospital, London, UK, photo by Clare Cooper Marcus.)

depression symptoms (McNeil et al., 1991). Exercise likewise mitigates depression in younger groups, including adolescents and children, as illustrated by Koniak-Griffin's research (1994) on pregnant adolescents. Importantly, several studies have suggested that exercise also tends to lower anxiety effectively, as do other procedures such as meditation and biofeedback (Brannon and Feist, 1997). Finally, there is evidence that physical activity can broadly reduce stress in adolescents and children.

Design Considerations for Exercise

There are several ways in which designers can capitalize on gardens as effective vehicles for fostering exercise. Because gardens are widely perceived as much more pleasant settings than most healthcare interior ward and treatment spaces (Cooper Marcus and Barnes, 1995), they can be designed and sited to serve as positive trip destinations that motivate increased patient walking and wheelchair movement. Even a small atrium garden, or a lounge with an attractive window view of an outdoor garden, might foster exercise by stimulating corridor trips that would promote patient emotional restoration as well as physical rehabilitation. To encourage longer patient trips involving greater exertion (and perhaps more restoration), ease of way-finding should be given considerable attention in design decisions for gardens. In regions with long cold winters or hot humid summers, it would be possible to plan corridor sequences in larger facilities to enable lengthy indoor walks that provide a continuous series of exposures to indoor nature features, atrium gardens, and window views of exterior nature settings. For on-site users of gardens, opportunities for deriving restoration through mild exercise can be increased by design that facilitates patient accessibility and independence, and provides features such as walking loops. While strenuous exercise is not possible or medically advisable for many patients, there may be instances when consideration should be given to creating spaces in gardens that enable adult patients to engage in comparatively strenuous exercise (aerobic and non-aerobic). Indoor physical rehabilitation settings might be designed so that patients are exposed to large window views of gardens or other attractive outdoor nature areas.

Designers of healthcare gardens for children should give particular consideration to providing spaces for stress-reducing physical activities and play. (See Robin Moore's chapter in this volume. See also a recent discussion of play equipment and barrier-free design for children's outdoor play spaces in

Figure 2-7   Three children run off steam in this outpatient facility while their parents and staff can keep a watchful eye on them from two adjacent pediatric waiting rooms. (Kaiser Permanente Medical Center, Vallejo, CA, photo by Marni Barnes.)

Shepley et al., 1998.) At the other extreme in age, elderly in nursing homes and assisted residential settings may derive especially important long-term restoration benefits (reduced depression) from garden design approaches that facilitate walking and other mild exercise. (See Deborah McBride's chapter in this volume.) Do elderly in assisted living or nursing homes comply better with physician instructions to take frequent walks if they have access to landscaped grounds or a large garden for walking, rather than a street with noisy traffic or a windowless shopping mall?

NATURAL DISTRACTIONS

A positive distraction is an environmental feature or situation that promotes an improved emotional state in the perceiver, may block or reduce worrisome thoughts, and fosters beneficial changes in physiological systems such as lowered blood pressure and stress hormones (Ulrich, 1992a, 1992b). In other words, positive distractions can be thought of as environmental design elements that effectively promote restoration from stress in patients, visitors, and healthcare staff (Ulrich, 1992b). Types of positive distractions that have received the most attention in healthcare include: comedy or laughter (Cousins, 1983); companion animals (e.g., Friedman et al., 1980; Beck et al., 1986); art (Kaye and Blee, 1997); music (e.g., Moss, 1988; Caine, 1991); and nature. This section focuses on the last of these, nature, giving particular emphasis to restorative influences of viewing settings dominated by such nature as foliage, flowers, and water. As will be evident from the findings surveyed below, there is mounting evidence that viewing certain types of nature scenes can significantly reduce stress. Accordingly, it seems very likely that one major way in which gardens in healthcare facilities can improve medical outcomes is by providing visual exposure to nature.

Theoretical Perspectives: Why Nature Is Restorative

The intuitive belief that viewing vegetation, water, and other nature can ameliorate stress dates as far back as the earliest large cities in Persia, China, and Greece (Ulrich and Parsons, 1992; Ulrich et al., 1991b). This traditional idea is echoed by a number of contemporary theoretical arguments, as widely different as cultural and evolutionary positions, that converge in predicting that most nature scenes tend to reduce stress, whereas many settings lacking nature hinder recovery from stress (Ulrich et al., 1991b; Hartig and Evans, 1993). One important category of theories emphasizes *learning* as the major mechanism by which people acquire restorative and positive responses to nature (Ulrich and Parsons, 1992). It has often been argued that people learn to associate restoration with nature settings, for example, during vacations in rural areas. On the other hand, people probably acquire stressful associations with urban environments because of such phenomena as traffic congestion, work pressures, and crime. *Cultural* explanations likewise emphasize learning, proposing that people are taught or conditioned by their society to have positive associations with certain types of environmental features and perceive others as negative or unsettling (Ulrich and Parsons, 1992). Several writers have contended that contemporary Western and East Asian cultures condition their urban populations to revere nature and to associate cities with stress (Tuan, 1974). However, in the face of steadily mounting empirical evidence showing broad similarities across diversely different cultures in terms of positive responses to nature, cultural and other learning-based explanations increasingly appear inadequate. (For a review of cross-cultural studies on responses to nature scenes, see Ulrich, 1993).

Alternatively, proponents of *arousal* and *overload* theories have proposed that built environments are often taxing or excessively stimulating, and accordingly, work agains restoration, because of high levels of visual complexity, noise, intensity, and movement (Berlyne, 1971; Mehrabian and Russell, 1974). Nature settings dominated by vegetation or water usually have lower levels of complexity and other stimulating properties, and hence should be more restorative (Wohlwill, 1983; Ulrich et al., 1991b). Arousal or stimulation theory has been tested directly as an explanation of stress-reducing effects of nature, and found to have certain merits but also major shortcomings (Ulrich, 1981; Ulrich et al., 1991b).

In recent years, authors have increasingly proposed *evolutionary* theories, partly because these explanations are easy to reconcile with the growing evidence that there can be high agreement across cultures and different socioeconomic groups in positive responsiveness to nature. Most evolutionary explanations have in common the argument that, as a remnant of two or three million years of evolution, modern humans may have a partly genetic readiness to respond positively to types of nature content (such as vegetation or water) and environments that were favorable to well-being and survival for premodern people (e.g., Appleton, 1975; Orians, 1986; Kaplan and Kaplan, 1989; Ulrich, 1983). Although most evolutionary writings have focused on aesthetic preferences for nature, an evolutionary perspective can also plausibly explain why certain types of nature scenes should have restorative or stress-reducing effects across diverse groups of people.

An evolutionary theory developed in detail elsewhere (Ulrich, 1993; Ulrich et al., 1991b; Ulrich, 1983) contends that acquiring a partly genetic or biological capacity for a restorative response to certain nature settings held major survival-related advantages for early humans. This capacity would have fostered emotional well-being and health, and enhanced survival chances in several ways, such as by promoting faster and more complete recovery from the negative stress effects of flight-or-fight responses that were essential for dealing with demanding situations and threats. A basic proposition is that the advantages of restoration were so critical for survival as to favor the selection of individuals with a biologically prepared disposition to quickly acquire and persistently retain restorative responses to certain nature settings. This conceptual perspective suggests that the several health-related benefits of restoration from stress should include, for instance, a shift toward a more positive emotional state, alleviation of deleterious effects of physiological mobilization (reduced blood pressure, reduced levels of circulating stress hormones, enhanced immune function), the recharging of energy, and gains in cognitive performance (Ulrich, 1993). It also follows from this theory that restorative responses to nature should occur fairly rapidly—usually within a few minutes rather than over several hours (Ulrich et al., 1991b). A further implication is that humans may have a biologically prepared disposition that motivates them, following a stressful experience, to seek out, approach, and spend time in nature settings with restorative properties.

This perspective also predicts that modern humans, as a partly genetic remnant of evolution, have a biologically pre-pared capacity for acquiring and retaining restorative responses to certain nature settings and content (vegetation, flowers, water), but have no such disposition for most built environments and their materials (Ulrich, 1993). Finally, these evolutionary arguments suggest that nature settings will tend to be especially effective in promoting restoration if they pos-sess the following characteristics: verdant plants, calm or slowly moving water, some spatial openness, parklike or savan-nalike properties (scattered trees, grassy understory), unthreat-ening wildlife (e.g., birds), and a sense of security or low risk (Ulrich, 1993).

Restorative Effects of Nature in Parks and Gardens

It will be recalled that a large body of research on nonpatient users of parks has found that restoration from stress is per-ceived as the most consistently important benefit. Recreation experiences are often complex and involve a number of coping mechanisms and types of experiences that ameliorate stress—including social support, physical exercise, and temporary escape. There are also indications in these studies that a major part of the restoration benefit often stems from simply viewing nature. In this regard, some urban park studies have found strong associations between users' restoration ratings and cer-tain nature properties of an environment, including vegetation, water, and savannalike qualities such as scattered trees, grass, and spatial openness (Ulrich and Addoms, 1981; Grahn, 1991). Schroeder (1986, 1991) found that the moods most commonly reported by users of a large arboretum near Chicago were serenity, tranquillity, and peacefulness, and such feelings were most often linked to areas having water, lush vegetation, large trees, flowers, and openness. In research using a different method, Francis and Cooper Marcus (1991) asked a sample of university students in California to identify settings they sought out during times when they felt stressed or depressed. A consid-erable majority of the individuals (75 percent) identified out-door nature settings that were rural or urban nature settings (e.g., wooded urban parks, places next to water features such as lakes or the ocean). The selection of nature dominated settings was corroborated by Barnes (1994) in a study of working adults living in urban and suburban areas.

A limited amount of park research has identified stress reducing effects of nature while controlling for other potentially restorative variables such as exercise and temporary escape. Hartig and his associates first produced stress in individuals with a demanding cognitive task, and then measured recovery effects of either (1) a forty-minute walk in an urban fringe nature area, (2) a forty-minute walk in an attractive urban area, or (3) reading magazines or listening to music for forty minutes (Hartig et al., 1991). Findings suggested that persons assigned to the walk in nature reported more positively toned emotional states than individuals assigned to the other two activities.

In their study of garden users in four healthcare facilities, Cooper Marcus and Barnes (1995, p. 5) found that the most frequently mentioned positive garden qualities were visual nature elements, especially trees, greenery, flowers, and water. Study participants strongly associated these nature features with beneficial influences on their moods—principally enhanced feelings of relaxation and restoration. In addition to prominently naming vegetation and water as promoting positive emotions, many respondents also mentioned other types of nature elements and qualities, including birds and squirrels, sunshine, and fragrances.

Restorative Effects of Viewing Nature: Findings for Non-Patient Groups

Findings from several studies on nonpatient groups such as university students suggest that simply looking at everyday nature, as compared to built scenes that lack nature, is significantly more effective in promoting restoration from stress. One early study focused on students who were experiencing mild stress because of a final course exam (Ulrich, 1979). A self-ratings questionnaire was used to assess restorative influences of viewing either a diverse slide sample of unblighted built settings lacking nature, or slides of undistinguished nature settings dominated by green vegetation. Results suggested that the nature views fostered greater psychological restoration as indicated by larger reductions in negative feelings such as fear and anger/aggression and much higher levels of positive feelings. Also, the scenes with vegetation sustained interest and attention more effectively than did the urban scenes without nature (Ulrich, 1979). Honeyman (1992) replicated this study but added a third stress recovery condition consisting of a sample of urban scenes *with* prominent vegetation. Her findings suggested that greater restoration was produced by the urban envi-

Figure 2-8   Example of a nature setting (urban park) found effective in promoting stress recovery (from Ulrich et al., 1991b).

ronments with vegetation than by the urban scenes without nature. In a study performed in Sweden using *unstressed* students (Ulrich, 1981), self-ratings data similarly supported the conclusion that everyday nature scenes promoted more positive emotional states and more effectively sustained attention than did townscapes with attractive buildings but without nature. In the same study, self-ratings results were broadly concordant with findings obtained by recording brain electrical activity (EEG) in the alpha frequency range (Ulrich, 1981). The brainwave recordings suggested that the undistinguished nature settings were significantly more effective than the built scenes in eliciting a relaxed yet wakeful state.

Nakamura and Fujii performed studies in Japan (1990, 1992) that also recorded brainwave activity as unstressed subjects viewed either vegetation or human-made objects. In an innovative experiment, they recorded the electroencephalogram (EEG) in a field setting while subjects viewed either a hedge of greenery, a concrete fence with dimensions similar to the hedge, or a condition consisting of part hedge and part fence (1992). Results showed that the ratio of alpha activity to beta activity was high when persons viewed the hedge; the ratio reversed, however, when the same persons looked at the concrete fence. These EEG findings were interpreted as suggesting that the hedge elicited relaxation or reduced stress whereas the concrete fence had stressful influences. In another intriguing experiment, Nakamura and Fujii (1990) analyzed the quantity of alpha rhythm recorded as unstressed subjects viewed: two types of potted plants, each with and without flowers (*Pelargonium* and *Begonia*); the same pots without plants; or a cylinder similar to the pots. Alpha quantities were highest when persons observed plants with flowers, second highest when subjects viewed plants without flowers, and lowest when looking at pots without plants (Nakamura and Fujii, 1990). (For a comprehensive survey of Japanese studies on people-plant relationships, see Matsuo, 1996.)

Hartig and his associates in Sweden (Hartig et al., 1996) performed a sequence of two experiments on psychological restoration; in one study participants were exposed to a stressor, in the other study subjects were not stressed. Participants in both experiments were assigned to a slide-simulated "walk" that progressed through either a nature area dominated by vegetation or urban streets lacking nature. Findings were broadly consonant with results obtained in the studies mentioned above—that is, in both experiments the visual nature "walk" engendered more positive emotional self-ratings than did viewing built environments. Further, the findings added to evidence that restorative emotional influences of viewing nature occur rather quickly—that is, can be detected within the space of a few minutes (Hartig et al., 1996).

Other studies have examined stress-reducing influences of nature using physiological measures as well as emotional self-reports. One controlled experiment monitored a battery of physiological responses in 120 stressed nonpatient subjects who were randomly assigned to a recovery period consisting of videotapes of one of six different nature settings (vegetation and/or water) or built settings lacking nature (Ulrich et al., 1991b). Results indicated that persons recovered from stress much faster and more completely when exposed to the nature settings. Greater recovery during the nature exposures was evident in lower blood pressure, muscle tension, and skin conductance. These physiological results showed that nature produced significant restoration by all physiological measure within only three to four minutes. (See Figures 2-8 to 2-10.) Further, affective self-ratings suggested that the nature settings produced significantly more restoration in the psychological component of stress, as evident in much higher levels of positive feelings and lower levels of fear and anger (Ulrich et al., 1991b).

In other research using physiological methods, Hartig (1993) studied a sample of Los Angeles area residents who were experiencing stress either because they had just driven in city traffic or had performed attentionally demanding tests. Findings obtained from blood pressure recordings and emotional self-reports converged in suggesting that recovery was greater—and occurred within only a few minutes—if persons were looking at a nature setting dominated by vegetation rather

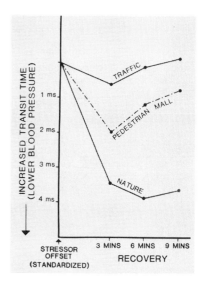

Figure 2-9 Systolic blood pressure (via pulse transit time) during recovery from stress in subjects exposed to nature settings (see Figure 2-8) or urban settings lacking nature (from Ulrich et al., 1991b).

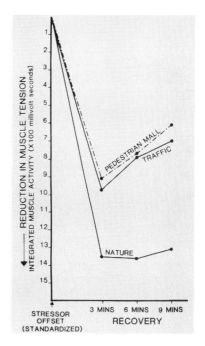

Figure 2-10 Muscle tension during recovery from stress in subjects exposed to nature settings (see Figure 2-8) or urban settings lacking nature (from Ulrich et al., 1991b).

that a built environment without nature. Hartig's study also included groups of unstressed participants who were similarly found to derive greater physiological and emotional restoration from contact with nature. While nature produced significant restoration in both stressed and unstressed persons, it is noteworthy that the greatest therapeutic effects in terms of positive physiological and emotional changes were found for people who initially were stressed (Hartig, 1993). Using methods similar to Ulrich et al. (1991b), Parsons obtained a pattern of physiological and self-report findings indicating that videotapes of preferred landscapes, some containing water, promoted greater stress recovery than less preferred outdoor settings (Parsons, 1991b).

In an extension of this line of research, a recent controlled experiment compared restoration in stressed subjects exposed to simulated auto drives (videotapes displayed on a 6 foot × 4 foot screen) that were comparable except for having either vegetation-dominated or built-dominated roadside environments (Parsons et al., in press, 1998). One hundred sixty subjects were randomly assigned to one of four nature-dominated or built-dominated ten-minute auto drives. Immediately following the drives, subjects arrived at "work" and were assigned stressful tasks consisting of mental arithmetic. Findings from physiological measures such as blood pressure suggested that built-dominated drives lacking nature, compared to nature/vegetation-dominated drives, slowed and hindered stress recovery during the auto "trips." Moreover, while performing the tasks persons were much less stressed (skin conductance, $p < .001$) if their earlier "drive" to work had been through a nature-dominated rather than built-dominated environment (Parsons et al., in press, 1998). In this study the effectiveness of nature in fostering stress reduction was impressive, considering that the drives lasted only a few minutes, the nature or built roadside content was visible to subjects only in narrow portions in the right and left peripheries of the "windshield," and the central portion of the windshield view in all drives was dominated by road surface and traffic. (For more detailed discussions of physiological research methods and findings concerning human responses to nature, see Ulrich et al., 1991a; Parsons et al., 1994; Parsons and Hartig, in press, 1999).

Other evidence suggesting restorative influences of visual contacts with nature has come from research on workplaces. For example, a recent office study using an experimental design found subjects' moods were more positive when plants were present than when not present (Larsen et al., 1998). A European study of 100 white-collar and blue-collar employees in diversely different work settings suggested that window views of nature appeared to buffer aspects of job stress and pos-

Figure 2-11 Many hospital staff can work an entire shift and never see the light of day. This staff break room has no views, nor is the lighting sufficient to support potted plants. (Photo by Clare Cooper Marcus.)

itively affect self-reports of general well-being (Leather et al., 1998). R. Kaplan (1993) found that office workers with a window view of nature reported feeling less frustrated and had higher life satisfaction and overall health.

While several studies have investigated stress reducing influences of settings containing water or comparatively large vegetation such as trees and shrubs, little work has focused on the role of flowers in fostering restoration. One of the few studies on flowers has been conducted by Adachi and colleagues (1998), who obtained affective self-ratings from unstressed subjects assigned to one of three room decor conditions: with floral displays (sweet peas), with green foliage plants, or without any floral or foliage displays. Findings suggested that the room condition with flowers had the most positive emotional influences, as indicated by significantly higher levels of feelings such as "relaxed," "composed," and "agreeable," and lower scores for feeling "discouraged" (Adachi et al., 1998).

Restorative Effects of Viewing Nature in Healthcare Settings

It seems likely that the restorative benefits of viewing nature are greatest when persons experience high levels of stress, such as those who are obliged to spend time confined in hospitals or other types of healthcare facilities (Ulrich, 1979). Evidence implying that nature can have important restorative influences across a diverse range of healthcare contexts comes from a recent interview study of groups of former patients in ambulatory care, acute care, and long-term care (MacRae, 1997). MacRae interviewed former patients living in different regions of the United States who varied in age and diagnosis category.

Patients' responses indicated that their most widely shared preference regarding the physical environment of healthcare facilities was for access to nature—including gardens, outdoor sitting and walking areas, balconies, views from patient rooms, indoor plants, and pictures of nature. Another study used a questionnaire to investigate preferences of patients who were severely disabled by accidents or illness and were bedridden (Verderber, 1986). These findings showed that patients assigned especially high preference to having a hospital window view of nature.

Findings surveyed earlier from studies of stressed non-patient groups suggested that even short-term visual contacts with nature—lasting only a few minutes—can produce significant restoration. This finding has similarly emerged in a few studies where stressed patients in healthcare facilities were exposed for short periods, such as five to fifteen minutes, to views of nature. In an early experiment, Katcher and his colleagues examined restoration from anxiety in groups of patients waiting to undergo dental surgery (Katcher et al., 1984). They found that visual contemplation of an aquarium with fish reduced anxiety and discomfort, and increased scores for patient compliance during surgery. Coss (1990) used an experimental design to evaluate the effects of viewing ceiling mounted nature posters on acutely stressed patients lying on gurneys waiting to undergo surgery. His findings suggested that patients assigned to "serene" arousal-reducing nature scenes had lower blood pressure than patients assigned to either stimulating, arousal-increasing outdoor scenes (e.g., a sailboarder leaning into the wind) or to a control condition of no picture. A pilot study by Heerwagen and Orians obtained heart rate data and affective self-ratings to assess the restorative effects of a nature scene on anxious patients in a dental fears clinic (Heerwagen, 1990). Both the heart rate and self-report data suggested that patients felt less stressed on days when a large nature mural was hung on a wall of the clinic waiting room, in contrast to days when the wall was blank.

In the United Kingdom, Stiles (1995) used questionnaire and observation methods to study hospital patients seated in a large waiting room during two different environmental conditions—with interior plants versus without plants. On days when the waiting area contained plants, patients rated the room as more restorative and pleasant—as indicated, for example, by substantially higher ratings for "relaxed," "unstressful," "welcoming," and "cheerful." Also, patients chose a different pattern of seating location when plants were present; that is, they positioned themselves where they could look at plants (Stiles, 1995).

Effects of Viewing Nature on Health Outcomes

The studies described above strongly suggest that even a few minutes of visual exposure to nature can significantly reduce patient stress. It is reasonable to expect that longer duration exposures to nature in healthcare facilities (several hours, a few days) could have comparatively persistent and perhaps larger restorative effects on emotional, physiological, and behavioral components of stress. If so, these stress mitigating effects in time probably would be associated with improvements in a number of health outcomes. In this regard, findings from a few studies of hospital patients suggest that prolonged exposure to window views and other visual nature can have important positive influences on health outcomes (Ulrich, 1984). One study of patients recovering from gall bladder surgery evaluated whether assignment to a room with a window view of nature might improve postsurgical outcomes. Data on recovery outcomes were obtained for matched pairs of patients who were similar for variables that could affect recovery such as age, weight, tobacco use, and previous medical history. The patients were assigned in a random manner to rooms that were identical except for window view: one member of each patient pair had a window overlooking a small grove of trees, whereas the other's window looked out on a brick building wall. Patients with the nature window view had shorter postsurgical hospital stays, tended to have fewer minor postsurgical complications such as persistent headache or nausea, and received far fewer negative evaluative comments in nurses' notes (e.g., "patient is upset," "needs much encouragement to do breathing exercises"). Moreover, the wall view patients required far more injections of potent narcotic pain drugs (e.g., synthetic morphine equiva-

Figure 2-13   Hospital window view of trees (from Ulrich, 1984).

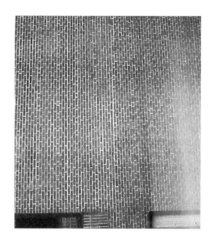

Figure 2-12   Hospital window view of brick wall (from Ulrich, 1984).

Figure 2-14   Pain drug intake of patients with brick wall window view versus tree view (from Ulrich, 1984).

Comparison of Analgesic Doses per Patient for Wall-View and Tree-View Groups					
	Number of Doses of Pain Drugs				
	Days 0-1		Days 2-5		Days 6-7	
Analgesic Strength	Wall Group	Tree Group	Wall Group	Tree Group	Wall Group	Tree Group
Strong	2.56	2.40	2.48	0.96	0.22	0.17
Moderate	4.00	5.00	3.65	1.74	0.35	0.17
Weak	0.23	0.30	2.57	5.39	0.96	1.09

lents), while the nature group took more oral doses of weak pain drugs such as acetaminophen (Ulrich, 1984).

Additional evidence of the importance of a nature window view comes from a case study based on participant observation of a cancer patient (Baird and Bell, 1995). The patient—a doctoral student in psychology—was hospitalized several times in various types of medical units as her disease became terminal. On every admission she expressed a clear and adamant preference for a room with a nature view over rooms with little view at all. On one occasion, upon initial admission to a bone marrow transplant unit, "the only view was of brick walls and neighboring buildings. After about three weeks, a room on the unit with a more natural view became available, and Carol chose to move to it immediately. Her affective state improved quickly, and optimism replaced despair" (Baird and Bell, 1995, p. 849). During the last stages of her illness, the patient evidenced strong positive attachment to a nature window with mountains and, ironically, a distant cemetery. In the patient's last weeks, she chose as her final resting place a plot in the cemetery in the nature area she could view through the window of her hospital room (Baird and Bell, 1995).

These findings are consistent with the notion that visual settings with prominent nature tend to reduce stress and improve outcomes in patients groups that include those experiencing stress accompanied by feelings of anxiety (fear, tension). Some investigators, however (Ulrich, 1984), have pointed out that the findings cannot be extended to all patient groups, such as many long-term patients in nursing homes, who may suffer from boredom or low arousal rather than from the anxiety and excessive arousal typically associated, for instance, with surgeries. Perhaps for certain patients a lively street setting with people might be more therapeutic than many serene arousal-reducing nature scenes (Ulrich, 1984). Limited empirical support for this interpretation has emerged from research by O'Connor et al. (1991) that focused on nursing home patients. They found that during the first month following admittance to a nursing home, patients with a window view of people had somewhat more favorable health outcomes than patients with a nature view lacking people. The pattern of findings changed, however, after the initial month—specifically, data for longer time periods suggested that the nature window view was associated with more positive outcomes than the view of people (O'Connor et al., 1991).

In other research on health outcomes, Ulrich and colleagues (1993) used an experimental design to investigate whether exposure to simulated nature views in intensive care units improved recovery indicators in heart surgery patients. At Uppsala University Hospital in Sweden, 160 patients who had undergone heart surgery were assigned to one of six visual stimulation conditions: two were nature pictures (either an open view with water and trees or an enclosed forest scene); two were abstract pictures (dominated by either rectilinear or curvilinear forms); and two were control conditions (a white panel, or no picture or panel). The pictures were large color photos mounted above the foot of the bed in the patient's line of vision. Results suggested that patients exposed to the open view of water and trees experienced significantly less postoperative anxiety than patients assigned to the other pictures and the control conditions. Moreover, persons with the water/trees view required fewer doses of strong, intravenous pain drugs. The enclosed forest setting with shadowed areas, however, did not reduce anxiety compared to the control conditions. Unexpectedly, the rectilinear abstract picture was associated with higher anxiety than the control conditions, indicating that psychologically inappropriate visual stimulation can some-times elevate rather than reduce anxiety in acutely stressed patients (Ulrich et al., 1993).

A study of patients suffering intense pain because of severe burns evaluated the therapeutic effects of an environmental dis-traction consisting of a videotape of scenic nature (e.g., forest, flowers, ocean, waterfalls) accompanied by a music soundtrack (Miller et al., 1992). The investigators found that use of the videotape during burn dressing changes benefitted the patients by significantly reducing both anxiety and pain intensity. The nature videotape almost certainly contributed to these improved outcomes, but the precise role of the nature scenery is unclear because of possible influences of the music soundtrack. Nonetheless, these findings bolster evidence from studies of sur-gical patients (Ulrich, 1984; Ulrich et al., 1993), suggesting that visual exposure to nature can mitigate the perceived intensity of pain and reduce patient needs for potent analgesic doses.

The possibility that exposure to nature can improve out-comes even in patients with late stage dementia, including Alzheimer's disease, has been supported by findings from a quasi-experimental study that examined levels of agitated aggressive behavior triggered by a shower bath (Whall et al., 1997). One patient group was assigned to being bathed in a nature room condition with recorded nature sounds (e.g., birds, babbling brooks) and large color pictures. A comparison group of patients received their baths in the same room without nature sounds and pictures. Ratings by trained observers revealed that the nature condition significantly reduced agitation.

NEGATIVE DISTRACTIONS IN GARDENS

In sharp contrast to nature and other positive distractions, negative distractions in gardens can be considered a subset of stressors that encompass unpleasant or disliked environmental elements or stimuli (visual, auditory, or olfactory). Negative environmental distractions are typically intrusive and demand attention, are often imposed on patients without possibility of personal choice or control, are appraised as stressful, and promote detrimental changes in emotional states and physiological systems (Ulrich, 1992a). Put simply, negative distractions tend to worsen rather than mitigate the stress experienced by patients, visitors, and staff in healthcare facilities. It is important for garden designers to be sensitive and cautious regarding potential negative distractions, because the presence of such distractions in a healthcare garden can reduce or even negate restorative benefits. As will be evident from findings surveyed in this section, there is preliminary evidence that negative distractions imposed on patients may, in certain scenarios, significantly worsen health outcomes.

Urban Noise

Intrusive human-made noises may frequently be negative distractions in healthcare facility gardens. Cooper Marcus and Barnes (1995) found that users of healthcare gardens reported they reacted negatively to incongruent mechanical sounds, for instance, from air conditioners or street traffic. This finding is paralleled by results obtained in research on nonpatient groups concerning the impacts of urban sounds on affective responses to nature scenes (Anderson et al., 1983). This work has shown that the presence of incongruent urban sounds (e.g., traffic, overhead jets) in nature settings such as city parks can have strong negative effects on users' evaluations. Barnes (1994) found that nonpatient subjects seeking solace in outdoor urban settings reported noises (traffic, other voices) as the primary "drawback" in the environment, disrupting their healing process. On the other hand, the presence of congruent or fitting nature sounds (e.g., birds, brook, breeze) often positively influences evaluations and affective responses.

A recent study by Mace and colleagues (1999, in press) is noteworthy because it indicates that restorative psychological effects of viewing nature can be substantially diminished or even negated by low-level intrusive human-made noises. In a laboratory experiment that approximated visual and auditory conditions at Grand Canyon National Park, nonpatient subjects were exposed to nature scenes with three background sound conditions: nature sounds (e.g., birds, brooks, breeze, natural quiet); background noise from a sightseeing helicopter at 40 dB; or helicopter noise at 80 dB. (By comparison, verbal conversation occurs in the 60–65 dB range.) Mace et al. (1999, in press) reported that even low level helicopter noise (40 dB) produced highly significant negative affective, aesthetic, and cognitive effects, including on self-ratings relating to restoration. Findings from these studies together imply that designers should attempt either to exclude intrusive urban sounds from healthcare gardens or mask them with nature sounds such as water. The presence of positive auditory qualities in healthcare gardens (e.g., quiet, bird sounds, breezes, moving water) may increase effectiveness in promoting restoration.

Smoking

As might be expected, there is some evidence indicating that *smoking* is an aversive negative distraction for many users of healthcare gardens (Cooper Marcus and Barnes, 1995). The fact that smoking increasingly is banned internationally within healthcare facility interiors may be putting smokers under more pressure to seek out gardens and other nearby outdoor spaces. Physicians are reluctant to ask certain patients, especially those with terminal illness, to stop smoking because the difficulty of giving up cigarettes would add to their stress. Shepley's (in press, 1998) post-occupancy study of an AIDS facility is useful for designers because it identified problems associated with a patio garden that served as a pleasant outdoor space immediately accessible to both smoking and nonsmoking patients. Her findings indicated that areas where smokers concentrated included just outside the entrance door to the patio garden, and under a tent that provided the only location sheltered from rain and direct sun. Nonsmoking patients who wished to use the space had to move through a cloud of smoke as they entered, only to find that the single sheltered area with seating also was occupied by smokers. Nonsmokers accordingly tended to avoid the space, leading Shepley to underscore the importance for designers of providing separate outdoor areas for smokers and nonsmokers (in press, 1998).

Sunlight: A Positive and Sometimes Negative Distraction

Sunlight can have distinctly healthful influences on many patients, but negative effects on others. Across a variety of settings (healthcare facilities, workplaces, classrooms), studies have found that persons prefer window views of nature settings illuminated by sunlight or clear lighting conditions, rather than cloudy conditions (e.g., Kim, 1997). Patients may respond negatively, however, if their windows are exposed directly to the sun, creating bright glare patches in room interiors (Boubekri et al., 1991).

Cooper Marcus and Barnes (1995) reported that at least 25 percent of the persons they interviewed in healthcare facility gardens mentioned sunlight as a garden quality that helped foster improved mood and restoration. Importantly, this notion has also received support from medical studies. A controlled study in Canada, for example, found that patients hospitalized for severe depression had shorter hospital stays if they were assigned to a sunny rather than a "dull" room (Beauchemin and Hays, 1996). It has been speculated that such depression-reducing influences of sunshine underlie the rather dramatic finding from another Canadian study that mortality of myocardial infarction (heart attack) patients was significantly lower if they were assigned to sunny intensive care rooms rather than to dull north-facing rooms in the same unit (Beauchemin and Hays, 1998). Additionally, an important healthful effect of outdoor gardens is implied by the fact that sunlight plays a key role in enabling humans to benefit from intake of vitamin D. Lamber-Allardt (1984), for example, found that serum vitamin D concentrations in groups of elderly were positively related to individuals' levels of outdoor exposure; serum vitamin D concentrations were low and inadequate in elderly with the lowest outdoor exposure, and highest and most adequate in those who spent the most time outdoors (Lamberg-Allardt, 1984). Because gardens are widely perceived as especially pleasant and preferred settings, they may entice many people in nursing homes and other healthcare facilities to spend additional time outdoors, resulting in more exposure to sunlight and hence improvements in emotional well-being and health.

These and other clearly beneficial effects notwithstanding, garden design approaches that emphasize opportunities for direct sun exposure but provide little or no access to shade should usually be avoided. Designers must keep in mind that many patients' medical conditions or treatments, including several commonly prescribed drugs (tetracycline, for example), markedly alter the body's response to sunshine, and often make patients acutely and negatively sensitive to direct sun exposure. This medical reality underscores the importance of providing adequate shaded areas in gardens for healthcare facilities, especially for sites in lower latitudes or higher elevations.

Differences in Designer Versus Patient Aesthetic Preferences

Some designers may unwittingly create gardens containing negative distractions if they focus exclusively on design qualities that please their personal aesthetic tastes. To explain why this effect can result, it is pertinent to mention that several studies conducted in different countries have found that the aesthetic preferences of artists and designers often vary widely from those of their clients or the general public (e.g., Devlin and Nasar, 1989; Melamid and Komar, 1994). Further, the types and styles of environmental design and art that many designers and artists personally prefer can be those that elicit distinctly negative reactions from the public. Accordingly, if a designer creates a garden to suit his or her personal tastes, and fails to consult or empathize sufficiently with patients, the visual outcome may be disliked by the patients and other potential users. To impose such a visual setting on patients without possibility of their personal choice or control would be to risk burdening them with a stressor.

The potential for designers and artists to miss the mark of patient and public tastes when selecting art for garden settings is implied by research on preferences for paintings and sculpture. Several investigators have reported that the majority of adults (85 to 90 percent) in North America, Europe, and Asia prefer realistic or representational art depicting nature (e.g., Winston and Cupchik, 1992; Melamid and Komar, 1994; Kettlewell, 1988). A considerable number of adults across different countries report that they dislike abstract paintings and sculpture. Importantly, the majority of the general public prefers art that produces positive feelings. For example, a study of a random national sample of Americans found that most adults strongly agreed with the statement: "I only want to look at art that makes me happy" (Melamid and Komar, 1994). The same study revealed that 77 percent of the public agreed that "art should be relaxing to look at." These findings are consonant with those from research on patient preferences for visual art in healthcare settings. Carpman and Grant (1993) showed a diverse collection of 71 color pictures to 300 randomly selected inpatients at the University of Michigan Medical Center, and asked patients to rate each picture for how much they would like to have it hanging in their hospital room. Results indicated that the patients consistently preferred representational nature scenes and disliked abstract art.

The art preferences of artists, designers, and persons seriously interested in art are, however, vastly different from those

Figure 2-15 A sculpture that might be considered interesting and attractive to a healthy individual may have a negative effect on others who are acutely stressed or mentally ill. This piece is installed outside the main entry of a locked psychiatric facility and has been perceived as a fish leaping from the upper floors, to its death. (Photo by Marni Barnes.)

of the general public. Most artists and experienced art viewers report liking visual art that is "provocative" or provides "challenge" (e.g., Winston and Cupchik, 1992). In direct contrast to the public, artists and experienced viewers reject the notion that art should make them feel happy or relaxed (Winston and Cupchik, 1992). Further, most artists and designers report liking a wide range of art styles, abstract as well as representational.

Ambiguous and Abstract Garden Features as Negative Distractions

Research advances in the behavioral sciences on the influences of emotional states on perception and cognition raise the possibility that acute emotional stress may make many patients vulnerable to detrimental, stressful reactions to certain abstract or ambiguous visual elements in art and design. Much evidence has accumulated during the last decade showing that persons' emotional states affect virtually all aspects of their thinking and remembering. One influential concept to emerge from this work is that of emotional congruence—the notion that when an individual is presented with an array of environmental information or stimuli, the subset that matches the emotional state of the perceiver will most likely be the focus of attention (Niedenthal et al., 1994). Related theory holds that a person encountering a designed environment will more readily and efficiently process, recognize, and remember information congruent with his/her emotional state (e.g., Bower, 1981; Singer and Salovey, 1988). Emotional congruence thus unifies internal emotional states with external stimuli; evidence suggests that fear promotes processing of the fearful, sadness the sad, and happiness the happy. Further, studies have suggested that the perceiver's emotional state can enhance recall of emotionally congruent memories. Sad feelings accordingly may tend to cue sad memories, whereas happy feelings cue positively toned associations and memories (e.g., Isen, 1987).

An important prediction of this theory and research is that the perception of ambiguous environmental stimuli might be biased such that "...the emotion-congruent elements of the stimulus are visually enhanced, or the elements are organized or combined in a manner that is congruent with the perceiver's emotional state" (Niedenthal et al., 1994, p. 109). Accordingly, designers who wish to create supportive gardens for healthcare facilities should be cognizant of a stark incongruity. The positive emotional state that the creation of art may engender within the artist and the highly negative state wrought by illness and stress upon their captive audience, may result in the same garden or work of art being experienced quite differently. The difference between designer/artist and viewer/user in a medical setting will tend to diverge even further as the level of ambiguity in the design increases.

Evidence of Negative Patient Responses to Ambiguity

A preliminary study of the influences of wall mounted pictures on psychiatric patients yielded insights concerning responses to ambiguous or abstract visual content compared to representational nature scenes (Ulrich, 1986b). Patients in a Swedish hospital were studied in a ward decorated with paintings and prints reflecting a wide variety of subject matter and styles. Interview responses suggested that patients responded positively to representational pictures dominated by nature (a nature landscape, a vase of flowers), but responded negatively to pictures having either ambiguous or unintelligibly abstract content. Figure 2-16 shows an example of an ambiguous print that could be perceived and interpreted in different ways. The print elicited negative interview responses from patients, whereas most of the staff gave positive reactions. Perhaps the negative emotional states of many of the patients (several were clinically anxious or depressed) biased their processing and associations in negative ways congruent with their feelings. The emotional states of the staff probably were comparatively positive, and accordingly they may have processed and interpreted the ambiguous picture content in an affectively equivalent positive manner.

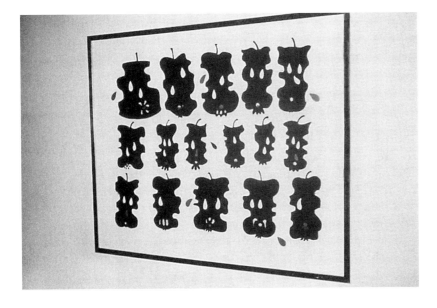

Figure 2-16   Ambiguous art print that elicited different responses from staff and patients (Ulrich, 1986b). Examples of staff comments:

"I think it's fun. Whimsical. I'd like to have it in my home."

"Funny little talking apple cores. Maybe some are sweating."

Examples of patient comments:

"Charred skulls. Drops of blood are flying."

"Wounded people. They're in pain and crying out."

Figure 2-17 An abstract print that was physically attacked by a patient (from Ulrich, 1986b).

The same study (Ulrich, 1986b) analyzed records kept during a fifteen-year period regarding incidents recorded by staff of negative patient responses and behaviors directed to the pictures. These events included unsolicited strong complaints to the staff and incidents when patients physically attacked pictures (such as tearing the picture from the wall and throwing it on the floor). The latter were dramatic actions given that these patients were considered unaggressive. (The ward was not locked.) Records indicated that seven paintings and prints had been targets of one or more attacks each, and all had ambiguous or abstract content. (See Figure 2-17.)

In the context of possible negative patient influences of visual ambiguity, it is pertinent to recall findings from a study that examined the effects of nature and abstract pictures on heart surgery recovery outcomes (Ulrich et al., 1993). Results suggested that patients exposed in intensive care units to a representational landscape photograph of water and trees had lower anxiety and required fewer doses of strong pain killers than patients assigned to control groups with no picture. By contrast, a highly ambiguous picture dominated by abstract rectilinear forms was associated with higher anxiety than measured for the control conditions. Moreover, several patients reported strongly negative affective reactions to the ambiguous rectilinear picture, necessitating its early removal. The heart surgery patients had no history of serious psychological disturbance, but similarly to the psychiatric patients they interpreted the ambiguous abstract picture in negative and sometimes frightening ways that appeared congruent with their negative affective states.

These findings from healthcare studies, together with the theory and research on emotional congruence surveyed earlier, influenced the development of the conceptual model depicted in Figure 2-18. The figure portrays hypothesized influences on stressed patients of exposures to "aesthetic" visual displays ranging from low to high in ambiguity (that is, that vary from being readily and clearly identifiable to highly uncertain or indeterminate). Figure 2-18 reflects the assumption that the content of a given visual display of nature, if presented in a realistic and clearly identifiable manner, will have restorative influences on both mildly and acutely stressed patients. (A realistic display of built content, however, may not be restorative.) Consistent with an emotional congruence perspective, Figure 2-18 predicts that as the ambiguity of stimuli or designed features increase, patients will increasingly process and respond in a stressful manner that matches their negatively toned emotional condition. This framework predicts that if a potentially restorative and positive stimulus, such as a verdant nature scene with water, is displayed unambiguously to a stressed patient, the scene will tend to have restorative influences even on acutely stressed patients.

This conceptual perspective may be useful in explaining certain isolated instances when ambiguous design features in healthcare gardens have unexpectedly elicited negative rather

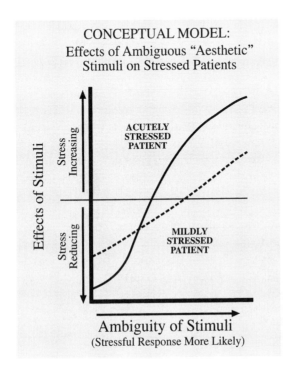

Figure 2-18 Conceptual model of effects of ambiguous environmental stimuli on stressed patients.

Figure 2-19 The Bird Garden, removed after negative patient comments.

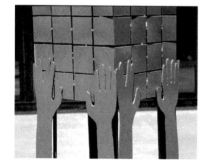

Figure 2-20 Closeup of one of the Bird Garden totems, that a patient interpreted as hands reaching out of a grave.

than restorative responses from patients. One documented example is that of a "Bird Garden" created to provide a therapeutic window view for cancer patients hospitalized in a leading medical center. Located on a rooftop courtyard surrounded by taller units housing patients, the Bird Garden contained ceramic tile and metal birds executed in representational and abstract styles. Other prominent features included several metal "totem" sculptures dominated by rectilinear or geometric abstract forms. Although termed a "garden," the space contained no greenery, flowers, or water. (See Figure 2-19.) The design for the Bird Garden was approved after a careful review process that included input from artists, the hospital's design department, nursing staff, and administrators (McLaughlin et al., 1996). It is clear from documentation concerning the process that the goal of all persons involved was to create a soothing, therapeutic visual distraction for patients.

Shortly after the Bird Garden was installed, anecdotal concerns were raised by nursing personnel about negative reactions by some patients (McLaughlin et al., 1996). As a result of these concerns, a survey was conducted to make possible an objective assessment of patient responses to the art installation. Questionnaire-based interviews were conducted with forty-six patients whose rooms overlooked the Bird Garden, and the nursing staff on the patient care units were surveyed. Twenty-two percent of the patients reported having an overall negative affective reaction to the Bird Garden (Hefferman et al., 1995). Open-ended comments indicated that many patients found the art installation ambiguous (for example, "Doesn't make any sense," or "What is it?"). This ambiguity may explain why some of the cancer patients responded in strongly negative ways that appeared affectively congruent with their internal duress. Although most patients gave positive or neutral responses about the Bird Garden, administrators deemed the percentage of negative reactions unacceptably high, and the decision was made to remove the installation. Consistent with the finest traditions and values of medical science, the arts program at the medical center has forthrightly disseminated information about the Bird Garden episode, thus enabling many other healthcare designers and administrators to gain important new knowledge.

CONCLUSION

This chapter has emphasized findings and theory derived from the types of scientific-experimental methods that are considered sound and persuasive by medical researchers and healthcare administrators. The survey has omitted the large literature on healing gardens based on intuition, anecdote, or informal methods that cannot be replicated or falsified. Particular emphasis has been given to the effects that passive contacts with healthcare gardens have on patient stress and other medical outcomes. The concentration on outcomes is justified by the fact that outcomes research is widely considered to provide the most credible basis for evaluating the medical effectiveness and cost-efficiency of particular medical treatments, technologies, and healthcare design approaches. There can be little question that the priority and resources accorded to gardens in healthcare facilities in the future will be largely shaped by the extent to which sound research demonstrates that gardens improve health outcomes, promote increased patient or consumer satisfaction with healthcare providers, and are cost-effective compared to alternatives such as not having gardens.

It is clear from the survey that research on healthcare gardens is at an early stage of development—only a small number of studies have used scientific-experimental procedures to investigate the potentially favorable influences of gardens on patient stress and other medical outcomes. One of the few findings to emerge in a fairly reliable manner from different studies is that certain types of nature views can have significant restorative effects on emotional, physiological, and behavioral components of stress in patients. It appears that even acutely stressed patients can experience significant restoration after only a few minutes of viewing nature settings with greenery, flowers, or water. Another potentially important finding that has emerged in at least three studies is that gardenlike scenes apparently mitigate pain, as indicated both by patient ratings of perceived pain and observed intake of analgesic medications. Despite these and other promising scientific findings, conspicuous research gaps exist in virtually all areas. For many important questions relating to gardens, there is no sound research yet available to inform the designer's or administrator's intuition, sensitivity, and experience.

The disadvantages associated with the shortage of studies on healthcare gardens are counterbalanced to a considerable extent, however, by major strengths and advantages arising from a large body of quality research on key related topics. Fortunately, designers and researchers concerned with gardens can take advantage of the comparatively well-developed and advanced research available on such issues as stress responses in patients, interventions that are effective for reducing stress, and links between stress and other health outcomes. The chapter draws heavily from this multidisciplinary resource to establish a more research-informed foundation for a proposed Theory of Supportive Gardens. The basic premise underpinning this theory is that the capability of gardens to improve health outcomes arises mainly from their effectiveness as stress reducing and buffering resources. The stress-centered conceptual framework contends that gardens in healthcare facilities should be effective in ameliorating stress and improving other outcomes to the extent that their environmental characteristics promote increased sense of control, social support, opportunities for physical movement and exercise, and access to natural distractions.

The overall state of knowlege on healthcare gardens is somewhat paradoxical. As noted, the area is limited by the shortage of rigorous studies that have examined directly the links between gardens and medical outcomes. Much is known, however, about effective "nonenvironmental" interventions for reducing patient stress and improving outcomes (for example, programs that provide social support for cancer patients or encourage walking by cardiovascular patients). Gardens in healthcare facilities can function as important and perhaps especially effective vehicles for fostering opportunities for such therapeutic experiences. Nature in gardens, apart from promoting restoration through its visual and auditory properties, largely accounts for why gardens are perceived as much more pleasant and attractive settings than the majority of healthcare interiors and other "built" spaces (Cooper Marcus and Barnes, 1995; Ulrich, 1993; Ulrich and Parsons, 1992). Because gardens stand out as exceptionally pleasant and soothing spaces in the often starkly institutional surroundings prevalent in healthcare facilities, they should be effective in enticing people to seek them out and spend time in them (Ulrich, 1983, 1993). In this way, gardens may indirectly stimulate increases in restorative and health promoting activities: if viewing a garden engenders relaxation and improved moods in patients, they may be more likely to engage in additional healthy activities such as talking with a friend or walking. Healthful effects of gardens thus may arise not only directly from exposure to nature, but also indirectly through the enhanced access to other important stress-reducing resources or activities that a well-designed garden provides.

If a researcher had seriously proposed two decades ago that gardens could improve medical outcomes in healthcare facilities, the position would have met with skepticism by most behavioral scientists, and probably with derision by many physicians. In recent years, however, the mainstream knowledge base and conceptual outlook of the medical and behavioral sciences has been altered by a flood of mind-body studies showing that psychological and environmental factors can affect physiological systems and health status. Knowledge in such fields as health psychology, psychoneuroimmunology, and behavioral medicine has now demonstrated that there need not be anything magical about the possible mechanisms and processes through which gardens in healthcare facilities should be capable of ameliorating stress and fostering gains in other outcomes. Accordingly, a balanced appraisal of the overall state of relevant knowledge suggests that cautious optimism is justified regarding the long-term potential for the role of gardens in healthcare facilities. What remains to be accomplished is the considerable but achievable task of generating a much larger body of research linking improved outcomes directly to these types of therapeutic conditions or interventions as provided by gardens in healthcare facilities.

Advantages of Gardens in Healthcare Facilities

Given the limited amount of scientific knowledge currently available on healthcare gardens, what advantages might be claimed as justifications for creating these settings? Put somewhat differently, in the event that a designer proposed a supportively designed garden for a healthcare facility, what benefits could a cost conscious administrator reasonably expect to achieve from the setting? On the basis of a broad assessment of the research that is both directly and indirectly relevant to healthcare gardens, we list the improved outcomes and other advantages that seem realistically attainable by a supportively designed healthcare garden. The list of advantages is not intended to be comprehensive.

PROBABLE ADVANTAGES

- Patients, visitors, and staff will experience reduction of anxiety/stress (very likely). Also, stress will be buffered in subsequent stressful episodes (likely).
- Reduction of depression (likely, especially if garden fosters exercise).
- Higher reported quality of life for chronic and terminal patients (likely, especially if garden fosters exercise).
- Reduced pain in patients (likely).
- Improved way-finding in healthcare facility (very likely, especially if garden has distinctive appearance and is in prominent location).

POTENTIAL OR POSSIBLE ADVANTAGES

- Reduced provider costs:
  - Patients need fewer costly strong pain doses.
  - Length of stay shorter for certain patient categories.
- Increased patient mobility and independence (if garden, for instance, serves as destination for walks and wheelchair travel).
- Higher patient satisfaction with facility and perhaps provider.
- Increased staff job satisfaction.

The improved health outcomes and other advantages listed above pertain to appropriately designed gardens. The chapter points out, however, that there is nothing inherently healing about any type of setting that is called a "garden." In fact, there is some evidence that inappropriately designed gardens can hinder stress recovery and may worsen other outcomes. The review of research findings and the discussion of the Theory of Supportive Gardens identified a number of supportive design strategies or characteristics. Examples of these supportive design considerations include: convenient way-finding to the garden; accessibility; access to privacy; seating that facilitates social interaction; exercise opportunities; and contact with nature. Concerning the last of these, nature contact, the research review suggested that gardens will tend to ameliorate stress effectively if they contain verdant foliage, flowers, nonturbulent water, parklike or savannalike qualities (grassy spaces with scattered trees), congruent nature sounds (birds, breezes, water), and visible wildlife (birds, squirrels). On the other hand, environmental qualities that tend to hinder recovery or even aggravate stress include: predominance of hardscape or starkly built content (concrete, for example); appraised risk or insecurity; crowding; cigarette smoke; intrusive urban or human-made sounds (for example, traffic, air-conditioning equipment, loud aircraft); and ambiguous design features or art works that can be interpreted in multiple ways.

Regarding ambiguity, theory and some empirical findings imply that designers should exercise caution before including ambiguous or abstract features in a healthcare garden. Patients suffering from acute stress might tend to be especially vulnerable to having stressful rather than positive reactions to ambiguous art or design. On the basis of emotional congruence theory, it is suggested that the negative emotional states of many patients may lead them to process and interpret ambiguous content in an affectively matching negative manner. However, positive feelings experienced by designers and artists may distort their responses to ambiguous features in emotionally congruent positive ways, conceivably making them more susceptible to misjudging the effect of ambiguous designs on stressed patients. Current research implies that the safest course for garden designers is simply to capitalize on the restorative, unambiguously positive qualities of most nature content and configurations.

REFERENCES

Abramson, L. Y., J. Garber, & M. E. P. Seligman (1980). "Learned Helplessness in Humans: An Attributional Analysis. In J. Garber and M. E. P. Seligman (Eds.), *Human Helplessness: Theory and Applications.* New York: Academic Press, pp. 3–34.

Adachi, M., L. E. Rohde, and A. D. Kendle (1998). *Effects of Floral Displays on Human Emotions.* Unpublished manuscript, Graduate School of Agriculture and Life Sciences, University of Tokyo, Japan, and Department of Horticulture and Landscape, Whiteknights University, Reading, UK.

Allshouse, K. D. (1993). "Treating Patients as Individuals." In M. Gerteis, S. Edgman-Levitan, J. Daley, and T. L. Delbanco (Eds.), *Through the Patient's Eyes: Understanding and Promoting Patient-Centered Care.* San Francisco: Jossey-Bass, pp. 19–44.

Altman, I. (1975). *The Environment and Social Behavior.* Monterey, CA: Brooks/Cole.

Anderson, L. M., B. E. Mulligan, L. S. Goodman, and H. Z. Regen (1983). "Effects of Sounds on Preferences for Outdoor Settings." *Environment and Behavior*, Vol. 15, pp. 539–566.

Appleton (1975). *The Experience of Lancsape*. London: Wiley.

Baier, S. and M. A. Schomaker (1985). *Bed Number Ten*. Boca Raton, FL: CRC Press.

Baird, C. L. and P. A. Bell (1995). "Place Attachment, Isolation, and the Power of a Window in a Hospital Environment: A Case Study." *Psychological Reports*, Vol. 76, pp. 847–850.

Barnes, M. (1994). *A Study of the Process of Emotional Healing in Outdoor Spaces and the Concomitant Landscape Design Implications*. Masters Thesis, Deptartment of Landscape Architecture, University of California, Berkeley.

Barnhart, S. K., N. H. Perkins, and J. FitzSimonds (in press, 1998). "Behaviour and Outdoor Setting Preferences at a Psychiatric Hospital." *Landscape and Urban Planning*.

Beauchemin, K. M. and P. Hays (1996). "Sunny Hospital Rooms Expedite Recovery from Severe and Refractory Depressions." *Journal of Affective Disorders*, Vol. 40, pp. 49–51.

Beauchemin, K. M. and P. Hays (1998). "Dying in the Dark: Sunshine, Gender and Outcomes in Myocardial Infarction." *Journal of the Royal Society of Medicine*, Vol. 91, pp. 352–354.

Beck, A. M., L. Saradarian, and G. F. Hunter (1986). "Use of Animals in the Rehabilitation of Psychiatric Inpatients." *Psychological Reports*, Vol. 58, pp. 63–66.

Berkman, L. F. and S. L. Syme (1979). "Social Networks, Host Resistance, and Mortality: A Nine-Year Follow-Up Study of Alameda County Residents." *American Journal of Epidemiology*, Vol. 109, pp. 186–204.

Berlyne, D. E. (1971). *Aesthetics and Psychobiology*. New York: Appleton-Century-Crofts.

Boubekri, M., R. B. Hull, and L. L. Boyer (1991). "Impact of Window Size and Sunlight Penetration on Office Workers' Mood and Satisfaction: A Novel Way of Assessing Sunlight." *Environment and Behavior*, Vol l23, pp. 474–493.

Bower, G. (1981). "Mood and Memory." *American Psychologist*, Vol. 36, pp. 129–148.

Brannon, L., and J. Feist (1997). *Health Psychology*, 3rd ed. Pacific Grove, CA: Brooks/Cole.

Burish, T. G., B. E. Meyerowitz, M. P. Carey, and G. R. Morrow (1987). "The Stressful Effects of Cancer in Adults." In A. Baum and J. E. Singer (Eds.), *Handbook of Psychology and Health, Vol. 5: Stress*. Hillsdale, NJ: Erlbaum. pp. 137–173.

Burnett, J. D. (1997). "Therapeutic Effects of Landscape Architecture." In S. O. Marberry (Ed.), *Healthcare Design*. New York: John Wiley. pp. 255–274.

Caine, J. (1991). "The Effects of Music on the Selected Stress Behaviors, Weight, Caloric and Formula Intake, and Length of Hospital Stay of Premature and Low Birth Weight Neonates in a Newborn Intensive Care Unit." *Journal of Music Therapy*, Vol. XVIII, pp. 180–182.

Calabrese, J. R., M. A. Kling, and P. W. Gold (1987). "Alterations in Immunocompetence During Stress, Bereavement, and Depression: Focus on Neuroendocrine Regulation." *American Journal of Psychiatry*, Vol. 144, pp. 1123–1134.

Carpman, J. R. and M. A. Grant (1993). *Design That Cares: Planning Health Facilities for Patients and Visitors*, 2nd. ed. Chicago: American Hospital Publishing.

Carr, S., M. Francis, L. G. Rivlin, and A. M. Stone (1992). *Public Space*. New York: Cambridge University Press.

Coffey, L. C., J. K. Skipper, Jr., and F. D. Jung (1988). "Nurses and Shift Work: Effects on Job Performance and Job-Related Stress." *Journal of Advanced Nursing*, Vol. 13, pp. 245–254.

Cohen, S. (1988). "Psychosocial Models of the Role of Social Support in the Etiology of Physical Disease." *Health Psychology*, Vol. 7, pp. 269–297.

Cohen, S. and S. L. Syme (Eds.) (1985). *Social Support and Health*. New York: Academic Press.

Cohen, S., D. A. J. Tyrrell, and A. P. Smith (1991). "Psychological Stress and Susceptibility to the Common Cold." *New England Journal of Medicine*, Vol. 325, pp. 606–612.

Cohen, U. and K. Day (1993). *Contemporary Environments for People with Dementia*. Baltimore: Johns Hopkins University Press.

Connelly, A. G. (1992). "An Examination of Stressors in the Patient Undergoing Cardiac Eelectrophysiologic Studies." *Heart & Lung*, Vol. 21, pp. 335–342.

Cooper Marcus, C. and M. Barnes (1995). *Gardens in Healthcare Facilities: Uses, Therapeutic Benefits, and Design Recommendations*. Martinez, CA: The Center for Health Design.

Cooper Marcus, C., and C. Francis (Eds.) (1998, second edition). *People Places: Design Guidelines for Urban Open Space*. New York: Wiley.

Cooper Marcus, C., C. M. Watsky, E. Insley, and C. Francis (1998, second edition). "Neighborhood parks." In C. C. Marcus & C. Francis (Eds.), *People Places: Design Guidelines for Urban Open Space*. New York: Wiley. pp. 85–148.

Corah, N. L. and J. Boffa (1970). "Perceived Control, Self-Observation, and Response to Aversive Stimulation." *Journal of Personality and Social Psychology*, Vol 16, pp. 1–4.

Coss, R. G. (1990). *Picture Perception and Patient Stress: A Study of Anxiety Reduction and Postoperative Stability*. Unpublished manuscript, Department of Psychology, University of California, Davis.

Cousins, N. (1983). *The Healing Heart: Antidote to Panic and Helplessness*. New York: Norton.

Devlin, K. and J. L. Nasar (1989). "The Beauty and the Beast: Some Preliminary Comparisons of 'High' versus 'Popular' Residential Architecture and Public versus Architect Judgments of Same." *Journal of Environmental Psychology*, Vol. 9, pp. 333–344.

Driver, B. L. and P. J. Brown (1986). "Probable Personal Benefits of Outdoor Recreation." In *President's Commission on Americans Outdoors: A Literature Review*. Washington, DC: Government Printing Office. pp. 63–67.

Driver, B. L. and R. C. Knopf (1976). "Temporary Escape: One Product of Sport Fisheries Management. *Fisheries*, Vol. 1, pp. 24–29.

Edgman-Levitan, S. (1993). "Providing Effective Emotional Support." In M. Gerteis, S. Edgman-Levitan, J. Daley, and T. L. Delbanco (Eds.), *Through the Patient's Eyes: Understanding and Promoting Patient-Centered Care*. San Francisco: Jossey-Bass. pp. 154–177.

Emery, C. F. and J. A. Blumenthal (1991). "Effects of Physical Exercise on Psychological and Cognitive Functioning of Older Adults." *Annals of Behavioral Medicine*, Vol. 13, pp. 99–107.

Evans, G. W. and S. Cohen (1987). "Environmental Stress." In D. Stokols and I. Altman (Eds.), *Handbook of Environmental Psychology*, 2 vols. New York: John Wiley. pp. 571–610.

Foxall, M. J., L. Zimmerman, R. Standley, and B. Bené (1990). "A Comparison of Frequency and Sources of Nursing Job Stress Perceived by Intensive Care, Hospice and Medical-Surgical Nurses." *Journal of Advanced Nursing*, Vol. 15, pp. 577–584.

Francis, C. and C. Cooper Marcus (1991). "Places People Take Their Problems." In J. Urbina-Soria, P. Ortega-Andeane, and R. Bechtel (Eds.), *Proceedings of the 22nd annual Conference of the Environmental Design Research Association*. Oklahoma City: Environmental Design Research Association, pp. 178–184.

Francis, M. (1989). "Control as a Dimension of Public-Space Quality." In I. Altman and E. H. Zube (Eds.), *Human Behavior and Environment: Advances in Theory and Research, Vol. 10: Public Places and Spaces*. New York: Plenum. pp. 147–172.

Friedman, E., A. Katcher, J. Lynch, and S. Thomas (1980). "Animal Companions and One-Year Survival of Patients Discharged from a Coronary Care Unit. *Public Health Reports*, Vol. 95, pp. 307–312.

Gatchel, R. J., A. Baum, and D. S. Krantz (1989). *An Introduction to Health Psychology*, 2nd ed. New York: McGraw-Hill.

Gerteis, M., S. Edgman-Levitan, J. Daley, and T. L. Delbanco (Eds.) (1993). *Through the Patient's Eyes: Understanding and Promoting Patient-Centered Care*. San Francisco: Jossey-Bass.

Gil, K. M. (1984). "Coping Effectively with Invasive Medical Procedures: A Descriptive Model." *Clinical Psychology Review*, Vol. 4, pp. 339–362.

Glass, D. C., and J. E. Singer (1972). *Urban Stress: Experiments on Noise and Social Stressors*. New York: Academic Press.

Grahn, P. (1991). *Om Parkers Betydelse* [On the Importance of Parks]. Göteborg: Graphic Systems AB.

Grant, C. (1994). *The Healing Garden: Incorporating Garden Experience in Hospitals and Other Health Care Facilities*. Unpublished thesis for Master of Landscape Architecture Degree. Department of Landscape Architecture, University of Georgia, Athens.

Hartig, T. (1993). *Testing Restorative Environments Theory*. Unpublished Doctoral Dissertation, Program in Social Ecology, University of California, Irvine.

Hartig, T., A. Böök, J. Garvill, T. Olsson, and T. Gärling (1996). "Environmental Influences on Psychological Restoration." *Scandinavian Journal of Psychology*, Vol. 37, pp. 378–393.

Hartig, T., and G. W. Evans (1993). "Psychological Foundations of Nature Experience. In T. Gärling and R. G. Golledge (Eds.), *Behavior and Environment: Psychological and Geographical Approaches.* Amsterdam: Elsevier/North Holland. pp. 427–457.

Hartig, T., M. Mang, and G. W. Evans (1991). "Restorative Effects of Natural Environment Experiences." *Environment and Behavior,* Vol. 23, pp. 3–36.

Heerwagen, J. (1990). "The Psychological Aspects of Windows and Window Design." In K. H. Anthony, J. Choi, and B. Orland (Eds.), *Proceedings of 21st Annual Conference of the Environmental Design Research Association.* Oklahoma City: EDRA, pp. 269–280.

Hefferman, M. L., M. Morstatt, K. Saltzman, and L. Strunc (1995). *A Room with a View Art Survey: The Bird Garden at Duke University Hospital.* Unpublished research report. Cultural Services Program and Management Fellows Program, Duke University Medical Center, Durham, NC.

Hester, R. T. (1984). *Planning Neighborhood Space with People,* 2nd ed. New York: Van Nostrand Reinhold.

Holahan, C. J. (1972). "Seating Patterns and Patient Behavior in an Experimental Dayroom." *Journal of Abnormal Psychology,* Vol. 80, pp. 115–124.

Holahan, C. J., R. H. Moos, C. K. Holahan, and P. L. Brennan (1995). "Social Support, Coping, and Depressive Symptoms in a Late-Middle-Aged Sample of Patients Reporting Cardiac Illness. *Health Psychology,* Vol. 14, pp. 152–163.

Honeyman, M. K. (1992). "Vegetation and Stress: A Comparison Study of Varying Amounts of Vegetation in Countryside and Urban Scenes." In D. Relf (Ed.), *The Role of Horticulture in Human Well-Being and Social Development.* Portland, OR: Timber Press, pp. 143–145.

Horsburgh. C. R. (1995). "Healing by Design." *The New England Journal of Medicine,* Vol. 11, No. 333, pp. 735–740.

Horsburgh, C. R. (1997). "Hospital Design Qualities that Facilitate Healing." *Journal of Healthcare Design,* Vol. IX, pp. 89–92.

Isen, A. (1987). "Positive Affect, Cognitive Processes, and Social Behavior." In L. Berkowitz (Ed.), *Advances in Experimental Social Psychology.* New York: Academic Press.

Janis, I. L. (1958). *Psychological Stress: Psychoanalytic and Behavioral Studies of Surgical Patients.* New York: Wiley.

Johnson, J., N. J. Christman, C. Sitt (1985). "Personal Control Interventions: Short- and Long-Term Effects on Surgical Patients." *Research in Nursing and Health,* Vol. 8, pp. 131–145.

Kaplan, R. (1993). "The Role of Nature in the Context of the Workplace." *Landscape and Urban Planning,* Vol. 26, pp. 193–201.

Kaplan, S. and J. F. Talbot (1983). "Psychological Benefits of a Wilderness Experience." In I. Altman and J. F. Wohlwill (Eds.), *Human Behavior and the Environment, Vol. 6: Behavior and the Natural Environment.* New York: Plenum. pp. 163–203.

Kaplan, R. and S. Kaplan (1989). *The Experience of Nature.* New York: Cambridge, University Press.

Katcher, A., H. Segal, and A. Beck (1984). "Comparison of Contemplation and Hypnosis for the Reduction of Anxiety and Discomfort During Dental Surgery." *American Journal of Clinical Hypnosis,* Vol. 27, pp. 14–21.

Kaye, C., and T. Blee (Eds.) (1997). *The Arts in Health Care.* London, UK: Jessica Kingsley Publishers.

Keeri-Szanto, M. and S. Heaman (1972). "Postoperative Demand Analgesia." *Surgical Gynecology and Obstetrics,* Vol. 134, pp. 647–651.

Kettlewell, N. (1988). "An Examination of Preferences for Subject Matter in Art." *Empirical Studies of the Arts,* Vol. 6, pp. 59–65.

Kiecolt-Glaser, J. K., C. S. Dyer, and E. C. Shuttleworth (1988). "Upsetting Social Interactions and Distress Among Alzheimer's Disease Care-Givers: A Replication and Extension." *American Journal of Community Psychology,* Vol. 16, pp. 825–837.

Kiecolt-Glaser, J. K., and R. Glaser (1991). "Stress and Immune Function in Humans." In R. Ader, D. L. Felten, and N. Cohen (Eds.), *Psychoneuroimmunology.* San Diego: Academic Press. pp. 849–867.

Kiecolt-Glaser, J. K., G. C. Page, P. T. Marucha, R. C. MacCallum, and R. Glaser (1998). "Psychological Perspectives on Surgical Recovery: Perspectives from Psychoneuroimmunology." *American Psychologist,* Vol. 52, pp. 1209–1218.

Kim, I.-K. (1997). *Subjective Responses to Daylight, Sunlight, and View in College Classrooms with Windows.* Unpublished doctoral dissertation, Department of Architecture, Texas A&M University, College Station, TX.

King, H. (1995). *Cross-Cultural Patterns of Institutionalization Among Hispanic and Anglo-American Alzheimer's Populations: The Case for Differential Design in Response to Diverse Needs.* Unpublished research paper. Department of Architecture, Texas A&M University, College Station, TX.

Knopf, R. C. (1987). "Human Behavior, Cognition, and Affect in the Natural Environment." In D. Stokols and I Altman (Eds.), *Handbook of Environmental Psychology.* New York: Wiley. pp. 783–825.

Koniak-Griffin, D. (1994). "Aerobic Exercise, Psychological Well-Being, and Physical Discomforts During Adolescent Pregnancy." *Research in Nursing and Health,* Vol. 17, pp. 253–268.

Kweon, B.-S., W. C. Sullivan, and A. R. Wiley (1998). "Green Common Spaces and the Social Integration of Inner-City Older Adults." *Environment and Behavior,* Vol. 30, pp. 832–858.

Lamberg-Allardt, C. (1984). "Vitamin D Intake, Sunlight Exposure and 25-Hydroxyvitamin D Levels in the Elderly During One Year." *Annals of Nutrition & Metabolism,* Vol. 28, pp. 144–150.

Langer, E. J. and J. Rodin (1976). "The Effects of Choice and Enhanced Personal Responsibility for the Aged: A Field Experiment in an Institutional Setting." *Journal of Personality and Social Psychology,* Vol. 34, pp. 191–198.

Larsen, L., J. Adams, B. Deal, B.-S. Kweon, and E. Tyler (1998). "Plants in the Workplace: The Effects of Plant Density on

Productivity, Attitudes and Perceptions." *Environment and Behavior,* Vol. 30, pp. 261–281.

Lazarus, R. S. and F. Cohen (1973). "Active Coping Processes, Coping Dispositions, and Recovery from Surgery." *Psychosomatic Medicine,* Vol. 35, pp. 375–389.

Leather, P., M. Pyrgas, D. Beale, and C. Lawrence (1997). "Windows in the Workplace: Sunlight, View and Occupational Stress." *Environment and Behavior,* Vol. 30, pp. 739–762.

Lee, I.-M., R. S. Paffenbarger, and C.-C. Hsich (1992). "Physical Exercise and Risk of Prostatic Cancer Among College Alumni." *American Journal of Epidemiology,* Vol. 135, pp. 169–179.

Lewis, C. A. (1996). *Green Nature/Human Nature: The Meaning of Plants in our Lives.* Urbana, IL: University of Illinois Press.

Mace, B. L., P. A. Bell, and R. J. Loomis (1999, in press). "Aesthetic, Affective, and Cognitive Effects of Noise on Natural Landscape Assessment." *Society and Natural Resources.*

MacRae, S. (1997). *Consumer Perceptions of the Healthcare Environment: An Investigation to Determine What Matters.* Preliminary report published by The Center for Health Design, Martinez, CA, and The Picker Institute, Cambridge, MA.

Malkin, J. (1992). *Hospital Interior Architecture.* New York: Van Nostrand Reinhold.

Matsuo, E. (1996). "Sociohorticulture: A New Field of Horticulture and its Present Status in Europe, the U.S.A. and Japan." *Journal of the Korean Society for Horticultural Science,* Vol. 37, pp. 171–185. (In English.)

McLaughlin, J., J. Beebe, J. Hirshfield, P. Lindia, and D. Gubanc (1996). "Duke University's Bird Garden." In *Proceedings of the 1996 Annual Conference of the Society for the Arts in Healthcare.* Durham, NC: Durham Arts Council and Duke University Medical Center. pp. 49–63.

McNeil, J. K., E. M. LeBlanc, and M. Joyner (1991). "The Effect of Exercise on Depressive Symptoms in the Moderately Depressed Elderly." *Psychology and Aging,* Vol. 6, pp. 487–488.

Mehrabian, A. and J. A. Russell (1974). *An Approach to Environmental Psychology.* Cambridge, MA: M.I.T. Press.

Melamid, A., and V. Komar (1994). "The Search for a People's Art." *The Nation.* March 14, pp. 334–348.

Miller, A. C., L. C. Hickman, and G. K. Lemasters (1992). "A Distraction Technique for Control of Burn Pain." *Journal of Burn Care and Rehabilitation,* Vol. 13, pp. 576–580.

Miracle, V. A., and G. Hovekamp (1994). "Needs of Families of Patients Undergoing Invasive Cardiac Procedures." *American Journal of Critical Care,* Vol. 3, pp. 155–157.

Moss, V. A. (1988). "Music and the Surgical Patient: The Effect of Music on Anxiety." *AORN Journal,* Vol. 48, pp. 64–69.

Nakamura, R., and E. Fujii (1990). "Studies of the Characteristics of the Electroencephalogram When Observing Potted Plants: Pelargonium Hortorum 'Sprinter Red' and Begonia Evansiana." *Technical Bulletin of the Faculty of Horticulture of Chiba University,* Vol. 43, pp. 177–183. (In Japanese with English summary.)

Nakamura, R. and E. Fujii (1992). "A Comparative Study of the Characteristics of the Electroencephalogram When Observing a Hedge and a Concrete Block Fence." *Journal of the Japanese Institute of Landscape Architects,* Vol. 55, pp. 139–144. (In Japanese with English summary.)

Nasar, J. L., B. Fisher, and M. Grannis (1993). "Proximate Physical Cues to Fear of Crime." *Landscape and Urban Planning,* Vol. 26, pp. 161–178.

Niedenthal, P. M., M. B. Setterlund, and D. E. Jones (1994). "Emotional Organization of Perceptual Memory." In P. M. Niedenthal and S. Kitayama (Eds.), *The Heart's Eye: Emotional Influences in Perception and Attention.* San Diego: Academic Press, pp. 87–113.

Nightingale, F. (1996) (1925, 1860). *Notes on Nursing* (Revised with Additions). London: Ballière Tindall.

O'Connor, B. P., H. Davidson, and R. Gifford (1991). "Window View, Social Exposure and Nursing Home Adaptation." *Canadian Journal on Aging,* Vol. 10, pp. 216–223.

Orians, G. H. (1986). "An Ecological and Evolutionary Approach to Landscape Aesthetics." In E. C. Penning-Rowsell and D. Lowenthal (Eds.), *Meanings and Values in Landscape.* London: Allen and Unwin. pp. 3–25.

Orr, R. (1992). "The Planetree Philosophy." *Journal of Healthcare Design,* Vol. IV, pp. 29–34.

Osmund, H. (1957). F"unction as the Basis of Psychiatric Ward Design." *Mental Hospitals,* Vol. 8, pp. 23–30.

Ott, P. J. and S. M. Levy (1994). "Cancer in Women." In V. J. Adesso, D. M. Reddy, and R. Fleming (Eds.), *Psychological Perspectives in Women's Health.* Washington, DC: Taylor and Francis. pp. 83–98.

Paine, R., et al. (1998, second edition). "Hospital Outdoor Spaces." In C. C. Marcus and C. Francis (Eds.), *People Places: Design Guidelines for Urban Open Space.* New York: Wiley. pp. 311–343.

Parkes, K. R. (1982). "Occupational Stress Among Student Nurses: A Natural Experiment." *Journal of Applied Psychology,* Vol. 67, pp. 784–796.

Parsons, R. (1991a). "The Potential Influences of Environmental Perception on Human Health." *Journal of Environmental Psychology,* Vol. 11, pp. 1–23.

Parsons, R. (1991b). *Recovery from Stress During Exposure to Videotaped Outdoor Environments.* Unpublished doctoral dissertation, Department of Psychology, University of Arizona, Tucson.

Parsons, R., and T. Hartig (1999, in press). "Environmental Psychophysiology." In J. T. Cacioppo, L. G. Tassinary, and G. Berntson (Eds.), *Handbook of Psychophysiology.* New York: Cambridge University Press.

Parsons, R., R. S. Ulrich, and L. G. Tassinary (1994). "Experimental Approaches to the Study of People-Plant Relationships." *Journal of Consumer Horticulture,* Vol. 1, pp. 347–372.

Parsons, R., L. G. Tassinary, R. S. Ulrich, M. R. Hebl, and M. Grossman-Alexander (in press, 1998). "The View from the Road:

Implications for Stress Recovery and Immunization." *Journal of Environmental Psychology.*

Pederson, C., and B. L. Harbaugh (1995). "Children's and Adolescents' Experiences while Undergoing Cardiac Catheterization. *Maternal-Child Nursing Journal,* Vol. 23, pp. 15–25.

Peterson, M. (1991). "Patient Anxiety Before Cardiac Catheterization: An Intervention Study." *Heart and Lung,* Vol. 20, pp. 643–647.

Proshansky, H. M., W. H. Ittelson, and L. G. Rivlin (1970). "Freedom of Choice and Behavior in a Physical Setting." In H. M. Proshansky, W. H. Ittelson, and L. G. Rivlin (Eds.), *Environmental Psychology: Man and His Physical Setting.* New York: Holt, Rinehart, and Winston. pp. 173–183.

Rabin, B. S., S. Cohen, R. Ganguli, D. T. Lysle, and J. E. Cunnick (1989). "Bidirectional Interaction Between the Central Nervous System and the Immune System." *Critical Reviews in Immunology,* Vol. 9, pp. 279–312.

Rubin, H. R., and A. J. Owens (1996). *Status Report: An Investigation to Determine Whether the Built Environment Affects Patients' Medical Outcomes.* Martinez, CA: The Center for Health Design.

Ruuskanen, J. M., and. T. Parketti (1994). "Physical Activity and Related Factors among Nursing Home Residents." *Journal of the American Geriatrics Society,* Vol. 42, pp. 987–991.

Sarason, I. G. and B. R. Sarason (Eds.) (1985). *Social Support: Theory, Research, and Applications.* The Hague: Nijhoff.

Schroeder, H. W. (1986). "Psychological Value of Urban Trees: Measurement, Meaning and Imagination." In A. F. Phillips and D. J. Gangloff (Eds.), *Proceedings of the Third National Urban Forestry Conference.* Washington, DC: American Forestry Association. pp. 55–60.

Schroeder, H. W. (1991). "Preference and Meaning of Arboretum Landscapes: Combining Quantitative and Qualitative Data." *Journal of Environmental Psychology,* Vol. 11, pp. 231–248.

Schroeder, H. W., and Anderson, L. M. (1984). "Perception of Personal Safety in Urban Recreation Sites." *Journal of Leisure Research,* Vol. 16, pp. 177–194.

Schulz, R. (1976). "Effects of Control and Predictability on the Physical and Psychological Well-Being of the Institutionalized Aged." *Journal of Personality and Social Psychology,* Vol. 33, pp. 563–573.

Schwarzer, R. and A. Leppin (1989). "Social Support and Health: A Meta-Analysis." *Psychology and Health,* Vol. 3, pp. 1–15.

Selye, H. (1956). *The Stress of Life.* New York: McGraw-Hill.

Shepley, M. M. (in press, 1998). "Designing for Persons with HIV/AIDS." *Journal of Architectural and Planning Research.*

Shepley, M. M., M.-A. Fournier, and K. W. McDougal (1998). *Healthcare Environments for Children and Their Families.* Dubuque, IA: Kendall/Hunt.

Shumaker, S. A. and S. M. Czajkowski (Eds.) (1994). *Social Support and Cardiovascular Disease.* New York: Plenum.

Shumaker, S. A. and W. Pequegnat (1989). "Hospital Design, Health Providers, and the Delivery of Effective Health Care." In E. H. Zube and G. T. Moore (Eds.), *Advances in Environment, Behavior, and Design, Vol. 2.* New York: Plenum. pp. 162–199.

Singer, J. A. and P. Salovey (1988). "Mood and Memory: Evaluating the Network Theory of Affect." *Clinical Psychology Review,* Vol. 8, pp. 211-251.

Singleton, D. (1994). "Two Community Hospital Gardens: A Therapeutic Assessment." In M. Francis, P. Lindsey, and J. S. Stone (Eds.), *The Healing Dimensions of People-Plant Relations: Proceedings of a Research Symposium.* Davis, CA: Center for Design Research, University of California, Davis. pp. 269–282.

Sommer, R. (1969). *Personal Space.* Englewood Cliffs, NJ: Prentice-Hall.

Sommer, R. and H. Ross (1958). "Social Interaction on a Geriatrics Ward." *International Journal of Social Psychiatry,* Vol. 4, pp. 128–133.

Spiegel, D., H. C. Kraemer, J. R. Bloom, and E. Gottheil (1989). "Effect of Psychosocial Treatment on Survival of Patients with Metastatic Breast Cancer.." *Lancet,* No. ii, pp. 888–891.

Steptoe, A. and A. Appels (Eds.) (1989). *Stress, Personal Control and Health.* Chichester, UK: Wiley.

Stiles, J. V. (1995). *Psychological Responses to Plants in a Hospital Waiting Area.* Paper presented at the Conference on Plants-People Research. The Hague, Netherlands.

Taylor, S. E. (1979). "Hospital Patient Behavior: Reactance, Helplessness, or Control?" *Journal of Social Issues,* Vol. 35, pp. 156–184.

Taylor, S. E. and L. G. Aspinwall (1993). "Coping with Chronic Illness." In L. Goldberger and S. Breznitz (Eds.), *Handbook of Stress: Theoretical and Clinical Aspects,* 2nd. ed. New York: Free Press. pp. 511–531.

Tinsley, H. E. A. and R. A. Kass (1979). "The Latent Structure of the Need-Satisfying Properties of Leisure Activities. *Journal of Leisure Research,* Vol. 11, pp. 278–291.

Tuan, Y. F. (1974). *Topophilia: A Study of Environmental Perception, Attitudes, and Values.* New York: Alfred A. Knopf.

Ulrich, R. S. (1979). "Visual Landscapes and Psychological Well-Being." *Landscape Research,* Vol. 4, No. 1, pp. 17–23.

Ulrich, R. S. (1981). "Natural versus Urban Scenes: Some Psychophysiological Effects." *Environment and Behavior,* Vol 13, pp. 523–556.

Ulrich, R. S. (1983). "Aesthetic and Affective Response to Natural Environment." In I. Altman and J. F. Wohlwill (Eds.), *Human Behavior and the Environment, Vol. 6: Behavior and the Natural Environment.* New York: Plenum. pp. 85–125.

Ulrich, R. S. (1984). "View Through a Window May Influence Recovery from Surgery." *Science,* Vol. 224, pp. 420–421.

Ulrich, R. S. (1986a). "Human Responses to Vegetation and Landscapes." *Landscape and Urban Planning,* Vol 13, pp. 29–44.

Ulrich, R. S. (1986b). "Effects of Hospital Environments on Patient Well-Being." *Research Report from Department of Psychiatry and Behavioural Medicine*, Vol. 9, No. 55. Trondheim, Norway: Department of Psychiatry and Behavioural Medicine, University of Trondheim.

Ulrich, R. S. (1992a). "Effects of Interior Design on Wellness: Theory and Recent Scientific Research." *Journal of Healthcare Design*, Vol 3, pp. 97–109.

Ulrich, R. S. (1992b). "How Design Impacts Wellness." *Healthcare Forum Journal*, Vol. 20, pp. 20–25.

Ulrich, R. S. (1993). "Biophilia, Biophobia, and Natural Landscapes." In S. A. Kellert and E. O. Wilson (Eds.), *The Biophilia Hypothesis*. Washington, DC: Island Press/Shearwater. pp. 74–137.

Ulrich, R. S. and D. L. Addoms (1981). "Psychological and Recreational Benefits of a Residential Park." *Journal of Leisure Research*, Vol. 13, pp. 43–65.

Ulrich, R., S. U. Dimberg, and B. L. Driver (1991). "Psychophysiological Indicators of Leisure Benefits." In B. L. Driver, P. J. Brown and G. L. Peterson (Eds.), *Benefits of Leisure*. State College PA: Venture Publishing. pp. 73–89.

Ulrich, R. S., O. Lundén, and J. L. Eltinge (1993). *Effects of Exposure to Nature and Abstract Pictures on Patients Recovering from Heart Surgery.* Paper presented at the Thirty-Third Meeting of the Society for Psychophysiological Research, Rottach-Egern, Germany. Abstract published in *Psychophysiology*, Vol. 30 (Supplement 1, 1993), p. 7.

Ulrich, R. S. and R. Parsons (1992). "Influences of Passive Experiences with Plants on Individual Well-Being and Health." In D. Relf (Ed.), *The Role of Horticulture in Human Well-Being and Social Development*. Portland, OR: Timber Press. pp. 93–105.

Ulrich, R. S., R. F. Simons, B. D. Losito, E. Fiorito, M. A. Miles, and M. Zelson (1991b). "Stress Recovery During Exposure to Natural and Urban Environments." *Journal of Environmental Psychology*, Vol. 11, pp. 201–230.

Van der Ploeg, H. M. (1988). "Stressful Medical Events: A Survey of Patients' Perceptions." In S. Maes, C. D. Spielberger, P. B. Defares and I. G. Sarason (Eds.), *Topics in Health Psychology*. New York: John Wiley. pp. 193–203.

Verderber, S. (1986). "Dimensions of Person-Window Transactions in the Hospital Environment." *Environment and Behavior*, Vol 18, pp. 450–466.

Ware, Cheryl. (1994) "Designing and Building Healing Gardens at Health Care Facilities." The Spink Corporation, Sacramento CA.

Warner, S. M., Jr. (1994). "The Periodic Rediscoveries of Restorative Gardens: 1100 to the Present." In M. Francis, P. Lindsey, and J. S. Stone (Eds.), *The Healing Dimensions of People-Plant Relations: Proceedings of a Research Symposium*. Davis, CA: Center for Design Research, University of California, Davis. pp. 5–12.

Waxman, H. M., E. A. Carner, and G. Berkenstock (1984). "Job Turnover and Job Satisfaction Among Nursing Home Aides." *The Gerontologist*, Vol. 24, pp. 503–509.

Weiss, C. S., C. S. Pato, C. G. McAllister, R. Littman, A. Brier, S. M. Paul, and A. Baum (1990). "Differential Effects of Controllable and Uncontrollable Acute Stress on Lymphocyte Proliferation and Leukocyte Percentages in Humans." *Brain, Behavior, and Immunity*, Vol. 4, pp. 339–351.

Whall, A. L., M. E. Black, C. J. Groh, D. J. Yankou, B. J. Kupferschmid, and. N. L. Foster (1997). "The Effect of Natural Environments Upon Agitation and Aggression in Late State Dementia Patients." *American Journal of Alzheimer's Disease*, September/October, pp. 216–220.

Whyte, W. H. (1980). *The Social Life of Small Urban Spaces*. Washington, DC: The Conservation Foundation.

Winkel, G. H. and C. J. Holahan (1985). "The Environmental Psychology of the Hospital: Is the Cure Worse than the Illness?" *Prevention in Human Services*, Vol. 4, pp. 11–33.

Winston, A. S. and G. C. Cupchik (1992). "The Evaluation of High Art and Popular Art by Naive and Experienced Viewers." *Visual Arts Research*, Vol. 18, 1–14.

Wohlwill, J. F. (1983). "The Concept of Nature: A Psychologist's View." In I. Altman & J. F. Wohlwill (Eds.), *Human Behavior and the Environment, Vol. 6: Behavior and the Natural Environment*. New York: Plenum. pp. 5–37.

Wortman, C. B. (1984). "Social Support and the Cancer Patient." *Cancer*, Vol. 53 (Supplement), pp. 2339–2362.

CHAPTER

3

Design Philosophy

Marni Barnes with
Clare Cooper Marcus

Where do landscape architects begin when creating a healing garden? The research presented in the previous chapter establishes the appropriateness of considering the exterior environment in medical facilities as part of the therapeutic milieu. The following chapters present the practical issues involved in a variety of healthcare settings and how to address the needs of specific populations. Before delving into the practical concerns, however, it is important to review the basic approaches to landscape design and to assess how these support or conflict with the sensitive creation of a healing space. J. William Thompson of *Landscape Architecture* has queried "...do they [landscape architects] yet know enough to shape such gardens so that they really help patients heal?" (1998, p. 67). Thompson is correct to raise the issue, for the specific demands of creating a therapeutic space requires an interface between two objectives, creating a *place* and facilitating a *process*. Trained in creating spaces, facilitating the process of healing is a recent addition to the job of the landscape architect. It is the interplay between sensitivity to the healing process and the development of a design that this chapter addresses.

The healing process is complex, and by no means fully understood, but there are basic attitudinal shifts that take place when an individual is stressed or otherwise in need of healing.

"I only went out for a walk and finally concluded to stay out until sundown, for going out, I found was really going in."

JOHN MUIR

87

These shifting emotions affect perception, and in turn influence a person's response to various environmental stimuli. Understanding how people *see* their environment, and how they react to it, is the most critical component of therapeutic design. This sensitivity to the "feeling" created by a space—what type of experience the user will have when viewing or occupying a garden—must be understood and incorporated into design decisions.

"Bridging the gap between what is internal and what is external is the function of the senses" (Lewis 1996, p. 7). This is only the first step, however, as the conveyance from the three-dimensional world—that which designers mold and shape—to the internal perceived world is not as simple or straightforward as just taking in the lines, forms, colors, and shapes that comprise our environment. What the individual experiences is enhanced or added to at two stages of incorporation into the human psyche. The first level of distortion is contained in what the individual observes, and the second in how it is interpreted.

Environmental psychologist William Ittelson and his co-authors (1974) address this when they discuss human perception. In summary, they state that there is a layer of "symbolic value" inherent in the environment. Part of the information picked up by our sensory organs—the sounds, sights, and smells in the environment—are external stimuli that are not directly identified by the conscious mind. They are cues that enter the psyche at a subliminal level. The meaning of these stimuli is felt more than deduced by thought. This symbolic communication is implicit in most environments and is an inherent part of observing the surroundings. To give one obvious example, an open gate is inviting, while a closed one says "keep out." This symbolism, which is primarily culturally determined, becomes part of how we define ourselves in relation to our environment (we are either included or excluded, as in the example); and thereby how we define our role in that environment (participant or observer/outsider). These symbolic meanings can be imbued by very subtle cues. But subtlety does not diminish the strength of the message; some of our deepest feelings are prompted by cues that bypass our conscious mind entirely.

Beyond this observed environment, a level of filtering takes place within the individual, automatically, often instantaneously, and without awareness. The translation from the observed objects to the internal perception of those objects is filtered by past experiences and present expectations, and therefore inherently incorporates our individual distortions (Ittelson et al., 1974). One poignant example of this aspect of

Figure 3-1 An open gate invites exploration and symbolizes inclusion.

perception is that of a 79-year-old woman whose husband had just died from cancer. This woman attended a bereavement group for family members, sponsored by the hospital. At the end of the session, a flower from the bouquet that had been on the table was given to each person as he or she left. This woman put her carnation in water when she got home, but in the morning found that it had wilted. She was so distressed by this that she became very angry and repeatedly expressed how uncaring and hurtful it had been to be given what she could only see as a dying flower. Her experience as a recent widow was one of death and abandonment, and she regarded this flower as embodying both of these messages—the death of the flower and the "abandonment" of the group by perpetrating such a hurtful act. She was so upset that she talked about it for several days and refused to return to any subsequent meetings. This illustrates that however supportive the intent is—in this case, the caring symbolized in the giving of a flower—the details and the implementation of that intent carry as much, or here, *more* significance than the intended message.

It is the delicate interplay between the real environment, the observed environment, and the perceived environment that becomes so critically significant in the design of therapeutic spaces. An understanding of these interactions must necessarily direct the vocabulary of the design as well as the implementation, if a healing benefit is to be obtained. Landscape architects must be aware of and control the symbolic meanings that may be contained within an environment, thereby being observed as part of it. It is equally important to learn about and design in relation to those meanings that may be projected upon the objects that we create, thus becoming part of the perception of that environment. One striking example of the symbolic meanings carried by an architectural object came to light as the result of an oversight on the part of a design team while creating a new cancer treatment center. This situation involved the unfortunate installation of a number of monolithic travertine slabs set at a tilting angle. These stone slabs rise from the floor to diagonally traverse the overhead space of a lower-level radiation waiting room and penetrate the glass building wall above. They continue, extending beyond the wall, up, out and over the adjacent plaza in a way that the medical staff and the city planner who reviewed the plans during the city's approval process perceived as resembling giant tilting gravestones. In reality, these are engineered, structural wall supports that are rectilinear in form and made from travertine tiles; from the interior, the physical cues are observed to be physically threatening—they look as though they could easily fall down in an

"Awakening in a state hovering between hibernation and sleep, I was able to focus long enough to detect a shimmering, light-reflecting mass of delicate white shapes out of the corner of my eye. From my bed this post-anesthesia stupor presented a respite from the recent chain of events which found me in a hospital bed, the repercussions of a poor decision to delay a surgical procedure following a miscarriage. The healing began with my awakening from the anesthetic to see the white dogwood blooming in profusion just outside my window. Over the next few days that glorious tree became an object on which I was able to focus and to remind me that there was still much beauty in the world I was fortunate to be returning to."

C. M., CALISTOGA, CA

Figure 3-2 The leaning pillars that penetrate the interior and exterior of this new treatment facility may be disturbing to some patients.

"Hospitals that are providing life-affirming surroundings for patients are not providing luxuries; these are essential ingredients of a positive patient attitude towards their recovery."

GERALD TURNER

earthquake—and from the exterior plaza, they are perceived as an emotionally threatening reminder of a bleak future.

This second level of filtering, that of interpreting one's surroundings based on personal experiences and expectations, is particularly relevant to design in medical facilities. Patients are vulnerable, partly because they are unwell and partly because they are in a stressful environment. Clinics and hospitals, even the best ones, serve to compound dependency, thereby increasing feelings of helplessness. This dependency tends to result in people feeling less confident than would normally be the case. Upon being admitted to an inpatient facility, patients are deprived of their ability to control their environnment, particularly in relation to access to privacy and the ability to make choices. Their lives are disrupted as they are removed from their social support network of family and friends; and their physical mobility and opportunities to exercise—even walking—are often severely curtailed. Because of these deprivations, as well as the intrusion of medical procedures themselves, the need for psychological escape and a desire for a positive distraction are intensified. Any depressive or anxious components in a person's emotional state will likely be projected onto the environment, as it is used to mirror the internal state—as with the widow just mentioned. In this vulnerable condition, people are more apt to perceive threatening or depressive messages in the objects around them.[1]

---

[1]Ulrich (Chapter 2) discusses fully the theory of emotional congruence in the process of perception.

The following chapters discuss common experiences of various patient groups, and suggest further ways to learn about, and to plan for, individual interpretations that are inevitably placed on the objects in the environment. It is clear, however, that there is an overarching principle. To create a supportive and healing environment for a vulnerable patient population, the symbolic meaning contained within the surroundings must be *unambiguously positive*.

Visitors and staff in medical facilities also tend to be coping with high levels of stress; these same mechanisms of perception apply to them. When they are "down" or stressed, what they see and what they will remember is the negative symbolism that they find in their surroundings. The attention of the landscape architect to the meanings conveyed in and through their design can enhance the intrinsic benefits of nature, as well as enable all to enjoy the support that a nonthreatening environment provides and the healing activities that may take place there.

This understanding of human perception, and particularly that of stressed or unwell populations, is the foundation for the following discussion on the philosophy of design—those principles and perspectives that are the underpinnings of the profession of landscape architecture. This review will assist the landscape architect to bring his or her approach into alignment with the goals of therapeutic design and refine, or if necessary, refocus his or her work. Following the presentation of three basic approaches to the design of therapeutic landscapes, the current research on nature and self-healing—primarily drawing upon the discipline of environmental psychology—is reviewed. This will introduce the designer to the uses and applications of research findings, so that these links can be better understood and utilized by the landscape architect.

DESIGN PERSPECTIVES

Like practioners of all other disciplines, landscape architects enter the profession for personal reasons, meeting their own needs through the application of their skills. In schools of design, they are taught the principles of spatial manipulation and the use and control of materials. These abstract ideas are most commonly taught in isolation from real-world factors, which are often said to hinder the creativity of the student. Some schools, however, do integrate information gathered from other disciplines into their programs. Aspects of the fields of environmental psychology and ecology are increasingly being taught under the rubrics of "people-oriented" and "sustainable design" practices. The need for such considerations is gaining recognition as exterior spaces become increasing limited and the expectations of, and demands upon, these spaces increase.

The relative merits of incorporating a knowledge base arising from another discipline have been discussed within the field for many years. Akin to the architectural debate as to whether form or function takes precedence, the split between landscape architecture as "art" and landscape architecture as a "service/craft" again moved to the forefront of attention in 1996 with the initiation of a conference intended to spark a dialogue within the landscape architecture-as-art segment of the profession—the Designed Landscape Forum. The coming together—hence, crystallization—of this element within the profession, although polarizing in some respects, has served to call attention to a basic philosophical divergence, which take on a great deal of significance in the arena of therapeutic landscapes.

It is these parallel thrusts—the increasing recognition of the need for the profession to perform a service to humanity as well as caring for the global environment and the mounting popularity of landscape architecture as an artistic endeavor—that form the backdrop of the design process at the time of publication of this book. Taking this opportunity to step back and assess the various approaches to landscape architecture will allow the designer to make conscious his or her biases, and to implement the design of therapeutic landscapes with clarity. For the purposes of this discussion, three broad philosophical approaches to the design of healing landscapes have been outlined: traditional approaches to design; the botanical/ecological approach to design; and the people-oriented approach. Each approach contains within it a range of stylistic perspectives.

In practice, few landscape architects operate exclusively from one perspective; most take a blended approach to their work. However, these differing perspectives, which serve as starting points when approaching the design of a landscape, influence the form and character of the final design. We will therefore examine these perspectives as discrete entities and consider how these have been, or might be, applied to the design of gardens in healthcare facilities.

Traditional Approaches

This approach incorporates three distinct and rather different subdivisions: designs based on historical precedents, designs incorporating regional attributes, and what we have called "statement art" (Figure 3-3). All of these subcategories repre-

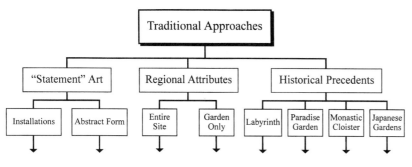

Fig. 3-3 Traditional Design Approaches to landscape architecture. Site examples are listed below each category.

sent a design philosophy that is part of the heritage of being a landscape architect. Many neophyte landscape architects are educated and trained how to approach their work from these perspectives and how to apply their vocabulary. This training can be blended with other concerns and foci, yielding a hybrid approach. But sometimes they are practiced in their pure form.

Historical precedents refers to those design approaches that have been with us throughout recorded history and continue to be drawn upon today. This category incorporates a range of design styles and traditions. For the purposes of this book, we are concerned only with the few of those precedents that are associated with rejuvenation and healing, specifically, the Labyrinth, the Japanese Zen and Tea Gardens, Paradise Gardens, and the Monastic Cloister Garden.

The Labyrinth, or unicursal maze, appeared in Greek mythology, and its derivation has also been traced to Egypt, appearing as early as 2000 BC. Representations of the classic pattern similar to the Cretan Labyrinth were carved in stone by many ancient cultures on many continents. This has been the most frequently used of all labyrinth patterns, and has been incorporated into the ritual celebrations and rights of passage of many European cultures. First appearing in stone, then adapted to the "turf maze," it has often been used for contemplation—traversing a symbolic journey to the center and rebirth, then back out again—and it is also used for symbolic cleansing. Scandinavian sailors used these labyrinths, often called "Troy-towns" from Greek mythology, before setting sail. By walking to the center and running quickly out, it was thought that evil spirits and bad weather were left behind (Campbell, no date). They have also appeared within cathedrals

Figure 3-4   A solitary 'traveler' is circling this labyrinth at California Pacific Medical Center, San Francisco, California, U.S.A.

"The human mind has an infinite capacity for expansion or contraction. Therefore humans can grasp vastness in the crack of a small stone."

ERAN BEN-JOSEPH

—notably in Chartres, France—and were originally walked as a substitute for a pilgrimage to the Holy Land. Today, they are reappearing in a few ecclesiastical and medical settings, and are used by individuals for walking meditations and also in some religious ceremonies.

One present-day installation of a classic Cretan Labyrinth is in the main entry of the California Pacific Medical Center in San Francisco, California. Here the pattern has been incorporated into the stone paving in the main plaza outside the hospital. People coming and going are often seen re-creating their own version of the 4000-year-old ritual, moving into the center and back out again. Perhaps in the slowing down of the pace of the day, or perhaps more internally, the symbolism of turning, turning, and turning again to "see" from all angles is helpful. Whatever the mechanism, the labyrinth still beckons people to leave their troubles at the its heart.

The concept of the Japanese Zen Garden appeared between 1185 and 1333—during the latter part of the Kamakura period (Ben-Joseph, 1987, p. 14). During this time, there was a move to reduce nature to its essential forms—as had long been captured in Japanese ink paintings—to bring together all of the elements of the landscape into "a picturesque 'image' that can be taken in at a glance" (Schaarschmidt-Richter, 1979, p 185). This type of garden became the focus of philosophical contemplation and a means of enlightenment. Often composed of stone and few plants—and thought of as a "dry" garden by Westerners—the Zen garden does not necessarily have be so. Planting can predominate, as long as the forms and placement represent the simple essence of nature.

Figure 3-5 A Zen Garden requires almost constant attention to maintain its purity of form.

Evolving from the Zen Garden, but distinct from it in that the creation was intended to serve a concrete function— that of preparing for the tea ceremony —is the Japanese Tea Garden, which was developed in the latter part of the eighteenth century (Schaarschmidt-Richter, 1979). Ben-Joseph describes the Tea Garden: "It is a conscious creation of psychologically oriented design…A breaking point from the outside world which produces aesthetic sensations conducive to the actual (tea) ceremony…" He goes on to quote Kakuzo Okakura's *Book of Tea:* "One who has trodden this garden path cannot fail to remember how his spirit, as he has walked in the twilight of evergreens overhead, over the regular irregularities of the steppingstones, beneath which lay dried pine needles, and pass beside the moss-covered granite lanterns, became uplifted above ordinary thoughts" (in Ben-Joseph, 1987, p 21).

The Japanese Tea Garden is difficult to translate to the medical setting, if the critical components are to be retained. The cleansing properties of the Tea Garden are primarily conveyed through the experience of traveling a set path of directed vistas, focal points, and places of contemplation. One of the components of this route are the "regular irregularities" in the path, causing the person to slow down, to look at the ground, enticing him or her to take in that minute level of detail and to get lost in the moment of their senses. A universally accessible path would, by definition, smooth out these irregularities and hesitations. Alternate mechanisms of slowing and focusing would need to be incorporated into the design. Would the feeling be lost for the patient who had to stay on a wider, smoother

Figure 3-6 Irregularities in the path and purposefully placed objects to draw attention into the moment are two components of a Japanese Tea garden.

path? Perhaps. The advantages to the visitor, to staff, and to able-bodied patients could still be provided by a secondary path, winding through the garden. The other components—directed attention to a sequence of focal points, the serene plantings, changes in scale, and so on—would benefit all who looked upon the garden. The more traditional Zen Garden is directly translatable to the medical setting in that it is designed for observation rather than participation. A moss garden, for instance, designed in the reductionist Zen style, would contain the meditative element in the context of a soothing green carpet. At the time of writing, the University of Florida Shands Cancer Center is the only facility that is known by the authors to have installed a Zen garden. While this garden style has not been observed or studied in a medical setting, the stillness of nature and the contemplative components of this classic design have provided a healing benefit for centuries.

Other types of historically established restorative gardens are the Islamic Paradise Garden and the Monastic Garden. Like the Japanese Tea Garden, these are walled spaces with set elements within. The origins of the Paradise Garden may be as early as 2500 BC, perhaps derived from the search of King Gilgamesh for everlasting life in the "Garden of the Gods," a place of "eternal and everlasting beauty, sustenance, and pleasure. There, the Tree of Life bears...fruit of imperishable beauty. These are the elements of hope, survival, and benefit, an oasis in an otherwise hostile environment" (Beckwith and Gilster, 1996, p. 45). Four significant elements of the Paradise Garden, as identified by Moynihan (*Ibid.*, p. 46)—the enclosing wall, water, canopy, and hill—have been adapted and incorporated into the Alois Alzheimer Center in Cincinnati, Ohio (presented as a case study in Chapter 9). The Paradise Garden has been more traditionally applied in one of the courtyard areas of the Woodlands Nursing Home in Lambeth, UK, where the garden maintains a more traditional arrangement, with a symmetrical design, a small fountain in the middle of cross-axes, and a formal bosk of trees. Unfortunately, the intensity of reflected light in this enclosed space—exacerbated by the fact that this is a recent installation—is quite high, creating a harsh transition from the adjacent day room. In such cases as this, where the sensitivity of patients' eyes or some other physical constraint is a factor, the replication of the precise design must be adapted to accommodate the patients' needs.

The Monastic Cloister Garden was an integral part of early monastic communities and hospices and the genesis of gardens in healthcare settings (see also Chapter 1). Paradoxically, the authors have been unable to find a present-day healthcare application of this classic garden form. Although the arrangement of planting within the Cloister Garden has changed over time (Gerlach-Spriggs et al., 1998), one consistent element has been the surround on all sides of a colonnade or arcade. It is this feature in particular that makes it most appropriate for a healthcare setting. Seemingly an ideal design for those who are unwell, the colonnade accommodates a variety of needs. The shadow cast by the overhanging roof serves to create a transitional space for those with visual impairment; those with mobility limitations can easily exercise by circumnavigating the garden; sheltered seating is easy to provide, thereby extending the use of the garden into the transitional seasons; and the walls and roof serve to trap and amplify the natural sounds within the garden. The low overhead creates a human-scale space, which, if carried on throughout the garden, can provide comfort to the people within. Still seen in religious settings, these gardens have as yet to be reapplied to the present-day medical environment.

Many of these gardens have been analyzed as to the components that influence human interaction and feelings (see e.g., Beckwith and Gilster, 1996, on Paradise Gardens, and Ben-Joseph, 1987, on Japanese Gardens). Also, due to their longevity, these garden designs could be said to have stood the test of time, repeated and adapted over centuries. They tap into deep memories, some culturally bound, others more universal. Providing solace and escape, as in the Monastic and Islamic gardens, or cleansing and release as with the Labyrinth and the Tea Garden, this bolstering of the spirit is believed to be healing to the mind and body as well.

As noted earlier, the direct "importing" of these gardens is difficult and may engender a number of problems. Vince Healy comments: "Producing an exact replica of one of these gardens —whether a Japanese tea garden or a cloistered European herb garden—would be costly ... to execute, [and] difficult to maintain ... [the key] is to integrate those concepts into settings where elements and use are familiar to everyday life" (Healy, 1986, p. 32). However, drawing from these ancient lessons when approaching the landscape design of present-day medical settings can provide a framework from which to begin; for these gardens are each walled,[2] protected, and imbued with power. As such, they are cultural archetypes for healing and restoration.

"... [Good garden design] employs the mind without fatigue, tranquilizes yet enlivens it and thus gives the effect of refreshing rest and reinvigoration."
FREDERICK LAW OLMSTED

---

[2]Although there is no physical wall around the Labyrinth, the pattern itself creates "walls" within the design, which dictate not only the path, but also the perception of one who is walking the Labyrinth. The visual rotations that are a part of walking the large radial turns of the arc, alternating with the tight 360-degree "returns," and the attention required to stay on the route, combine to keep the mind directed and focused, "inside the walls."

Figure 3-7   This second floor courtyard provides seating, but the undulating paving causes problems for all but the most agile.

Adapting these classic garden styles to meet the present-day requirements of a healthcare setting requires creativity and adaptability, as some of these gardens can incorporate the accessibility and mobility demands of a medical setting more easily than others. The high level of attention to detail in both the planning and the maintenance required by such designs becomes a commitment and the dedication of resources becomes a statement on the part of the hospital. The garden can be a vehicle for the facility to visibly depict the degree of attention that, hopefully, is directed to all matters within the medical facility.[3]

Another aspect of the traditional approach to landscape architecture, that of using the *regional attributes* of a particular setting, can be drawn upon for inspiration and can form the basis for design decisions. Such themes can be developed and used throughout a site, both inside and out. This is often done to provide a sense of identity for the organization or institution and can run the gamut from master site planning, to interior detailing and corporate logos. Incorporating local icons or attributes can offer a sense of cohesion and connection with the surroundings.

Two examples of such an application are the designs of St. Mary's Hospital on the Isle of Wight, UK, and the Leichtag Family Healing Garden at the San Diego Children's Hospital in California; interestingly, both have adopted a water theme. St. Mary's Hospital is on an island off the south coast of England. Here the water theme runs throughout the entire hospital in art mosaics, tapestries, tile work, murals and so on. It is an impressive display, much enjoyed by the local populace. However, this concept became the driving force at the expense of some basic practical issues in a few locations. One such area is a small courtyard where the undulations of the flooring become three-dimensional, resulting in insecure footing and a very awkward traverse for those who venture out to the benches set in this undulating "sea." In San Diego, the theme of waves and beaches is used only within the Leichtag Family Healing Garden. Here it is represented in the paving materials that swirl throughout most of the site, in the adaptation of the beach umbrella into fanciful bench arrangements, a seahorse fountain, and so on. The portrayal of the theme prompted extensive use of blue and green concrete representing the ocean and

[3] Jain Malkin speaks of the new client's need to evaluate a healthcare setting. Because patients have virtually no access to any substantive way to evaluate the quality of care, the level of detailing in the environment and the quality of the maintenance—which are representative of the caring given to the physical surroundings—become the visible indicators of a facility's overall quality of care (Malkin, 1992).

areas of crushed fines for the sandy beaches. These depictions in turn limited the planting to small "islands" and the "cliff tops"—symbolized by the concrete and stone seat wall planters. This limited amount of greenery—which studies in gardens at medical facilities in California indicate is the most frequently mentioned beneficial element of a garden (Cooper Marcus and Barnes, 1995)—is a missed opportunity. Fifty percent of those interviewed in the garden requested more "trees, greenery, and vegetation" (Whitehouse, 1998). Another simple oversight that could have been incorporated into the theme, if therapeutic benefits had been more fully understood, is that the "beach" within the garden could have been represented by a free-form sandbox, which would have provided a wonderful activity area (see also the case study in Chapter 7).

Figure 3-8 *Swirls of blue concrete and fixtures representing sea animals are used in this garden to convey a water theme. (San Diego Children's Hospital, California, U.S.A.)*

There are several advantages to using a regional approach, particularly if the concept is applied in a more realistic form rather than veering toward the abstract. By incorporating element(s) from the surroundings, the transition from the community at large to the medical setting is bridged. This familiarity can enhance the level of comfort for the users. In addition to providing inspiration and an integrated design theme, this approach can enhance marketing and fundraising by providing a readily accessible "tag" to be used in its promotion. If, however, the attribute is taken to extreme abstraction, the benefit of familiarity is lost, and the possibility for negative meaning to be imbued upon the objects is increased.

Examples of *statement art* are installations that are created with the intent of conveying a message or making a mark on the land. The artistic concept is of paramount importance—indeed, it is sometimes the only focus of the piece. Issues of use, and even accessibility, are often of minimal significance. In installations, the statement often takes an abstract form. The manipulation of the natural to look unnatural, or conversely the use of constructed objects to represent living things, is frequently applied when practicing in this realm. For it is in the trick of the eye or the confounding of the brain that the statement is often made.

One medical setting where this approach has been applied through the construction of artistically placed walls is in three courtyards at the West Dorset Hospital in England. Here the arcing walls, made from rough-cut stone, rise from the ground and recede again, slicing in and out of the courtyard patios. While dry stone walls are common to the regional landscape of northern England, they are not a familiar sight in Dorset; in addition, the undulation of the walls sets them quite apart from any natural form. Though the emergency helicopter pilots are able to appreciate the interesting pattern that is created within

Figure 3-9   Three courtyards echo each other's curving stone walls, creating an artistic statement at West Dorset Hospital, UK.

the footprint of the hospital, from the building windows, the courtyards appear hard, sparse and illogical. The planting is minimal—strips of low shrubbery at the base of the walls and a few trees—and the design relies upon the architectural statement of the dramatic walls to achieve the designer's intent. The courtyards are sloped, and a bench or two is set in each one, offering those who are adequately ambulatory the choice of sitting outside and the opportunity to challenge themselves to a stroll up the incline. The healing benefits of strolling in fresh air and the escape from the medical surroundings may be augmented by the diversion of attention caused by the uniqueness of the artistic statement. Unfortunately, known benefits have been lost in the making of this "design statement," for greenery and wildlife have been abandoned for the sake of the art piece.

Additionally, risks have been increased because landscape abstractions (similar to abstract art) are designed to evoke interpretations, and often a wide range of reactions will arise from any given piece. While this may be stimulating and interesting among a healthy and unstressed population, it is a high-risk proposition in a vulnerable population. With people who are in a depressed, anxious, or otherwise negative frame of mind, the likelihood that the perception of the piece will be negative is quite high. When healing is a goal, providing a feeling of safety and protection is a therapeutic necessity. Ambiguity leaves too much room for negative perceptions.

Is "statement art" an appropriate approach to hospital garden design? Are there advantages to this type of landscape in a medical setting? If done with attention to the characteristics that minimize negative perception and to the sought-after healing qualities mentioned throughout this book, it could be therapeutic. Without this level of attunement, however, the garden becomes simply a benefit in terms of its aesthetic marketability. The administration may be able to use it to attract donors or more clientele—especially if the designer is well known; and the designer may be able to do the same. The users, however, will most likely come up short, as the degree of emphasis on the "statement" seems to be inversely related to the level of sensitivity to the users. At best, it is likely to be a lost opportunity for support or relief, and at worst, will trigger an experience that increases stress and inhibits innate healing abilities.

As is evident throughout this discussion, the traditional tools and approaches that are a part of the landscape architect's philosophy may help, or hinder, the professional's ability to successfully create a healing space. Other avenues are open to the designer, however. These are discussed next.

Botanical or Ecological Approaches

A second cluster of approaches to the design of outdoor spaces in healthcare settings grows out of the fields of botany and ecology. This cluster can be divided into those gardens with a focus on the use of medicinal plants and those that are designed to be sustainable (Figure 3-10).

Sustainability is a concept that is difficult to define, and the variations on its implementation are many. The design team may define it in several ways, ranging from the use of native plants to companion planting, organic maintenance practices, permaculture, and so forth. The intent of this approach is to create an ecosystem within the built environment that is in harmony with nature's own support systems, one that will return what it takes, so that the life cycle may continuously flow without depleting the resources of the environment. This concept

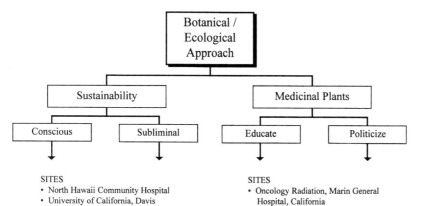

Figure 3-10 Botanical and Ecological Approaches to landscape architecture. Site examples are listed below each category.

"Our eyes do not divide us from the world, but unite us with it. Let this be known to be true. Let us then abandon the simplicity of separation and give unity its due. Let us abandon the self-mutilation which has been our way and give expression to the potential harmony of man-nature. The world is abundant, we require only a deference born of understanding to fulfill man's promise.... To do this he must design with nature."

IAN McHARG

"Nature eliminates a surplus and compensates for deficiency."

TAO TE CHING

may be applied in such a way as to be consciously brought to the attention of the user, through a plaque or literature. More often, however, designers incorporate this approach into their philosophy believing that even if the user's conscious mind is ignorant, the healing will take place at a subliminal level.

The Gardens of Makahikilua, at North Hawaii Community Hospital, have not yet been constructed; however, the plans indicate a very comprehensive application of ecological principles, extended to include humans in the ecosystem. Elements of this garden include a Self-sufficient Hawaiian Garden; a Biointensive Mini-farm; Mini Orchards designed for research in permaculture; thematic gardens including the Garden of Hope and the Garden of Four Noble Plants and Three Friends; and patient room gardens entitled Botanical Lace gardens. Designed to be spiritually healing as well as physically therapeutic, the intent of these last is described by the designer: "Together, the gardens form a 'Botanical Lace' to moderate temperatures; pump oxygen; create privacy, a lovely view and the sounds of nature; muffle noise and pollution; and create an easy focal point for patient contemplation and relaxation" (O'Neill, 1996, p. 94).

When this approach is applied, the belief is that the individual using the space can perhaps relax, or feel better taken care of, in an environment where the focus has been to promote the health of all living things. If the design intent goes unmentioned, the benefit is thought to be experienced at a deeper level of awareness; and the natural environmental harmony that has been sustained, or perhaps restored, is believed to extend to all species in that environment. The advantages for the designer and client include knowing that the negative impact a constructed landscape can have on the surrounding ecosystem is minimized and perhaps—especially if the site was previously built upon—the garden will also improve the local conditions by increasing both the carbon dioxide - oxygen exchange and the diversity of plant and animal life. The larger community is likely to benefit from this low-impact treatment of the land and may, as in the previous example, have the opportunity to become directly involved, by volunteering in the garden—thereby reaping social and perhaps therapeutic benefits themselves.

The use and labeling of *medicinal plants* is a widely used component of contemporary healing gardens in healthcare settings. There are two streams within this design application. First is the promotion of education among the users: the idea being that seeing the natural plant form of the drugs used in medical treatment brings these chemicals into the realm of the knowable, and demystifies them. This incorporation of the drugs' sources into the immediate surroundings brings a degree of familiarity, which may serve to increase the patient's level of comfort with a treatment that otherwise may feel intrusive and alien. A second—and in this author's opinion a rather counter-productive—trend that has appeared in some gardens is to use the naming of the plants to call attention to the diminution of the earth's biodiversity and the fragility of our planetary sustainability. Although this latter has not been observed as the major emphasis of a garden in a healthcare setting, in those gardens where planetary sustainability is raised as an issue, the message may be too depressing for vulnerable users.

One healing garden where this approach was employed is adjacent to an oncology radiation waiting room at Marin General Hospital in California. The garden can be entered, but due to its size and to mobility limitations within the garden, it functions predominantly as a viewing garden. An annotated copy of the plan of the garden is displayed on a pedestal, which is set to prop open the door on nice days. A handout of small, beautifully crafted black-and-white images of plants, which are gathered together into a leaflet, describes the plants in the garden and their connection to the medical world. The staff and patients are very pleased with the garden, and it has been reported that at least one patient has been known to collect what she believed to be "healing waters" from the fountain. Clearly, the transformation of this previously neglected court-yard has had a beneficial impact; what remains unknown is what part(s) of this design are healing—is it the fountain, or the lush summer greenery, or the naming of the plants?

Drawing upon the lessons of current research, it is likely that the primary advantage provided by labels in a garden is in the reading of the names and the engagement of the intellect—serving as a distraction, albeit it a short one. This may help to lift one out of a depressive reverie or otherwise uncomfortable state and facilitate the opportunity for a subsequent change in mood. However, sensory stimulation also serves this purpose (Barnes, 1994; Kaplan and Talbot, 1983). Bringing the treatment into the realm of the familiar may help some people, but for those who are seeking a complete getaway, the presentation of this information may be experienced as an intrusion.

People-Oriented Approach

A third basic orientation to healing landscapes that directs the goals and areas of emphasis for the landscape architect is one primarily based on the interaction between humans and their environment. Three perspectives fall within this approach (see Figure 3-10). At the present, knowledge based on personal experience or clinical practice are the two predominant perspectives. The approach based on *personal experience* has

"While our five month old son lay so ill in Boston Children's Hospital, we went several times to the spacious garden for some much needed respite from the nightmare going on all around us. To be sure, the garden gave us a tiny, welcome glimpse of natural life, the only piece of nature for many blocks around. But we must have wanted the garden to reflect the wholeness and natural beauty that our child was trying so hard to embody. Ultimately, we could not find the oasis we craved from the scientific, diagnostic drama because it had such an organized, labeled, hands-off, distant feeling, not unlike the attitude inside the building. Most of the times we sat or ate in the garden, helicopters landed regularly on the roof with ear piercing, soul shattering intensity, bringing emergencies to the hospital. It seemed as if both the soul of nature and of the child were subjected to the same forces of man, and in the end, neither benefitted."

B. W. AND R. R.,
TAOS, NEW MEXICO

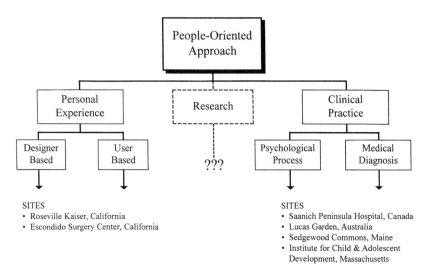

Figure 3-11 People-Oriented Approaches to landscape architecture. The underdeveloped category of research based design is shown in dashed lines. Site examples are listed below the other categories.

arisen out of a desire on the part of hospital clients to work with designers who are familiar with the experience of patients in medical settings and are informed in their decision making. Consequently, there are growing numbers of landscape architects who are drawing on their own medical experiences for inspiration and applying their personal knowledge of health issues to the design process. Applying personal knowledge has its advantages in that a designer may represent a group of like-minded or psychologically similar individuals. To the extent that such a landscape architect can act intuitively and implement gardens that would be healing to her or him, a portion of the population will be served.

Other designers may base their work on the conception of what the experience of a patient under treatment *might* be. The Escondido Surgery Center in southern California is one site where the empathetic understanding of the experience of a patient going through surgery has been the guiding inspiration for the creation of a series of healing spaces. Here the landscape architect designed six gardens, each representing a physiological arena in the surgical procedure: reception, separation, anesthesia, awakening, recovery, and reunion. Using the steel and glass of the modern building to symbolize the precision of surgery, the atriums and courtyard gardens were designed with softer elements and hand-built stone walls to represent the contrast of human touch. Water elements were incorporated to draw wildlife into the courtyards, and the site features were hand-finished, with the intent of representing and conveying to the observer the high level of caring attention that is practiced throughout the facility (Six Metaphysical Gardens, 1995).

While designing from personal experience is no guarantee of success, the advantages of this more human approach to design can be substantial. The focus of the design is automatically upon the experience of the user in the space. Whether derived from one's own medical experience or an empathetic creation, the design will most probably address issues of stress reduction, physical comfort, accessibility, distraction, and escape, as these are universal issues among patients. The potential drawbacks lie in the implementation of these concepts. Based on a single experience, or an imagined one, the methods used may be fitting to a greater or lesser number of people. What is healing for one individual is a good start, but it stops short of confident implementation of a landscape designed with the greatest potential to heal.

The other direction that informed, people-oriented design has taken is that of drawing upon *clinical practice* and applying the knowledge gained there to the process of landscape design. There are currently two sources of clinical information: that based on a specific disease or diagnosis and that arising from psychological and developmental criteria. Alzheimer's facilities are some of the best-known institutions to have taken advantage of information gained through studying a specific medical diagnosis. Designers are aware of the patient's need to pace, of their diminishing capacity for memory, their increased agitation, and their reduced ability to make choices, and this awareness has led directly into landscape design decisions. A path for pacing with no dead-ends (which might increase agitation), few forks necessitating decision making, and a plant palette that evokes the memories of childhood are now standard practice in the design of Alzheimer's gardens (see Chapter 9 for a comprehensive discussion of designing for Alzheimer's facilities).

Figure 3-12   This garden at an Alzheimer's facility incorporates several areas of interest without prompting wayfinding difficulties for confused residents. (The Nature Room, The Lodge at Broadmead, Victoria, B.C., Canada.)

Figure 3-13   Up in the branches of this stately cedar these adolescent boys have found a private hide-away.

Figure 3-14   Water in the landscape can evoke a multitude of sentiments. Crossing a stream can represent the trials of a journey, cleansing, or a symbolic rebirth.

Recreational spaces for children have long embodied the lessons of developmental psychology in the design of play equipment. This approach is readily translated into gardens at medical facilities, where the design should incorporate subareas that allow the user to select his or her activity and location based on the developmental stage of growth that needs attending. A child who needs protection may seek an enclosed womb-like area for safety, while another, exploring issues of mastery, may choose exhilarating equipment to challenge himself or herself. Adults may also seek out areas of comfort that often relate to a specific developmental stage. Addressing these needs in a garden setting is only now arising, as the concept of therapeutic gardens is gaining in popularity. Examples are elements that may provide psychological sustenance might be: bridges, which represent change, transition, and growth; a winding path, representing a journey through the past or the anticipation of the future; water for its symbolic meaning as the source of life or for its cleansing and soothing abilities; and so forth. A developmentally based approach accommodates as many different needs as is appropriate to the size and constraints of the space.

Sedgewood Commons in Maine, presented as a case study in Chapter 9, is an example of a design based on both the medical diagnosis of Alzheimer's disease and on a theory of psychological development. The landscape architect incorporated in his design an application of a theory of psychological regression that has been observed in this progressive disease. In this three-tiered facility, he designed gardens that move back in time for each stage of the disease, addressing the developmental needs and preferred activities of each period of accessible memory.

The advantages of applying knowledge from clinical disciplines to landscape design are in the application of specific information regarding the relevant needs of a given patient population. Arising from the observation of groups of people, rather than from the experiences of an individual, the applicability is also relatively generalizable within that diagnosis group. The focus remains on the experiences of the user, while the sensibilities of another discipline are applied to increase the potential healing benefit of a design that incorporates this perspective. Although this procedure comes a long way toward achieving maximum therapeutic benefit, the link to design applications is not explicit. There is room for misinterpretation and misapplication of information as it is translated into design goals. For that reason, best practice today should involve the incorporation of *research* that links emotions with environment and therefore is directly applicable to the design of the landscape.

It is the observation of the authors of this book that research being conducted on this topic is underutilized—even as greater and greater amounts of information are emerging. The following section is an introduction to the application of research to the design process. By looking at this overview, the designer and client will be able to identify some of the various approaches to environmental research, and how they can inform design decision making.

RESEARCH

There is a growing source of information on therapeutic environments being gathered through empirical research on the relationship between healing and exposure to nature. With the notable exception of post-occupancy evaluations, these sources have barely been tapped by the design professions, and their application to the design of landscaped spaces is negligible. This is a serious oversight in the effort to create spaces that are as beneficial as possible. For although the definitive answer to what exactly is healing about gardens and greenery is not agreed upon, a growing number of studies address just that question. Landscape designs based on such information, termed "hypothesis design" by Hartig (Chapter 12), could and should apply knowledge about the connection between healing and the natural environment.

More and more disciplines are beginning to recognize the influence of the environment on physical and mental health. These disciplines (see Figure 3-15) are now beginning to address this connection by studying the effect that our surroundings have on a number of factors—or processes—which indicate how an individual may be reacting to his or her environment. Currently, however, the largest body of directly relevant research is not being utilized in the design process to any significant degree. It is the goal of this discussion to demystify the available research and thereby increase the accessibility of this information source.

The discussion that follows describes the methods most commonly used in relevant research, the relative reliability of these methods, and what those studies that deal directly with the exterior environment can reveal to the designer. Each type of study presented is discussed in relation to the specific areas where there is the potential for a direct contribution to landscape architecture.

The methodologies used in empirical research on human interaction and the environment generally involve one or more

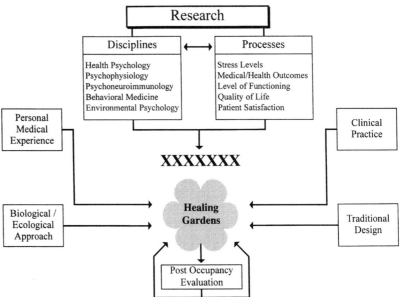

Figure 3-15 The variety of approaches to designing healing gardens in medical facilities. Research from a variety of disciplines is becoming increasingly available – but remains disconnected from the design process.

of the following ways of gathering information: self-report, observation, and physiological measures. Self-report includes interviews with users, questionnaires, analysis of essay and journal writing, and the like. Observation is just that: watching individual actions, mapping routes—and over time, trends—recording demographic information about the user, and finally, relating the behavioral recordings to observations of the environment (e.g., the relative attraction of sun versus shade in seating arrangements or the predominance of people choosing to be near a water feature or a vending machine). Physiological measures are the recording of physical and chemical changes within the body that are linked with emotion. Heart rate and blood pressure are two well-known physiological measurements. Also frequently measured in this context are the acidity of sweat (galvanic skin tests) and, in sedentary situations, brainwaves and minute changes in facial expression (flickering of eyelids, movement of smile muscles, etc.).

Depending on the type of information/data sought, these different techniques will produce varying degrees of accuracy. The most reliable way to record behavior is to observe it. To ask people to recall their behavior, or to try to predict their behavior in a given, imagined situation is much less accurate. However, if the information seeks not just "what" an individual does, but "why," observation alone is insufficient in that it requires the recorder/observer to place an interpretation upon everything that is recorded. A subject's thoughts and feelings, previous actions, subsequent emotions, and other potentially relevant information remain unknown. For example, in the roof garden at Alta Bates Medical Center (case study presented in Chapter 5), the most highly used area of the garden was a covered alcove just outside of the elevators. This space was the only covered spot in the roof garden, and it contained the only vending machines. The numbers of people choosing to sit and stand in this area can be "observed," but were people here because of proximity to the elevator? Because they were under a roof? Because they used the machines? Because it was protected from the wind? Or for some other reason? This information is not revealed through observation alone. In this case, the addition of self-report increases reliability, though it is still susceptible to distortion. Self-report incorporates thoughts and feelings into the database, but all information gathered in this manner is filtered through the subject's interpretation and then reiterated by the individuals involved. In addition to the internal distortions inherent in perception, the results may be skewed due to the subject's desire to please the tester/interviewer, by giving what they believe to be the "right" answer, or to present themselves in a desirable manner. This tendency is slightly less apparent in journal analysis because when the information is being written down, the involvement of the tester is more remote and the desire on the part of the subject to please is less evident.

Physiological measures do not help to establish why a behavior is observed, but they do definitively assess what emotional responses are occurring. By directly measuring physiological responses, the filtering of the conscious mind of both the subject and the tester is bypassed. Specific and reliable information can be gathered about emotions aroused within quite a narrow time frame—hence specific environmental stimuli can be linked to specific emotional responses. The collection of data through the review of medical records containing a mix of medical/physiological information and behavioral commentary can also be used in the evaluation of the effects of the environment on a patient population.

The studies discussed below can contribute to the process of making informed decisions about design. One or a combination of the aforementioned methodologies can be used in these research procedures. The form that these studies take are either laboratory experiments, quasi-experimental studies in the outdoors, surveys about restorative experiences, or postoccupancy evaluations of gardens in medical facilities. With a basic understanding of the methods and their degree of relevance to the various factors involved in design, landscape architects can utilize these studies to make research-based decisions in their creation of a healing garden.

"Wilderness Studies" is the name given to a growing number of quasi-experimental studies that investigate the relationship

Figure 3-16 *Time alone observing nature is a strong antidote for stress. Whether it is the antics of a squirrel, or the play of light on still water, absorption into nature's gentle side helps us to slow down and take time to heal.*

Figure 3-17 *This site was selected by a wilderness study participant for a three day solitary fast. The combination of rugged beauty, exposure to the elements, and the protection from people passing along the trail offered by the granite outcropping matched this individual's psychological needs for both serenity and challenge.*

between humans and remote natural settings. This research approach focuses on the psychological changes within individuals as they spend time in undeveloped natural wilderness areas. There are many contributors to this arena; some of the more well-known authors are associated with the Outward Bound Organization (e.g., Bacon, 1983), which conducts wilderness trips for personal growth. Terry Hartig and associates (e.g., Hartig et al., 1991) and Rachael and Stephen Kaplan and their students (e.g., Kaplan and Talbot, 1983; Kaplan and Kaplan, 1989) have studied this aspect of emotions and the environment. This research addresses several areas that have implications for landscape architecture. For example, the following journal entries made during a personal growth wilderness trip reveal three levels of interaction with the environment: (1) landscape preferences, such as what types of areas and individual may be drawn to and why ("For my three-day solo, I chose a granite rock jutting out into the lake. Exposed, rugged, with a forked pine outside my tent, I was protected from three sides and had a front-row seat for every sunset!"); (2) psychological processes ("I was glad to have time to reflect on my leap of faith into a second career; and when the frog dropped from the sky and landed on my head, I began to believe in miracles!"); (3) social factors ("Being alone in the wilderness has never been scary for me, but when I realized that I am more afraid of the two-leggeds than the four-leggeds, I realized why I am so uncomfortable in the city.")[4] The frequency and patterning of these types of comments, in relation to various environmental characteristics, indicate which changes in behavior and attitude may be associated with the surrounding environment. Applied to the designed landscape, these indicators of sought-after landscape qualities, and the emotions that surface in these settings, give an indication of the types of stresses and the types of solutions people are able to address when surrounded by nature.

The Restoration Survey category of research includes research based on self-report, regarding where individuals go when they are seeking emotional solace. Carolyn Francis and Clare Cooper Marcus (1991) were the first to explore this arena, with studies incorporating the analysis of the places selected by subjects for sought-after experiences, and a comparison of indoor and outdoor selections. Empirical research by Barnes (1994) follows from this to analyze "built" and "natural" outdoor sites for distinctive qualities as well as similarities. In addition to corroborating the elements cited in the Francis and Cooper Marcus study, the complexity of emotional healing was addressed and a process of emotional restoration became evident.

---

[4]These are journal entries from a "vision quest" wilderness trip in 1984, incorporated in a paper by Barnes (1983).

The following examples of responses elicited by the Barnes study (1994) demonstrates how this growing body of research addresses landscape preferences in regard to the affective qualities of space ("I wanted a place that would be private, so I could cry, yet close to people, so I wouldn't feel so alone"); psychological processes ("The pounding of the surf absorbed my screams; catharsis happens when it all comes out like that.") and self-selected activities ("It was the challenge of the hike through the rugged and rocky terrain that exhausted me, and my anger came out as sweat through every pore."). These surveys link stress reduction and emotional restoration with behaviors, physical landscape elements, and (as in Barnes, 1994) design goals. From the more general information gathered in the wilderness studies, the restoration survey research begins to identify specific qualities and characteristics that are described as "healing" by the subjects studied.

Simulated laboratory experiments that are relevant to landscape architecture are primarily based on viewing pictures or videos of outdoor scenes, though some studies include auditory cues as well. Contrasting pairs of images are often used to measure and compare the reactions prompted by the experience. Roger Ulrich and students (e.g., Ulrich, 1979, 1981) and Terry Hartig (e.g., Hartig et al., 1996) are major contributors in this field where physiological changes are recorded as participants are subjected to stresses and potential recovery experiences. The areas addressed through these studies that are relevant to landscape architecture are: speed of recovery from stress, duration of recovery, arousal of fear and pleasure reactions, and landscape preferences. Physiological measures are also used in quasi-experimental "naturalistic studies." These are conducted in the outdoors with the subjects' physiological changes being monitored by mechanical recording devices (e.g., stopping to take blood pressure readings at specific intervals along a route through an arboretum). This procedure has the advantage of incorporating all of the senses in the experimental trial; however, it is harder to eliminate confounding variables. The application of this information to landscape architecture is in providing statistically reliable data on the instantaneous, and often subconscious, reactions to environmental stimuli. It is through these two avenues that the finer gradations of what is healing (birds singing versus a bamboo windchime, or moving water versus a standing pool) can be assessed. Because the landscape architect has discretion over such matters down to this level of detail, this is a valuable resource for the fine-tuning of a garden and developing the greatest potential therapeutic benefit.

Post-occupancy evaluations are studies conducted in a designed setting—in this case, a landscape—with the goal of

Figure 3-18 The Post Occupancy Evaluation is one form of research that is readily applicable to landscape architecture. Conducting P.O.E.s should become standard practice in all healing garden installations. (The Comfort Garden, San Francisco General Hospital, California, U.S.A.)

assessing the advantages and limitations of that space for its users and non-users. Data collection most often incorporates observation and self-report gathered through interviews with the users. In medical settings, the additional means of checking medical records is available, and in other residential settings such as nursing homes, behavior reports can be used. Post–occupancy evaluations address frequency and duration of the use of a space, user preferences, behaviors, site analysis, and user recommendations. A post-occupancy evaluation may be expanded to incorporate the collection of additional information, such as emotional state and mood change, as in Cooper Marcus and Barnes (1995). Often, the analysis of the data results in the formulation of recommended changes and future guidelines (e.g., Cooper Marcus and Barnes, 1995; Perkins and Barnhart, 1996). The applicability to landscape architecture is twofold: it can be used as a self-checking mechanism to determine if design intentions were achieved; or it can serve as an assessment/evaluation of a space to formulate recommendations for change and guidelines for other similar spaces.

This last mechanism, the postoccupancy evaluation, is the only research method that is currently being channeled directly into the design of therapeutic gardens. Although it is a valuable source of information, by its very nature, it must come *after* a garden is installed. While a postoccupancy evaluation may lead to more informed design of future gardens, this procedure of trial and error is not the most expedient. The information from all of the types of studies mentioned here—as well as the increasing amount of information coming from research in other disciplines—needs to be linked to the design process. This can be done only by the incorporation of research into the knowledge base and design perspective of the landscape architect. For the designer to remain ignorant of the significance of this resource is to relinquish the ability to comprehensively design a successful therapeutic space, and to thereby undermine the true integration of aesthetic and functional considerations.

CONCLUSION

"Design directs perception through space.
Therapy guides healing over time.
Therapeutic design is the guidance of healing through space and time."

M. B.

The designing of a healing garden truly is the intertwining of two conceptual components: a *process* of healing and a *place* in which it is supported. This, of all the types of projects a landscape architect might take on, absolutely necessitates the adoption of a people-oriented perspective and the informed application of the available research. The spatial manipulations and the use and control of materials that are the domain of the landscape architect must be wielded to serve the therapeutic process. In so doing, the influence of the landscape architect expands to incorporate considerations of emotion, support, sustenance, and health. In this rich and comprehensive arena, a pleasing aesthetic is only one of the design goals. Whatever approach is applied to the design, it *must serve* the user and his or her healing experience.

REFERENCES

Bacon, S. (1983). *The Conscious Use of Metaphor in Outward Bound.* Denver, CO: Outward Bound School.

Barnes, M. (1993). "Emotional Healing in the Wilderness and its Implications for the Built Environment." Unpublished Paper. Berkeley CA.

——— (1994). *A Study of the Process of Emotional Healing in Outdoor Spaces and the Concomitant Landscape Design Implications.* Masters Thesis, Deptarment of Landscape Architecture, University of California, Berkeley.

Beckwith, M. and S. Gilster (1996). "The Paradise Garden: A Model for Designing for Those with Dementia and Alzheimer's Disease." *Journal of Therapeutic Horticulture,* Vol. 8, pp. 45–52.

Ben-Joseph, E. (1987). *The Humanistic Aesthetic Principles of Japanese Gardens and Their Application in Contemporary Outdoor Design.* Masters Thesis, Department of Landscape Architecture, Chiba University, Japan.

Betrabet, G. (1996). "The Garden as a Restorative Environment: A Theoretical Perspective." *Journal of Therapeutic Horticulture,* Vol. 8, pp. 15–20.

Bloomer, K. and C. Moore (1997). *Body Memory and Architecture.* New Haven, CT: Yale University Press.

Campbell, Scott (no date). *Mazes and Labyrinths: The Search for the Center.* Public Broadcasting System Presentation, USA.

Chang, A. (1965). *The Tao of Architecture.* Princeton, NJ: Princeton University Press.

Cooper Marcus, C. and M. Barnes (1995). *Gardens in Healthcare Facilities: Uses, Therapeutic Benefits and Design Recommendations.* Martinez, CA: The Center for Health Design.

Cooper Marcus, C. and C. Francis (1998, second edition). "Post-Occupancy Evaluation." In Cooper Marcus, C. and C. Francis (Eds.) *People Places: Design Guidelines for Open Space.* New York. Wiley.

Engler Efrati, M. (1989). *Archetypes in Landscape Experience: Understanding Human Response in Natural Places.* Masters Thesis, Department of Landscape Architecture. University of California, Berkeley.

Fisher, A. and D. Kingham (1991). *Mazes.* Princes Risborough, UK: Shire Publication.

Francis, C. and C. Cooper Marcus (1991). "Places People Take Their Problems." In J. Urbina-Soria, P. Ortega-Andeane, and R. Bechtel (Eds.), *Proceedings of the 22nd Annual Conference of the Environmental Design Research Association.* Oklahoma City: Environmental Design Research Association.

Gerlach-Spriggs, N., R. E. Kaufman, and S. B. Warner Jr. (1998). *Restorative Gardens: The Healing Landscape.* New Haven, CT: Yale University Press.

Hartig, T., A. Böok, J. Garvill, T. Olsson, and T. Gärling (1996). "Environmental Influences on Psychological Restoration." *Scandinavian Journal of Psychology*, Vol. 37, pp. 378–393.

Healey, V. (1986). "The Hospice Garden: Addressing the Patients' Needs Through Landscape, Part 2." *The American Journal of Hospice Care*, Nov./Dec., pp. 32–36.

Holborn, M. (1978). *The Ocean in the Sand*. Boulder, CO: Shambhala.

Ittelson, W., H. Proshansky, L. Rivlin, and G. Winkel (1974). *An Introduction to Environmental Psychology*. New York: Holt Rinehart & Winston.

Jung, C. G. (1964). *Man and his Symbols*. Garden City, NY: Doubleday & Company.

Kaplan, R. and S. Kaplan (1989). *The Experience of Nature: A Psychological Perspective*. Cambridge, MA: Cambridge University Press.

Kaplan, S. and J. Talbot (1983). "Psychological Benefits of a Wilderness Experience." In Altman and Wohlwill (Eds.), *Behavior and the Natural Environment*. New York: Plenum. pp. 163–203.

Lao-tzu (1929). *Tao Te Ching*. Shanghai, China: Ssu-pu-ts'ung-k'an Commercial Press.

Lewis, C. A. (1996). *Green Nature / Human Nature: The Meaning of Plants in Our Lives*. Urbana, IL: University of Illinois Press.

McHarg, I. (1969). *Design with Nature*. Garden City, NY: The Natural History Press.

Malkin, J. (1992). *Hospital Interior Architecture*. New York: Van Nostrand Reinhold.

Mehrabian, A. (1976). *Public Places and Private Spaces: The Psychology of Work, Play and Living Environments*. New York: Basic Books.

Messervy, J. (1990). *Contemplative Gardens*. Charlottesville, VA: Holwell Press.

Minter, S. (1993). *Healing Garden: A Natural Haven for Emotional and Physical Well-Being*. London, UK: Headline Book Publishing.

O'Neill, C. (1996). "The Healing Gardens of Makahikilua: The Landscape as a Healer." *Journal of Therapeutic Horticulture*, Vol. 8, pp. 92–96.

Perkins, N. H. and S. Barnhart (1996). A map of the special places at Homewood. Guelph, Ont., Canada: Homewood Health Centre Grounds Master Plan.

Schaarschmidt-Richter, I. (1979). Translated by J. Seligman. *Japanese Gardens*. New York: William Morrow and Company.

Segal, F. (1988). "Wilderness Experience: A Phenomenological Study." Ph.D. Dissertation, Department of Psychology, California Institute of Integral Studies, Berkeley.

Six Metaphysical Gardens: "The Escondido Surgery Center" (1995). American Society of Landscape Architects' Professional Awards Program.

Thompson, J. W. (1998). "A Question of Healing." *Landscape Architecture*, Vol. 88, No. 4., April.

Turner, G. and J. Major. *Humanistic Healthcare*. Ann Arbor, MI: Health Administration Press.

Ulrich, R. S. (1979). "Visual Landscapes and Psychological Well-Being." *Landscape Research*, Vol. 4, No. 1, pp. 17–23.

——— (1981). "Natural Versus Urban Scenes: Some Psycho-physiological Effects. *Environment and Behavior*, Vol. 13, pp. 523–556.

——— (1984). "View Through a Window May Influence Recovery from Surgery." *Science*, Vol. 224, pp. 420–421.

Ware, C. (1994). "Designing and Building Healing Gardens at Health Care Facilities." Sacramento CA: The Spink Corporation.

CHAPTER

4

Acute Care General Hospitals: Typology of Outdoor Spaces

Clare Cooper Marcus

In the course of evaluating more than seventy hospitals while researching this book, it became apparent that there are many different types of outdoor space in contemporary medical settings. Few are specifically designated as "healing gardens," but many are well-used by hospital staff, visitors, and patients for this purpose.

This section provides an overview of these different types of outdoor spaces observed in hospitals visited during 1995–1998 in the United States, Australia, Canada, and England. A definition of each type of outdoor space is followed by one or two examples of actual places visited, observed and critiqued in terms of their location, design, and use. Every garden was visited for a minimum of thirty to sixty minutes, some for much longer. Photographs were taken and a description of the setting and its use was written in situ. All these visits were made on weekdays between 11:00 A.M. and 2:00 P.M., during warm weather. This proved to be a most useful exercise, as these observations expanded our understanding of hospital outdoor space and informed the kinds of design recommendations presented in the next chapter. When published literature is

"I work in ICU, which is like a hell hole. For the first four hours I just run. Sitting out in the warm sun is like therapy to me. I can relax, gather my thoughts. I feel like I have my head screwed on straight."

(MALE NURSE)

115

sparse—as is the case with hospital outdoor space—there is no substitute for analytical field observations.

LANDSCAPED GROUNDS

This type of open space consists of extensive landscaped areas between buildings. It is often used as a walking route between buildings, as a setting for eating or waiting, and as a space for ambulatory patients or those using wheelchairs. This is the most spacious type of outdoor area reported in this typology, is sometimes described by users as "a park" or "a campus," and is often the hub of a hospital complex.

ADVANTAGES

- Can tie together a variety of buildings into a campus-like setting.
- Can provide a variety of landscapes from manicured lawns and flower beds to natural woodland or meadows.
- Can serve a variety of users and activities.

DISADVANTAGES

- Maintenance may be costly.
- Often piecemeal in development, the relationship between spaces, as well as interior-exterior connections, may be lacking in cohesiveness.

Figure 4-1   Landscaped grounds with a lake offer a complete contrast to the hospital interior, and draw patients, staff, and visitors outdoors. A looped path is accessible to people with a range of abilities. Conservatories at the ends of wards offer views to the lake and grounds. (St. Mary's Hospital, Newport, Isle of Wight, UK.)

St. Mary's Hospital, Newport, Isle of Wight, England

When a new hospital building was added to this nineteenth-century medical complex, the designers proposed a redesign of the central outdoor space. It is a spacious area with a lake in a depression where building materials for the original Poor Law Hospital were quarried. The area around the lake was relandscaped with lawns, paths, seating, new trees, two bridges, and two "pads" for the eventual location of gazebos. It is used by outpatients waiting for appointments, by staff walking between departments, by visitors or volunteers pushing wheelchair-bound patients, and by townspeople as a park where children may be brought to feed the ducks or watch a family of swans who have taken up residence on the lake. It is a very attractive, naturalistic space and is as different from an interior hospital environment as any nearby space could be. Obviously the provision of such a space is a rarity given the urban locations of most hospitals. St. Mary's is able to incorporate this parklike setting because it is located on a spacious site on the edge of a small country town.

Ottawa Health Sciences Center, Ottawa, Ontario, Canada

A group of medical facilities on the outskirts of Ottawa, Canada, share an extensive area of landscaped grounds. These facilities comprise Children's Hospital of Eastern Ontario, Ottawa General Hospital, The Rehabilitation Center, The Eye Institute, and Ottawa Regional Cancer Center. Collectively they are referred to as the Ottawa Health Sciences Center. The largest of these institutions is Ottawa General, which began as three sick beds in a small wooden cottage in 1845. Now a 464-bed teaching hospital offering primary, secondary, and tertiary care, Ottawa General moved to its present site in 1980.

The medical institutions that comprise the Ottawa Health Sciences Center are grouped in a horseshoe shaped campus off Smyth Road. On the outer ring of the U are access roads, parking lots, emergency department entries and a helicopter landing pad. The whole of the inside of the U consists of landscaped grounds, patches of natural woodland, paths, seating areas, and patios with chairs and tables off cafeterias. Creative manipulation of the topography, clumps of evergreen spruce and pine trees, and plantings of deciduous trees provide visual buffers partially screening one institution from another. Meandering paths through this central green campus provide pleasing walk-

Figure 4-2   Staff enjoying a lunchtime walk in the extensive grounds shared by a number of medical institutions. The grounds include landscapes that are designed and maintained (left) as well as patches of the original Ontario bush landscape (right). (Ottawa Health Sciences Center, Ottawa, Ontario, Canada.)

ing routes from one building to another, or settings for lunch-hour walking and jogging. Elevated covered walkways connect all the buildings at the second floor level and are highly used during the winter.

Particularly attractive in this green complex are patches of natural woodland, preserved when the Health Center was constructed. Since these areas are skirted by footpaths, one can see into these patches of the original "bush" landscape of eastern Ontario, with their dense masses of trees and saplings, rotting logs, patches of swamp, rocks, wild flowers, and birds' nests. While the density of underbrush, rocks, and roots would make it difficult to go into these woodlands, paths and seating are sensitively placed so that one can peer in while walking or sitting nearby. Research indicates that hospital staff and patients want to be outdoors in a setting as different from the institutional interior as possible (Cooper Marcus and Barnes, 1995). The landscaped grounds at Ottawa Health Science Center provide an exemplary setting, ranging from beds of tulips and manicured lawns to portions of the original Ontario wooded landscape, all within easy reach of hospital interiors.

LANDSCAPED SETBACK

A landscaped setback is an area in front of the main entrance to a medical center, usually comprising lawns and trees, and often required by zoning regulations. This is a space akin to the front yard of a house, providing a buffer-separation between a building and the street. Also, like a residential front yard, this space is not usually intended to be used, but rather to provide a visually pleasing setting on approaching the entrance.

ADVANTAGES

- May evoke a familiar, comforting image at a hospital entrance.
- Provides offices or rooms at the front of building with some privacy from passing vehicular and pedestrian traffic.
- If designed well for sitting and conversing, may provide an appreciated, usable outdoor space.

DISADVANTAGES

- Because often not intended for use, its lack of seating, pathways, and so on, may be frustrating for staff or visitors who want to use it, especially if this is the only available outdoor space.
- If the integration of landscaped setback, vehicular and pedestrian approaches is not carefully thought through, the result may be a confusing approach to the building.

Figure 4-3   Landscaped setback at a small hospital. This space is not designed to be used. (Novato Community Hospital, California.)

Main Entry, Alta Bates Medical Center, Herrick Campus, Berkeley, California

The four-story stucco buildings of Alta Bates Herrick Campus face onto the busy street of Dwight Way, a few blocks from downtown Berkeley. A wide flight of brick steps with planters full of flowers leads up to the main entrance. On either side of the south facing steps an area of lawn, about 25 feet deep, provides a setback for the building. It is punctuated by a few trees and small flower beds. Larger street trees cast shade on parts of the lawn. There are no pathways, seats, litter containers, or other cues to suggest this area might be used. This is the only green outdoor space at this facility, and might well be used if it were designed appropriately. Ironically, on the opposite side of this building is a sparsely used, shady paved plaza, overprovided with benches, and with none of the green and colorful image provided by this Dwight Way setback (see description on page 133–134).

Charing Cross Hospital, London

Charing Cross Hospital is a very large, modern, high-rise medical facility, relocated from its original site in central London to

Figure 4-4 Entrance to a large urban hospital where the arrangement of pedestrian and vehicular access, bicycle and car parking, seating, sculpture, and water features creates a somewhat confusing entry experience. (Charing Cross Hospital, London, UK.)

its present location in the inner suburb of Fulham. The front entrance of this hospital—like many others observed in the United States and the United Kingdom—is an example of poorly integrated uses. An entry path leads directly from Fulham Palace Road to the main entrance, clearly indicated by a large canopy and the hospital name. Since many people come to the facility by bus, this clear and direct pedestrian entry is appreciated. What is unfortunate is the lack of integration of elements in this area which is both a place of movement (pedestrian and vehicular), and a place of repose (sitting, waiting, talking). These competing elements include a roadway, parking for autos and bicycles, setback landscaping, water features, sculpture, and seating. The setback landscaped area of grass and trees that separates the hospital site from the busy traffic on Fulham Palace Road is fenced along the road (which is desirable), but is also fenced so that people cannot access it from the main entry path. There are two handsome reflecting pools bisected by the main entry path, but the seating is so arranged that you have to sit with your back to the water. This is unfortunate since viewing water has a calming effect on people in a potentially stressful situation. A striking sculpture by Henry Moore—"Reclining Figure"—is so positioned in one of the reflecting pools that the only way to really look at it is to pick your way through parked bicycles, or to swivel sideways on the fixed benches. Finally, the entry path is relatively narrow, and those walking to the entrance have a feeling of "running the gauntlet" as they pick their way between two opposite rows of people *facing* the pathway.

All the elements are here for a pleasing, therapeutic space—grass, trees, water, sculpture, seating, pathway—but their arrangement leaves something to be desired. This is doubly unfortunate since this is the most easily accessible outdoor space in this huge medical facility. A large sunken courtyard near the main entrance is off-limits for everyone except those in a rehab program; a large area of grass, trees, and a few benches located at the back of the hospital has no signs indicating its location and is sparsely used.

THE FRONT PORCH

Most hospitals have some features at the main entrance that are analogous to the front porch of a house. These might include an overhang or porch roof, a turnaround for vehicle pickup and drop-off, seats, directional signs, a postbox, phone, bus stop, and so on. The first view of a hospital at its entrance can be a critical element in setting the mood of a person about to enter. Is it reassuring, calm, welcoming—or confusing, busy, and disturbing? The combination of pedestrian and vehicular access, along with a pleasant place to sit and wait to be picked up by a car or taxi, presents a design challenge, met with varying degrees of success.

Figure 4-5 Visitor wheels relative out for a smoke in the front porch of a large suburban hospital. (Glendale Adventist Medical Center, Los Angeles, California.)

ADVANTAGES

- Provides visual cue to main entrance.
- Overhang may scale down size of building.
- Sensitively located seating provides amenity for those waiting to be picked up or waiting for bus.

DISADVANTAGES

- May be overused—creating congestion—if it is only outdoor seating area provided.
- May be underused if main access to hospital is via parking under building.
- May be confusing if vehicular and pedestrian needs are not sensitively integrated.
- Often raises conflict of smoking just outside the entry—an unpleasant experience for many who are traversing the space.

Main Entrance, Alta Bates Medical Center, Ashby Campus, Berkeley, California

The front porch seating at this medium-sized community hospital is sensitively located just to one side of the main entrance, where there is a lushly planted pocket space. People passing back and forth on the adjacent sidewalk or walking in and out of the hospital go by this small seating area, but do not go through it. Hence, people seated here—as if in an eddy off the mainstream—experience some degree of seclusion, yet can easily see if a taxi or a friend's car arrives. The seating is in the form of comfortable, wooden garden benches with backs. "No smoking" signs ensure that nonsmokers will not be bothered by one of the frequent uses of spaces just outside a hospital entrance (and many other public buildings), that is, employees coming out for a quick smoking break.

Hammersmith Hospital, London

The main entrance of Hammersmith Hospital is centrally located in an elegant brick and stone building with a copper-green clock tower dating from 1904. A half-moon shaped entry plaza is paved in warm-colored brick with plenty of comfortable wooden benches and an eye-catching central sculpture—"Cycle of Life" by Sarah Tombs. The space is punctuated by a few brick planters with shrubs and cherry trees and by attractive old London lamp standards with glass globes. A double row of black iron bollards separates the plaza from a narrow, one-way access

Figure 4-6 An attractive and functional front porch to a hospital with planting, seating, lighting, sculpture, and a clearly defined drop-off drive. (Hammersmith Hospital, London, UK.)

road that permits easy drop-off for patients and visitors. This access lane and the entry plaza are in turn separated from the busy traffic on DuCane Road by a wrought iron fence and brick wall, and a row of chestnut trees.

This is a well-used space. On a typical day, a few in-patients are taking in the sun; staff sit and talk on breaks; patients are dropped off from vehicles; patients and visitors wait to be picked up. There are virtually no other outdoor seating areas on this large urban hospital site, which makes the entry plaza especially appreciated; the space is a model of a well-organized, humane, uncomplicated, and welcoming entrance that may well inspire confidence in those entering the hospital.

Whittington Hospital, London

In contrast to the preceding, the entrance of Whittington Hospital is a model of "how not to do it." This is an old hospital in North London, with a confusing mix of nineteenth century and contemporary buildings. This mix in itself is often inevitable when old hospitals have to expand and modernize on a tight urban site. But in this case, the confusion is exacerbated by a main entrance that is institutional, busy, unwelcoming, and lacking in amenities. The main entrance and the Accident and Emergency entrance (often separated) are adjacent here, so there are traffic problems involving ambulances and patients being dropped off from cars. The drop-off road is so poorly designed that some vehicles have to back up to get out. There is nowhere to sit comfortably anywhere near the entrance so that people waiting for a ride have to stand or perch on a low wall at the base of a directional sign. A steeply sloping lawn across the road is used by younger people willing to sprawl on the grass, but is certainly no substitute for seating at the entrance. Finally, a colored locator map at the main entrance shows buildings with key letters, many of which do not appear on the legend! Overall, the confusing, if not nerve-racking, experience of entering this hospital must surely affect people's moods: as a visitor commented, "If it's this confusing at the entrance, what must it be like inside?"

ENTRY GARDEN

This is a landscaped area close to a hospital entrance that, unlike a "front porch," is a green space with a garden image, and unlike a "landscaped setback," is designed and detailed for use.

ADVANTAGES
- The garden is visible and accessible.
- Makes more aesthetic use of part of site that might otherwise have been paved for parking.
- Provides a pleasing image on entering hospital environment.
- Allows use by ambulatory inpatients who want to watch the world go by.
- May successfully double as a public park, and costs of maintenance devolve onto a city department.

DISADVANTAGES
- Without sensitive planting, may be too exposed to nearby parking and entry road.
- Depending on the garden's size and location, may impede access to the main entrance.
- Space for garden may have to compete with parking provision.
- High visibility of space may deter inpatients in hospital garb from using it.

Main Entrance, Marin General Hospital, Greenbrae, California

East of the new main entrance to this medium-sized community hospital is a landscaped area with mature palms, live oaks, and eucalyptus, and paths zigzagging up to an upper parking lot and the old hospital entry. The trees screen out much of the hospital building; the views out from this area are of hillsides covered with native trees and the more distant slopes of Mt. Tamalpais. It has a quiet, green, park-like feeling. Nine tall Washingtonia palms border a small circular seating plaza. Around this are lawns, ivy-covered slopes, and a flower bed with every species neatly labeled. Two other benches, up-slope from the palm circle, offer a more sunny location. From the circle seating, nearby parking is barely visible, and traffic on a street that gives access to the hospital is heard only intermittently. Due to a steeply sloped site and the configuration of the buildings, this is the only outdoor space at Marin General, and it appears to be well-used.

Entry Park, St. Thomas' Hospital, London

St. Thomas', founded in 1551, is one of the oldest hospitals in London. The hospital moved to its present site in 1868. It was built in a series of pavilion-wings, following the principles pioneered by Florence Nightingale. In the 1980s, part of this hospital was demolished, new multistory wings constructed, and a large garden/park created over a new parking garage. This outdoor space now forms a highly used amenity shared by the hospital and the general public. It is easily visible and accessible from one side of a broad pathway that leads to the main entrance of the hospital.

Figure 4-7 The attractive and highly used entry garden to a central London hospital is enjoyed by staff, patients, visitors, and local office workers. (St. Thomas' Hospital, London, UK.)

"It is two days after surgery, I am sitting in the garden. I feel the breeze on my face, blowing my hair. It feels so good! No smell of disinfectant out here; no chrome bars, linoleum floors, rattle of trolleys—just the smell of grass, starlings chirping, a squirrel collecting acorns and racing up the rutted trunk of an oak tree.... Figures move quietly between buildings. Shadows of olive, plane, alder, and maple make patterns on the concrete path.... L. arrives to take me home."

(C. M.) BERKELEY, CALIFORNIA

The garden is divided into two levels. The upper level, accessed from near the hospital entrance, consists of a broad pathway with raised flower beds, areas of raised lawn and ground cover on either side. Ample seating is available in the form of wooden park benches, backless benches, and concrete seat walls. Most of the seating faces striking views over the River Thames to Big Ben and the Houses of Parliament. On some summer days, barbecued food is available for hospital staff and the general public.

Many carry this food, or their own brown-bag lunches, to the lower, larger segment of the garden—a large square bounded by low walls, seating, and raised flower planters. In the center is a spacious, raised lawn with a central pool and fountain. Between the square lawn and the peripheral seating, a broad pathway enables people to perambulate around the square without intruding on those who are seated. In many ways, the design is typical of the familiar London square with the exception of very large trees, precluded because it is sited over a one-story parking garage.

This is clearly a very well-used and successful space. Hospital staff, a few inpatients—some in wheelchairs—tourists, office workers, construction workers, hospital visitors and outpatients sprawl on the grass, eat their lunches while seated on the concrete edge of the raised lawn, or on one of many comfortable benches, read magazines and smoke, doze on the grass, and chat with friends. There is plenty of space so that people alone, couples, or larger groups can find comfortable places to be. The fact that this attractive large space is bounded on three of its four sides by public rights of way (a Thames-side walk, the entry path to the hospital, and Westminster Bridge Road) makes it appear more as a public park than a hospital garden and, judging by age, role, and style of dress, attracts a very wide range of users. It serves as a visible connecting link between the hospital and the wider community.

Entry Garden, Homerton Hospital, East London

Homerton Hospital is a new two-story complex located in a working class inner suburb of East London. It is built on the "nucleus" principle of hospital design, promoted by the U.K. Department of Health. Natural light penetrates the low-rise building via many interior courtyards and via many long indentations in the footprint, somewhat akin to the spaces between pavilion wings in nineteenth century hospital buildings.

At Homerton Hospital, one long indentation penetrates deep into the complex, providing space for an entry garden

Figure 4-8   A linear entry garden with vine-covered arbors for sitting and viewing. Inpatients in hospital garb feel comfortable sitting here. (Homerton Hospital, East London, UK.)

flanking the main pedestrian entrance to the hospital. A wide paved walkway leads slightly downhill to a major entrance, and via two T-shaped extensions, to minor entries and doors leading directly into wards. The main walkway is flanked by narrow lawns, low shrub planting against the walls of the two-story hospital, and a number of brick- paved, wooden arbors, over-hung with thick plantings of grape vines and jasmine, forming sheltered seating areas. The theory of "prospect and refuge" describes how humans seem genetically predisposed to feel most comfortable when seated with protection at their back and overhead ("refuge"), and a view out to the front ("prospect"). The arbors at Homerton Hospital form particularly attractive seating spaces, with the backs of benches protected by the hospital walls, arbor beams and columns, vines, and trailing vegetation. With views out to passing pedestrians walking by, the arbors are psychologically comfortable enclosures. Unfortunately, the actual number of benches provided is many times fewer than could have been located in these attractive spaces. Of the ten arbors, only five are furnished with benches. These are the familiar, six-foot wooden park benches that permit a maximum of two people to sit on each of them. The arbors are spacious enough that two or three such benches, or a variety of individual chairs and benches could have been placed in each. Thus there is a situation where many more seated people could have been provided for, in a range of groupings. This is especially unfortunate since: (1) doors from ground floor wards open onto this entry garden and seating areas are easily accessible for ambulatory inpatients; (2) the fact that wings of the hospital "embrace" this linear garden means that inpatients in hospital garb feel comfortable coming out into a space that is definitely "hospital territory" and not a public space; (3) the almost-constant stream of people walking in and out of the hospital via this linear garden (in this poorer section of London, many people come by foot) provides an interesting, people-watching distraction for patients who come to sit outdoors; (4) potential sitters, wandering and hovering around the few benches available, waiting for someone to leave, give a clear indication that many people *want* to sit here who cannot; and (5) a number of interior courtyards (potential alternative seating areas) are kept permanently locked and labeled "Private."

COURTYARD

This is a space that forms the "core" of a building complex like the hole in a donut. It has walls on all four sides and may be located at grade or on a roof. (An outdoor space on a roof with views out is considered, in this typology, to be a roof garden or roof terrace.) Ideally, a courtyard should be immediately visible or apparent upon entering the hospital so that visitors and patients know that it is there. When a cafeteria occupies one or more sides of the courtyard, it can function as an outdoor eating place.

ADVANTAGES

- Semiprivate and secure; surrounded by hospital building.
- Brings light into the core of the building.
- Depending on location, may be easily viewed and accessed.
- Shielded from wind; buildings likely to provide shade.
- Likely to be of human scale.
- Can be used to provide way-finding cues from the interior.
- May provide attractive views from windows of offices or patient rooms.

DISADVANTAGES

- Depending on its size, location, and design, may create a "fishbowl" experience for those using it.
- If lacking an adequate buffer—planting or structural— adjacent rooms may need to keep blinds drawn for privacy.
- Sounds may intrude into the rooms or from rooms into the courtyard.
- If many courtyards are provided, there may not be the budget or interest in keeping them all well maintained and accessible, as was unfortunately the case in many hospitals observed.

Figure 4-9 Visitors taking a rest and an employee doing paper work in the small courtyard of a community hospital. (Novato Community Hospital, California.)

St. George's Hospital, London

St. George's is a large London teaching hospital dating back several centuries, which moved to its present site in an inner suburb of southwest London in 1980. It forms a large complex of two- to six-story buildings with outdoor spaces of varying size and quality. By far the most successful in terms of being used by a variety of people is a very attractive courtyard between the St. James and Grosvenor wings. The courtyard is rectangular in shape, approximately 150 × 75 feet, and completely enclosed by one- to six-story buildings. It is easily accessible from one end of the rectangle where a busy corridor bounded by doors and floor-to-ceiling glass permits a pleasant view of greenery for those who are just passing by.

A central feature of the courtyard is a large lily pond with goldfish, bordered by a pathway, low planting, a sprinkling of one-story tall trees, and several benches (see image on jacket of book). The water can be enjoyed in two ways. At one end of pond, a jet provides views and sounds of falling water, partially masking the noise of a nearby air-conditioning unit. At the opposite end, the water is still, reflecting waterside planting and the sky, and with glimpses of goldfish swimming beneath the surface. At this end (most distant from the entrance) is a raised wooden deck and mini-plaza with a variety of seating in the form of wooden park benches and wooden picnic tables and benches. Sun reaches into the space from mid-morning to mid-afternoon. The green atmosphere is enhanced by ivy and climbing plants on several walls; three fire escape doors, which might have marred the image, have been nicely screened by brick walls covered with trellises and climbing vines.

This is a verdant, peaceful oasis within a large, busy, probably stressful, urban hospital setting. The number of people (staff, patients, visitors) drawn into it is some indication of its success. While a number of alternate spaces are available, this is the only one that combines an accessible, restful milieu with *places to sit!* The other outdoor spaces on this site include an entry plaza that also has plenty of benches but that is bounded on all four sides by traffic; an unkempt planted courtyard with a few garden chairs that is permanently locked; and a large lawn area near the entrance that has three prominent sculptures, but only one, hidden-away bench! Although the latter area draws younger staff willing to sprawl out on the grass in their lunch hour, the courtyard with the lily pond and ample seating is clearly the resting place of choice for less-than-youthful staff, visitors, and patients in wheelchairs.

Figure 4-10 A visitor-family enjoying a stroll beside the lily pond in a hospital courtyard. (St. George's Hospital, London, UK.)

At mid-afternoon on a warm September day, two male employees enjoy a smoke, a cup of coffee, and conversation sitting on a bench and looking into the pond; a young man (a visitor?) reads a newspaper in the sun; a nurse eats a brown-bag lunch while seated at a picnic table; two young women (office staff?) smoke and laugh while seated on a bench on the deck; a middle-aged couple push an elderly woman in-patient in a wheelchair—with difficulty— over some cobbles, sit opposite her talking, and offer her a can of Guinness (which she eagerly accepts); two nurses come out for a break and a smoke; a teenage boy in a wheelchair is pushed by his mother to a space beside the pond and she draws up a stray plastic chair so she can sit beside him; a couple brings a tray of food from the cafeteria (one floor and two hundred yards away) and settles down at the picnic table; a woman finishing a sandwich feeds crumbs to some sparrows and pigeons.

(FIELD NOTES, ST. GEORGE'S HOSPITAL, C.C.M., SEPT. 10, 1997)

On a hot Saturday morning, a hospital chaplain greets an Indian patient and his mother; they move to a large bench where all three can sit together. A mother wheels her toddler daughter in, attached to tubes, and feeds her a banana while seated on the edge of the pool. A father guides his small son and a trolley-IV around the courtyard and tries to interest him in the goldfish swimming in the fountain pool. He seems too ill to be interested. The surging water masks the sounds of conversation and its pulsing evokes the effect of waves breaking on a beach. Water lily leaves quiver in the apse end of the pool. The sight and sound of the water is quite hypnotic and is the focus of attention of all who enter the courtyard.

(Field notes, Royal Brompton Hospital, C. C. M., Sept. 4, 1997)

Royal Brompton National Heart and Lung Hospital, Sydney St., London

This small courtyard garden is immediately visible from the entry-foyer of this newly built hospital in Chelsea. The courtyard is rectangular, approximately 30 × 100 feet, and bounded by four and five story buildings. The most dominant feature—both aurally and visually—is a bronze fountain designed by Philip Kimberley (a researcher in the hospital). Its shape is based on a section through the ventricles of the heart; water surges through mimicking the heartbeat. A bubble fountain in the adjacent foyer feeds a rill directed toward the pool and fountain outside. The spring inside the building symbolizes the source of life that flows to nourish life outside.

The landscape architect chose to introduce a feeling of formality and serenity in this high-sided courtyard by including rounded, apse ends to the large central pool. This form is echoed in the raised beds at either end of the court, and in the rounded backs and arms of four wooden benches. To provide an attractive setting in all seasons, plant material is limited to a harmonious mix of evergreens (boxwood, laurel, fuschia, liriope, and ferns—among others), plus groupings of single begonias for color. Boston ivy is rapidly covering the brick walls to a height of five stories—a feature repeated from the old Brompton Hospital, which previously stood on this site. This vertical green element does much to tone down what could have been a pit-like experience in this high-sided court without

Figure 4-11 A small, well-used courtyard in a rebuilt urban hospital. The fountain's shape is based on the ventricles of the heart, and water pulses mimicking the human heartbeat. (Royal Brompton National Heart and Lung Hospital, London, UK.)

trees. Sun strikes the walls of ivy and penetrates to portions of the courtyard. Windows at ground level, which might have experienced some lack of privacy, are curtained or partially screened by the Boston ivy. Comfortable seating in the plant-filled foyer is also within hearing distance of the soothing fountain surges.

Linneaus Physik Garden, Santa Rosa Community Hospital, Santa Rosa, California

The Linnaeus Physik Garden at Santa Rosa Community Hospital is a good example of what can be done in a long, narrow, leftover space in the midst of an evolving medical complex of old and new buildings. It is bounded on three sides by older, two story hospital buildings, and on the fourth side by an open, arcaded corridor providing access to administrative offices. It is not near the main hospital entrance, nor are there any directional signs indicating its location. However, on approaching the cafeteria, it is glimpsed through corridor windows.

The courtyard is approximately 40 feet wide and 120 feet long. The dominant aesthetic effect is provided by five two-story-high maple trees arranged in a line along one long edge of the court. Under each is a raised planter of flowers bordered by a square bench. These provide seating places with a variety of views and varying degrees of shade. Between the trees, and in a few other locations, are simple wooden picnic tables with movable benches, popular with groups of two or more who carry food out from the nearby cafeteria. During peak-use hours, some of these tables are in deep shade, some in dappled shade, and some in full sun—providing plenty of choice depending on people's tolerance for the sun. Since summers in Santa Rosa can be very hot, the provision of shade is essential. On the opposite, long side of the court are three sets of wooden garden seats with upholstered cushions—each set is a pair of chairs, with a small table between and an adjustable umbrella overhead. These are very popular and are in use both before and after the lunchtime users have left the picnic tables. Benches are often moved from one of the picnic tables so that users of these padded chairs—reading, eating, chatting, smoking, dozing—can sit with their feet up.

The well-placed maples provide needed shade and—not incidentally—attract a lot of birds, whose songs and chirping provide soothing background sounds. Planters beneath the maples and along the edges of the court are filled with flowers; baskets of flowers hang from the roof of the arcaded corridor.

Figure 4-12   This well-used courtyard occupies what was a leftover space between buildings in an evolving medical complex. Tables, benches, and padded chairs offer a variety of settings for conversation and relaxation. (Linneaus Physik Garden, Santa Rosa Community Hospital, Santa Rosa, California.)

Two of three entries to the courtyard are down flights of six steps; beside these are overflowing planters of star jasmine, so that one's entrance into this space is marked by strong fragrance. Elsewhere in the plaza, star jasmine climbs the walls of the adjacent building so that people using the upholstered seating areas are aware of the scent.

This court was dedicated as the Linnaeus Physik Garden in 1986, when the hospital auxiliary installed six planters along the two long sides of this space, filled with medicinal herbs and plants from Central and South America, Europe, North America, Africa, India, and China.

The negative features of this space include the view of dumpsters and storage bins at one narrow end, and the ever-present sound of air-conditioning units attached to windows, blocking out the sounds of a small corner fountain for all but those sitting close to it. The black asphalt surface of this court is not especially pleasing, particularly where roots of the maples have caused cracks and heaving.

PLAZA

Plaza spaces in hospitals are outdoor areas that are predominantly hard-surfaced, but furnished for use. They may include trees, shrubs, or flowers in planters, though the overall image is not of a green space, but of a paved urban plaza.

ADVANTAGES

- Low plant maintenance and irrigation costs.
- A small place can be designed for relatively heavy use.
- Patients using wheelchairs, walkers, or crutches may be able to move easily in this space.

DISADVANTAGES

- May have few of the qualities that many people perceive as therapeutic in outdoor spaces—an overall green and/or colorful setting, a garden or oasis image.
- May evoke the image of a shopping mall or corporate office plaza rather than a space for peaceful, stress-reducing, passive enjoyment.
- Reflected heat from hard surfaces may be a deterrent to use.
- Light-colored, paved surfaces may create glare problems, especially for the elderly.

Hospital outdoor space needs to be carefully considered along with the design of hospital buildings. When a multistory building was added to this large urban hospital, a garden was designed over a new parking garage. (St. Thomas' Hospital, London, UK.)

A small sunken courtyard provides a quiet seating space and green outlook from the waiting area of a cancer center. (Comprehensive Cancer Center, Good Samaritan Hospital, Portland, OR.)

A hospital located on a naturally wooded site is designed so that patient rooms have views into the trees. (St. Michael Medical Center, Texarkana, TX, photo by James F. Wilson.)

A rehabilitation unit looks onto a variety of outdoor areas: a games court; a picnic area beside a flower planter; mowed lawns; and a patch of the original wooded landscape of the region. (Rehabilitation Center, Ottawa Health Sciences Center, Ottawa, Ont., Canada.)

The staff member who worked at this desk in a hospice facility greatly appreciated the view out to the garden. (Hospice House, Portland, OR.)

The view from this patient's room onto the landscaped grounds at a psychiatric facility played an important part in her recovery. (The Retreat, York, UK.)

Each patient room at this hospice facility has a view into a semi-private patio and to the gardens beyond. (San Diego Hospice, San Diego, CA.)

This glass-sided corridor provides attractive views onto the surrounding natural landscape for people passing by, and for outpatients sitting in waiting areas. (Victoria General Hospital, Victoria, B.C., Canada.)

The views into this hospital courtyard from the main foyer and stairs alert people to its existence; doors to the courtyard from a small foyer café provide easy access. (West Dorset Hospital, Dorchester, UK.)

A well-used courtyard at a busy urban hospital. Windows in a corridor connecting two wings provide attractive views in, and announce its presence. (St. George's Hospital, London, UK.)

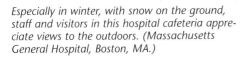

Especially in winter, with snow on the ground, staff and visitors in this hospital cafeteria appreciate views to the outdoors. (Massachusetts General Hospital, Boston, MA.)

This glass roofed veranda is an attractive transition from interior to exterior. The covered seating area provides a "safe" place from which to view the garden, for patients who are not ready to venture further afield. A combination of moveable chairs and benches provides opportunities for both solitude and social interaction. (The Retreat, York, UK.)

Glass doors and full length windows serve to connect the interior with the exterior, and to encourage use of the garden; the wide, smooth path can accomodate gurneys and leads both to near and distant patios, in both sun and shade. (California Pacific Medical Center, Garden Campus, San Francisco, CA.)

This two level structure provides a bridge to facilitate direct access to the garden from patient rooms. Clinics and meeting rooms open on to patios below. (Lambeth Community Care Center, London, UK.)

A meandering path up to a remote parking lot at this community hospital has ample seating along the way. A circle of palms provides a quiet spot for this visitor to enjoy the sunshine. (Marin General Hospital, Greebrae, CA.)

A comfortable length for lounging, these whimsical benches were designed to be moved around to suit the users' needs. (San Diego Children's Hospital, San Diego, CA.)

Gently curving benches allow for comfortable conversations without forcing intimacy. The circular backless bench at the base of the oak allows individuals to face inward and talk or outward to observe passers by. (Kaiser Permanente Medical Center, Walnut Creek, CA.)

A combination of seat-walls, benches, and grass for lounging accommodates a large number of people at lunch time. This garden overlooking the Thames serves as a public park as well as outdoor space for a hospital. (St. Thomas' Hospital, London, UK.)

A visitor and her hospitalized grandmother relax in a lush flower garden. (Stanford University Medical Center, Palo Alto, CA.)

A hospital garden provides an essential casual space where patients and visitors can chat in privacy: mother and son beside a lily pond in a courtyard-garden. (St. George's Hospital, London, UK.)

A teenage patient and two friends spend time in a hospital garden that doubles as a public park in the center of London. (St. Thomas' Hospital, London, UK.)

A husband and wife visit an elderly relative, while she enjoys a sip of Guinesss. (St. George's Hospital, London, UK.)

One of the chief assets of a garden is that it provides an environment in complete contrast to the sights, sounds, smells and textures of the hospital interior. This is appreciated by patients and visitors, but especially by staff: an office employee has brought some paperwork to do outside. (The Anniversary Garden, Glendale Adventist Medical Center, Glendale, CA.)

The Attending Physician of a hospice ward takes a break in the shade in a garden he helped to design and build. (Memorial Garden, Laguna Honda Hospice, San Francisco, CA.)

Two nurses enjoy lunch and conversation in a courtyard garden. (Santa Rosa Community Hospital, Santa Rosa, CA.)

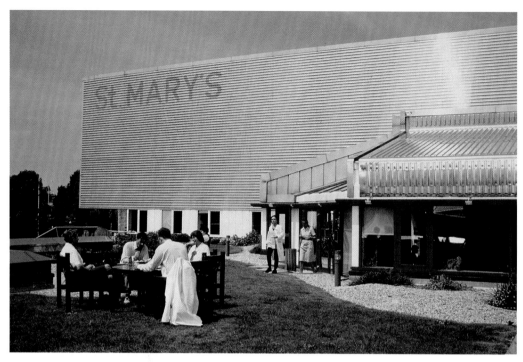

Hospital staff often work in highly stressed situations and appreciate taking breaks outdoors, here on a roof terrace outside the cafeteria. (St. Mary's Hospital, Newport, Isle of Wight, UK.)

. . . here beside a tree-lined walkway. (St. Michael Medical Center, Texarkana, TX, photo by James F. Wilson.)

. . . here chatting to the gardener outside of an outpatient clinic. (The Comfort Garden, San Francisco General Hospital, San Francisco, CA.)

Small spaces can be put to good use. The planting and overhead corridor screen this promenade from the adjacent busy street. Hospital staff and visitors enjoy using the space to read, smoke, eat, and stroll. (Kaiser Hospital, Los Angeles, CA.)

A narrow courtyard between old and new wings of this hospital provides a welcome space for quick breaks and getting away. The liquidambar trees offer varying degrees of shade, important in this hot climate. (Santa Rosa Community Hospital, Santa Rosa, CA.)

This forgotten space was completely refurbished through the volunteer efforts of the clinic staff. A sponsored bicycle ride to a German sister city provided the funding for this practical and attractive space. (Hartington Wing, Royal Chesterfield and North Derbyshire Hospital, Chesterfield, UK.)

The acute care waiting room opens up onto this simply designed but well used courtyard. (El Camino Hospital, Mountain View, CA.)

Research indicates that natural elements and plants provide significant restorative benefits. These elements can be successfully arranged and designed in a variety of ways: an orthogonal courtyard design. (Kaiser Medical Center, Vallejo, CA.)

A traditional garden with lawns, trees, and meandering pathways. (Boston Children's Hospital, Boston, MA.)

An informal flower garden. (The Comfort Garden, San Francisco General Hospital, San Francisco, CA.)

A roof garden with flower beds and planter-edge seating. (Alta Bates Medical Center, Berkeley, CA.)

A lily pond with fish in a hospital courtyard provides a soothing contrast to the building interior a few steps away. (St. George's Hospital, London, UK.)

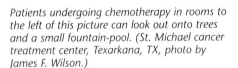

A two-story high waterfall provides a soothing sound in this hospital courtyard and is also audible from many staff offices. (West Dorset Hospital, Dorchester, UK.)

Patients undergoing chemotherapy in rooms to the left of this picture can look out onto trees and a small fountain-pool. (St. Michael cancer treatment center, Texarkana, TX, photo by James F. Wilson.)

A quarry that provided material for an old Poor Law hospital on this site was filled with water to create a lake in the grounds of a new facility. Walks around the lake are enjoyed by ambulatory patients, visitors, staff, and local townspeople. (St. Mary's Hospital, Newport, Isle of Wight, UK.)

Art in the garden can take many forms. Granite columns set among river rocks and pampas grass on a roof terrace at Harrison Memorial Hospital, Bremerton, WA.

This joyful fountain sculpture marks the entry at San Diego Children's Hospital, San Diego, CA.

Funded by the local arts commission, "The Companion Piece" uses granite slabs to create an artistic statement. (San Francisco General Hospital, San Francisco, CA.)

The "Magician's Hat and Cloak" was created by volunteers outside the windows of this hospital. The lighting of the candles extends the visibility of the snow sculpture into the long winter nights. (Hesttoniemi, Tailcurinhattu, Finland, photo by Helinä Kotilainen.)

Designing for children, and the child in all of us, is particularly relevant in medical settings. Set between 2 pediatric outpatient waiting rooms, this maze allows children to run off steam. The activities can be supervised by parents and staff inside. (Kaiser Medical Center, Vallejo, CA.)

This second floor garden provides a view to the entry rotunda below, as well as colorful artwork which incorporates kinetic sculpture. (San Diego Children's Hospital, San Diego, CA.)

The opportunity for exploration and discovery are particularly welcome in this long-term care facility. Children of visiting families can entertain themselves in the garden for extended periods of time. (California Pacific Medical Center, Garden Campus, San Francisco, CA.)

A small bear sculpture has provided the opportunity for someone to make their own artful contribution to the garden by placing flowers in its mouth. (Boston Children's Hospital, Boston, MA.)

As the world population ages, designing for the elderly becomes increasingly important. Comfortable seating, reduced glare, and ways to mitigate heat and cold are basic elements that support the use of outdoor spaces. (Oak Bay Kiwanis Pavilion, Victoria, B.C., Canada.)

A garden can allow residents to feel useful when designed to promote participation. This woman cuts and arranges flowers for the common rooms, everyday. (Judson Retirement Community, Cleveland, OH.)

Loss of short-term memory often accompanies aging. The integration of familiar features from childhood into the garden can stimulate fond remembrances and become a vehicle of connection between memory impaired residents and their visitors. (Alzheimer's Unit, Chemainus Health Care Centre, B.C., Canada)

Views into this garden from a wide seating corridor, on left, and a cafe to the right of this picture are much appreciated by the elderly residents, especially those who are less mobile. (Jewish Home for the Aged, San Francisco, CA.)

The stress-reducing qualities of nature can be brought into the hospital: trees and garden-style benches inside the light-filled foyer of an urban hospital. (Medical Center of Central Massachusetts, Worcester, MA.)

Plants and stained glass in a solarium-stairwell. (Lambeth Community Care Centre, London, UK.)

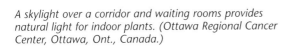

A skylight over a corridor and waiting rooms provides natural light for indoor plants. (Ottawa Regional Cancer Center, Ottawa, Ont., Canada.)

Bringing nature indoors is especially important in regions where there are long, cold winters. Tropical vegetation flourishes in this interior garden used by visitors, staff, and patients. Patient rooms also enjoy a green outlook. (Royal Alexandra Hospital, Edmonton, Alberta, Canada.)

Playrooms, corridors, stairways, and elevators look down onto the large atrium of this children's hospital with cafe seating, a fountain, and murals of outdoor scenes. (Hospital for Sick Children, Toronto, Ont., Canada.)

Patients and relatives enjoy visiting together in this indoor garden-cafe. A barrel-vaulted glass ceiling lets ample daylight into this two-story space. Street lamps, garden furniture, and arbors complete the image of being "outdoors." Patient rooms look down onto the greenery from the second level. (Lloyd Wilson Garden Rotarium, Glenrose Rehabilitation Hospital, Edmonton, Alberta, Canada.)

Figure 4-13 An uncomfortable, barely used seating plaza outside the waiting area of a cancer clinic. Hard edges; the predominance of concrete, travertine, steel, and glass; benches placed awkwardly opposite each other; and huge tilting travertine slabs reminiscent of tombstones do nothing to foster a sense of comfort and security for patients.

Seating Plaza, Alta Bates Medical Center, Herrick Campus, Berkeley, California

This is an L-shaped seating plaza located outside the Comprehensive Cancer Clinic waiting area. The space can be entered from one of three doors in the clinic, or via steps and ramp from an adjacent street. It is about four feet above street level. Both arms of the L are approximately 75 feet long; one is 50 feet wide, and the other is 25 feet wide.

The feel of this space is of an overly designed and probably expensive space, but one that is rather cold and hard. It is located on the north side of a mid-rise hospital building. There is a predominance of slick surfaces and sharp edges: twelve concrete, over-scaled box-shaped tree planters; travertine paving, now stained by water draining from the planters; the windows and stucco walls of five-story buildings on three sides; the sloping glazed roof of a below-ground waiting area; steel benches; and a row of seven travertine slabs that tilt up into the plaza and down into the waiting area beneath. These latter, in particular, create a disturbing sense of imbalance in the space, and—unfortunately—are reminiscent of tombstones.

The planting in this space does nothing to offset the overall hard appearance. Twelve small Japanese maples are delicate and appropriate to this north-facing space but are completely overshadowed by the size of the adjacent building and the dominant hardscape. Eight small pittosporum trees in planters along the raised street edge also do little to create a green setting.

The seating here is also unfortunate—six-foot maroon, steel benches placed across from one another between the large raised concrete planters. Though the benches are reasonably comfortable to sit on (with backs and arms), their number and placement suggests seating for large numbers of strangers at a bus terminal or shopping mall. Considering the stressful nature of waiting in an Oncology Department, it would have been more appropriate to provide short wooden benches or movable chairs, so that a person alone, or with a friend, could sit in a semiprivate location. The eight benches could, theoretically, seat sixteen people—an obvious overprovision in this small setting. Unfortunately, sitting alone in a field of benches evokes a lonely feeling, with so many empty seats in view.

ROOF GARDEN

This is an area on top of a hospital building that is designed and landscaped for use by patients, staff, and visitors, and—in some cases—for viewing from offices and hospital units. It has views out in several directions and is clearly in a rooftop location (unlike an enclosed courtyard, which may also be on a roof).

ADVANTAGES

- Captures space that might otherwise be unused.
- Private to people in the hospital; it is unlikely that people "just walking by" would use it.
- Has the potential for expansive views to the surrounding urban or natural landscape.

DISADVANTAGES

- Structural problems may preclude the use of large trees or water feaures.
- Exposed to elements: may be more windy than spaces at ground level, or enclosed courtyards.
- Depending on the orientation and height of any adjacent buildings creating shadows, temperatures may be uncomfortably hot or cold.
- Heating/air conditioning units often vent on roofs, creating intrusive mechanical sounds.
- Unless well signed, visitors and patients may not know of its existence.

One example of a roof garden is described and analyzed in the case study section of the following chapter (Alta Bates Medical Center, pp. 169–176).

ROOF TERRACE

Unlike a roof garden, which is located on *top* of a building, a roof terrace is usually on the side of a building forming a long narrow "balcony" to that building. It is usually a linear space, predominantly hardscaped but with some garden elements (planters, seating, etc.).

ADVANTAGES

- Captures space that might otherwise go unused.
- Potential for expansive views.

DISADVANTAGES

- Depending on location, may be too exposed—too hot, cold, or windy.
- Unless carefully designed, use of terrace may intrude on privacy of people in adjacent rooms.

The Gardens, Harrison Memorial Hospital, Bremerton, Washington

Harrison Memorial Hospital is situated on a forested ridge overlooking water and the distant Olympic Peninsula in a small port city west of Seattle. It is a 297-bed acute care hospital, opened in 1965, renovated and expanded in 1985. An attractive roof terrace named "The Gardens" was constructed on the first floor over a mechanical department and surgery unit, and opened in 1995.

The main hospital entrance leads directly into a large foyer and waiting area, from which there is access onto the roof terrace. The clear connection between inside and outside permits visitors, staff, and patients to select one of three environments, depending on the weather and their preference for type of seating and thermal comfort. When seated inside in the waiting area, there are attractive views out to the terrace and to distant mountains on the skyline. Stepping outside onto a glass-roofed deck, one can pull a light garden chair up to a table. Large glass panels between this deck and the open terrace provide shelter from the wind on a cooler day, and permit unimpeded views out to the terrace and "borrowed" landscape beyond. Finally, it is simple to carry a chair out to the open terrace and be more fully *in* the garden, with views and the sound of a gushing fountain. These different, easily accessible environments furnished with movable seats provide users with a sense of control—something lacking in most hospital settings. The same wood decking extends out from the covered area into the terrace proper, providing an easy surface to negotiate for those who may be infirm or elderly (See Color Insert).

"[The garden] helps build relationships. Every one who comes up, we've gotten to know each other…. It's a place to meet people. I feel very fortunate to have this. Sometimes, in the evening, the sun is setting. It's a wonderful experience. I have a lot of pride in this garden. I tell patients about it, and new employees when I'm orienting them."

(FEMALE STAFF MEMBER)

Research on hospital garden use indicates that people who are stressed experience a positive change of mood when spending time in a garden that is a sensorially rich environment. At Harrison Hospital, beyond the deck, is a semi-abstract landscaped area of flat river rocks; mounded areas planted with low-growing grasses, heather, liriope, and tall dense clumps of pampas grass; blocks of basalt; and from a simple fountain water gushes out of a stone block onto a bed of black pebbles. It is a restful place. The sound of the fountain can be heard throughout the garden; pampas grass sways in the wind; the leaves of golden bamboo cast shadows on a wall. The colors are muted, yet soothing in their complementary range of hues: the yellow-beige spikes of pampas grass echo the same color in the walls of the building; mounded grass, river rocks and concrete edging provide shades of grey; the light brown of timber decking is picked up in the weathered vertical columns of basalt; golden bamboo and a variegated liriope provide shades of acid green; the deep green of a strawberry ground cover is echoed in the dark green of traditional garden furniture.

A sense of restfulness in the garden is further enhanced by distant views of the Olympic Range. The 4-foot wall bounding the outer edge of the terrace fortuitously blocks off views of nearby houses (though not, unfortunately, nearby telephone lines), but permits uninterrupted views of near- and middle-distance trees and the distant mountain range.

The garden terrace certainly draws people out but in small numbers and once there, use is rather limited. There is little to engage children. In fact, what they would most like to do—examine the pebbles, climb over the low wall, explore and so on—is specifically prohibited by notices warning, "No access beyond this point," and, "Please stay on the path and deck areas. Do not walk on the plants, rocks, or wall. Please supervise children." Because of structural issues, approximately half the 12,000 square foot area cannot be accessed. Visitors with children quickly leave. The verbal notices create a rather negative, controlling tone, at odds with the contemplative mood created by the design and the words on the entry door: "The Gardens. Dedicated on March 17, 1995 to honor Harrison patients, family, and friends. May they find a place of refuge, a source of tranquility, and a wellspring of hope."

The garden cannot be explored; it has a "hands-off" setting; it's a garden to *look at*, not *be in*. Also, very loud jarring messages over a loudspeaker on the deck interrupt the meditative quality of the space. Elements of the abstract design may be disturbing to some. A stone path leads from the fountain back toward the hospital building and terminates at a building wall. A low stone wall extends like an arrow across the curvilinear

On a warm October afternoon, two staff members enjoy a quiet bag lunch together on the covered deck and stay there talking for forty minutes. A grandmother with two small children comes out to the garden. The children run to the fountain and the grandmothers warns them to go no further. They leave after a few minutes. A man and a small girl enter the garden and are attracted to the fountain. They leave after a few minutes. An elderly man and a young woman walk out, look at the view, examine the bamboo leaves, and leave. Three staff members sit at a table in the sun for fifteen minutes, apparently having an informal meeting. A young man and a woman, apparently staff members, sit at a table in the sun for fifteen minutes, talking and drinking coffee. Later, an older woman, her coat on to provide protection from a late afternoon breeze, sits at the same table with a thermos and a book for twenty minutes, then returns inside to her office.

(FIELD NOTES FROM HARRISON MEMORIAL HOSPITAL, C. C. M., OCTOBER 7, 1998).

plots of rocks and planting, ending abruptly at the fountain and preventing access beyond the wall.

Despite these drawbacks, this roof terrace does provide an attractive, soothing place where friends or colleagues may eat, talk together, or spend time in quiet contemplation. Certainly, a place for such activities is sorely needed in a hospital setting.

Promenade, St. Mary's Hospital, San Francisco, California

This is an excellent example of a roof terrace. A view out is immediately visible from the main lobby, drawing one to a large glazed wall and the discovery of this terrace. Its outer edge is bounded by a long concrete planter filled with blue agapanthus and trailing rosemary. Paralleling the planter edge is a long walkway used for strolling outdoors and bounded by planters with seat-high concrete ledges. Off the walkway and forming the most prominent features of the terrace are two brick-paved seating clusters, bounded by planters filled with shrubs and flowers and shaded by pittosporum trees. The seating, with curved backs, is made of wood slats and is quite comfortable. It is arranged in right-angled clusters so that three or more people can sit together comfortably and converse.

This terrace provides ample greenery with seating in attractive, semiprivate settings where people eat lunch, read, doze, or talk with colleagues. The greenery can also be enjoyed by people working in offices looking out onto the terrace. The terrace seating is far enough away from the windows that the privacy of neither space is compromised.

"This is my first time here. I've been admiring the trees, the landscape, the quietness, the birds. It's really relaxing—when I'm not having a contraction!"

(WOMAN IN LABOR)

Figure 4-14 A roof terrace with a clear route for strolling, and attractive seating clusters offering places to sit or lay down in the sun or shade. (St. Mary's Hospital, San Francisco, California.)

Perimeter Terrace, Davies Medical Center, San Francisco, California

This is an unfortunate example of this type of open space. It wraps around the south and east sides of a central high-rise hospital building and is accessible by steps and a ramp adjacent to the main entrance and directly from a second floor lobby. Surfaced with cement, this is a stark, glaring space with almost nothing to tempt people to stay. There are a number of small, poorly maintained trees in concrete tubs, completely out of scale with this extensive terrace and the height of the building. A few round concrete planters with seating ledges around them punctuate the space but offer little shade and provide seating that is uncomfortable.

So much more could have been made of this space, especially since on its east side it has magnificent views over downtown San Francisco. The relative nonuse of the terrace is confirmed by the fact that the hospital administration has seen fit to place two large round bicycle storage containers here, further marring the aesthetics of the space.

HEALING GARDEN[1]

This is a category that includes outdoor or indoor garden spaces in hospitals that are specifically designated as healing gardens by the administration and the designer.

ADVANTAGES

- Users can expect that some thought has been given to creating an environment that is therapeutic.
- Presence of a healing garden may convey message that the institution has a wholistic approach to medical care.

DISADVANTAGES

- Some staff members may not embrace the wholistic approach to medical care and may question the appropriateness of a healing garden.
- Users may be confused as to appropriate behaviors in the garden.

---

[1]Healing gardens and meditation gardens are identified as separate categories within this typology. A few hospitals studied had gardens that were specifically designated as one of these types. All of them had plaques identifying and dedicating the space.

One example of a healing garden is described and analyzed in the case study section of the following chapter and in Chapter 11, "Getting It Done" (Good Samaritan Medical Center, Phoenix, AZ).

Healing Garden, Oncology Department, Marin General Hospital, Outpatient Medical Building, Greenbrae, California

This is a small (15 × 25 feet) garden in what otherwise might have been an unused space. On one side is a restricted waiting area for Oncology Radiation, with floor-to-ceiling glass so that the garden forms a pleasing green outlook. Two-story, cedar-shingled walls and the windows of several offices look out and down into this space, but during the spring and summer the feeling while seated in the garden is not of being in a fishbowl because of very lush planting that seems to surround and enfold you. In the winter, however, the vegetation—much of it decidu-ous—is sparse. The plants—many tropical and shade-loving—are predominantly species that have healing properties. Short paths leading to two seating blocks at either end of the garden are made of concrete stepping-stones set in moss and are unfor-tunately difficult to negotiate by those who are unsteady on their feet. An unusual water feature—a grooved stone channeling a small stream down into a hollowed rock—provides a soothing sound. This is a very small, quiet and soothing space that feels "filled" when occupied by one person, but which benefits many who look out at it from the waiting area.

Figure 4-15   Water feature in the Healing Garden of a hospital oncology department. (Marin General Hospital, Outpatient Medical Building, Greenbrae, California.)

MEDITATION GARDEN

This is a small, very quiet, enclosed space specifically labeled with a plaque as a meditation garden by the administration and/or the designer.

ADVANTAGES

- Provides a space for those in a hospital setting who want to be very quiet and contemplative.
- By its name, precludes other, possibly distracting, activi-ties (eating, smoking, etc.).

DISADVANTAGES

- If it is visible from indoor spaces, one night feel self-con-scious, in a fishbowl. It is quite probable that only one person at a time might use such a space, depending on its size and its design.

- Given its designation, one might feel self-conscious about using it for other quiet activities that are not meditation, such as reading or writing.

Meditation Garden, Marin General Hospital, Outpatient Medical Building, Greenbrae, California

"You can come out here and meditate whether it's work related or stuff I'm dealing with at home. I can come out here and think about things and then go back in and be more productive...."

(STAFF MEMBER)

This is a small (15 × 25 feet) court/garden space entirely enclosed by the two-story cedar-shingled walls and windows of the building. The garden has low planting around its edges; an attractive stone wall; a fountain trickling into a bed of black pebbles; and a path of decomposed granite looping around the fountain. There are four comfortable wooden benches, each long enough for two people, though they do not have backs.

The small size, greenery, and sound of falling water set the stage for what may serve at times as a contemplative space. It is close to the waiting area and is labeled on the entry door as a Meditation Garden. However, the windows of five offices open onto this garden and in warm weather, with windows open, the inevitable conversations and occasional laughter are intrusive. There is also something of a self-conscious, "fishbowl" feeling while sitting in such a small space with minimal screening.

Meditation Garden, El Camino Hospital, Mountain View, California

This garden in a community hospital was donated by two couples—each of whom had lost a family member and had yearned for some place to go and sit quietly while in the hospital setting. The garden is approximately 40 × 60 feet and is enclosed by two-story buildings on two and a half sides. The entry is from a landscaped walkway through the half side that is open. The end that is not bounded by buildings is enclosed by trees and shrubs, screening the garden from lawns at the front of the hospital and a distant entry road.

The garden is dominated by four large weeping willows, which provide a green canopy, the sound of rustling leaves, and moving shadow patterns on the ground. Beneath the willows are shade-loving shrubs and ferns, scattered rocks, a dry stream bed of pebbles, and a Japanese lantern.

A concrete pathway—wide and smooth enough for a wheelchair or gurney—leads from the garden entry to seating under a wooden-roofed gazebo in the middle of the garden. Lighting in the gazebo and along the entry path permits use after dark—a thoughtful amenity in this area of hot summer nights. Windows from the Dialysis Unit on one side permit views out for the patients and staff inside. Reflecting glass in these windows creates an impression that the garden is larger than it is and eliminates the feeling of being in a fishbowl when in the garden. Two bird feeders hanging outside these windows encourage birds into the garden, which are then visible from inside and outside. There are also views into the garden from a staff lounge and a patient waiting room. Half-closed blinds in these windows permit some privacy for those inside and out.

Some of the drawbacks of this garden include: the low hum of an air-conditioning unit that competes with the pleasing sound of moving leaves; benches that have no backs or armrests and that form long right-angled arrangements, suggesting socializing rather than lone contemplation; and the central gazebo, which suggests larger gatherings. There is one additional short metal bench with back and arms on which sits, incongruously, a green-metal sculpted frog—a whimsical element more suited to a children's garden than to a place of meditation. The presence of an outdoor porch (with tables and chairs) off a staff recreation room at one end of the garden is also unfortunate, as the laughter and conversation of staff on breaks conflicts with the need for peace and quiet in the garden.

Overall, this is at most times a soothing, quiet milieu that feels quite separate from the hospital. Though not far from the main hospital building, the garden's location off a minimally used path is a drawback that has impacted its use. However, unlike the case of many other hospitals visited, the volunteers at the front desk *do* know of the garden's existence, and will escort people to it. The therapeutic benefits of such a space could have been enhanced with a greater variety of plant materials, engaging the eye to explore textures and colors while in the garden. This green, shady garden raises a question about the desired milieu for meditation. Although there is a pleasing rhythm of forms and textures, the planting remains primarily monochromatic. Perhaps this visually "quiet" environment is conducive to a contemplative mood, if that is what is desired; for someone seeking more engagement with the environment, it might be perceived as boring. More research is needed to reveal the qualities of an environment that would support a contemplative mood.

The Sherri Hinderstein Memorial Garden, Kenneth Norris Cancer Center, University of Southern California, Los Angeles, California

This garden, designed as part of a new oncology center at a large teaching hospital, is one of few visited whose location was clearly indicated by prominent signs in the main corridor. The

Figure 4-16   Seating and sculpture in the meditation garden of a cancer center. (Sherri Hinderstein Memorial Garden, Kenneth Norris Cancer Center, Los Angeles, California.)

garden has a clear sense of entry: the corridor leading to it terminates in a semi-outdoor "porch" with a dedication plaque and bench. Turning left, one enters the garden and the initial view is of three tall slabs of burnished concrete, black wire trellis boxes for vines to grow on, and an expanse of compacted, crushed fines. One's first image is of striking visual elements that are arid, hard-edged, and human-made. The tall concrete slabs, though perhaps intended to evoke a mysterious, towering presence, may unfortunately be interpreted by stressed cancer patients as tombstones.

The structural layout of this garden was inspired by the work of Kudriashe, a Russian constructivist painter. The space consists of a series of terrace stepping down to a chain-link boundary fence facing a street. Each terrace consists of a wide expanse of crushed fines and a narrow planting bed bounded with granite curbs; all the beds are planted with irises. The terraces are bisected by radiating wire-mesh "walls," which will eventually be covered by mandevillia, trumpet vine, and bougainvillea. Flowering trees include chorisia and jacaranda. There are plenty of comfortable wooden benches, but the garden provides limited visual variety. A small water feature near the entry consists of a polished, flat-topped, black rock with water spilling over the edge into a large steel grate. Unfortunately, it cannot be heard from any of the benches.

The overall image of this garden is somewhat arid due to the large expanses of buff-colored fines, selected by the designers to enhance the sensory experience of walking on this surface, and watching shadows play across it. One apparent conflict with its designation as a Meditation Garden is a secondary entrance into it from an adjacent café.

VIEWING GARDEN

With space and budget limitations, some hospitals incorporate a small garden that cannot be entered but can be viewed from inside the building.

ADVANTAGES
- Brings light into the building interior.
- Introduces greenery into a small area.
- Can be viewed from indoor seating, sheltered from rain, and in a heated/air-conditioned space.
- Low maintenance costs compared to accessible and used spaces.

DISADVANTAGES

- Greenery, flowers, and so on, cannot be viewed up close, touched, or their fragrances enjoyed.
- A fountain or birds—if present—cannot be heard.
- Hospital users cannot walk, stroll, or sit in garden.
- Inaccessibility of the garden may be frustrating for some —"Look, but don't touch."

Central Atrium, John Muir Medical Center, Walnut Creek, California

A small, square (approximately 30 × 30 feet) garden can be viewed through floor-to-ceiling windows from a large, plushly furnished foyer-atrium and from three adjacent corridors in this modern, suburban medical center. For much of the year, the weather in this region is either very wet, or excessively hot. A viewing garden is thus a quite suitable amenity. Flowers and ferns grow in square concrete planters of varied heights. There is a small fountain in the center and two fifteen-foot high trees. The garden was designed and is maintained by a local garden club.

The garden provides a green outlook for people waiting in the foyer or passing by in the corridor. The trees are well selected, with delicate foliage that moves in even a slight breeze. The fountain, with a number of very thin falling jets, offers a view of water, but a fountain with more visible water would have been a better choice, considering that people cannot hear it. More lush, colorful, and varied planting would have made this a more attractive feature.

Figure 4-17 A small atrium garden viewable from the entry foyer and corridors in a suburban hospital. (John Muir Medical Center, Walnut Creek, California)

THE VIEWING/WALK-IN GARDEN

This is a variation of the viewing garden in which a space that is —in terms of spatial extent and use—a garden to look out at from inside the hospital can also be entered and sat in by a very limited number of people. Such a space is usually viewed or entered from a waiting area or corridor. (It is also a variation of a courtyard, but is defined separately here because, unlike a courtyard, it is designed for very limited use).

"I work in the operating room. We have no windows; it's very cold with artificial light. This is the complete opposite—it gives me a lift to come out in the natural light."

(STAFF MEMBER)

ADVANTAGES

- Provides a soothing green outlook for people waiting or passing by.
- Provides a very quiet sitting place since few people are present.
- The relative lack of use ensures that users of any adjacent offices or patient rooms will not feel that their privacy has been unduly intruded upon.
- Brings light into the hospital interior.

DISADVANTAGES

- People sitting in the space may feel that they are in a "fish-bowl," being stared at, or if they are talking, that they are bothering people in adjacent rooms.

Interior Gardens, St. Mary's Hospital, Newport, Isle of Wight, England

Three small courtyard spaces seen through windows off the main ground-level corridor of this new community hospital could be characterized as viewing gardens. One has seating in it and is thus described in this section.

A door opens off the corridor and one steps into a space that is approximately 60 × 60 feet in size. Almost half the total area comprises tiled paving in a wavelike design, echoing a water theme used throughout the interior and landscape design of this hospital, located as it is on an island. Beyond the paving (as you view it on entering) is low shrubbery that acts as a buffer between the garden and the windows of offices/patient exam rooms on the other three sides of the square.

While the paving design is an attractive feature viewed from the corridor or from the two floors above, the detailing and furnishing of this space are less successful. There is one seating element comprising a circle of seats arranged in a sociofugal design (i.e., the seats face out, away from each other). This means that any more than two people entering the space together cannot easily converse while seated. Such a seating arrangement is suitable where strangers are sitting next to each other (e.g., a subway stop) but is not as appropriate where visiting families or coworker/colleagues are the likely users. There is no seating in several other half-moon-shaped paved areas that are bounded by shrubs, locations that would have been very appropriate as private seating spaces for one or two people. Also limiting the use of this garden is an inordinately high and awkward step up/step down entrance sequence. The paving rises and falls in wavelike undulations (on a vertical dimension), which echos the water theme, but is a bizarre choice in a hospital where elderly or infirm people would find this space difficult, if not impossible, to use.

The Atrium Garden, Stanford University Medical Center, Stanford, California[2]

At ground level in a new building complex of this large medical center and medical school, there are two walk-in/viewing gardens accessed from a major corridor at grade and viewed from three corridors, open stairways, and small waiting areas above. The gardens are very visible from inside through floor-to-ceiling glass. Beside one of these gardens, the corridor widens out to a spacious, tiled waiting area with comfortable leather armchairs. Thus this garden can easily be enjoyed by a number of people sitting inside.

The garden is roughly triangular in shape and is accessed by doors off the corridor-waiting area. It is approximately 115 feet long and 45 feet wide at its widest point. There are seating clusters in two areas, each with concrete paving and furnished with five handsome wooden garden benches with backs and arms, plus a litter container. The two clusters at either end of the garden are linked by a narrow, winding concrete path that enables a brief walk through the garden. Around each cluster are a number of silver birch trees, three stories high. These provide some sense of enclosure to those seated, and the soothing sound of leaves rustling as well as a green outlook for those in offices and patient rooms in the floors above . At most times of the day, there is a choice of seating in the shade or in the sun.

The planting in the gardens is exemplary for the effect intended, that of a colorful "cottage garden." There are underplantings of shade-loving ferns, camellias, azaleas, and impatiens beneath the birches; massed plantings of blue agapanthus,

---

[2]Despite the name, this garden does not constitute an atrium as we have defined it.

Figure 4-18 An attractive flower garden with space for a few people to sit in, and visible from a wide corridor and waiting area. (Stanford University Medical Center, Stanford, California.)

pink and white roses, white and blue petunias, white cosmos, white and pink dahlias, pink penstemon, blue lobelia, and blue delphiniums. Birches in two corners and cherry trees in the third act as a backdrop.

While one side (nearest the corridor) is obviously planned for use—with seating clusters and pathway—the other two sides are faced by the windows of offices and patient rooms. The depth of the garden and the height and variety of planting ensure complete privacy for those inside. Although a distant air-conditioning unit can be heard, the overall experience in this garden is of being very remote from the hospital atmosphere. This space accommodates a variety of people and activities. Some of those observed included people on their own, reading and eating, groups of visitors talking, an elderly patient in a wheelchair with a companion looking at the flowers and dozing, and small children exploring in the shrubbery. This human-scaled, secure, and enclosed setting, with the sound of moving leaves and views onto a wonderful variety of plants, flowers, leaves, shadows, and textures—is a true oasis experience.

A TUCKED-AWAY GARDEN

This type of garden is not often encountered but is worth mentioning since in some medical settings a space set *apart* from the building may be the only outdoor space available. If "advertised" and reasonably accessible from the hospital, such a setting can provide a welcome outdoor experience.

ADVANTAGES

- Can make good use of otherwise "leftover" space on the site.
- A short walk to the garden can provide a welcome separation from hospital activities.

DISADVANTAGES

- Without good signage, may be sparsely used except by those "in the know."

The Anniversary Garden, Glendale Adventist Medical Center, Glendale, Los Angeles, California

Founded in 1905 as the fifty-bed Glendale Sanitarium (on another site), the Glendale Adventist Medical Center has expanded into a large acute care general hospital on its present site near the Ventura Freeway in Los Angeles.

A short walk from the hospital lobby, over a bridge spanning a garage entry, brings you to the Anniversary Garden—so named because it was donated by the Hospital Volunteers on the occasion of the hospital's 75th anniversary in 1980. The garden is approximately square with a one-story medical office building on one side; a 5-foot wall on a second side; and 5-foot railings and a gate on the two sides from which you approach the garden. Although there are no signs to the garden within the hospital, once you approach it, the trees and the sounds of water beckon you.

Figure 4-19 Nurse taking a break beside a small waterfall and pool in a garden tucked away in between buildings at a large hospital. (Glendale Adventist Medical Center, Los Angeles, California.)

The major feature of this garden is a rock-bordered koi pond with water cascading into it from three corners of the garden. The soothing sounds of falling water pervade the space. Seating is provided under a wooden trellis; on a slightly raised wooden deck above the pool; and in several other scattered locations. The seating materials are of wood, heavy plastic, and fake stone. Whereas the latter would be inappropriately cold in many climates, these seats feel pleasantly cool in the hot climate of the Los Angeles basin.

A variety of native trees, including pines, American sweet gum, camphor, evergreen pear, bottle brush, gingko, carrotwood, and southern magnolia, provide deep and dappled shade. Trees approximately two stories high around the periphery of the garden subtly screen out the view to three- to six-story hospital buildings which, while not enclosing the garden as in a courtyard, form a background element on most of the four sides. Where a gap between the buildings permits a distant view to the San Gabriel Mountains, a gap in the trees allows garden users sitting under a trellis to enjoy this vista. There are, however, too many and too wide a variety of trees in this garden and a few could do with being removed or well-pruned.

Approximately half the total area is hard surfaced, with exposed aggregate and red brick insets; it is in a free-form shape that easily permits walking around the garden and approaching close to the pond.

Somewhat at odds with the quasi-Japanese feel to this space is the use of europs daisy, yellow gazania ground cover, bougainvillea and climbing roses. Flimsy one-foot fencing around all of the areas planted with ivy, gazania, and juniper seems unnecessary as it is unlikely anyone would walk across these ground covers.

An attractive feature of this garden is an entry porch comprising 6-foot stucco walls with a wooden arbor. It allows a brief funneled view of the garden before stepping completely into it. Unfortunately, looking back at this feature from within the garden, the walls seem rather stark and could have been softened with vines. The garden appears to be well used, especially by the staff for eating lunch, taking a quiet break beside the waterfall, or bringing paperwork to do outdoors at one of a few well-used tables.

BORROWED LANDSCAPE

Views out onto gardens or natural landscape can provide an important stress-reducing experience for hospital patients, staff, and visitors. Where a natural or designed landscape abuts the site of a new or remodeled hospital, it is very important that windows from patient rooms, waiting rooms, and single-loaded corridors are positioned so as to take advantage of these views to "borrowed landscape."

ADVANTAGES

- A green outlook can be provided with no expense of land acquisition or maintenance to the hospital.
- Wildlife or people using the space may provide a pleasing diversion, particularly for inpatients.
- An experience of nature is close at hand, even in inclement weather.
- Views out are complemented by daylight coming in.
- May provide a useful orientation element.

DISADVANTAGES

- Unless designated as a park or greenbelt, the space may eventually be built over.
- If ambulatory access to the space is not possible, may be frustrating to some people.

Figure 4-20   Taking advantage of "borrowed landscape." the patient rooms in this building look out over an urban greenbelt. (Scottsdale Memorial Hospital North, Scottsdale, Arizona.)

Scottsdale Memorial Hospital North, Phoenix, Arizona

Patient rooms on the east side of this multi-story hospital built in the mid-1980s look out over the Scottsdale Green Belt and Trail, a beautiful shallow valley that has been preserved as a ten-mile trail connecting the community of Scottsdale with the University of Arizona campus. Green lawns are punctuated by lavender-flowering jacaranda trees and eucalyptus. The valley is populated with rabbits, quail, and passing joggers and cyclists, and provides a pleasing view from inpatient rooms.

Victoria General Hospital, Victoria, British Columbia, Canada

A glass-roofed, glass-sided corridor, approximately 200 feet long, connects the main entrance to a secondary entrance at the opposite end of the building, and connects the North and South Towers (containing patient rooms) at the ground floor level. Through the glass are views to a segment of completely wild landscape—moss-covered rocks, ferns, patches of grass, shrubs, brambles, and oak trees. The hospital is located on the edge of a city in a rocky, forested milieu.

Figure 4-21 The glass sides and roof of this main corridor at an edge-of-town hospital allow people walking by, or sitting and waiting (left of picture), to look out at the natural wooded landscape. (Victoria General Hospital, Victoria, BC, Canada.)

As you enter the main entrance, you can see the length of this corridor and out to greenery beyond at the other end of the hospital building. Light floods into the building and waiting areas along the corridor are oriented toward the views out to the natural wooded landscapes. An added attractive element in the landscape around this hospital are the many tame rabbits, a mix of wild and domestic breeds, that populate the space.

NATURE TRAILS AND NATURE PRESERVES

"I feed the squirrels and birds. I have two blue jays who come down to eat peanuts—and there's George the squirrel; (you know) I speak fluent squirrel. I can recognize baby squirrels even though they're now grown. I've even come here on my day off!"

(FEMALE STAFF MEMBER)

Although a rare amenity in a hospital setting, an accessible nature trail or nature/wildlife preserve can provide a welcome outdoor experience, especially for staff on their lunch hour.

ADVANTAGES
- Can take advantage of the natural landscape surrounding a hospital when it is located in a out-of-town setting.
- A wide variety of species provides interesting views for hospitalized patients.
- Can provide an exercise route that may entice staff outdoors during breaks.
- Can provide an educational and community resource.

DISADVANTAGES

- May not be as usable by inpatients as a courtyard or entry porch.
- Depending on the local climate, may not be usable all year.
- May raise issues of supervision, especially in secure units.

Urban Wildlife Preserve, University of California, Davis, Medical Center, Sacramento, California

A four-acre wildlife preserve was opened in 1997 after a participatory design process involving members of the medical community, and teachers and students from an adjacent elementary school. It is designed to be a combination of habitats including riparian, oak woodland, and open grassland. All plants are native to California, and labeled plants with medicinal and healing qualities are used at the main entry. The range of habitats is intended to attract and accommodate a diversity of animal species. Features include walking paths, sitting areas, an outdoor classroom, a historic ruin, an arroyo, and a wildlife pond (doubling as storm water detention and irrigation runoff collection). A sense of discovery is achieved through the inclusion of curvilinear paths, mounds, tall grass and scattered mass plantings. Some wildlife areas are protected by restricted access. This is a good example of hospital outdoor space doubling as a community, educational resource.

Naval Hospital, Bremerton, Washington

A nature trail runs through portions of the forested environs of this 1980s high-rise hospital. The longest portion runs along a valley floor with towering conifers, ferns, shrubs and wild flowers. The trail surface of bark mulch, fallen leaves, and pine needles is a resilient material for walking or jogging on. The trail is signed and offers a locale close to the hospital that is a complete contrast to the interior.

Unfortunately, the overall route of this trail is fragmented and unclear. Portions running through the forest terminate in parking lots and access roads, with no indication where the trail continues. A short portion leading to a tidal marsh terminates in a muddy dead-end. There are no places to sit and enjoy a rest or a picnic lunch on any portion of the trail. There are no signs inside the hospital indicating its presence; nor are there any mentions of the trail in a hospital brochure handed to staff and patients, even under sections headed "Stress Management" and "Fitness." In short, this is a potential outdoor amenity that is neither developed nor used to its full potential.

Figure 4-22 *A nature trail provides an exercise route for the staff in the wooded landscape around a high-rise hospital. (Naval Hospital, Bremerton, Washington.)*

Mayo Clinic, Scottsdale, Arizona

The Mayo Clinic in Scottsdale is a new edge-of-town, upscale, outpatient clinic building with an interior furnished and decorated in the image of a hotel. Three to four minutes' walk from the main entrance is a nature trail set in the natural desert landscape of this region. The trail is a looped path that takes about fifteen minutes to walk, and has plant labels and several informative panels about the local geology and wildlife. There are two drinking fountains en route (with warm water!), and several rosy-concrete benches that are not in the shade and were already too hot to touch at 10:00 A.M. in early April.

The trail does not appear to be much used, despite the fact that there are leaflets available describing it and volunteers lead guided walks twice a week. There are no signs to alert you to its presence as you drive by it to the building entrance, nor any signs within the hospital. Such a trail might work better if it started right at the clinic entrance, rather than a few minutes walk down the entry road. It is possible, too, that the climate renders it unusable much of the year, especially for many older retired patients newly arrived in the southwest and unused to the excessively hot climate.

ATRIUM GARDEN

In latitudes where the climate precludes sitting or strolling outdoors through much of the year, an indoor garden—either heated or air-conditioned—can provide an attractive substitute. Numbers of medical facilities in very hot regions (e.g., Florida and the southern United States), or very cold regions (Canada, Scandinavia) incorporate a solarium or an atrium, furnished with appropriate trees, plants, and seating.

ADVANTAGES

- Simulates an "outdoor" green experience during times of inclement weather.
- Provides a space that is undoubtedly part of the hospital's territory and is secure.
- The space is usually very visible and accessible.
- The inside of hospital is flooded with daylight.

DISADVANTAGES

- Heating, or cooling, of space increases energy costs.

- Plants may need special care, or entail high maintenance and replacement costs.
- Difficult growing conditions may mandate use of plastic plants.

Royal Alexandra Hospital, Edmonton, Alberta, Canada

This very large, regional medical center has two impressive atrium spaces. The first is encountered a few paces from the main entrance. A barrel-vaulted glass roof arches over a large rectangular space approximately 50 feet wide and 200 feet long.

The space is six stories high and is bounded by patient rooms, offices, single-loaded corridors, and corridor seating areas looking down into the space through planters and unobtrusive blue-green mesh. The same blue-green tone is picked up in the atrium steel-mesh seating, small tables, movable chairs, the background color of way-finding signs, and accent tiles in the gray and cream tiling of the atrium floor. Railed cut-outs in the atrium floor allow daylight to access the cafeteria below.

The overall feel of this atrium is of an indoor plaza rather than a garden. Plants in pots and three small palm trees provide green accents, but the predominant visual experience is of the soaring glass and steel roof, light tiled floor, anodized railings, mesh seating, and street lamps. There is a quiet hum of sound from the cafeteria below and from three glazed elevators that "swish" up and down one segment of the six-story space. Staff and visitors walk through and some stop to look at a concession table selling jewelry. Few seem to use the space for sitting in.

From the first atrium, a wide curved stairway and an oil painting of a gesturing hand leads you up to a second atrium, approximately 40 feet wide and 180 feet long. Another vaulted glass roof allows light to shine in, supplemented by flood lights in the evenings. On one long side of the atrium are windows to six stories of patient rooms; on the other are single-loaded corridors—some glassed in, some open with cascading plants that trail down into the atrium garden.

Unlike the first atrium, this is a garden oasis. A large sinuous planting area is bounded by 18-inch high, yellow brick edging. Ficus trees and palms grow up to four stories high; under them are lush plantings of monstera, umbrella-plant, Norfolk Island pine, sansevieria, spider plant, and cactus. Staff come here to eat lunch; visitors and patients to find a private place to talk. Blue-green mesh seating is fixed in the brick planter edge in three curvilinear groupings, each one partially screened from the next by the thick planting (See color insert).

Figure 4-23 This glass-roofed six-story plaza-atrium brings daylight and a sense of the outdoors into this northern latitude hospital. (Royal Alexandra Hospital, Edmonton, Alberta, Canada.)

Figure 4-24 Hospital designed on the shopping-mall model. A glass-roofed, twelve-story atrium brings daylight to a row of shops and an "outdoor" café. (Walter C. MacKenzie Health Sciences Center, University of Alberta Hospitals, Edmonton, Alberta, Canada.)

Walter C. Mackenzie Health Sciences Center, University of Alberta Hospitals, Edmonton, Alberta, Canada

The Walter C. Mackenzie Health Sciences Center is a very large building—part of a major university hospital and medical school—housing emergency, day surgery, and outpatient clinics, rehab and psychiatry facilities, along with labs, offices, and classrooms attached to the medical school. Two huge atrium spaces span the center of the building—each twelve stories high. The initial impression is of an immense, confusing shopping mall. Steel-trussed bridges crisscross the atria at many levels; huge duct pipes loom in and out and down the walls like the insides of a ship; people are moving about at multiple levels. It is not a restful space, though it would be a fine place to explore if you were an energetic ambulatory patient or a youngster in a wheelchair.

The first atrium you encounter on coming through the main entrance has the frenetic energy of a neon-signed shopping mall. There is a cafeteria counter with a large area of "outdoor" seating, flower and gift shops, a hair salon, a news and candy store, ATM machines, public phones, and an espresso cart. Looming above, glass-enclosed corridors sprout cascading greenery and house-sized windows are adorned with window boxes. There is little here to suggest you are in a hospital; the walls above could be those of a hotel or an apartment house. Then you spot a white-coated figure, a patient in hospital green trailing an IV pole, and a discreet sign to "Emergency." This is not just a shopping mall.

At one end of this long space, red-tiled steps lead up beside a waterfall to a smaller cafe space at second and third levels, the chairs and tables looking down from balcony spaces into the main atrium. As the pace of the day slackens and the crowds in the ground level cafe start to thin out, the place begins to feel more comprehensible, less frantic. But then, looking more closely, you realize that the peace lilies and hydrangeas, the pink-tinged caladium leaves, the magenta bougainvillea cascading down beside the waterfall, the ficus trees and the trailing ivy are all *synthetic!* The only living plants are the flowers for sale in the florists' shop. One may feel a little tricked; what seemed like a big greenhouse full of plants is nothing but glass, steel, and plastic.

A second atrium, parallel with the first, houses a large cafeteria. Multi-globed street lights, colorful banners and wall hangings create the impression of a single-story space although the atrium actually soars twelve floors above. The table areas are carpeted—reducing noise—and furnished with attractively upholstered wooden furniture. Off a corridor that connects the two atria are an art gallery, a bookstore, and a volunteer-run kiosk for stamps, film, and lottery tickets.

The most restful space in this whole medical complex is a fourth floor atrium—a carpeted open space with light movable chairs, peripheral planting in buff-tiled planters, three attractive white-painted steel mesh arbors with seating inside and bougainvillea growing over them. This is the only space in this hospital with *real* plants! Large, semitropical plants fill the peripheral planters (sansevieria, peace lily, montera, umbrella plant) and four four-story high ficus trees grow in the center of the space. Children can run around; people in wheelchairs can easily move about; the glass barrel vault of the roof is only six stories above. This is a quiet, backwater space where families can visit, people can read quietly. The arbor spaces are particularly pleasing, the mesh of small leaves above and the semicircular benches plus movable chairs, create a restful, human-scale space—a place to get away from the almost frenetic hustle and bustle of this busy regional hospital.

Figure 4-25   A quiet fourth-floor atrium in a busy hospital, with arbors, plants, and movable seating, provides a place to rest in an indoor garden even when there is thick snow and subzero temperatures outside. (Walter C. MacKenzie Health Sciences Center, University of Alberta Hospitals, Edmonton, Alberta, Canada.)

"After an appointment with the breast surgeon, I sit in the hospital garden: distant sound of an air conditioner and overhead plane. A breeze blows my hair over my eyes. People are moving through the garden: a pink-coated volunteer pushes a patient in a wheelchair; a purple ressed woman sits pensively in the shade and stares across the garden at me. An acacia casts a deep abstract shadow onto the grass; the top branches of an olive sway gently, as if breathing.... I always feel nurtured by this garden—birds, leaves, shadows, breeze, solid tree trunks, starlings foraging.... The natural world continues, ever changing, merging, molding, emerging, singing—urging us to reach deeply into our own inner nature, where all is well—all is very, very well."

(C. M., BERKELEY, CALIFORNIA)

CONCLUSION

This typology, while probably not exhaustive of all possibilities for outdoor space at a hospital, provides an overview of the most frequently occurring categories and their pros and cons. Hopefully, it will encourage hospital administrators and designers of new or remodeled medical facilities to take a second look at what is possible, and perhaps, create a needed garden in what might have been a leftover space or bleak courtyard. As time goes on, and there is greater awareness of the need for healing gardens, designers and their clients will no doubt find categories to add to this list, and expand our knowledge of the best locations and design of usable hospital outdoor space.

REFERENCE

Cooper Marcus, C. and M. Barnes (1995). *Gardens in Healthcare Facilities: Uses, Therapeutic Benefits and Design Recommendations.* Martinez, CA: The Center for Health Design.

CHAPTER

5

Acute Care General Hospitals: Case Studies and Design Guidelines

Clare Cooper Marcus
and Marni Barnes

A cute care hospitals are those local and regional institutions we all associate with the word "hospital." They are the places where we might have gone for an appendix operation; to visit a friend recovering from an accident, to give birth to a baby, or to have a child checked out after a fall at the playground. They are often in large building complexes with multiple departments. We may have entered them as inpatients, outpatients, visitors, or employees. Rarely do they incorporate gardens, and if they do, the garden seldom rates an appearance in way-finding directions.

A brief history of the provision of outdoor space in these types of hospitals appears in the Introduction to this book (Chapter 1). In this chapter there are two sections: case studies and design guidelines. In the case study section, the outdoor spaces of five acute care hospitals are described and analyzed as to their design and use. These hospitals are: Kaiser Permanente Medical Center, Walnut Creek, California; Alta Bates Medical Center, Berkeley, California; San Francisco General Hospital, San Francisco, California; Good Samaritan Medical Center, Phoenix, Arizona; and St. Michael's Health Center, Texarkana, Texas.

The second part of this chapter consists of design guidelines for outdoor spaces at acute care hospitals. A discussion of these guidelines and recommendations as to their use appears in the introduction to that section of the chapter.

CASE STUDIES

Central Garden, Kaiser Permanente Medical Center, Walnut Creek, California

Description and History of the Facility
Kaiser Permanente is the largest Health Maintenance Organization in the United States. The first Kaiser Medical Center was built to serve the employees of the Kaiser Permanente Cement Plant in California. From those humble

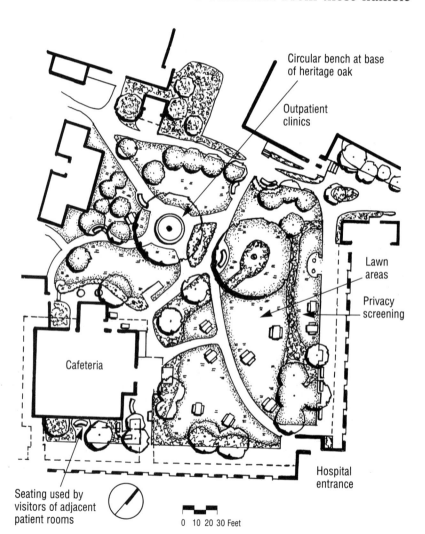

Figure 5-1 Site plan of Central Garden at Kaiser Permanente Medical Center, Walnut Creek, California.

beginnings, it has grown to provide medical services in most of the western portion of the United States and is expanding into the rest of the country.

The Walnut Creek campus was opened in 1953. In 1960, a two-story medical office building was constructed, followed by a cafeteria/office building in 1966. Another four-story acute care facility with offices was built in 1969; a parking garage in 1975; and a three-story addition to that in 1984. Due to the insistence of the Walnut Creek City Council, these structures were built around a central outdoor space in order to preserve several old, magnificent oak trees. During the first thirty years of operation, the outdoor space remained virtually untouched, occupied in part by a two-story house, one of the original farm buildings on the site. In the 1970s, the landscape architecture firm of Babcock and Assoc. (Berkeley and Lafayette) was contracted to landscape the area as a trade-off (again prompted by the City Council) for the construction of the multistory parking garage.

Two post-occupancy evaluation studies have been conducted in this garden. One, in 1991, was undertaken by graduate students in architecture and landscape architecture at the University of California, Berkeley, under the direction of Clare Cooper Marcus (unpublished). The second was undertaken in 1995 (Cooper Marcus and Barnes, 1995). The results of both were very similar and both inform the following account. (Where statistics are quoted, the date of the relevant study is indicated.)

In 1997–1998, Kaiser Walnut Creek conducted a major building program that impacted the central garden; new multistory buildings extended into the garden, resulting in approximately a 20 percent loss of green area. This unfortunate loss of space and the resulting changes in the atmosphere of the garden could provide an opportunity for a comparative study to be conducted between the two—before and after—spaces. This would be a valuable addition to the growing body of research on the therapeutic benefits of gardens in medical facilities.

Description of the Garden

At the times of the 1991 and 1995 studies, the central garden at Kaiser, Walnut Creek, was designed around the two heritage valley oak trees. The garden forms a central focus to the hospital community; its large old trees, varied vegetation, lawns, and paths create an environment that ties together the buildings of varied heights, materials, and styles that surround it. Sitting in the garden, one is aware of the buildings, but only partly. Windows, walls, and doorways are glimpsed through the foliage. The atmosphere is of an urban park; the buildings it serves are not far away, yet are somehow visually removed.

Figure 5-2   One of the protected valley oaks that form the core of the well-used garden at Kaiser Permanente Medical Center.

Figure 5-3   A path that crosses the open space from a multistory parking garage to the main lobby brings many people through the garden.

An outpatient waiting for her appointment felt "rested spiritually" in the garden:
"It's a privilege to be here. Look at this incredible oak tree — it's a universe in itself."

The location of the garden at the center of the hospital complex is important in a number of ways. First, it is very accessible to everyone; you can't help seeing it and knowing it is there. It is very easy to walk into it — however briefly — from any department or building; walking through the garden is the quickest route between buildings; hence even those staff or visitors with little time to spare can enjoy the outdoor environment, as a break from sterile corridors and stairways.

The garden is crisscrossed with wide concrete paths; it is anchored at one corner by the main hospital entrance while a multistory parking structure is situated diagonally opposite. At the time of the evaluation studies, single-story wards encompassed the east and south edges of the space, with windows and sliding glass doors leading directly into patient rooms. These wings were home to post-op patients, and some pediatric and orthopedic patients. The length of stay was sometimes as high as three weeks; however, the average stay was reported to be three days. These patients' rooms were buffered from the garden by a wide, covered arcade. Low shrubs separated the arcade from the large expanses of lawn, while allowing a view for people in their beds into the limbs of the trees beyond. The other two sides of the courtyard were bounded by a four-story outpatient medical building to the north, and the two-story cafeteria building and a temporary building housing the outpatient EKG Center to the west.

The plants and trees were sensitively chosen to provide a wide variety of visual interest — from the delicate white trunks and branches of silver birches near the pharmacy to the shiny dark leaves of a white-flowering magnolia, the wind-tossed leaves of sycamore, alder, and olive, the blue spikes of agapanthus, and feathery pink blooms of a flowering eucalyptus. The deeply serrated trunks and wide spreading gnarled branches of the two valley oaks, which form the core and canopy of the garden, are reminders that not long ago this was open wild country. These two trees — and especially the one with a wide circular bench beneath it — feel like aged and stately elders, lending a sense of nurturance and history to this much-used setting.

As wind or soft breezes blow through the garden, leaves move, revealing subtly different colors and textures on their undersides. The sound of wind through leaves and branches creates a soft "white sound" that helps mask the distant hum of air conditioners and freeway traffic. As well as providing the sensory pleasures of the sounds and sights of growing things in a garden setting, such a place can also provide a habitat for other creatures. At Kaiser Walnut Creek, there are brown squirrels, starlings, robins, blue jays, sparrows, and butterflies and more. While there is relatively little nighttime use, the garden still functions as a walking route between buildings after dark, and on balmy summer evenings, some inpatients come outdoors to meet with their visitors in relative privacy. Two types of lighting adequately provide for artificial light at this time: tall, brown-painted steel light posts blend with the trees and almost go unnoticed during the day; shoulder-height light fixtures are slightly more noticeable, but their brown steel shafts also blend in with the predominant brown and green tones of the garden. At night, these latter fixtures, with small "bubble" lights shining downward, subtly light up the pathways without shining upward into people's eyes.

Uses of the Garden

The most numerous users of the garden are hospital employees. Identifiable by their hospital garb or ID badges, employees spend brief coffee and smoke-breaks outdoors between 10:00 A.M. and 11:00 A.M., and then come out in larger numbers and for longer periods of time during the lunch hours (12:00 P.M.–2:00 P.M.). Shortly before noon, a barbecue is often set up near the cafeteria; employees collect their lunch, or arrive with brown bags, and cluster at tables set on a covered patio and out on the grass. Often a group from the same department will sit together at a picnic-style table, chatting and laughing while enjoying their lunch. Others may seek a quieter spot, further from the cafeteria, to sit and read.

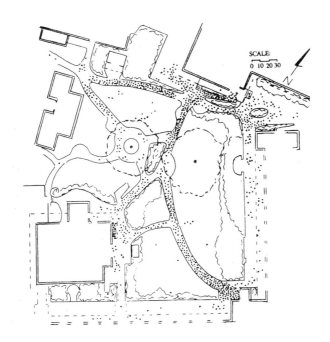

Figure 5-4 The principal users of the garden are those passing through. Dot map shows aggregation of eight hours of observations (summer, 1995).

Visitors to the hospital use the garden most of the day. They are more noticeable before and after the lunch period when employee use is at its peak. Most are using the garden to sit and wait for appointments or for a prescription to be filled. They tend to use two areas of the garden less frequently used by employees: two benches near the entrance to the pharmacy, and a circular bench under the smaller of the two huge oak trees. The children of visitors and outpatients, and children outpatients, are a third group of users. As might be expected, they use the garden more actively than adults, running or rolling on the grass, balancing on benches, sometimes exploring the shrubbery. While adults enjoy the garden as a quiet respite from work or waiting rooms, children particularly enjoy the freedom of movement and exploration permitted in the garden as compared to the more regulated atmosphere indoors.

The smallest group seen outdoors in terms of numbers are inpatients; nevertheless, this is undoubtedly an important environment for them too. It is not uncommon at any time of day to see patients propelling themselves—or being pushed—in wheelchairs; patients trying out crutches or a walker, or trailing an IV on a stand. The relatively small size, semiprivate nature, and (most of the year) warm temperature of the garden make it an ideal setting for recuperating patients and those seeking a break from their rooms.

There are three basic types of use of the garden: walking through it, sitting in it, and looking out at it. In terms of total numbers throughout the day, the most frequent use is by people passing through—walking to the cafeteria to pick up lunch, wheeling trays of files between departments, walking from the parking garage to the pharmacy or the main hospital building, pushing a wheelchair-using patient for a touch of sun and fresh air. Smooth concrete pathways allow easy movement from building to building by reasonably direct routes. The quiet, totally pedestrian nature of the garden allows even frail, slow-moving patients to feel unpressured, and lets the parents of young children feel relaxed about their children running off the paths. Of the 1,251 people recorded during the two mornings and two afternoons of observation in the 1995 study, 506 walked through without lingering, while 745 either stopped to talk or sat eating, waiting, having a smoke, or purposefully passing the time by strolling through the grounds or playing. Those who came into the garden with the intention of staying awhile sought out a place to sit down. A lot just came to relax, often on a work-break. Many came out to eat lunch, often carrying food from the cafeteria to one of the outdoor tables on the lawn. Sitting and talking was another important activity; this

A visitor to this medical facility remarked while in the garden:

"I like the openness, the grass, birds, the breeze. Although there's a lot of people around, there's a quietness about it. It reminds me of a campus."

included chatting with fellow workers on a break, visiting with a patient in the hospital, or holding a work-related meeting. This latter is a small but significant aspect of outdoor use. Picnic tables in the garden offer a setting where employees can discuss a patient case or work issues in relative privacy.

The relaxed use of the garden by so many throughout the day is made possible by the provision of a range of seating. With its simple array of outdoor features, the garden at Kaiser, Walnut Creek, is a refreshing example of how to make a public outdoor space work, with relatively low budget furniture that nevertheless responds to its users' needs sensitively.

The garden contains six types of seating. Fixed, semicircular wooden benches located just off the main paths are often used by people reading, children playing, or others just sitting, relaxing, talking with friends, or waiting. Under one of the large oak trees, an attractive large-radius circular bench is especially popular with both employees and visitors. The design and location of the bench allow you to choose to sit in sun or shade, facing in or facing out. Several concrete stools and tables are clustered in niches off the central lawn, creating semiprivate outdoor seating. Often the employees acquire these spaces during one of their short breaks of ten to twenty minutes. But the furniture in most demand are the residential-scale wooden picnic tables and benches located in various spots, in sun and shade, throughout the garden. The tables are relatively easy for two people to lift and move; they are shifted from shade to sun and vice versa, depending on the time of day, or sometimes are moved into a cluster for an informal employee birthday lunch or baby shower. Finally, metal mesh patio tables and chairs are located on the terrace off the cafeteria.

The provision of such a variety of seating, in terms of design, setting, and movability, allows most people to find a place to sit according to their needs. Interviews in 1991 revealed three shortcomings: employees wanted *more* tables and benches near to the cafeteria—it is not uncommon at lunchtime to see people with laden trays searching for a place to sit outdoors. Some wanted a few more options for sitting *alone* in a secluded spot; these included employees who wanted a break from human contact, and some people visiting acute care patients who needed a quiet break. Finally, a few elderly visitors and outpatients remarked on the lack of benches with arm rests and backs, which make outdoor seating more comfortable.

A total of fifty people were interviewed in the garden (1995); two-thirds of them were women. Of those interviewed, twenty-seven were staff, eleven were visitors, eight were outpatients, and four were inpatients. Almost half reported using the garden

Figure 5-5   Two volunteers enjoy a private conversation in the garden.

every day or several times a day; a third used it "occasionally." With the presence of picnic tables, ample seating, and an adjacent cafeteria, it is not surprising to find that one-fifth reported spending periods of more than thirty minutes in the garden, and nearly three-fourths took breaks of ten to thirty minutes.

While "relaxing" appeared high on the list here and in all the case study gardens, at this Kaiser facility a higher proportion than elsewhere reported using the garden for eating, visiting with a patient, watching their children play, and attending an outdoor meeting. Almost half reported there were no impediments to their using the garden, and most of the remainder—as at other sites—reported weather and work as the only serious impediments.

The garden was highly regarded and appreciated by everyone interviewed, especially by staff, who were thankful for the contrast between the indoor and outdoor environments. A woman employee who comes out once or twice a day to relax, talk, eat, stroll, or visit with a patient responded, "You can get away from the fluorescent lights, sounds, and smells of a hospital; listen to the birds, the breeze. It's a tremendous place to unwind."

Several people felt it looked like a park or "a country club." Employees especially appreciated its tranquillity. "I like it when I do swing shift; at dusk you could imagine this is your backyard. I like the tranquillity. It has a certain peace about it."

Visitors and outpatients appreciated having a relaxing place in which to wait, and a woman inpatient remarked,

Figure 5-6 People interviewed in the garden spoke enthusiastically of its relaxing atmosphere, the trees, birds, squirrels and lawns. Staff particularly appreciated its tranquility compared to the hospital interior.

I really hate hospitals a lot. I get tired of my room. It's so much nicer out here—I like seeing the grass and hearing the birds. I come out several times a day to sit or stroll or have a smoke. My favorite time is the evening when everything is really quiet.... It's much better than sitting inside and watching the boob tube.

When asked if people felt any different after spending time in the garden, the most frequent and consistent response was: "Yes —more relaxed." A garden and a hospital are almost polar opposites on a continuum from controlled to natural, from stressful to relaxing. It is small wonder that staff and employees felt so passionately about this garden in the midst of their work environment. "I feel more calm, more relaxed. If you want to get away from things, just sit under a tree and reflect—things usually get better." "It's very soothing because it's so different from the interior of the building, which is stressful. This is a complete opposite." "I'm back to being me again. This is absolutely my little spot to get centered and heal myself."

Visitors and patients both felt strongly about how this place facilitated a change in mood. An outpatient, who told us she brought visitors from Europe to show them what a nice hospital looks like, remarked: "It doesn't feel, smell, or look like a hospital. Coming to a hospital scares and worries people. Being in the garden before or after visiting the doctor is good, regardless of what you find out. I feel more relaxed."

People had no trouble connecting their change in mood with specific characteristics of the garden, even if—as some said—they hadn't consciously thought about this before. For many it was a whole range of elements, such as this visitor to the hospital named: "... the landscaping, the birds. You can get a cup of coffee, sit back, and look at the trees. Every time I come, it's a different season. It takes your mind off whatever you're here for."

A female inpatient interviewed near her room particularly liked "Listening to the birds; it's quiet here. I like to see other people sitting and relaxing on the benches. I can't get out there, but it's neat; it's really relaxing."

The huge valley oaks elicited a lot of positive comment, particularly their size, their great age, the wildlife they harbored, and for some, the memories they evoked. A male security guard who patrolled the garden liked the tranquillity and peace "... and the large trees, when the wind blows through the branches. It's a sound I got used to a kid growing up in the Arizona countryside."

For others it was the oasislike quality of the space that helped evoke a change in mood. A male employee, who comes

Figure 5-7   Hospital expansion in 1997–1999 encroached on the garden and eliminated some much-loved outdoor space.

out to sit and eat several times a day, feels calmer as a result and attributes that to "the trees, the grass, birds, animals—it's like an oasis among the concrete, yet it's close to whatever you need. You have to stay conscious because you can get into a mood and forget about the time."

This space is not large by park standards, yet people *experienced* it as spacious: because of the planting that screened some of the surrounding buildings; because—by hospital standards—it is a large open space; and because, for some, it provided a contrast to the small spaces in which they live and work. A female employee confided:

> When I work evenings, I come here two hours early and just *sit* here! In my life, this is a vast space. I live in a little condo, work in a little office in surgery. This is like a vast open space to me! The patients come out here all the time—pregnant women waddle around. They say, 'This is such a great space, so soothing. Who'd believe this was here?'

Finally, for a few people, it is not so much the trees, the fresh air, animals, and openness that helped to change their mood, but the companionship and good spirits of other people in the garden, particularly, it seemed, the gardeners. One employee who admitted, "I'd be out here all day long if I could," added "The gardeners keep us laughing all the time. They do such a good job, keeping the garden. It's a joy to have them out there." In creating a garden for therapeutic outcomes it would pay not only to design it with care, but also to select maintenance staff for their sensitivity and good humor.

When asked (in 1995) if there was anything in the setting that needed to be changed, just under half of the respondents wanted no changes in the garden. Others wanted to see planting improvements—especially more flowers—and a few specifically requested a fountain or birdbath. Some people identified practical items such as a drinking fountain or more tables and seating.

Compared with the other sites observed, Kaiser provided well for smokers. A small three-sided, roofed structure with comfortable chairs inside was erected in 1995 for the convenience of smokers who need to come outside. While this looks onto the center of the garden, the smokers don't annoy non-smokers by sitting next to them on a garden bench.

Hospitals are obviously associated in most people's minds with illness, accidents, death. It is clear from observing—and talking with—people in the garden at Kaiser, Walnut Creek, that the presence of *life* just outside is enormously therapeutic. The trees, the birds, the squirrels, children playing—all remind people that "life goes on." Several patients and employees mentioned the fact that the garden made this Kaiser facility unique and that they used—or had taken a job at—Walnut Creek specifically because of its soothing milieu.

In order to gain some measure of what the garden meant to people, in the 1991 study we posed the question: "How would you feel if this outdoor area was built over?" We were surprised at the emotions raised by this hypothetical situation. Most responded with sadness or anger and a few with horror. "I would be devastated." "It would be just terrible." Many showed considerable emotion at the idea of losing this resource, especially hospital employees who use it frequently for breaks or for walking through. One employee who had worked in many medical facilities since 1959 rated this—because of the garden—as one of the best. And a male employee who used the garden every day, sometimes to do work-related reading, summed it up:

> I work in the operating room—no windows. The diurnal cycle is interrupted. Out here, it's open to the sky. It fits with the holistic idea of what I think health care is. It's not only medicine and physical treatment; you also have that part that's unique to the individual called the soul. This garden helps to revive that."

ADVANTAGES

- Historic—and therefore protected—native oak trees provide a beautiful atmosphere, help with orientation and way-finding, and serve as a meeting place.
- Variety of planting creates a visually stimulating milieu.

- Before recent construction, glass doors from patient rooms facilitated easy visiting, especially with restless children.
- Proximity of the cafeteria maximizes use and therefore potential benefit from the garden.
- The central location assures that everyone knows of the garden's existence.
- Screening planting offers a degree of privacy between the patient rooms and the majority of the garden.
- Variety of types and location of seating options provides for many users.
- The large amount of seating provided for small groups (two to eight) is well-utilized by staff and visitors.
- The size of the garden permits children freedom to run and climb trees—as in a park—without parents' worrying about disturbing others.
- The paths are used by post-op and maternity patients for exercising.
- The high level of maintenance and frequent rounds of security guards seems to indicate a high level of commitment to the care of the garden and the people in it.
- Lighting adequate for nighttime use is provided.

DISADVANTAGES

- A greater variety of plant species, especially flowering shrubs, would serve to increase the seasonal interest in the garden.
- Before recent construction, people walking along the paved arcades could pass very close to ground-level patient rooms. The addition of planting-islands between doors would have allowed patients more privacy without losing the benefit of the access or the view.
- The vast majority of the seating has no back to lean against. Chairs and benches designed for people in a frail condition would be a valued addition to the seating options.
- There are few spots for solitude in the garden. Before recent construction, the space was large enough to accommodate some areas designed for solitary reflection, but since redesign of the garden in 1997, this is no longer so.
- The destruction of part of this well-used and highly valued space belittles the importance of a garden's role in the therapeutic milieu of a medical facility.

Alta Bates Medical Center, Berkeley. California,

Description and History of the Facility

Alta Bates Medical Center is a complex of buildings, three to six stories in height, set in a neighborhood of single family homes, apartments, and medical office buildings in south Berkeley. It is named for Alta Alice Miner Bates, who first settled in Berkeley in 1904, and nursed patients in her parents' home as there was no hospital in the community at that time. In 1905, at the request of local physicians, and with plans drawn up by her contractor-father, she constructed an eight-bed nursing facility and school for nurses on Dwight Way, called the Alta Bates Sanitarium. In 1908, due to the population expansion in Berkeley after the 1906 earthquake, the facility moved to large three-story buildings at its present site on Webster Street. In

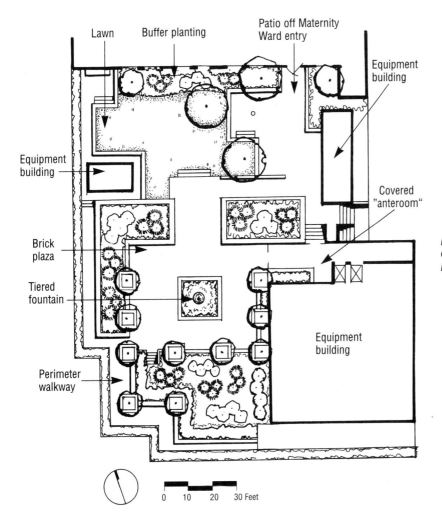

Figure 5-8 Site plan of the Roof Garden, Alta Bates Medical Center, Berkeley, California.

1928, its name was changed to Alta Bates Hospital and six-story buildings were added. Care was taken through setbacks and landscaping to ensure that the buildings blended into the residential neighborhood. When the old buildings were replaced by modern facilities in the 1980s, a generous setback from Ashby Avenue was dedicated to lawns and trees.

The roof garden—dedicated to the Alta Bates Volunteer Auxiliary—was opened on the third floor of one of the new buildings in 1983. It is accessed from elevators located at the end of a long corridor that jogs its way from the main lobby through the different additions and finally to the elevators. Upon finding the remote elevators, only an enigmatic "R" button in the elevator indicates the garden's presence. Access from the main elevator bank in the center of the structure is prohibited, as the garden shares the third floor with the maternity ward, and due to a recent policy change, that ward is now a security unit; the general public is not allowed to pass down the hall to the garden. There is no indication on any way-finding maps of how to reach the roof garden, nor are there signs anywhere directing people to it. Even the volunteers at the information desk in the main lobby did not know how to direct the authors to the garden when we first visited.

Description of the Garden

The roof garden is located on the southwest corner of the hospital complex, three floors above the ground. On the north side, it is bounded by the facade of the adjacent five story wing containing patient rooms and offices. To the west and south the views are expansive, overlooking residential neighborhoods and

Figure 5-9 A roof garden at Alta Bates Medical Center is used by staff for taking breaks and eating lunch, but most patients and visitors do not know it is there.

beyond to a panoramic view of San Francisco Bay, the Golden Gate Bridge and the islands and hills of Marin County. To the east, the wooded residential Berkeley Hills can be seen between and above the one story structures housing elevator shafts and equipment that are within the garden.

The garden consists of four distinct subareas. Upon emerging from the elevator one walks out into a small covered area, with a few plastic patio chairs tucked into the corner. This small "anteroom" to the garden proper is well-used because it is near the elevators, contains vending machines, and is sheltered from the heat and wind as well as rain.

This covered area opens onto a sunny square brick plaza bounded by raised planter beds that are edged with a concrete seat-wall. Punctuating the perimeter of this patio are eight higher planting boxes containing small carob trees. These boxes separate the seat-wall into segments, providing back support for someone sitting sideways and allowing separate groups of people to claim a spot for themselves without feeling too close together. In the middle of the plaza is a square planted with annual flowers, in the center of which sits a small tiered fountain. On the structure bounding the eastern edge of this plaza, two ornate columns and a crest that formed the entrance to the 1928 hospital building have been incorporated into the wall.

The second major section of the roof garden is four steps below the plaza and has more of a "garden" quality to it. A small brick and concrete patio is set outside a door into the maternity wing. It is bounded by seating height concrete planters on one side and by a raised lawn on the other. Residential style patio tables, topped with umbrellas and surrounded by chairs have been set out on this patio. The lawn is larger than either the plaza or the patio—covering approximately one fifth of the accessible roof area—and feels generous. Three Japanese maple trees are set into the lawn and offer filtered shade on hot days. A planting bed runs beneath the patient windows, providing separation from the lawn and filtered screening for the patients inside. The flower bed is planted with shrubs and vines; scarlet and purple climbing bougainvillea has grown up the facade to provide a splash of color on the wall and to create a privacy buffer between the roof garden and patient rooms.

The last and most secluded section of the garden consists of a narrow walkway—with alcoves set back into the raised planters—on the west and south perimeter of the roof garden. Since this section is separated from the other areas by the shrubbery, from here one's awareness is directed toward the panoramic view. Movable garden chairs are carried here for private sitting, viewing, and conversation.

A female employee who uses the garden every day responded:

"It's a place for meditation and relaxation. It is tranquil. Because I work in the radiation department in the basement, I feel like one of the Mole People; I come out for sun. It's a big mental, emotional lift…"

Figure 5-10   Staff eating lunch out-doors. In summer, the heat, glare, and lack of shade cause problems.

The background hum of a large air-conditioning/heating unit is quite evident as you exit the elevator, though it is not unduly intrusive everywhere in the garden. One is aware of birdsong, and in the plaza area, of the sounds of the fountain. On a breezy day, the rustle of trees and vines is a soothing back-drop for garden users. The garden is high enough above the street that traffic cannot be heard. Apart from the sounds of an occasional plane or helicopter, the roof garden is very quiet and peaceful. When seated in most parts of the garden, the views over the city are screened by planting, and one has the sense of being in a secluded city garden.

Use[1]

The roof garden at Alta Bates is relatively underused.[2] In eight hours of observation at Alta Bates during the spring of 1995, only 154 people came into the garden. This relatively low usage can be explained by a number of factors: this roof garden is a "terminus" location—you go there to be there rather than pass-ing through it on the way to somewhere else; a roof garden tends to be more exposed to the elements than a garden at ground level; the garden at Alta Bates is not publicized and is only visible from a few rooms on three wards.

The most frequent pattern of use was for a person to find a place to sit while he or she had a smoke or ate a brown bag

---

[1]A postoccupancy evaluation of this garden was conducted in 1995 and is report-ed more fully in Cooper Marcus and Barnes (1995).

[2]Some of the photos in this book were taken prior to the introduction of security features in the maternity ward. These show more people than are typical today.

lunch or a snack from the vending machines. Since the cafeteria is three floors down and catty-corner across the complex, it was very rare to see people arrive with a meal on a tray. Those arriving for a short break tended to cluster around the vending machines beneath a building overhang; it was here that most socializing took place. Those coming to the garden for a longer period tended to sit alone on the concrete seating bounding the main, brick-paved plaza, or to walk very purposefully to a favorite seat or bench in more remote and hidden corners of the garden. The latter apparently came to be alone and often dozed, sunbathed, looked at the view, or were lost in thought. Sixty percent came to the garden alone; 21 percent came in pairs, usually to eat lunch together. The 18 percent observed in groups usually did not arrive together but either arranged to meet here or bumped into each other while taking a break.

Thirty-six people who were spending time in the garden were interviewed; half were male and half female. Of these, twenty-nine were staff and employees, three were visitors, two were outpatients, and two inpatients. The garden was used predominantly by staff. A third of those interviewed reported using the garden several times each day, and an additional 25 percent came once a day. The primary use of the garden was either for quick break with a drink or a cigarette (almost one-half used the garden for a less-than ten-minute break); or for a longer visit of ten to thirty minutes, usually at mealtime. When respondents were asked what they did in the garden, the most frequently cited activities were relaxing, talking, eating, strolling, and "outdoor therapy."

When interviewed, many respondents referred to the pleasing contrast between the garden—open, sunny, colorful, "natural"—and the environment inside the hospital. For example, a man whose wife had just given birth had come to the garden three times that day. "I feel more relaxed. It's mostly because there aren't too many people out here. I'm a solitude kind of person. The sunlight is nice. The waiting room with fluorescent light sucks the energy out of you."

For many people, the garden provides an escape from work and the stress of constant interaction with people. A male employee who uses the garden every day remarked: "It's an excellent area for relaxation even if it's only for a short time.... Five minutes out here is better than an hour in the cafeteria. Its calming influence creates a sense of separation from the hospital that a recreation room wouldn't provide. It's a complete getaway. ..."

Patients come seeking a place to get away as well. They also can use the garden for exercise. It provides an attractive desti-

Figure 5-11   Light, movable chairs are popular and enable people to use the planter edge as a table, and to create a small private space. At the time of a post-occupancy evaluation study (1995), there were only five of these chairs—and 300 linear feet of concrete planter edge seating.

A female employee who visits the roof garden two or three times a week remarked:

"I'm at peace—you can see the birds and the water. I feel a sense of meditation; I feel better. Breathing the fresh air helps clear my head even if I need to scream or run in place. It's getting away from people, from work. The air helps me revive. ..."

nation, to help motivate one to get out of bed. A circuit through the garden involves both steps and ramps, as well as various surface textures, and is therefore well suited for improving stamina and balance. The abundance of seat-wall provides a resting spot as often as needed. A woman outpatient who, on this visit was waiting for an appointment, recalled a previous time when she practiced walking on the lawn as an inpatient recovering from an accident: "When you're in the hospital it's easy to get caught up in that whole sick vibe. When you come out here it's life, a surrender—that you're still breathing, you're still alive."

Most people knew quite well what components in the garden helped them to feel better. Overall, aspects of planting (flowers, "greenery," colors, seasonal changes) were by far the most often cited. The fountain, though small, is centrally placed and audible from seating places in the main plaza section and was mentioned by several people. Importantly, it also offers water to birds, some of which have made nests and raised their young in the roof garden. A woman employee who comes to the garden to relax, stroll, eat and "center myself" was especially articulate about what characteristics helped change her mood.

> The most important thing for me is the fountain because I love the sound of water and it attracts birds. Then, there's the greenery and flowers. And a third component—the design is pleasing to the eye: there's a combination of shapes and sizes; the brick gives a warm feel. ... I like the nooks and crannies so you can have a place to be alone. As an employee in health care, you're constantly giving, interacting. It's important to have a place to recharge ...

An outpatient who was in the garden for the second time in one day also appreciated the birds, the fresh air, the greenery, the wind blowing, but especially the colorful flowers. Yet another woman employee said that some of the flowers took her back to her childhood and their colors made her think about dress material for her granddaughters.

The fact that many of our respondents used the words "more productive," or implied such when discussing their mood changes, is a strong indication that such outdoor spaces are not merely "cosmetic extras," but should be intrinsic components of every working environment. The health of the staff is as important as that of the patients. One male doctor who worked part-time at another hospital remarked that at the other facility, there were plants but no places to sit. "Here I sit and smoke *one* cigarette and I don't need another to relax me." While smoking is certainly not beneficial to health, if the garden enables an

Figure 5-12   A staff member enjoys a quiet smoking break and looks at the view of San Francisco Bay.

employee to relax with one cigarette rather than two, that is certainly an improvement.

One of the disadvantages of the garden was the small number of movable chairs. There was more than 300 linear feet of concrete planter-edge seating , but only five movable chairs! When more than two people sit side by side on a seat-wall, conversation becomes problematic. To accommodate three or more, movable chairs are required to complete the social circle. Additionally chairs with backs are more comfortable, and they can be moved to adjust to the weather and the degree of privacy/sociability desired.

Other design factors that inhibit use are the lack of elements to ameliorate the wind or bright sun. Rooftops tend to be windier than the adjacent ground level areas. A screened section of the garden, offering shelter from the prevailing winds, would have been a welcome addition. Given that it is usually breezy in the garden, it is warm enough to sit outside, fully exposed, little more than one-half of the year. When it is sunny, depending on the time of day, the glare from the walls and patio can be an issue as well. The choice of trees in the main plaza — short, squat carobs — was a poor one; they appear to be unhealthy and create very little shade.

While staff were certain of the garden's benefits to themselves, they also felt strongly about its value for patients. A female employee, who thought of the garden as a "natural haven in an unnatural setting," remarked on the need for cost-effective gardens for patients and staff. A male employee who used to bring patients out for certain therapies finds that now time doesn't allow it. He believes the garden is an important setting for people who are dying. "We've brought patients out here to die because the family asked for it. They were able to die in peace without the critical care setting. When the family decides to 'let go,' we'll jump through hoops to let a patient come out here to die."

ADVANTAGES
- Stunning vista provides a distant escape.
- Plenty of seating is provided by the seat-walls.
- Subspaces in the garden allow one to get "lost."
- Fountain attracts birds.
- Universally accessible (in regard to mobility within the garden).
- Buffer between adjacent patient rooms and peering eyes.
- The relative lack of people was appealing to those who sought solitude.

A healthcare employee who uses the garden every day to relax, eat, meditate, and exercise, summed it up by saying:

"It's like time has stopped, like a vacuum, a quiet space. I'm really glad it's here; it gives me an 'out.' I close my eyes and listen to the water like I'm hearing a stream or a brook. ... I can get away from the downstairs hustle and bustle. It's the best thing about this hospital."

DISADVANTAGES

- Out-of-the-way location results in underutilization.
- Lack of signage exacerbates poor usage.
- Not convenient to the cafeteria.
- Inadequate shelter from the elements.
- Carob trees appear unhealthy.
- Not enough movable chairs.

The Comfort Garden, San Francisco General Hospital, San Francisco, California

Description and History of the Facility

The first buildings designated as San Francisco General Hospital were erected on this gently sloping site at the base of Portrero Hill in 1872. Outbreaks of bubonic plague, the spread

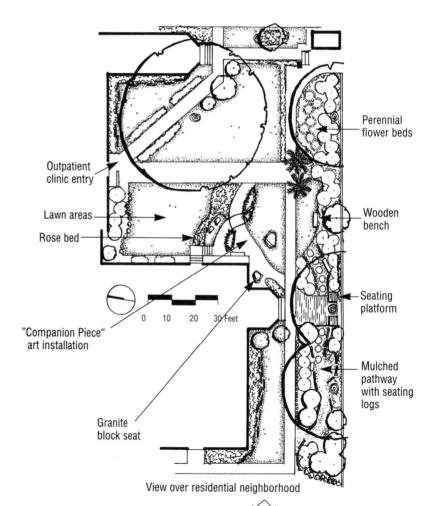

Figure 5-13 Site plan of the Comfort Garden, San Francisco General Hospital, SanFrancisco, California.

of TB, the earthquake of 1906, and the influenza epidemic of 1918 brought about severe overcrowding in this—and many other—San Francisco hospitals. Most of the present buildings were constructed from 1915–1920, designed by city architect Newton Tharp in an Italianate style, laid out with green lawns and bright flowering plants to add to the attractiveness of the structures. Early photographs depict lawns, shrubs, paths, and palm trees between the buildings.

The Comfort Garden is a small (approximately 100 × 160 feet), well-used outdoor space in the sprawling campus of the hospital. It was dedicated in June 1990 as a "living memorial" to hospital employees who had died. A plaque in the garden, recording its inception, concludes with the words: "It is meant to be a place of solace where nature's beauty can bring you comfort."

Description of the Garden

The garden is located adjacent to Buildings 80 and 90— adjoining six-story brick buildings with rows of sash windows looking out over the outdoor space. These buildings house a variety of clinics, including those for TB, HIV, methadone maintenance, family health, and child abuse. None of the buildings adjacent to the Comfort Garden contain inpatient beds. However inpatients are occasionally brought through the garden to appointments in these clinics. The garden is bounded on one side by these buildings; at its eastern end by a low hedge; while a vine-covered fence separates it from 22nd Street.

The feeling of this garden area is of a residential scale, green and colorful retreat. Three very large trees—one cedar, and two Monterey pines—are almost as tall as the buildings. Several lawn areas are bounded by concrete paths and flower beds. Most of the paths are designed for easy, direct pedestrian movement, but one made of granite fines and another formed with sawed-off rounds of redwood set in bark mulch, are clearly designed for more casual strolling. The latter winds through the lushly planted garden bed where shrubs and flowers can be viewed at close quarters; and was added as the gardeners responded to the desire people had to get in amongst the plants. When asked to describe the garden, some users referred to it as "an oasis." We suspect that this image is evoked by two things: the lush and colorful planting and the relatively enclosed feeling of the garden.

This is clearly a garden that has been created—and is maintained—with love and care. (See also the case study in Chapter 11, "Getting It Done.") Tree stumps have been arranged to border flower beds; an arbor has been created out of branches pruned from nearby trees; salvaged rocks and old tree roots have been placed among the perennials; and annuals are tucked

A female visitor who comes once a week and waits in the hospital garden for a friend while he's at an appointment, remarked:

"It's pretty, it's relaxing. . . . Visual beauty lifts my spirits. I feel that any plant life has a big effect on people . . . I've come out here and picked flowers for a friend who is dying because I didn't have any money, and it made her feel better."

Figure 5-14   The Comfort Garden at San Francisco General Hospital provides a green retreat near the entrance to several busy outpatient clinics.

Figure 5-15   A long border of flowering perennials forms a colorful focus in the garden, beside an entry path leading from the street and bus stop to the clinic entrance.

in here and there, adding to the colorful display. There are no weeds, nor is there any litter, yet the garden has a casual rather than a manicured appearance.

While most of the Comfort Garden has a "country cottage garden" image, a portion of it was changed in 1994 to add a more formal sculptural element. This section was designed by Peter Richards and is entitled "Companion Place—a complement to the Comfort Garden." It is composed of curving, intersecting paths bounded by granite curbs and surfaced with crushed fines, five large granite blocks that double as sculpture and informal seating, and three eyelet-shaped flower beds planted with large billowy feather grasses.

Within and beside the informal perennial border that runs the length of the garden, there are a variety of places to sit. Two wooden benches with backs and arms are a perfect size for two people to occupy for a private conversation, or for one person to claim by sitting lengthwise with his or her feet up. Under one of the large pine trees the gardeners have built a simple wooden platform. This enables up to four people to sit with their backs against the tree, their feet up, and their lunch or book beside them. It is pleasantly informal, flexible in use, and far enough away from a path to be relatively private. Also providing informal seating are a row of large tree stumps forming an edge along a portion of the flower border. Though set along a strolling path, the feeling of these seats is one of being tucked into the planting, and remote from others passing by.

On a sunny day in spring and summer during the peak-use hours (11:00 A.M.–2:00 P.M.), approximately 85 percent of the garden is in the sun. However, this part of San Francisco can be quite windy. Even if it is sunny, on a breezy day, the comfort-difference between sitting in the sun and in the shade is quite marked. Fortuitously, both garden benches and all the granite seating blocks are in the sun almost all day. The wooden-platform seating, underneath a large Monterey pine, is in shade most of the time. Thus only on the hottest days is this a comfortable place to stop for an extended time.

Use[3]

Typical users of the garden were staff members who came out alone or in pairs, on a break or to enjoy lunch; and visitors or patients who sat for a while, sometimes smoking or drinking, or who lay dozing on the lawn. It was not uncommon at lunchtime to see staff members come out and look around for a vacant bench and find them all full. Two-fifths of those interviewed reported staying in the garden for thirty minutes or more when they came out. There was no significant difference between staff and outpatients/visitors regarding the use of the garden or the length of time they stayed. Compared to those who spend time *in* the garden, a much larger number enjoyed it while walking through, on their way in and out of the adjoining buildings. On the weekends, when the clinics are closed, neighboring families were observed to come and picnic and play ball on the lawn.

A total of fifty people who were spending time in the garden were interviewed. Of these thirty-one were men and nineteen were women; twenty-four were employees, twenty were outpatients, five were visitors, and one was an inpatient. When asked how often they used the garden, close to half said "up to twice a week." A substantial number use the garden at least once a day. Every person interviewed responded that they came into the garden to relax; three-fourths also came to eat or drink; and more than half to talk, stroll, or partake of their own "outdoor therapy."

For most people who spent time in it, the garden facilitated a change in mood that was positive. They left after a medical appointment, or returned to work in the hospital feeling less stressed, refreshed, more content. A young female employee reported: "My level of stress goes way down. I'm a lot more relaxed; I go back to work refreshed...." A male outpatient

Figure 5-16   The gardeners have made good use of donated plants, and of materials "scavenged" from elsewhere on this large medical campus.

Figure 5-17   Small garden-style benches enable people to claim a spot for a quiet break alone.

---

[3]A post-occupancy evaluation of this garden was conducted in 1995, and is reported more fully in Cooper Marcus and Barnes (1995).

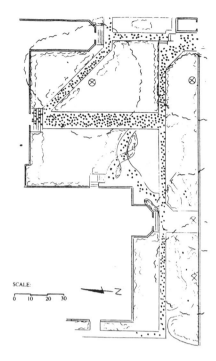

Figure 5-18 Many people enjoy the garden every day as they walk between buildings. Dot map shows aggregation of people passing through during eight hours of observation (summer, 1995).

remarked: "It's a good escape from what they put me through.... I enjoy the air, the feel of the sun, the privacy.... It gives me the strength to deal with things." When asked, "Do you feel any different after you have spent time in the garden?" half said that they felt calmer, more relaxed, less stressed; these comments were made by both staff and outpatients. A significant number of respondents, primarily outpatients, also reported feeling "better," "stronger," "more positive." When asked to describe the garden, people said: "...a little bit of heaven," "a paradise," "like a garden in someone's home."

The social opportunities offered by the garden were valued as well. It served as a gathering place for support groups from the clinics, and was also used casually by patients. Two outpatients who were interviewed remarked: "It's a place where you can come and think.... I feel more comfortable when I'm around other people who are ill or recovering—they're in the same position as me." Several of those interviewed spoke of this as "their garden." This was true of staff—to whom the garden is actually dedicated—but also true of outpatients from both the methadone clinic and the HIV clinic as well.

A small number of people interviewed complained that the garden is "too noisy." Indeed, there is a fair degree of background noise in this setting: cars and buses driving past on Portrero Avenue; the occasional car accelerating uphill on 22nd Street; and the sounds from a large air-conditioning unit on an adjacent building.

ADVANTAGES

- Colorful and casual planting changes through the seasons.
- Residential scale contributes to the psychological comfort of users.
- Smaller benches are in keeping with the scale of the garden and a feeling of intimacy.
- Being located outside of busy clinics promotes high use, thereby maximizing potential benefits.
- Families from the surrounding community use it as a public park.
- People were drawn by the memorial aspect of the garden—finding it a safe place to cry.
- The gardeners respond to the needs of people and plants.

- This is a setting that inspires many people to feel it is their own special garden.

DISADVANTAGES

- Noise from equipment and the city traffic.
- The limited amount of seating often filled up at lunchtime.
- Softer seating was requested—something with padding.
- No movable chairs, limiting the flexibility/expandability of seating arrangements.
- The only seating for groups of more than two or three was on the lawn.
- Some issues arose during interviews regarding people smoking and bringing dogs.

Healing Garden, Good Samaritan Regional Medical Center, Phoenix, Arizona[4]

Brief Description of the Facility and Its History[5]

Good Samaritan is a regional medical center of 575 beds serving patients throughout Arizona and the Southwest. It was founded in 1911 and expanded to its present site in 1982. The buildings comprise four linked, twelve-story, white-clad, curvilinear towers located near downtown Phoenix.

Within view of the main foyer of the hospital, there is a rooftop courtyard that was opened in the Fall of 1996 as a healing garden. Before its conversion to a garden, this 20,000 square foot space was an unappealing concrete courryard with columns on two sides and a few spindly olive trees in concrete planters. The only reason people used it was the presence of a coffee cart and a few chairs and tables. It was also a smoking area.

In July 1994, Sandra Brown (Director of Patient Relations) contacted Barbara Crisp, project architect for The Orcutt/ Winslow Partnership, about redesigning the courtyard. The hospital had recently established a Healing Environment Committee inspired by Planetree; some of the nurses were doing Touch Therapy and a Dog Therapy program was in place. The fact that these programs existed indicated an awareness about the broader issues of healing. With the support of Steve Seiler (CEO and VP), Crisp asked the Healing Environment

---

[4]Also see an account of this garden in Thompson (1998).

[5]A fuller account of the process of design development, funding, and implementation appears in Chapter 11, Getting It Done.

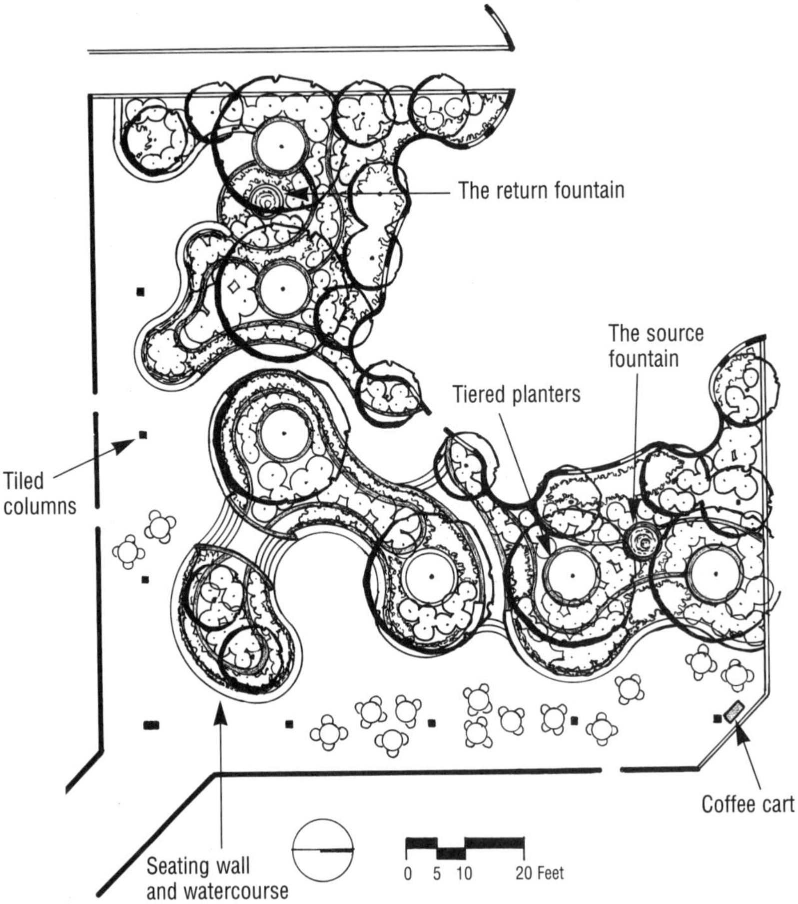

Figure 5-19   Site plan of the Healing Garden at Good Samaritan Medical Center, Phoenix, Arizona.

The return fountain

The source fountain

Tiered planters

Tiled columns

Coffee cart

Seating wall and watercourse

0   5   10   20 Feet

Committee to read Diane Ackerman's *A Natural History of the Senses* as a means of educating them to the importance of multisensory experience within healing environments.

The initial budget assigned to the project was $60,000; an additional $750,000 was raised by donations from hospital auxiliary, medical staff, and the annual "candlelight capers."

A collaborative design team joined Crisp early in the design process to continue the development of the garden. The initial team included landscape architect Christine Ten Eyck and tile artist Joan Baron. Design work was accomplished in collaborative charettes[6] at the schematic and design development phases, with input from the Healing Environment Committee. Two additional team members were added during the construction drawing phase—landscape architect, Kristina Floor, and metal sculptor, Joe Tyler.

[6]Architectural term for an intense brainstorming session.

Figure 5-21   The well-used coffee corner, tiered planters, and columns decorated with colored tiles.

The Healing Garden

The garden courtyard is bounded on three sides by two-story buildings, and on the fourth side by a twelve-story tower, with porthole windows, that looms up in one comer of the garden. While the tower could have been an oppressive presence, it is not, as upon entering, one's attention is immediately drawn to an attractive water feature opposite the entry doors from the main foyer. The water feature, symbolizing "The Cycle of Life," begins in a low fountain pool ("The Source"), symbolizing birth; it feeds into a rocky artificial stream bed ("The Water Course") that flows through the gardens behind a continuous winding seat-wall, ending in a quiet, contemplative pool ("The Return"), symbolizing the end of life. The water, which is easily heard and touched, flows swiftly in some segments of The Water Course, slower in others, symbolizing the active and quieter phases of life. The winding passage of The Water Course at seating height maximizes the number of people sitting privately, or in family groups, who can sit close to the soothing presence of moving water, particularly appreciated in the hot climate of the Southwest.

The existing structural system dictated that a series of terraced planters be designed to accommodate the varying allowable weight of soil, concrete, and plant materials at different locations on the deck. The continuous seat-wall holds the bermed earth that slopes from the tower building throughout the site, allowing plants and water to be within reach of all visitors. The curvilinear wall offers a variety of seating and gathering opportunities for families and staff or for more private consultation and individual reflection. The terracing also provides a three-dimensional sculptural view from above, for the

Figure 5-22   A mother and child spend time in the garden while another child receives treatment.

patients confined to rooms in the adjacent tower building. In addition, the change in elevation provides a series of low steps for the warm-up and cool-down exercises of the cardiac rehabilitation patients in an exercise therapy program.

The raised beds that step up behind the seat-wall and water-course are planted with a variety of low water-use, low maintenance plants or shrubs indigenous to the desert environment. Some of these have historical medicinal properties and were used by indigenous cultures of the region. Species were selected to provide color, blooms, and fragrance at different seasons, and to attract hummingbirds and butterflies into the garden. Due to the over-structure location of the site, palo brea trees, which can grow to thirty feet across, were planted over the columns where a greater soil depth for the trees could be accommodated.

Art was a fully integrated healing aspect of the project from its inception. The tile artist transformed nine 2 × 2 × 12 unattractive existing concrete columns that bound the site on two sides. The columns are covered with colorful mosaics of ceramic, glass, and shells. Some are decorated with spiritually uplifting phrases — one must walk around the column to read the whole quotation. Others are decorated with donated "Wisdom Circles." Each column is different and reflects the garden concept — the Cycles of Life. The metal sculptor came on board during the construction process to design and fabricate two 12 × 12 egress gates based on the desert willow tree.

The site is fully accessible and can accommodate wheelchairs, walkers, gurneys, and wagons; all modes of transportation have been observed there. The coffee cart facility in the old courtyard was a well-liked amenity, so the redesign created a coffee counter with movable chairs and tables in the corner where people enter and within view of the main foyer. Although the presence of people talking and laughing may seem incompatible with a Healing Garden, the contemplative pool ("The Return"), with its semicircular perimeter seating, is located out of sight and hearing distance of the coffee corner, and is thus a setting available for those who want to be alone, or to talk quietly with a colleague or friend.

The garden-courtyard is well used: by visitors and inpatients who come together to enjoy a coffee or stroll; by visitors waiting for an outpatient who is at an appointment or undergoing a test; by staff, for breaks, lunch, or small group meetings; by physicians and hospital chaplains meeting with family members. A fairly large expanse of flat concrete allows beds to be wheeled out on occasions. Another, less direct form of use, is visual access. Outpatients attending a cardiac care unit can exercise on the StairMasters while looking out onto the garden via floor-to-ceiling glass windows. An intriguing monitoring device secreted in the tree canopies permits telemetry cardiac patients to continue to be monitored in the garden when exercising outdoors.

Members of the Phoenix Symphony play in the garden periodically, providing an added amenity. The hospital receives many requests for use of the garden by a variety of people and organizations (weddings, receptions, cocktail parties, fund-raisers). To conserve the integrity and intent of the garden, however, the hospital has made a policy against such public uses. A future plan for creating windows in the second and third level tunnel corridors that link to the tower building on the north and west sides of the garden and at surgery ICU waiting will permit more people to have visual access to the garden from above.

Figure 5-23 *A family waits beside the Water Course while a relative undergoes surgery.*

The overall response to the garden has been very favorable, especially as a place of respite for patients, staff, and visitors. There were elements of resistance in the beginning, due to the perception that operating capital was being spent on a garden versus providing someone's salary or new equipment during turbulent times in the medical community. Once people saw what the garden did for people, however, they were convinced that it was important and viable in the healing process.

The design was driven by the desire to create a mentally, physically, and spiritually healing environment. The creation of a multisensory, interactive environment for all users based on sight, sound, smell, taste, and touch was critical to the success of the design. The purpose of the garden is best stated by CEO and Senior Vice President, Steve Seiler:

> The Healing Garden has brought to life what a "healing environment" is. It represents not the completion of a garden, but the beginning of our efforts to blend the science of medicine and the curing of disease, with the healing of people. It is a remarkable living symbol of what we are moving the organization towards.

The following patient testimonies about Good Samaritan's Healing Garden capture its essence in a profound and meaningful way:

> I am suffering from HIV and coming here makes me forget some of my problems and fears. Thank you so much. God bless you.

> My daughter has been here sixteen times since she was six weeks old. She is now three and is post liver transplant. For so long we had nowhere to go and enjoy the outside and now we do. It is very peaceful. You did a wonderful job.

ADVANTAGES

- Sound of water is heard in many parts of the garden.
- Water can be touched.
- Plant palette appropriate to region.
- Many plants have historic medicinal properties from local indigenous cultures.
- Plants attract birds and butterflies.
- Plants reflect changing seasons.
- All plants are labeled.
- Variety of seating is available— movable chairs, planter-edge seating.
- Choice of places in sun or shade.
- Variety of subspaces allow visitors to be private and alone, or with a small group.
- The garden is available for all patients—as well as staff and visitors.
- It is open twenty-four hours a day—significant in a hot climate where people may want to go outdoors at night
- Choice is available among a variety of milieus, from convivial coffee corner to quiet contemplative pool-side seating.
- Attractive, colorful ceramic tiles brighten up structural columns. One with uplifling sayings that have to be read while circling the column adds to the interactive nature of the garden.
- One column has "wisdom circles" that people can donate, permitting users to leave their mark in the garden (all columns will eventually have wisdom circles).
- Garden is easy to see and approach from the main entry lobby of the hospital.
- Views exist down onto garden from patient rooms above.
- Garden has strong support from administration, who seek to evaluate its use.

DISADVANTAGES

- The extent of concrete slightly detracts from the garden feel of this courtyard.
- There is too much glare. Tinting the concrete floor surface and planter edge seating—for instance, with a southwestern earth tone or rosy tint—would have reduced the problem. An integral color concrete with a rose tint was used, but it has faded considerably since construction.

St. Michael Health Center. Texarkana, Texas

BY JAMES BURNETT (LANDSCAPE ARCHITECT)

Description of the Facility and Its Setting

St. Michael Health Center Campus includes a 695,000 square foot hospital and attached professional medical offices, and an eighty-bed specialty hospital that includes skilled nursing, rehabilitation, day care and a fitness center. Utility easements and an extensive flood plain limit building possibilities at the 52-acre site. The design addressed these issues through two strategies. First, different buildings are linked by a single entry drive that traverses the woodland and terminates at the Hospital, the major facility on the site. The second means of site unification is the triangular composition of the Hospital entry, which extends its arms to the landscape beyond. The Specialty Hospital and the main Hospital facility anchor the site, permitting more flexible uses to occur on the remainder of the land.

The charge given to the design team by the Sisters of Charity and the administration of St. Michael was to establish a model facility that would set the standard for all future Sisters of Charity institutions. The design emphasizes a core Sisters of Charity value: creating an environment that recognizes healing is possible even when curing is not. The landscape is intended to complement the hospital by providing a healing environment, harnessing the powers of nature. The design is one of

Figure 5-24   The entry to St. Michael Health Center, Texarkana, Texas, is a grove of 60-foot pine and oak trees, which help to scale down the six-story bed towers and provide a comfortable entry with walking paths and a fountain. (Photo by James F. Wilson.)

simplicity and order, thereby allowing a focused environment for personal healing.

History of the Facility and Gardens

The Office of James Burnett, Houston, the landscape architect, worked as an equal partner with architect Kirk Hamilton in developing the master plan. The landscape development was solely the responsibility of the landscape architect. The response of the architecture to the landscape, and of the landscape to the architecture, has been reciprocal: the building massing is subordinated to the larger landscape ideas, and the plantings adjacent to the buildings are direct outgrowths of the building's geometries.

General Description of the Outdoor Spaces

The approach to the landscape site development is to preserve and enhance the natural attributes of the setting and to create a harmonious relationship between the hospital and the site. This was a critical objective to the client, as this project is the first of its scope and size in the community. Care was taken not only to make the project unimposing but to develop a level of fine, human-scale detail.

The order of the Texarkana pine forest is complemented throughout the site in the form of bosques and allées, which enrich the quality of the built areas. Maximum seasonal color is afforded through the use of flowering trees and shrubs planted in key locations around the loop road. The courtyard areas near the building are heavily developed with special paving, seating, fountain features, potscapes, and landscape planting. The courtyards are designed as break areas so that people may experience an outdoor environment more healthy and healing than is typical in medical institutions. A path system further unites the site, reaching from the buildings to a pond edge and throughout many of the undeveloped areas of the site. The pond also functions as an irrigation reservoir. Through this efficient use of water resources and by using a select palette of proven plant materials, the opportunity for a maintainable and healthy landscape was created.

St. Michael Cancer Treatment Center–Shirley Burnett Peace Garden

The Shirley Burnett Peace Garden is designed primarily as a viewing garden for those patients who are undergoing chemotherapy treatment. The garden is designed to give the patient an interesting view that changes not only seasonally, but hourly as the patients may be in the room for up to eight hours

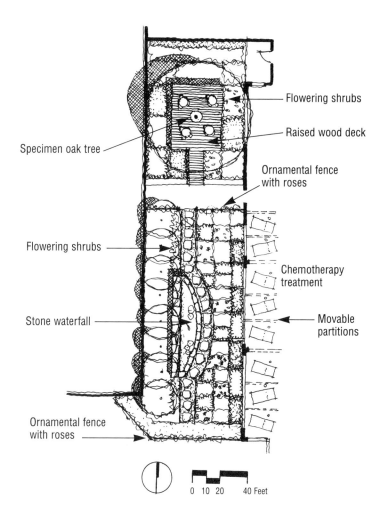

Figure 5-25   Site plan of the Shirley Burnett Peace Garden, St. Michael Health Center.

for treatment. A series of bird feeders attract different species throughout the day. The water feature is designed as a biologically sound waterfall and is home to lilies and koi, which are visible to the patients. The planting offers a wide range of seasonal blooming plants, providing change on a periodic basis for the patients. Texarkana offers an optimum climate for roses, and the court has a series of climbing rose demonstration areas to help screen views into the treatment areas. The garden was designed in a straightforward simple way, while remaining rich and interesting. It works in association with the forces of nature to offer an alternative view for the patients who are undergoing this often painful therapy.

ADVANTAGES

- The garden is designed specifically for cancer treatment patients who face onto the garden.

- The garden has good light all day long (good for blooming plants, waterfall, lilies, koi, etc.).
- The patients enjoy garden watching (birds, fish, plants) as an alternative to watching TV.
- The architect has designed a partition system that allows group viewing or private viewing and lets the patient make the choice.

DISADVANTAGES

- The heavy glazing limits a clear view to the garden. Low E (energy efficient) clear glass should be used when gardens are designed specifically for viewing to avoid reflection, distortion, and glare.

Dining Court

The dining court at the St. Michael Health Center is adjacent to the main dining facility in the middle of the complex. It is surrounded by structures on all four sides and primary access is from the dining hall. The design of the garden is focused on providing outdoor terraces for dining, meetings, and special occasions. The court is created to provide a number of seating options for both small and large groups. The movable teak furniture, with its comfortable seating cushions, provides great flexibility in seating combinations. Benches are located in a few private locations for one or two visitors. Evergreen hedges separate areas for privacy much like partitions do in an office setting. The large gathering area in the center of the court is marked with a donor recognition wall—which was anticipated and designed into the landscape concept. The wall represents recognition for all those, past and present, who have given to the St. Michael Foundation. The wall is eight feet tall and is sited to be seen from the dining hall as well as from a number of other vantage points. The donor wall doubles as a fountain, adding a cooling effect and a soft splashing sound in the court. It is a significant marker for all those who visit this popular location on campus, closely tying the community to the foundation through the spirit of giving. The view from floors above reveals the symbol of the Sisters of Charity carved in the granite paving, symbolizing the care and commitment of the hospital in the community.

ADVANTAGES

- Due to its prime location, it is frequently used by all who visit and work at the hospital.
- The court is often in shade, which makes the hot summers tolerable.

- The variety of spaces offer flexibility for having special events.

DISADVANTAGES

- The visual link from the dining room to dining court is not as direct as it could be.
- The heavy glazing limits a clear view to the garden. Low E (energy efficient) clear glass should be used when a garden view is desired.
- The dining court has a canyon feel as it is surrounded by multilevel buildings on all sides. Having an open side or a more transparent bridge link would have given the space a more comfortable and expansive feel.
- For safety reasons, the water feature/donor wall has been surrounded by a post and chain system, which distracts from the beauty of the space.

Garden of Balance

The Garden of Balance is located between the Medical Office Buildings and the Medical Surgical Bed Tower. It is a large garden area that is composed of a raised earth feature and an amphitheater as centerpieces for the space. The amphitheater represents the carving out of earth while the raised feature was made from material excavated for the amphitheater. The juxtaposition represents the balance one strives for when recovering from an illness. The raised earth offers a seat-wall surround, which provides a place from which to look outward to the other

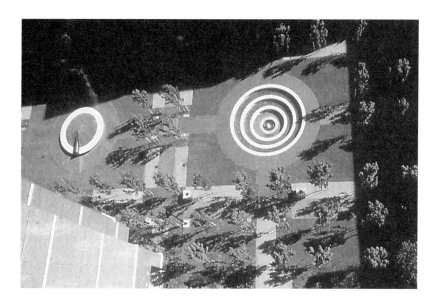

Figure 5-26   The Garden of Balance contains an amphitheater fountain court and a raised earth seat-wall garden, providing a variety of seating and gathering opportunities. (Photo by James F. Wilson.)

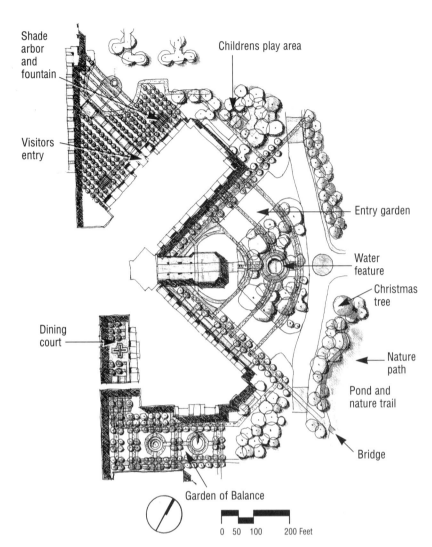

Figure 5-27 Site plan of the hospital gardens at St. Michael Health Center.

garden areas. A black granite wall extending to the edge of the seat wall is a sundial that marks the date of the sisters' arrival to the Texas coast from Ireland some 130 years ago. This arrival is celebrated each October in the garden by the sisters, staff and community.

The amphitheater has overscaled steps that are designed at seat height, focusing on a center water feature. It can accommodate a large group for special events (poetry reading, musical performance, or hospital gathering). The central water feature adds sound and visual interest to the court. The edge of the Garden of Balance is planted with pear trees, which provide shade and seasonal color for the benches beneath them.

ADVANTAGES

- The garden is large enough to host big events with unobstructed views.
- The space has great variety.
- The landscape architect and the architect worked closely to scale the space appropriately and comfortably for the large buildings that surround the garden.
- The garden has an open end with long views to the lake and adjacent woodlands.

DISADVANTAGES

- The garden is underutilized due to its location and limited access.
- The garden is not easily found by visitors.

Pond and Nature Trail

The pond and nature trail are located near the front door to the hospital and are popular attractions on the campus. The pond, which supports fish and wildlife, is used as an irrigation reservoir and is recharged through the use of a well. A perimeter walking path of granite gravel weaves through the natural landscape and along the pond edge. Near the midpoint of the pond, a bridge crosses the water, and a covered pavilion provides a stopping point for walkers. The pond and path are heavily used by patients, visitors, staff, and community. A large spruce tree marks one end of the pond and is decorated at Christmas. Other seasonal events include a fishing tournament and an annual Easter egg hunt.

Figure 5-28 The two-acre pond near the main entry is designed to offer a waterside nature path with a bridge and covered pavilion. (Photo by James F. Wilson.)

ADVANTAGES

- The pond offers a natural counterpoint to the structured gardens and is very close to the main waiting areas.
- The nature path is quiet private and contemplative.
- The nature path offers a community amenity.

DISADVANTAGES

- The pond is close to the loop road and traffic can become a distraction.

St. Michael Specialty Hospital

The eighty-bed freestanding Speciality Hospital is sited on a heavily wooded site near the main entry to the campus. The interior facing gardens are structured and designed to provide comfortable shady areas for patients to view and access.

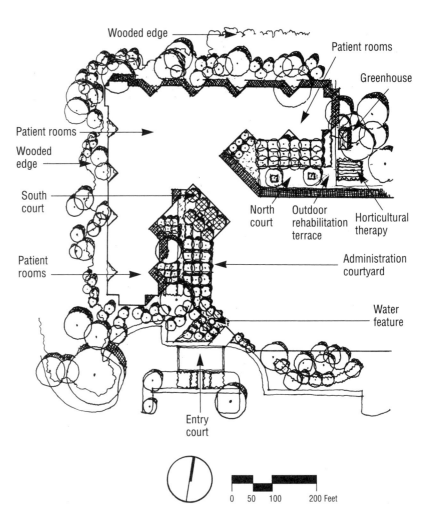

Figure 5-29   Site plan of the Specialty Hospital at St. Michael Health Center.

The north court offers an a outdoor terrace for some patient therapy activities as well as shaded seating areas for relaxing. The adjacent greenhouse and raised garden plots are designed to support the horticulture therapy program.

The south court is designed as a view garden both from the patient rooms on the west and the administration functions on the east. It has a small circular water feature at the entry drop-off to help reduce stress and provide a comfortable and welcome entry statement. A crushed fines walk leads one through the garden to a larger fountain terrace. This sunny court is a popular area for dining although not directly connected to the dining facility.

The perimeter view gardens are designed to preserve the natural vegetation and enhance the views with supplemental plantings. Dogwoods, redbuds, and numerous seasonally blooming shrubs and wildflowers were strategically located to maximize views from patient rooms. Bird and squirrel feeders have been a positive addition, attracting wildlife for patient viewing.

Patients, families, and staff respond to the healing environment provided at St. Michael Hospital. "I'm a convert" says Dr. Henry Camey, whose wife has been a patient at the new campus. "I didn't think that nature made that much difference, but believe me, it makes all the difference in the world" (*Capsule Magazine*, summer, 1994). "I've seen a drastic improvement in patients here," said Sister Damian Murphy, the director of pastoral care at St. Michael. "The average rehab patient is home now in two to three weeks compared to about six weeks or more in the old facility" (*The New York Times*, December 29, 1994).

Figure 5-30   A small fountain and bench in a shady location near the entry to the Specialty Hospital. (Photo by James F. Wilson.)

ADVANTAGES

- The low scaled buildings are intimately connected to the surrounding gardens.
- The architect worked to provide covered terraces on the second level so that those who are less ambulatory can still view the garden and natural woodlands.
- The gardens are easily accessed from a number of doorways.
- The gardens provide variety: sunny south court versus shady north court; natural view gardens with wildlife versus controlled courtyards with fountains and people.
- A horticulture therapy program has been developed and is an integral part of the facility.

DISADVANTAGES

- The views from the beds are not as direct as they could be.
- The heavy tinting on the windows detracts from the beauty of the gardens and woodlands.
- More attention to sun shading devices on sunny walls and clear glass on the north facing gardens could have made the indoor/outdoor connection much stronger.
- Greater planting diversity would help attract wildlife into the interior courts (birds, butterflies, etc.).
- Biologically sound water features that are "alive" could help add greater fascination to the center (i.e., koi, frogs, lilies, etc., add interest over a traditional chlorinated fountain feature).
- Dining would be more successful located adjacent to one of the garden courts and not facing the parking area.

DESIGN GUIDELINES: SOURCES, USE, AND ORGANIZATION

The following guidelines are presented as suggestions and recommendations, rather than as hard and fast "rules." They are derived from several sources: (1) from research on nature-viewing and stress reduction as presented by Ulrich in Chapter 2 of this volume; (2) from the findings of post-occupancy studies of existing hospital gardens (and in particular, Cooper Marcus and Barnes, 1995); (3) from published work on the design and use of public outdoor spaces (in particular, Carr et al., 1992; Cooper Marcus and Francis, 1998; Paine et al., 1998; Whyte, 1980); (4) from field visits and observations by the authors of outdoor spaces at seventy acute care hospitals in the United States, Canada, and England (1995–1998); and (5) from common sense. Though the last may seem a surprising and "unscientific" source, observations of obvious mistakes and missed opportunities in many hospital gardens prompted us to include some recommendations that are just common sense, but that are, nevertheless, often overlooked.

We made no attempt to prioritize these guidelines, or to indicate how conflicts between two or more of them—as occasionally may happen—can be solved. Each site is unique, each cultural and climatic setting different from another. We are not setting out to "tell the designer what to do." Rather, these recommendations are presented as a summary of what we know at this point in time. Hopefully, a designer setting out to create a healing garden will find useful reminders and guidance in the pages that follow, while putting into the final design their own particular creative slant.

Design guidelines are intended as aids, not as constraints on creativity. However, the particular needs of the *users* of healing gardens demand that designers and their clients pay close attention to what we currently know about stress, nature, and health. A hospital garden is not a suitable locale for frontier-breaking, innovative solutions, nor is it necessary to reinvent the wheel. There is still much to learn, but there is a lot we already know. These guidelines are presented in the hope that they will assist those responsible for the financing, designing, and administration of healing gardens in the hospitals of the twenty-first century.

The guidelines that follow are organized into the following broad categories:

1. Planning the hospital site
2. Awareness of outdoor spaces
3. Views to outdoors
4. Physical access to outdoor space

5. Site planning within the garden
6. Planting
7. Furnishings
8. Maintenance and administrative policies

1. PLANNING OF HOSPITAL SITE

Plan the provision of usable outdoor spaces from the start of the design process. A professional landscape architect needs to be on the team from the beginning to assist in the determination of outdoor space location, orientation, function, and ambience, and to assess microclimates, accessibility, and anticipated user-groups. The landscape architect can also be invaluable in coordinating the phasing of outdoor construction; determining a realistic budget for construction or ongoing maintenance; analyzing context and overall image. The worst situation is to think about outdoor spaces after building design and parking provision are finalized.

    Use excavated material on the site. On a new or expanding site, consider utilizing material excavated for the foundations of new buildings to create changes of elevation in the outdoor spaces. Where the area is large enough to create swales and low hills, an interesting landscape can be created for walking through as well as looking out at. Tall trees planted on the crests of these hills will maximize the number of stories of nearby hospital buildings from which people can look out into (not just down onto) elements of nature.

    Take advantage of views and access to existing green space when siting and planning hospital buildings. An ideal location is a medical facility that looks out over a public park,

Figure 5-31 Grading and planting in the landscaped grounds of a large medical complex provide visual interest for those passing through or looking down onto, the outdoor space. (Ottawa Health Sciences Center, Ottawa, Ontario, Canada.)

nature preserve, open greenbelt, or body of water. While patients in hospital garb may not feel comfortable in a public space, the green area can provide attractive open views from patient rooms, and it may be used by staff and visitors. The Scottsdale (Arizona) Memorial Hospital North, for example, is bounded on its east side by a wide greenbelt in a shallow valley, containing a bicycle and jogging trail linking Scottsdale to the University of Arizona campus at Tempe, ten miles away. Patient rooms have very attractive views onto the (irrigated) grass, jacaranda and eucalyptus trees, passing cyclists and joggers, and—close by—an abundant population of quail and rabbits.

When the hospital looks into a natural or designed landscape, create some single-loaded corridors where one side looks out to the outside. This enables staff, visitors, and ambulatory patients to see out to the natural world while moving around in the hospital setting. Places where this corridor opens up to a seating or waiting room area will enable people to sit and look outside, even in inclement weather, and offer a substitute to the standard TV-and-magazines waiting room experience. Floor-to-ceiling glass, plus a partial roof of glass, will provide an even greater connection to the outside—views to sky, clouds, and birds.

Consider incorporating a sense of history. When an old hospital is being replaced by more modern buildings, consider retaining some historic elements to be incorporated into a garden or outdoor space. At St. Luke's Hospital in Phoenix, AZ, for example, a small shed/cottage sits in one of the outdoor spaces, a remnant of an era when some patients were housed in tents and cottages on the hospital grounds. At West Park Hospital in Toronto, Ont., Canada, the ruins of an old stone farmhouse have been left in the spacious grounds of this former sanitarium. The original farmhouse, with four beds, was the nucleus of what became the Toronto Free Hospital for the Consumptive Poor (1904). The ruins are today an attractive destination for rehabilitation patients using wheelchairs (see Fig. 1-14).

Provide a variety of outdoor spaces. Since there are likely to be multiple users (staff, inpatients, outpatients, visitors), with a range in ages, including children, the planning of a new hospital should include consideration of a variety of outdoor spaces. These need to be varied as to location—near cafeteria, near main entrance, and so on; type—roof terrace, courtyard, and so on; and design image—a hard-surfaced balcony or terrace with a view for wheeling out gurneys; an attractive viewing garden where people waiting for appointments or for items in the pharmacy can sit and look out at greenery, a ground-level or roof area that has the immediate imagery of "a garden," and

Figure 5-32 An historic element in the hospital landscape. A seating alcove, dating from 1760, was removed from London Bridge in 1832, and purchased by the hospital in 1861 for ten guineas as a shelter for convalescing patients. (Guy's Hospital, London, UK.)

that is furnished and detailed for quiet contemplation, eating a brown-bag lunch, meditation, strolling, and so on.

In one British hospital (West Dorset County Hospital), three courtyards employ the same design of curved rock wall inclines with minimal planting. Commissioned as part of an "Art in Hospitals" project, the walls were intended to "flow" in and out of the courtyards, giving the impression that the three were one continuous space. This was perhaps a worthy artistic goal, but in the wrong place. A hospital with a limited number of outdoor spaces needs to foster variety so that staff, in particular, can have a selection of environments when they choose to sit outside for a break.

Provide at least one space where users will feel they can "get away" from the outside world and the hospital environment. Interview-surveys with hospital outdoor space users indicate that most people are looking for a peaceful, secluded milieu where the senses are stimulated by greenery, flowers, birdsong, fresh air, and so on. Such sensory stimulation seems to trigger a calming and relaxed mood (Cooper Marcus and Barnes, 1995). Outdoor spaces designed to optimize therapeutic benefits need to have a degree of enclosure or separation from the outside world. An entry lawn, landscaped setback, or busy front entry plaza are not appropriate as the only spaces available for outdoor use.

Provision of an outdoor space next to the dining area is essential. Except for the front lobby, more people gather in a dining area than in any other hospital space. A garden, courtyard, or roof terrace next to the cafeteria can draw people into the fresh air, offering a choice and allowing them to take best advantage of their free time. Also, in most hospitals, this is the only space where one can eat and smoke.

In long-term care wards, staff monitoring of outdoor spaces from inside is especially critical. While use of outdoor spaces by long-term patients with family visitors is a common occurrence, it is important that ambulatory patients be able also to venture out alone. A patio or garden off a staffed day room or one visible from a nursing station is often a good solution.

Provide outdoor spaces that the hospital staff can temporarily "claim." Nursing staff reported the desire to get away at times from the stress and tension of dealing with patients (Paine, 1984). Many of the activities that staff do to relax—smoke, talk in groups, eat—may conflict with the patients' need for rest outdoors or are something that the patients are prohibited from doing. This does not mean, however, that a "staff only" outdoor space is needed or even desired. Instead, judicious screening and space planning can create a number of semipri-

Figure 5-33 A glass shelter in a hospital garden in San Francisco protects people from the wind, and facilitates the garden being used for more hours of the day and more months of the year. (California Pacific Medical Center, Garden Campus, San Francisco, California.)

Figure 5-34 Mechanical noises can be a disturbing intrusion in hospital gardens. The noise from an adjacent air conditioning unit virtually obliterates the quiet sounds of this small fountain. (Santa Rosa Community Hospital, Santa Rosa, California.)

vate spaces that groups of staff colleagues can temporarily "claim" during a break from work.

In cold to moderate climates, plan the outdoor spaces with a protected or high sun exposure. This allows more use of the outdoor space in the cool early spring and late fall and enables winter use on warm days. In hotter climates, a shady location may be desirable for protection from harsh sun or extreme heat. The goal should always be to maximize the amount of time the space can be used, throughout the day and throughout the year.

Keep intrusive noises to a minimum. Most users of hospital outdoor spaces go there to get away from the sounds, smells, and activity of the indoor environment. Outdoor relaxation is particularly enhanced by views of greenery, quietness, and being able to hear birdsong and falling water if a fountain is present (Cooper Marcus and Barnes, 1995). Ulrich (Chapter 2) quotes research to indicate that intrusive human-made noises may frequently be negative distractions in healthcare facility gardens, and that the restorative benefits of viewing nature can be substantially diminished or even negated by such intrusions. Among the most frequently experienced intrusions in hospital gardens are the sounds of air conditioning units, recycling pumps, street traffic, and emergency helicopters. The sounds of an attractive small fountain at a Santa Rosa (California) community hospital, for example, are almost totally masked by rushing air extruded from an air conditioning unit right next to it. In a courtyard at Middlesex Hospital (London, UK)—the only outdoor space in a very large multistory, inner-city facility—the soothing natural sounds of birdsong and water falling in a fountain are all but obliterated by the loud noise of a major air conditioning unit, unfortunately located in the courtyard. When locating heating, ventilation, and air conditioning units, make sure that users' enjoyment of a nearby roof garden, or other outdoor space, is not compromised by intrusive noises.

Avoid missed opportunities. Visits to more than seventy hospitals revealed all too many missed opportunities in existing hospital environments: a courtyard with adjacent, ground-level windows too high for outpatients in a waiting room or staff in their offices to be able to see into it; a site plan that put all the outdoor space in a spacious, for-show front lawn that nobody used; a meditation garden where the surrounding open windows of staff offices, ringing of telephones, buzz of conversation, and sounds of laughter rendered the space unusable. It is critical that the whole design and client team be cognizant of the importance of outdoor spaces and all the ramifications of their location and design.

Coordinate design intentions, administrative policies, and maintenance budgets to maximize the creation of usable outdoor space. There is often a lack of communication between the designer of a space, the administrative staff who will eventually determine how and when it is used, and the maintenance staff responsible for its upkeep. This is true in many institutional settings, and is particularly problematic in the case of hospital outdoor space. When spaces are designed for use but are kept locked, or are open but unfurnished, or are usable but badly maintained, patients and staff are likely to

Figure 5-35 A missed opportunity at a large urban hospital. This stark, glaring roof terrace has almost nothing in it to tempt people outside. Poorly maintained trees are completely out of scale with the setting; concrete seating is uncomfortable; there is no shade; two large bicycle storage containers fill the space.

experience frustration, which can only lead to more stress in an already stressful environment.

A particularly egregious case was observed in a West London hospital at Wexham Park. The facility was designed with many courtyards abutting the corridors, including the only outdoor seating area off the cafeteria. A few of these spaces are attractively planted and open to access but have no benches in them; a few are obviously intended for use with benches and movable chairs, but are remarkably unattractive and poorly maintained; others are accessible and minimally furnished but have noisy HVAC units protruding into the space; still other attractive green spaces have no access doors. Certainly budget for landscaping is an issue in every hospital design, but it is regrettable that a large number of trees were planted in this hospital's parking lot, while potentially restorative spaces for sitting in are poorly landscaped, minimally furnished, and/or kept locked. After several hours observing this hospital on a warm summer day, the authors finally observed the only people using an outdoor space: several young female staff members dragged metal chairs outdoors to a sidewalk near the Maternity Entrance where they sat and smoked, looking out over a parking lot and entry road.[7]

2. AWARENESS OF OUTDOOR SPACES

Figure 5-36 A sign inside or outside a hospital, indicating the presence of a garden, is a rarity. This was one of very few encountered in field visits to more than seventy hospitals. (El Camino Hospital, Mountain View, California.)

Field studies reveal that potential users' knowledge, or lack of it, about the existence of a garden space is one of the most critical factors in its use. The location and visibility of such spaces is very important. All patients and visitors should be aware upon their entry to the hospital that outdoor spaces are available for them to use during their visit. Where possible, outdoor space should be visible from the main entrance or there should be clear and prominent directions as to its location. This will encourage visitors to take patients outdoors, thereby freeing staff from doing do.

Provide maps and directional signs in the hospital, especially at elevator lobbies and front entries, to direct people to the outdoor spaces. Or just a notation of "garden" on prominent fire-escape maps would suffice.

Provide a map in the patient's information packet. This will inform the patients of their location in the hospital, the proximity of outdoor spaces, and the routes to such spaces.

Offer a tour of the outdoor spaces for patients who pre-plan their hospitalization, for example, for elective surgery

[7]Inpatients at this hospital do have access to patios off the wards. The courtyards discussed above are those potentially accessible to staff, outpatients, and visitors.

or maternity care. These tours are effective marketing and advertising strategies for hospitals wishing to tell patients about features that differentiate a particular hospital from others. At one hospital studied, the outdoor space was included as part of the introductory tour of the maternity ward, and it always impressed prospective users (Paine, 1984).

3. VIEWS TO OUTDOORS

A view to an outdoor space can effectively advertise its presence, leading to more use. If it is possible to see a courtyard or garden from a lobby, cafeteria, or major corridor, many people will be aware of it, leading either to spontaneous use or to a decision to visit the space later.

Views are also important in their own right. Planning for outdoor space should certainly include consideration of the views created from patient rooms, offices, and corridors. Views out to nature from the corridors of a surgical ward, for example, are especially important since many patients are encouraged to get up and stroll as much as possible. Pausing to view the outside world and nature through corridor windows can be psychologically therapeutic.

A number of studies have begun to supply empirical evidence for what most people would assume from common sense to be fact: that windowlessness in hospitals is a significant form of sensory deprivation (Ulrich, 1984; Verderber, 1982; Wilson, 1972). Studies of hospitals have joined those of windowless offices (Ne'eman, 1974), schools (Larson, 1965), and factories (Manning, 1963) to reinforce the psychological importance of windows to the building's occupants:

> The window aperture symbolizes openness and freedom. For the hospital patient, windows are considerably more than panes and frames. They are a break in the walls which symbolize isolation from the environment outside the hospital. Through them, patients and staff may perceive the serenity of nature, the intensity of urban life, the transformation of one season to the next, the diurnal pattern of day becoming night, observe people and activity and, likewise, be observed by the passing world and experience an active involvement in it (Verderber, 1982, pp. 476–477).

Clearly, if the purpose of rehabilitation is to reintegrate the patient into society, then a view out to the real world of nature, city, pedestrians, animals, birds, and clouds is bound to have some therapeutic effect. Ulrich (Chapter 2) discusses research studies that indicate the stress-reducing effects of viewing

"With Mother in the ICU two days before she died—a narrow room, lined with machines blinking and beeping out the remaining hours, while doctors talk about maybe regrowing the bone marrow, even though she had made up her mind to go.

"I sat in that room for hours at a time, just to be there if she awoke and wanted something. In that small, anxious room, I felt the presence of a dense tree outside one window behind me, shading that narrow space from the western sun and admitting live, flickering light that bathed my back and enlivened the page before me with wonderful fluid shapes and shadows of moving branches and leaves. The sort of thing she always noticed and loved. The play of light helped me do the breathing practices, the gentle inward smiles that Buddhism offers to relieve this and all kinds of suffering in the world. Practices that became a part of me after that.

"That tree was my Bodhi tree. I can still feel its deep comfort. Yet, for the life of me, I cannot remember what kind it was—a redwood, a broad-leafed tree? She always cared about the Latin names. It may not matter. And I shall never know because—when memories pulled me back five years later—the tree had been cut out to make way for a new emergency wing at the Queen of the Valley Hospital."

(L.D.) NAPA, CA.

Figure 5-37 A view out to a garden or courtyard from the main foyer to a hospital effectively announces its presence. (West Dorset Hospital, Dorchester, UK.)

nature. These studies support Ulrich's earlier suggestion that "location and design decisions for some activities and institutions—such as high stress work places and hospitals—should assign considerable importance to providing 'through the window' contact with nature" (Ulrich, 1979, p. 22). The importance of providing windows and views with some interest value can hardly be questioned, but designers need to consider the available alternatives when determining who gets the most restorative views. If the patients' rooms can be arranged to look onto either a hospital courtyard, or a park, hills, or a body of water lying beyond the hospital, the latter may be preferable. In such a case, a (less-favored) view of a courtyard may be more valuable from a lounge, waiting area, or corridor.

Locate windows or glass doors to a usable outdoor space next to elevator lobbies, and main entries. More patients and visitors pass through these areas than through any other hospital spaces, and so views from these sites provide an excellent opportunity to advertise an outdoor space. Select glass with consideration of views; heavy, reflective glazing distorts colors and images.

Where doors must be solid, locate some windows adjacent to the entry to an outdoor space. This allows a user to examine the space before going outdoors, to determine who is present, whether a comfortable place to sit is available, or how the weather looks. Being able to orient oneself to a public place before entering it frequently contributes to its use.

Provide windows in patients' rooms, therapeutic settings, and staff offices. The therapeutic effect of natural views on recovering patients, coupled with the recognition that those

Figure 5-38 An attractive view out to a terrace and garden from a patient's room. Even when lying in bed, patients can look out to the tops of trees and an expanse of sky. (Lambeth Community Care Center, Lambeth, London, UK.)

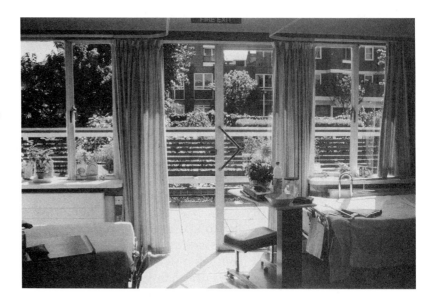

most impaired by windowlessness are the chronically ill, the paralyzed, and visually impaired patients, indicates that views from patients' rooms onto natural settings, trees, greenery, or water should be given the highest priority. The staff, in offices, lunch rooms, meeting rooms, and so on, will also benefit from the stress-reducing quality of such views. Ideally, a window should allow views of close-in details and open sky, even from a near-horizontal position. The design of Lambeth Community Care Center (UK) is particularly successful in this regard. Twenty inpatient rooms open onto a terrace that looks out onto an award-winning garden. The rooms have floor-to-ceiling glass facing the garden, so that even when horizontal, a patient has a view to the sky and the tops of tall trees.

Open views to wildlife. Views out from a hospital setting to birds and wildlife can reassure patients of the natural order of life, of life going on. At Victoria General Hospital in British Columbia, Canada, an extraordinary number of rabbits live in the wild and manicured landscapes that surround the hospital. Views out from the cafeteria and from some patient rooms are animated by views of large and small animals feeding, playing, dozing in the sun. They appear—from their wide color range—to be a mixture of wild and domestic rabbits. Many have become quite tame and hang out fearlessly around a hospital entrance and a patio off the cafeteria. (Their burrows are quite evident in the wild, sloped areas that skirt the hospital buildings.) Birdfeeders outside patient room windows are also much appreciated, especially by those spending longer periods in the hospital.

Provide windows that ensure the patient's ability to see out while at the same time minimizing the potential for others to see in. Windows should have a sill height of between 20 and 30 inches, to allow bedridden patients and those in wheelchairs to see out. However, when windows look onto a courtyard or pathway, care must be taken to avoid the patients' feeling "on stage," owing to people looking in. Windows should not directly overlook public areas or should be screened. This can be accomplished through planting, which allows a filtered view while maintaining privacy, or through lattice work, interior blinds, and so on.

Create outdoor spaces at least 30 feet wide where windows are directly across from each other. Users of any small courtyard spaces may be very conscious of a "fishbowl" effect, of being stared at by people inside. A space at least 30 feet wide provides enough area for a table, gathering area, and planting (or other visual screens) against the windows. Twenty feet is also the approximate distance at which views from one window across the outdoor space into another window become unclear. This distance gives sufficient privacy to all concerned and is

"I was in the antepartum ward for one and a half months trying to hold onto a painful pregnancy that had taken me six years to conceive. I was fearful and anxious. Looking out my hospital window to the large Douglas fir trees and meadows where wild bunnies hopped out helped me to focus beyond my immediate pain. Three months after my daughter's birth I was able to carry her out of the hospital to see the bunnies and trees that had been part of our survival."

(L. T. H.) VICTORIA, B.C., CANADA

especially important where a hallway with windows looks across the outdoor space into patients' rooms or staff offices.

Provide vertical, as opposed to horizontal, apertures. Rooms with narrow, small, or horizontal windows tend to be disliked as much, if not more, than windowless rooms. Rooms with too few windows create needless perceptual barriers, especially for those confined or bedridden for long periods of time. Where possible, design vertical windows, but do not make them too narrow; allow distant, middle-ground, and close-up views to be taken in simultaneously (Verderber, 1982). When possible, the bed should be placed no more than 12 feet from the window so that a patient can have maximum benefit from the view.

Create balconies or terraces with views to a garden. Balconies or roof terraces with a view into a garden can add to the use of an outdoor space, especially for those on gurneys or in wheelchairs or those on upper floors who cannot easily access the garden proper. These spaces need to be of ample size and have wide doors so that visitors and volunteers can easily assist patients who wish to be outdoors. An old attractive garden at California Pacific Medical Center's Garden Campus was much appreciated by patients, staff and visitors at a chronic, long-term care ward, as beds could be wheeled out onto a wide balcony with views to the greenery below (Cooper Marcus and Barnes, 1995).

Provide opportunities for contact with nature indoors. Since it is traditional for visitors to bring flowers or plants to hospital patients, place a small shelf for vases where the patient can directly look at them. It is not satisfactory to place flowers on a bedside cabinet since this is often used for books, magazines, and so on, and is usually positioned behind the patient's

Figure 5-39 Smooth concrete paths permit staff and visitors to push patients in wheelchairs through this attractive garden in a suburban hospital. (Kaiser Permanente Medical Center, Walnut Creek, California.)

head when he or she is sitting up. It is therapeutic for longer term hospital patients to view birdfeeders just outside the window, or to care for indoor plants and to be able to see them from their beds. When possible, provide shelves or table space for plants near the windows, yet make sure that the plants will not block the view outdoors for patients in bed or in wheelchairs and will not interfere with blinds or curtains.

4. PHYSICAL ACCESS TO OUTDOOR SPACES

The entry to an outdoor space should be easily accessible in order to maximize the number of people who will use it. Physical access deals with door type, location, and design of entrances, and surfacing materials.

Do not create an outdoor space solely for visual use if it can also be used in other ways. A space that could be used to sit or walk in but that is presented only as a visual amenity is often seen by staff members as a waste of time (Paine, 1984). On the other hand, an outdoor space that is located or dimensioned so as to be physically unusable should still be given considerable attention for the views it may provide for people sitting in a waiting area or passing by in a corridor. The many courtyards punctuating the corridors of Britain's "nucleus" and spine-and-pavilion hospitals, while criticized elsewhere in this chapter, *do* provide useful orienting devices and relieve the look of long interior corridors.

Locate the main entry to an outdoor space so that it is accessible to those most likely to use it. If the space is intended for general use, place the entry in a public area easily reached from corridors and elevators throughout the hospital. On the other hand, if it is a more specialized outdoor space, the easiest way to limit the number of people who use it is to install the entry off the relevant room or hallway; for example, an outdoor space for physical therapy might be sited off a rehabilitation unit, or a quiet garden for visitors might be near the intensive care unit. Hospital staff, patients, and visitors are reluctant to walk through areas of the hospital beyond their assigned ward or visiting area, and so only those with immediate access to it will use such outdoor spaces. At North Derbyshire Royal Hospital (United Kingdom) a staff lounge was moved ten feet across a hallway next to a garden. Staff report they now use the outdoor space much more because it is so convenient to get to and it feels like "theirs."

Install doors that are appropriate for the use of the space. *Automatically opening doors:* An automatically opening

Figure 5-40 An unfortunate choice of paving in an attractive, small court-yard serving a maternity ward makes it less accessible for patients who feel unsteady on their feet.

door provides the easiest access, as most patients could use it. There are fewer difficulties coordinating the movement of accessory medical equipment attached to the patient while going through this door. However, staff may worry about patients' wandering outdoors unsupervised. The patients' security, especially that of patients with cognitive dysfunction, is an important concern. This type of door, therefore, is best for areas where there is supervision or where the patients' conditions do not require it. *Sliding glass doors:* A sliding glass door, assuming there is not a raised threshold, is the second easiest door for patients to use, as no pushing or bracing is required. It also provides visual access to the space. *Push-bar doors:* A push-bar is heavy and requires pushing and bracing; and thus patients in a weakened condition or in wheelchairs cannot open them unassisted. It can also be difficult coordinating medical equipment attached to the patient when using this kind of doors. *Self-locking doors:* Self-locking doors inconvenience the people using the outdoor spaces. Staff at all the hospitals with such doors were observed circumventing the problem by propping the doors open with trash containers or wood wedges or by taping the bolt shut. Denied access can be very frustrating. If a door is kept locked it should be clearly labeled to avoid the experience of entrapment that comes with rattling a locked door. All doors must meet ADA requirements governing thresholds, dimensions of opening, hardware, kick plates for manual swinging doors, and needed maneuvering space.

Provide paving that does not inhibit movement. Paving with deep grooves, heavy aggregates, or large joints (such as mortared stone or large aggregate concrete blocks) should be avoided, as it is difficult for people using wheelchairs, gurneys, or walkers. Even fine joints can cause problems for attached medical equipment such as IV units, which have small wheels and are top-heavy. The ADA identifies brushed concrete, or similar surfaces, as appropriate, slip-resistant, and accessible.

It is particularly important, when considering paving, to take account of *who* will be using the space, and how. A Healing Garden in Phoenix, Arizona (Good Samaritan Medical Center) has, at first glance, what appears to be rather too much hard surface, but this was intentional; it allows not only patients in wheelchairs, but some in beds, to be wheeled out to enjoy the trees, plantings, running water, and hummingbirds. A small, delightful garden off the maternity ward in a British hospital (West Dorset County Hospital) is attractively planted and detailed, but—unfortunately—is paved with rounded pebbles set in cement, a most unsuitable surface for women in the last stages of pregnancy who may feel unsteady on their feet. Some other courtyards in this hospital, while attractive in every other regard, are floored entirely with deep gravel, making them virtually unusable except by the very able and determined.

Avoid glare. The reflections or glare, from light concrete in particular, are especially troubling to older people and to immune-compromised patients treated with medications causing photosensitivity.

Provide handrails to support weakened and recovering patients. Patients may want to use, and may benefit from using, the outdoor space, even if they have limited strength or stamina. A combination of ADA regulation handrails and judiciously placed benches enables such use.

Make major walkways wide enough for two gurneys to pass (at least five feet). The outdoor space will be used more often if it is easy to move into and out of. If lots of maneuvering is required, patients and staff may not want to bother.

Limit grade changes in the most highly used outdoor areas. For people whose mobility is impaired in any way, even a slight grade change may prove difficult. The best solution is to offer routes of varying incline, so patients can choose an appropriate challenge or work on gradually building up their strength. The slope of a walk must not exceed 1:20 (if a section is steeper than this, it is considered a ramp, and applicable ADA requirements must be met). Cross-slope may not exceed 1:50, as it poses great difficulty to wheelchair users.

Enable the outdoor area to be used during as much of the year as possible. Where snow or ice is likely to make walkways slippery, install melting devices to clear the walkway. Being able to go outdoors in the winter, even for a few moments, can be an important respite from "cabin fever."

Where possible, creat an entryway at grade so that the outdoor space is free of ramps or steps, and provide maneuvering space around the door. Ramps near doors inhibit the patients' use of a space. Patients in gurneys or new to a wheelchair cannot independently maneuver up a ramp. Also it is difficult to coordinate a patient and accessory medical equipment such as an IV up and down a ramp, to stop at the door, and then move through the door. A generous landing at the door offers maneuvering space for bringing people and their things (food tray, medical equipment) outdoors. ADA requirements for maneuvering room, which vary by door type and approach, are generally inadequate in a hospital setting.

Install a walking path. A walk in a garden or natural outdoor space can provide relief from the hospital setting and have physiological and psychological benefits for those in sedentary occupations, or recovering from surgery. Where there is room,

Figure 5-41 A roof terrace with movable furniture off a ward provides a welcome outdoor extension. Attention to details would have enhanced patients' experience: the height of the balustrade blocks views to attractive landscaped grounds for those who are seated; the aluminum capping to the balustrade creates an annoying problem of glare.

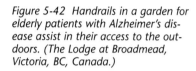

Figure 5-42 Handrails in a garden for elderly patients with Alzheimer's disease assist in their access to the outdoors. (The Lodge at Broadmead, Victoria, BC, Canada.)

two types of walking should be accommodated: the brisk walk and the contemplative stroll. The former requires a clear, circular route, smooth surfaces, width for passing, resting places en route, changing views, and a mix of sun and shade. A path for a contemplative stroll, on the other hand, might have the same characteristics as above but be slightly narrower, follow a more circuitous route, and allow for a sense of mystery and exploration. The former is aimed more at physiological restoration, the latter at psychological restoration.

In smaller outdoor areas such as a courtyard or terrace, make sure that there is ample room for people to stroll without intruding on the personal space of those who are seated. In a modest courtyard in the interior of Middlesex Hospital (London, UK), two-thirds of the total area is a broad paved area for strolling, with comfortable seating placed against the periphery of the courtyard, and the inner one-third of the space is occupied by a rectangular garden of lawn, flower beds and a small fountain. There is a comfortable distance between those seated and those strolling by so that neither group feels they are intruding on the other.

5. SITE PLANNING WITHIN THE GARDEN

So far, these guidelines have dealt with the overall location of outdoor spaces on a hospital site, the integration of building and outdoor space planning to enhance people's awareness of usable gardens, views to the outdoors, and physical access to—and within—usable garden areas. This section includes recommendations on the site planning within the garden itself. Noteworthy, these guidelines must be used in conjunction with recommendations on circulation (see previous section) and those regarding planting, furnishing, and maintenance (see sections that follow).

Program each outdoor space carefully. Consider *who* is most likely to use it, at what *time of day,* in what *size groups,* for which *activities,* and design overall plan and details accordingly. A human-focused design should work for everyone—staff, visitors, patients, children, adults, seniors, the able-bodied, and people with handicaps. A garden should not discriminate.

Provide garden users with choice. Ulrich has urged the importance of hospital garden users having a sense of control, since this contributes to reduced stress. Fundamental to a sense of control is ease of way-finding to, and in, the garden; and ease of usage—including accessibility and independence for persons using walkers, crutches, wheelchairs, or pulling an IV pole. Another significant means by which a garden user can exercise control is in being able to make *choices.* The design should permit people to make choices among: several walking routes; different seating arrangements (sitting alone vs. sitting in a group); different experiences while seated (e.g., a panoramic view, middle distance view, close-in view); different microclimates (sun, dappled shade, deep shade); utilizing different kinds of outdoor spaces (cafeteria patio, strolling path, meditation garden, etc.).

Provide a setting that is nurturing, calming, and familiar. A hospital garden is not a place to create a visionary landscape, or to "break the mold" in terms of design motifs. People who are sick, or who suffer from physical or mental impairments, need an environment to be in or look out at that is comforting (see also Chapters 2 and 3). This means one that is unambiguously positive, a result that may be provided through surroundings that are *familiar* and that may remind patients of

Figure 5-43 Hospital patients appreciate gardens that are calming and familiar. This small garden of a traditional design of lawns, trees, and flower beds is much loved by outpatients attending several adjacent clinics (for AIDS, Methadone Maintenance, Child Abuse) and by the staff. (The Comfort Garden, San Francisco General Hospital, California.)

happier times. The body is more likely to heal when a person is relaxed and stress levels are low.

Ulrich has pointed out the contrast between artists' and the general public's view of art. Many artists believe that art should offer a challenge, and reject the notion that it should produce positive feelings in a broad audience. The public, on the other hand, prefers art that elicits positive feelings. This disparity is especially significant in the stressed atmosphere of a hospital. Research indicates negative reaction and negative associations by hospital patients to abstract and semiabstract art, positive reactions and associations with familiar representational landscapes. Parallels can be drawn with regard to garden designs. When feeling healthy and unstressed, an individual may enjoy the challenge and excitement of abstract and ambiguous paintings—or garden designs. But in a hospital setting, gardens need to evoke familiar and comforting images, and their design should not be based on abstract or futuristic motifs or be "used" by client, donor, designer or hospital to "make a statement."

Consider using materials that would be familiar in the locality. Most people visiting a hospital feel some degree of anxiety. Providing an outdoor setting that has some familiar elements can be reassuring. This is achieved, for example, in the central (and only) courtyard in a rather drab London hospital (Middlesex) by providing paving typical of old-style sidewalks, and the same wooden benches found in London's parks and squares.

The layout of the garden needs to be easily "readable," to minimize confusion for those who are not functioning well. This is especially true in units for the elderly and those

Figure 5-44 People using this garden-courtyard in a large urban hospital may find the space a little more "familiar" since the paving is identical to that used on city sidewalks, and many of the benches are the same as those used in city parks. (Middlesex Hospital, London, UK.)

patients with psychological impairment. Focal elements for orientation, such as a central feature, marked entry treatment, clear path system, and set boundaries, help to reduce confusion and anxiety.

In creating a garden in a courtyard, consider the walls around it as part of the garden design. The walls and windows surrounding and defining a courtyard space can add to, or detract from, the overall aesthetic of a courtyard garden. At a London hospital (Brompton Heart and Lung Hospital) the potentially pitlike experience of being in a small, deep courtyard is alleviated by a thick mass of Boston ivy growing up the walls and catching the sun. A courtyard at West Dorset County Hospital (UK) has on one side an eye-catching, two-story waterfall cascading over rocks into a brick-edged pool, bounded with thick plantings of bamboo, pampas grass, and other evergreen shrubs. It creates a soothing ambience. However, the opposite side of the courtyard is bounded by a huge area of windows with red and blue trim, and views through them onto a major stairway detailed in yellow—the whole creating a jazzy, almost garish, aesthetic in complete contrast to the rest of the courtyard. In the courtyard of a new Oncology Center at Maidstone Hospital (UK), a water feature, seating, and tall ornamental grasses create a potentially restorative setting. However, the space is entirely surrounded by glass—corridors on two sides, waiting areas on the other two sides—so that when sitting in the courtyard one has the uncomfortable feeling of being stared at; the soothing message of the design is negated by its location.

Create subspaces. Where there is sufficient room, divide the space so that there are subareas of varying size and levels of privacy. Some users come alone and seek a space in which to sit that is comfortably private, while others may desire distraction and social interaction.

A central gathering space. Where the hospital grounds are sufficiently large, it may be helpful to provide some sort of gathering place for special outdoor events—for example, a barbecue, an ice cream social, a musical event, fund-raising. This space should be paved, with adequate fixed seating and room for temporary seating. A gazebo/bandstand structure can be a welcome component for use as a speaker platform or stage for special events, and as a place for sheltered seating on regular days. A gazebo, unlike a stage, does not appear "empty" when not in use and can provide a useful orientation cue.

Add an entry element. Where appropriate, provide an entry element (gate, trellis, porch) to evoke a sense of anticipation on entering the garden, and a sense of departure on leaving.

Figure 5-45 A curving wall successfully divides this large courtyard into two gardens. One side is for public use; the other is part of a secure psychiatric ward. This high wall is designed with a trellis on one side and a smooth surface facing the secure unit, to reduce the risk of elopement. (Photo by Marni Barnes. Stanford Medical Center, Stanford, California.)

Figure 5-46 Seating needs to be provided for groups, and for people sitting alone. An inpatient in hospital garb enjoys a quiet, private moment outdoors. A trellis overhead and a wall at his back make this a psychologically comfortable setting. (Homerton Hospital, East London, UK.)

Figure 5-47 A gazebo in a garden provides a sense of being in an outdoor room with overhead protection and views out. (Alzheimer's Patient Unit, West Park Hospital, Toronto, Ontario, Canada.)

Create a sense of enclosure. Where possible, create a frame or sense of boundedness to an outdoor space to provide a sense of enclosure, security, and separation from the interior hospital environment. This may be achieved by means of a wall, fence, dense planting, or building edges.

Include overhead protection. Some people sitting outdoors find that a sense of enclosure overhead, at approximately ceiling height, evokes a sense of protection and security. This may be provided by an actual structure—a gazebo, a garden house, a cloister, a trellis—or by a tree.

An even greater sense of protection is provided where seating under an overhead "ceiling" is placed against an edge—wall, planting bed, fence, or other vertical element—which creates protection from the back, our most vulnerable side. An almost archetypal sense of security is created in a cloister where a person seated has actual built protection overhead and at their back, but has a view "out," usually to a garden. However, care should be taken when creating a cloister-type space to build it with sound absorbing materials or details. One such space in an Arizona hospital provides attractive seating in the shade but also creates such echoes that normal conversations could be heard several tables away.

Provide a panoramic view. Where a distant view can be seen from a hospital outdoor space, make sure that seating is located so that the view can be seen and that planting frames the view. Research on restorative environments indicates that people who are upset or stressed feel particularly calmed on contemplating a distant panorama. It seems that this experience can help people to see the "big picture," or to "get things into perspective" (Francis and Cooper Marcus, 1991).

Consider the views of people in wheelchairs or on gurneys. When designing vistas, plantings, views out of the garden, fountains, and so on, take into account the eye-level perspective of a person who is seated in a wheelchair or propped up on a gurney.

Design the garden as much for viewing into (from indoors) as for being in. Since views *out* are very important, consider how the garden will appear from a nearby window when selecting planting, planning vistas, and so on.

The interior and exterior spaces should complement each other. If patients near an outdoor space have private rooms, exterior areas for social interaction and observation should be a priority. If nearby units have an open, multiple-bed floor plan, more areas for private conversations and withdrawing from social interaction need to be provided.

6. PLANTING

Planting should provide sensory interest and relieve the hospital's institutional aspects. Plants provide a more normal home-like environment and may help relax patients.

Ulrich (Chapter 2) cites considerable evidence supporting the proposal that viewing nature, even for just a few minutes, can significantly reduce symptoms of stress. While "nature" is a broad term, all the research cited defined a nature scene as one dominated by *greenery* (trees, shrubs, grass, plants), sometimes with water (lake, pond, stream, fountain), and /or flowers being present. Nature scenes—both actual or depicted in paintings or photographs—tended to fall into the category of savannah-type landscapes (open green with clumps of trees); or a clearing in a forest occupied by a meadow or lake. All of these components suggest the traditional idea of an oasis or garden. This is not to suggest that an arid or desert landscape, a prairie, a dense forest, or rocky terrain (or a garden design based on any of these), could not be restorative; but at present there is no research evidence to support such a claim.

Save existing mature trees on site. Mature trees provide immediate visual interest; they also create shade and a sense of space, and can provide attractive environments for birds and squirrels. For most people, trees evoke a sense of permanence, which is especially important in a hospital setting where patients and visitors experience little sense of permanence and often high levels of anxiety. Two immense valley oaks in the central garden at Kaiser Medical Center, Walnut Creek, California,

"Flowers are restful to look at. They have neither emotions nor conflicts."
SIGMUND FREUD

Figure 5-48 A comforting experience of being "in nature" is enhanced when plant materials are varied by size, texture, form, and color. A quiet seating area on the roof terrace of an urban hospital. (St. Mary's Hospital, San Francisco, California.)

create shade, visual interest, wildlife habitat, a sense of history, and are much loved by all who use this hospital environment. (Cooper Marcus and Barnes, 1995).

Where an outdoor area is bounded by high buildings, select and locate trees so that their canopy will bring down the scale of the surroundings. In a high-rise urban hospital where users of a courtyard or atrium may experience the space as "pit-like," it is very important to create a lacy, green ceiling effect, which will allow some sunlight through, yet will provide an overhead canopy of human scale. This effect is best created with the species with considerable horizontal spread, or with a vine-covered trellis. At Middlesex Hospital in Central London, the experience of sitting in a courtyard entirely surrounded by four- to eight-story nineteenth century buildings is considerably softened by the presence of three medium-to-large trees. Without these, the experience of looking at a formal rectangle of lawns, flower borders, and a fountain would be much less pleasurable. The trees also create a habitat for birds, whose singing provides a welcome respite in this very urban context.

Provide a variety of plant materials. Provide lush planting that is varied and eye-catching so as to suggest the image of a garden. Contrast and harmony in texture, form, color, and arrangement of plant materials provide a variety that holds people's attention and helps to draw their focus away from themselves and into the exterior world. Over and over, trees, plants, and greenery were cited as the most significant helpful characteristic in reducing stress when users of four California hospital gardens were interviewed about the beneficial effect of being outdoors (Cooper Marcus and Barnes, 1995).

Aim for a degree of visual variety without verging on visual clutter. Someone who is stressed and seeks some respite in a hospital garden will appreciate some visual variety to engage the eye, but may not appreciate *too* much variety in a small space. A small courtyard at a British hospital (West Dorset County Hospital), while pleasantly scaled and furnished, was aesthetically uncomfortable in that it had too great a variety of ground surfaces (stone pavers, cobbles, and red brick in four different patterns), and of plant materials (more than twenty-five species). On the other hand, a meditation garden at a U.S. hospital (Norris Cancer Center, Los Angeles) had only one species of perennial (iris), though several different types of trees. With only one type of low flowering plant, this garden appears colorful for a short period in the year, and rather monochromatic for the rest of the year. A balance needs to be struck between these two extremes. A monoculture of one or two plants may lead to boredom rather than stress reduction.

"… what would the world be like without the beauty of flowers? [It] touches us on a deep, natural level. It speaks to our hearts and souls, our essential natures. It pleases our minds and emotions with harmony, balance, unity, and peace. It calls to our spirits, and we respond with natural joy. While our culture seems obsessed with style and fashion, it also seems to grossly underestimate the importance of real beauty."

Veronica Ray

Plant densely rather than sparsely, with many varieties of trees, shrubs, and flowers. Carpman et al. (1986) reported:

> When people look at a scene, they seek a sense of involvement and a richness that gives them reason to continue viewing. For instance, a densely planted area provides greater visual interest than a sparsely planted one. In one [hospital-based] study, scenes with a greater number of trees were consistently rated higher than those with fewer trees. The ratings increased in a linear fashion as the number of trees increased. Trees were seen as a source of visual interest as well as a source of beauty, shade and color. Absence of planting was characterized as "bare" and "boring" by some respondents (*ibid.*, p. 220).

Figure 5-49 A plant palette in which flowering perennials are represented by only one species results in a garden that is somewhat monochromatic through much of the year. (Norris Cancer Center, University of Southern California, Los Angeles, California.)

Offer a variety of sunny and shady areas. Many hospitalized patients are extremely sensitive to temperature and so must have many options from which to choose in order to be comfortable. If the outdoor space has been situated to maximize sun exposure, the designer should add features that will supply varying degrees of shade. Unless the climate is especially hot and bright, people usually prefer a dappled shade, such as that provided by a small-leafed tree or a trellis. Changes in light intensity also serve to create the experience of transition and movement from "room" to "room."

Include a variety of flowering shrubs, trees, and perennials. There are few people who are not cheered by flowers. In a study of four hospital gardens where users were asked what elements helped elicit a positive mood change, flowers ranked prominently in the responses and lack of color was often mentioned. Flowering trees, shrubs and perennials that change through the year, or through the day, reinforce people's awareness of life's rhythms and cycles. Colors provide a noninvasive stimulus which is helpful in facilitating a shift in consciousness.

When selecting plant materials, research which particular species might have special sacred or evocative meanings for the cultural and age groups being served. For example, elderly people in a particular region may have great fondness for certain garden flowers no longer "in fashion." Certain plants may have sacred or healing significance for particular minority groups in the region. In a healing garden at Good Samaritan Medical Center, Phoenix, Arizona, medicinal plants traditionally used by local Native Americans form an important component of the plant palette.

Select plant materials native to the locality. With the wide range of plants available plus the advantages of irrigation, we often use materials in our gardens whose origins are widespread. To help create a sense of place in a hospital garden, con-

Figure 5-50 Plants native to the locality are featured in this garden near to the main entrance of a desert-region hospital. Alternative outdoor spaces on the site include shady, lush courtyards and an expanse of irrigated lawn. (Scottsdale Memorial Hospital North, Scottsdale, Arizona.)

Figure 5-51 A tree that invites touch. (San Diego Hospice, San Diego, California.)

sider creating one area with native plants, labeled for easy identification. In Scottsdale Memorial Hospital North (Arizona), an attractive space close to the main entry features rocks, sculpture, square concrete seating pods, and a wide variety of cacti, all labeled. Other spaces available in this setting include shaded, lush patios and irrigated lawns. No matter what a person's environmental preference, he or she could most likely find a place in which to feel comfortable.

Choose plants with strong fragrances. The sense of smell is one of the least affected by old age, or by diseases such as AIDS. Hospitals frequently have an immediately noticeable odor that may evoke fear or apprehension in some patients and visitors, recalling childhood or other traumatic hospital experiences. People interviewed in hospital courtyards and roof gardens often remarked how good it felt to smell trees, grass, shrubbery, and flowers as a respite from the prevailing antiseptic odor in the hospital building (Paine, 1984; Cooper Marcus and Barnes, 1995). Consider using fragrant herbs, trees, shrubs, and perennials.

Consider planting and details that have tactile qualities. This might include touchable plants and blooms, water that invites touch, and opportunities to walk on and handle different surfaces—brick, wood, stone, grass, and so on.

Select some plants whose foliage moves easily. Leaves that move in even a slight breeze draw people's attention to patterns of color, shadows, and light, described by interviewees as soothing and meditative (Cooper Marcus and Barnes, 1995). Consider plants that bring wind into the visual and audible realms, such as ornamental grasses and some forms of bamboo. Trees with these characteristics might include poplars, willow, quaking aspen, and birch. Watching leaves move and at the same time listening to them can have a particularly mesmerizing effect, helping to reduce stress.

Consider the outdoor environment as a setting for wildlife. Plant species that attract butterflies call attention to the ephemeral, serving as a gentle reminder of the preciousness of life. Mature trees may provide a habitat for birds and squirrels. Certain flowers and shrubs are attractive to hummingbirds. Shallow fountain pools often attract birds for drinking and bathing. A winter birdfeeder may attract birds into the garden during that season.

Formal interviews and informal conversations with users of many hospital gardens recorded the affection that many feel for wildlife that has taken up residence: the squirrels in two mature oaks at Kaiser Medical Center, Walnut Creek, California; the pair of swans on the newly formed lake at St. Mary's Hospital, Isle of Wight, UK; the rabbits that populate the gardens and natural landscape around Victoria General Hospital, British Columbia, Canada; the hummingbirds that found their way across downtown traffic to the blooms in a new healing garden at Good Samaritan Medical Center in Phoenix, Arizona.

Install a lawn area where feasible. Case study interviews found that people in hospitals respond very positively to the sight of lush green grass. It has a powerful visual image; it may be symbolic of the "home front lawn," and therefore familiar and reassuring; it is a versatile surface for children, patients, visitors, and staff; and the smell of newly mown or watered grass is particularly evocative (Paine, 1984; Cooper Marcus and Barnes, 1995). A large lawn forming the centerpiece of an entry garden at St. Thomas' Hospital, London, is highly used, especially by staff on their lunch hour, as a place to sprawl, picnic, doze, sunbathe, and read. Laying on grass on a warm day gives people the excuse to take a needed nap, where they might feel more self-conscious doing so sitting on a bench.

Care must be taken always to provide a path (suitable for wheelchairs and IV poles on wheels) through or around any lawn area so that it is usable by inpatients. Amazingly, areas of lawn without pathways were observed in some hospitals. Such an amenity might be appropriate in a neighborhood park, but not in a medical facility.

Provide buffer planting. Where offices or patient rooms border a garden, create a planting buffer of sufficient distance and depth so that people walking or sitting in the garden do not feel that they are intruding on the privacy of those indoors.

Figure 5-52 A lawn in the entry garden of a large London hospital is a popular place for members of staff to take a break. Some people may feel less self-conscious lying down on grass than they would, say, on a bench. (St. Thomas Hospital, London, UK.)

"A salute to grass. It is so adaptable; fine for sitting, napping, sunbathing.... Like chairs, it provides a limitless choice of arrangements."
W. H. WHYTE

Figure 5-53 Lack of maintenance can render parts of a garden unusable, such as this path in a hospice garden. Plant selection should be made with projected maintenance budgets in mind.

Provide green outlook from upper floors. When offices and/or patient rooms look out and down onto a garden space, plant fast-growing, tall trees with a relatively narrow horizontal spread so that upper rooms have a green view.

Design with projected maintenance levels in mind. Appropriate plant selection, with special attention given to maintenance requirements, correct placement in the garden, and projected maintenance budgets, is one of the essential elements of a therapeutic garden environment, as dying and unhealthy plants have a negative psychological impact on those observing them.

Avoid a very low maintenance garden, however. A garden that is designed to be "tough" and to require little maintenance will not provide as therapeutic an environment for staff—in particular—who enjoy observing the changing seasons, changing plantings, and who may have beneficial relations with the gardening staff. Shrubs, trees, and flowers are labor intensive compared to structures and patio spaces. Yet it is these green, growing things that appear to offer the most restorative value. Appropriate fertilizing, selective thinning rather than shearing, and the use of seasonal color contribute to the healthy and natural qualities listed as significant by the users of hospital gardens.

7. FURNISHINGS

Site furniture makes the space usable. Without it, people's choices are limited, and they are likely only to look around or walk through a space and then leave. Site furniture should enable a space to be used by as many people as possible throughout the year.

Design to facilitate social support. Ulrich (Chapter 2) presents evidence for the importance of social support in mitigating the effects of stress. Since being a patient, an employee, or a visitor to a hospital is frequently a stressful experience, it is essential that outdoor space design contribute in its own way to facilitating social support. This can be achieved: by offering subspaces that can be "claimed" by a couple or a group; by providing seating arrangements that facilitate private conversation; by execising care in planting and design details so that talking does not disturb others who may want to use the garden as a private retreat. In one London hospital, the soothing tones of a fountain completely masked sounds of conversation between people on benches placed quite close to each other in a small courtyard.

It is especially important that the designer be aware of cultural differences in the size of family groups that come to visit

Figure 5-54 Social support helps miti-gate the effects of stress. It is important that a hospital garden provide settings for quiet conversation. (Alta Bates Medical Center, Berkeley, California)

an inpatient, and may wish to spend time in the garden and find suitable seating. Observations of Native American visitors in a hospital garden in Arizona and of Latino visitors in a hospital garden in California suggest that groups of six or more are not uncommon.

Offer seating of as many types and forms as possible. Without adequate seating, people cannot stay outside. Many people using hospital outdoor spaces are alone or in small groups of two to four. Some seating should consist of movable chairs, which people can adjust for group size, sun, shade, wind, or desired views. In a comprehensive study carried out at the University of Michigan Hospitals, 200 randomly sampled patients and visitors indicated a strong desire to be able to choose from a *range* of seating options (Carpman et al., 1986, p. 203). This study also found a preference for chairs and benches made of wood, rather than wire or concrete, and for seats with backs and armrests for support. Carpman suggested that any seating provided should be comfortable for an hour or more if it is truly to support the activity potential of an outdoor space. Observations in another hospital garden study suggest that short, garden-style benches are preferred over long park or bus stop style benches (Cooper Marcus and Barnes, 1995).

Right-angled seating allows a comfortable distance and ori-entation for conversation. Fixed linear seating, by requiring companions to angle their heads or bodies toward one another, may cause discomfort, and makes group interaction virtually impossible. Fixed opposite seating, in which companions

"Fixed individual seats deny choice. The designer is saying you sit here and you sit there. This is arrogant....People are much better at this than designers."

W. H. WHYTE

Figure 5-55 *A variety of places to sit in this hospital garden, which doubles as a public park, permits many people to enjoy the space, varying by age, gender, connection to the hospital, and so on. (St. Thomas' Hospital, London, UK.)*

directly face one another, or circular inward-facing seating creates a "room" effect that may deter users who arrive after the space has been appropriated.

People in hospitals, as in other semipublic places, do not necessarily want to interact with strangers or intrude on others' privacy. In four case studies of California hospital outdoor spaces, staff and employees were found to be predominant users, and many expressed a desire to get away from constant human interaction and be outside alone (Cooper Marcus and Barnes, 1995). Backless benches or planter-edge seating allows people to lie down to take a nap or sunbathe, as was frequently observed in summertime use of hospital gardens, especially by staff (Cooper Marcus and Barnes, 1995).

Fixed seating in a linear arrangement allows strangers to sit comfortably, relatively close to each, avoiding eye contact. This kind of arrangement is made even more psychologically comfortable if those seated have something engaging to look at— passing pedestrians, attractive planting, or a distant view. If the need for seating and the dimensions of the outdoor space demand that two rows of seating look across at each other, it is essential either that they be at least 30 feet apart, or that planting forming a filtered screen at seated eye-level is placed between the opposite rows of seating.

Coordinate seating materials and design. Seating materials will be influenced by the garden image, budget, and local microclimate. Where the outdoor temperature is marginal for part or most of the year, wood seating would be most appropriate since it absorbs warmth more easily than other materials. When the climate is oppressively hot for part of the year, metal seating should be avoided and stone or concrete might be employed. The latter materials can feel pleasantly cool on a hot day, if located in the shade.

Around some of the seating, use planting to create a sense of enclosure. Seating partly enclosed by planting, or on the edge of an open space, provides a degree of privacy for those wanting to be alone, or who want to observe from a distance. People gain a sense of security from sitting with something at their back, and in some type of enclosure. In a University of Michigan Hospitals study (1986), people preferred seating surrounded by a combination of shrubs and trees. Such seating will be enjoyed if oriented to a view of activity in such a way that one can observe without feeling observed in return. A particularly attractive and popular seating arrangement at Homerton Hospital (London, U.K.) consists of wooden garden benches (with backs and arm rests) nestled into a series of brick-paved wooden arbors draped with jasmine and grape vines. Sitting inside evokes the experience of being in your own private room, with the added plus of a view out to a busy pedestrian entry walk to the hospital's main entrance.

Seating at another London hospital is not so successful. In each of two large landscaped courts, west and east of the busy main entrance to St. George's Hospital, there is a small, very private paved area, almost totally surrounded by high, unkempt shrubs. Inside each is a single bench. While the experience of sitting here is of being in a private oasis, the fact that there is only *one* bench in each means that, once that single bench is occupied, no one else enters the space. This is espe-

Figure 5-56 A concrete bench would be quite unsuitable in a cool climate or where most of the users are elderly, but on a hot afternoon in the shade in a semi-tropical climate, it can have a pleasant cooling effect. (Glendale Adventist Medical Center, Los Angeles, California.)

Figure 5-57 Picnic benches in the garden of this suburban hospital are highly used, especially by staff, who sometimes come outdoors for group meetings. (Kaiser Permanente Medical Center, Walnut Creek, California.)

cially unfortunate since there are no other benches in these large courts and people have to sprawl on the grass or pull out chairs from inside the building. Creating a private sitting space is fine as long as there are enough of them.

Provide some bench and table arrangements. Tables allow more activities, including eating, reading, and writing, to occur in a space. They also function as markers to establish territory, as people will seldom intrude on a table in use. Observations at a California hospital where picnic tables were provided in a green, lush outdoor space, indicated that groups of medical staff particularly appreciated such furniture for informal staff meetings (Cooper Marcus and Barnes, 1995). Because the average group tends to contain four or fewer people, long tables such as eight-foot picnic tables are not as useful as are four-foot tables. Accessibility for wheelchair users is increased where one side of the table is not blocked by a fixed seat or bench. Wood tables (as opposed to metal or concrete) have the advantage of having a surface that does not have to look clean; however, the uneven surface may cause difficulties for people trying to write. Umbrella tables with movable chairs are another popular option, providing shade and a semiprivate grouping, especially appreciated near a cafeteria. Adjustable umbrellas allow people to control the amount of sun or shade, so important to those who feel unwell, or who are taking certain medications.

Provide weather-mitigating features. Wind shelters, heat-reflecting surfaces—or alternatively, shade-producing arbors and gazebos—help to mitigate the climate and maximize throughout the year the use of the garden.

Orient some fixed seating to views and sun. Where there is a view, make sure that some seating faces that direction to facilitate psychological movement out of the space. If the exterior space is a roof garden or terrace, the edge rail, balustrade, or planter should be sufficiently low or transparent so that people seated can take in the view. Where there is not a ready-made view, a sense of mystery and movement can be created by designing smaller-scale glimpses and intriguing focal points within the garden, to draw the users' attention and, sometimes, facilitate a change in perspective. Orientation to the sun, especially between approximately 11:00 A.M. and 4:00 P.M., is also important in areas with moderate to cool climates.

Provide unusual or memorable items in the outdoor spaces. Basic site furniture makes the space usable; unusual items make it memorable. Such things as water fountains, aviaries, extraordinary views, and artwork are popular with patients and staff, offer a contrast with the hospital environ-

Figure 5-58 Umbrella tables on a roof garden with little shade provide a pleasant spot for staff members to eat lunch. (Alta Bates Medical Center, Berkeley, California.)

ment, and can lead to spontaneous conversation between strangers. Providing one or more eye-catching and unique features by which people will identify a garden serves to anchor memories of the garden and the restoration achieved there. Unusual items attract patients to a space, and they may return to show these features to visitors. For example, one year after an aviary was removed from a courtyard at a California hospital, the staff still remembered it and felt that it had given a great deal of enjoyment to the patients (Paine, 1984).

However, great care must be taken in selecting appropriate artwork. Tall slabs of stone or travertine may be fashionable in landscape design, but are quite inappropriate in a hospital garden because of their association with gravestones. Semiabstract sculptures of birds in a space overlooked by cancer patients in a North Carolina hospital were perceived by some as vultures, were intensely disliked, and had to be removed. Ulrich (Chapter 2) describes the theory of emotional congruence—the notion that when faced with an array of environmental stimuli, those that mesh with the emotional state of the perceiver will most likely be the focus of attention. The more stressed people feel, the more they yearn for simple, familiar images and forms; and the more they will be distressed by negative or ambiguous images. A garden for hospital patients is not a suitable locale for puzzling, abstract pieces, or for avant-garde art that would be more comfortably located in a corporate or museum forecourt.

Provide an element of whimsy. Working—or being a patient—in a hospital is serious business. A hospital garden can be an ideal setting for introducing elements that may evoke a smile, a chuckle, or be a source of comment and conversation. Decorated tiles, sculpture, bas-relief, water elements, topiary—any of these, or several in combination—might be employed with the conscious goal of causing people to stop and smile. Humor is known to reduce stress levels, and even the slight facial movement of a smile creates beneficial psychological response.

In a few hospital gardens visited the written word is successfully and subtly incorporated into the design. In the Healing Garden (Good Samaritan Medical Center, Phoenix, Arizona), existing columns are decorated with inspirational quotes in tile. In a very different setting (The Bird Garden at West Dorset County Hospital, UK) in a lushly planted courtyard with a "secret garden" feel, fragments of poetry inscribed on stone are half hidden in the greenery and on the walls behind it.

Provide textures in contrast to those encountered inside the hospital. Most textures used inside a hospital are

Figure 5-59 A touch of whimsy in a hospital garden. However, this seated frog might have been more appropriate outside a children's ward, rather than in a meditation garden, pictured here.

Figure 5-60 The sound and sight of moving water is always appreciated in hospital gardens. In this case, the fountain is inspired by the shape of the ventricles of the human heart, and its sound replicates the human heart beat. (Royal Brompton National Heart and Lung Hospital, London, UK.)

smooth, man-made, easily cleaned, and indestructible. The exceptions would be sculpture, woven wall hangings, paintings, and so on—hence their great importance. Patients may enjoy a contrast in an outdoor patio or garden environment. These might include rock walls or individual rocks; logs or wood beams for planter construction; tiled surfaces; plants inviting touch; wooden picnic tables; concrete stools, and so on.

Where possible, provide a water feature. A fountain, pool, fish pond, waterfall, or man-made stream is a particularly welcome feature in an outdoor space intended for healing, rest, and contemplation. Research on restorative places suggest that the sights and sounds of water are particularly soothing to people who are stressed or upset (Francis and Cooper Marcus, 1992; Barnes, 1994). Unlike children in Victorian England, a fountain should be both seen *and* heard. The therapeutic value of water, especially in a hospital setting, is doubly enhanced if it engages our hearing and our sight. Hence a bubble fountain or one where a very delicate sound can only be experienced by a person sitting right next to it should be questioned. In a post-occupancy study of a hospital roof garden, a small fountain was particularly appreciated for its sound, and because birds were attracted to drink and bathe in the water (Cooper Marcus and Barnes, 1995). The shape of a fountain in a small courtyard at the Royal Brompton Heart and Lung Hospital (London, UK) is based on sections through the ventricles of the heart, and water surges through it, replicating a human heartbeat. Since the courtyard is relatively small (approximately 30 × 100 feet), and benches consequently are quite close to each other, the sound of the fountain has both a soothing, almost hypnotic, effect, and functions to mask the sounds of conversation.

An attractive lily pond fills up approximately half the space encompassed by a courtyard at St. George's Hospital (London, UK). A path encircling the pond is a popular place to stroll while looking at the water, the lilies, and the goldfish that swim beneath the surface. A jet of water falling into the pond at one end provides an experience of listening to water; the opposite end of the pool, with a slightly raised wooden seating deck, allows for a different experience where one can watch the fish, or the reflections of clouds and waterside plants. Everyone who enters the courtyard—at least for some of the time—looks at the water. (See photo on jacket of this book.) The presence of multistory buildings bordering the courtyard is less obvious, or potentially oppressive, because of the presence of the lily pond.

In the center of a large, square lawn in the entry garden at St. Thomas' Hospital (London, UK) is a large fountain. It is noticeable that those who choose to lay down on the grass on

Figure 5-61 A lily pond with still and moving water is the central feature of a well-used courtyard in a large, inner-city hospital. (St. George's Hospital, London, UK.)

warm days (mostly nursing staff on breaks) do so close to the fountain, presumably because its sounds are soothing, and because it masks the noise of traffic passing nearby on the approaches to Westminister Bridge.

To maximize the benefit of the water feature, provide seating in semiprivate "niches" near to the water for those who wish to meditate, nap, or view the water in seclusion. Seating for groups eating lunch, chatting, or holding an informal meeting might be placed further away so that the atmosphere of contemplation evoked by water is not intruded upon.

In an attractive courtyard at West Dorset County Hospital (UK) a two-story high waterfall cascades down across local Purbeck stone into a pool at its base. Three wooden garden benches are positioned by the pool, and in other locations, and there are never more than a few people in the courtyard at a time. A snack bar just off the courtyard provides for groups eating together, whose conversation might intrude on the restorative benefits of the outdoor space.

Make sure that where an air conditioning unit or a recycling pump is located nearby, it is soundproofed or the sound is masked so that mechanical noise does not intrude on the aural space of those enjoying the sounds of moving water.

Provide a drinking fountain outside and a bathroom within or next to the outdoor space. These are basic amenities for any outdoor space and are necessary except for a short visit. They are particularly important for patients and visiting children. Make sure that the drinking fountain can be used by children and people in wheelchairs, as well as by standing adults, possibly on crutches, and that the water control is simple (requiring minimal manipulation and strength).

Place trash containers near all doors and outdoor social areas. Trash containers permit easy disposal of food and paper products, particularly important where the climate and garden design encourage eating outdoors. A form of litter frequently observed were cigarette butts; smoking is not allowed inside hospital buildings and so it is done outdoors. Where a smoking area is provided, include plenty of easily maintained ashtrays.

Provide adequate, attractive lighting. Nighttime lighting maximizes the therapeutic benefits by allowing people to use the space safely after dark, or to look out at the garden from indoors. This is especially important in regions with balmy evening temperatures when people would want to be outside after dark, and in cooler climates where up-lighting of trees in all seasons can provide an attractive view from inside the building.

Figure 5-62 Ornamental grasses and bamboo beside an eye-catching waterfall and pool in a hospital courtyard. (West Dorset Hospital, Dorchester, UK.)

Provide electrical outlets. Electrical outlets allow the garden to be used for hospital parties or other sponsored functions. These may encourage use of the garden by those who don't often go outside, publicize its existence, enable fund-raising events to take place outdoors. Since most hospital gardens are funded by private donations, this latter function is important.

8. SECURITY, MAINTENANCE AND ADMINISTRATIVE POLICIES

While a design team will have prime responsibility for the creation of a hospital garden, responsibility for its ongoing maintenance and use will fall on the facility management and gardening staff. It is essential that their concerns be ancticipated and addressed in the design of the garden, and that management and maintenance staff be represented in brainstorming meetings throughout the design process. Not only will this ensure that the designers are made aware of issues pertinent to management and maintenance, but also that the staff of these departments feel a part of the process and buy into the whole idea of a garden at an early stage. Case studies of hospital gardens indicate that this is essential to the ongoing support and care of hospital outdoor spaces.

Educate employees about the existence and therapeutic benefits of exterior spaces. Our field studies revealed that awareness of the garden space is one of the most critical factors in its use. We found that even where there was an outdoor space, people at the information desk were often not aware of its existence, or were mistaken about accessibility (The extreme situation was in one hospital where it took 45 minutes and several exasperating trails of misinformation before access could be attained to a locked roof garden that was "open to the public"). Installing signs that direct people to the space, labeling the gardens on posted maps, and listing them in the resource handbook at the information desk would go a long way toward promoting their use and reaping their rewards.

Encouraging the medical staff to promote the use of exterior spaces will increase the use of gardens by patients and visitors and extend a ripple of beneficial effect to everyone. Scheduling events and meetings in the garden incorporates the restorative benefits of a garden into the work schedule.

Consider use of volunteers to take patients outdoors. In a time when money is limited, creative thinking can lead to increased benefit. Recruitment and use of volunteers to take patients outside gives relief to the staff as well as to the

Figure 5-63 Hospital gardens need to be well maintained and open for use. Dying plants or "Keep Out" notices do not convey a positive message.

patients. Some patients cannot physically move to or through the space by themselves, nor does the hospital staff want them left there unattended. Having a trained volunteer in an outdoor space may enable patients to use it freely without a regular medical staff member being present. Alternatively, perhaps a part-time supervisor could be hired to be on duty during those times when patients are most likely to use the space. The supervisor should have a comfortable location from which he or she can easily see the patients, with a connection to the hospital communications system for emergencies.

Maintain garden. Maintenance is important in terms of both the physical safety of the site and the therapeutic potential. The view of a poorly maintained garden does not instill confidence in hospital patients concerning the care *they* will receive from hospital staff. If the design of a hospital building creates a large number of "holes" to be designed as courtyards, yet the landscaping and maintenance budgets do not allow for sufficient high-quality exterior design and on-going care, the potential of these spaces may backfire. The Department of Health (UK) has sponsored many hospital buildings that are termed "nucleus," or "harness," or "spine-and-pavilion" buildings. Many courtyards and spaces between long pavilion wings allow daylight to penetrate the buildings, and natural cross ventilation to occur. Some such hospitals have created some beautiful, usable outdoor spaces in these courtyards (for example, West Dorset County Hospital). In others, unfortunately, initial planting and subsequent maintenance are substandard. At Newham Hospital in East London, while the courtyards are to human scale in terms of their dimensions and height-to-width ratios, their planting and detailing is unimaginative and their maintenance and upkeep is poor. Plants are dying; weeds and brambles have overgrown many of the original shrubs; benches are broken; paving slabs are uneven; styrofoam cups and cigarette butts litter the ground. Many courtyards cannot be entered; their doors kept permanently locked. Florence Nightingale's pleas for more daylight and cross-ventilation in hospital wards have been heard, but the visual and functional potential of those open spaces has been completely overlooked.

Where garden maintenance budgets are inadequate (which is probably the case in the hospital described above) consideration should be given at the design stage to putting in very low maintenance planting. Alternatively, volunteers from a local garden club might be approached to maintain the outdoor spaces, or local youth-training programs might be approached to use hospital outdoor space as a locale for teaching landscape maintenance.

Use organic methods. Encouraging birds, butterflies, squirrels, and so on—another aspect of the garden that is high on the list of significant qualities—is easier if organic practices are employed. Undocumented but also relevant may be the detrimental effect of the use of chemicals and pesticides on the health of the people in the garden, especially those who are physically unwell. Hand weeding, mulching, companion planting, appropriate spacing of plants, and integrated pest management all reduce the need for the use of chemicals.

Maintain a comfortable milieu. Interest, variety, the fact that "someone cares" about the garden, were mentioned by users of hospital gardens; pristine lines, perfection, and aesthetic excellence were not (Cooper Marcus and Barnes, 1995). Maintenance should be geared toward providing a friendly, comfortable, welcoming space rather than toward excessive neatness and perfection.

Keep gardens open. Appealing gardens, designed with seating but behind locked doors, are as bad or worse than nothing at all. The frustration of rattling locked doors increases the stress levels of newcomers to the facility, and the emotional cost would be greater, and longer term, for those who may be confused or disoriented. Gardens that are designed for use should be kept available.

Take advantage of the fact that communication can be easier in an exterior space. Interviewees in one study mentioned that the gardeners provided companionship (Cooper Marcus and Barnes, 1995). The head gardener at one of the study sites remarked on the public relations service he provided, by listening to people vent and express their dissatisfactions. The casual nature of being in the garden can enhance communication; acknowledging this and capitalizing on it would benefit the entire organization.

Include storage space. Storage space in the garden is important for ease of maintenance, and for specialized functions and therapy. Movable chairs, small tools, holiday decorations, maintenance tools, and therapy equipment need to be easily accessible. At one hospital, the lack of such a storage space made it virtually impossible to perform therapeutic activities outdoors.

Set up smoking and nonsmoking areas. Smoking is not only prohibited inside hospitals but also in some outdoor spaces where this activity might bother other people. Since some staff, patients, or visitors may want to smoke in the hospital environment, it is essential to identify areas which are appropriate. At Kaiser Medical Center, Los Angeles, it is a second story courtyard surrounded by tall buildings where movable chairs and tables, and adjacent vending machines form a reasonably pleasant setting. In some hospitals, smoking is permitted at the main entry where people may be waiting for buses or taxis and where patients using wheelchairs can be wheeled out to a semipublic outdoor space. At other hospitals, smoking at the main entry is specifically prohibited since it depicts what some would see as an "unhealthy image." At Kaiser Medical Center, Walnut Creek, California, smokers have been provided with a roofed, three-sided "shack" enabling smoking in all weathers. Clearly this is a touchy issue, and locations for smoking must be discussed with the administration when planning a range of outdoor spaces in a hospital setting.

Provide a telephone for emergencies. To facilitate calling for assistance in the event that a medical emergency or security problem occurs in the garden, a house phone should be installed near an entrance. Because a phone may sometimes be used for private conversations, it should be located—or shielded—so that a conversation does not intrude on the privacy of those in the garden.

Provide pagers for staff who may want to spend time outdoors. Staff using hospital gardens may need to be contacted in the event of an emergency or phone call. A public-address system, typical of hospital interiors, can be very disruptive of the restorative experience of being in nature. Providing pagers would permit staff to take restorative outdoor breaks while on call.

CONCLUSION

As noted elsewhere in this book, these recommendations are intended as performance guidelines, not as hard-and-fast prescriptions. We have not attempted to prioritize these recommendations, as each setting will have different requirements. In additions, the details of specific plant materials, cultural icons, climatic-related features and so on, are not covered in these generic recommendations. It is our intention that the basic concepts within these guidelines be as relevant in Scotland as they are in Australia.

Finally, no set of design recommendations is fixed in stone. As more research is conducted, these guidelines may need to be modified or expanded. Until such time, however, we feel confident that they provide a solid base for the design of restorative outdoor spaces for the enjoyment of all in healthcare settings.

REFERENCES

Ackerman, D. (1995). *A Natural History of the Senses.* New York: Vintage Books.

Barnes, M. (1994). *A Study of the Process of Emotional Healing in Outdoor Spaces and the Concomitant Landscape Design Implications.* Master's Thesis in Landscape Architecture, University of California, Berkeley.

Carpman, J. R., M. A. Grant, and D. A. Simmons (1986). *Design That Cares: Planning Health Facilities for Patients and Visitors.* Chicago: American Hospital Publishing.

Carr, S., M. Francis, L. G. Rivlin, and A. M. Stone (1992). *Public Space.* Cambridge, UK: Cambridge University Press.

Cooper Marcus, C. and M. Barnes (1995). *Gardens in Healthcare Facilities: Uses, Therapeutic Benefits, and Design Recommendations.* Martinez, CA: The Center for Health Design, Inc.

Cooper Marcus, C. and C. Francis (1998). *People Places: Design Guidelines for Urban Open Space.* (2nd ed.) New York: Wiley.

Francis, C. and C. Cooper Marcus (1992). "Places People Take Their Problems." In J. Urbina-Soria, P. Ortega-Andeane, and R. Bechtel (Eds.), Proceedings of the 22nd Annual Conference of the Environmental Design Research Association. Oklahoma City: Environmental Design Research Association.

Larson, C. T. (Ed.) (1965). *The Effect of Windowless Classrooms on Elementary Schoolchildren.* Ann Arbor: University of Michigan Architectural Research Laboratory.

Manning, P. (1963). "Daylighted or windowless design for single-story factories?" *Light and Lighting,* 56, pp. 188–192.

Ne'eman, E. (1974). "Visual aspects of sunlight in buildings." *Lighting Research and Technology,* 6, pp. 159–164.

Paine, R. (1984). *Design Guidelines for Hospital Outdoor Spaces: Case Studies of Three Hospitals.* Master's Thesis in Landscape Architecture, University of California, Berkeley.

Paine, R., C. Francis, C. Cooper Marcus, and M. Barnes (1998). "Hospital Outdoor Spaces," in *People Places: Design Guidelines for Urban Open Space.* (2nd ed.) New York: Wiley.

Raven, A. (1994). "Patients Discover the Healing Power of Gardens," *New York Times,* Living Arts Section, p. B1, Dec. 29.

Ray, V. (1996). *The Zen of Gardening: A Down-to-Earth Philosophy.* New York: Berkley Publishing Group.

J. W. (1998). "A Question of Healing." *Landscape Architecture,* Vol. 88, No. 4, April.

Ulrich, R. S. (1979). "Visual landscapes and psychological well-being." *Landscape Research,* Vol. 4, No. 1, pp. 17–23.

——— (1984). "View through a window may influence recovery from surgery." *Science,* Vol. 224, pp. 420–421.

Verderber, S. F. (1982). "Designing for the therapeutic function of windows in the hospital rehabilitation environment." In *Knowledge for Design*, P. Bart et al. (Eds.). College Park, MD: Environmental Design Research Association.

Whyte, W. H. (1980). *The Social Life of Small Urban Spaces.* Washington, DC: Conservation Foundation.

——— (1988). *City: Rediscovering the Center.* New York: Doubleday.

Wilson, L. (1972). "Intensive care delirium, the effect of outside deprivation in a windowless unit." *Archives of Internal Medicine*, 130, p. 225–226.

CHAPTER

6

Psychiatric Hospitals

Naomi Alena Sachs

This chapter focuses on outdoor spaces in psychiatric healthcare facilities. These outdoor areas can comprise one or sometimes a combination of the following: a large, freestanding psychiatric hospital, where the grounds are at least several acres; a small, specialized mental health facility, where the outdoor space is often more limited, and is sometimes enclosed by the buildings that make up the facility; a psychiatric ward or unit in a general hospital, in which the grounds are usually quite small (a courtyard or a rooftop garden), and are often shared with the rest of the hospital. The structure and character of the outdoor space in mental healthcare facilities is often connected to the time period in which the institution was built; and the way that it is used presently and has been used in the past is usually linked to broader social and medical trends in psychiatric care.

This chapter begins with a historical overview of the use of outdoor space in psychiatric hospitals and units, focusing on the history of Europe and the United States. A literature review summarizes information related to the topic of outdoor space in psychiatric care, and discusses some of the disciplines that have contributed to issues of design. Although several of the healthcare facilities in the case studies care for special populations such as the developmentally handicapped (mentally retarded), children, and the aged, this chapter has not included a literature review on these specific groups. Six case studies give an in-depth review and analysis of mental healthcare facilities with exemplary outdoor spaces: Butler Hospital (Providence, RI) and The Retreat (York, England) are classic examples of hospitals built in the late eighteenth through the early nineteenth centuries with grounds designed in the pastoral English landscape style; Whitby Mental Health Centre (Whitby, Ont., Canada) is a hospital set in a landscape similar to Butler Hospital, but with a newly constructed building that features separate enclosed courtyards for each patient care unit; the Sub-Acute Treatment for Adolescent Rehabilitation Services (STARS, San Leandro, CA) is a newly constructed, specialized care institution for teenagers, where the buildings of the facility surround and enclose the primary outdoor space; and The Blackthorn Garden Project, where outpatients engage in gardening as part of their therapy. The last case study, on Homewood Health Centre (Guelph, Ont., Canada), discusses clinical empirical research that has taken place at the facility and provides important indicators about the use of outdoor space by both patients and staff.

A set of design guidelines follows the case studies. Information from the previous sections of the chapter (historical research, review of relevant literature, and research on mental healthcare facilities with exemplary outdoor spaces) are distilled into the guidelines that may be used by designers, healthcare providers, and administrators to aid in decisions for the design of their specific care facility.

HISTORY

Europe

The idea of the outdoors as restorative is not new or even modern. People's connections with and use of both "natural" and designed environments for physical, mental, and spiritual well-being has been well documented. This notion of "nature as healer" has waxed and waned over the centuries, as has the institutionalized use of the outdoors as a therapeutic component of healthcare. Less common has been the deliberate use of the outdoors for the amelioration and/or cure of mental illness. The degree to which the outdoors is utilized by psychiatric care facilities as a therapeutic tool has fluctuated, usually in connection with the broader cultural zeitgeist. As early as the fifteenth century, physicians included outdoor recreation as a distinct part of a planned therapeutic program. Again, in the mid eighteenth to the early nineteenth century, outdoor spaces were highly valued for improving the mental health of psychiatric patients, and hospitals were designed for easy access to the surrounding grounds. Windows were directed outward, gardens were planted, and farming programs were implemented in order to allow patients' contact with the natural environment around them. In the twentieth century, scientific advances in healthcare, as well as a complex interaction of sociocultural and economic forces, have led to the neglect and even denial of the outdoors as part of a therapeutic milieu. Generally, the value of the outdoors as salubrious for people with psychiatric problems has been seen as strongest when two ideologies are present: when psychiatric care is focused on the patient as a unique individual, so that the quality of the patient's total social and physical environment is viewed as important to his or her well-being; and when the natural environment is seen as something favorable for the physical and mental well-being for all people. At the present time we are in another "upswing," in which gardens and nature are once again being seen as not only beneficial, but essential for the health of people, particularly those suffering from psychiatric and other illnesses.

Though most hospital design reform did not come until centuries later, the Hospital at Zaragua, Spain, set an early example that many later designers would look to and emulate. The common "treatment" during the early 1400s in Spain and throughout Europe was to classify mental patients as prisoners, confining and often beating them. At Zaragua, however, patients followed a very different routine of eating together, then doing household chores and work in vegetable gardens, farms, and vineyards. The most violent patients were kept locked in their cells, but even they were spared the beatings and physical restraints typical elsewhere (Warner, 1995b). It took the rest of Europe (including many other parts of Spain) 300 years to come to the same conclusions that the designers and administrators at Zaragua had reached in the early fifteenth century.

The European Romantic Movement of the eighteenth century was the gestation period for much of that century's hospital reform. The therapeutic connection between medicine and the outdoors coincided with the revival of pastoralism; gardens (and nature in general) came to be thought of once more as places of bodily and spiritual restoration. Romanticism was "an all-pervasive cultural movement that sought to unite human emotions with morality and nature," (Warner, 1995b, p. 25); and much like the Renaissance of the fifteenth century, this movement had a profound impact on almost every aspect of life—including science, education, art, and medicine—in Europe at that time (*ibid.*).

Figure 6-1 This aerial photo (c. 1960) of The Retreat, York, UK, shows the buildings and extensive grounds. Encouraging clients to go outdoors has been accomplished in many different ways over the facility's 200-year history. Seen here are a farm area, bowling green, cricket pitch, and tennis courts, as well as several smaller more protected courtyards. (Photo courtesy of The Retreat Archives, York, UK.)

Two of the first asylums built specifically for mental patients, which embodied the new trends of the Romantic movement, were the Schleswig Asylum (1792–1820) in Germany, and The Retreat in York, England (1796–present). Schleswig Asylum's buildings and surrounding grounds took the form of a country hospital, with gardens planted in the open English landscape style. The Retreat was a small institution directed by William Tuke and his son, Samuel. Built of brick "on a hill with a fine view in all directions," the hospital provided several areas where patients could venture outdoors, or could see outside from indoors. In front of the hospital were decorative and vegetable gardens, enclosed by a high fence. At the back were exercise grounds enclosed by "the requisite 8-foot walls," designed to seem less imposing by being built on a slope. Inside of the building, all windows were free of bars, allowing patients unobstructed views outward (Thompson, 1975, pp. 72–73). In 1813, Samuel Tuke's *Description of The Retreat* was published, and became an influential model for hospital designers and practitioners in England and many countries.

In France in 1785, a book was published of "instructions on the manner of governing the insane," among which were the stipulation for pure air and water; "promenades of trees to give [the patients] some sense of freedom yet protect them from the sun;" and several groups of buildings only one story high, with each group built around its own square court, and with an arcade on all four sides (Thompson, 1975, p. 54). In the following year, Louis XVI ordered the reconstruction of the Salpêtrière, one of the largest insane asylums in France. Prior to reconstruction, the Salpêtrière was a living nightmare of poor physical design and inhumane treatment of its patients. The new design for the Salpêtrière followed many of the above-mentioned recommendations, including several separate outdoor areas planted with allées of trees, each meant for a particular mental affliction: "The melancholy were to console themselves among the trees of the central garden, while the senile could walk around the periphery under the lindens" (Thompson, 1975, p. 56). Before its reconstruction in 1822, the Bicêtre in Paris kept most patients in locked cells. Only the paying patients had a bed to themselves, heat in the room, and access to an outdoor courtyard where they were allowed to stroll. In the newly built Bicêtre, the loges, or cells, faced a court "overlooking quincunx and a flower garden," and an open courtyard encircling the loges was known as the "fairweather promenade" (Thompson, 1975, p. 56). Innovations in both the physical environment and in treatment were copied everywhere throughout Europe.

Philippe Pinel (1745–1826) is known as the first psychiatrist in France, and is especially remembered for his instrumental role in converting psychiatric care institutions from prisons to hospitals. Having directed at the Bicêtre and the Salpêtrière, Pinel was the first to refer to the type of patient care used at The Retreat at York as "moral treatment." The goal of the moral treatment was to resocialize the patient by creating a social and physical environment that would allow his or her own resources for reasonable behavior to reassert themselves. Pinel built upon the writing of Samuel Tuke and proposed a threefold reform: first, the abolition of all forms of physical punishment and physical restraints; second, careful observation and classification of patients according to their symptoms; and third, a regular routine in a restful setting that resembled activities of the outside world. Parts of these routines included farming and gardening, as well as daily walks outside. Pinel's book, *A Treatise on Insanity* (1800), both reflected and propelled improvements in the treatment and physical environments of the mentally ill (Warner, 1995b).

After the passage of the Lunacy Act (1845) requiring the countries of England, Wales and Ireland to provide asylums, John Conolly wrote *The Construction and Government of Lunatic Asylums* (1847), in which he called for a change in the prevailing asylum design and management practices. Part of the cure Conolly recommended included the outdoor environment: "The external aspect of an asylum should be more cheerful than imposing, more resembling a well-built hospital than a

So well organized is the program for patients that nearly every hour of every day is filled with occupational and recreational activities. These include classes in hobbies and avocatons, such as modeling and industrial work, literary and current events groups, parties and dances, concerts and entertainments, bowling, movies, cooking and serving, gardening and forestry work, as well as nature walks during which the wealth of woodland and shore surrounding the Hospital unfolds before the studious observer. A glance at a typical week's program in the summer shows group hikes and lawn sports, sun bathing, baseball games, horseshoe pitching, tennis, croquet, a lawn party, picnic supper on the riverbank, ward games, a swimming party ... ."

BUTLER HOSPITAL INFORMATIONAL BROCHURE, 1944, QUOTED IN RUGGLES place of seclusion or imprisonment. It should be surrounded by gardens, or a farm," (Conolly, 1847, p. 14, as quoted in Taylor, 1991, p. 135). In 1870, the British Commissioners in Lunacy, influenced by Pinel, issued a pamphlet advising that there should be at least one acre for every four patients, "to allow agricultural employment, exercise and recreation—such land to be in the sun and to the south of the asylum," (Taylor, 1991, p. 148). During this period, many newly built asylums provided open space for exercise and recreation, as well as for gardening and agriculture. Examples of these hospitals are numerous and they share many of the same characteristics. The City and County Asylum at Hereford (1871), for example, contained extensive south-facing airing grounds, which looked much like formal English gardens. In addition, smaller yards and four separate exercise grounds offered further opportunity for outdoor recreation. Even asylums for the criminally insane had airing courts. If the hospitals for the poor and the criminally insane were a great improvement, those for the rich were even more grandiose: The Manchester Royal Lunatic Asylum in Cheadle (1848-1849) was set on a 52-acre site replete with pleasure and airing grounds, a bowling green, and a kitchen garden; the avenue and grounds contained 18,000 trees and shrubs. At the Holloway Sanitorium in Virginia Water, in addition to a Winter Garden, "the grounds were laid out with a cricket ground and pavilion, bowling green, tennis courts, and landscaped walks around entire south and east areas of the site," (Taylor, 1991, p. 159).

Figure 6-2 Oakwood, in Maidstone, Kent, UK, a typical nineteenth century mental hospital set in spacious grounds, was closed in 1990. (Photo by Clare Cooper Marcus.)

The United States

Seventeenth-century colonial America was far behind Europe in its treatment of the mentally ill. "Demoniacal possession was the common explanation of most forms of mental disorder, and the scourge, rack, the stake and the gallows were the common methods of treatment," (Deutsch, 1949, pp. 24–25). The mentally ill were usually kept in workhouses or prisons. In New York in 1736, the Poor-House, Work House, and House of Correction of New York City kept the poor, the criminal, and the mentally ill all under one roof. The "mildly insane" worked along with other inmates, and the "unruly" were imprisoned in the cellar, which was built for them alone *(ibid.)*.

In general, only the very wealthy mentally ill were able to obtain adequate treatment. One of the first agitators for better state hospitals for the insane poor in the United States was Dorothea Linde Dix (1802–1887). She toured entire states, calling attention to the treatment of the mentally ill and making recommendations to the state legislature. She has been given credit for starting state hospitals in over 30 different states, including Butler Hospital (Case study, pp. 251–260) (Kiesler and Sibulkin, 1987). Another organizer, Horace Mann, worked with Dix to turn the public's attention to the philosophy of public welfare. As the writings and actions of people such as Dix and Mann gained popular acceptance and support, states rapidly began to build mental hospitals.

The influential psychiatrist Thomas Kirkbride (1809–1883) dictated much of the hospital design in the early and mid 1800s, and the designs reflected those European hospitals like The Retreat at York and the Bicêtre. Kirkbride, who acquired many of his ideas from his European predecessors such as the Tukes and Pinel, was the first leading advocate of "moral treatment" in the United States. The hospitals built during this time period were relatively small, usually situated on pieces of land slightly removed from the city, on which farming and many other outdoor activities took place as part of the daily routine. In Philadelphia in 1851, Kirkbride was one member at a meeting for the Association of Medical Superintendents of American Institutions for the Insane. At this pivotal meeting, several of the "26 Propositions" drafted related to the function of the outdoor environment:

- "I. Every hospital for the insane should be in the country, not within less than two miles of a large town, and easily accessible at all seasons."
- "II. No hospital for the insane, however limited its capacity, should have less than fifty acres of land devoted to gar-

dens and pleasure-grounds for its patients. At least one hundred acres should be possessed by every State hospital…"

- "IV. No hospital for the insane should be built without the plan having been first submitted to some physician or physicians who have had charge of a similar establishment, or are practically acquainted with all the details of their arrangements, and received his or their full approbation."
- "X. No class of room should ever be constructed without some kind of window in each communicating directly with the external atmosphere."
- "XVI. The wings should be so arranged that, if rooms are placed on both sides of a corridor, the corridors should be furnished at both ends with movable glazed sashes, for the free admission of both light and air."
- "XXV. The wards for the most excited class should be constructed with rooms on but one side of a corridor, not less than ten feet wide, the external windows of which should be large, and have pleasant views from them."
- "XXVI. Wherever practicable, the pleasure grounds of a hospital for the insane should be surrounded by substantial wall, so placed as not to be unpleasantly visible from the building."

(Goshen, 1967, pp. 518–522)

Many of the psychiatric hospitals built during the moral treatment heyday of the early and mid 1800s had grounds designed in the English landscape style, with rolling hills, groves of trees, paths throughout, and formal, more intimate gardens closer to the buildings. This style was a copy of the grounds at hospitals like The Retreat at York, but was also a reflection of a larger trend in the United States toward the parklike English landscape. It was during this same period that Frederick Law Olmsted was advocating public open spaces set within or near city limits. Olmsted believed that "pastoral park scenery, with a gracefully undulating greensward and scattered groves of trees, was a powerful antidote to the stress and artificiality of urban life." He felt strongly that such scenery promoted a sense of tranquility (Tishler, 1989, p. 41).

Frederick Law Olmsted and both of his sons designed hundreds of grounds for hospitals and asylums throughout the United States (Beveridge and Hoffman, 1987). Other landscape architects, including H. W. S. Cleveland, were also employed by

Figure 6-3 Butler Hospital, Providence, RI, was opened in 1847 and is still in operation. Its extensive grounds, based on an "English pastoral" model, are enjoyed today by in- and outpatients, and by staff (as here) walking on their lunch hour.

mental hospitals during this time in the design and construction of the grounds. In 1871, Cleveland developed a plan for the Iowa Hospital for the Insane, in which he involved patients in the therapeutic planting of native trees and shrubs on the asylum grounds (Tishler, 1989).

Ironically, the American reform movement begun in the 1830s by Dix was so successful that it mushroomed into a system of hospitals that no longer fulfilled the goals the original movement set out to accomplish. As individual states took over the costs of treating the mentally ill, local agencies were eager to save on expenses by emptying their jails and almshouses and shipping the insane to the newly built asylums. With the increasing demand for mental hospital beds, buildings became larger and more hastily constructed; by 1880, the average mental hospital housed over 500 patients and many had over 1,000 patients. Furthermore, the state hospital was a bureaucratic institution run as an extension of the government, which "depersonalized and regulated the environment for patients, interfering with the basic premises of moral treatment," (Kiesler and Sibulkin, 1987, p. 31). As hospitals became larger and more heavily populated, patients' access to the outdoors became increasingly restricted. Individual attention was hardly foremost in treatment, and patients were lucky if they even had access to a window to see outdoors, much less were accompanied outdoors for walks or other recreation. Caretakers reverted to the use of physical restraints for many patients, and "chemical restraints"—drugs such as opium, morphine, and chloral hydrate—also began to be used more heavily, even as early as the nineteenth century (Kiesler and Sibulkin, 1987).

Problems with the rapid growth in patient population led to the adoption of "cottage" and "colony" plans in the late 1800s. In 1885, the State Asylum at Kalamazoo, MI, became the first colony system in the United States. The Asylum added 250 acres to its already existing property and built smaller buildings to house the various types of patients, classified and segregated according to their mental illness. Patients farmed the land, and had easier access to the grounds due to the smaller size of the individual buildings. This type of "farm colony" became a popular alternative to the monolithic institutions that had sprung up so rapidly earlier in the century (Deutsch, 1949). For a time, this design plan alleviated some of the problems of overcrowding and lack of access to the outdoors.

The increase in use of occupational therapy, including horticultural therapy, in both mental and general care hospitals was a positive outcome of the aftermath of World War I. As discussed above, occupational therapy in the form of work programs, including farming and gardening, had long been part of the moral treatment in mental hospitals in Europe and the United States. In 1911, Dr. Herbert Hall published his observations of a workshop he had set up in Gloucester, MA, in which mental patients worked side by side with craftsmen. He concluded that the work had strong therapeutic effects on the patients, and his example was soon followed by other doctors and nurses throughout the country. The flood of disabled veterans returning from the war gave occupational and physical therapy movements the push toward validity that they needed to become viable additions to hospital rehabilitation programs. In Europe, many hospitals added gardening to their occupational therapy programs, with the intent that veterans would "turn their thoughts from their experiences of destruction toward acts of creation" (Warner, 1995b, p. 59). The practice of horticultural therapy caught on quickly in the United States, and by 1920 Red Cross volunteers were setting up truck gardens at veterans hospitals, and the Federal Board for Vocational Education was offering disabled soldiers courses in garden work (*ibid.*).

It was in private mental hospitals, however, that the relationship of occupational, physical, and horticultural therapy programs began to be established as part of the patients' therapeutic regimen in the form of "milieu therapy." Psychiatrists like Dr. Harry Stack Sullivan (1892–1949) and Karl Menninger (1895–1990), combining past research on moral treatment with newer Freudian concepts, began to reexamine the physical and

Figure 6-4 Whitby Hospital (Whitby, Ont., Canada), which opened in 1919, consisted of residential cottages, a significant change from earlier prisonlike asylums. Inpatients worked in over 400 acres of farm land, vegetable gardens, and orchards until the practice was stopped in the 1950s. A new facility— Whitby Mental Health Centre— replaced the cottages in 1996 (see Figure 6-11). (Photo by Clare Cooper Marcus.)

social hospital environment as a critical component in patient care and treatment. By World War II, milieu therapy—the process of paying attention to all aspects of the patient's hospital environment, "and the practice of having all a particular patient's staff consult together as a team"—had become a well-respected form of treatment to which many mental hospitals were turning (Warner, 1995b, p. 60). It is ironic that at a time when such exciting innovations as occupational and horticultural therapy programs and milieu therapy were gaining acceptance within some already existing hospitals, newly designed and built hospitals were turning farther away from an architecture that allowed for this type of patient care.

In 1948, Albert Deutsch's *Shame of the States* was published, in which he exposed deplorable, inhumane conditions in mental hospitals all over the country:

> The writer heard state hospital doctors frankly admit that the animals of nearby piggeries were better fed, housed and treated than many of the patients in their wards. He saw hundreds of people shackled, strapped, straight-jacketed and bound to their beds; he saw mental patients ... crawl into beds jammed close together, in dormitories filled to twice or three times their normal capacity (Kiesler and Sibulkin, 1987, p. 36).

Deutsch's exposé spurred public outcry, and led to the formation of the National Institute of Mental Health in 1949. In 1955, the Mental Health Act passed, which led to the Joint Commission on Mental Illness and Health. The Commission pressed for an improvement of care, suggesting decreasing mental hospital size. One solution was decentralization, in which community mental health centers would serve the mentally ill who were transitioning from the hospital back into society. The Commission urged that mental hospitals be used for acute care, and that community organizations be used to transition and monitor patients after discharge. The recommendation argued for more active rehabilitative treatment (as opposed to the custodial care of the past 100 years), deinstitutionalization, and aftercare whenever possible. This transition to decentralization, now viewed by many as the norm, was not easy.

> The dominant cultural trends in the United States during the fifties, sixties, and seventies did not support these reformers' goals. Americans remained frightened by the mentally ill. Attempts to locate half-way houses and clinics in residential neighborhoods met ferocious opposition. Citizens associated such places with drugs, crime, violence, and loss of the sales value of their homes (Warner, 1991, p. 49).

Community centers, halfway houses, and other small-scale mental healthcare facilities were never built in adequate numbers, and thus the financial strain on older and larger psychiatric hospitals was great. These institutions, financially strapped and often architecturally ill-equipped to deal with new advances in psychiatric care, certainly would not focus on "extra" amenities such as horticultural therapy and roof or courtyard gardens.

In addition to the restructuring of psychiatric care, changes in American medicine also strongly influenced the way outdoor space came to be excluded from patient care. In the 1920s, important pathogenic and bacteriological discoveries led to an increased focus on science by American medicine. Moral treatment (which was environmentally and behaviorally based) and the importance of the patient's physical environment—both in and out of doors—receded into the background. In 1961, Dr. John Gray became one of the leading American psychiatric spokesmen, claiming that "mental patients were really physically ill with a brain disease" (Kiesler and Sibulkin, 1987, p. 32). This belief that mental illness was a physical disease led to the conclusion that it could be cured with medicine and science. Occupational therapy was seen as ineffective; psychiatrists concluded that, for those patients who were in hospitals waiting for their cure, all that could be done for them in the interim was to provide custodial care. Psychiatric hospitals became "holding cells" more than places for a wide variety of both physical and occupational therapies. As this position (the antithesis to the moral treatment) became the accepted point of view, the importance of experiential therapy and patients' relationship to their environment diminished significantly.

Another important change in the care of mental patients in the past few decades has been the inclusion of psychiatric units in general hospitals. The first United States psychiatric unit in a general hospital was established in 1924 at the Henry Ford Hospital in Detroit, MI. The idea of units in general hospitals was slow to catch on, but once it did, it spread rapidly across the country: "The widespread acceptance of this idea has now made it literally true that any general hospital design without a psychiatric unit will be obsolete before it is even finished" (Lebensohn, 1965, p. 3). Though most psychiatric units are generally designed to house incoming patients until they are assessed and sent to more appropriate locations, they help take the burden off of hospitals designed for more intensive, long-term care.

Despite moves toward hospital decentralization and the inclusion of units within general hospitals, mental hospitals have continued to be built as large structures, often removed

"After the 1906 earthquake, psychiatric patients in the Napa State Hospital had to be housed in tents because of heavy damage to the building. Physicians and administrators at the hospital were astounded to find immeasurable improvement in their patients' health under these somewhat unusual circumstances. When the building was repaired and the patients were moved back, their behavior deteriorated; they reverted to their more disturbed and bizarre behavior."

ALBERT MEHRABIAN

from the environments around them. Similar to other trends in healthcare since the 1950s, increasing emphasis has been placed on technology and medication to remedy mental illness. Hospitals built within large metropolitan areas have been high-rises with little or no access to the outdoors, including windows that are often sealed to keep hot and cool air in and smog and pollution out.

Only in the past thirty years has this trend slowly begun to reverse. The late 1950s and early 1960s saw the beginning of a new academic discipline, environmental psychology, that was closely linked with the concept of milieu therapy. Early research in this field was mostly limited to small, measurable factors such as color, quality of light, sound, and room size, and was almost solely restricted to the indoor environment. Nevertheless, the groundwork laid during this era has been critical in fostering interest in outdoor spaces as part of the therapeutic environment. Environmental psychology was one of the first interdisciplinary approaches to hospital design in which teams of psychiatrists, psychologists, designers, sociologists, and other researchers and administrators collaborated with designers to create institutions that would better serve their patients. Viewed as a new, revolutionary idea three decades ago, environmental psychology is beginning to be accepted by most healthcare professionals.

Many newer psychiatric hospitals and units still utilize outdoor space only if there is money left over, or if a donor specifies such a project. Most hospitals do not pay the same attention to integrating outdoor spaces into their site design as they pay to the design of patient units, common rooms, cafeterias, and other interior spaces. This ignorance of the potential of the outdoor spaces is partially due to the dearth of research and scientific evidence "proving" that such design would positively affect both patient and staff quality of life; it is also due to the scattered nature of the information that does exist.

LITERATURE REVIEW

Literature on the use of outdoor space as a therapeutic tool in psychiatric care is scarce. Within the disciplines of environmental psychology and environmental design, researchers have touched on aspects of this topic, but few have directly addressed the issue of the link between outdoor environments and patients struggling with mental illness. This review focuses on literature published after 1950, following the genesis of envi-

Figure 6-5 Although psychiatric wards in general hospitals now provide much in- and outpatient care, some large psychiatric hospitals with extensive grounds are still in operation. (Napa State Hospital, CA, photo by Clare Cooper Marcus.)

ronmental psychology. Before this time, little had been written or documented on the connections between physical space (indoors or out) and psychiatric health. The literature reviewed in this section comes from three different types of publications: those related to the academic disciplines of environmental psychology and clinical psychology (journals such as *Environment and Behavior, Journal of Environmental Psychology, Journal of Clinical Psychology, Journal of Consulting and Clinical Psychology*); academic and design-focused branches of the discipline of environmental design (*Architecture, Architectural Record, Landscape Architecture, Progressive Architecture*); and practical healthcare-oriented literature *(Health Facilities Management, Hospitals, Hospital and Community Psychiatry, Modern Hospitals)*.

Within the discipline of environmental psychology, the focus has been almost exclusively on hospital interiors. Researchers have documented the effects of color, sound, light, furniture arrangement, and other architectural variables on psychiatric patients (DeVries, 1968; Drew, 1971; Griffin et al., 1969; Holohan and Saegert, 1973; Kasmar et al., 1968; Moos et al., 1969; Rosenblatt, 1970; Zeller, 1969). In the Ohio State Hospital's *Bibliography of Materials Useful for Change in Mental Hospitals* (1973), among thousands of articles listed, only two alluded to the study of the outdoors in their title. To date, almost all of the articles and books offering specific physical design recommendations for psychiatric care facilities have failed to include any mention of the outdoors in their discussion of the environmental milieu (Baker et al., 1959; Bayes and Francklin, 1971; Canter and Canter, 1979; Cox and Groves, 1981; Falick, 1981; Gulak, 1991; Izumi, 1965, 1968; Osmond, 1966; Osmond and Izumi, 1971; Sivadon, 1970; Whitehead et al., 1976; "Architecture for Psychiatric Treatment," 1991; Bopp et al., 1996). While there has been a small sample of literature that at least cursorily mentions outdoor space in the design of mental hospitals (Bailey, 1966; Davis et al., 1979; Good et al., 1965; Haun, 1961; Miller, 1981; Selland, 1988; Smith, 1958), it has been only in the past decade that researchers have begun to study specific correlations between the use of the outdoors and mental health at psychiatric institutions (Barnhart, 1996; Langer, 1987, Larsen, 1992; Perkins, 1998).

Within the fields of environmental psychology and environmental design, there have been numerous academic studies by researchers documenting the salutary psychological effects of nature and the outdoors on human beings, as well as studies of people's preferences for specific outdoor environments (Barnes, 1994; Francis and Hester, 1990; Francis and Cooper Marcus,

1991; Hartig et al., 1991; Kaplan, 1973; Kaplan and Kaplan, 1989; Relf, 1992; Ulrich, 1979, 1981; Ulrich, 1986). However, the vast majority of this literature focuses only on people from "the general population," not on those with mental or even physical disabilities. Researchers such as Roger Ulrich have documented the physiological effects of the outdoor environment on people with physical health problems (Ulrich 1984, 1986; Ulrich et al., 1991). In addition, two influential books have been published that speak to the need for outdoor spaces in healthcare facilities, and that offer specific guidelines for designers (Carpman et al., 1986; Cooper Marcus and Barnes, 1995). However, neither of these books specifically discusses psychiatric hospitals or units and the concomitant design issues that might need to be addressed.

Most of the literature that at least mentions the outdoor space(s) of psychiatric hospitals is from either design-related (mostly architectural) publications, or from healthcare publications. Typical of architectural reviews of psychiatric hospitals has been the complete disregard for anything outside of the building (including views out of the windows). A few design-related articles have appeared that either do focus on the hospital's outdoor environment, or discuss the outdoor spaces in at least as much detail as the indoors ("The Butler Hospital Extension," 1979; "Designing for Patients...," 1995; Hammerslough, 1997; Kelius, 1993; Kuntz, 1979; McLaughlin and Boerger, 1981; "Menninger Foundation...," 1981; Miller, 1981; Noakes, 1994; Radley, 1997; Reed, 1995; "California Licenses New...," 1984; "*Garden Design's* Golden...," 1995/1996; "Village Not...," 1993; Wiser, 1993; "135-Year Old Hospital ...," 1979).

Two of the earliest articles on outdoor space in psychiatric hospitals were spurred by the redesign of Butler Hospital, which involved the addition of a new patient wing. In 1979, *Architectural Record* and *Hospitals* both reviewed the new wing, lauding the design for its incorporation of the hospital's beautiful grounds. This wing included an atrium with lush plantings, a cafeteria with windows along the length of one wall providing views out to the grounds, as well as windows in every room and unit with views outward. In *Architectural Record*, ("The Butler Hospital Extension," 1979), much of the article focused on the architects' efforts to "bring the outdoors in," and the positive review had much to do with the architects' perceived success. Furthermore, most of the article's graphics highlighted aspects of the design that attempted to incorporate views and access outdoors into the patients' indoor experience. In the *Hospitals* article as well ("135-Year Old Hospital...," 1979), the author praised the architects' design, particularly their efforts to provide better access to the hospitals' beautiful and extensive grounds.

It should be noted that discussing the outdoor space of a mental hospital does not automatically mean that the outdoor space (or the hospital itself) is successful as a therapeutic environment. The most dramatic example is Architectural Review's look at Richard Meier and Associates' new Bronx Developmental Center ("Bronx Developmental Center," 1978). This building, which had been slated to be a center for the treatment of developmentally handicapped people, was never used as such; parents and other caregivers were so outraged at the lack of attention to the needs of the users that they protested and refused to move in. The author of the *Architectural Review* article did not see the insensitivity of the design. The finishes of "fine aluminum skin...[and] gleaming silver wings" were lauded as beautiful and state-of- the-art. The outdoor courtyards were also praised:

> Between gleaming silver wings there is an elaborate garden full of concrete conceits, like this lectern and Greek theater ... the garden is crossed by bridges that link the two sides of the centre's life—the treatment blocks and the residential blocks. High gloss, smooth finishes and a rational plan are not the elements always associated with domestic comfort. It will be difficult for the patients to feel that they are anywhere but inside an institution. But at least they can be comforted by the knowledge that they inhabit an extremely refined example of architectural design," ("Bronx Developmental Center," 1978, p. 98).

Two other articles reviewing architectural designs that failed to provide healthy positive outdoor spaces were published in 1993 and 1994. Tony Noakes' discussion of three new buildings in Birmingham, AL, includes the treatment of the outdoor space (Noakes, 1994). He commends the designers' attempts to include outdoor spaces that would be meaningful and therapeutic, and bemoans the design/build decision, which led to skimping on the detailing of the landscaping, making the outdoor spaces much less inviting. Noakes points out that the details of landscaping are too often left for last, which then inevitably inhibits the facility's function as a cohesive whole. In "Village, Not: The Unfulfilled Promise of Yale's Psychiatric Institute" (1993), the author points out the many flaws in the new design that make the facility less therapeutic than originally intended. Several of the failures have to do with the designers' treatment of the outdoor spaces, such as the sparsely planted courtyard, the lack of wheelchair accessibility to the gym's mezzanine, and the lack of private outdoor spaces for the staff: "The courtyard is a popular place for relaxation—and a gymnastic challenge to those who have scaled that fence. The courtyard's nooks and crannies were criticized because they make it difficult for staff members to monitor patients" ("Village, Not..." 1994, p. 101).

In recent years, the idea of nature as therapy has been recognized, and even embraced, by people outside of the specialized fields of horticultural therapy and environmental design. Designs for "healing gardens" have been publicized in landscape architecture, popular garden design, and even more mainstream magazines and newspapers (Dannemaier, 1995; Goode, 1995; *Garden Design's* Golden..." 1995/1996; Hammerslough, 1997; Radley, 1997; Raver, 1994; Reed, 1995; Warner, 1995; "Winning Big," 1997; "Sanctuary," 1996). Many hospital administrators are currently requesting designs for such healing gardens for their roofs, courtyards, and other outdoor spaces. It is the author's hope that this groundswell will encourage more serious academic research focusing on the links between psychiatric healthcare and outdoor space in care facilities. Until then, designers must make inferences from related literature, history, and perhaps most importantly, from present-day examples that integrate interaction with the outdoors as part of the therapeutic milieu.

CASE STUDIES

Butler Hospital, Providence, Rhode Island

Description of the Facility and Its Setting
Butler Hospital is a private, for-profit mental healthcare center that serves clients of a wide range of racial, ethnic, and socioeconomic backgrounds from Rhode Island, Massachusetts, and Connecticut. The hospital is located on the scenic East Side of Providence, ten minutes from downtown. The 110-acre campus runs from an affluent residential neighborhood on the west end of the property to the banks of the Seekonk River to the east. The grounds are still characterized by the English or "parklike" landscape in which they were originally designed, with rolling lawns and groves of trees interconnected by streets and pathways leading to the various outlying buildings. Natural woodlands border much of the grounds. Many of the original buildings still stand on the campus, some dating back to the mid and late 1800s. As part of a major renovation and

"It is the wish of the Trustees to make the grounds in their wooded portions a typical example of a New England forest and many native trees and flowers that had disappeared are being returned to their native settings. Probably there is no patient who has ever been at Butler Hospital who does not feel that the grounds have contributed in large part toward peace of mind and ultimate recovery."

BUTLER HOSPITAL: THE STORY...

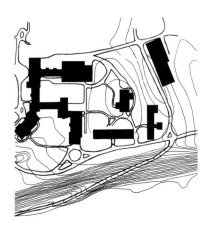

Figure 6-6 Original 1912 site plan of buildings, road, and topography at Butler Hospital, Providence, RI. (Courtesy of National Park Service, Frederick Law Olmsted National Historic Site.)

expansion project in 1978, two of the original buildings were connected to a new wing that houses the inpatient program and the cafeteria. The atrium connecting these buildings is furnished with indoor plants, benches for sitting, and a small fountain. Almost all of the rooms, in the newer wing as well as in the older buildings, have windows that look out onto the grounds. The staff/visitor and the patient cafeterias both face outward through a series of windows with a view of the lawn and woods.

Butler Hospital consists of four specific comprehensive programs, all of which take place within its campus: the Outpatient Specialty Program, Partial Hospital Program (similar to a day hospital), the Inpatient Specialty Program, and the Alcohol and Drug Treatment Services. There are seven separate inpatient units to care for patients' specific needs; these are the Senior and Neuropsychiatry Program, the Developmental Disabilities Program, the Children's Program, the Adolescent Program, the Alcohol and Drug Program, Mood and Psychotic Disorders, and the Intensive Treatment Unit.

History

Butler Hospital was not only the first hospital in Rhode Island for mental healthcare, but the first hospital of any kind in the state. When a tract of farmland for construction of the hospital was purchased in 1844, the design of both the buildings and the land surrounding the facility was seen as an essential component of the restorative treatment of the hospital's patients. The hospital trustees enlisted the consulting services of architect-psychiatrist Dr. Luther V. Bell for the design of the hospital, and he visited several countries to study the most up-to-date examples of mental institutions. Plans for the new hospital called for a spacious building for 130 patients, "containing wide, bright, high-storied galleries with rooms on one side faced by windows on the other" (Ross, 1972, pp. 9–10). This building type was an improvement over the traditional low, narrow, prisonlike galleries flanked by poorly lighted sleeping rooms. One psychiatrist wrote that instead of looking out onto doors punctuated by white walls, "poorly calculated to relieve the tension of confinement, or divert the thoughts to healthier channels," the patients would gaze out on the surrounding countryside: "In every direction the eye rests on dense groves which give to the landscape an air of retirement and repose exceedingly appropriate to the character of the establishment" (Ross, 1972, pp. 9–10). On December 1, 1847, Butler Hospital opened its doors to receive its first patients.

Although the farm was in poor condition when bought by the trustees, it was still used as a vehicle for occupational therapy; patients grew fruits and vegetables and raised dairy cattle for the production of milk, not only for the hospital, but also for sale in the greater Providence area. In the early years, especially, monetary rewards from the farm were low; nevertheless the farm provided food and milk for the patients and served as an outlet of work that contributed to the patients' well-being. In 1848 the trustees reported:

> But even if [the farm] hardly paid its way, it is a thing of some value certainly, that, during the season, this large household receives all its vegetables fresh from the ground and milk at all times of the best quality and besides, furnishes employment to the patients which, in promoting the bodily and mental health, is of incalculable value (Roelker, 1944, p.12).

In 1859, "The Duncan Improvement Fund" was established for the purpose of improving the grounds of the hospital. The trustees hired the landscape architect H. W. S. Cleveland to examine and design the grounds. In the Trustees Report of 1868, Chairman Amos D. Smith stressed that "to dress the garden, and to keep it," was of great importance. A greenhouse was donated in 1879, and in 1881 a stable was built on the grounds of the hospital, from which "fine carriages set out with matched teams to take the patients for drives about the grounds and surrounding countryside," (Butler Hospital: The Story ..., 194-, pp. 8–9). In 1901, the original greenhouse was replaced by a larger structure, which contained a wide variety of plants. One hospital doctor wrote of the new greenhouse:

> Roses and carnations have grown in this new conservatory in such luxuriant profusion that patients have been attracted to it during the year as to a delightful resort. *Indeed it would be difficult to overestimate the value of this addition to our resources of treatment, so large a factor has it been in cheering the sick and promoting welfare* [italics author's] (Roelker, 1944, p. 25).

During the years 1895-1912, John Charles and Frederick Law Olmsted, Jr. were employed as landscape architects for the hospital, providing topographic and planting plans for both old and new portions of the hospital grounds (Beveridge and Hoffman, 1987, p. 64). Today these landscape and recreational features may seem more like luxuries enjoyed at a spa or resort rather than at a mental institution. However, one must keep in mind that since drug- and psychotherapy were still in the early devel-

Figure 6-7 View of the enclosed patient courtyard at Butler Hospital with gazebo and a covered walk from the inpatient units. Buckets of tomato plants, grown by the patients, are part of the occupational therapy program.

opment stages, physical and recreational therapy were used as ways to resocialize patients. However, even at that time, the degree of emphasis on recreation at Butler was more than people were accustomed to. Consider, for example, this quote from an informational brochure written by the hospital's superintendent in 1944:

> To the visitor this all may seem a far cry from the ordinarily accepted methods of treatment. But when one realizes how much, in these days of rapid transportation and the development of machinery for every task, we tend to neglect the natural interests and beauties all about us and to concentrate on events and activities that cause tension and at times almost confusion, it can easily be understood why a quiet walk in the country with the appreciation and knowledge of natural beauties can help one to relax, turn one's thought outward, and produce a calm and an interest that is most health-giving. With this new appreciation and understanding of natural beauties and their development and utilization, many patients will return to their homes with an added vocational resource which will help them to keep well with an improved pattern of life (Ruggles, 1944, pp. 8, 9, 12).

Description of Outdoor Space

Today the grounds of Butler Hospital retain much of their original pastoral quality. The quarter-mile drive from the entry at Blackstone Boulevard to the main building is surrounded on both sides by over 100 acres of rolling lawns, groves of conifers, and the original forest beyond. Historic buildings, New England stone walls, and a wide variety of specimen trees and shrubs punctuate the vast expanse of green. Squirrels, rabbits, and birds are a common sight, as the landscape provides an excellent habitat for small wildlife species. By the time one has driven the short road from the entrance to the main building, one feels much farther from downtown than the actual ten-minute drive.

Most of the grounds (including the main entrance) are not fenced in or guarded; the sense of separation is obtained through the distance from the neighbors and the thick screen of natural woodlands. Recently, however, two new outdoor areas have been enclosed with a high cast-iron fence, allowing outdoor access to patients who might not otherwise be able to go out unsupervised. One of these spaces, accessible through the atrium or through the inpatient treatment units, is approximately 30 × 100 feet and features a gazebo, three park benches, and several movable plastic chairs. The other enclosed outdoor space, adjacent but separate to the one above, is accessible through the Children's Program unit, and is primarily a playground with a variety of play equipment.

A paved, handicapped-accessible pathway loops around the entire main building, and is furnished intermittently with park benches and plastic chairs where one can stop and rest. Within this loop and closest to the hospital are several areas where patients, visitors, and staff go to be outside. A covered (roofed) smoking porch and a small lawn area with picnic tables and a volleyball net are located close to the building. In good weather, this is one of the most heavily used outdoor areas, by smokers and nonsmokers, staff, patients, and visitors—on their break, visiting with friends or family, or waiting for group therapy. Even in the colder months, the roofed smoking porch is often still crowded with people. The staff cafeteria opens out onto a small paved eating area with two or three picnic tables, where staff members and visitors often sit, particularly during lunch hours. Several of the outpatient exits open onto the grounds, where small groups of people sit on the lawn, steps, or movable plastic chairs. At the main entrance to the hospital, the steps leading to the front door are a popular place for visitors, patients, and staff to sit on a break or while waiting outside for a ride.

Use of the Grounds

PATIENTS

Almost all inpatients use the hospital grounds, for different activities and under varying levels of supervision. Whenever possible, the physical therapy program involves outdoor activities such as volleyball, badminton, Frisbee, bocce ball, strolling, and "powerwalking." Clients from the Intensive Treatment Unit, who are often lacking in concentration and slowed down or disoriented due to medication, go outside for walks more than other groups. Going outside, even just for a walk or to sit on a bench, may be particularly important for these patients, since many of the other more rigorous activities are difficult or impossible. Geriatric and neuropsychiatric patients, though less mobile, enjoy being outside, sitting on benches and observing the world around them. Because their needs in terms of mobility and safety are so different from the other patients at Butler, the hospital is planning to install a separate courtyard directly accessible from the geriatric unit.

Interaction with the outdoors is particularly important for children as inpatients. Since their length of stay is generally longer, more varied stimulation is needed than with adults. As often as possible, staff takes groups of children outside, either to the playground for games and sports, or for nature walks on the grounds. For many children, Butler Hospital may be their first experience with nature; it can be very exciting, imparting a

Figure 6-8 Plastic chairs, kept outside in warm weather at Butler Hospital, allow patients, visitors, and staff to arrange seating for personal reflection or for small conversation groups.

sense of discovery and wonder. Patients collect objects such as acorns, robins' eggs, and leaves during their walks, and they often bring these curios back to the unit. The secluded pastoral setting, with its wide open green spaces bordered by tall trees, creates a space that feels open and free, yet at the same time sheltered and safe; here children may begin to explore and rebuild their lives. On a more practical level, running around outside helps children "blow off steam," which in turn helps them focus on "paper-and-pencil" activities once they are back inside the unit.

Unfortunately, aside from the loop around the hospital and the secondary roads through the campus, there are few paths for people to use. Paths through the woodlands surrounding the property do exist, but they are underutilized because the current small staff-to-patient ratio and the distance from the hospital make it easy for patients to run away. Because staff are discouraged from taking patients along the woodland trails, the loop around the hospital is often the only option, especially for patients who are less mobile (and who may need this type of exercise the most). In general, there is a strict hospital protocol regarding "grounds." For example, staff who take individual or groups of patients for walks outside must have walkie-talkies connected to hospital security, and depending on the patients' level of observation, there must be a certain staff-to-patient ratio on any such outings. At the present time, most patients cannot go outside without one or two attending staff members. This puts the burden of taking patients outside on an already limited staff of nurses and social workers.

Shorter patient stays, a current trend in most U.S. psychiatric care institutions, has had a significant impact on how outdoor space is used. The nursing and social work staff have long employed the incentive of going outdoors as a way to reward positive patient behavior. When patients' stays were longer, getting to go outside—first with a nurse or therapist, and then on one's own—was a major behavioral incentive, as well as a large motivating factor in a patient's role in her or his own recovery. Now that stays are so much shorter (some even just one to two nights), there is less of an opportunity for patients to "work up to" the grounds privilege. An interesting side effect of the reduced length of stay and reduction in number of staff is that as patients get to go out less, the privilege of going outside becomes more precious.

VISITORS

For visitors, too, Butler Hospital's grounds are important. They help to assuage feelings of fear and anxiety when visiting the

Rachel, a former patient, recalled: "For some reason, one of my clearest memories is of sitting on the lawn just outside the building, writing in my journal. It must've been pretty late in my stay, since I would have had to "earn" privileges to go outside by myself, unsupervised. At a certain point it doesn't matter how nicely the ward might be decorated, it's still filled with people who are in a lot of pain—sometimes that was just as depressing as what I'd come in for! Going outside by myself was the best way to escape, to get a break from that. To smell the grass, feel the air, to be reminded that there was also beauty in the world that somehow counteracted all that ugly pain."

Figure 6-9 The enclosed Children's Program Unit's playground at Butler Hospital. The black cast-iron fence blends in well with the surrounding greenery, and is in character with the building and grounds.

hospital. The parents of a former patient sum up the feelings of many friends and family members:

> When our daughter was admitted to Butler, we were so scared. We lived an hour away from Providence, and so had no idea what kind of a place this hospital was. When we drove up the next day, as soon as we entered the grounds we felt some relief—it was spring, everything was in bloom—we felt buoyed by the beauty of the surroundings; that "first impression," however superficial it may have been, gave us hope that our daughter was in a safe place where she could begin to heal.

It is critical to have a setting somewhere outside the hospital where patients can walk and visit with their family members or friends. Along the "loop," as well as in nodes closer to the building, benches and movable plastic chairs provide places for people to sit and visit with each other in a somewhat private setting, removed from the hospital.

EMPLOYEES

For Butler's employees, the hospital's outdoor spaces and scenery provide a restorative environment that reduces stress and adds to their quality of life. Many employees take advantage of the pathways for walking or jogging. One group of interns commented:

> We do something outside every day. It's like a little vacation. Often when we get off work we go jogging around the grounds and out to Blackstone Boulevard—it's wonderful to work in a place that is so beautiful that you actually want to stay after

your work day is over! It's unbelievable what a difference it makes—out of all the places I've interned, this is by far the greatest.

The beauty of the grounds and the opportunity to use the grounds for outdoor activity enables staff to cope with the high stress of the work: "It's an emotionally draining job, so it's nice to get out and away from what's going on inside—you feel much more balanced after being outside."

Weaknesses in Butler's Use of the Outdoors as a Therapeutic Environment

Clearly most of the staff and visitors at Butler Hospital are happy with the grounds as they are now—they enjoy the pastoral views and the peaceful atmosphere. There are, however, areas in which the landscape could be changed to maximize its therapeutic potential. As mentioned above, patients would surely benefit from the availability of more easily accessible paths close enough to the hospital for security monitoring purposes. These paths might have destination points instead of merely "going in circles" as the one around the main building does now. Suggested destinations might be any number of theme gardens—sensory, butterfly, water, children's discovery—to which people could walk, and in which people could sit, play, even garden. The hospital would also benefit from a gathering and seating area for groups larger than three people—at this time, there is no such place, unless people are willing to sit on the lawn.

Winter, and poor weather in general, poses another set of difficult problems for the hospital. For four to six months out of the year, cold or danger from wet or icy pavement prevents many patients from venturing outside. Butler Hospital does offer more (indirect) access to the outdoors in winter than many other cold-weather institutions; the majority of buildings have windows that face outward, offering patients and staff natural light and a view of the outdoors when they are unable to go outside. In addition, the small atrium between the old and new wings brings a little of the outdoors inside. Nevertheless, direct access to the outdoors—even during the cold and icy months— is important, and more rigorous attempts at making winter outings possible would surely enhance patients' quality of life.

Budget cuts have affected the landscape at Butler; the grounds crew is the smallest it has been in years, and is restricted by time and financial contraints to mowing the lawn, pruning shrubs and trees, and planting annuals at the most visible building access points. Any exposure patients get to horticultural therapy is often due to the interest of one person. For example, Barbara Ostrove, one of the occupational therapists, has a strong personal interest in gardening; therefore, many of her activities with patients involve plants and nature. For example, she has engaged patients from the Children's Unit in planting tomato seeds and growing the plants to harvest tomatoes. The patients were enthusiastic about the project, were excited when the seeds sprouted, and became eagerly involved in the daily watering and care of the seedlings.

Butler Hospital is a good example of a late nineteenth century mental hospital: The main and auxiliary buildings stand on a large piece of property, slightly removed from downtown, which has been landscaped in the English pastoral style. Butler has been successful at keeping up-to-date with patients' needs in terms of the overall physical plant, while at the same time maintaining the bucolic campus atmosphere. Patients, staff, and visitors alike enjoy and benefit from the naturalistic setting and the opportunities for outdoor activity. In some ways, however, the hospital seems to be "resting on its laurels" with its reputation as a beautiful environment in which to obtain treatment. There is no doubt that the grounds are lovely, and they certainly provide visual stimulation and the opportunity for outdoor recreation. Yet if the administration is serious about using the grounds to their full therapeutic and restorative potential, they will need to do more than fund the grounds crew to mow the lawns and prune the hedges. There need to be more outdoor spaces specific to patient needs that staff can use as part of the occupational and physical therapy programs. Horticultural therapy would be an excellent addition to the

Figure 6-10 Patients reclining on the lawn at Butler Hospital.

existing occupational and physical therapy programs, and there need to be more opportunities, during as much of the year as possible, for patients to access the outdoors. Furthermore, there must be more ways for patients to go and be outdoors by themselves in a safe, secure environment. There are many opportunities to implement design changes that can go a long way toward increasing quality of life for patients, staff, and visitors alike. Unlike many other psychiatric healthcare institutions, where there is little or no room to utilize the therapeutic benefits of outdoor space, Butler Hospital has a strong foundation on which to build. Butler has the potential to be a prime example of a hospital that actively uses its outdoors for the best possible patient care.

ADVANTAGES

- Beautifully landscaped grounds provide peaceful, restful views from indoors and out.
- Path looping around the hospital is handicapped accessible and easily walkable.
- Two enclosed (fenced) outdoor spaces provide access from the hospital, one for adults, one for children.
- Windows in patient units, cafeteria, and administrative offices offer views outside.
- Atrium with indoor plants, benches, and a fountain brings outdoors inside.
- Outdoor activities are a large component of physical and occupational therapy programs.

DISADVANTAGES

- No "destinations," few places other than the "loop" on which to walk.
- Enclosed outdoor areas need further development—not enough ways for patients to go out on their own, not much for adults to do.
- No outdoor area for large groups to sit in.
- Cold and inclement weather prohibits outdoor activity.
- Little use of extensive woodland path system due to security issues.
- Small staff ratio makes it difficult to take patients out as often as needed.
- No horticultural therapy program.
- Budget restrictions strongly limit grounds maintenance to anything but upkeep.

- Existing outdoor spaces do not always accommodate patients with specific needs—that is, those who are wheelchair bound, have decreased motor skills, need higher levels of supervision, and so on.

Whitby Mental Health Centre, Whitby, Ontario, Canada

Description of the Facility and Its Setting

Whitby Mental Health Centre (WMHC) is located in the suburbs of Whitby, 50 kilometers (approximately 30 miles) east of Toronto, on 86 acres of land bordering Lake Ontario. Whitby provides assessment, consultation, treatment, and rehabilitation to individuals suffering from serious mental illness, with the goal of achieving the earliest successful community reintegration at the most independent level. Although the average length of stay is six months, there are patients who stay longer, some for many years. The hospital serves a catchment area of 2.2 million people, from the Municipalities of North York, Scarborough, and East York, the Regional Municipalities of York and Durham, and Victoria County. Opened in 1996, WMHC is a 500,000 square foot, low-rise facility with 325 beds. It contains eight interconnected buildings that are separated by easily accessible landscaped courtyards and linked by 1,400-foot-long interior corridors on the first and second floors. There are fourteen patient care units and two outpatient units, each with an outdoor courtyard designed specifically for the needs of the patients in that unit. The hospital is intended to serve as a microcosm of the outside world, with a hierarchy of spaces on a continuum from private to public. Starting with the private patient care units, each area becomes more public: the semipublic interior corridors (called "Main Street") lead to the more public areas such as the cafeteria and the outdoor courtyards, which lead to the very public realm of the grounds beyond the landscaped courtyards.

Features within the building reflect the designers' commitment to a connection with the outdoors. All of the patient care units have been positioned on the outer edge of the building, so that each bedroom, the communal areas, and most of the corridors and offices have windows with views outward. Each unit also has a "solarium," which is especially welcome in inclement weather. In summer, many units open the doors leading to their courtyard to allow in fresh air as well as easy access outside. The southwest-facing wall of "Lakeview Cafeteria" is composed almost entirely of windows, which look out onto a patio and courtyard, and to the grounds and Lake Ontario beyond. Within the cafeteria, three 15-foot tall ficus trees help to add greenery during the long, grey winters.

History

Until recently, Whitby Mental Health Centre comprised a group of cottages set within a bucolic landscape that patients, staff, and visitors could use and enjoy. Due to deterioration of the original facility, however, a new plan for the hospital was developed and subsequently built, and Whitby is now the newest psychiatric facility of its kind in North America.

The original Whitby Mental Health Centre, constructed between 1913 and 1926, was a significant change from the dark, prisonlike facilities of previous asylums. In 1911, the architect James Govan visited many hospitals throughout the world to see examples of the most humane and modern hospitals. Upon his return, he worked with an advisory committee of psychiatrists, physicians, and government officials on his design. The provincial government purchased 640 acres of wooded and fertile farmland in 1912, and construction began in 1913. It was Govan's advisors who stipulated that patients have views to the outside, and that "all wards in all cottages receive some form of direct sunlight, even during the shortest days." Govan's final design featured sixteen cottages, each housing about seventy patients, situated in a villagelike setting amongst winding treed avenues. The main group of cottages faced southwest, near the shore of Lake Ontario: "Patients who had formerly been housed in dark facilities had access to fresh air and sunshine in an environment that was conducive to healing." ("Feature Supplement: Whitby…" 1996, p. 1). In addition to the cottages, Govan's design provided for a wide array of support buildings, including staff residences, maintenance facilities, and several facilities for recreation, including greenhouses and a nursery. The hospital was opened as "Ontario Hospital Whitby" in 1919, and from opening day, every bed was filled. By 1927, Whitby's official capacity was listed at 1,542 beds (ibid.).

A patient- and staff-operated farm that provided supplies for the facility opened with the hospital. Over 400 acres were used for farming, and 135 acres nearby were rented to grow additional grain crops to feed the livestock. The farm housed cattle for milk, pigs and chicken for meat, as well as a 75-acre vegetable garden and extensive fruit orchards. An on-site cannery was used to can and pickle fruit and vegetables for the winter months. Male patients, sometimes as many as 200 per day, worked in the fields and gardens under the guidance of farm staff, and were paid with tobacco rations. Use of the farm provided occupational therapy for the patients and kept hospital costs down.

Figure 6-11 Whitby Mental Health Centre (Whitby, Ontario, Canada), opened in 1996. The open space in the foreground is part of a greenbelt with bicycle and foot paths, open to the public and to some of the inpatients.

By the late 1950s and early 1960s, social and medical trends marked the beginning of the end of farming at Whitby. Social and union labor attitudes regarding patient labor were changing; the public began to feel that it was unfair to make patients work while they were being treated. Medical treatment had shifted from a heavy emphasis on occupational therapy and recreational activities to more intensive drug therapy and individual counseling. By 1964, Whitby's farm operations had ceased, and in 1969 all farm stock was sold at a public auction.

As early as 1955, building inspectors reported that the hospital was badly in need of repair due to overcrowding. A combination of physical deterioration and changes in the hospital program led to the need for a new facility. In 1989, "user groups" were formed to develop a plan of requirements that would then be used by designers for the construction of a new, larger facility. A major goal of the design program was that the new facility reflect the homelike quality of the old facilities' cottages, but not be so comfortable that patients would be inclined to stay indefinitely. Also important in the design was the idea of the outdoors as an extension of the indoors. It was deemed essential that patients, staff, and visitors have easy access to the outdoors; even in months when it was too cold to venture outside, people should continue to have visual linkages through windows overlooking Lake Ontario and the surrounding landscape. There were three primary reasons for emphasizing a connection with the outdoors: use of the outdoors would hopefully increase patients' motivation through both passive observation of nature and active recreation; visual and physical access to the outdoors would help reduce the institutional feeling of the hospital, and contribute to a homelike atmosphere; and finally, even basic pleasures like access to sunlight and fresh air were seen as beneficial amenities for patients.

The chosen architects for the new facility were the Architectural Consortium of Crang & Boake of Toronto, Cannon of Grand Island, and Moffatt Kinoshita of Toronto. Their final design placed an "emphasis on user wellness, achieved by providing views of the outdoors, natural light and a clear sense of orientation in all public, staff and patient areas" ("Feature Supplement: Whitby...," 1996, p. 12). Whitby Psychiatric Hospital was renamed Whitby Mental Health Centre in October 1994, and was opened as such in September 1996.

Description of the Outdoor Space

In 1991, Mary Jane Lovering of Vertechs Design, Inc., was hired as the landscape architect. Lovering's goal was to create simple, low-maintenance landscapes that would provide color and visual interest with vegetation. The overall design approach was intended to reflect the residential style of the area's neighborhoods by having a front entry to the building and a back door to each courtyard. In an attempt to avoid overstimulation, hardscaping materials were to be kept to earth tones and other subtle colors, much like the building itself. The subtlety of the design was intended to instill a feeling of calm, quiet, and continuity.

Although the new building was designed to reflect the residential style of the hospital's original cottages, it is actually too monolithic a structure to successfully carry out this goal. In order to fit all modes of care under one roof while still keeping

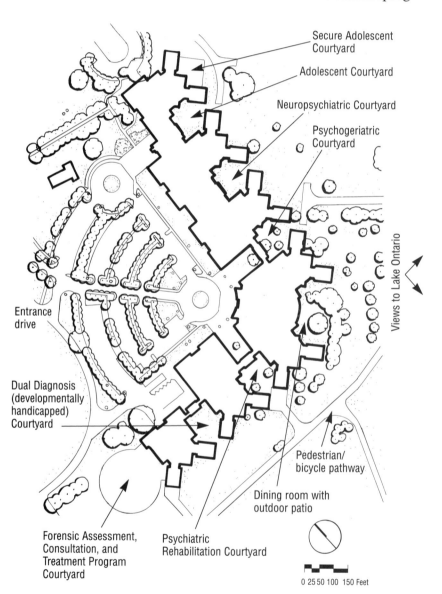

Figure 6-12 Site plan of Whitby Mental Health Centre.

Figure 6-13 Windows along both sides of the main corridor (Main Street) look outside onto courtyards. The enclosed courtyard in the foreground features one of the apple trees preserved from Whitby's original orchard. (Photo by Clare Cooper Marcus.)

the building height low to provide easy outdoor access, the architects resorted to creating the sprawling structure that is now Whitby Mental Health Centre. Dense plantings both in front of the hospital and within the courtyards provide a break in color and texture from the buildings' regularity and size, and from the tans and greys of the building facade and outdoor furnishings. An extensive system of pedestrian and bicycle paths surrounding the facility has been maintained and upgraded for patient use, and serves as an invitation to members of the Whitby community to use the hospital's grounds.

Within the grounds at Whitby, courtyards are attached to each care unit, as well as to the admitting area and the cafeteria. Each courtyard is designed specifically for the patient population of the unit it serves, yet the courtyards share certain characteristics. All courtyards are handicapped accessible, and all have barbecue grills, which are used quite frequently in the summer. All courtyards use similar building and paving materials as well. Furniture is bolted to the ground so that it cannot be picked up and thrown or used as a weapon. During the warmer months, many client activities are held outdoors. In addition to more traditional outdoor activities such as volleyball and badminton, people often have barbecues and picnics outside; therapists pull tables into the adjacent courtyard for occupational therapy; and counselors conduct psychiatric interviews with patients outdoors.

Each courtyard differs according to the specific needs of the patients. Some courtyards are enclosed with a subtle grey

Figure 6-14 The STEP (Schizophrenia Treatment Evaluation Program) courtyard, serving mostly young and physically able patients, has a large swath of lawn to facilitate casual lounging, BBQ picnics, and active outdoor recreation. (Photo by Clare Cooper Marcus.)

cast-iron fencing, and others are completely open to the grounds beyond; some of the fenced courtyards are kept locked at all times, and others are less restricted. The landscaping within each courtyard is also specific to the needs of the patients on each adjoining unit. For example, the Schizophrenia Treatment Evaluation Program (STEP) courtyard serves a younger and more physically active and able population. In this courtyard, it was important to provide a "backyard" feeling, as well as to give opportunity for casual lounging and active games. Thus it is a larger space, with more grass and less pavement. Since the STEP patients are under less strict surveillance, this courtyard is enclosed but not locked. In the Dual Diagnosis Service, patients are developmentally disabled but generally have the motor skills and physical needs of most young people. Here, again, more grass is provided to allow room to run or lounge around, or to engage in games and other group activities. The Neuropsychiatry Unit houses patients with organic neurologic diseases (such as Pick's and Huntington's disease) and with accident-related neurologic problems, which often stem from attempted suicide, such as carbon monoxide poisoning, head injuries from falls, and gunshot wounds. In this unit, many patients have restricted motor capabilities, so more paving is provided. Much of this locked courtyard is filled with arbors and trees, not only to provide shade but also to allow patients a feeling of security even when they are in the larger, more open environment of the outdoors. In all courtyards, shade helps to mitigate the photosensitivity side effect caused

Figure 6-15 Patients in the Neuropsychiatric Unit often have restricted motor capabilities; hence their courtyard is mostly paved to allow easy movement. Raised planting beds in the sun and terrazzo tables and chairs under a pergola allow patients seating opportunities in either sun or shade. (Photo by Clare Cooper Marcus.)

by many antidepressant and antipsychotic medications. In the Psychogeriatric Unit, too, shade is important since elderly people are more sensitive to the sun and to glare. Within the interior courtyards, several mature apple trees remain from the original orchard. These trees provide shade and are also a symbolic connection to the old farm. Groupings of plants at courtyard entrances from the outside grounds are intended to give each courtyard its own identity, since the spaces themselves are architecturally similar. The variety in vegetation gives patients visual cues to identify their personal unit. It may be that the vegetation is still not varied enough, especially to those who are not familiar with plants' subtleties in leaf, bark, or other characteristics. Since the plantings are still new and young, it remains to be seen how effective they will be in terms of providing wayfinding cues. The vegetation planted in and around the courtyards has two other qualities important in psychiatric care settings: it is both nontoxic and durable—able to stand up to the wear-and-tear that emotionally disturbed patients often inflict on both plants and building materials.

The Forensic Assessment, Consultation and Treatment Program (FACT) consists of two medium security inpatient units, housing twenty people each, and a consultation and outpatient service. The Forensic Assessment Unit, on the second floor, evaluates mentally ill offenders with regard to their fitness to stand trial and face criminal responsibility. The Forensic Treatment and Rehabilitation Unit, on the first floor, provides a comprehensive, multidisciplinary service for mentally ill offenders who stay at Whitby once they have been determined to be "not criminally responsible."

The FACT units and their outdoor courtyard differ from the other courtyards at Whitby because of the significantly higher level of security and surveillance. These units, situated at the end of the building, are also more removed from the activities of the rest of the hospital. Half of the FACT courtyard is surrounded by a 20-foot high bricked wall, topped with smooth cylindrical caps that are impossible to scale. Though the walls seem imposing, they look far less institutional than the traditional barbed and razor wire usually found atop prison and other high-security walls. The other half of the courtyard is fenced off similarly to other Whitby courtyards, with the exception that the fences are higher, and are given a "buffer zone" on the outside by a low wooden fence, preventing possible direct contact between those within and those on the outside of the courtyard. This high fence allows views out to Lake Ontario, and also allows views in from the various pedestrian and bicycle paths surrounding the hospital.

The FACT courtyard is larger than the others, and includes basketball courts and a small running track. The ground is paved with asphalt instead of concrete pavers, since pavers could potentially be picked up and used as weapons. The furniture is bolted to the ground, as it is in the other units. Cameras are placed along the edge of the courtyard to enable staff inside to monitor patients. Unlike some of the other units, in which patients may be able to wander out from the unit to the courtyard freely at certain times of the day, patients in the forensic unit must always be let out and then accompanied by a staff member. The courtyard is planted primarily with trees and turf. The trees, numbering twenty in all, will provide shade once their canopies fill out. The limbs will be pruned up to prevent patients from climbing the trees or breaking limbs off. Turf provides a softer alternative to the asphalt, and is a place where people can sit and rest or participate in group activities.

The issue of visual permeability is an interesting one, for the FACT unit and for other units at Whitby. Early in the design phase, researchers found that members of the Whitby general community would be more comfortable if the courtyards were enclosed with fences rather than walls; the community felt less cut off from the hospital, and the design committee also felt that patients would benefit from the extended views outward. Issues of confidentiality and safety were discussed by the community, hospital staff, administration, and patients. They decided that a greater degree of visual permeability was important, and that clients' confidentiality would not be violated.

Figure 6-16 View of the FACT (Forensic Assessment, Consultation and Treatment) Unit courtyard from second floor of FACT Unit's common area. Half of the courtyard wall is "open," affording views out to Lake Ontario. A mix of pavement and turf facilitates a variety of activities. (Photo by Clare Cooper Marcus.)

Since the facility is still so new, it remains to be seen exactly how the openness of the courtyards will play out over time.

Surrounding Grounds

Outside of the courtyards, the landscape has been kept as close to prebuilding conditions as possible. As part of this plan, the designers made a commitment to save most of the existing trees, many of them indigenous to the site; thousands of trees were preserved. Part of the larger landscape design involves a series of pedestrian and bicycle paths around the lake, which some patients are allowed to use, and which the public of Whitby and neighboring towns are also encouraged to use. The land borders Lynde Marsh, a conservation area that provides habitat for a wide array of wildlife. The opportunity for recreation and wildlife observation has been, and will continue to be, a draw for the public. It is the designers' hope that as people use the site, they will gain a deeper appreciation of the area, which may foster a long-term sense of investment and stewardship. The fact that some of the Centre's land was deeded to the town of Whitby during the planning phase provides a concrete sense of ownership in addition to the more emotional or symbolic feeling of stewardship.

The newly built Whitby Mental Health Centre is still in its infancy, and therefore conclusions are difficult to make. Many of the trees that will eventually offer shade have several years to grow before their branches will provide such respite; many of the plants originally installed may need replacing as the maintenance crews and landscape architects discover what best withstands the site's conditions, both in terms of climate and in terms of wear and tear from the patients. The plants used may be too subtle in color and form to be successful as way-finding cues within the various courtyards. Mary Jane Lovering says of the landscape design: "This is just the bare bones." In time, she would like to see more features added to the outdoor plan, such as gardens or planting beds for growing flowers, fruit, and vegetables; birdhouses and birdfeeders to invite wildlife closer to the patients; and a fountain for one of the more heavily used courtyards. Administrators are currently working to add horticultural therapy to the existing recreational therapy programs. The decision both to invite the public onto the hospital grounds and to enclose the courtyards with visually permeable fences instead of walls raises issues of privacy and confidentiality, which, despite careful consideration, may eventually create problems for patients and staff. Overall, the hospital and its design team must be commended for their commitment to creating an environment that embraces and utilizes the outdoors for both passive and active therapeutic benefit.

Advantages

- Views outside from most rooms and corridors, including cafeteria.
- General public allowed on grounds—gives public a sense of ownership; reduces societal fears about mental illness.
- Individual courtyards for each care unit, specific to that unit's needs.
- Retention and incorporation of many original trees on-site.
- Planting of many new trees.
- Simple, low-maintenance planting
- Conscious use of nonpoisonous plant material.
- Some patients have access to surrounding grounds/public space.
- Horticultural therapy program is in development stage.

Disadvantages

- Plant palette may be too subtle for nondesigners to detect planting distinctions intended as way-finding cues.
- Shade provided in some courtyards may not be enough for patients with real photosensitivity, especially in early years before trees fill out.
- Patterns created on ground by trellis shadows may be disorienting to some patients.
- Large degree of visual access from outside of courtyards may create issues of privacy and confidentiality.

Sub-Acute Treatment for Adolescent Rehabilitation Services, San Leandro, California

Description of the Facility, Its History, and Setting

The Sub-Acute Treatment for Adolescent Rehabilitation Services (STARS) is a community-based facility designed for adolescents who have serious emotional disorders located on ten acres within the grounds of Fairmont Hospital in San Leandro, California. Youngsters between the ages of twelve and seventeen are treated in a secure, campus-style facility. Patients are admitted to STARS for three problems: trauma, severe emotional disturbance, and/or failed lower levels of care. The facility is designed to house up to 48 live-in clients who are cared for by 124 staff members. The average length of stay is one year.

STARS is supported in large part by the Short-Doyle program of Alameda County, a state funding mechanism that directs county mental health dollars toward programs that provide medically necessary services to the county's most seriously and persistently troubled patients. In addition, STARS is supported by state and federal monies through MJ Gross and Associates, a private nursing company. Like its sister care facilities in Torrance, Long Beach, and San Bernardino, CA, the STARS model was thoroughly researched by trained psychologists before implementation, both in terms of physical design

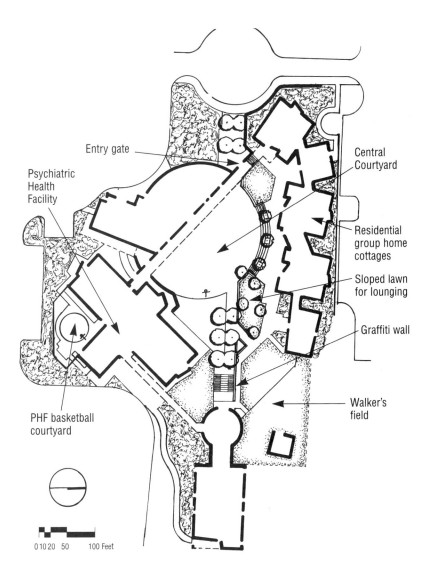

Entry gate

Psychiatric
Health
Facility

Central
Courtyard

Residential
group home
cottages

Sloped lawn
for lounging

Graffiti wall

Walker's
field

PHF basketball
courtyard

0 10 20 50   100 Feet

Figure 6-17 Site plan of Sub-Acute Treatment for Adolescent Rehabilitation Services, San Leandro, CA.

and as a continuum of care. Though similar in program design, these other facilities are not housed in a state-of-the-art facility designed to support clinical treatment programming. The STARS facility architect, John Boerger of The Design Partnership, worked in concert with Alameda County and the STARS Administrator, Peter Zucker, an experienced psychologist and hospital administrator, in designing both the indoor and outdoor spaces. A landscape architect was brought in to work out specific technical details such as grading, drainage, and planting plans once the design of the buildings and main courtyard were finalized.

The stated goals of STARS are social interaction, student-focused activities, education, and rehabilitation therapy. These are achieved by the coordination of the facility's four basic components—The Psychiatric Health Facility (PHF), Residential Group Home, Intensive Day Treatment Program, and an on-site Non-Public School—all which function within the small, gated campus. The PHF, specifically designed for acute care, is a locked residential treatment unit licensed by the California Department of Mental Health. This sixteen-bed unit provides a high-security environment for assessment, evaluation, and treatment. Many clients are admitted to the STARS program through the PHF after an attempted suicide, severe acting out, or an elopement (escape or attempted escape) from a lower care facility. The PHF is an inpatient facility with the added benefit that, once the youngster is ready, he or she may transition to an adjoining group home within the same campus. The fact that the PHF is part of the larger STARS facility is also useful when a youngster in the Residential Group Home needs higher security intervention for a short period of time.

The second and less acute level of care is the Residential Group Home, which is licensed by the California Department of Social Service. This group home is a large, elongated building comprising four open/unlocked eight-bed group home "cottages" with connecting corridors in between. Each tan, wooden shingled cottage has its own kitchen, group lounge, bathrooms, and laundry area, and each pair of contiguous cottages shares one nursing station. The focus within the group homes is on the tasks of daily living and on work that develops initiative and industry.

The Intensive Day Treatment Program is a key rehabilitative component: State certified by the Short-Doyle/Medi-Cal program, the day treatment program operates seven days a week, providing rehabilitation activities and therapy groups. The program serves up to forty-eight residents as well as eight to ten community-placed adolescents who attend the program as a day hospital. The state-certified Non-Public School provides education for fifty-five severely emotionally disturbed students, some who come from outside of the facility. This school, also located within the campus in a brick-red schoolhouse on axis with the main entrance, functions cooperatively with STARS therapists and staff, parents, and local school districts.

Description of Outdoor Space
STARS is not only a new facility in the physical sense, but also in the programmatic sense — it is an experiment in mental health-care that involves providing all aspects of care on one campus. The aim is to provide comprehensive continuous care for adolescents, thus avoiding the "revolving door" problem that has plagued mental health patients and practitioners for years. Since the program and the site itself are so new, it is difficult to gauge how well they will work, and how well they will stand up over time. Since its opening in 1997, reception by clients, parents, and members of the San Leandro community has been positive. There are two elements of the design, which are becoming the norm for this kind of facility. One is the placing of value on outdoor space as an important environmental factor — at least as important as the indoors of the building — in client care. The second element, which stems from this higher regard for outdoor space, is a design in which the buildings of the healthcare center surround an open outdoor space, creating a central courtyard. If implemented well, this design allows for easy access and visibility from the buildings. It also alleviates the need for fencing material around the outdoor space which,

Figure 6-18 The campus of Sub-Acute Treatment for Adolescent Rehabilitation Services (STARS). Group home cottages, a school, and treatment facilities surround and enclose a central courtyard. The central gathering space is easily accessible and visible from all buildings. (Drawing by The Design Partnership, San Francisco, California.)

in addition to being costly, can add to a client's feeling of being "caged" or locked in. While there are certainly other design alternatives, this central courtyard model is being utilized by many designers, particularly in urban settings where space is limited and privacy and confidentiality are paramount.

The primary outdoor space within the campus is the Central Courtyard. It is here, through a locked gate, that most visitors, staff, and clients first enter the campus. The Central Courtyard is surrounded by the buildings that make up STARS—the group home cottages, the activities building, the PHF, and the school. John Boerger, the architect, designed the campus with the intention that the outdoor area be a gathering space for clients and staff, which would be easily accessible and visible from the surrounding buildings. A low, concrete retaining wall, decorated with brightly colored ceramic tiles by local artist Johanna Poethig, greets visitors as they enter from the parking lot. This wall begins outside of the locked entry gate, and continues into the Central Courtyard. The tiled wall and landscaped terraces of lawn and trees surround the lower paved area, creating an informal amphitheater. The circular asphalt-paved ground area is a fairly large unprogrammed open space (approximately 4,500 square feet), which is used during graduations, group meetings, and other large public events in addition to everyday activities such as basketball and outdoor art therapy classes.

One might surmise that the size of the Central Courtyard, combined with its bowl shape and enclosure by the STARS buildings, would create too much of a "fishbowl," in which nothing other than very public activities could take place. Due to the placement of the stairs, terraces, and trees, however, peo-

Figure 6-19 Views from the STARS Central Courtyard: amphitheater steps and a sloping lawn enclose the Courtyard and provide a variety of seating for programmed activities and casual recreation. Group home cottages are in the foreground, the non-public school in the background.

ple are able to find within that large space smaller, more intimate niches. Like many adolescents, STARS clients often prefer and seek out the most private of spaces, where monitoring from indoors and even from within the courtyard is difficult. A 5-foot concrete "graffiti wall," built along the entry ramp to the school, serves as a vertical surface for students to draw on. Because of its height and placement, the wall has also become popular because it is one of the few places where clients can hide from monitors' view. While the staff have had to take extra precautions in monitoring this area, the administration has decided that the wall does not pose enough of a risk to necessitate its removal.

Walker's Field, the second-largest outdoor space, is an open, grassy area between the school and the cottages. The field was not part of the original campus design, and was fenced off and inaccessible from the courtyard. When the adolescents complained that they had no large, unpaved surface on which to play and hang out, they suggested obtaining and reworking the adjacent land for that purpose. Once the land was acquired, the adolescents were employed to regrade and then plant the field with sod. Planting beds have been created along the edges of the field and are used by students for science projects and other school-related activities such as growing vegetables and herbs. While the number of plants in these beds is small, there is the potential for a larger and more formal horticultural therapy program. Because Walker's Field is not as easily visible from the surrounding buildings, the fenced entrance to this area is kept locked, and is unlocked and opened as needed for picnics, volleyball, and school activities.

Because of the need for high security within the locked Psychiatric Health Facility, residents of the PHF are not allowed to enter the Central Courtyard without supervision. There is, however, a small 1,000-square-foot courtyard on the exterior of the complex directly adjacent to and accessible only from the PHF. Although it can be seen from the nurse's station inside the building, this paved courtyard is generally kept locked, and is only opened at certain times of the day. Unfortunately, the courtyard itself is less than inviting. Paved entirely with asphalt and equipped with one basketball hoop attached to the building, this area serves as a small space for shooting hoops. The absence of trees or a covered arcade or pergola is problematic, as there is little respite from the hot sun in summer and fall and from rain in winter and spring. Aside from the basketball net, there are no furnishings such as benches or tables and, unlike the rest of the STARS facility, there is little plant material to mitigate the harshness of the asphalt. The small PHF courtyard is a sharp contrast to the rolling San Leandro hills in which the campus is nestled. These northern California foothills are covered with annual grasses, which are a deep green in winter and spring, and a golden brown in summer and fall. The grasses are laced with wildflowers such as California poppy and lupine, and the hills themselves are interspersed with trees such as the native coast live oaks and soft chaparral of coyote bush and coffeeberry. The windows of most of the buildings, particularly the schoolhouse and the cottages, face both inward toward the courtyard and outward to the San Leandro hills, so that from indoors one still has a positive connection to nature.

Use of the Outdoor Space

As would be expected, the greatest amount of outdoor activity takes place within the Central Courtyard. It is here that most public events such as assemblies, games, barbecues, and performances take place. In addition, the courtyard is where clients go to hang out with other kids, meet with a counselor, visit with family members or friends, or just be alone. The large swath of turf closest to Walker's Field is a popular sunbathing area, and clients often bring their radios outside to add music to the scene. Because it is large and yet well-defined by both the architecture and the landscaping, the courtyard tends to be a relaxed area in which both programmed and unprogrammed activities can take place. Significantly it is also the place where the least amount of psychotic behavior—or acting out—occurs.

A heavy emphasis is placed on therapeutic recreation in the form of occupational and physical therapy. Thirteen full-time activity staff and a full-time director coordinate and facilitate the daily activities, many of which take place outside, both on campus and off. Physical therapy consists of ball games, swimming, and even a ropes course. Clients also hike in the surrounding hills once or twice a week. Art therapy, music therapy, and rehabilitation therapy all use the outdoors in parts of their programs; whether clients hold an outdoor concert or merely pull tables out into the central courtyard during art class, the staff are aware of the therapeutic effect of fresh air, direct light, and the absence of walls and roofs. Another part of clients' occupational therapy is a vocational and prevocational program. Adolescents who wish to work during their stay at STARS are employed by the facility to do any number of tasks, including indoor and outdoor maintenance and food service. Some outdoor maintenance jobs include cleaning the Central Courtyard and tending to the trees, shrubs, and perennials within the campus. The manager of Facility Physical Plant supervises the landscape and other maintenance work crews.

Figure 6-20 The entry gate to STARS is characteristic of the facility's residential scale.

The vocational program allows clients to earn money for their work, and also instills a sense of stewardship for the physical plant.

More than most groups of clients, adolescents generally need a large amounts of space and stimulation. The question arises whether the campus is large and varied enough to hold emotionally disturbed adolescents for an entire year. Will the Central Courtyard and Walker's Field be sufficient? Unfortunately, the very site plan that makes the courtyard an enclosed and easily supervised space makes the development of any other future outdoor spaces on site more problematic. Thus far, STARS administrators have been receptive to clients' needs and have been successful at adapting their surroundings.

ADVANTAGES

- Setting in the hills—quiet and beautiful, yet still near to downtown San Leandro.

- Central Courtyard as a concept and a space is successful in providing casual and programmed use; ability to claim "intimate niches" within larger space has been appreciated.

- Walker's Field provides a larger open green space for activities like badminton and volleyball, as well as for gardening and science projects.

- Good balance of hard and green spaces.

- Windows within buildings all look out, either to courtyard, to hills beyond, or both.

- Activities including sports, art, and even hiking acknowledge importance of outdoor space.

- Opportunities for vocational training with landscaping and other outdoor work.

DISADVANTAGES

- Site space itself is relatively small—may become a problem for clients housed on site for an entire year.

- Free access to all spaces (except for PHF residents) does not offer the opportunity (behavioral incentive) for clients to earn "grounds" privileges, as at some other facilities.

- Courtyard outside of the PHF is bleak, could easily be improved without compromising safety of residents and staff.

- Asphalt surface of Central Courtyard is drab and is already in need of repaving.

- Graffiti wall poses a potential security risk, acting as a place for people to hide.
- No horticultural therapy program.

The Retreat, York, England
By Marni Barnes

Description of the Facility

The Retreat is a 200-year-old psychiatric facility on the outskirts of the city of York, in northern England. Run under the auspices of the Society of Friends (Quakers), it is a registered charity that offers an extensive array of inpatient and outpatient services and draws residents from all over the United Kingdom. There are a total of 165 beds and the services are clustered into four main categories. (1) Specialist Services, including residential facilities and treatment for individuals with eating disorders, substance misuse, post-traumatic stress disorder and other acute care conditions. (2) Services for Elderly People with a Mental Illness, incorporating both a long-term residential care unit and respite services to relieve at-home care takers. (3) Rehabilitation Services for individuals suffering from an enduring mental illness. This service includes help with social behavioral skills as well as mastering self-medication and daily living skills. One component of this area of service is a three bedroom resettlement house on the grounds, which serves as a halfway house in the progression toward independent living. (4) Psychology and Counseling for inpatients and outpatients with a range of mental disorders. The outpatient component is housed at the Tuke Center and is also a training institution for psychotherapists and counselors (Thomson, 1996, pp. 6–7).

The philosophy of the retreat embraces spiritual values as a part of life.

> We believe that spiritual values at The Retreat should find expression above all in respect for each person as a spiritual being. It is not enough to balance the chemicals in the bloodstream, it is not enough to address the emotional needs of patients and their families, it is not enough to share information and decisions with patients as they are able—though all these things may be good and necessary. We have to work with the hunger for meaning, the in-built sense of direction and the qualities of hope, fortitude and compassion, which each can bring to bear on their own problems and those of others. ...

> We affirm the value of working for, and with, people whose spiritual nature is hardly able to find expressions because of the degree of damage to their physical structure or their state

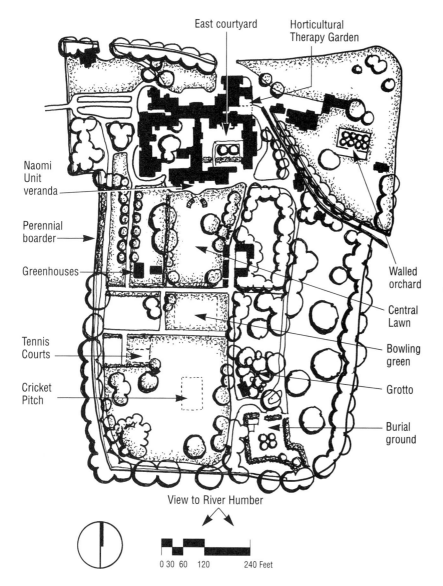

East courtyard

Horticultural Therapy Garden

Naomi Unit veranda

Perennial boarder

Greenhouses

Tennis Courts

Cricket Pitch

Walled orchard

Central Lawn

Bowling green

Grotto

Burial ground

Figure 6-21 Site plan of The Retreat, York, England.

View to River Humber

0 30 60   120   240 Feet

of emotional trauma. We believe that a wide range of therapies should be available, which address the whole person rather than the illness, and which encourage creative exploration. ... [in that regard] We believe that beauty and peacefulness are important. (Britton, 1995, pp. 30–31)

The extensive grounds of The Retreat provide a large dose of "beauty and peacefulness." The site is bordered on three sides by medieval "stray-land," once protected as grazing pastures for freemen living within the city walls of York, and now preserved as public open space. Slightly mismatched but appealing one- and two-story brick buildings are clustered at the north end of a large and gently sloping site. Each ground floor ward has access to a garden area off a main corridor or dayroom. In addition to the inpatient wards at The Retreat, the regional office of the English National Board of Nursing and a nursing home (Lamel Beeches) are housed on the present site, as is the outpatient psychotherapy and counseling service (Tuke Center), and the Resettlement House to assist those making the transition from an inpatient stay to living independently.

History

The Retreat was designed in the late 1700s by John Bevans, a London architect, and was taken through construction by architect Peter Atkinson of York. It was built by the Quakers as an inpatient psychiatric facility on a ridge of land overlooking York's medieval Minster and city walls.

Originally eleven and a half acres, The Retreat opened in May of 1796 with two inpatient wards with separate walled gardens, one for men and one for women, and a working farm on the site. The size of the property has expanded and contracted throughout the years as ideas in psychiatry have changed, and the resulting requirements have evolved.

The farm was an integral part of The Retreat when it opened and it produced most of the food for the facility. Believing in the treatment value of participation, the administration had patients work the farm fields and tend the animals alongside the staff.

In the late 1800s the grounds were levelled into 5 terraces to maximize the potential for the patients' recreational activities. The gardens between the main buildings, used primarily by long-term patients, were flattened to create courtyards on this upper level and to provide better seating areas and easy strolling. The acute care facility (Naomi Ward) with its verandah, and the Respite Center occupy the second terrace, which in turn, overlooks the recreational grounds and old farm site on the lower terraces (see site plan, Figure 6-21).

In 1912, a rockery was created on the east end of the lower terrace. Subsequently the rockery was let go until it was restored in 1989. Presently, it is somewhat hidden. Only apparent to those who look off of the path through the shrubbery, its appealing rock formations draw those who are curious. This requisite of discovery and exploration exudes a sense of secrecy and privacy, rare in institutional settings.

In 1927, The Retreat purchased the adjacent Garrow Hill estate, which now houses the outpatient services of the Tuke Center for Psychotherapy and Counseling, along with an old

Figure 6-22 Providing areas for exploration and discovery draws patients into the garden at The Retreat and keeps them engaged with their surroundings. This rockery is an unusual feature that provides the feeling of a complete getaway from the wards. (Photo by Marni Barnes.)

walled orchard, and a "natural garden" running the length of the original parcel of land.

In the early 1930s legal interpretations regarding enforced labor and confined populations precipitated the cessation of patients working on the farm, and resulted in the grounds being used primarily for recreational purposes. The farm area was transformed into lawn with a central allée of cherry trees. Only one old greenhouse and a few raised beds remain. The introduction of television and other indoor entertainment in the late 1950s led to changes in lifestyle, and the demand for outdoor recreational activities diminished. This shift has been exacerbated by the recent advances in psychotropic medications, which has resulted in much of the patients' time now being spent quietly in the dayroom, or engaged in indoor pursuits, thus further reducing the patients' use of the grounds.

Referring to the changes in the grounds and their uses, the current estate manager, David Mitchell, remarked: "Just about anything you can think of we have tried here, at least once in the last 200 years!" This cyclical pattern of treatment modalities (and use of the grounds) is evidenced by the return to a program of participatory gardening with the development of a horticultural therapy program as a component of the occupational therapy unit. A purpose built horticultural therapy garden was installed adjacent to that department in 1990. At the time of writing, plans are being made to transform the old walled orchard into an organic garden for occupational therapy and casual use by interested long-term patients.

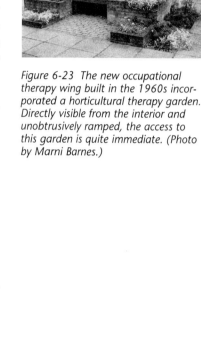

Figure 6-23 The new occupational therapy wing built in the 1960s incorporated a horticultural therapy garden. Directly visible from the interior and unobtrusively ramped, the access to this garden is quite immediate. (Photo by Marni Barnes.)

Figure 6-24 The veranda immediately outside the acute care ward commands a view of the grounds and provides a way for patients to see their environment before leaving the security of the building. This is a highly used space, in contrast to the lawn below, which is too big and open for the comfort of some patients. (Photo by Marni Barnes.)

Description of Outdoor Space

The present-day grounds consist of 38 acres. As the city of York expanded beyond its medieval walls, the original view from the front gates of the historic embattlements and Minster has been lost; however, the land to the south of the buildings, with its gentle slope down to a hedgerow of mature lime trees, chestnuts, and beeches on the boundary, still provides a striking view. While benefiting from a sense of separation and protection provided by the treed boundary, one can still gaze to the pastures beyond. The sky above this scene is an equal contributor to the beauty of the vista, providing changing clouds and intensities of hue in accordance with the season. This provides a backdrop of pastoral elegance when looking out over the grounds from the terrace at the back of the acute ward or the respite center, as well as from the upper story windows of the main building.

The veranda located on the terrace to the south of the acute ward is a comfortable and well-used space. The wood bench seating follows the undulation of the bay windows in the facade of the building, creating a mix of single and multiple seating set at 135-degree angles to each other. This combination is ideal for conversation and yet minimal eye contact is demanded. There is much else to gaze at and the proximity and orientation of the chairs allows for either an easy flow of social interaction, or for solitude, as desired. The verandah is covered with a frosted glass roof which provides shelter in inclement weather and softens the light at midday. One end of the verandah has tables, again with a mix of seating combinations and the addition of light plastic chairs scattered about.

The grounds today are extensive and are composed of many elements. The original parcel, now the terraced middle strip of the property, contains the cottage, which has become the Resettlement House, and several other brick buildings and walls remaining from the days of the farm. These walls now partially edge a central lawn area and add an air of formality to the middle terrace. The fourth terrace is home for the bowling green and tennis courts, while the fifth and lowest terrace holds a cricket pitch, a small Quaker burial ground (where patients may choose to be buried), and the Rockery. Two asphalt paths run down either side of the gardens to the bottom terrace, one down the allée of cherry trees, and the other up past the resettlement house and other outbuildings. There are connecting paths at the top of each slope between terraces, creating several circular routes of various lengths. The greatest change in elevation is at the foot of the verandah on the second terrace, where an old and elegant brick stairway descends from the buildings to the central lawn below.

Separated from the building and verandah by a tarmac drive, a perimeter planting of roses and a 5-meter drop in elevation, the central lawn and lower terraces seem remote. This provides a sense of protected isolation for people on the terrace, but there is no complementary gesture to welcome one into the garden to explore. During the site visits, only a single bench was visible from the verandah, approximately 50 meters to one side of the lawn, under a row of mature trees. It seemed just too far and too isolated to be a safe initial destination. There were actually some other benches quite near, however, but they were tucked into the slope, and hidden from view. There is also ample seating along the paths, and still more benches surrounding the bowling green and set out on the perimeter of the lower terrace, but these too are not evident from the building or verandah. The quantity and variety of seating spaces is one of the assets of this garden, but it is only after venturing down into the grounds that the benches became visible, and the benefit of offering a close and comfortable destination is lost.

There are smaller garden spaces contained within the form of the building (the original Men's and Women's gardens), which are visible from the dayrooms of the long-term wards, and which are dedicated to their use. They have been made more accessible by the addition of ramps, which, although functional and necessary, have encroached into the space so as to seemingly drop one down in the middle. A cluster of chairs and a table have created a "patio area" at the base of the ramp on the east side garden, which serves to offset this feeling. Young trees have been planted, which will in time increase the sense of privacy in these spaces surrounded by windows.

Figure 6-25 Garden benches are ideally suited for private conversations. Here a patient talks with a nurse while seated in the front garden. Beyond is a view of York Minster. (Photo courtesy of The Retreat Archives.)

Figure 6-26 Bulbs heralding the coming of spring can symbolize hope for a brighter tomorrow. Several patients at The Retreat commented on the beautiful flowers throughout the grounds, and the significant role that the outdoors was playing in their recovery. (Photo courtesy of The Retreat Archives.)

More than 34,000 bulbs are planted on the grounds, some lining the path through the allée of flowering trees, some in the annual flower beds throughout the site, and a most in a 7-acre field on the east side, which becomes a carpet of daffodils in the springtime. There is a long perennial bed bordering the old farm site on the west side of the property and a smaller lawn hedged with English laurel, for special functions. There were many majestic elms on the grounds that were lost to Dutch elm disease in the early 1980s. This, combined with trees that are past maturity, has given rise to a long-range plan to maintain and rebuild the tree population. As this plan is implemented, the lawn areas will of necessity be broken up by the new plantings.

The gardens are a valued part of this institution. Beauty and peacefulness are regarded as an integral part of the healing environment, and the grounds and gardens provide much of this atmosphere. The history of the grounds has been chronicled by the Estate Manager, David Mitchell, and significant components of the past can be seen in the landscape. The remnants of the original formal gardens add charm, yet the concept of a garden in decline is one that merits further investigation in regard to the potential psychological impact on those in an emotionally fragile state. Perhaps, like the experience of witnessing the changing seasons and the "death" of winter, an old garden can instill a sense of life's patterns, and the timelessness that accompanies them. Certainly the gardens at The Retreat do convey an element of rooted timelessness and history. On the other hand, perhaps, because they are creations of human hands, the wooden arbors, in their deteriorating state, and the remaining brick elements, "lost" by their isolation, carry a different message. None of the patients interviewed mentioned this aspect of the grounds (though one interviewee who was an avid gardener did mention her distress about the health of a few beautiful old trees that are in decline). Perhaps it is the subjective view of an American in an English landscape that raises this issue, but this author wonders if in the broken world of mental instability, this aspect of an old garden may play a role in its perceived safety.

Use of Outdoor Space

While the farming component of the gardens has disappeared, the grounds department continues to propagate and grow all of their annual plantings, as well as some fruits and vegetables for the kitchen. The central lawn is the setting for an annual Summer Gala and other fund-raising garden parties. The grounds are open to the public with the five gardeners on staff keeping an eye out for questionable behavior.

Tennis matches are arranged upon occasion by staff for the acute care patients and the cricket pitch is cared for and used by the local pub team. But the gardens are primarily used for strolling by the more mobile patients from all of the wards and clinics. The Estate Manager, David Mitchell, commented that the grounds are not used as much by the long-term residents as they could be because mobility issues make going in to the garden a "one-on-one" staff to patient experience. However, the grounds do provide a restful view for those who are more confined.

Patients in Naomi Ward (who tend to be more oriented and agile than residents of the long-term wards) have a sign-out board. After having attained an adequate degree of recovery, they are able to come and go from their building. A few patients have bicycles and local shops are within the limits of their travels. Most often, however, the board is used to sign out to the garden.

Interviews with three women on this acute ward were arranged by the staff. Two of the patients were in their late teens and one was in her early twenties. The two teenagers used the garden almost every day, each on her own. One, who had been in residence for six months, had developed a favorite route through the garden which she took each day. The second woman had been readmitted a week previously, and she spent her time wandering and exploring the "nooks and crannies" and finding new/old favorite places every time. Comments such as "a garden makes it worth living" and "flowers give me hope" indicate how the garden augments these patients' more traditional therapeutic treatment. Illustrating how important the garden is to them they discussed the significance of the view from their bedroom windows (See Color Insert), especially "in the beginning when we were not able to go out." They also spontaneously described a room on the ward that faces a brick wall rather than the gardens. "Everyone on the ward hates that room, we all talk about how we would go crazy if we had that room." The longer term resident also remarked on how wonderful one staff member is, who used to take her outside for strolls when she was confined to a wheelchair. This, she said, "made all the difference in my recovery; I would not have begun to get well."

These women reported that everyone on the ward likes to sit on the verandah and watch the weekend cricket matches in summer, and even if there is no activity in the garden, the orientation of the building is such that they can watch approaching thunderstorms and — sometimes — incredibly spectacular lightning.

The third patient sought the interviewer out because she is an avid gardener. She loves having the large expanse of grounds, especially since her family brings her dog every day, and she

Figure 6-27 This walled orchard, reminiscent of the "Secret Garden" in the children's story by that name, is being developed into a horticultural therapy garden for longer term patients. It is one of several delightful surprises on the grounds of The Retreat. (Photo by Marni Barnes.)

romps and plays with him in the garden. Like the other two women, she also commented on the significance of the view out her bedroom window and has rearranged the furniture in her room to be able to see a beautiful atlas cedar from her bed. This patient knows the healing power of nature firsthand, and feels strongly that the outdoor space at The Retreat is "underutilized."

This patient-gardener would like to work in the garden while she is staying at The Retreat, and does not think that it is an option. She expressed some concern that she would put someone out of a job if she asked if she could help, and instead, suggested that an organic garden be planted specifically for patients to work in — and thereby work out their problems. She was delighted to hear that one was being planned for the walled orchard.

The walled garden is a beautiful setting, although it is rather remote from the main buildings. The success of this as a patient garden will be dependent upon support through programming and staff allocation. A garden that could be worked would provide the many benefits of horticultural therapy, and would also serve as a destination for people out for a stroll. Participating and observing the activity there could make this one of the most utilized components of the garden.

When asked, all three women interviewed felt that the central lawn area was a little forbidding. The two teens thought that it was "almost too big." They certainly didn't want it any bigger, because it would be like a playing field at school and they agreed that this would be most disconcerting to them. The avid gardener thought the space boring, and slightly intimidating, saying that when her dog runs into that area, she prefers to walk near the walls. She recommended planting more trees to break up the space and provide interest. The size of the open space is rather daunting, in that the proportions are grand, and thus evoke the sense of one's own fragile qualities. This, combined with the exposure to eyes gazing from the terrace and windows behind, make this an underused space. Fortuitously, the long-range plan for tree planting will provide the added interest and psychological security lacking in this central lawn area.

The gardens are a valued component of this facility, contributing to a sense of serenity, so important in the confusing internal world of the mentally ill. Equally important, they serve as a private place to visit with guests, as well as a safe place to be alone.

ADVANTAGES

- A philosophical approach that recognizes the value of nature.
- The pride in and care taken of the grounds — they are well maintained.

- Staff encouragement to use the garden.
- Visibility of the gardens from the common areas of the wards.
- Long-range planning to maintain tree population and health.
- Large number of benches set throughout the property, most of which are movable and can be arranged (by two people, as they are heavy) to meet changing needs.
- Grounds provide areas for both privacy and social interaction.
- Wide asphalt paths throughout most of the site.
- Paved circular routes of various lengths available.
- Proximity of the verandah to the acute ward.
- The interest provided by weekend cricket matches in the summer.
- Open-door policy regarding use by surrounding community.
- Expansive vistas from the wards.
- Visibility of the garden courtyards from the common rooms of the long-term units.
- Ramps added to improve accessibility in courtyards.

DISADVANTAGES

- The present lack of visible features and/or comfortable seating, to pique one's curiosity and provide destinations within easy reach, encouraging use of the garden.
- Need for areas of more human scale within sight of the acute ward, increasing the psychologically perceived safety of venturing into the garden.
- No universally accessible paths with curbs and railings, improving accessibility to physically impaired patients and their guests, who may be unaccustomed to handling wheelchairs.
- Lack of universally accessible circular paths in the courtyards to encourage independent use by long-term residents.
- Forgotten "eddy spaces" created by courtyard ramp additions may be disorienting to confused patients.
- Minimal exterior space at the same grade as the long-term common rooms for those who have very limited energy or those who may need closer visual monitoring by staff.

Blackthorn Medical Centre, Maidstone, Kent (UK)

By Clare Cooper Marcus

Description of the Facility and Its History

In a suburb of Maidstone, Kent, in the southeast of England, is a remarkable example of a medical facility combining conventional and complementary[1] medicine, addressing both physical and mental illness, and with specialized indoor and outdoor environments designed for healing. In 1983, a local general practitioner, Dr. David McGavin, became increasingly concerned that there were some patients he just could not help—those with chronic, complex, and life-threatening conditions. Sometimes termed in general practice "heart-sink" patients ("Your heart sinks when they come in"), these are patients who cannot be helped by conventional medicine, who keep coming back for help, and who become increasingly passive and helpless regarding their condition.

Casting around for something to offer these patients, Dr. McGavin met an art therapist, Hazel Adams, whose methods were grounded in the anthroposophical teachings of Rudolf Steiner. She started working with some of Dr. McGavin's "most difficult" patients, and within a few months improvements were evident. A counselor and other creative therapists joined the group. A new kind of primary care medical practice was born.

For some years, three general practitioners and several therapists worked out of an old medical office. As the practice grew, the environment became increasingly chaotic; art therapy took place after-hours, on a board thrown over the examination couch. The staff determined that they needed a purpose built building where the physical environment itself had healing properties. After an energetic program of local fund-raising, the present building was opened in December 1991, designed by Vladimir Radish of Camphill Architects (Aberdeen, Scotland) on anthroposophical principles. The design goals were simple but profound: the building was to offer a gesture of care and of "uprightness"—people who come to it must be called upon to use their own healing powers. In contrast to mainstream medicine and popular beliefs about ill health, anthroposophical medicine sees illness as a gift and healing as a conscious process of spiritual development. Thus, healing must engage the will of the patient (Leviton, 1988).

Located on a quiet residential street in the Maidstone suburb of Barming, the exterior view of the Blackthorn Medical Center immediately communicates that this place is "different."

---

[1]The term for alternative medicine in Europe.

The subtle pink stucco walls, the rhomboid-shaped windows, the profusion of roses around the entrance—these features both attract your attention and put you at ease. It is clear that this is a different kind of medical practice.

The heart of the building is a spacious, two-story waiting area with comfortable furniture, specially commissioned woven wall hangings, and a restful view out to an upward-sloping garden with grass, shrubs, trees, flowers, and a flow-form water feature. On the lower floor is a reception desk, the offices of the four GPs who make up this practice, and a large eurythmy therapy studio doubling as a meeting room. On the upper floor, accessed by a graceful staircase and views out to the neighborhood, are rooms for Steiner-based art therapy, music therapy, counseling, and rhythmical massage. All therapists are trained in the Rudolf Steiner tradition concerning health, illness, and development. There are approximately 7,000 patients in the practice, and at any one time, 150 of them may be actively receiving therapy. Approximately 30 percent of the patients are referred by GPs or consultants outside this particular practice. The conditions that seem to respond best to this combination of conventional and complementary treatment are multiple sclerosis, multiple environmental disorders, cancer, Parkinson's disease, and mental illness. The National Health Service is so impressed with the results of these therapies that it funds—via the local health authority—70 percent of their costs at Blackthorn. The remaining 30 percent is covered by an active local program of fund-raising organized through the Blackthorn Trust. The Blackthorn staff meet regularly with the staffs of five other centers comparable to Blackthorn, located in Stroud, Shrewsbury, Bristol, Maidstone, and Aberdeen, to share their experience and to plan a research project to gauge the effects of this approach on chronic illness, the role of the community, and the importance of teamwork in a combined conventional and complementary practice.

Figure 6-28 The Blackthorn Garden Project, Maidstone, Kent, UK. View of part of the garden and the café. (Photo by Clare Cooper Marcus.)

The Blackthorn Garden Project

A unique, successful, and inspiring component of the integrated program at Blackthorn is the Garden Project. Initiated in 1991 and directed by Tijno Voors, the project provides rehabilitation through work for people with a range of mental and physical conditions that have not responded to conventional medical approaches.

The site of the Blackthorn Medical Center backs onto the extensive grounds of a huge nineteenth century mental hospital (Oakwood), which was closed in 1990. The Garden Project comprises 22 acres of land, part of which is leased from the former mental hospital. The facilities comprising the Garden Project consist of:

- A quiet flower garden with trees, lawns, and benches used by patients and members of the community, and for fund-raising events
- A greenhouse and lath-house (left over from the mental hospital) where house and garden plants are raised for sale
- Extensive vegetable gardens
- A café serving daily vegetarian lunches of organic produce raised in the gardens to about sixty staff, patients, coworkers, volunteers, and other people from the local neighborhood
- A kitchen where the meals are cooked and bread is baked for sale in the community
- A craft hut

Everything in the garden is used. Vegetables are used in the kitchen; bedding plants and cut flowers are raised for sale; dried flower arrangements, pressed flower cards, nature-photo cards, massage oils, herbal preparations, jams, and chutneys are all produced and sold via the crafts program. And, of course, what is left over is recycled in compost.

The garden has three main objectives: "to provide rehabilitation and community support for people who have not responded to other treatments; to create an environment which encourages social integration and cultural activity; and to encourage all the various disciplines involved in community care and mental healthcare to meet and work together more effectively and efficiently" ("Community Care," 1995, p. 6). Individuals are referred to the Garden Project from the Blackthorn Medical Center, by other GPs, as well as by local psychiatrists, social workers, and psychiatric nurses. They are taken on as coworkers, rather than as patients or clients, and work alongside project staff and community volunteers. "Blackthorn Garden aims to restore, through work, a sense of usefulness and meaning, rebuild confidence and self-esteem, and to emphasize the strong and healthy side of the coworker, rather than just focusing on their illnesses" (ibid., p. 6).

At any one time, sixty coworkers are engaged in the Garden Project, working from one to three days a week at tasks they select with the staff. Some do heavy gardening tasks (digging, hoeing); others perform lighter tasks (harvesting, weeding, greenhouse work); some work in the cafe planning, preparing,

Figure 6-29 The aim of the Blackthorn Garden Project is "to restore, through work, a sense of usefulness and meaning" to coworkers who garden, prepare and serve meals, bake bread, and produce crafts. (Photo by Clare Cooper Marcus.)

or serving meals; others work in the craft hut alongside volunteers. Depending on the coworkers' condition or mood, they can work alone or with others. All gather for lunch in the café together with staff, visitors, and members of the local community. Coworkers are struggling with a range of conditions, from schizophrenia, chronic states of anxiety, depression, and school phobia, to a variety of chronic physical illnesses such as cancer, multiple sclerosis, and cerebral palsy.

Most of the coworkers live in the local community. At first, they received no pay for their work, but now that the project is "on its feet," each receives a nominal £10 a week. Some move on to other paid employment after a period in the garden; others are more or less permanent as there is little chance for improvement of their condition. Two other medical practices based on the Steiner approach—those at Stroud and Bristol—are currently developing garden projects inspired by the experience at Blackthorn.

A two-year study evaluating the Blackthorn Garden Project by the Sainsbury Center for Mental Health was published in 1995 (Nehring and Hill, 1995). During the first year (1992–1993), fifteen men and sixteen women joined the project, ranging in age from fifteen to sixty-one years. On joining the project, coworkers agree to work on specified days in the garden, kitchen, bakery, or cafe. In the first year, coworkers on average attended 74 percent of their contracted time; in the second year, this rose to 82 percent. Interviews with coworkers revealed that most appreciated the relaxed, caring atmosphere and the sense of being valued as part of a community. The companionship, routine, attractive surroundings, supportive staff, and opportunity to do meaningful work all contributed to coworkers' positive experiences:

> Working in the Blackthorn garden has made me feel part of a family, increased my self-confidence, and communication skills. ...

> I have become more optimistic about the future and more confident within myself.

> The project had a very important effect on me last year, in giving me a new focus at a time when I felt in despair.

> Looking at nature—realizing it is God's creation—peace—preserving the plant garden for the future. People who are ill supporting each other, the staff giving their support, making new friends, understanding each other better, a place of security like a retreat.

While the two-year evaluation found no dramatic improvements in the functioning of coworkers (as indicated by standardized mental health tests), it concluded that for many, the Garden Project provided a very valuable social/physical setting where they could find relief from distressing symptoms and distractions from worries. As one coworker remarked: "It is better than being given pills and told to come back in a week's time. ... It gives people a sense of identity, something useful to do ...."

It is ironic that this approach of providing people with psychological problems "something useful to do" was at the heart of treatment in large mental institutions in Europe and North America from the mid-nineteenth to the mid-twentieth centuries. Farm and garden work provided healthy outdoor tasks, as well as producing food for consumption, until public opinion (" 'They' shouldn't be made to work.") and the unions put a stop to this practice. Inspiring projects such as that at Blackthorn are causing people to rethink the therapeutic value of work, while its location on the same site as a primary care medical center helps to reduce the stigma attached to mental health problems. As an informational brochure on the Blackthorn Garden states:

> Working the land, living by the seasons, growing plants, preparing good food and serving others in a simple and light-filled environment offer the conditions that encourage rehabilitation. A respect for all that lives helps to cultivate the healthy and responsive side of each person, however ill she or he might be. In such a climate, illness falls into the background and true character shows through.

Homewood Health Centre, Guelph, Ontario, Canada[2]
By Nathan H. Perkins, Professor of Landscape Architecture

Description of the Facility and Its History
The Homewood Health Centre, established in 1883, is a 320,000 square foot psychiatric hospital located on 55 acres of maintained and naturalized grounds along the Speed River in Guelph, Ont., Canada. Six historic and architecturally significant buildings house 312 in-patient beds with about 2,000 admissions per year. Homewood provides a wide range of in- and out-patient psychiatric programs including ones for eating disorders, addictions, and survivors of trauma, as well as specific programs and therapies directed at mental illnesses such as bipolar disorders, schizophrenia, and Alzheimer's. Homewood has a number of complementary programs such as shiatsu, massage therapy, recreation therapy, and an internationally recognized and respected Horticultural Therapy program. All of the complementary programs are offered as integral components of other programs.

In the late nineteenth and early twentieth centuries the original Homewood buildings were sited on a high river terrace on the agricultural fringe of Guelph. As the hospital developed and expanded, structures were added to the north of existing buildings and later linked with connecting corridors. The result is a grouping of six distinct period buildings, ranging from brick with ionic colonnades, mullioned windows, and deep verandahs, to native rough cut limestone with elaborate roof brackets and distinctive regional decorative elements. Outstanding views are afforded from the hospital to the woodlots, open spaces with recreational fields and gardens, and small structures such as a gazebo and a clubhouse.

Access to the hospital in the early Homewood era was along carriageways that followed the river and ascended the terraced hills in gentle curves. The modern internal road circulation system follows the original carriageways, and the roads remain narrow and without curbs. In the 1920s a major city road, Delhi Street, was built on the uphill side of the hospital and this is now the primary route to the hospital. The result is an awkward situation in which the back of the hospital complex is the public face oriented to the street. Numerous modifications to the hospital have followed with main entrances, entry courtyards, and pedestrian walks designed to reorient the hospital to the street.

---

[2]This case study differs from others in this chapter in that a number of post-occupancy studies provide very detailed information regarding the perception and use of outdoor space.

The hospital, once on the periphery of the city, is now enveloped by primarily residential neighborhoods on two sides and is linked to a health corridor with a large medical hospital and outpatient clinics located nearby.

The Outdoor Space

The Homewood landscape is truly outstanding with large blocks of second growth forests framing open areas of lawn and ornamental planting beds with specimen trees. Although there are lingering traces of an English pastoral landscape characteristic of a sanitarium of the early twentieth century, the visual character of Homewood is now dominated by extensive woodlots with dense understory vegetation. The topographic change from the hospital complex to the river is substantial, with an approximately 15-meter fall in two distinct terraces. By accident rather than intent, the hospital grounds today are characterized by near-building formal plantings, including annual flower beds, becoming progressively more natural and less formal as one moves away from the hospital toward the river. Slightly removed from the hospital are two century-old and historically significant mansions. The first was used for years as a home for the medical superintendent and family and is now a daycare center for Homewood employees. The other, Riverslea, is an exceptional example of a Richardson Romanesque style stone mansion built by one of Guelph's founding families, and is presently used for conferences and meetings.

The hospital and circulation (pedestrian and vehicular) are the major organizing elements for the entire site. Narrow paved roads connect the hospital and its prominent position at the top of the hill to the "Manor Green" and "River Green" below. There are no paved sidewalks except those immediately adjacent to the hospital, so patients and staff use the roadways or packed gravel paths in the woodlots below for walking.

During the first half of this century, extensive areas on the grounds were devoted to recreational activities such as lawn bowling, croquet, and tennis, as well as for extensive vegetable gardens and a complement of chicken coops and dairy cattle barns. Patients grew their own food, collected eggs, and milked cows as part of their program; vestiges of these activities can still be discerned on the grounds. Maintenance expenses and changing therapeutic directions led Homewood to replace these activities and facilities with a baseball field and outdoor volleyball court. In tracing the changes of the Homewood landscape over the last fifty years, it appears that the landscape has evolved in tandem with the use of the grounds. Formal recreation activities requiring high maintenance and single-use

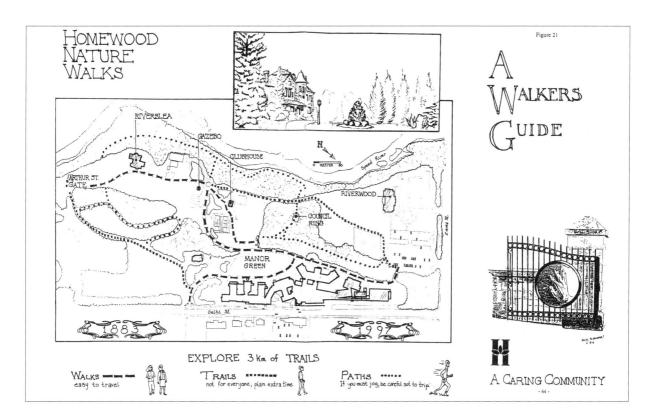

areas, such as lawn bowling, have been replaced by activities such as strolling or bird-watching, which occur primarily in the woodlots or along the paved roadways.

By the early 1990s, decades of reduced maintenance had resulted in woodlots increasingly dominated by the exotic and invasive Norway maple and much of the infrastructure such as stairs and roadways was in disrepair. Formal annual flower beds were reduced in size when the on-site greenhouse was demolished in the 1980s, and tree and shrub planting and maintenance declined. These changes clearly affected the aesthetics of the Homewood landscape and resulted in changing patient and staff use of the grounds. Although Homewood has a horticultural therapy program with formal gardens and raised planting beds, the gardens are distant and downslope, making it difficult for physically challenged patients to get to them. Most importantly, outside of a few major pathways, the Speed River and much of the natural landscape has become virtually inaccessible as Norway maple has come to dominate the woodlot understory.

Figure 6-30 A "Walker's Guide" handed to inpatients and staff at Homewood Health Centre, Guelph, Ont., Canada, to encourage them to use the extensive grounds of this psychiatric facility. (Perkins and Barnhart, 1996c).

Users

Although most of Homewood's patients are from Ontario, Canada, Homewood markets its services throughout North

America and there is a small international patient population. One of the main emphases of Homewood marketing is hotel services—amenities such as full-service dining rooms and hotel-quality rooms—as well as the beautiful natural setting of the hospital.

Many inpatient programs are of fixed duration, during which time patients are offered a highly structured daily routine including group and individual treatment, recreation activities, and opportunities to select from a range of personal entertainment options. Almost all of the patients at Homewood are self-admitted, although there is a small crisis unit for limited-term patient stabilization. On average, there are between 300 and 400 patients and almost 600 staff members at Homewood each day. Patients in most programs are allowed visitors, and on any given day 50 to 100 visitors may be at Homewood.

The grounds of Homewood are used extensively by patients, staff, and visitors from May to November. Daily walks are required in some treatment programs, and recreation activities as well as horticultural therapy sessions are well-attended complementary programs. Many staff members use the grounds during lunch and breaks, and visitors often meet with patients outdoors. Although use of the grounds by patients, staff, and visitors is high, the large area and variety of activities taking place on the grounds make it difficult to understand what specific activities people are engaged in and, perhaps more significantly, why users are choosing to engage in them. For years, this lack of information has made it difficult to direct planning and design efforts for the Homewood landscape that would support and enhance patient use of the natural environment.

In 1996, a master planning process was initiated based on the understanding that patient behaviors and experiences within the environment need to be central in the design of therapeutic outdoor settings. Four applied research studies were conducted over a six-month period to determine how patients behaved in and experienced the natural environment at Homewood. The objectives of these studies were: (1) to assess the existing use of the grounds by patients and staff through surveys and structured behavioral observations; (2) to understand patients' behavioral and visual preferences using a custom-designed computer survey; (3) to develop a "special places" map of the site based on patient and staff interviews and mapping exercises; and (4) to link patients' expected experiences while viewing a video with physical qualities of the special places in order to create a planning and design framework applicable to the entire site.

Studies and Results

Each of the studies built on results from the previous studies to create a logical and defensible process through which hospital executives, clinicians, and support staff could better understand the link between the physical environment and patient behaviors and experiences. Numerous constraints on the collection of information from psychiatric patients were addressed through the design of two computer-based, stand-alone surveys that presented rich visual images of the Homewood environment and collected subject responses in a range of formats. The results of these studies as well as a comprehensive biological and physical analysis of the entire site were used to create a master plan for the hospital intended to be used in the planning, design and maintenance of physical settings that supported desirable and healthy psychiatric patient behaviors and experiences.

A series of structured behavioral observations were conducted over a two-week period in which patients and staff were unobtrusively observed in nine near-building locations (e.g., courtyards, patios, entrances, parking areas), as well as in several areas removed from the hospital. Observations were designed to collect information on the time of day, frequency, and duration of use. User behaviors were documented using ethograms (predefined categories of behaviors) in which individual and group behaviors were identified, mapped, and summarized (Perkins and Barnhart, 1996a).

Patients and staff used the areas near the buildings for short periods of ten to twenty minutes during four peak periods during breaks between programs or following meals, generally for smoking. As a result, the near-building areas such as the courtyards, verandahs, and major entrances that received sun were intensively used, yet only for relatively short periods of time, leading to overcrowded spaces. Some of these spaces were furnished with picnic tables, and, in addition, patients brought chairs out of the building to sit on. At times, so many people were in a courtyard or clustered around an entrance that entering or exiting the building became difficult.

Summaries of the observations taken in areas farther away from the buildings clearly showed a different set of behaviors. For example, an area of well-maintained grass with a southern exposure, known as The Manor Green, located a short distance from the busy social courtyards, was used primarily for passive, solitary pursuits such as sunbathing and reading. In general, the farther the setting was from the hospital, the more passive and solitary were the behaviors observed. Although this was not particularly surprising, the observations substantiated a widely held assumption that patients and staff used the natural areas of the grounds, which were furthest away from the hospital, to "get away," "find some peace and solitude," and to "walk alone or with significant others."

The results from this study indicated which behaviors were being expressed in specific settings. A subsequent analysis of the settings themselves helped to establish the attributes of a setting that might support a particular behavior. What was not determined was whether there were behaviors not being expressed because of an unsupportive setting. To answer this question, a second study was designed to test patient and staff preferences for a wide range of both settings and behaviors.

The goal of the second study was to link patient's preferences for certain environmental settings with their preferences for certain behaviors. Numerous constraints, such as patient confidentiality issues, meant the investigators could not interview or meet with some patients directly. In addition, varied patient abilities to respond to certain forms of surveys led the investigators to develop a stand-alone, touch-screen computer survey that would meet confidentiality guidelines and be available to respondents in a secure ward.

Images of typical settings found near the hospital were digitized and arranged to present two constructs that were felt to best characterize the outdoor environment; these were Built–Natural and Open–Enclosed. Over a two-week period, a self-selected sample of 37 patients and 37 staff from the addictions program completed the survey. The sample contained 42 percent of the patients and 75 percent of the staff in the unit. The mean age for the patient sample was 37. Ages ranged from 23 to 70 for 9 females and 28 males.

The results of the survey showed that patients and staff expressed clear preferences for specific settings in which to engage in specific behaviors. Natural settings were consistently preferred by patients and staff for a wide range of behaviors. However, about 20 percent of the patients preferred only built settings, such as patios and courtyards, porches, and other settings with little vegetation present. By and large, these 20 percent of patients preferring highly built settings could not be distinguished by diagnosis or other characteristics from the majority who preferred natural settings.

"Enclosed" outdoor settings, such as paths through woodland, were generally more preferred for behaviors best characterized as active (e.g., walking, strolling with others), while open settings were linked to passive behaviors such as sitting, reading, and smoking. In general, patients and staff preferred natural-enclosed settings, such as woodlot trails, for getting away and natural-open settings for relaxing and engaging in solitary activities. These results were, in general, consistent with an earlier study of schizophrenic patients' visual and setting preferences conducted at the London Psychiatric Hospital in London, Ont. (Larsen, 1992).

The goal of the third study was to ascertain not only *which* settings patients and staff preferred but *why* they preferred them. A series of individual and group meetings were held in which both patients and staff were asked to identify "special places" on a map of Homewood. In addition, patients were asked to provide a brief written description of why they found those places to be special. Although some patients required assistance, most found the activity to be an enjoyable and refreshing break from their daily routine.

More than 120 people participated from 7 community meetings representing the major psychiatric programs at the hospital. The information collected consisted of the types and locations of "special places" and comments on why these places were considered special. The written descriptions were summarized and a basic content analysis was conducted. Approximately fifty identifiable special places were mapped along with more than forty different adjectives or statements describing qualities of those places (Perkins and Barnhart, 1996b). Although a large number of locations were identified, a few places were frequently listed by a number of patients, such as a popular woodlot trail and a grove of spruce trees near the hospital.

A common element of virtually all the special places listed was a clear reference to how the place made the individual *feel*. For example, a place under a large maple on the Manor Green made six patients feel relaxed and comfortable; for two patients, the river walk evoked a feeling of being in a cathedral. Very few of the patients used place names or referred to the architectural or spatial qualities of the place.

The adjective descriptions for each special place were summarized. Based on a striking pattern of responses, each special place was categorized as one of the following:

A Place of Meaning   The setting or object held a special significance for what it represented to the individual: for example, a memorial garden.

A Place of Behavior   The setting or object held special significance because it was enjoyed for a certain activity: for example, a spruce grove that is valued because it is a nice place to eat lunch.

A Place of Experience   The setting or object held special significance because it led to a sought-after feeling or experience: for example, sitting under a special maple tree "makes me feel peaceful."

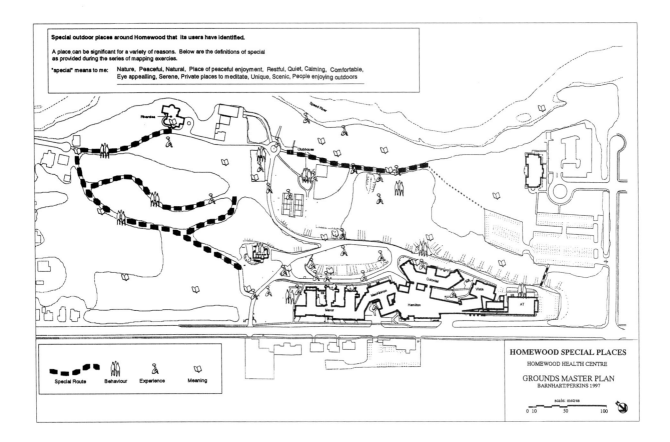

Figure 6-31 A sample of patients and staff at Homewood Health Centre were asked to locate and describe places on the grounds that were special to them. These fell into three categories: Places of Behavior (enjoyed for a certain activity); Places of Experience (enjoyed for the feelings aroused); and Places of Meaning (significant for what they represented). (Perkins and Barnhart, 1996b).

Both patients and staff had no difficulty identifying many "special places" throughout the grounds. Most of the patients were quite articulate in describing why specific places were selected, using a range of adjectives. It was expected that "special places" would generally be found in accessible areas, yet a number were removed from the hospital and walking routes. The majority of identified locations were natural settings that patients linked to specific personal experiences (e.g., helping a fellow patient overcome a personal crisis), or contained unusual physical forms or spatial qualities (e.g., the larch snag in a remote location where one patient went to read). One of the most significant locations was a circle of cedars 15 meters in diameter. Many patients described this area as spiritual and groups of patients would often hold "healing" ceremonies within the circle.

It was evident that many patients had deep and personal attachments to specific settings based on their individual experiences. Many places that might have been overlooked or deemed common by the investigators, such as individual trees within a woodlot, were identified by patients and staff as places meriting recognition in planning and design. This study also provided necessary background information for developing the virtual tour discussed below.

The goal of the fourth study was to create and test a means for patients and staff to view a number of settings throughout the grounds from within the hospital. Many patients in the hospital were not familiar with the range of settings on the grounds or were in programs that restricted access to the grounds during the initial period of their residence. It was found that these patients, when granted unsupervised access to the grounds, did not take advantage of that freedom because of their lack of familiarity with the variety of settings the grounds offered. The result was that patients were not using the grounds because they were not informed, and the grounds were not receiving adequate attention because few patients appeared to be using them.

A digital, photographically realistic program was created to portray the Homewood grounds. The program allowed viewers to have a sense of control in moving through the grounds as well as the ability to "look around" within settings. Eighteen of the locations identified in the special places survey were photographed using a digital camera on a rotating panoramic mount. The camera and panoramic mount "captured" a set of twelve digital images that could be "stitched" together to form a seamless 360-degree panorama called a QuickTime Virtual Realty Movie (QTVR). Viewers of QTVR Movies could choose what they were looking at by panning horizontally or vertically as though they occupied the center of a photographically realistic cylinder. Multiple QTVR movies, called "nodes," were then linked together, enabling the viewer to experience movement within the hospital environment by moving from node to node.

The purpose of the module was to present a simple, user-friendly way for people to select any node and not be confused by the computer interface. Using the Virtual Tour as a research instrument, a study was conducted to examine the link between attributes of environmental settings and people's expected experiences within those settings (Yeats, 1997). Thirty-two subjects (sixteen staff and sixteen patients) volunteered to participate in the study. Each subject was asked to describe the experiences (e.g., tranquil, distressed, etc.) they would expect to have if they were actually in the setting displayed using the Virtual Tour. Each subject was asked to "visit" all eighteen settings. Although a list of adjectives was provided as an aid, subjects were encouraged to respond using any words that might come to mind. The investigators recorded each subject's verbal responses for each node as well as what direction the subject was viewing within the node.

The results of the study indicated that most settings clearly promoted a set of commonly shared expected experiences among staff and patients. Even when some patients and staff were not familiar with a particular setting, they were able to quite clearly describe what experiences they would expect to have and indicated that they would make choices to seek out those places that best supported their desired experiences. Although there were some minor differences, both staff and patients generally used the same adjectives to describe their expected experiences for specific settings. For example, settings rated as natural, enclosed, less complex, highly textured, and small in scale were always described as settings in which patients would expect to feel "calm," "relaxed," "tranquil," and "at peace." Settings rated as complex—whether natural or built—and lacking unity or organizing form were expected by patients to elicit feelings of "nervousness," "coldness," and "discomfort." These findings allowed the investigators to link actual qualities of the physical setting with likely patient and staff experiences that could, or would, be derived from the setting. Settings from around the hospital were categorized and organized using patient expected experience information.

The outcome of all of these studies was a better understanding of patient and staff behaviors within the existing environment and a better understanding of how psychiatric patients experienced the diverse natural environments at Homewood. Based on this information, a series of twelve design principles was used to create a master plan specifying steps in planning and designing a range of settings—settings that would elicit, support, and enhance certain desirable patient behaviors and experiences (Perkins and Barnhart, 1996a).

Information, such as "A Walker's Guide to the Homewood Community" (Perkins and Barnhart, 1996c; see also Figure 6-30), is now given to all new patients encouraging them to explore and discover these settings. Informal monitoring has shown patient use of the natural environment has increased and a wider range of settings is now being used. Interviews with staff and patients have determined that newly designed settings do indeed elicit the patient experiences that were predicted (Perkins, 1998).

Much of the existing literature on person-environment interactions is relevant to the planning and design of therapeutic landscapes for psychiatric patients. At Homewood, hospital executives, staff, and even the design consultants were unaware of the extensive body of information available and therefore rarely included the whole natural environment in planning and design. Using an environment-behavior framework, Homewood has moved beyond designing specific gardens for specific therapeutic programs, and has begun a process of evaluating both the interior and exterior environment in total. In the final analysis, the research conducted in the course of creating the Homewood Health Centre Grounds Master Plan (Perkins and Barnhart, 1996d) provided the guiding principles that are now used by the Homewood staff to better care for their patients. The philosophy adopted by Homewood, and one that will reap future rewards, is one of creating places for experiences based on a better understanding of the experiences derived from places.

ADVANTAGES

- The landscape at Homewood is recognized by hospital executives, staff, and patients as a major asset in therapeutic programs as well as a source of staff satisfaction.
- The Homewood landscape and peripheral woodlots act as a buffer between the hospital and surrounding residential and institutional areas, creating a general sense of enclosure and privacy.
- The size of the landscaped grounds affords both the flexibility and the opportunity to create a number of behavioral settings without conflict (e.g., places of solitude and repose as well as places of high activity).
- The diversity of the grounds (e.g., woodlots and open spaces) offers a diversity of use and experience opportunities for patients and staff. Setting diversity is essential to allow patients and staff to select those settings that best meet their perceived behavioral and experiential needs (from settings for smoking to settings for spiritual/ceremonial experiences).
- The transition from buildings to landscape, progressing from built to natural, offers patients and visitors a continuum of choices along a gradient of natural settings.
- Key concepts such as setting diversity, behavioral niches, experience settings, and patient behavioral and setting choice have been used successfully to integrate physical design issues with desired patient behavioral and experiential outcomes.
- Patients and staff have information about the range of settings afforded at Homewood, increasing the likelihood that they will make appropriate choices from the range of settings.
- Program leaders have a better understanding of what places at the hospital might be most appropriate for their patients' specific needs.

DISADVANTAGES

- Allocation of resources for maintenance of the existing landscape is more difficult to "sell" to hospital executives and foundation members, who are generally more enthusiastic about tangible changes to the environment such as new structures or gardens.

- The sheer size and complexity of the environment makes it difficult to develop design standards that provide consistency in signs, furnishings, walkways, plants, and so on, while striving for a diversity of settings.

- Although it is generally accepted that the natural environment is a valuable resource in patient care and staff satisfaction, specific measures and outcomes of the positive effects afforded by the natural environment have not been placed in comparable units so that trade-offs among competing decisions can be made.

DESIGN GUIDELINES

"… when designing for other people, particularly the psychologically handicapped, it is not the designer's perception of the environment but his perception of how the people for whom the facilities are designed need to perceive this environment. There is need for humility which permits not only the necessary awareness but the sensitivity and understanding as to the significance of environmental needs for these handicapped people. There is no place for arrogance and esoteric aesthetic ventures if one is really concerned about the welfare and literally the psychological life of these people,"

H. OSMOND AND K. IZUMI

Most of the design guidelines for acute care general hospitals can be equally well applied to psychiatric hospitals and units. In this section, those design guidelines that are more specific to the needs and issues of psychiatric healthcare are discussed.

Design for the needs of the client. It is critical in psychiatric healthcare settings to keep the focus on the patients and their needs. Architects and other designers often wish to create designs that express their own personalities, that set them apart from their predecessors and colleagues, or that function just as much as a means of artistic expression as a space for people to inhabit. As Clifford Moller iterates, "The true goal of architectural design, a beneficial interaction of space and personality, is all too frequently obscured by a hectic striving for 'originality,' which usually results in bizarre forms totally unrelated to spatial [and emotional] needs" (Moller, 1968, p. 138). Ego must not get in the way of the primary goal, which is to serve the people who are using the psychiatric health center's space by providing a welcoming, restorative environment that is conducive to personal growth and recovery.

Collaborate with other designers and with clients. Site planners, architects, and landscape architects, as well as psychologists and other healthcare providers, must collaborate throughout the entire design process. Design of the outdoor space is not simply the concern of the landscape architect, who is often (unfortunately) brought in long after the site and building plans have been developed. Especially in urban areas, where the hospital building(s) may enclose a courtyard, it is the architect, ideally in concert with other members of the design team, who ultimately determines the form of the outdoor space and its relation to the surrounding buildings. Working with hospital administrators, staff, and patients can provide insight for a design that is tailored specifically to a group's needs. Involvement of the community adjacent to the healthcare facility is also important. Mental illness still has a strong stigma, and there are many people who are afraid of those with psychiatric health problems. The more the designer and the facility can work with and inform the public, the greater the potential for a strong and positive relationship once the facility has been built. During the design of the Whitby Mental Health Centre, for example, user groups consisting of designers, healthcare providers, and members of the Whitby community were essential in the beginning decision-making process. Because the citizens of Whitby were included in the design process, they now have a positive connection with the hospital and the surrounding site.

Treat the outdoor space as one part of a cohesive whole. A discovery path, a butterfly garden, or a bench for resting, all may work individually, but if they do not work in concert with the whole, the point is lost:

> ... in the design of environments for the psychologically handicapped, particularly for those who suffer from certain perceptual distortions and are unable to compensate for these, it is not simply a matter of correlating good features in a particular room or space, or even within the entire building, purely on a visual basis as in the case with the usual architectural approach. Very complex perceptual considerations enter into the picture ... (Osmond and Izumi, 1971, p. 32).

Perhaps equally as important as the coherent arrangement of objects in the outdoor spaces is the relationship of the outdoors to the indoors, the building to the surrounding site. When planning the outdoor space, provide as many visual and programmatic connections to the indoors as possible, so that all spaces within the hospital will function best for the care of the patient.

Bring the outdoors in. The benefits of windows and other architectural elements that connect people inside to the world outside have been well documented. With psychiatric patients, such connection is all the more critical because they are often unable to leave the building. Ideally, all patients would be

Figure 6-32 View from waiting room to accessible private garden in outpatient psychiatric facility. (El Camino Hospital, Mountain View, CA, photo by Marni Barnes.)

allowed to venture outdoors when and if they so desired. However, this is not always possible. Sometimes inclement weather alone—for example extreme cold, pouring rain, or extreme heat—prevents patients (and even employees) from going outdoors. Depending on the degree of security needed by the patient, the staff-to-patient ratio, and the setup of the outdoor space, there may be times when going outside is simply not feasible. Especially in settings where a patient may feel "trapped," and may even be in the facility's care against his or her will, it is critical to provide some type of access to the outside world. Something as simple as a window that allows a view outside, particularly onto a natural area, a courtyard, or an interesting street scene, can give the patient a feeling of escape. Irving Goffman, after observing patients in a psychiatric ward in the late 1950s, wrote the following:

> The vicarious consumption of free places was one of the most poignant instances of make-do in the hospital. Patients in seclusion would sometimes spend time looking out the outside window, when this was within reach, or out of the Judas hole in the door, vicariously following the activity on the grounds of the ward. Some male patients in back wards would vie with each other for possession of a window sill; once obtained, the sill was used as a seat, the patient curling up in the window, looking outside through the bars...and in this way somewhat removing himself from the ward and somewhat freeing himself from its territorial restriction (Goffman, 1961, pp. 237–238).

While they do not replace the actual experience of being outside, indoor areas such as atria, solaria, glassed-in porches, and greenhouses provide "in-between" spaces, which are especially welcome during days or even seasons when outdoor activity is undesirable.

Provide easy access from the indoors to the outdoors for patients, visitors, and staff. Depending on the clients' needs and program, voluntary access to a courtyard or grounds may not be appropriate. However, it is still important to inform potential users of the whereabouts of the facility's outdoor spaces, as well as how to get to them. Views from the indoors, along with clear signage and brochures with the areas clearly marked, are all excellent "advertisements" for rooftops, courtyard gardens, and trails. At the Homewood Health Center in Ontario, Canada, patients and visitors are given a map of the hospital and grounds, in which many possible outdoor sites are clearly shown. At Butler Hospital in Providence, RI, the path

A staff member at an old psychiatric facility remarked: "These grounds are beautiful. You do better if you get out and clear your head. I walk almost every day, at least once, even when it's cold out, even in the snow. Going outside calms me down, it centers me, and it helps me enjoy my job. I like my job, but it can get very stressful... the grounds are a great perk of working here."

Figure 6-33 Lawn area for bowling and socializing at an inpatient psychiatric facility. Exercise is an important component of treatment. (North Staffordshire Hospital, Stoke-on-Trent, UK, photo by Marni Barnes.)

that loops around the main building, as well as some of the benches along this path, can be seen as one approaches the main entrance, and act as an invitation to the passerby.

Design for specific needs when possible. If the designer knows who the patients are or will be, it is helpful to provide spaces specific to those patients' needs. For example, in a study on schizophrenic patients' preferences for outdoor environments, researchers found that the patients had a greater preference for outdoor spaces with a high degree of enclosure and complexity (Larsen, 1992). At Whitby Mental Health Centre, the courtyards adjacent to each of the various units are designed with the patients of that specific unit in mind. Treatment of the ground plane is one example of this "tailoring": In courtyards where patients have poorer motor capabilities, more paving and less lawn is provided to allow for easy wheelchair access and navigation. In courtyards for younger and more mobile clients, larger areas of lawn can be used for lounging, picnicking, and sports. Designers musts understand the needs of the individuals and groups for whom they are designing—not only the general disorder, such as schizophrenia, but the particular group in the specific locale.

In cases where patient-specific design is not possible (often because clients with many different illnesses will share the same space), it is important to draw upon available research on the landscape preferences of people with a range of psychiatric disorders. Generally, it appears that people with mental health problems are attracted to many of the same types of spaces that most people are attracted to, and for similar activities (for example, smaller niches for private conversation or personal

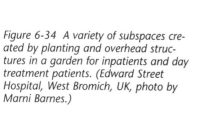

Figure 6-34 A variety of subspaces created by planting and overhead structures in a garden for inpatients and day treatment patients. (Edward Street Hospital, West Bromich, UK, photo by Marni Barnes.)

reflection; larger, open areas for recreation and exploration). In addition, mental patients, similar to people who do not have psychiatric illnesses, generally prefer "natural" over "built" environments. Especially for the mentally ill, ordered nature is preferred over something that seems completely "wild." Some degree of enclosure is generally preferred, but complete enclosure can make patients uncomfortable.

Provide a variety of spaces and experiences. Whenever possible, provide a variety of spaces and destinations for patients, visitors, and staff. For areas farther away from the main building, "destinations" such as an herb garden, a water feature, or a grove of trees can help to draw people into the surrounding landscape. Even at the STARS facility (San Leandro, CA), where space is relatively limited, clients have at least three spaces that they can occupy: the Central Courtyard, Walker's Field, and (on supervised outings) the San Leandro Hills surrounding the site. A hierarchy of spaces—usually radiating out from the building and becoming less enclosed and less specific as to function—can assist clients in exploring their surroundings and beginning to come out of themselves. This is often an important step in the recovery process. The Therapeutic Garden in Wellesley, MA, designed by Douglas Reed (case study, Chapter 7), provides another excellent example. The acre of land adjacent to the Institute for Child and Adolescent Development is set up as a sequence of spaces that are designed to correspond, symbolically and physically, with the stages of a child's recovery. "The garden elements combine to form a sequence of both introverted and extroverted spaces, corresponding directly to the stages of recovery: a narrow, dark, cave-like ravine for safety; an upland woodland for exploration; steep and shallow slopes for climbing to get views; and a large sunny glade for running and playing" (Reed, 1995, p. 21).

Allow for a variety of experiences, even in small areas. Just as important as the provision for many separate spaces is the facilitation of a variety of options and experiences within a single space. This is key on sites with only one outdoor area, such as a rooftop garden or an enclosed courtyard. With careful planning, even a small courtyard can allow the user several areas and experiences to choose from: intimate nooks for solitary reflection; nodes for groups of two or three people to meet; pathways for wandering and discovery; larger open areas with seating for groups of people (often useful for group therapy, family meetings, and staff meetings). A courtyard with a basketball hoop, or a lawn with a badminton or volleyball net can facilitate group, one-on-one, or individual physical activity; it is of course best if the spaces are large enough that more than one activity can take place at one time. Open, unprogrammed areas such as patios or ball courts, when adjacent to occupational, art, or music therapy rooms, can allow staff and patients to pull chairs and even tables outside. At the John George Psychiatric Pavilion (San Leandro, CA), a covered, paved patio outside of the therapy units is often used during scheduled program hours, and is used as a casual seating area for patients and visitors during "off" hours. Swaths of lawn can function as flexible spaces for passive, active, social, and solitary recreation. At Butler Hospital, a small lawn area just off the "smoking porch" is set up with two picnic tables and a volleyball net. During lunch, employees sit at the picnic tables. At other times of the day, recreation groups use the net for volleyball or badminton. At still other times, people sit on the lawn or at the picnic tables to read, write, or converse.

Figure 6-35 A garden courtyard provides a quiet and private setting for informal counseling. (Stanford University Medical Center, Stanford, CA, photo by Marni Barnes.)

Balance privacy and safety. Designers continue to grapple with the seemingly conflicting needs of patients for both a secure environment and an outdoor space in which they can achieve some form of "escape" or separation from the indoor routine. Especially for patients who cannot be out of sight of nurses or other staff, it is important to create outdoor spaces that, while still visible from a nurse's station or dayroom, provide a sense of separation and privacy. This can be accomplished by the manipulation of the space and the materials—plants, topography, hardscape, furniture—within that space. For example, "rooms" can be created with seats, planters, or low bushes. In hospitals where clients do not have access to easily monitored outside areas, it is paramount that programs such as physical, occupational, and horticulture therapy incorporate "going and being outside" into the routine. For hospitals that care for patients with a range of safety needs, it is best to provide a hierarchy of outdoor spaces, which clients can work up to as they progress in treatment. At both Butler Hospital and the Whitby Mental Health Centre, fenced courtyards are surrounded by acres of open grounds, which patients can use for recreation when they are allowed and able. At Butler Hospital, going outside alone (without an attending staff member) is one of the most powerful behavioral incentives used by the staff.

Provide at least one space where the layout is "readable" by the user. For some patients, leaving the building may be a challenge, emotionally and/or physically. Especially in areas directly adjacent to the building, where patients under the most acute levels of care will venture most often, the design should be simple enough for the patient to "read" and navigate. Simple does not have to mean boring. If a strong framework is established, the use of planting, seating arrangements, and overhead structures can create plenty of variety to stimulate the senses. If it is possible to provide a hierarchy of spaces as one gets further from the building, it may also be appropriate to allow these spaces to become less planned or formal. By providing a "staging area" from which the rest of the garden might be safely surveyed, the fear of venturing further is minimized. The verandah at The Retreat is an excellent example of such a space. Research also indicates that, when patients are allowed to wander on their own, they tend to retreat to spaces that are farther away and more secluded. Often these are very "natural" places, such as the grotto at The Retreat, and paths in the woods at Homewood.

Avoid "fishbowls". In psychiatric hospitals and units where complete enclosure is often necessary for patients' safety, many designs feature a building or a series of buildings that surround a courtyard. This type of design reduces the need for fencing around the periphery of the facility. To allow in the greatest amount of light and allow views outward, patients' windows are often oriented toward the courtyards. It is important to "buffer" these windows, both for the privacy of the users inside, and to lessen the "fishbowl" effect for people outside. Ideally, this buffer would permit a sense of privacy for those both inside and out, while still allowing people inside to have a visual connection with the outdoor space. Two solutions are changes in grade, where the outdoor area is slightly lower than the patients' windows, and buffer planting, which both visually and spatially (physically) screens windows. Plants do not need

Figure 6-36 Entry structure, sundial and trellis walks provide orientation cues in a garden for patients. (Edwards Street Hospital, West Bromich, UK, photo by Marni Barnes.)

to completely block a window to facilitate a feeling of privacy; their screening foliage or branches can be partially transparent rather than completely opaque.

Provide separate spaces for staff. It is helpful for hospital staff to have some type of outdoor "room of their own" where they can be with other colleagues, away from the view of patients and visitors. In *Progressive Architecture*'s review of the Yale Psychiatric Institute ("Village, Not…," 1993), the author's observations of the facility's failure to provide separate spaces for staff contributed to the negative assessment of the Institute:

> …nurses and therapists are desperate for private spaces where they can relax. There are no closed staff lounges and no private outdoor spaces. On the basement level, a makeshift terrace (known as "the moat") is the staff's only outdoor retreat. It is not wheelchair accessible and is in fact not supposed to be occupied because it is surrounded by walls of lead-coated copper, a material kept out of reach throughout the building (*ibid.*, p. 103).

The John George Psychiatric Pavilion (San Leandro, CA) has a separate courtyard for employees, which is separated from the patient courtyard by clear glass blocks that allow light, but not views, in. The courtyard is planted with trees and a few flowers, and is furnished with tables and chairs. A separate space does not have to be this elaborate—Butler Hospital's staff and visitor cafeteria is separate from the patient cafeteria, and its doors open onto a small slab of concrete furnished with wooden picnic tables. Even though this space is not fenced off from the general campus, it is distant enough from the main path to provide a feeling of privacy where staff can hold informal meetings, eat their lunch, and regroup.

Keep in mind possible ways in which materials might be perceived. People with mental health problems often see everyday objects differently, and this can be disorienting and even scary. For example, knots in a wooden door may look like eyes, or like the face of a monster. The shape or shadows of trees uplit at night may look menacing. Since each person sees different patterns and shapes, it will not be possible for the designer to "cover all the bases," to avoid using anything that might potentially be scary or threatening. However, it is helpful to keep in mind that people being treated for mental health disorders may be more sensitive to certain patterns, shapes, or textures. One way to address this issue is to conduct "focus groups" to get a feel for how materials are received by the intended user population. Focus groups are yet another example of how working closely with the client, patients, and staff can help designers to

Figure 6-37 Informal garden with simple benches used by staff and coworkers at the Blackthorn Garden Project. Planting creates visual interest and seclusion. (Blackthorn Medical Centre, Maidstone, Kent, UK, photo by Clare Cooper Marcus.)

Figure 6-38 The formal placement of these benches provides a secure setting with a brick wall at one's back and a long view down this main pathway. (The Retreat, York, UK, photo by Marni Barnes.)

make educated, sensitive decisions for beautiful, safe, and restorative outdoor spaces.

Use materials that are durable and, if safety is an issue, impossible to use as a weapon. People with mental disorders tend to "worry" the environment around them by touching, pulling, rubbing, and otherwise physically interacting with it. This behavior is often an unconscious stress-reducing technique, in which case damage is usually minimal. At other times, a patient may act out on her or his physical environment, in which case damage can be more severe; therefore, it is wise to use materials that are durable. The designer should also be conscious of objects in the landscape (chairs, pieces of sculpture, even loose stones or pavers) that might potentially be used as weapons. At the Whitby Mental Health Centre in Ontario, Canada, all furniture is bolted to the ground to avoid the risk of a patient damaging it or hurting another person. Potentially injurious objects that are easy to break and/or confiscate should be avoided, particularly in areas where there is danger of patients' attempting to cause themselves or others harm. For example, at one hospital, a patient attempted suicide by cutting her wrists with the broken glass of her bedroom lightbulb. With all of this in mind, it is nonetheless very important that the designer try her or his best to provide a setting that, while safe and secure, does not appear institutional; materials should still look and feel pleasant. If objects such as benches or tables are secured in some way, the implementation should be subtle.

Provide a water feature. If economically and logistically feasible, a water feature in the outdoor environment can greatly enhance the quality of the space. As landscape architect Anne Spirn writes, "Water is a source of life, power, comfort, and delight, a universal symbol of purification and renewal. Like a primordial magnet, water pulls at a primitive and deeply rooted part of human nature" (Spirn, 1988, p. 119). Depending on how it is used, water can function in many different ways. It can act as a focus for reflection and meditation, a gathering point, and a tactile way for people to engage with the outdoors. Wildlife is attracted to water, which provides visual, auditory, and seasonal interest. Water makes a pleasant sound and mitigates annoying noises such as traffic, air conditioners, even other people's conversations. At the Institute for Child and Adolescent Development's Therapeutic Garden in Wellesley, MA, water runs through the entire garden, acting as a connector and drawing children into the environment: "As they follow the rill on its journey through the landscape, children are drawn into the garden's different areas. One juror [in a design competition] commented, 'I can just imagine...a child putting something—a leaf, a stick, a sailboat—in this trough and watching it make its way through the landscape'" ("Winning Big," 1997, pp. 46–47). In San Francisco, a home for autistic youngsters overlooks the San Francisco Bay. Several of the residents spend much of their days watching the water—the waves, the boats, the reflections of the sun—and it has a significant calming effect. One client also has a fountain in his room, where he can hear and interact with the water whenever he chooses. On a larger scale, water can be used for educational and recreational purposes: wading, catching pollywogs, swimming, and boating are all exciting activities that engage patients with their environment and encourage exploration and discovery.

Of course, the way water is used on a site must be tailored to fit the needs and limitations of the users. If there is danger of patients falling into or tripping over a water feature, it should be enclosed, raised, or otherwise separated to avoid accidents. Some hospital nurses are upset if patients have any physical access to a water feature, arguing that it is a clean-up nuisance at the very least, and at worst, dangerous. Nurses sometimes object to the trickling sound of water, which they say inhibits some patients' bladder control. Such conflicts of interest are not uncommon, and should be addressed by the designer early in the process.

Provide temporal cues. People grappling with mental illness often have trouble with their sense of time, and are comforted by clues that help them to grasp the time of day, the day of the week, even the time of year. The John George Psychiatric Pavilion (San Leandro, CA) and Whitby Mental Health Centre (Whitby, Ont., Canada) both have large clock towers that are visible from the main courtyards; Butler Hospital (Providence, RI) has a sundial near the main building's entrance. In areas like New England, seasonal changes are quite obvious due to changes in temperature, foliage, and precipitation. In areas where seasons are less easy to discern, it is helpful to provide other types of cues. For example, in Northern California, the hills are green in the winter and spring and brown in the summer and fall; views toward these hills provide seasonal cues as well as visual interest and a connection with the cycles of nature. Another example would be the use of trees: many bear fruit, lose their leaves, and flower in relative accordance with the "traditional" seasons. The more the designer can find out about regionally traditional temporal and seasonal indicators (both natural and built) of an area, the better he or she can utilize them within the design.

Sun and glare: Provide plenty of options for shade; reduce confusing shade patterns; reduce glare. Many

Figure 6-39 A flow-form water feature in a garden used by medical and psychiatric patients. (Blackthorn Medical Centre, Maidstone, Kent, UK, photo by Clare Cooper Marcus.)

Figure 6-40 Flowering trees and shrubs in the grounds of a psychiatric facility reveal the changing of the seasons. View to York Minster in the background provides the opportunity for psychological excape. (Photo courtesy of The Retreat Archives, York, UK.)

antipsychotic and antidepressant medications have the side effect of heightening photosensitivity: patients are more susceptible to the sun's brightness and its harmful ultraviolet rays. Older patients, even without such medications, are often more sensitive to sun and bright light. Whenever possible, provide options for patients so that they can be in the sun for short periods of time, and can then move to the shade when they choose. Orienting shelter structures, benches, and trees to block or let in the sun at specific times of day can also help: afternoon sun is generally much stronger and harsher than morning sun. Shade can be dense, under a solid roof, canopy, or a heavily foliaged tree, or it can be moderate, under a planted pergola or a tree with finer textured foliage.

The designer should be cautious, however, of creating strong shadow patterns on the ground; for example, pergolas and arcades, especially if not heavily planted, often make dark linear shadows on the ground. These patterns can be disturbing and disorienting to patients. Glare from shiny or lightly colored paving (including standard grey cement) should also be avoided. One relatively inexpensive solution is colored concrete. Concrete tinted in buff or earth tones reduces glare and also provides a more visually attractive, less institutional character to the outdoor space.

Use plants that are pleasing to more than one sense. There are many plants that, in addition to being visually stimulating through color, texture, and shape, engage the other senses as well. Plants that are soft (or even sticky) to the touch, that are fragrant, and that make interesting sounds in the breeze all provide a richer sensual experience in the outdoor environment.

Figure 6-41 Staff and patients usually enjoy getting outdoors. This tea party was one of several types of programmed activities at a psychiatric facility that encouraged social interaction in the 1930s. (Photo courtesy of The Retreat Archives, York, UK.)

They also encourage patients to explore and experience the world around them in a variety of ways. In addition, plants can sometimes by used symbolically: Many herbs and other plants that have been used over time and in various cultures as antidotes for depression and other mental illnesses. Designs that include such plants, particularly in educational gardens with labels or some other form of information, can perhaps give a garden more meaning.

Avoid poisonous vegetation. Most plants are harmless if eaten, and many are even beneficial. However, poisonous plants do exist, and a designer working on a planting plan should fully research plants' toxicity before including them in the design. Though this guideline is important in most healthcare settings, the use of nonharmful plants is of particular importance in a mental healthcare environment, where patients are more inclined to touch and pick plants, and to chew on or eat the foliage, bark, and berries. This is especially important when small children use the space, as patients or as visitors, since their bodies are more susceptible to smaller doses of poison. Plants vary in terms of their level of toxicity, as well as what parts are toxic; for example, hydrangea flowers are toxic, but the leaves are not. There are several sources for designers to use in researching specific plants (e.g., Moore, 1993; Wise, 1986).

Avoid plants that are irritating to the touch. Designers often use thorny or bristly plants as natural barriers in the landscape. This is good practice for some designs, but not in a setting where people are less able to discern what is thorny before they actually grab hold of, climb, or walk into the planting. A small number of plants (in addition to the well-known poison oak and

As a former practitioner, I am as keenly aware as any practicing architect that somewhere along the line one has to make decisions and commitments. However, there are already too many stereotyped solutions for…facilities for the care and treatment of the mentally ill. These facilities are not service stations for cars or bus-stops to be reproduced from a set of standard plans or existing prototypes, if we are really concerned about people as persons who happen to suffer from a variety of mental illnesses. There is no single solution to even a single situation.

H. OSMOND AND K. IZUMI

ivy) are also irritating to the skin, and they should be avoided for the same reason. Some plants, such as thyme, attract an inordinate number of bees when they are in bloom; these plants, particularly in heavily used areas, should be avoided. Many people have strong feelings of fear when it comes to insects that sting, and some are highly allergic to stings.

All of these guidelines are important factors to take into account when an outdoor space for psychiatric healthcare is being planned. However, these guidelines are not meant to serve as a checklist for good outdoor space design. As with all good design, the beauty of a site—its sense of place, its ability to evoke feelings of calm, of joy, of awe—must come from the designer's commitment to creating a truly therapeutic environment. The designers—be they a full team of architects, landscape architects, administrators, and patients, or a small group of garden-club volunteers—must be able to balance the very real and legitimate concerns raised in this chapter with the more difficult task of making places that do, indeed, lift the spirit toward wellness and recovery.

REFERENCES

"Architecture for Psychiatric Treatment" (1991). *Progressive Architecture*, Vol. 72, No. 1, January, pp. 126–127.

Bailey, Roger (1966). "Needed: Optimum Social Design Criteria." *The Modern Hospital*, Vol. 106, No. 3, March.

Baker, A., R. L. Davies, and P. Sivadon (1959). "Psychiatric Services and Architecture." World Health Organization Public Health Papers, Geneva.

Barnhart, Steven (1996). "Examining the Relationship Between Behavioural and Environmental Setting Preferences Among Patients and Staff at a Psychiatric Hospital." MLA Thesis, University of Guelph, Guelph, Ont., Canada.

Barnes, Margaret (1994). "A Study of the Process of Emotional Healing in Outdoor Spaces and the Concomitant Design Implications." MLA Thesis, University of California, Berkeley.

Barnhart, S., N. H. Perkins, and J. FitzSimonds (In Press). "Examining the Relationship Between Behavioural and Environmental Setting Preferences among Patients and Staff at a Psychiatric Hospital." *Landscape and Urban Planning*.

Bayes, Kenneth, and S. Francklin (1971). *Designing for the Handicapped*. London: George Godwin Ltd.

Beveridge, C. E., and C. F. Hoffman (1987). *The Master List of Design Projects of the Olmsted Firm, 1857–1950*. Boston, MA: National Association for Olmsted Parks.

Bopp, J. H., D. J. Ribble, J. J. Cassidy, and R. A. Markoff (1996). "Re-Engineering the State Hospital to Promote Rehabilitation and Recovery." *Psychiatric Services*, Vol. 47, No. 7, July, pp. 697–698, 701.

Britton, Rachael (1995). "Spiritual Values at The Retreat." The Retreat Annual Report, York, UK, pp. 30–31.

"Bronx Developmental Center" (1978). *Architectural Review*. Vol. 163, No. 972, February, pp. 95–98.

Buhyoff, G. J., J. D. Wellman, J. Harvey, and R. A. Fraser (1978). "Landscape Architects' Interpretations of People's Landscape Preferences." *Journal of Environmental Management*, Vol. 6, pp. 255–262.

Butler Hospital Annual Report (1970). Providence, RI.

"Butler Hospital: An Overview" (1996). Informational Brochure, Butler Hospital, Providence, RI.

"The Butler Hospital Extension" (1979). *Architectural Record*, Vol.166, No.5, October, pp.124–126.

Butler Hospital: The Story of Its Growth, Portrayal of Its Facilities and the Methods Used in Restoration of Mental Health (194-). Providence, RI: The Butler Hospital Hobby Print Shop.

"California Licenses New, Freestanding Chemical Dependency Hospital" (1984). *Hospitals*, Vol. 58, September 16, pp. 87–88.

Canter, D. and S. Canter (1979). *Designing for Therapeutic Environments: A Review of Research*. New York: Wiley.

"Care in the Community" (1994). *Architect's Journal*, Vol. 200, No. 22, December 8, pp. 25–34.

Carpman, J. R., M. A. Grant, and D. A. Simmons (1986). *Design That Cares: Planning Health Facilities for Patients and Visitors*. Chicago, IL: American Hospital Publishing.

Community Care (1995). United Kingdom. Nov. 30–Dec. 6.

Cooper Marcus, C. and M. Barnes (1995). *Gardens in Healthcare Facilities: Uses, Therapeutic Benefits, and Design Recommendations*. Martinez, CA: The Center for Health Design, Inc.

Cox, A. and P. Groves (1981). *Design for Healthcare. The Butterworths Design Series for Architects and Planners*. London: Butterworth and Co.

Dannemaier, Molly (1995). "Healing Gardens." *Landscape Architecture*, Vol. 85, No. 1, January, pp. 56–78.

Davis, C., I. D. Glick, and I. Rosow (1979). "The Architectural Design of a Psychotherapeutic Milieu." *Hospital and Community Psychiatry*, Vol. 30, No. 7, July, pp. 453–460.

"Designing for Patients—Redeveloping De Bijtjes Hospital" (1995). *World Hospitals and Health Services*, Vol. 31, No. 3, pp. 22–26.

Deutsch, Albert (1948). *The Shame of the States*. New York: Harcourt, Brace, and Co.

———— (1949). *The Mentally Ill in America*. New York: Columbia University Press.

DeVries, D. L. (1968). "Effects of Environmental Change and of Participation on the Behavior of Mental Patients." *Journal of Consulting and Clinical Psychology*, Vol. 32, pp. 532–536.

Drew, C. J. (1971). "Research on the Psychological Behavioral Effects of the Physical Environment." *Review of Educational Research,* Vol. 41, No. 5, December, pp. 447–465.

"Evaluation: A Mental Health Facility, Its Users and Context" (1971). *AIA Journal,* Vol. 67, No. 2, February, pp. 38–41.

Falick, J. (1981). "Humanistic Design Sells Your Hospital." *Hospitals,* February 16, pp. 68–74.

"Feature Supplement: Whitby Mental Health Centre" (1996). *Whitby Free Press,* Durham Business News, September.

Frances, M. and R. Hester (Eds.) (1990). *The Meaning of Gardens.* Cambridge, MA: MIT Press.

Francis, C., and C. Cooper Marcus (1991). "Places People Take Their Problems." Proceedings of the 22nd Annual Conference of the Environmental Design Research Association, Mexico.

"Garden Design's Golden Trowel Award for 'Best Healing Garden'" (1995/1996). *Garden Design,* December/January, p. 64.

"General Information" (1997). Whitby Mental Health Centre brochure. Toronto, Ont., Canada.

Goffman, I. (1961). *Asylums.* Garden City, NY: Anchor Books.

Good, L. R., S. M. Siegel, and A. P. Bay (1965). *Therapy by Design: Implications of Architecture for Human Behavior.* Springfield, IL: Charles C. Thomas.

Goode, E. (1995). "The Nature of Health." *Mirabella,* No. 72, May, pp. 82–84.

Goshen, C. E., M.D. (1967). *Documentary History of Psychiatry.* New York: Philosophical Library.

Griffin, W. V., J. H. Mauritzen, and J. V. Kasmar (1969). "The Psychological Aspects of the Architectural Environment: A Review." *American Journal of Psychiatry,* Vol. 125, No. 8, pp. 93–98.

Gulak, M. B. (1991). "Architectural Guidelines for State Psychiatric Hospitals." *Hospital and Community Psychiatry,* Vol. 42, No. 7, July, pp. 705–707.

Hammerslough, J. (1997). "The Children's Hour: A Garden Offers Time to Heal." *Garden Design,* June/July, p. 50.

Haun, Paul (1961). "Architectural Considerations." In L. Linn (ed.) *Frontiers in General Hospital Psychiatry.* New York: International University Press. Chapter 5, pp. 67–81.

"Historical Note" (1994). From An Invitation to the Centennial Celebration of Butler Hospital. Providence, RI, May 10.

Historic Display (1997). Whitby Mental Health Centre. Toronto, Ont., Canada.

Holahan, C. J. (1982). *Environmental Psychology.* New York: Random House.

Holohan, C. J. and S. Saegert (1973). "Behavioral and Attitudinal Effects of Large-Scale Variation in the Physical Environment of Psychiatric Wards." *Journal of Abnormal Psychology,* Vol. 82, No. 3, pp. 454–462.

"Information Guide" (1996). Whitby Mental Health Centre. Toronto, Ont., Canada.

Izumi, K. (1965). "Special Considerations of Design." *Mental Hospitals,* Vol. 16, pp. 20–23.

Izumi, K. (1968). "Architectural Considerations in the Design of Places and Facilities for the Care and Treatment of the Mentally Ill." *Journal of Schizophrenia*, Vol. 2, No. 1, pp. 42–52.

Hartig, T., M. Mang, and G. W. Evans (1991). "Restorative Effects of Natural Environment Experiences." *Environment and Behavior*, Vol. 23, No. 1, pp. 3–26.

Kaplan, R. (1973). "Some Psychological Benefits of Gardening." *Environment and Behavior*, Vol. 5, pp. 145–162.

Kaplan, R. and S. Kaplan (1989). *The Experience of Nature: A Psychological Perspective*. Cambridge, MA: Cambridge University Press.

Kasmar, J. V., W. V. Griffin, and J. H. Mauritzen (1968). "Effect of Environmental Surroundings on Outpatients' Mood and Perception of Psychiatrists." *Journal of Consulting and Clinical Pscyhology*, Vol. 32, No. 2, pp. 223–226.

Kelius, J. S. (1993). "A (Dining) Room with a View: Cafeteria Takes Advantage of Grounds." *Health Facilities Management*, Vol. 6, No. 4, April, pp. 10–11.

Kiesler, C. A., and A. Sibulkin (1987). *Mental Hospitalization: Myths and Facts About a National Crisis*. Newbury Park, CA: Sage Publications.

Kuntz, E. F. (1979). "Menninger Foundation Plans New 166-Bed Adult Psychiatric Hospital." *Modern Healthcare*, Vol. 9, No. 10, October, pp. 50–53.

Langer, L. L. (1987). "Therapeutic Landscapes: Preferences for Psychiatric Patients." MLA Thesis, University of Guelph. Guelph, Ont., Canada.

Larsen, L. (1992). "Nature as Therapy: An Assessment of Schizophrenic Patients' Visual Preferences for Institutional Outdoor Environments." MLA Thesis, University of Guelph, Guelph, Ont., Canada.

Lebensohn, M. D., and M. Zigmond (1965). "Facilities and Organization." In M. D. Kaufmann and M. Ralph (eds.), *The Psychiatric Unit in a General Hospital: Its Current and Future Role*. New York: International University Press.

Leviton, R. (1988). *Anthroposohpic Medicine Today*. Hudson, NY: Anthroposophic Press.

McLaughlin, H. P., and J. Boerger (1981). "Recreation Areas and Skylights Bring Outdoors Into Psychiatric Unit." *Hospitals*, Vol. 55, February 16, pp. 145–148 and 171.

"Menninger Foundation" (1981). *Progressive Architecture*, Vol. 62, No. 1, January, pp 156–157.

"Mental Health Unit Serves Many Needs" (1980). *Hospitals*, Vol. 54, No. 4., February 16, pp 126–134.

Miller, J. A. (1981). "Health Professionals Surveyed for Psychiatric Hospital Design." *Hospitals*, February 16, pp. 129–133.

Minter, S. (1993). *The Healing Garden*. Rutland, VT: Charles E. Tuttle Company (lists some medicinal and symbolic qualities of herbs and other plants).

Moller, C. B. (1968). *Architectural Environment and Our Mental Health*. New York: Horizon Press.

Moore, R. C. (1993). *Plants for Play*. Berkeley, CA: MIG Communications (list of poisonous plants, also plants that stimulate other senses).

Moos, R., R. Harris, and K. Schonborn (1969). "Psychiatric Patients and Staff Reaction to Their Physical Environment." *Journal of Clinical Psychology*, Vol. 25, pp. 322–324.

National Health Service Estates (1992). "Health Building Note 45: External Works for Health Buildings." Her Majesty's Stationery Office.

National Health Service Estates (1993). "Environments for Quality Care." Her Majesty's Stationery Office.

Nehring, J. and R. G. Hill (1995). "The Blackthorn Garden Project." The Sainsbury Center for Mental Health.

Noakes, T. (1994). "The Mind's Eye: Birmingham's Pioneering Approach." *Architecture Today*, No.52, October, pp. 29–32 and 35–36.

Ohio State Hospital, Cleveland Research Department (1973). *A Bibliography of Materials Useful for Change in Mental Hospitals: Architecture, Institutional Settings, and Health*. Monticello, IL: Council of Planning Librarians. October, pp. 183–464.

"135-Year-Old Hospital Retains Grace in Update" (1979). *Hospitals*, Vol. 53, No. 18, September 16, pp. 60–64.

Osmond, H. (1966). "Some Psychiatric Aspects of Design." In L. B. Holland (Ed.) *Who Designs America?* Garden City, NY: Anchor Books.

Osmond, H. and Izumi, K. (1971). "The Mentally Ill: The Problem of Design Guidance." In K. Bayes *Designing for the Handicapped*. London: George Goodwin Ltd.

Pastalan, L. A. and D. H. Carson (1970). *The Spatial Behavior of Older People*. Ann Arbor, MI: University of Michigan Press.

Perkins, N. H. (1996). "Summary of Patient and Staff Interviews." Unpublished manuscript.

——— (1998a). "Psychiatric Hospital Landscapes: A Case Study of Homewood Health Center." March

——— (1998b). "Post Master Plan Review." Unpublished manuscript.

Perkins, N. H. and S. Barnhart. (1996a). "Summary of Behavioural Observations of Patient and Staff Use of the Homewood Grounds." Guelph, Ont., Canada: Homewood Health Centre Grounds Master Plan.

——— (1996b). "A Map of the Special Places at Homewood." Guelph, Ont., Canada: Homewood Health Centre Grounds Master Plan.

——— (1996c). "A Walker's Guide to the Homewood Community." Guelph, Ont., Canada: Homewood Health Centre.

——— (1996d). "Homewood Health Centre Grounds Master Plan."

Pinel, P. (1800). *A Treatise on Insanity*. Reprinted in D. N. Robinson (Ed.) (1977). *Significant Contributions to the History of Psychology 1750-1920*. Washington, DC: University Publications of America.

"Plan #336-26, Butler Hospital, Providence, RI" (1912). By Olmsted Brothers, May 6, 1912. From the Olmsted Plans and Drawings Collection, courtesy of National Park Service, Frederick Law Olmsted National Historic Site, Brookline, MA.

Radley, S. (1997). "Healthcare Guidance." *Landscape Design,* No. 257, February, pp. 19–21.

Raver, A. (1994). "When Hope Falters, Balm for the Soul." *The New York Times,* December 29, pp. C1, C6.

Reed, D. (1995). "The Therapeutic Garden." *Art New England,* August/September, p. 21.

Relf, D. (Ed.) (1992). *The Role of Horticulture in Human Well-Being and Social Development: A National Symposium. 19-21 April 1990, Arlington, VA.* Portland, OR: Timber Press.

Roelker, W. G. (1944). "A Layman's Narrative." *A Century of Butler Hospital, 1844-1944.* Boston: The Merrymount Press.

Rosenblatt, D. (1970). "Physical Plant, Staff Morale and Informal Ideologies in Mental Hospitals." In L. A. Pastalan and D. H. Carson, *The Spatial Behavior of Older People.* Ann Arbor, MI: University of Michigan Press.

Ross, E. (1972). "Butler Hospital: The Role of the Insane Asylum in Urbanizing America." Undergraduate Paper, Brown University, Providence, RI.

Ruggles, A. H., M.D. (1944). "The Achievements of Five Superintendents." *A Century of Butler Hospital, 1844-1944.* Boston: The Merrymount Press.

"Rx: Environment: Building Types Study 589: Mental Health Care Facilities" (1983). *Architectural Record,* Vol. 171, No. 7, June, pp. 85–103.

"Sanctuary" (1996). *Design Quarterly,* No. 169, Summer.

Selland, T. (Ed.) (1988). *Health Facilities Research Bibliography 1979–1986.* Washington, DC: The Health Facilities Research Program.

Sivadon, P. (1970). "Principles of Psychiatric Design." *World Hospitals,* Vol. 6, pp. 96–101.

Smith, C. W. (1958). "Architectural Research and the Construction of Mental Hospitals." *Mental Hospitals,* Vol. 9, No. 6, June, pp. 39–42.

"Special Report on Psychiatric Units in General Hospitals" (1959). *Modern Hospital,* Vol. 93, November, pp. 80–93.

Spirn, A. W. (1988). "The Poetics of City and Nature: Towards a New Aesthetic for Urban Design." *Landscape Architecture,* Vol. 7, No. 2, Fall, p. 119.

STARS (1997). Informational brochure. Sub-Acute Treatment for Adolescent Rehabilitation Services, San Leandro, CA.

STARS website: www.starsinc.com.

Taylor, J. (1991). *Hospital and Asylum Architecture in England, 1840-1914: Building for Healthcare.* London: Mansell Publishing, Ltd.

Thompson, J.D. and G. Goldin. (1975). *The Hospital: A Social and Architectural History.* New Haven, CT: Yale University Press.

Thomson, D. (1996). "Report by the Chief Executive Officer." The Retreat Annual Review, York, England.

Tishler, W. H. (Ed.) (1989). *American Landscape Architecture: Designers and Places.* Washington, DC: The Preservation Press.

Ulrich, R. (1979). "Visual Landscapes and Psychological Well-Being." *Landscape Research,* Vol. 4, pp. 17–23.

———— (1981). "Nature Versus Urban Scenes: Some Psychological Effects." *Environment and Behavior,* Vol. 13, No. 5, pp. 523–556.

———— (1984). "View Through a Window May Influence Recovery from Surgery." *Science,* Vol. 224, pp. 420–421.

———— (1986). "Human Responses to Vegetation and Landscapes." *Landscape and Urban Planning,* Vol. 13, pp. 29–44.

Ulrich, R., R. F. Simons, B. D. Losito, E. Fiorito, and others (1991). "Stress Recovery During Exposure to Natural and Urban Environments." *Journal of Environmental Psychology,* Vol. 11, pp. 201–230.

"A Village of Healing" (1990). (Cover story) *Architecture,* Vol. 79, No. 3, March, pp. 115–121.

"Village, Not: The Unfulfilled Promise of Yale's Psychiatric Institute" (1993). *Progressive Architecture,* Vol. 74, No. 6, June, pp. 100–103.

Warner, S. B., Jr. (1991). "Restorative Gardens: Recovering Some Human Wisdom for Modern Healthcare." July. (Unpublished report).

———— (1995a). "Restorative Landscapes." *Landscape Architecture,* January, p. 128.

———— (1995b). "Restorative Gardens: Recovering Some Human Wisdom for Modern Design." July 20. (Unpublished report).

Whitehead, C., G. Ellison, S. Kerpen, and D. Marshall (1976). "The Aging Psychiatric Hospital: An Approach to Humanistic Redesign." *Hospital and Community Psychiatry,* Vol. 27, No. 11, November, pp. 781–788.

"Winning Big" (President's Award of Excellence) (1997). *Landscape Architecture,* Vol. 87, No. 11, November, pp. 44–47.

Wise, T. (1986). *Gardens for Children.* Sydney, NSW, Australia: Kangaroo Press.

Wiser, S. (1993) "On the Cutting Edge: Designing Canada's Newest Psychiatric Hospital." *Competitions,* Vol. 3, No. 4, Winter, pp. 6–13.

Wohlwill, J. (1983). "The Concept of Nature: A Psychologist's Point of View." In I. Altman and J. F. Wohlwill (Eds.) *Behaviour and the Natural Environment.* New York: Plenum Press. pp. 5–38.

Yeats, T. (1997). "Exploring the Experiential Qualities of Landscape Settings at a Psychiatric Hospital." Unpublished Masters Thesis. University of Guelph, Guelph, Ont., Canada.

Zeller, E. V. (1969). *Psychiatric Treatment Environment and Function.* Topeka, KS: The Environmental Research Foundation.

CHAPTER

7

Healing Gardens
for Children

Robin C. Moore

As a vehicle for healing children, gardens have special significance because of the way in which children relate to the world through play and their attraction to nature (Moore and Wong, 1997). Play is the child's way of establishing authentic relationships with the social and physical world. Play is also a right as guaranteed in Article 31 the Convention on the Rights of the Child (CRC, United Nations, 1989).

WHAT IS A CHILDREN'S HEALING GARDEN?

Insights about the significance of relationships between childhood, play, and nature have an extensive history. One needs only to think of names such as Montessori, Pestalozzi, Steiner, Froebel, and Dewey to realize that the legacy of more than a century of child development theory and practice can help us understand the role of children's gardens as places of healing. Through playful interactions with people, natural objects, and materials, the child learns in a special boundless way that stimulates the development of mind, body, and spirit. Children's interactions with the physical environment are intimate and immediate. This makes garden settings especially satisfying because they are diverse, constantly changing, multisensory, and alive. The "compressed nature" of gardens, regarded by

Figure 7-1   Healing gardens for children are a new type of nature-based, protected haven for children and youth that can incorporate the creative roles of professional staff and volunteers. Through caring for the garden together comes healing. Watering the garden at Lucas Gardens School, Canada Bay, Australia. (Photo courtesy of Lucas Gardens School.)

researchers as a healing agent (Olds, 1985), counteracts boredom, stimulates children's innate curiosity, and offers a huge range of experiential choice compared to synthetic environments (Moore and Wong, 1997).

Healing gardens have special significance as places where the inner life of the child can be integrated with the external world, where children can find both stimulation and solace. British child psychiatrist and pediatrician Donald Winnicott (Winnicott, 1971) called this experiential domain the child's "potential space," where, through play, children can work through internal conflicts, express fears, and communicate desires nonverbally. Winnicott's notion of "potential space" (resulting from a lifetime working with children and families) lends powerful support to the idea that playful garden settings can serve as therapeutic or healing environments for children, their parents, and caregivers.

HISTORY OF CHILDREN'S HEALING GARDENS

The field of specialized landscapes designed for children has been evolving for more than fifty years and has much to contribute to advancing the healing role of children's gardens. An early pioneer was the British landscape architect Lady Allen of Hurtwood. In the mid-1940s she visited the Emdrup Adventure Playground in Copenhagen, which was developed by the Danish landscape architect C. Th. Sørenson. Adventure playgrounds expressed the revolutionary concept that children could create their own community through hands-on manipulation of the physical environment, facilitated by trained playleaders. Lady Allen was so impressed that she led a successful movement to establish similar facilities in London neighborhoods serving families traumatized by the bombs, "doodlebugs," and firestorms of World War II. Later, she extended the movement to include children with special needs, beginning in London in the 1970s with the founding of the Handicapped Adventure Playground Association, now known simply as HAPA, whose play professionals work outdoors to promote the health of children with special needs. Allied developments include children's farms, where there is a strong focus on animals. (See Brett et al., 1993, and Westland and Knight, 1982, for more information on these and other specialized landscapes for children.) Most children's farms have a strong commitment to inclusion of children of all abilities, including activities such as therapeutic horseback riding.

"I used to work at another hospital without any gardens; it was just a tall stark building; there was not even a place to go outside. You're there in the hospital and you know you're there. There's no escape. At hospitals like that, the patients' families have to visit them in their rooms; there's no place else to go; it's got to be depressing and make them feel trapped in their illness. Here, with the gardens and all the outdoor places, it's so much better."

(STAFF MEMEBER)

A search of the literature on healthcare facility design related to children indicates that healing gardens for children are a very recent development in the medical field. Lindheim et al. (1972) propose design guidelines for children's hospitals and emphasize the importance of children's play, the outdoor environment, and experience of nature—themes reiterated in the design guidelines book by Olds and Daniel (1987). A decade later, in a comprehensive treatment of healthcare facilities for children and families, Shepley (1998) reemphasized the importance of play, calling it a "healing activity" (p. 109), though she notes in her literature review that there is "no scientific research on children's outdoor health facility play spaces" (p. 106). The significance of the natural environment can also be inferred by Ulrich's research findings in relation to adults (see Chapter 2) and it is assumed that similar positive health correlations apply to children.

In the world of practice, landscape architects have begun to have an impact on hospital design. A volume edited by Marberry (1997) contains a chapter by James Burnett on the therapeutic effects of landscape architecture in hospital design—although the concept is not related to children specifically. In the mainstream landscape architecture profession, the topic of healing gardens has only very recently received visibility. In 1995, it was the cover theme of the January issue of *Landscape Architecture* (Volume 85, Number 1, pp. 56–79). Of the six built projects presented, one was specifically designed for children. This was a series of playful courtyards in the Children's Hospital and Health Center, San Diego, CA. The Healing Garden in the same institution, included in this chapter, was absent, as it was not yet constructed.

Figure 7-2 Through the planting design the landscape architect created passageways between areas with a sense of mystery and discovery; the garden is never revealed entirely from any vantage point, encouraging the child to move through its sequences of spaces. (The Garden Path of the Therapeutic Garden, Wellesley, MA, photo by Douglas Reed.)

Figure 7-3 Two children explore a Sensory Garden and play at "getting lost" at Lucas Gardens School in Sidney, Australia. (Photo courtesy of Lucas Gardens School.)

The history of the general field of children's environments suggests five basic assumptions about child development, play, and the outdoor environment that can be usefully applied to children's healing gardens:

1. *Outdoor play.* Outdoor play, in and of itself, is a critical factor in healthy child development.

2. *Environmental quality.* Through design, the quality of the outdoor play environment can critically affect the range and depth of play activity and the attractiveness of the site to children. Both Sørenson and Hurtwood understood that environments for children had to be designed in a way that liberated children's freedom of engagement with their surroundings. This was a radical departure from the still dominant notion of fixed equipment playgrounds, later challenged by Simon Nicholson in his celebrated "theory of loose parts" (Nicholson, 1971).

3. *Significance of nature to child development through play.* Nature can be designed into the environment in such a way that children can have intimate contact with the basic elements of life: sunlight, fresh air, soil, water, plants, and animals. Emdrup Adventure Playground in Copenhagen was surrounded by a protective, bermed, buffer of native species. Gardening, working, and playing with plants provided constant opportunities for children to participate in the processes of life (Moore, 1996; Moore and Wong, 1997).

4. *Trained play leadership.* Play leadership and playful staff intervention can extend the range, challenge, and creativity of both indoor and outdoor experience far beyond what might be possible in undirected situations. In Denmark, playleaders are called "social pedagogues" and receive their training in much the same way as classroom teachers, except they are oriented to working in community leisure centers, youth clubs, and playgrounds. In the United Kingdom, play professionals are called playworkers and work in afterschool care, summer holiday play schemes, playgrounds, hospitals, and toy libraries. In French- and Spanish-speaking countries, "animators" work as professionals in creative nonformal education, embracing childhood culture and the arts in playful social production. Child Life Specialists in United States are a closely allied profession working in children's healthcare facilities. Child Life Specialists "advocate for a comprehensive understanding of the child [and]...col-

laborate within a multi-disciplinary team to support growth and development of children, adolescents, and their families" (*Child Life Volunteer Handbook* (no date), p. 1). Child life specialists work through play and informal recreation because of the individual freedom offered, in contrast to the invasive medical protocols endured by the child over which she or he has no control.

5. *Indoor-outdoor links.* The ease with which children can observe nature from inside and/or move easily from indoors to outside significantly affects the positive impact of the natural environment on their quality of life. Indoor-outdoor links can be further facilitated by playleaders, therapists, horticultural therapists, Child Life Specialists, and special educators.

CHILDREN WITH SPECIAL NEEDS, REHABILITATION OR HABILITATION

Healing gardens must accommodate children of many types, including those in the process of rehabilitation: children temporarily disabled because of an accident, or recovering from a severe operation, or from an overwhelming psychologically traumatic experience. Other children may have a terminal disease, in such cases the healing garden functions as a refuge of peace and tranquillity for child and loved ones as the inevitable unfolds. As in an adult hospice setting, the goal here is to provide the highest quality of life rather than a cure.

Other children able to benefit from healing gardens are those with permanent and profound physical and mental impairments who are not "recovering" from anything. This has led Swedish professionals to embrace the concept of "habilitation"—an approach designed to build on the specific potentials of the child, as opposed to rebuilding (rehabilitation) something that never existed. The last decades have seen a shift in thinking about previously termed "handicapped children." In the United States, where the disability rights movement has been so strong, the term "handicapped" was replaced by "disability" and "people with disabilities," and more specifically "sight disabilities, " learning disabilities," "mobility disabilities," and so on. "Children of all abilities" is a common phrase used nowadays in speaking of any mixed group of children. Such thinking has helped to move both the professional community and the public away from stereotypical notions of the "helpless handicapped," shut away from the rest of society in segregated facilities. Children of all abilities tend more and

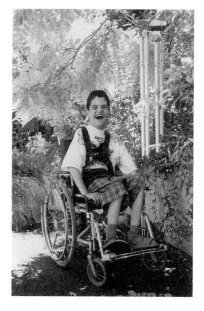

Figure 7-4 *Through playful interactions with people, objects, and materials, the child learns in a special boundless way that stimulates the development of mind, body, and spirit. Child playing with the tuned wind chimes in the Sensory Garden at Lucas Gardens School, Canada Bay, Australia. (Photo courtesy of Lucas Gardens School.)*

Figure 7-5   Healing gardens are places where children can lose themselves, release worries and concerns generated by the controlled environment of the health institution, and become restored to a more tranquil state of mind. Two children relax in the Sensory Garden at Lucas Gardens School. (Photo courtesy of Lucas Gardens School.)

more to be integrated and "included" in everyday life. The notion of "ability" assumes that all children have abilities or potential competencies and skills. Healing gardens then become the vehicle for discovering new skills and practicing and enhancing old ones.

Another group to be considered consists of "at risk" children, whose development may be permanently impaired because of negative influences in their everyday environment, such as poor nutrition, physical abuse, verbal abuse, sexual abuse, promiscuity, overcrowded and substandard housing, or drugs. These ills are often a consequence of poverty and are spreading in the world as global economic restructuring and information technology produce more and more unemployment or underemployment (Christoffersen, 1994). There is, too, the general concern expressed by many childhood professionals concerning the "boxed-in" lives of middle-class children, whose activities are becoming rigidly structured and increasingly restricted in time and space (Frost and Jacobs, 1995). As these problems of stress and deprivation become more severe, the restorative and therapeutic benefits of specially designed childhood landscapes will become more pertinent—far beyond their role in healthcare.

In a "playing and learning" garden created some years ago in an urban elementary school in Berkeley, California (Moore and Wong, 1997), institutional asphalt was replaced with running water, woodland, and wildflower meadows. Butterflies and birds filled the air with colorful movement and song. As a result, dramatically positive changes occurred in the children's social behavior and their feelings about themselves and their school. The garden was a place to escape from the rigors of the classroom and find freedom of expression, a place where children were in control of their environment instead of being controlled by it. The garden was aptly described in a follow-up interview with an adult former student as "compressed countryside." She summed up her overall feeling as "intense peace"—not the kind of language normally associated with a city schoolyard.

These schoolchildren were not in need of "healing" in the medical sense; even so, many of the impacts on the children's behavior could be defined as "healing," socially and psychologically. The garden became a "special friend" to individual children and to the children as a whole, giving them a sense of identity and belonging. Their naturalized schoolyard became the vehicle for positive bonding between children and institution—a process that could apply equally well to institutions such as hospitals, where children inhabit a very alien environment containing few positive cues from everyday life.

The Berkeley garden also supported a summer creative arts program (Project PLAE) for groups of mixed-ability children (some of them with severe impairments), and provided a powerful stimulus for inclusion, tolerance, and understanding. The community artists who animated the program loved working there because the garden offered creative support for the children's wide spectrum of needs. Although the space was not used for formal therapy, the many years experience working with the children and studying their behavior provided powerful insights concerning the therapeutic, rehabilitative, and habilitative effects of the garden—a research grounding for the present chapter (Moore, 1996).

Every type of institution dealing with children could offer similar outdoor natural settings, allowing children to escape into their own private world. This is particularly true of medical and rehabilitative institutions where children go to have frightening, mysterious things done to them, over which they have no control. Gardens are places where children can lose themselves, release the worries and concerns generated by the controlled environment of the health institution, and become restored to a more tranquil state. Healthy development requires a counterbalance of freedom of experience and expression to help the child recompose his or her inner self. For all children, healing gardens offer broad therapeutic potential to help them retain their good health or restore health they may have lost.

"We sometimes get a classroom of kids from a local school to spend some time with our kids and the natural place to go (I mean that in more than one way!) is the garden. When the convalescent kids could see the normal fifth-graders exploring the garden, it had an amazing effect on them; I saw so many of them looking more engaged and alert and happy than I usually see them, as if they were able to experience more through watching the more active children."

(STAFF MEMBER)

Figure 7-6   Child enjoying gardening activity in the Garden Play program at Children's Memorial Center, Chicago, IL. (Photo by Roberta Hursthouse.)

GARDEN THERAPIES

Play Therapy

In the well-developed, contemporary play therapy literature (Gil, 1991; Landreth, 1991; van der Kooij and Hellendoom, 1986), there is almost no mention of outdoor, natural environments as appropriate, therapeutic settings. A major exception is the pioneering work in Sweden of Ivonny Lindquist. In 1956 she started a play therapy program as a nursery school teacher in the University Hospital of Umea. In the foreword to her book, *Therapy Through Play* (Lindquist, 1977), John Lind, head of the Pediatric Clinic of Karolinska, Stockholm, emphasized that "Children need to get out into the open. If they are confined to the ward," and he theorized that "the longing to get out gradually vanishes. Life outside the window … is no longer real" (*Ibid.*, p. viii), For children who could not go out for medical reasons, Lindquist found ways of connecting the outside world to the children, especially to those with long-term illness. She tells a story of how much she learned from the positive reactions of one particular boy with cancer—in response to Lindquist's bringing in seasonal natural objects (flowers, mosses, mushrooms, and berries) and arranging them into a "miniature, enchanted wood." One day, she brought a branch of bilberries. "When the bilberries had ripened … [we] spread them out on a newspaper on his cot and pretended he was out in the forest picking bilberries. He picked them carefully, one at a time, got his arms and hands covered in juice but his whole face was one big sunny smile." Lindquist describes how the event became "a landmark in time," with the child referring to other events as having happened before or after "I picked bilberries" (*Ibid.*, p. 22).

In 1973, the Karolinska Pediatric Clinic of Stockholm embraced Lindquist's ideas about the therapeutic effects of play and nature and started a three-year pilot project. The results demonstrated that play therapy, with parents' active cooperation, cut the average time spent in hospital by children (Lindquist, 1977). The results also showed a positive effect on children's mental health. By 1977, all hospitals in Sweden were required to make proper arrangements for children to participate in the same kind of activities provided in pre-schools and leisure centers. In the opinion of John Lind, Head of the Karolinska Pediatric Clinic, play therapy was one of the major improvements in pediatrics" at that time *(ibid.)*.

In a 1977 monograph produced by the Swedish Department of Social Welfare, reporting on the Karolinska project, the outdoors was presented as important because it is where the child could move, breathe fresh air, feel it on his or her cheeks. A therapist told a story about a boy who was standing in the entrance talking with her, looking at the sleet outside. Suddenly, he went outside, saying "I'm going out to feel it" and lifted his face to the precipitation (translated from the Swedish original and reported in Sarkissian et al., 1980).

The same translated excerpt in Sarkissian et al. (1980) articulates the case for the importance of the outdoors by stressing that outside, children have a sense of control. They get a rest from hospital smells, feel the security of a familiar environment, experience greater freedom, relate to the staff in a more relaxed atmosphere, have an opportunity to withdraw from the constant human interactions inside, engage in boisterous games and loud noises that cannot occur indoors, run, let off steam, ride wheeled toys, playfully explore the "unprepared" open-ended world of nature (pinecones, flowers, leaves, grass, stones, bark, fruits, soil, and water).

The smell of the outdoors is particularly significant because it contrasts so strongly with the alien smell of medical facilities. The aroma of a space wraps around and envelopes a person. It is very subtle, like birdsong or music. Humans have a common positive appreciation of some smells (roses, for example, or lavender). Soothing effects in both body and mind are generated by the biochemical reaction to these pleasurable odors (Lawless, 1997). For the same reason, we abhor other smells—no one likes the smell of rotten eggs.

Horticultural Therapy

Horticultural therapy has developed extensively in recent years, and covers a wide range of contexts and clients, including children with special needs. Lindquist paved the way for the strong connection that we now see between play therapy and horticultural therapy—well-illustrated by the Children's Memorial Hospital, Chicago, case study presented later in this chapter. A powerful illustration has also been presented by Hoffman and Castro-Blanco (no date). They describe the case of four-year-old Eric, diagnosed as having a speech-language impairment, a variety of behavioral problems, and depressed affect. He participated in twice-weekly horticultural sessions for fifteen weeks with a horticultural therapist in the preschool greenhouse. The authors describe in detail how Eric engaged initially in "free play," and then gradually "adopted" the plants, showing concern for them. Through caring for his own garden he was able to verbalize feelings about his troubled family situ-

"I work with a recreational therapist out there with the kids from the convalescent hospital. We take a whole group out there, sometimes as many as fifteen to twenty kids, a few times a month. It is so nice because the kids seem to respond out there. They respond to the bright colors, the water, the shadows, and sunlight. I think it can be calming for some of the kids, but also stimulating, too."

(STAFF MEMBER)

ation. He often commented that caring for the plants made him "feel good." By the end of the program, Eric's in-class behavior had improved markedly. He also exhibited an improved affect and capacity to express empathy and nurturance. The authors concluded that horticultural therapy is especially appropriate for working with young children to help enhance their social skills by providing a neutral or positive milieu for expressing nurturing and prosocial feelings. At the same time, it provides children with an enhanced sense of competence and self-esteem.

Animal Therapy

The emotional and therapeutic impact of animals has been well documented (Kellert, 1996; Moore, 1984; Myers, 1998). Gardens can facilitate contact with animals by providing habitats for wildlife. Butterfly gardens are a common example. Planting to attract birds is another strategy. A wonderful example of more comprehensive programming around animals was developed at the Buenos Aires Zoo by a team of doctors from the Neuropsychiatric Hospital for Children and Youth. The program, called Care-While-Caring, teams up ten- to eighteen-year-olds with mental disorders with zoo staff in various aspects of animal care. In this sense, the whole zoo can be viewed as a therapeutic environment.

Figure 7-7   Children having fun blowing bubbles via a touch-activated bubble machine in the Sensory Garden at Lucas Gardens School. (Photo courtesy of Lucas Gardens School.)

Nature as Therapy

It is generally recognized that many adults view nature as a restorative, therapeutic environment in their everyday lives. Experience of nature is nutrition for the human sensory system—our mechanism for perceiving and understanding the physical world. If one of the sensory channels is damaged or nonexistent, other channels will pick up the slack. Blind people often have extraordinary acoustic perception. In the field of disability, multisensory stimulation has become emphasized as a therapeutic strategy using light, color, movement, sound, and fragrance (Hutchinson and Kewin, 1994). Aromatherapy—the application of essential oils to improve health and well-being (Lawless, 1997)—has grown out of a long folk tradition (dating back to ancient Egyptians) and has received more acceptance in recent years. The therapeutic effect of music (popularized as the "Mozart Effect") is also receiving attention (Campbell, 1989).

Garden settings are important for children because they live through their senses. As they explore their surroundings through play, they engage in development processes that can be extended, enhanced, and facilitated by adult professionals. This is well understood by progressive educators (Dewey, Steiner, Pestalozzi, Hodgkin, Bruner—discussed in Moore and Wong, 1997, Chapter 17), who all agree that children's learning must start with primary experience of the real world. Cognitive development must resonate with real experience; if not, learning becomes an ungrounded abstraction, without meaning to the child.

"It's a peaceful place; it gets you, or patients, out of the hospital. It's wonderful; it's a great idea. You use so many of your senses, especially if you take a kid, [to] smell, touch, see, hear. It's a good place to bring kids; you can watch over them."

(STAFF MEMBER)

New Professional Roles

The recognition of the role of the senses in therapy, the importance of primary experience with nature, and the recent movement of horticultural therapy away from its vocational training and medical roots, now holds the potential for collaboration with landscape design in the creation of new types of nature-based, protected havens where professional staff act as hybrid therapist/playleaders. New types of interprofessional, interdisciplinary teams are required to design these environments. To do this effectively, play professionals must have extensive knowledge of plants, animals, and gardening; horticultural therapists need to be well versed in the role of play and child development; and landscape architects need to understand how they can design environments to support the creative roles of play professionals and horticultural therapists. The pioneering examples discussed in this chapter show promise in this direction. In presenting these cases, the author has had to rely pri-

"The garden is an additional tool for therapy. Sometimes when I work with these kids, it can get pretty emotional for them. I can take them out there for a break, to go relax and refocus; it helps the children collect themselves. If the child comes in anxious, sometimes I will start out there, it is a way to decrease their anxiety."

(STAFF MEMBER)

marily on professional judgments of best practice rather than empirical evidence; because, so far, investigations that would provide such evidence have not been conducted.

POTENTIAL USERS OF A HEALING GARDEN

A key dimension in the design of a children's healing garden is the range of users that will need to be accommodated. They include the following:

Figure 7-8   Mother and child patient playing with Seahorse Fountain, Leichtag Family Healing Garden, San Diego Children's Hospital. (Photo by Marni Barnes.)

- Parents and child before or after a routine hospital visit. The garden needs to engage both adult and child.
- Parents and siblings of a child undergoing surgery. The garden needs to engage siblings and be restorative for stressed parents.
- Parents of a child who comes regularly for treatment for a chronic condition, for example, dialysis. The garden needs to provide an uplifting respite for the parents while the child is being treated.
- Parents who bring an inpatient child in a wagon/wheelchair to the garden. The garden needs to give the parents an opportunity to interact with the child outside the hospital setting, in a place where diversions and distractions abound. Opportunities need to be provided to attract even the most severely sick children to forestall the possibility of parental disappointment and depression if the child does not show much interest.
- Parents of a child who is in a crisis situation in the hospital or grieving parents. The garden needs to provide quiet, private corners and peaceful sanctuaries.
- Staff during lunch breaks. The garden needs to work for staff seeking stimulation and novelty, as well as those seeking peaceful restoration.
- Teens, who may enjoying hanging out in the garden. As boisterous behavior may well disturb other users, either the garden needs to be large enough to accommodate adolescents or separate space must be provided for them elsewhere.
- Child seeking diversion from hospital fears or from the emotions of stressed parents. The garden needs to contain many choices and natural diversity, as well as features and materials that a child can manipulate or change.

TYPOLOGY

The typology that follows has been generated in large part from work in the field and in particular from the case studies documented below. The typology is best presented in terms of user groups, types of relationships, depth of interaction between users and the garden landscape, and the institutional context (whether directly connected to a medical facility or not). Within this framework, five types of healing gardens for children have been identified; an example of each is presented as a case study

.

1. *Formal therapeutic garden.* Accent on explicit, defined, garden-based approach to therapy, most likely targeted toward a specific area of therapeutic need, requiring therefore a custom-designed landscape to accommodate particular therapeutic strategies. Example: The Therapeutic Garden at the Institute for Child and Adolescent Development, Wellesley, Massachusetts.

2. *Nonformal play and horticultural therapy garden.* Accent on active participation by children (and parents) in the gardening process. Emphasis on diversity and freedom of choice by the individual child to act on the garden environment in many ways. This freedom serves to balance the medical environment over which the child has no control. The therapy programs are usually developed by child life specialists with strong links between indoor and outdoor spaces. Example: Garden Court at Children's Memorial Hospital, Chicago, Illinois.

3. *Informal, strolling garden.* Focus on de-stressing, exploration, restoration, meditation, prayer, and relaxation (for children, parents, and staff). Accent on providing a diversity of informal settings for walking, privacy, sitting, socializing, and sensory interest (color, texture, fragrance, butterflies fluttering, birdsong). High quality aesthetic surroundings, including special child-landscape features. Examples: Prouty Garden at Children's Hospital, Boston, Massachusetts; Leichtag Family Healing Garden, Children's Hospital, San Diego, California.

4. *Community-based, multiuse, multipurpose garden.* Accent on diverse "habilitative" program serving several populations, most likely embracing a range of formal, nonformal, and informal programming approaches, as listed above. Commonly includes joint use of facility by community groups. Highly developed example: Lucas Gardens School, Canada Bay, New South Wales, Australia.

CASE STUDIES

A search of best practice in children's healing gardens was conducted. Five examples representing the different typologies were selected:

Name	Institution	Location	User Groups	Typology
Therapeutic Garden	Institute for Child and Adolescent Development	Wellesley, MA	Traumatized children, and therapists	Formal therapeutic garden
Garden Court.	Children's Memorial Hospital	Chicago, IL	Hospitalized and outpatient children; parents, siblings, caregivers; Child Life Specialists; volunteers	Nonformal play and horticultural therapy
The Prouty Garden	Children's Hospital	Boston, MA	Hospitalized and outpatient children; parents, siblings, caregivers; hospital staff	Informal strolling garden
The Sensory Garden	Lucas Gardens School	Canada Bay, New South Wales, Australia	Severely impaired children; parents, siblings, caregivers; teaching staff, therapists; volunteers; community groups	Community-based, multiuse, multipurpose garden
Leichtag Family Healing Garden	Children's Hospital and Health Center	San Diego, CA	Hospitalized and outpatient children; parents, siblings, caregivers; hospital staff	Informal strolling garden

Information was assembled through interviews with designers and institutional staff, site observations, and institutional archives. Key questions included the history of the garden, location, climatic zone, design, site function, user groups, special garden settings, institutional support, and activity programs. In one case (Leichtag Family Healing Garden), there was a formal post-occupancy evaluation study to draw from.

Therapeutic Garden at the Institute for Child and Adolescent Development, Wellesley, Massachusetts

Located in a residential neighborhood, the one-acre therapeutic garden was designed as an integral part of a nonprofit agency dedicated to treating traumatized children and training professionals. The garden is used for individual and group therapy sessions. The Therapeutic Garden received the ASLA President's Award of Excellence in 1997 (*Landscape Architecture*, 1997).

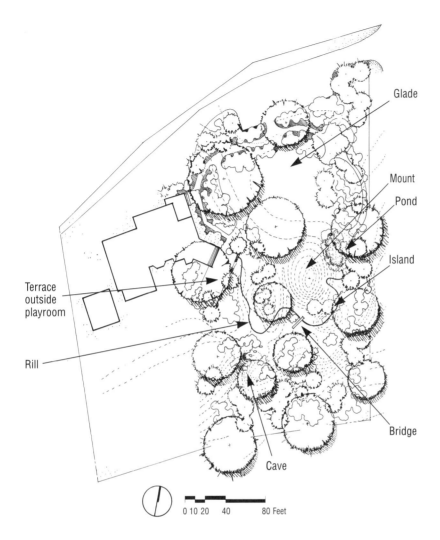

Glade

Mount

Pond

Island

Terrace
outside
playroom

Rill

Bridge

Cave

0 10 20   40   80 Feet

*Figure 7-10   Site plan of the Thera-
peutic Garden, Institute for Child and
Adolescent Development, Wellesley,
MA.*

History and Philosophy of the Garden

The Institute for Child and Adolescent Development specializes
in treating emotional, learning, and behavioral disorders that
can develop when children suffer hidden trauma (witnessing
tragedies such as illness, violence, or death, involving someone
close to them). Such children can develop fear for their own
safety, display learning and emotional problems, lose hope and
trust in the future, and develop violent behavior. Untreated,
these behaviors interfere with learning and the development of
body image, leaving a child unable to regulate feelings, to use
fantasy creatively, or to give positive meanings to experiences.
For designer Douglas Reed, the Therapeutic Garden expresses
the fundamental idea that human growth and development is

rooted in childhood and engagement with the landscape. By forging connections with plants, rocks, and water, the child gains a deeper sense of self within the surrounding physical and spiritual universe.

Sebastiano Santostefano, clinic director, describes the therapeutic role of the garden in the clinic's mission statement (Santostefano, no date):

> For every mental knot there is a corresponding body knot, and vice versa, since the mind and body are not two, but one. To untie body knots, or traumatic "body memories," the child should freely enact body symbols while participating within a healing therapeutic relationship....Each of us have (sic) observed a child climb to the top of a rock and, with body erect, experience the power of the meaning "up." Or we may have observed a child crawl into a "cave" formed by the branches of a bush and experience the body as a protective enclosure within which the child finds refuge and fends off attack. In these examples, the body's "memories" are available and participate in the meanings the child experiences. But when trauma strikes, the child's mind draws a mental boundary between the mind and the body, splitting off bodily meanings from awareness. While the boundary is successful in isolating painful, embodied meanings from awareness, the meanings are neither experienced, nor revised, but remain underground, unnamed and forever active. In recent years...a shift [in psychoanalysis] has occurred...toward emphasizing interactions between therapist and child within which meanings are constructed and revised...the child manipulates the therapist to become a figure and voice representing his unconscious embodied meanings. As child and therapist engage each other within the metaphor set by the child, the embodied meanings are gradually enacted, elaborated and revised. The concept that emotional conflict is resolved through negotiations between child and therapist suggests that the therapeutic setting contains symbolic equivalents of a caretaker-child relationship...The unique sequence of sensory and symbolic experiences provided by the microcosm of nature in the therapeutic garden invites and enables the child to journey into the outer reaches of his/her inner self.

To explore how Santostefano's theories could be turned into landscape form, psychologist and designer visited designed landscapes together, and assembled and discussed images of relevant landscape prototypes. These prototypes included man-made landforms, like Indian mounds and garden mounts, and natural forms like coastal dunes, forms that evoke feelings of being protected and embraced by the earth. They investigated the sensual and spatial qualities of plants, especially those with large leaves that create internal spaces; thickets, like bamboo

Figure 7-11   Within dunes, there is a powerful sense of being embraced and protected by the earth. View of Mount and Ravine in the Therapeutic Garden. (Photo by Douglas Reed.)

and swamp azalea; and plants with unusual tactile qualities, like the paper-bark maple. They looked at images of water-courses ranging from natural streams to more abstract forms. Since water had been the principal formative force of the existing site, and is a strong symbol of life and recovery, it became a basic theme in the design of the garden. Careful sculpting of the site and additions to the existing topography, combined with a very thoughtful planting design, created a sense of mystery and discovery.

Description

In a 1997 presentation Reed explained how:

> the design expresses the narrative of a watercourse that weaves its way through the site linking a sequence of spaces that correspond to stages of a child's recovery.... [They include] archetypal landforms carved by water, a cave-like ravine for safety and security, an upland wooded plateau for exploration, a mount for climbing, an island for seclusion, a pond for discovery, steep and shallow slopes that invite risk, and a large sunny glade for running and playing. A play terrace provides the threshold from the Clinic's playroom into the garden. A low fieldstone seat wall retains the terrace and defines the entrance into the adjacent ravine. The paving breaks apart into a checkerboard of individual stones and grass squares to express freedom of movement into the garden. (Reed, 1997, p. 13).

He continued to explain how the watercourse originates on the terrace in a low green-granite basin, spills over the basin's edges, emerges from stainless-steel pipes, splashes into an eight-inch-wide, steel-sided rill that meanders through the central ravine, and ends in the pond. Vegetation is layered and combined with the landforms to create patterns of light and shade and a mix of intimate and expansive spaces. The garden is never fully revealed from any one vantage point, which encourages the child to move through its sequences of spaces.

The garden is used year-round, even when there is snow on the ground. The diversity of plants provides for interest throughout the year. There is very little annual planting. The garden is not an intensely manicured landscape and requires only normal pruning and lawn care. The filter on the recirculating pump must be cleaned out periodically, and the pond once a year.

Wheelchair access could be an issue as there is no hard-surfaced accessible route through the garden and no direct access from the play terrace. However, a nonpower-wheelchair user could come down the side of the house into the garden, and

Figure 7-12 An eight-inch-wide, steel-sided rill that meanders in the central ravine, past various landforms, and flows into a pond. "Water became for us in the design of the garden a strong symbol of life and recovery" (Reed, 1997). Rill in the Therapeutic Garden with Clinic beyond. (Photo by Douglas Reed.)

with assistance could navigate the central part of the garden across the lawns. Indeed, one of the staff who uses a wheelchair manages to navigate the garden successfully.

Physical safety issues have so far not arisen. The children explore the landscape, climb on the granite field stones, and interact with the pond—"that's what its about," commented Reed, "so I don't see liability being an issue. There is nothing unsafe in this type of landscape used under such close supervision."

Use

The Wellesley therapeutic garden is used for one-on-one therapy sessions between therapist and child and for group therapy. The principal therapeutic expression is the interaction between child and landscape. It is a place where children can be challenged to explore and take risks. "Landscape invites risk," Reed commented. "A ravine may feel protective and comfortable, climbing up a hill is more challenging, deciding to cross the bridge from one place to another—from here to there, is another type of challenge or stage of a journey" (Reed, 1997). In an effort to understand the role of the garden in treatment, the clinic staff document each child's behavior on a map of the garden, tracking the children, identifying patterns over time.

Reed (1997) recalled a story that Santostefano tells of a four-year-old boy who spent the first two years of his life in a sealed and sterile bubble, isolated from any human contact. He was mute and immobile. After two years with Santostefano he finally overcame his fear enough to venture outside the clinic. Eventually, he found his way through the garden to the cave, where Santostefano sat and played with him. One day the child darted out of the cave to the lower branches of a nearby pine and pressed his hands against the needles. "Ouch! Pinchy!" he exclaimed and then raced back to rejoin Santostefano in the cave. In this situation, the landscape evoked basic emotions in the child and provided metaphors for two vital experiences, one of safety and security, the other of menace and pain.

How is such a healing garden to be evaluated? It is a very private place. Everything that takes place there is confidential, accessible only to the professionals working with the children. However, in the classic tradition of clinical psychology, reported cases of healing, compiled and interpreted by the psychologists, lend weight to the conviction that the primary experience of nature is fundamental to individual health—and by implication to society and culture—indeed to human life itself. Thus we gain insight into the more global significance of nature from the experiences of individual children in a designed one-acre New England microcosm of the whole.

Figure 7-13   "Each of us have (sic) observed a child climb to the top of a rock, with body erect, experience the power of the meaning 'up'" (Santostefano, no date). View from the Garden Path in the Therapeutic Garden. (Photo by Douglas Reed.)

ADVANTAGES

- Custom designed to serve specific therapeutic needs.
- Variety of environmental settings.
- Active, supportive staff.
- Low maintenance.
- Research site for gaining insights about interaction of children with the "near landscape," potentially transferable to other child-landscape contexts.

DISADVANTAGES

- Wheelchair access may be difficult. Walker access may not be possible.

Garden Court and Garden Play Program at Children's Memorial Medical Center, Chicago, Illinois

The Garden Court is located in a sub-basement open courtyard of the 250-bed Medical Center facility. The bulky, nine-story buildings cover a triangular site occupying more than a city block bounded by busy arterial streets on two sides. The Garden Court was designed by Roberta Hursthouse, who is also the horticultural therapist. In 1997, the Garden Play Program (a more friendly term than "horticultural therapy") was recognized by the Chicago Botanic Garden's "Planting with Pride Urban Gardening Competition" as the Best Overall Horticultural Therapy Garden. The program serves all patients and their families.

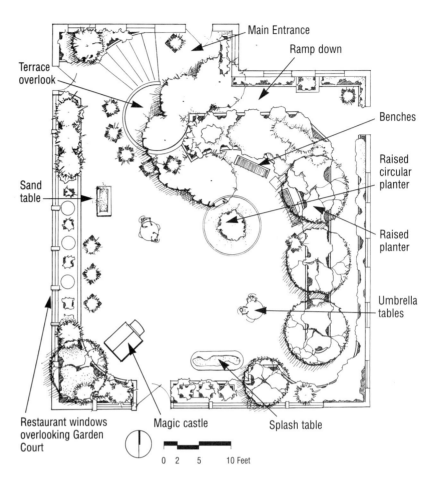

Main Entrance

Ramp down

Terrace overlook

Benches

Raised circular planter

Sand table

Raised planter

Umbrella tables

Restaurant windows overlooking Garden Court

Magic castle

Splash table

0 2   5   10 Feet

Figure 7-14   Site plan of the Garden Court, Children's Memorial Medical Center, Chicago, IL.

The original hospital was founded in 1882, by Julia Foster Porter in memory of her son Maurice, who died of acute rheumatism at age 13. In 1905, the hospital moved two blocks to its present site, in Chicago's Lincoln Park neighborhood, twelve miles north of downtown. Children's Memorial is the pediatric training facility of Northwestern University Medical School; its mission includes pediatric healthcare delivery, research, education, and advocacy for the general well-being of all children. Children's Memorial offers a full range of medical services in the Chicago region to children from infancy through adolescence. Special areas include cardiac treatment, leukemia and solid tumors, spina bifida, perinatal care, cystic fibrosis, hearing loss, orthopedic problems, and psychiatry. The average length of stay is 3 days; the range of stay is 24 hours to 180 days. Many chronic patients are accommodated as both in- and out-patients.

History and Philosophy of the Garden

The original Garden Court was built for passive use when the new hospital was built in the 1940s. In 1984, the Child Life staff initiated development of the Garden Play Program and redesign of the Garden Court as a cooperative project between the Child Life Department and the Chicago Botanic Garden outreach program. Normally, the Botanic Garden provides horticultural therapy interns for twelve months to an institution to help get the program established. In the case of Memorial Hospital, such an unusual learning opportunity was provided that the Botanic Garden continued to be involved for a second year (1985). Roberta Hursthouse, who had been an intern with the Botanic Garden some years earlier, became involved from the beginning as the horticultural therapist, working closely with the Child Life Department, family support services, and pastoral care program. Material costs of the garden and program are still supported by the voluntary Women's Board of the hospital through grants, donations, and special events. In 1997 a modest redesign and upgrading of the Garden Court was planned, including the creation of a new, more convenient at-grade entrance from the adjacent volunteer services.

In 1996–1997, the indoor/outdoor Garden Court horticultural therapy program served 584 school-aged and teen patients, their siblings and parents, through 29 "Garden Play" sessions with an average attendance of 21.

Description

The Garden Court is located one floor below street level and is completely surrounded by the Medical Center building—six stories high on two sides and nine stories high on the other two. The size is approximately 40 × 40 feet. Lack of direct sunlight severely limits the variety of plants that can thrive in the courtyard space.

A very positive aspect of the Garden Court is that it is clearly visible from the hospital's street level entry lobby. Visitors see the sunken Garden Court in full view through large plate glass windows. At the lower level, the hospital restaurant directly overlooks the space. The restaurant (exclusively used by the hospital community) has no direct access to the garden because of security issues and concerns about litter. Nonetheless, visitors get an immediate visual introduction to the Garden Court and are motivated to use it, with or without a child.

The Garden Court entrance is 2 feet above grade and flows into a small circular space offering an elevated view out over the whole court. From this point, able-bodied visitors descend a curved flight of six stairs. In additional to wheelchairs, the

"It's too loud for me in the playroom and the music hurts my head. I'm tired of crutches. The garden looks pretty. Is it quiet out there?"

(ORTHO-REHAB, INPATIENT)

Figure 7-15 Garden Play activity starts in patient's rooms with Child Life Specialists during the cold season. Plants are transplanted in the Garden Court, which children can observe from the ward windows. (Photo by Roberta Hursthouse.)

Garden Court is accessible to "transport carts" (across between wheelchair and gurney). Children using either vehicle must use a long ramp around two sides of the courtyard and separated from it by a large elevated, L-shaped planter. As Roberta Hursthouse commented, "able-bodied siblings leap straight down the stairs into the court, leaving their patient brother or sister to take the long way round via the ramp with nurse or parent." This situation will be improved by the at-grade entry in the renovation plan.

Other planting beds, pots, and movable planters occupy the other two walls of the court. Considering the climatic limitations, there is a impressive diversity of permanent trees, shrubs, and ground covers, particularly selected for both their early- and late-blooming characteristics. A large circular planter is located in the central open area of the court. Although attractive, this planter occupies too much space and is difficult to use by children as its sides are too narrow to sit on or to support garden tools. Most of the soil surface is beyond the reach of children using wheelchairs.

Park-style benches nestle in the curve of the large planter. Among the evergreens, two charming small stone sculptures greet the children. One is a child smelling flowers, the other, a pair of animal cubs of indeterminate species snuggled up to each other. Facilities include a splash table with water syringe, bubble machine, two sand tables (preschool and wheelchair accessible), an activities table, and a bucket table, any of which can be set up to suit the needs of individual children. For the rare child flat on his or her back, a canopy of redbud trees provides sensory interest. There are also windsocks and windchimes—an acoustic landscape that emphasizes the needs of children with sight impairments. In the "Magic House" (manufactured by Kompan, a Danish play equipment company) children can "act out" medical situations through dramatic play.

Tables with cafe-style umbrellas allow the courtyard to be used even under a light sprinkle of summer rain. "Everything in the environment is very mobile and adapted for indoor-outdoor use," noted Roberta Hursthouse. "Sometimes, the sand tables are put into storage so that the Court always looks different."

Use

The mission of the child life program at Memorial Hospital is to advocate for each child, to interpret hospital procedures to the young patients in a developmentally appropriate way, and to create situations where children can have mastery and control over their lives and seek restoration, in contrast to the medical environment where much of the time they have things

"We love it! We are here almost daily. It is wonderful to have a place to go. This has a nice, secluded feeling of containment. The diversity in here; there is so much to look at and observe; it's wonderful!"

(MOTHER OF INPATIENT)

done to them over which they have no control. Within the matrix of permanent plantings, the courtyard is designed to support mastery via horticultural therapy activities and a variety of other wheelchair accessible free play opportunities, including water play, sand play, medical play, story time, crafts, music, art therapy—"anything the children want to do in the different playgroups," commented Roberta Hursthouse. Volunteers have a critical role assisting children in customizing appropriate physical arrangements. The Garden Play Program is particularly significant as it offers an opportunity for all children to directly affect their surroundings through their own efforts and ideas. "With cut flowers and leaves, the children create little landscapes in trays." In a sense, these gardens reverse the work of the caregiver. It now becomes the child who must care for a living thing back in his or her hospital room. Garden Play moves freely back-and-forth between indoors and outdoors. with a specially prepared horticulturally sterile planting mix[1] is used to bring the planting experience to the bedside of children who are too sick to go outside or when the weather does not permit outdoor activity. Planting activity can be done by children in bed, flat on their backs, by holding a mirror above the bed while the child works on a "bed tray." Once the growing season is under way, plants are transplanted by the staff in planters in the Garden Court (early March). Children can see them from some of the rooms and share them with their parents.

Therapeutic play groups are organized on Friday mornings for preschool and school-aged children four years old and above for one-and-half hours. The children are free to come and go between groups, including Garden Play. All children are welcome. Whatever they choose is fine—or they can choose to say "no." Toddlers are supervised by parents. The program is developmentally based. In winter it is held once a month and in summer every other week (possibly increasing to once a week in the future).

---

1. The planting mix is called "Promix." It is a horticulturally sterile mixture of peatmoss and pearlite. When dry, it has fewer microorganisms than the normal air we breathe. The mixture is prepared outside the hospital, imported, and used in moistened form on the same day, before the microbes multiply. In addition to the planting mix, much care is taken to ensure there are no sharp corners or edges on any of the planting pots, and planting implements so no cuts or scratches will occur. Anything that children can throw is removed. Physical surveillance is very tight. Planters have removable liners that are replaced with each planting cycle. A whole protocol has been established for dealing with planting structures in the hospital. Everything inside must be sterile, horticulturally speaking. New liners must always be on hand to reline the accessible planters when new patients participate and plants must be replaced. It is an ongoing cycle.

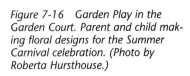
Figure 7-16 Garden Play in the Garden Court. Parent and child making floral designs for the Summer Carnival celebration. (Photo by Roberta Hursthouse.)

Roberta may see children several times, especially if they return to the hospital for repeat visits. Sometimes garden activity can be used to rechannel the energy of particularly dominant children; for example, by encouraging them to share their experiences by giving away flower arrangements to children who cannot come down to the Court.

Each Christmas season, a joyful feeling is presented by the Garden Court full of light and color glistening on fresh snow; the whole courtyard is decorated with lights and special installations (in 1997, a family of reindeer was created from white birch trunks and branches). Through the year, the garden accommodates many special social events, some of them for fund-raising, such as summer carnivals, floral design programs, and cookouts that can attract up to 300 people.[2]

Use of the garden varies according to the season. Sometimes, it is too cold to go out until the second week of June. Once the weather is warm enough, there is an afternoon teen program in the Garden Court focused on creative self-expression and career exploration. One teen boy learned floral designs when he was a patient and then found a job for the summer with a florist in his neighborhood. Not all Court users are strictly children or youth. A small number of users are in their 20s because they have cystic fibrosis and have been patients at the hospital most of their lives. There are also teen mothers with babies being treated in the hospital. The garden must satisfy their needs too.

---

[2]In 1998, a new Family Life Center opened, including a new playroom, reference material, solarium, and a new home for the Garden Play program.

During the summer it is in use from early morning and hours expand until late at night—when it becomes a tranquil sanctuary for parents dealing with their anguish, stress, and sorrow. Parents walk around or sit in the garden in the evening with and without child or siblings. "It is a place for restoration that is emotionally accessible, a place that is truly healing," Roberta recounts. A garden of any type provides a common point of reference. It helps people feel they do not have to carry their burden alone. All share this place of unburdening, of release, of communication with life and therefore with a sense of hope, recovery, and rebirth.

"One day a mother came with her daughter who had not walked since she had had an accident—she didn't want to," Roberta reported. "No motivation. The mother asked for help. Her daughter chose to participate in the floral design activity. To help the mother feel at ease, I suggested she join in. She got so engrossed she stopped paying attention to her daughter. Suddenly we were both aware she was up, walking around, watering the plants. It was a magic moment that so well illustrates what happens when a child is allowed to start controlling her life again. I see myself as a facilitator to help children explore and create, rather than guiding them through preestablished therapy. This would negate the basic premise of the Garden Play Program." The garden can be used by all children except those from the hematology and oncology departments, as their medical conditions make it impossible. The garden is not sterile enough for these children—they have their own play therapy on their floor, inside.

Regarding safety aspects of the program, Roberta reported that all plants used in the program are carefully researched as nontoxic and hypoallergenic.[3] She recommended impatiens and begonias. Small animals are also accepted and celebrated in the garden. As no pesticides are used in the garden, ladybugs, for example, are prolific. The Child Life Program obtained clearance from the medical staff to handle them. Birds from the inner city enjoy making the Court their home; for example, a pair of mourning doves are currently nesting there. "Children enjoy the idea of someone watching us," Roberta commented.

The sensorial impact of the gardening program is especially emphasized, as hospitals are dominated by negative sensorial experiences and periods of confined boredom. "Many children have never experienced gardening in their lives," reflected Roberta. "Working with them is so charged and energizing.

"They think my son is autistic, and we are just waiting for the news from his developmental evaluation. Waiting out here is better than inside; he does great out here. He has such a lot of energy, too much, maybe, to be inside for long periods of time. He's a lot happier out here, and he seems to fit in better, too."
(MOTHER OF OUTPATIENT)

Figure 7-17 Examining ladybugs in the Garden Court Garden Play program. (Photo by Roberta Hursthouse.)

[3]Careful checks for toxic plants have been made using the AMA guide as a reference, as well as consultants at the Chicago Botanic Garden.

I know it is healing." For Roberta, the garden is an "invitation to hope," an "antidote to despair." It is a place where children are challenged to do something different. The garden says to the child "you can do this" as a starting point. They rise to the challenge in comfortable steps. The staff is there to facilitate and encourage (never to coerce!) what is developmentally appropriate and medically safe. Issues that are medically challenging get resolved in the garden. It is an invitation, a starting point in the healing process.

ADVANTAGES

- The Garden Court is used by a well-developed, highly professional, inside-outside, Child Life and horticultural therapy program that fully exploits the potential of the garden space.
- A fully developed protocol with medical authorization has been implemented for the planting activities.
- Fully enclosed and protected from external city environment.
- Diverse plantings relative to microclimatic constraints.
- Flexible, adaptable space. Can be reconfigured rapidly using movable trays and tables.
- Overhead protection is provided by market umbrellas.
- The garden is highly visible as you enter the hospital.
- The garden is overlooked by the hospital fast food restaurant.
- Wildlife is encouraged to make their home in the garden (ladybugs, birds, etc.)
- Multisensory elements, such as windsocks and windchimes, are integrated into the landscape.
- There are no limits on "opening hours." The garden can be used any time of the day or night—especially by parents.

DISADVANTAGES

- Because the Garden Court is completely enclosed, it is difficult to make major changes; for example to add or remove large trees. Doors and elevators must be negotiated. The large, circular planter is going to be removed, but it will be very costly and disruptive.
- Lack of sunlight during much of the year, blocked by surrounding hospital building
- No night lighting.

- "Bluestone" paving looks beautiful but does not work well with IV poles (they are on their own carriage and must be pushed alongside a child using a wheelchair or transporter). The surface is not sufficiently smooth. The paving will be replaced with a synthetic safety surface (not native rubber as some children have severe rubber allergies.)

- Lack of at-grade entrance. Existing ramp segregates wheelchair users. Planned renovations include a new at-grade entrance from the Volunteer's Services area.

The Prouty Terrace and Garden, Children's Hospital, Boston, Massachusetts

Children's Hospital, Boston, is one of the premier hospitals for children in the United States. It is located in the Longwood medical and academic section of Boston, along with several other large urban medical facilities.

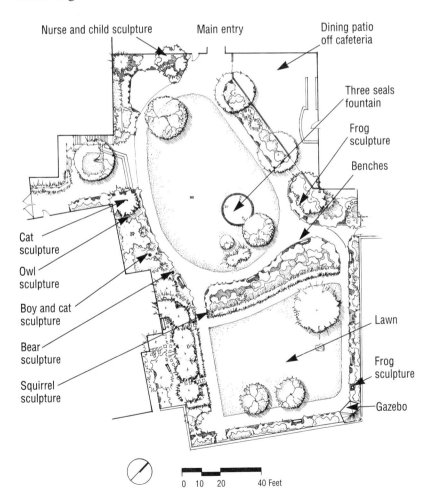

Figure 7-18 Site plan of the Prouty Garden, Children's Hospital, Boston, MA.

"It gives you some peacefulness. You can go there and sit, get away from it all; there is more hope in the garden. It's different from a chapel, where you go to pray, to try to find some acceptance. When a person is so sick, critically ill, or is dying, people go to the chapel. The garden is for healing. You feel closer, you feel more hope, more uplifted. It is a place of hope."

(STAFF MEMBER)

History of the Garden

The garden was opened in 1956 and completed in 1987, but the origin goes back to the 1920s, with Mrs. Prouty's interest in two old hospital wards. She had lost a second child and was contemplating adoption when Dr. Richard Smith, her pediatrician and Chief of Pediatrics at Children's, took her to see a twelve-bed ward in need of rehabilitation. He suggested that instead of a child, she "adopt" the shabby ward and try to improve its appearance. Success in this led her to take on a second twelve-bed ward and dedicate both to her two deceased children. When the wooden ward building was torn down in 1953 and replaced with the present building, Mrs. Prouty was asked if she would like to sponsor a garden.

Mrs. Prouty liked the idea and contacted Olmstead Brothers, the Boston landscape architecture firm, to design the garden. At her request, they modeled it after the walled garden and terrace of the Museum of Modern Art in New York. The final design was executed by Boston landscape architects Shurcliff and Merrill. The garden opened on October 4, 1956, and four years later was awarded a gold medal by the Massachusetts Horticultural Society for a "well executed court garden." As you enter the garden from the Farley Building, a simple bronze plaque to the right reads: "This Terrace and Garden in Memory of Anne and Olivia Prouty." The trust fund that was established by Mrs. Prouty still supports the equivalent of a full-time gardener. Credit for the garden's successful early planting is due to the efforts of late Colonel William Smith, former Director of Resources at Children's, who donated many valuable plants from his own garden.

Description

The garden is accessed from a corridor on the first floor of the hospital (one level above the main entrance). Unfortunately there are no specific signs indicating its existence, only a few small signs to "Garden Elevator" and a small sign naming the garden at the entrance. The half-acre, roughly rectangular (190 × 120 feet) garden is enclosed by hospital buildings ranging from three to six stories on the north, south, and west, and by the single-story hospital library and a garden wall flanked by an adjacent six-story building to the east. While the strong sense of enclosure offered by largely high-rise buildings might have created a pit-like space, the relatively large extent of the garden, plus the presence of several large trees screening the buildings, ensures that the garden feels like a quiet, well-kept urban oasis. The tall, solid, light brick garden wall, shrouded in espaliered climbing hydrangea, pyracantha, and wisteria, charms the visitor and seems to shut out the world beyond.

The garden comprises three large, and several small, sub-spaces. Large areas are an oval lawn with a fountain-pool set off-center; a paved cafeteria terrace looking over the oval lawn; and a square lawn to the rear separated from the oval lawn by a perennial border and low yew hedge. The smaller subspaces consist of a number of seating clusters set around the edge of the garden, looking out over the lawns. The straightforward circulation system provides enough choices that a staff member out for a stroll, or a parent pushing a child in a wheelchair, has a variety of visual experiences. A gray asphalt path circles the oval lawn, another runs around the square lawn. The two paths link together, forming a broad figure-eight with views on one side onto open lawns, and on the other onto richly textured shrub and perennial planting.

The many small sculptures set into the planting beside the pathways and on the lawns are an especially attractive feature of the garden. Circulating around the garden counterclockwise from the main entrance, one encounters sculptures of a nurse and child, small figures of a goose, a cat, an owl, a boy holding a cat, a bear, a squirrel, two frogs, and a fox, half-hidden in the shrubbery, and small life-size figures of a rabbit and birds set on the lawn. Children taken out into the garden take great delight in finding and naming these figures, more so because they are half-hidden. On one day in mid-November, yellow chrysanthemum flowers picked from the snowbound, fading perennial border had been placed (most likely by a child) in the mouths of the bear and the fox, and in the arms of the boy.

Figure 7-19   View across main lawn toward fountain and birch grove at the Prouty Garden. Hospital ward building to the right. (Photo courtesy of Boston Children's Hospital.)

"I think for the parents with the chronic kids, having the garden is a real plus. They are here a lot and the hospital is more like a second home to them, so the space here is that much more important, especially when you consider the amount of stress they must be feeling."
(Staff member)

Figure 7-20 "Boy and Cat" sculpture peeking out from a Prouty Garden shrub border, welcoming children and parents, adding a point of interest, a subject of conversation, and a sense of identity for the users. (Photo by Clare Cooper Marcus.)

There are plenty of places to sit, including nine concrete backless benches set just to the side of the peripheral walkway; several clusters of movable garden chairs and tables set in more private, tree-screened corners; fixed wooden seating in a corner gazebo; many attractive green-painted metal chairs and tables on the cafeteria terrace. In the summer, the lawns are also used for sitting or sprawling in the sun. Whether one is part of a group of workmates sharing a picnic lunch, a visitor sitting alone, or two stressed parents needing a place for privacy, the garden offers many varied options.

The planting in the garden adds immeasurably to its charm and oasislike milieu during all seasons. Several very large trees—a ginkgo, a white pine, a dawn redwood, several cryptomeria, and white birches—seem to scale down the height of the multi-story buildings around. Complementing these at a lower height are a great variety of smaller trees, including flowering dogwood, Japanese maple, carnelian cherry, magnolia, hemlock, and flowering cherry. Deciduous and evergreen shrubs, including rhododendron, azalea, hydrangea, juniper, holly, lavender, mountain andromeda, and mountain laurel form an understory beneath the peripheral trees, their colors changing with the seasons. Among the larger trees are several rare specimens, including one of the most unusual, the metasequoia or dawn redwood. In addition, there are seven cryptomerias (evergreens seldom found as far north as Boston), Japanese katzuras; and a tall, stately tulip tree. At least one of every variety of tree, shrub, and plant bears an identifying tag giving both its common and Latin names. A glass framed plan of the garden with every plant identified is an interesting feature of the cafeteria patio that overlooks the garden.

The garden's colors are at their brightest in the spring with the early blossoming of crocuses, daffodils, and lavender Mongolian azaleas. Later come the tulips, the pink clusters of Carolina rhododendrons, and the reds, whites, and yellows of the late-blooming azaleas. In May, pansies, marigolds, petunias, and dahlias appear, as well as various unpretentious little flowers with common names especially appealing to children: Johnny jump-ups, Jacob's ladders, Dutchman's breeches. By mid-May the garden is filled with flowering trees: dogwood, both pink and white, cherries, crab apples, and silverbell.

The garden is managed by the Office of Facility Planning and Space Planning through a Garden Committee which oversees the condition of the planting, requests replacements, and manages the garden horticulturally. They also define appropriate uses and establish rules. The resident hospital architect is a member of the committee and is personally involved on a daily basis.

Use

The garden is intended to serve the children at the hospital, their siblings, parents, relations, and hospital employees. From early spring to late fall, the grounds are populated not only with children but also with visitors, lured into sitting a while on the stone benches and garden chairs placed in both sunny and shady spots. The garden is well-used on warm days by staff on breaks and during lunch hours, and by parents taking a break from a sick child's bedside. On a warm spring day, up to 150 people may use the garden. Spring, summer, and fall are obviously the peak seasons, but even in winter (and under snow) staff take walks in the garden or pass through it when moving from one building to another. On-site observations indicated hospital staff as the most frequent users—eating a brown bag lunch, taking a break or a walk. Because the garden can be viewed from the attractive cafeteria terrace and the hospital library, the staff know of its existence and are drawn to it in warm weather.

The next most numerous group observed were parents waiting for a child undergoing surgery or treatment. With a few hours to spend and probably in a tense mood, the garden-as-green-oasis provides a welcome respite from the hospital environment. To anxious parents and patients alike, the garden is a merciful refuge, as well as a pleasant place to wheel recuperating children. Parents with siblings of a hospitalized child find the garden a welcome place to let well children explore and let off steam.

In terms of raw numbers, inpatient children may be the least frequently observed users because hospital stays are so brief these days, and a because a child who is in for a longer stay is likely to be too sick to go to the garden. However, the garden is used by many children at some point during their stay in the hospital, including postoperative, oncology, psychiatric, general medical, and general surgical patients.

There are no special staff assigned to the garden. It can be used by any resident patient or outpatient accompanied by a child life specialist, parent, or volunteer (Child Life runs a training program for volunteers). The garden is also used for patient parties and has been the scene of many special events. A tree lighting ceremony, held in the garden every Christmas, is watched through hospital windows by children and staff. Summer programs have included gardening, "arts in the garden," groups of musicians, magicians, traveling zoos, circuses, and community actors playing to the children. At the time of writing, these programs had been discontinued due to potentially harmful particulates into the air caused by construction activity.

"I feel like I am not in the hospital anymore when I am in the garden. I feel more relaxed. It is an escape. It is so nonhospital; nothing in there is like the hospital; it feels so open, so bright and colorful—the fresh air, the breezes—it's great to get out of the sterile cave."
(STAFF MEMBER)

Figure 7-21   Users of the cafeteria and hospital medical library have a view out into the Prouty Garden. (Photo by Clare Cooper Marcus.)

Children can interact physically with the landscape to a limited degree. They can smell and pick the flowers, but there are no facilities for them to plant flowers or vegetables. As children move around, they discover different secret corners where they can explore and hide. The animal statues add to the sense of discovery—some are placed on pedestals so that children being wheeled on the meandering paths in beds or wheelchairs can more easily see them. The raised deck of the gazebo provides a lookout that is accessible by a ramp.

The garden has southern exposure and an excellent microclimate; its winter temperature can be ten degrees warmer than the streets surrounding the hospital. "Even in winter on a nice sunny, calm day it can be very comfortable out there," reported Charles Smith, hospital architect. For that reason, children use the garden in the winter and sometimes even come out to make snow people there.

The garden is very secure, as one must enter through the hospital; there is plenty of cross-traffic between the surrounding hospital buildings that also overlook the space. Many eyes watch over it. It is well lit at night. The formal pool is about twelve inches deep and without a guardrail. "Although some safety experts may regard this as hazardous, there have been no incidents with the pond as far as I am aware in all the years I have been here," commented Charles Smith.

The only use conflict that occasionally arises is when the psychiatry patients try to use the garden for recreational activities such as football. This is an appropriate activity for the participating patients, but the garden is too small, and other users are disturbed. Occasionally children climb the trees, which is sometimes seen as problematic by the staff because it damages the trees. It would be nice if a specific climbing tree with low-slung branches could be designated. The worst maintenance issue seen by the staff is the daily cleanup after lunch on the cafeteria terrace when all the napkins and paper plates blow around in the wind.

ADVANTAGES
- Southern exposure provides excellent microclimate.
- Endowment fund provides for appropriate maintenance.
- Flat terrain is easily accessible.
- Animal sculptures.
- Fountain and pool.
- Diversity of plantings.
- Overlooked by cafeteria and medical library.

- Many different exploratory subspaces for discovery, contemplation, and privacy.
- Used by whole hospital community.

DISADVANTAGES
- Child Life-sponsored programs have been discontinued.
- Little hands-on engagement of the children, no planting activity.
- Occasional conflicts between active recreational uses and passive users.
- No directional signs to the garden in the hospital building.

Gardens at Lucas Gardens School, Canada Bay, New South Wales, Australia

History and Philosophy of the Garden
Lucas is a special education facility located in a suburban community outside Sydney, administered by the Department of Education of New South Wales, and linked to a nearby residential pediatric hospital. The original school dates from 1938. Because of falling enrollment it closed in 1985, was renovated and opened as a school for children with multiple disabilities in 1987. The single-story school buildings enclose a series of courtyards where the gardens (opened in 1989) have been developed over several years. The original layout of the gardens was provided by Good Manors, Landscape Architects. The facility is managed by school principal Jeanne Stratford, who came up with the idea of creating gardens in the existing cracked and pot-holed asphalt courtyards. Unusable because they were very hot in summer and full of puddles in winter, thus inhibiting mobility, the courtyards were renovated with the help of the local Rotary Club. At first, some of the staff wanted to use the funds to buy a minibus, but Jeanne argued that the children could not go somewhere every day. She wanted to create a "somewhere" right on the school site, "to bring nature into our midst," as she put it. A design was developed and implementation continued over several years.

About 50 percent of the children are transported to the school each day from the nearby hospital where they are permanent residents because of the severity of their disabilities. Most of these children use wheelchairs or cots. The other half of the children, also with severe, multiple disabilities, live with their families in the community.

"We had something really stressful happen just prior to coming here; we came here to debrief. It is a good setting to get away from the hospital stress, to feel more peaceful."
(STAFF MEMBER)

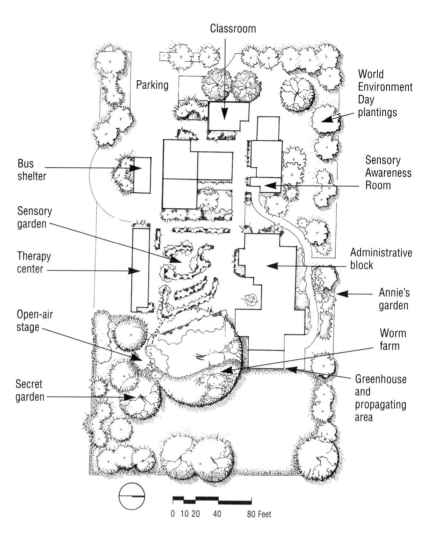

Figure 7-22 Site plan of Lucas Gardens School, Canada Bay, New South Wales, Australia.

Classroom

Parking

World Environment Day plantings

Bus shelter

Sensory Awareness Room

Sensory garden

Therapy center

Administrative block

Annie's garden

Open-air stage

Worm farm

Secret garden

Greenhouse and propagating area

0 10 20   40   80 Feet

Community Involvement

Initially, the community was threatened by the idea of a school for "disabled" children coming to the neighborhood. Jeanne's strategy was to use the garden project to bring the community together in a "double healing process." First, it helped the community to recover from the loss of closure of the original school and to accept the new facility and its students. Second, the garden celebrated the healing of the children. "I worked deliberately with the garden as a catalyst, as an upbeat project to bring the community together." Jeanne commented. Churches and local businesses contributed financially and the garden won an award for community involvement. When the movie, "The Secret Garden," was released, a show featuring Lucas' "secret garden" (a walkway featuring native Australian plants) was televised. "Now there are secret gardens all over," Jeanne observed.

Description

The Sensory Garden is the centerpiece of Lucas Gardens School. Surrounded on three sides by the school buildings, it was created by constructing a series of curving, raised planters that enclose several activity stations and provide ample space for permanent plantings emphasizing sensory stimulation. Activity stations include a texture table where children can explore a variety of natural objects, and a splash table—both designed for children either standing or using wheelchairs.

A swinging garden bench provides a quiet retreat where staff and children can snuggle up. Benches on the sides of the planters provide further resting spots. In addition to the colors, fragrances, and textures of the plants, the garden is "dressed" each day with wind chimes, windmills, colorful windsocks, flags, banners, and more than fifty cue-signs carrying messages such as "Listen to the bird song" or "Find the spider web." Part of the garden has been allowed to grow into a junglelike area with large vines hanging down where children can explore and get "lost." "It is a challenge, they enjoy it," explained Jeanne. Most recently, a "no dig" garden has been installed, made of newspaper, straw, and sand.

Figure 7-23 Music therapist uses the healing garden setting to work with one of the children. (Photo courtesy of Lucas Gardens School.)

One side of the Sensory Garden is bounded by a building containing a splinting and plastering clinic, a wheelchair assessment clinic, and a physical and occupational therapy center. Activities spill out into the Sensory Garden "to extend the idea of therapy as caring for the soul and spirit of the children," commented Jeanne.

Related facilities include a shade house, a compost area, a big grassy "paddock," an outdoor concert stage, a potting shed, and an area for propagating native plants for projects in the community. "Our philosophy is to always give back to the community," said Jeanne. "It's a key commitment, and very good public relations."

An earthworm breeding farm in the Palm Garden was developed as a community project and fund-raising activity. It started out as a vocational project with students and gradually grew into something bigger. The farm is so prolific that it supplies earthworms to several local organizations and municipalities and is destined to be a major breeding source for New South Wales. So far, several thousand dollars have been raised through sales. Purchasers receive a kit, a list of do's and don'ts, and a set of materials. About 200 schools have received kits from the earthworm farm, which also attracts several visitors a day.

Theme areas include the Palm Garden, the Secret Garden, a native plant area, butterfly- and bird-attracting plants, and World Environment Day gardens. A huge South African Kaffir plum (*Harpophyllum kaffrum*—used as the Lucas logo—shelters part of the garden and provides a symbol of guardian strength for the Lucas community. Most likely the tree was planted in the 1800s when the site was one of the first farm leases in convict times.

Use

Lucas's gardens are designed for children with special needs, including behavioral disorders, and multiple physical, intellectual, and sensory disabilities. Some of the children have complex medical conditions or terminal illnesses. Some have gastrotubes fitted. Others have had an accident or an illness later in life. For Jeanne, the gardens were created to provide opportunities for children to be challenged, to be alone, to be together, or to be with parents and special friends.

WORKING WITH CHILDREN. Most of the work with the children is one-on-one. "The garden is the first place we take children to get their spirits up when they come back from surgery," Jeanne noted. She explained that even though some of the children are quite mobile, supervision is not much of an issue. Even children with intellectual disabilities, who might try to run away, are often "held" by the garden. "Once a child becomes independently mobile they have a wonderful feeling of freedom to explore, going from space to space, enveloped by grown-up plants. All you can hear are their voices. We challenge children by calling their names. They can't see you but must find you—like hide-and-go-seek."

Figure 7-24 Drawing (1991) of the Sensory Garden by Jennifer Porter, a staff member, showing the elements of the design.

"Lovely things happen," reported Jeanne. "Rielly couldn't hold his head up when he came to school. Now he's mobile in the garden, along walkways, in the bushes, in his chair, head up. He has a big head, too—hydrocephalic. When he first started, we doubted that he could even travel to school. Now he's just out and about in the garden!"

Teachers, teacher's aides, and therapists use the garden for program activities, including mobility training. They bring children from other schools where they work for visits, as a treat. The garden is a nice place to have lunch. For volunteers—including high school students fulfilling their community service requirements—the gardens are an attractive and enjoyable place to work. For Jeanne, "the overall diversity of the gardens and the cue-signs [for the helpers] make it easy to come up with stimulating ideas to engage the children's interest." One of the staff summed up the garden as a place of healing as "seeing the faces of happy children experiencing life in a memorable way."

SENSORY REACH. Much of the garden landscape is at wheelchair height. The chimes and windmills are low so that children can reach out and activate them. Old birds' nests are put on lower branches so that children can see into them, feel them, and understand how they work. The environment is designed to stimulate mobility, to encourage children to reach out, to touch, to explore, to be challenged, to go beyond their own limits. Each morning a group of children pick flowers for the classrooms and foyer.

Sensory stimulation is a key dimension. "The gardens work like a sensory treasure hunt," Jeanne explained. "We have a 'listening map' showing what can be heard in different spaces. Smell is very important, especially the memory of smell. Children arrive in the morning along a scent trail covered with climbing roses, wisteria, and star jasmine. We call it our 'fragrant greeting.'" Jeanne and her staff worked with the Asthma Foundation to choose plants that do not trigger asthma or allergies and that are very user-friendly. As a result, the garden is planted mostly with bird- or insect-pollinated plants rather than wind-pollinated plants.

"I feel more relaxed out here. It is the water, the sound of the little windchimes. The sound of the leaves in the breeze. The colors, it is bright, cheerful."
(STAFF MEMBER)

ANIMALS. As farmyard animals are difficult to accommodate permanently, Lucas brings in a farmyard once a year with goats, cows, ducks, and chickens. Birds inhabit the site permanently, including a pair of native doves, plovers, and a cockatoo. "We have all kinds of snails, bugs, beetles, and other insects," Jeanne reported. "Butterflies are prolific, together with magnificent spiders and their webs. We don't use insecticides, although we

7-25   View of a section of the Sensory Garden showing several "activity rooms" and one of the wheelchair/standing frame tables (far right). Notice the banners, windsocks, and giant butterflies (far right). They respond to breezes and add movement and color to the garden. (Photo courtesy of Lucas Gardens School.)

have to be careful with bee and wasp stings. I knock the wasp nests down at night when I see them."

A PLACE FOR FAMILIES. The intricate, sheltered spaces of the garden are more conducive to nursing, and holding a child than the impersonal, public hospital wards. As a result, more parental visiting happens in the garden than at the hospital. "Siblings are the same way," commented Jeanne. "One of a pair of twins was brain-damaged at birth [and they were not relating to each other]. Now, the two boys can play together here and have a lovely time. Children and parents realize this is a special place, value it greatly and feel they can share it with each other."

When a child passes away from a terminal illness or disability, a "memorial plant" is chosen by the parents and staff. Jeanne told the story of Tanya. "She had a lovely smile and lots of white, curly hair. Her tree is a frangipani. The blossom has a golden center, white petals around it, and a beautiful perfume. Memorial plants are a therapeutic part of the healing process. Sometimes a parent will come back and say, 'Oh, I just came by to prune Susie's rose,' and I'll say something like 'Oh, great, good to see you.'"

A COMMUNITY PLACE. Part of the philosophy of the garden is that it is open to the community. It is used by visually impaired students from the local school system and high school wheelchair users for plant identification and experimental projects. Other students use the facility for environmental education and arts and crafts activities—at the same time, learning about the Lucas children. "We get lovely thank you letters," commented

Jeanne, "saying how much they enjoyed their visit and how lucky we are to have such a beautiful facility."

Mildly physically disabled young people engage in "work experience" at the site. Jeanne told of a young man recovering from cancer who had had a nervous breakdown and could not face going back to his formal horticultural studies. "When he first started with us he couldn't get on a bus without getting off at the next stop. After nine months he was able to face the world again. We're like an employment agency for people with that kind of problem, especially in the area of horticulture. It is a gentle place for them to start back again." The juvenile court occasionally refers young people to the garden who have been in trouble with the law. One such person appeared in court with pictures of himself working in the garden. The judge was so impressed he gave him a second chance. "The garden turned his life around," Jeanne commented.

A nursing home reading group meets in the garden on nice days. Jeanne noted the value of the garden for Alzheimer's patients because they don't get lost. Reflecting on the importance of plants, she recalled talking about a daphne flower. "One of the Alzheimer's ladies overheard me and said, 'Daphne, that's my name.' She had not said it for fifteen years!"

"Weekend passes" are issued to casual users of the garden. A local community group uses it for composting and runs courses on Sundays. Several groups host educational and horticultural activities at the garden. The Rotary Club uses the nightlit gardens for their Christmas party. The Therapy Center opening was attended by 400 people, all of whom were accommodated in the garden with space left over.

Jeanne noted that in more than ten years the garden has never been vandalized. "We've had bricks through the school windows, but the garden has never been touched. Local children and skateboarders play here at the weekend. Neighborhood residents bring newspapers and refreshments and take it easy."

The Lucas gardens are well known in the region. They have been featured as an exhibition garden on the Great Garden Tour of Sydney and have been written up in environmental magazines. "When visitors come by, they are always impressed by what they see," noted Jeanne. "Everyone on the staff is proud of it. The school psychologist calls it 'my beautiful oasis.' The garden has led to many good things happening at this school, way beyond what it cost. I walk out there some evenings at the end of the day and say 'good on ya, garden—you had to be!' The joy of sharing nature with people makes it all worthwhile."

A fund-raising fair for the garden is held once every two years with all the stores in town participating. Fruit is harvested, brandied, and given to family and friends as "thank yous." Spices and herbs are sold and used to make spiced vinegar. Lavender is used to make lavender satchets called "dream pillows."

MAINTENANCE. The maintenance regime for Lucas Gardens is very modest. A gardener comes one day a week. A fluctuating group of volunteers cares for the plants. According to Jeanne, "Mostly, the garden takes care of itself—it has to. Survival of the fittest is our philosophy. We mulch a lot and focus on native plants."

ADVANTAGES

- Community-based, which results in high visibility and strong community support.
- Includes fund-raising components such as an earthworm farm.
- Multiuser groups. Enriches lives of children and other users.
- Attractive place for volunteers.
- Encourages family involvement. Symbolizes high quality of life even after the passing of a child.
- Emphasizes sensory stimulation.
- Provides a great diversity of hands-on activity choices.
- Supports intimate connections with the indoor spaces of the facility.
- Universally designed to accommodate the needs of a wide variety of user groups.
- Low maintenance, "survival of the fittest" landscape approach.

DISADVANTAGES

- Relies on the leadership of a single individual to maintain the momentum and integrity of the evolving vision (as with most visionary projects).

Leichtag Family Healing Garden, Children's Hospital and Health Center, San Diego, California

By Clare Cooper Marcus

Children's Hospital is the principal hub for pediatric health care in the San Diego region. It accommodates over 200,000 inpatient and outpatient visits annually. The Cancer Care Center treats 400 children annually. Two-thirds of the patients are under four years of age. Over 60 percent have no medical insur-

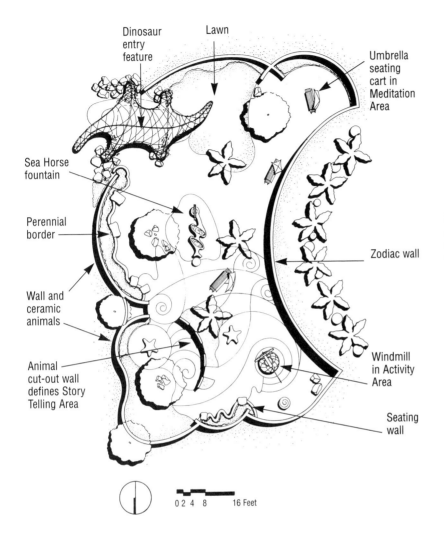

Dinosaur
entry
feature

Lawn

Umbrella
seating
cart in
Meditation
Area

Sea Horse
fountain

Perennial
border

Wall and
ceramic
animals

Animal
cut-out wall
defines Story
Telling Area

Zodiac wall

Windmill
in Activity
Area

Seating
wall

0 2 4 8   16 Feet

Figure 7-26   Site plan of the Leichtag Family Healing Garden, Children's Hospital and Health Center, San Diego, CA.

ance and are covered by the state health plan. Patients represent the cultural breadth of the area. Principal groups are Asian, Hispanic, Caucasian, and African-American.

History and Philosophy of the Garden

The Leichtag Family Healing Garden opened in 1997. Its development involved a complex process of discussion, team-building, design brainstorming, and fund-raising, led by Delaney, Cochran & Castillo, Landscape Architects. It began with the idea of a garden envisioned by the hospital's Bereavement Committee in the late 1980s. In 1993, with the creation of a Healing Environment Steering Committee, the focus of the garden shifted and it became part of an overall healing environment program which also encompassed redesigned waiting areas and a performing arts program. The primary stakehold-

"My son was only in the hospital for 17 hours and then he died. Later there was a memorial service here for the children who have died, for their parents. The memorial service was beautiful, very meaningful. Someone had brought flowers, and let the petals drift gently in the grass in the breeze. It was a way to share our grief with others who had also experienced this loss and it was healing, it helped with this process of healing. My son and I had really bonded when we were outside so it was especially meaningful for me to be outside in a memorial for him."

(BEREAVED MOTHER)

ers for the garden (landscape architect, Vice President for Facilities, parents, staff, child-life specialists, etc.) brainstormed its goals and worked together as the design evolved. After considerable fund-raising efforts, the garden was completed and dedicated in July 1997. (See Chapter 11 for a more detailed account of the process of creating this garden.)

Description

The garden is located behind the hospital, on its northwest side. There are signs to the garden (in English and Spanish) beside the elevators off the main lobby. It is visible from the nearby elevator lobbies and stairways on several floors of the hospital. The garden is completely enclosed with curvilinear, brightly painted, 4- to 7-foot high walls and is entered under a large tubular steel structure. Bougainvillea is planted at the base of this frame and will eventually cover what is intended as a huge, vine-covered dinosaur nicknamed "Sam" At present the vines have grown only 4 or 5 feet up the four dinosaur "legs" and the structure doesn't particularly convey "dinosaur," but it nevertheless provides an eye-catching gateway entrance.

The curvilinear walls serve a number of purposes: they define and enclose the space; they curve around and create a number of child-scale "rooms"; the colored surfaces (orange, deep blue, purple, green, yellow) provide a vibrant backdrop for the ceramic animal, fish and insect figures with which they are decorated and for the perennials that are planted around the edges of the garden against the walls. The wall you first see on entering is deep blue in color and has colored glass set into it in patterns of the constellations, which glow as the afternoon and evening sun shines through them. Other walls are decorated with ceramic figures or encompass steel panels with animal cut-outs.

In the center of the garden is a ceramic tile sea horse fountain, which jets two long spouts of water into two raised ceramic-tiled pools. The sound can be heard throughout the space. There are a variety of ground surfaces; starting with painted concrete under the entry dinosaur; around the fountain, and extending into the areas most distant from the entry. In other locations, the curvilinear edge of painted concrete gives way to expanses of beige-colored crushed fines, and to patches of lawn. All the surfaces are easy to walk on and to pull a wagon across as inpatient children can be brought by family members to the garden in brightly painted wagons.

Vertical features in the garden consist of trees and structures. Among the latter are a blue-painted steel windmill, with birds inside the structure that flap their wings as the windmill

Figure 7-27   Leichtag Family Healing Garden, view from above looking over dinosaur entry, Zodiac Wall beyond. (Photo by Marni Barnes.)

turns; the dinosaur; the concrete walls; and yellow umbrellas hanging over three movable bench "carts." Tree planting consists of palm trees inside the garden and just outside its walls, as well as several deciduous species.

There are plenty of spaces to sit, varying by location, material, view, and sense of enclosure. Around part of the perimeter are seat-height planter walls backed by plants and with several seating rocks set into the planter edge. Two ceramic-tile starfish seats and one ceramic-tile "mushroom" provide casual seating for a person alone, or a parent and child. Three highly colored bench "carts" with shade umbrellas provide seating for two or three people and are—theoretically—movable, but are actually too heavy.

The designers chose to focus on a seaside beach theme in the creation of this garden, with an emphasis on appropriate colors (blue, sandy yellow), appropriate textures (sandy decomposed granite), and ceramic sea creatures. The overall feel of the garden seems appropriate to southern California: sandy-colored surfaces, the sounds of a splashing fountain, palm trees, bird of paradise plants, shadows cast on walls, Mediterranean colors. In the cool of the afternoon, it is a pleasant place to be—close to the hospital, yet seemingly far-removed.

Use

A postoccupancy evaluation of this garden was conducted in the summer of 1998, employing behavior mapping, tracking, and interviews with adult and child garden users and nonusers.

(Center for Child Health Outcomes, 1998). The majority of garden users reported going to the garden to relax and rest, to cope with worries, and to get away from stress; 90 percent reported a positive change of mood after visiting the garden.

A father of a child in intensive care remarked: "This is a better place to wait than the waiting room. We couldn't stand being in there, wondering if she'd make it. This is quiet and peaceful: the greenery, the colorful flowers, the sound of water." The mother of an outpatient replied: "For my son, this garden is wonderful. He's autistic, and the garden seems almost built for him. He loves the waterfall. He is very visual, and also working at learning the names of things, like animals. He does a lot better out here than he does inside a waiting room, so it is less stressful for me...." A staff member responded: "I feel happier and less stressed out. I think it's mostly the running water, the bright colors. [But] I think it needs more hands-on stuff for kids to do."

"What a contrast this is from a normal hospital waiting room! I think this could be an excellent spot for therapy sessions. I told my son's specialist about this, and brought her out here; she loved it too! She had never been out here! She said she could do her two-hour therapy sessions out here very easily."

(MOTHER OF OUTPATIENT)

Features mentioned as helpful included the soothing sound of running water; the sense of "escaping the hospital"; the fresh air and breezes; and the flowers. Half reported that the garden increased their willingness to recommend Children's Hospital to others. For one staff member, the presence of the garden convinced him to take a job at the hospital: "It really helped me like this place...I was really impressed...I mean, if they take this level of care, to put in gardens for the families and staff like this, for healing...I decided this was the place for me to do my [pediatric] residency."

However, the garden was significantly underused. Nearly half of all garden users would enter, walk quickly around, and leave in less than five minutes. While the sea horse fountain and the parasol benches attracted users, other areas of the garden were unused. The whole garden was empty for long periods of time.

Some people found the colors and hard surfaces jarring; two-thirds of children interviewed wanted "more things to do" in the garden. The majority of users recommended changes such as adding more trees and greenery, creating a vegetation screen to create a private corner (for therapy, grieving parents, etc.), and building a wheelchair path to the central paved area.

"I even got out there to the gardens once for a whole five-minute break! The volunteers said I should go on down there. It was nice to get out of here, away from all the smells and the stress. But my son has been in too bad shape to go out. It would be better for him than watching TV all day. He needs some color. I am tired of being stuck in this room I wish we could get more sun, wind, air. It has healing value."

(MOTHER OF INPATIENT)

Ninety-five percent of the families surveyed in the hospital building (N=23) had never been to the garden, and 48 percent did not know of its existence. Clearly, one barrier to use is lack of knowledge about the garden. Other barriers included "too far to go"; confusion over its purpose—for example, who and what it is for; and the medical model of treatment, that is, staff focusing on the physical illness with less attention to the emotional needs of patients and families. One staff member responded: "What's so healing about the healing garden? I just don't get it!" This latter comment suggests the need for greater understanding of the potential benefits of healing gardens.

Based on this study and other, informal site observations, the garden seems to serve parents and children as a brief diversion before or after routine hospital visits. When parents and children must visit the hospital regularly for treatment of a chronic condition—for example, for dialysis—the parents and any siblings might come to the garden for an uplifting respite while the ill child is being treated. However, the same environment that appeals to a child may not be restorative for stressed parents, since there are no private get-away spaces, and the intense colors and forms, which attract children, may be too "busy" for an adult seeking quiet solace. Parents of a child in a crisis situation in the hospital may similarly have difficulty finding a peaceful corner in this garden. A bench located in what was intended as a quiet, meditative corner is exposed to everyone who enters the garden. Thus any desire for a private, contemplative spot needs to be accommodated elsewhere on the hospital grounds in a calmer, less visible space.

For parents who bring inpatient children to the garden in a wagon/wheelchair, there are opportunities to interact outside, away from the indoor associations of the hospital, in a space where diversions and distractions abound. The child may or may not be able to be engaged, depending on the severity of the illness.

For staff eating lunch outdoors, the garden works well for those seeking a sociable space, visual stimulation, novelty, and movement (in contrast to the necessary sterility of indoors). For staff wanting to unwind in peace and quiet, the garden may not provide a sufficiently restorative experience—because of the lack of privacy and the predominance of hardscape rather than green nature.

Adolescents obviously enjoy hanging out and "messing around" (stopping the fountain jets, hanging off the dinosaur structure, etc.), but this type of activity conflicts with those users seeking peace and privacy. The attraction of the windmill and dinosaur for climbing have resulted in "no climbing" signs being attached to those features. These more active pursuits might need to be accommodated somewhere.

For the child who seeks diversion from hospital fears or from the emotions of a stressed parent, more diversity is required. While the garden is clearly welcoming to children, there are not enough opportunities for the child to be engaged and interested for long periods. This would require installation

Figure 7-28   Grandmother and child playing "peek-a-boo" through the Animal Wall. (Photo by Clare Cooper Marcus.)

"I think the garden would get more use if they put signs around that invite kids to touch some of the plants, or smell them, or pick them; for example, Touch me, I am soft or Smell me, I am lavender. If children should not touch something, make it a friendly sign, say Look at me, but don't touch me please. Have the kids in O.T. make the signs, or [have] the convalescent kids help make them (even if all they do is paint the signs). Then the kids could bring their parents to the garden and show off their work."

(STAFF MEMBER)

of more features or materials that children could move, manipulate, or change. With these present, their attention would be more strongly engaged, ensuring a more positive outcome from a garden visit.

A security guard reported that the staff often came to the garden to eat their lunch. The guard remarked: "It's a nice place, but I don't know why they had to put all this dirt in here; it should have been lawn." (He was referring to the crushed fines.) This remark sums up what may be a typical adult reaction to a space that is designated a "garden" but whose appearance most resembles a colorful beach scene.

ADVANTAGES

- Easily accessible from hospital.
- Entry clearly marked with sign and dinosaur armature.
- Strong sense of enclosure suggests security and a distinct sense of place.
- Strong colors provide a cheerful setting.
- Sounds of fountain, heard throughout most of the garden, are soothing.
- Form of fountain, fanciful starfish seating, ceramic figures on walls, and so on, communicate "This is a place for children."
- Walled subspaces draw children in to explore.
- Plenty of places to sit.
- Variety of perennials to examine with informative labels; plants attract humingbirds.
- Trees and windmill cast interesting, attractive shadow patterns on vividly colored walls.
- Light shining through individual glass balls in the zodiac wall add an attractive and distinct punctuation to the space.
- Small ceramic figures on walls and cutout animal figures are child-scale, can be touched, and engage children's attention.
- Holes in the wall stimulate classic peek-a-boo and note-passing play activities.

DISADVANTAGES

- Too much variety of color and materials in such a small space; can be emotionally draining, the opposite of restorative. There are few places for the eye to rest.

- There are no places for an adult to be private and decompress, or for a child to semi-hide and be alone. These are experiences that people may seek in a healing garden.

- Not enough shade. The trees selected do not create much shade. The umbrellas over the movable benches create shade only for those sitting on those benches. The garden is too hot to use at the height of summer.

- While an armature shaped like a dinosaur creates a striking entry feature, it is so much bigger than the children that most do not recognize what it is supposed to be, and a few are frightened by it.

- The zodiac wall, while an attractive feature, is not understood or recognized by most garden users.

- When a breeze is not moving the windmill, the feature does not seem to be noticed by children.

- The seahorse fountain engages children as soon as they enter, but some parents seem concerned as to whether children are "allowed" to touch and play with the water.

- What engages children the longest is "manipulative play" (e.g., digging in sand, piling up blocks, turning over rocks, picking up sticks). Unfortunately, the garden provides few opportunities for manipulative play, except for the fountain pool.

- The lawn area is too small. Once a family "occupies" it, no one else can use the space.

- The "mobile" benches are too heavy to move.

- The steel legs at one end of each bench have a tendency to sink into the compacted crushed fines, creating a seat that slopes uncomfortably.

- People using the area of the garden intended as a private meditative corner are most "on view" to those entering the garden, and while seated in that space, the sounds of a nearby freeway compete with the restful sounds of the central fountain.

- There are no litter containers and users have requested them.

DESIGN GUIDELINES FOR CHILDREN'S HEALING GARDENS

The following design guidelines are based on the findings of the primary case studies as well as additional, unpublished case study material (as referenced).

Figure 7-30   View of the Chicago Garden Court from the main foyer of the hospital, showing raised beds, shade trees, and accessible play tables. The garden is decked out with pumpkins celebrating the fall harvest. Main entrance is on the left, hidden by the tree. Users can gather on the circular terrace (around an umbrella table in the summer): descend the steps (far left), if ambulatory; or turn sharp left down a ramped pathway behind the planter. (Photo by Roberta Hursthouse.)

1. Site Planning

Orient the garden site to receive year-round sun and shelter from winter winds. Many users refer to healing gardens as "green oases." Plants are the most highly valued feature and provide the essence of "healing" in healing gardens. But plants need sun to grow. Children need outdoor spaces warmed by the sun in spring, fall, and winter (to a greater or lesser degree, depending on the latitude).

The Chicago Garden Court was overshadowed all winter by the surrounding hospital buildings and children could not use it until June. The Boston garden, on the other hand, faced south and had almost no overshadowing and could be used year-round.

Site the garden on level terrain. Anything but a very modest degree of topographical variation in the garden site will give difficult if not impossible access problems.

The difference in level between the access floor and garden levels of the Chicago garden resulted in a ramp that consumed a significant proportion of the courtyard area. The ramp meant that children using wheelchairs and transporters had to enter the courtyard by a separate route. In contrast, other case study sites offered access without such hindrance—except Wellesley, but that is a private clinic working with only one child at a time.

Conserve natural features of the site. Natural features, such as mature trees, rock outcroppings, and watercourses, should be conserved as they provide natural identity to the site and potentially useful amenities (e.g., shade, in the case of trees). Conserve as much topsoil as possible, to give the new plantings the best possible start in life.

The identity of the Lucas Gardens was greatly enhanced by the huge, old plum tree that symbolized the whole garden and was used as the logo for the school. The natural topography of the Therapeutic Garden was extended and designed as a major element in therapeutic use of the garden.

2. Location

Locate garden so it is overlooked by patient rooms. For children who cannot go outdoors, the window view into the garden is critically important. Child life specialists are then able to make the connection between inside and outside by physically importing natural elements from the garden as well as visibly transplanting plants prepared by the child indoors. Chicago Children's Memorial worked very effectively in this way, using the horticultural therapy program to activate the indoor-outdoor link.

Locate garden adjacent to playroom. Adjacency of garden and playroom will save time and energy on the part of Child life specialists and horticultural therapists who must move items of equipment and play materials back and forth. The Wellesley clinic was designed so that the therapist and child could move easily from the playroom out into the sequence of spaces in the Therapeutic Garden. The Lucas gardens were ever present to the user populations and highly accessible from the interior spaces. This surely explains in part the great diversity of activities supported by the gardens. In other cases (Leichtag, for example), the garden is some distance from wards and playroom, thus the garden is used more formally and becomes "a place to go" or "destination." The other San Diego courtyard and roof gardens offer more direct indoor/outdoor connections.

Locate garden so that it is visible from public use facilities such as entrances, waiting areas, and cafeterias. When the garden is visible from the entrance, it reinforces a friendly, welcoming message to patients and visitors—especially if it is the first time they have been to the hospital. In both the Boston and Chicago case examples, the garden was overlooked by the hospital's public restaurant. Both gardens communicated their presence and gained beneficial exposure through the visual adjacency.

3. Security

Locate hospital garden so that it is fully enclosed on all four sides and inaccessible from the public surroundings of the facility except through the security-controlled entrance of the hospital. If the garden is used by the community,

"My granddaughter has been in ICU and we have been with her, for five days now. We just now saw this place from a window, we don't have much time because we want to be with our baby but it is nice to be out here for a break."

(GRANDMOTHER OF INPATIENT)

apply principles of defensible space (single entrance, overlooked by administrative office, audio signal of each coming or going, electronically controlled gate, etc.). Children, parents, and other users of the garden must be protected from intrusive, unwanted social interaction. An interesting exception to this principle was Lucas, which in a suburban location is open to public access at all times and to community use after hours. During the day, the high level of outdoor activity and staff presence in the garden meant that there were always active eyes on the lookout for anything unusual or inappropriate.

4. Microclimate

Provide shelter from the summer sun. Children have sensitive skin that can easily be damaged by overexposure to the harsh summer sun. Children with limited mobility are especially vulnerable as they cannot get away quickly from direct sun. Plenty of shady areas need to be provided. Filtered light works best at many latitudes. Deeply shaded, dark areas are not attractive and because of the low illumination, do not function well as activity settings. The Boston site offered users several retreats sheltered by shade trees. The Lucas gardens used trees, many large shrubs, pergolas and arbors to create a wide variety of shade conditions. The San Diego Children's Hospital garden provides only minimal shade and is often too hot to use at the height of summer. However, good lighting at San Diego enables use in the cool of the evening.

Provide for the penetration of spring, winter, and fall sunlight. Use south-facing orientations (reverse in southern hemisphere) for activity areas. At many latitudes, outdoor activity spaces are more attractive and comfortable if direct sunlight is allowed to penetrate. Tree species should be chosen and shade structures designed and positioned in relation activity spaces oriented toward the sun, to allow sunlight to penetrate during temperate and cold seasons. As the trees leaf out, these same spaces will be protected from direct sun during the hot season. These general principles of design for human comfort are supported by many research studies of public use of urban open space (Cooper Marcus and Francis, 1998).

Provide shelter from precipitation. In the middle part of the year when the weather is warm or hot, children enjoy being outside, even when it is raining, provided that the activity space is sheltered. A light, impervious roof will serve this purpose and allow children to continue with their activity and to be exposed to the sensory enjoyment of the elements.

Figure 7-31 Tranquillity Corner, Shriners Children's Hospital, Tampa, FL. The gazebo is surrounded by a mixture of shrubs, perennials, and annuals, including species that attract butterflies. A lake is in the background. (Photo by Noelle Vallet.)

No case studies were identified where this need was explicitly addressed. It is exemplified by best practice in nursery school design, especially in regions where year-round precipitation is high. An excellent example is offered by the University of British Columbia Childcare Services buildings. Their ample extended classroom terraces are covered by a translucent, ultraviolet light-resistant fabric that lets the light through, while keeping the rain off (*PlayRights*, 1994).

5. Entering and Exiting

Make all entrances welcoming and child-friendly. Children, especially first-time users, should feel comfortably at home and welcomed into the garden with some friendly gestures. This can be achieved by the placement of artifacts such as sculpture, benches, playful archways, permanent color, or colorful plantings. Lucas Gardens School welcomed their users with a fragrant, covered walkway. The San Diego Healing Garden welcomed users with a tiled sign and a dinosaur-shaped entry feature. The Therapeutic Garden attracted children with an elegant, spring-like water feature that fed the rill leading children through the garden. Water has been used as a welcoming symbol of healing throughout the history of landscape architecture from Babylon to Boston. A powerful idea, not implemented by any of the case studies, is to engage the children themselves in developing ideas for permanent elements and/or temporary displays or installations. New York Botanical Garden Children's Garden and the Michigan State University 4-H Children's Garden and the main entry to San Diego Children's Hospital all use topiary figures as playful, welcoming elements—possibly inspired by children's ideas or characters from children's literature.

6. Accessibility/Usability

Provide accessibility to children using wheelchairs, transporters, walkers, cots, and gurneys. Children in hospitals and other medical facilities use different types of mobility devices. Gardens should be universally designed to provide an equally stimulating experience to children of all abilities. For example, make sure as much of the experiential landscape as possible is at the height of these devices. Also, design for children lying on their backs on gurneys.

In the design and management of Lucas Gardens, much care was given locating interactive artifacts at wheelchair height. In the Garden Court, a large shade tree was located to

"I viewed the garden initially out of a window. I would use this, if possible, for consults. It would be nice to be away from the distractions of the hospital, and the kids would probably be more relaxed out here too."
(STAFF MEMBER)

function as something interesting overhead to look up at. Lucas Gardens installed wind-sensitive artifacts such as flags and banners to serve the same purpose.

Provide usability for children with sensory impairments. The needs of sight- and hearing-impaired children should be balanced and met in ways that are nonintrusive for other children. Sight-impaired children need acoustic, tactile, and fragrance cues for orientation and way-finding. Hearing-impaired children need visual cues. Following eye surgery, children may be temporarily blind. Permanently blind or sight-impaired children may also be patients at the health facility. As a preventive measure, the design of the garden should be checked for protruding objects. Pathways should be designed with strongly delineated edges to facilitate easy, safe movement by children with sight disabilities. Plantings should emphasize year-round fragrance to coincide with the visual way-finding structure of the garden; for example, reinforce the perceptual impact of a central nodal point with a heavily scented species.

Signage should be considered in relation to hearing-impaired children as they are more dependent on the visual sense. Iconographic rather than verbal signs should be considered for preliterate children. Harsh, high frequency noises (metal furniture scraping on a hard surface for example) should also be avoided as such noises can be very uncomfortable especially for the hearing-impaired. Hearing-impaired children have difficulty discriminating complex acoustic dimensions, therefore the acoustic landscape should be low key and simple in form. Lucas Gardens provided many examples of these considerations through the use of windchimes, banners, fragrant plants, and cue-signs to guide parents and volunteers.

Provide a clear hierarchy of pathways. Primary paths should provide for relatively direct travel through the garden—especially for users with sight impairments. Secondary and tertiary pathways can be designed to be progressively more indirect with an accent on exploration and discovery. Pathway systems in both Prouty Garden and Lucas Gardens had a hierarchical structure.

Provide smooth, even surfaces to all primary pathways. Main pathways should be constructed of concrete—a material that can be tinted and inlaid with ceramic tile for aesthetic enhancement. In the Garden Court, it was almost impossible to use an IV stand outdoors because of the unevenness of the stone surface. At the Leichtag Healing Garden, some of the decomposed granite surfaces are being replaced with concrete to permit easier movement for children in wheelchairs.

Figure 7-32   Jeanne Stratford and a child explore the texture of the paperbark tree in the Sensory Garden at Lucas Gardens School. (Photo courtesy of Lucas Gardens School.)

Provide access for large scale equipment required for major renovation and repair. The design of healing gardens should take into account the need for access for maintenance vehicles and occasional heavy equipment. The major renovation planned for the Garden Court was delayed and possibly compromised because there was no way to bring heavy equipment into the courtyard to demolish and remove obsolete items.

7. User Group Territories (Children, Adolescents, Parents, Staff, Visitors)

Provide for use by different groups, if appropriate, by allocating different spaces or through time-sharing. In casually used gardens, territorial use is likely to be a more common issue as there is no structured program, or control of access to the garden. In the Lucas Gardens, there was an impressive amount of conflict-free joint use because it was carefully programmed. In the Prouty Garden, conflicts were mentioned between boisterous adolescents and users seeking quiet contemplation. In a smaller nonprogrammed garden, this could become a serious issue that must be considered at the design programming stage. In some cases, it may make sense to provide facilities for adolescents in their own garden space.

Provide spaces for grieving and highly stressed families. Parents, siblings, and relatives need secluded spaces where they can be in contact with life and restore their inner balance. Natural spaces immediately communicate the regenerative processes of life. They encourage people to discover positive

Figure 7-33 Staff and children getting "in touch" with natural objects around the wheelchair/standing frame table in the Sensory Garden. (Photo courtesy of Lucas Gardens School.)

"There was one family I helped once. The child was dying and had to be taken off life support. The family wanted to spend some time outside with their baby, and they wanted to be alone and have some privacy. I contacted security and they cleared the garden for this family to go spend a half-hour with their child. The family was able to be by themselves out there; I think it really helped them to come to terms."

(STAFF MEMBER)

attitudes to confront adversity, to "swallow the bitter pill." Benches, the sound and movement of water, screens of plants, and places that are elevated, that give a sense of perspective (prospect and refuge), are features that can support the restorative process.

Provide differentiation of spaces for preadolescent/adolescent groups, if relevant. Adolescent groups prefer to have their own spaces where they can hang out away from adults. This is a very subtle design problem. Any space identified or labeled for use by adolescents is in fact unlikely to be used by adolescents, who often need to react against adult rules and policies.

8. Supervision

Provide a comfortable social environment with plenty of places for parents and staff to sit and share the space with children. "Supervision" from the point of view of "monitoring of behavior" is not a big issue in children's healing gardens as many children are engaged one-to-one with staff members or participate in close-knit activities with more than one staff member. Lucas Gardens exemplifies best practice in this open-program approach.

9. Attracting Trained Volunteers

Create an environment that is attractive as a place of work for volunteers. Provide a wide range of choice and diversity of settings and options for relating to children and parents.

Most healing gardens rely on volunteers to help maintain them and to work with the children. The provision of a high quality environment is a major incentive to attract and retain committed volunteers. The Prouty Garden, Lucas Gardens, and the Garden Court supported this principle.

10. A Range of High-Quality Social Settings

Provide a broad range of settings to accommodate children being together as well as children being able to withdraw from the group to be alone. Children in hospital and other medical environments have a wide range of social and psychological needs that are constantly changing as the group of patients changes. It is fundamental to the role of the outdoor environment that each child has freedom to find her or his own most comfortable and enjoyable setting. Choice of setting is critical, as exemplified by all the case examples studied, espe-

"The first time I visited the garden with a patient, I just wanted us to be outside; I had a high-risk case—gang related—that I felt it important to go to an outside, out of the way, to a safe place."

(STAFF MEMBER)

Figure 7-34   The watercourse in Wellesley's Therapeutic Garden is the central organizing element of the garden. It originates on the terrace in a low green granite basin, spills over the basin's edges, and emerges from stainless-steel pipes in a fieldstone seating wall. Play Terrace with Water Basin. (Photo by Douglas Reed.)

cially where plants provide the main source of change and cyclical interest.

Provide a choice of settings for children, parents, and siblings to be together. A choice of settings that range from private to public should be provided. They should be of different sizes to accommodate a variety of groups. Consider the variety of mobility devices the children will be using. Prouty and Lucas illustrate best practice in nonprogrammed and programmed spaces, respectively. The Leichtag Family Healing Garden, while visually engaging, does not offer a sufficient variety of places to *be* in the garden.

Provide settings where special events/entertainment can be held or staged. Consider the possibilities for creating programs of special events and entertainment for children and their families. Many special events are best accommodated by a space that is custom designed for good audience-performer relations. A modest, multipurpose amphitheater can be an appropriate solution if space is available. Alternatively, an area in the garden can be designed to be converted into a temporary stage and presentation setting.

Whether temporary or permanent, the space should be designed to support theatrical accouterments such as backdrops and wings. Performance areas should be orientated facing the sun for good illumination. The sun should be behind the audience, who should be protected by permanent or temporary shade. In the case study sites, events such as birthday parties were organized by child life specialists (in the Garden Court);

"It is not so private out there for them [bereaved parents, patients in therapy for abuse issues, etc.]; maybe there could be a planted area in that screened-off place in the garden—no more walls, please, just a nice planted area, perhaps with a climbing rose bush or jasmine, something green and pleasant."

(STAFF MEMBER)

other events were presented by professional groups from the community (in Prouty, for example); yet others were annual social occasions of support groups (in Lucas, for example); or semiannual memorial services for children who have died (Leichtag Family Healing Garden).

11. Accommodation of Different Patient Types

As much as possible, design healing gardens to include all possible patient types. Requirements should cover the range of different patients served by the medical institution. These may include but are not limited to children in the following categories: Postoperative, oncology, and psychiatric patients; children with emotional, learning, physical, sensory, and developmental impairments—temporary and permanent; long-term, resident children. These categories are not necessarily exclusive, and should be used as a basis for discussion with child life specialists and medical staff about the functional requirements to be accommodated by the design. This approach was used for the redesign of Garden Court.

12. Accommodate Needs for Both Challenge and Rest

Provide a range of physical/social settings so that all individuals can explore and discover their own level of challenge. In order to grow, children need to be challenged. Practitioners in the field of childhood disability emphasize the many ways to challenge a child besides the stereotypical idea of gross motor physical challenge (Moore et al., 1992). One child may be challenged by the idea of simply going outside. Another will need to overcome shyness in playing with other children. Yet another will find planting a flower in a pot a new and awesome experience. And so on.

Other children, perhaps recovering from surgery or a severe illness, seek rest rather than challenge. They need quiet, peaceful corners to recuperate. The only way to accommodate this great variety of needs is by including as much physical diversity as possible (see guideline 14 below)—so that all individuals can find their own comfort level of activity.

13. Child-Nature Interaction

Provide as many options as possible for children to have primary experience of nature, that is, to interact through their senses and/or through hands-on activities. The essence of a healing garden from the perspective of children is for them to experience directly the sensory richness and living quality of nature. Diversity and change are the key criteria. The natural setting should contain the greatest diversity of plants possible, selected for their collective year-round performance from early spring to late fall. At any time of year there should be a new natural event happening in the garden. Select species that produce flowers, fruit, and other parts that can be harvested and used by the children directly as play objects.

Lucas Gardens provided an excellent example of this approach. All case examples illustrate the importance of this guideline in a variety of ways, from the structured sequence of experience in the Wellesley garden to the multiple interactive possibilities of Lucas.

Provide opportunities for planting. One of the most meaningful activities for a child undergoing the stress and anxieties of medical treatment is to be able to intervene in the cycle of life—to start a new life, to plant a seed. The feasibility of such activities is dependent on institutional commitment to facilitate and support planting activities, the blessing of the medical staff, and the presence of trained horticultural therapists to run the program.

The Chicago and Lucas gardens illustrate this principle and demonstrate the powerful, positive impact on the well-being of patients. Chicago's Garden Court demonstrates the wealth of possibilities when these criteria are satisfied. Lucas demonstrates the rich possibilities of a community-based facility. (See Moore et al., 1993, for design guidance.)

Provide opportunities for harvesting. Harvesting is the natural consequence of planting. However, except for long-term residents, individual children are not able to experience the full cycle of harvesting the results of their own planting—particularly vegetables and flowers. Vegetables are not as feasible in a medical environment. Flowers certainly are. An appropriate strategy is to provide opportunities for harvesting by children or staff in every season of the year. Children gain much enjoyment from any type of harvesting activity, for example, gathering pussy willow, other budding branches, and daffodils in the spring. As with planting, to be successful, harvesting activities require institutional commitment, the blessing of the medical staff, and trained horticultural therapists to facilitate the activity.

In Sweden, everyone brings home birch branches from the forest to enjoy the bright green leafing-out indoors to help endure the end of long winters. Lucas children cut flowers daily to decorate the foyer entrance and classrooms. Fall arrangements of dried seedheads and grasses are equally inviting.

Many craft and recreational activities can be offered around harvesting of plants. At Lucas, the staff also harvest seed heads and other plant parts for the children to play with and explore as a sensory/language experience.

14. Diversity of Natural Settings

Provide as wide a range of natural settings as possible within the constraints of climate and available space. Consider the following major categories:

Vegetation. There are many methods of bringing vegetation into a garden setting—groundcovers, raised beds, planters, pots of many types, annual-filled tubs, arbors, trellises, arches, vine-covered fences, moss- and vine-covered walls, hedges, topiary, perennial borders, herbs, bulbs, shrubs, trees of various sizes, and many other techniques. Plants should be selected for seasonal interest (early flowering, late color, long flowering season)—very important for long-term hospitalized children, as Ivonny Lindquist discovered many years ago (Lindquist, 1977). Other key criteria for plant selection are sensory variety (fragrance, texture, wind effects), play value (fruits/nuts, seeds, and foliage that can be used a play props, places to hide), "nature's bounty" (edible fruits/nuts, herbs), shade qualities, screening (visual buffers and wind screens), wildlife habitat value (birds and butterflies in particular), erosion control properties, and drought tolerance and general hardiness. The issue of toxic and allergy-triggering properties of plants must also be considered. (See Moore, 1993, for additional plant selection guidance.)

Animals. Animals are particularly fascinating to children and can offer a powerful therapeutic effect (Myers, 1998). At the other end of the age spectrum, it is interesting to note that domestic animals are becoming recognized as a way of improving the well-being of nursing home residents through the Eden Alternative strategy (Thomas, 1996). In relation to children, nondomestic animals are also significant. In this regard, vegetation areas function as *de facto* animal habitats. Consider possible habitat conditions for amphibians, insect life, and birds; think about aquatic habitats for fish, dragonflies, and damsel flies (Moore and Wong, 1997). Think about species connections to the classics of children's literature that may relate to storytime. Birds were present in all case study sites, and ladybugs are a feature of Garden Court.

Water. Water is a traditional garden element. Research shows it is a popular play material and a strongly remembered childhood experience (Moore and Wong, 1997, Chapters 4 and

Figure 7-35 Close-up of fountain (with three bronze seals squirting water) and birch grove. (Prouty Garden, Children's Hospital, Boston, photo courtesy Boston Children's Hospital.)

16). In healing gardens, water is even more significant as it is the source of life. It is not difficult to imagine including a naturalistic fish pond, perhaps elevated to avoid children falling in. The chosen solution will depend on many factors. Colleagues who use environmental autobiography as a teaching/training method with university students attest to the frequent mention of aquatic experiences as powerful childhood memories. In the Wellesley garden, water is the real and symbolic thread that weaves in and around the landscape forms and plantings, leading the patient, symbolically, on the road to recovery. The many ways of designing water into a garden setting are exemplified by the hard-edged, linear Wellesley rill; the decorative Prouty fountain; the modest splash tables in Garden Court and Lucas, and the seahorse fountain in the Leichtag Family Garden. (For further design guidance on vegetation, animals, and water, see Dannenmaier, 1998; Guiness, 1996; Moore et al., 1992; Rivkin, 1995.)

15. Hands-On Activity

Provide attractive movable items that will engage children in their use of the garden. One of the fundamentals of children's play is the desire to manipulate the environment. Small wagons that can be moved around or a sandbox with toys will be sources of delight for patients and well siblings.

At the Children's Garden at Legacy Emanuel Hospital, Portland, Oregon, brightly colored watering cans left casually in the garden encourage children to collect water from a faucet and water the plants.

Provide a range of appropriately scaled, accessible multipurpose settings for hands-on activity as well as for social gatherings of different types. When the garden supports an active program component, spaces for group activity with the therapist or child life specialist must be provided. The design of these settings must be fully discussed with the relevant staff with regard to location, size, flexibility (fixed or movable furniture), seasonal variation, and so on. Where possible, activity settings should be designed to also serve the social functions described above.

16. Integrating the Arts

Provide opportunities for artists to contribute to both the design and programming of the garden. Inclusion of artists on the design team and the integration of temporary and per-

"I can see how some people might enjoy the garden, like families with young children. Maybe what would be ideal would be to have two gardens, the one we have and then one drastically different, with the classic greenery, a stream running through, perhaps some fish, more like a tranquil Japanese garden."

(STAFF MEMBER)

manent works of art into the garden will add aesthetic richness and symbolic meaning to the garden experience. Consider designing gardens to explicitly attract horticultural therapists, community artists, playworkers, and animators desiring to work with the children (see Moore and Wong, 1997). Gardens that are sufficiently interesting will attract volunteer artists. All the case study sites met this guideline in various ways. Wellesley made the water feature into an elegant work of art. Garden Court and Lucas both displayed windsocks and other hanging works. Lucas used wind chimes. Prouty installed a series of animal sculptures in the landscaping. The Leichtag Family Healing Garden could be considered as a work of art in its own right.

17. Storage

Carefully estimate and fully provide for storage needs outside. Storage is one of the most commonly overlooked needs in the design of spaces for children. Location next to activity areas and size (which should be then multiplied by two, one is tempted to add) should be carefully considered by the Child Life and horticultural staff. The more that items to be used outdoors can be stored outdoors close to their use locations, the more richness and diversity will be added to the program.

18. Maintenance

Match the level of required garden maintenance to the ability to support the costs by the institution. Whatever type of garden is installed, it will require some level of maintenance. It is reasonable to assume that the institution will commit an appropriate amount of maintenance support; otherwise the idea of implementing a healing garden will not be feasible.

In each of the case studies, maintenance was an issue and was addressed in different ways. Wellesley established a trust fund to carry the cost; Garden Court was maintained by the staff, but was facing the issues of major renovation in an inaccessible interior courtyard; Prouty had a trust fund that supported a full-time gardener; Lucas had a part-time gardener and relied heavily on a variety of community volunteers, which worked well because of the strong community ethos of the project; the Leichtag Family Healing Garden is maintained with assistance from volunteer-members of a local botanical society.

REFERENCES

Brett, A., R. Moore and E. Provenzo (1993). *The Complete Playground Book*. Syracuse, NY: Syracuse University Press.

Campbell, D. (1989). *The Roar of Silence: Healing Powers of Breath, Tone, and Music*. Wheaton, IL: Theosophical Publishing House.

Center for Child Health Outcomes, Children's Hospital and Health Center, San Diego (1998). "Leichtag Family Healing Garden: Post Occupancy Evaluation." (Unpublished paper).

Child Life Volunteer Handbook (no date). Chicago, IL: Children's Memorial Hospital.

Cooper Marcus, C. and C. Francis (Eds.) (1998). *People Places: Design Guidelines for Urban Open Space*, 2nd ed. New York: Wiley.

Dannenmaier, M. (1998). *A Child's Garden: Enchanting Outdoor Spaces for Children and Parents*. New York: Simon & Schuster.

Frost, J. and P. Jacobs (1995). "Play Deprivation: A Factor in Juvenile Violence." *Dimensions of Early Childhood*, Vol. 23, No. 3, pp.14–21.

Gil, E. (1991.) *The Healing Power of Play*. New York: Guilford Press.

Guiness, B. (1996.) *Creating a Family Garden: Magical Outdoor Spaces for All Ages*. New York: Abbeville Press.

Hoffman, E. and D. Castro-Blanco (no date). "Horticultural Therapy with a Four-Year-Old Boy: A Case Report." Psychology Department, St. John's University, Jamaica, NY (reprints from E. Hofman, Ph.D., 60 Wesleyan Road, Smithtown, NY 11787).

Hutchinson, R and J. Kewin (1994.) *Sensations and Disability*. Chesterfield, Darbyshire, UK: ROMPA.

Kellert, S. (1996.) *The Value of Life: Biological Diversity and Human Society*. Washinton, DC: Island Press.

Landreth, G. (1991.) *Play Therapy: The Art of the Relationship*. Muncie, IN: Accelerated Development, Inc.

Landscape Architecture (1995). Vol. 85, No. 1, pp. 56–79.

——— (1997). Vol. 87, No. 11, November.

Lawless, J. (1997). *Aromatherapy*. New York: Barnes & Noble.

Lindheim, R., H. Glaser, and C. Coffin (1972). *Changing Hospital Environments for Children*. Cambridge, MA: Harvard University Press.

Lindquist, I. (1977). *Therapy Through Play*. London: Arlington Books.

Marberry, S. (Ed.) (1997). *Healthcare Design*. New York: Wiley.

Moore, D. (1984). "Animal Facilitated Therapy: A Review." *Children's Environments Quarterly*, Vol. 1, No. 3, pp. 37–40.

Moore, R. (1993). *Plants for Play: A Plant Selection Guide for Children's Outdoor Environments*. Berkeley, CA: MIG Communications.

——— (1996). "Compact Nature: The Role of Playing and Learning Gardens in Children's Lives." *Journal of Therapeutic Horticulture*, Vol. VIII, pp, 72–82.

Moore, R and H. Wong (1997). *Natural Learning: The Life History of an Environmental Schoolyard*. Berkeley, CA: MIG Communications.

Moore, R., S. Goltsman, and D. Iacofano (Eds.) (1992). *The Play For All Guidelines: Planning, Design, and Management of Outdoor Play Settings For All Children*, 2nd ed. Berkeley, CA: MIG Communications.

Myers, G. (1998). *Children and Animals: Social Development and Our Connections to Other Species*. Boulder, CO: Westview Press.

Nicholson, S. (1971). "The Theory of Loose Parts." *Landscape Architecture*, Vol. 62, No. 1, pp. 30–34.

Nygaard Christoffersen, M. (1994). "A Follow-Up Study of Longterm Effects of Unemployment on Children: Loss of Self-Esteem and Self-Destructive Behavior Among Adolescents." *Childhood*, Vol 2, No. 4, pp. 213–220.

Olds, A. R. (1985). "Nature as Healer." In J. Weiser and T. Yeomans (Eds.), *Readings in Psychosynthesis: Theory, Process, and Practice* Toronto, Ont.: Ontario Institute for Studies in Education. pp. 97–110.

Olds, A. R. and P. Daniel (1987). *Child Health Care Facilities: Design Guidelines & Literature Outline*. Washington, DC: Association for the Care of Children's Health.

PlayRights. (1994). Vol. XVI, No. 3 and 4, pp. 32–33.

Reed, D. (1997). Places of Sanctuary: The Domestic Garden & the Therapeutic Garden. Paper presented at the *Garden as Sanctuary Symposium*, School of Environmental Design/State Botanical Garden/Humanities Center, University of Georgia, Athens, Georgia, February 14, 1997.

Rivkin, R. (1995). *The Great Outdoors: Restoring Children's Right to Play Outdoors*. Washington, DC: NAEYC.

Santostefano, S. (no date). "Mission Statement."

Sarkissian, W., C. R. Spagnoletti, and C. Isam (1980). *The Design of Medical Environments for Children and Adolescents: An Annotated Bibliography*. Monticello, IL: Vance Bibliographies.

Shepley, McCuskey, M. (1998). *Healthcare Environments for Children and Their Families*. Dubuque, IA: Kendall/Hunt Publishing.

Thomas, W. (1996). *Life Worth Living: The Eden Alternative in Action*. Acton, MA: VanderWyk & Burnham.

United Nations (1989). "The Convention on the Rights of the Child." New York: UNICEF.

van der Kooij, R. and J. Hellendoom (Eds.) (1986). *Play, Play Therapy, Play Research*. Lisse, Netherlands: Swets & Zeitlinger.

Westland, C. and J. Knight (1982). *Playing, Living, Learning: A Worldwide Perspective on Children's Opportunities to Play*. State College, PA: Venture Publishing.

Winnicott, D. W. (1971). *Playing and Reality*. New York: Basic Books. Chapter 8, "The Place Where We Live."

Nursing Home Gardens

Deborah L. McBride

This chapter examines how the design of nursing home gardens affects the social, physical, and emotional health of nursing home residents. A review of research, observations of the use of nursing home outdoor spaces, and interviews with staff and residents of nursing homes were among the methods used. A set of design considerations was formulated based on behavioral and social science research on the physical health, individual behavior, and social processes of the elderly. These concepts were evaluated through interviews with nursing home residents and qualitative observation of nursing home gardens. The chapter concludes with case studies of five nursing homes gardens and a set of design recommendations.

THE ROLE OF NURSING HOMES

Nursing homes care for seniors suffering from chronic problems that prevent them from caring for themselves and for whom there is no adequate alternative source of care. According to the American Association of Retired Persons, over 1.7 million people live in nursing homes in the United States today (AARP, 1997). It is estimated that the number of people living in nursing homes will increase to 5.3 million in 2030 (Zedlewski et al., 1990). People over the age of 65 accounted for 13 percent (34 million) of the population in 1997, and are projected to surpass 20 percent (70 million) by the year 2030. In addition, the number of people 85 and older, the group most likely to suffer from chronic illness requiring nursing home care, is expected to increase from just over 1 percent of the population in 1997 to 5 percent by the middle of the next century (Horgan, 1997). Similar demographic trends are found elsewhere in the Western industrialized world.

Residents of nursing homes are generally considered to fall into one of three groups: the active elderly; the frail elderly, who need help with daily activities such as getting dressed; and the infirm elderly, who need constant medical care. Because of an image problem, nursing homes today often prefer to be called "nursing care units," "care centers," "homes for the elderly," "homes for the aged," or "skilled nursing facilities." All these terms, however, refer to facilities that have the capability of providing 24-hour nursing care to the elderly.

Nursing homes are designed to protect vulnerable people. This protection can, however, have harmful effects common to other forms of institutionalization. These harmful effects result from the residents' isolation from family and friends, their lack of autonomy and their increased passivity (see also Ulrich, Chapter 2). A lack of affection between caregivers and residents also has a detrimental impact (Spivack, 1984). Studies have found some nursing homes to be sterile, and dehumanizing. Observations suggest that nursing home residents spend much of their time "doing nothing" (see Figure 8-1). Though this passive behavior may be accompanied by self-reflection, boredom is a frequent complaint of nursing home residents. Significantly, research has shown that activities that take place in outdoor spaces associated with nursing homes can slow, and even reverse, the mental, emotional, and physical deterioration that often accompanies institutionalization (Brody, 1977).

HISTORICAL BACKGROUND

In 1821 a study was undertaken by the Massachusetts General Assembly to investigate the causes of poverty. The reaction to this study led to the creation of the first institutional solution to indigence in the United States, the almshouse (sometimes called the poorhouse or poor farm). These government supported facilities developed rapidly and spread throughout the United States. The poor, the aged, the disabled, and the criminal were all housed together in these institutions with minimal standards of cleanliness and comfort. After 1865 specific groups moved into separate institutions such as orphanages for the young, mental hospitals for the insane, and workhouses for the

Figure 8-1 Research has found that nursing home residents spend much of their time in the facility "doing nothing." This resident is fortunate to have a window from which he can gaze out upon flowering shrubs.

able-bodied, leaving the elderly in the almshouses (Binstock et al., 1996).

Between 1865 and 1935 three forms of institutional care were available to the elderly in the United States: (1) poorhouses or poor farms, based on earlier public almshouses; (2) private group homes for the elderly, organized by charitable institutions; and (3) private boarding houses (McClure, 1968).

Architecturally, the typical poor farm was a large rectangular structure, two or three stories high, with separate male and female wings, usually set back from the road in a grove of trees. County and municipal governments, hoping that these institutions would become self-supporting, created work programs for the residents in the vegetable gardens and fields that surrounded these buildings.

Charitable institutions, which were founded at the turn of the century by immigrant groups and religious organizations, housed much more homogeneous populations than public poorhouses and were the forerunners of modern nonprofit nursing homes. A good moral character, a sound mind, and good physical health were often requirements for entrance. The small scale of some of these facilities allowed for the design of a variety of minor spaces that took advantage of the outdoors, such as porches, bay windows, and balconies (see Figure 8-2).

Figure 8-2   The Home for the Friendless (later called the Protestant Home) was Minnesota's first private nursing home. It was created by a group of Protestant churchwomen. It moved into this building in St. Paul in 1883. (Photo courtesy of Minnesota Historical Society.)

Figure 8-3   The Protestant Home of St. Paul, Minnesota constructed this building to house the infirm elderly in the early 1900s. (Photo courtesy of Minnesota Historical Society.)

Between 1900 and 1940 the number of elderly grew from 4 percent of the population to 6 percent. As the demand grew larger, more institutional buildings were constructed. Red brick pillared buildings with large lawns were common. Unprecedented poverty among the elderly was caused by the Depression, when over seven and a half million elderly lost their jobs. The resulting political pressure led to the passage of the Social Security Act of 1935. This public pension system gave the elderly the resources to provide for their own care in private nursing homes and resulted in the closing of many public poorhouses. These early nursing homes were often called "homes for the aged" or "rest homes" and distinguished themselves from boarding houses by providing basic medical care (Vladeck, 1980).

A great deal of diversity was observable in the outdoor spaces of American nursing homes built during the first half of this century. "Not-for-profit" nursing homes were often placed on spacious lots in the suburbs with extensive landscaping, so that land could be set aside, tax free, for future expansion (see Figure 8-3). For-profit nursing homes, which were often located in urban areas, frequently had minimal land set aside for landscaping in order to maximize the use of land for buildings and reduce the cost of real estate.

In 1946 the Hospital Survey and Construction Act was passed by Congress, lending money to nonprofit and public agencies to construct hospitals. In 1954 the Act was expanded to include nursing homes. This revision placed nursing homes in the same category as other health related facilities and removed them from their association with the welfare system. As nursing homes became the last step on a continuum of medical care, changes in the physical form of nursing homes ensued. The nursing home became a specialized hospital for the chronically ill. The resulting "medical model" of nursing home architecture reflected the social policy toward the elderly in the United States. Outdoor spaces were neglected in the belief that the medical setting itself was sufficient.

During this time nursing homes received more money for bedfast than for ambulatory residents. The result was that many nursing home operators preferred bedfast residents and little was done to get frail older people out of bed. Late in the 1950s, however, the idea of rehabilitating the elderly took hold. Social workers and others concerned about the lack of activities for residents began to encourage mobility and occupational therapy for residents. As resident mobility increased, multipurpose dayrooms, where residents could walk and sit, were added to homes. However, beliefs concerning the importance of observation of residents by nurses meant that most residents of nursing homes were not allowed to go outside unaccompanied. This was not the result of a regulation, but rather of caretakers' fears that any untoward consequences would be judged as neglectful or substandard care (Kane, 1995). Outdoor spaces were, therefore, generally minimized and little effort was made to make the spaces accessible to residents.

Government nursing homes, which were frequently built on public property during the 1960s, were often located on spacious lots. These were commonly unadorned, expressing tight financial controls in their simple planting. Characterized by large, manicured lawns (unbroken by plantings or monuments), the grounds of these institutions represented safety, order, cleanliness, and efficiency. Large lawns were popular because they were easy to maintain, reduced construction costs, and simplified supervision of residents while they were outdoors.

Congress passed the Social Security Act Amendment in 1965, creating Medicare and Medicaid. These are still the major source of funding of nursing homes. In 1967 the Moss Amendments to the Hill-Burton Act created the first federal standards for nursing homes receiving federal funds. The standards for most nursing homes required 24 hour nursing care and a supervising registered nurse and addressed issues of safety.

Throughout the 1970s nursing homes of less than 100 beds were forced to expand or close because of the cost of meeting the new medical standards. In 1975 a Certificate of Need procedure, by which states regulate the number of healthcare facilities, was made mandatory by many states. Designed to minimize overbuilding of nursing homes, control costs, and ensure fireproof and well-equipped homes, these certification procedures provide state agencies with the tools to control the architecture of nursing homes.

Figure 8-4 The expansion of the Hospital Survey and Construction Act in 1954 to include nursing homes resulted in many medical model nursing homes being built by counties. Green Acres Nursing Home was built by Chicago Country in 1954 and remodeled and enlarged in 1956 and 1959. (Photo courtesy of Green Acres Nursing Home Archive.)

Architecturally, many nursing homes built during the 1960s and 1970s borrowed the imagery of small rural hospitals (see Figure 8-4). However, the image of a hospital is not liked by many elder people, who fear institutionalization and who prefer a homelike environment (Wheeler, 1982; Rowles, 1983; Willcocks et al., 1987; Dovey, 1985).

By the mid 1990s, the medical model nursing home was being replaced by homes that borrowed the imagery of the European manor, the English bed-and-breakfast home, the Spanish colonial revival, or the Mission revival traditions, depending on the region. Large porches, steep roofs, and compact massing that began to appear in this period gave a residential quality to many nursing homes.

The country manor style is very popular in some nursing homes because, for people of north European background, it symbolizes the stability, security, and graciousness of an earlier era. The adoption of this style by nursing homes was originally fueled by a desire for connection, status, and permanence in a rapidly fluctuating society (Gowans 1986). The bed-and-breakfast hotel style is a variant of the country manor or cottage style of housing. This style was made popular in the United States by Andrew Jackson Downing in the 1800s. For the dominant culture, a cottage hung with vines and roses and surrounded by a well-kept garden was a symbol of the moral force of the mother and the family. A lawn with a bed of flowers or a clump of trees in the shape of an oval or crescent or other geometric forms was the creation of an upwardly mobile middle class seeking to affirm gentility. These gardens were of particular importance to women, who used them as escapes from the confines of their lives, where they could establish their own identities (Hill, 1995). Intimate landscapes and familiar plants such as roses are frequently requested by nursing home residents today (Stoneham and Thoday, 1996).

In the last twenty years long-term care has changed dramatically. Prompted by the growing population of older adults, the high cost of nursing home care, and the preference of the elderly for staying in their own homes or noninstitutionalized care, healthcare providers are experimenting with new models of long-term care. Assisted living communities are the fastest growing components of long-term care today. These communities allow the elderly to live independently by providing assistance in the activities of daily living within self-contained living units. Continuing care communities provide residents with different levels of care on one site as their needs change, thus reducing the forced relocation of residents due to their changing medical needs, and the resulting "transfer trauma." Nursing home designers are beginning to borrow ideas from other milieus,

Figure 8-5   Arizona's Sun City West, with a population of 24,800, is one of the largest retirement communities in the United States. Accommodations vary from studio apartments to three-bedroom houses. This recently opened assisted living community illustrates the popular country manor style of architecture, which is used to represent upper class status by designers.

including the mall and hospitality industries. Recently major hospitality providers such as the Marriott Corporation, have entered the long-term care market. Using their expertise in providing hospitality, they are adding health and social services in high service assisted and nursing care arrangements (see Figure 8-5). The nursing home industry, however, continues to grow in size and importance relative to other providers of long-term care (Harrington, 1991). Recent innovations in nursing home design include using regional and local design imagery, renovated buildings, new forms of community integration, and memory enhancing designs. One approach that has gained popularity is the Eden Alternative, which began at the Chase Memorial Nursing Home in New Berlin, New York, and stresses the importance of interaction with nature in many forms. Animals and plants are incorporated in the home, as are facilities for visiting children (Thomas, 1996).

RESEARCH

Researchers studying nursing homes have identified a number of principles with regard to the relationship between residents and the design of their surroundings. These include the importance of a homelike environment, privacy, sensory stimulation, socialization, family visits, outdoor activities, comfort, security, and accessibility.

Providing nursing home residents with a *homelike environment* can encourage feelings of connectedness, bondedness, and identity between the residents and their living place. In contrast to the institutional associations of some nursing homes, the concept of "home" carries with it connotations of safety, familiarity, privacy, belonging, and caring (Dovey, 1978; Rubinstein, 1989; Howell, 1985). Colorfulness, lawn, comfortable chairs, small scale, and quiet evoke the ideal cozy home garden. The incorporation of mature trees, historical stylistic references, and traditional vegetation is a visual metaphor for a security, stability, and roots (Gowans, 1986; Dovey, 1985).

Providing residents with *privacy* is a goal of outdoor spaces at nursing homes because privacy has been found to contribute to resident comfort in group residential facilities, which, in turn, promotes resident interpersonal support and independence (Timko and Moos, 1990). The negative impact of lack of privacy within institutional settings has been described by researchers including Willcocks et al. (1987) and Moos and Lemke (1990). Residents interviewed by Firestone et al. (1980) viewed the nursing home as an insecure place with insufficient interior privacy and excessive accessibility to residents by staff. Privacy can be increased by limiting visual access into spaces where residents sit and reflect. Utilizing landscape elements to create a spatial hierarchy, separating public, semipublic, semiprivate, and private spaces increases privacy (Carstens, 1985).

In addition to controlling visual intrusion, privacy measures should permit residents to control the amount of unwanted auditory stimuli. Noise control is one of the biggest problems in nursing homes. A British study identified a peaceful atmosphere, specifically a quiet, tranquil environment without the ringing of call bells, doors banging, and general staff noise, as the most important characteristic influencing resident satisfac-

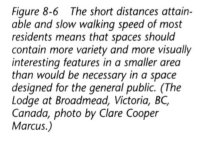

Figure 8-6   The short distances attainable and slow walking speed of most residents means that spaces should contain more variety and more visually interesting features in a smaller area than would be necessary in a space designed for the general public. (The Lodge at Broadmead, Victoria, BC, Canada, photo by Clare Cooper Marcus.)

tion with a home (Bartlett, 1993). The provision of outdoor space where environmental demands are minimized, and therefore stress is reduced, can be a very significant factor in the quality of life of residents.

Providing opportunities for residents to manipulate natural objects and observe seasonal changes can encourage residents to use the environment as a source of positive *sensory stimulation*. The sensory stimulation resulting from interacting with nature can be a beneficial distraction from the mundane routines of the home. A predictable, structured, and visually rich environment is recommended for people with visual impairments (Wolanin and Fralich Phillips, 1981).

The mobility impairments of many residents mean that more landscape elements designed to add interest and pleasure are needed—and they should be placed at shorter intervals—in order to compensate for the reduced distances some residents can comfortably walk (Carstens, 1985). The short distances and slow walking speed of most residents means that spaces should contain more variety and more visually interesting features in a smaller area than would be necessary in a space designed for the general public (See Figure 8-6). Activity and movement in the landscape, such as water features, animal activity, or kinetic sculptures, are highly valued by residents (Cranz, 1987).

Outdoor spaces provide opportunities for pleasant smells such as fragrant plants and fresh air. Plant materials should be used to create opportunities for visual, tactile, and olfactory experiences. The principles for selection of plant materials include providing contrast of light and dark, using bright col-

Figure 8-7 Courtyards, which feel sheltered and enclosed while still preserving a view, are the outdoor spaces most popular with residents. Dappled shading from the fine-textured trees and the covered trellis protect residents from a sharp change in temperature when leaving the building. (Jerry L. Pettis Veterans Memorial Medical Center, Loma Linda, CA.)

ors, varying the size of plant materials, incorporating recognizable themes, and relating the content to the background of the residents. Changing plantings can provide seasonal highlights as well. Outdoor spaces should offer "reality cues" by reminding confused and chronically ill residents of the season, time of day, and weather (Carpman and Grant, 1993).

Animals give residents something to nurture, something spontaneous to react to, something to interact with on an emotional level, and something to touch. Hendy (1987) reported that live pet visits increase desirable behaviors in nursing home residents such as smiling and alertness. Outdoor spaces can be designed to house animals and to provide opportunities to walk or play with nursing home pets (Thomas, 1996).

Studies on the life review process confirm the importance of reminiscence as a form of therapy for the elderly and as a preparation for death (Ott, 1993). The need to reminisce has been identified as of prime importance in improving the psychological condition of geropsychiatric patients (Blankenship et al., 1996). Sensory reminiscence has been found to be an important mode in the life review process and the validation that accompanies it (Ott, 1993). Ott reported that using aids that evoked a variety of sensory modes (seeing, hearing, touching, tasting, feeling, and remembering) helped depressed, withdrawn, unsociable, or isolated individuals process and develop resolution. Reminiscences of gardens brought about by the sensual experience of plants may be a starting place for work with the elderly as they look for continuity and meaning in their lives.

The *social climate* of nursing homes has been linked to the health and well-being of their residents (Lemke and Moos, 1986). Positive, close social relations are a major determinant of informants' valuations of the quality of life in such facilities (Najman and Levine, 1981; Green and Monahan, 1981). Socialization gives residents a sense of connectedness to a home and reduces the loneliness of residents. Regnier (1995b) believes that the most important goal in designing for the elderly is to enable people to create friendships.

Nursing home residents need exposure to a continuum of social groups, from solitude to larger gatherings. A variety of social spaces needs to be provided for residents, ranging from small spaces where residents can be alone to large spaces for many people. Nursing homes are often criticized as lacking spatial variety. The uniform size and shape of spaces in nursing homes can make them appear institutional, dull, and lifeless. In Bartlett's (1993) in-depth interviews with residents, staff, and health authority officers at five English nursing homes, she

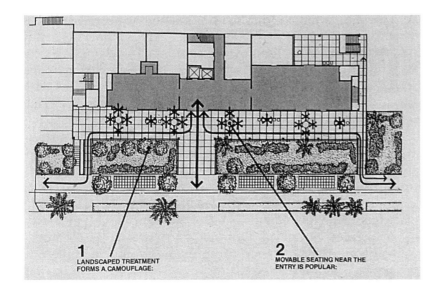

1 LANDSCAPED TREATMENT FORMS A CAMOUFLAGE:

2 MOVABLE SEATING NEAR THE ENTRY IS POPULAR:

Figure 8-8   The most popular places to sit in a nursing home are in sheltered areas, close to the building entrances, where there is a view of people entering and leaving the buildings. This entry garden is very popular with residents, who are visible from the interior of the home as well as from the road as they sit outside (from Regnier, 1985).

noted the importance of gardens to the social environment. An absence of accessible shared spaces leads to feelings of confinement and contributes to the dependency of residents. She found that, "Without access to this facility [the grounds] the world of informants was usually confined to the bedroom and the often mundane routine of the nursing home" (*Ibid.*, p. 115)

Sheltered, comfortable seating that encourages eye contact can increase socialization (Sommer, 1970). High activity areas are popular places for sitting and watching. Typically, the area nearest the entrance of a nursing home is the most congested and popular area, where residents are most likely to congregate. In her survey of 280 residents at 8 public housing units for the elderly in New Jersey, Cranz (1987) found that people wanted to sit where there is action, usually near the street. Her research indicated that the most popular sitting areas for residents were those that provided views of both on-site and neighborhood activity.

Adaptability of seating allows residents to arrange social groups as they desire. Seating in which residents inside the home and those outside the home can see each other is popular. However, seating that creates excessive visual closeness can be uncomfortable (Regnier, 1985). Osteoporosis can reduce the mobility of the neck in elderly people. The difficulty turning the head from side to side makes it difficult for people seated next to each other to interact. Right-angled or U-shaped seating allows several people to sit at a comfortable conversation distance without feeling too enclosed and has been shown to increase socialization.

Figure 8-9   This resident is getting her exercise outdoors. The path is wide enough for two people to walk abreast or pass, even with walkers or wheelchairs. There are no inhibiting steps or grade changes to impede her progress. There also is a variety of fixed and movable seating available under a canopy of mature trees. The large plate glass windows serve to bring the outdoors in, so that even on days when the weather is poor, the garden remains visibly accessible. (Eden Home, New Braunfels, TX.)

The quality of care in a nursing home has been associated with the continuing *involvement of family members.* Barney (1974) has demonstrated the role of outsiders, relatives, volunteers, or representatives of religious groups, in assuring a high quality of care. Outdoor spaces can strengthen the ties with family members and the community by providing space and activities for socializing.

Visiting a relative in a nursing home can be a disturbing experience and the design of nursing homes often fails to support family members and make them feel welcome. In Bartlett's study (1993) although visits from friends and family were looked forward to, the residents saw the nursing home as a poor place for socializing. Family visits often improve with increased visual privacy. Small outdoor spaces separated by plantings, walls, planters, or distance can provide limited visibility and promote social interactions.

Also significant in this regard is the location of the nursing home in relation to public outdoor space. The proximity of a park where family members can take a resident confined to a wheelchair can provide a significant positive emotional experience for a resident.

Designing the grounds of a nursing home so as to encourage *outdoor activities,* such as exercise and therapy, can forestall the inactivity that often accompanies aging. Many studies documenting the lifestyle of residents in nursing homes found it to be largely one of inactivity. Bartlett's (1993) informants described their primary activities as sleeping, just sitting, or watching TV. Being inactive and dependent created feelings of uselessness and low self-esteem. Barriers to residents going into the garden included residents' feeling that they would be too unsteady on their feet, that their incontinence would cause embarrassment, or that it was too much trouble to ask the staff to help them go out (Bartlett, 1993).

Cardiovascular disorders, muscular weakness, osteoporosis, dizziness, and decreased input from the muscle and joint receptors can lead to problems in walking among older adults. The 1985 National Nursing Home Survey (US Department of Health and Human Services, 1985) found that less than half of nursing home residents can walk unassisted and 10 percent are at least partially paralyzed. The inability of residents to walk may lead to decreased mobility, social isolation, and passivity. Activities that provide moderate physical activity, such as walking, are encouraged to prevent the deterioration in the older person's ability to perform the activities of daily living such as washing and dressing themselves or going to the bathroom unassisted (Richman, 1969).

In a study of public housing designed for the elderly, Cranz (1987) found that 22 percent of the residents used outdoor recreation areas for activities. Although Cranz concluded that elderly residents experience reduced physical ability and prefer designs that represented visual variety combined with physical passivity (Cranz, 1987), many researchers feel that designers of extended care facilities should design to stimulate the activity level of residents, particularly walking (Carstens, 1985). A recent report by the American Hospital Association (1991) described the optimal patient unit as providing interesting areas for ambulating and a tangible goal outside the patient's room to encourage walking. Different lengths and difficulty of routes will provide choice to residents with different needs.

While some residents may be very active, the number of people in wheelchairs in nursing homes has increased significantly in the last decade. The ambulatory person may spend as much as six hours sitting in the same chair and nonambulatory residents may spend up to twelve hours (Regnier and Pynoos, 1987). Sitting in a wheelchair for many hours can cause pressure ulcers, flexion contractures, and nerve paralysis (Hartigan, 1982). In addition to providing ambulatory goals to encourage residents to walk outside, gardens need to be designed for ease of use for those using wheelchairs and provide outdoor physical therapy areas to help residents build skills and strength.

Comfort, the physical ease in doing a task or being in a particular place, is important in the design of nursing home gardens because it affects the independence, autonomy, competence and self-esteem of residents. Comfort can be maximized by careful attention to the location, siting, and circulation of outdoor spaces at nursing homes. In general, the environment should be constructed to reduce physical demands on nursing home residents (Kiernat, 1985). However, some research indicates that interactions with the environment can play a major role in eliciting intelligent behavior, and that coping with environmental complexity contributes to mental function (Christenson, 1990). Thus outdoor spaces at nursing homes need to be designed with an appropriate level of environmental complexity, which will allow residents to function at their maximum physical and mental capabilities.

An important consideration in the design of outdoor spaces for older people is orientation. Confused residents have difficulty orientating themselves. Landmarks or other prominent features can help older persons to locate themselves in the environment. Outdoor objects and furniture, such as pergolas, benches, or arbors, groupings of plants or statues, or any unique feature can help older adults to remember when to

Figure 8-10 Nursing homes brochures stress the importance of a homelike environment. But while "homelike" is often interpreted as meaning that the facility is decorated in a noninstitutional way, on another level it also means an environment designed to maximize functioning. Sturdy handrailings provide needed support for residents who may have mobility problems. There can be contradictions between the optimally safe environment, a therapeutically supportive one, and an aesthetically pleasing one. This is an example of a particularly successful resolution of these design dilemmas. (The Lodge at Broadmead, Victoria, B.C., photo by Clare Cooper Marcus.)

stop, where to sit or turn. A looped path, which eliminates dead ends, combined with unique features can aid confused residents in achieving a better sense of orientation (Osterburg, 1987). In addition, older people may have difficulty remembering the location of features they cannot easily see or distinguish. If a resident cannot find a poorly marked toilet, the risk of incontinence is increased and with it a resident's sense of dignity and independence is diminished. Easy access to toilets from the garden therefore will encourage residents to use the garden.

One aspect of designing for outdoor use is understanding how the environment will be perceived by residents. The placement of signs at or slightly below eye level is needed to compensate for spinal changes, which may produce dizziness when an older person looks upward. The average eye level of a seated person is 43 inches (Panero and Zelnik, 1979). In addition, age related reduction in peripheral vision means that very large graphics will be out of the visual field (Bowersox, 1979).

The design of seating is of great consequence in determining the ability of residents to use it. A study done by Finlay et al. (1983) found that 77 percent of the residents who previously needed help getting out of a chair were able to do so independently from a chair that had arms at a height at least 10 inches above the seat and a seat that was between 16 and 17 inches from the floor. In addition, providing an opening under the front edge of the seat allows one foot to be placed underneath so that a person is able to push up to a standing position, greatly improving stability.

Figure 8-11 These teak chairs are an adequate height and have desirable arms that extend beyond the front edge of the seat. They are heavy enough to be stable, even on the uneven surface of this crushed fines patio. Arranged in a small grouping, remote from the building, this is a likely spot for a family visit, or for a few staff members on a break. As the tree matures, the patio will have a canopy overhead, providing a sense of containment, as well as summer shade. (Woodlands Nursing Home, Lambeth, UK; photo by Clare Cooper Marcus.)

A study of types of chairs and visitor comfort in waiting rooms conducted at the University of Michigan Medical Center found that armrests are important because they give the people who use them a sense of territoriality and separation from people they are sitting next to (Carpman and Grant, 1993). The inclusion of chairs along a pathway, allowing for occasional stops, will increase the ability of a person with limited mobility to move about in the nursing home. Rocking behavior is often seen in disoriented adults and can be encouraged by providing rocking chairs, porch swings, and gliders. These provide kinesthetic appeal and give a residential feel to outdoor areas (AOTA, 1983).

An important physiological change with age is an increased susceptibility to glare. Glare, such as sunlight reflecting off metallic or plastic, may cause problems for residents. Placement of sun screens and vegetation to prevent direct sunlight from being in the line of sight and limited use of water in bright light settings will help reduce glare. Moving from an indoor area to an outdoor area can cause problems for older people because of the longer length of time it can take their eyes to adjust (Hatton, 1977). An arbor, porch, or overhang is an important transition space from indoor to outdoor light levels. A foyer or lighted entryway can help provide consistent lighting and provide time for visual recovery when entering or exiting an outdoor area.

Visual access to outdoor space from indoor areas so that residents can see what the weather is like, who is in the area, and how crowded it is before entering will affect how readily residents will enter an outdoor space and use it (Carpman and Grant, 1993). Providing windows onto outdoor spaces creates opportunities to preview the space before entering it and provide ease of monitoring of residents by the staff.

Security, defined as the freedom from risk, danger, concern or doubt, and the maximizing of physical safety, should be a major design consideration in the design of outdoor spaces at nursing homes. Providing secure outdoor areas can increase mobility, which has been shown to impact other psychological attributes such as control, privacy, independence. and self-esteem.

Safety and security are frequently mentioned by nursing home residents as characteristics of nursing homes that influenced their quality of life (Weidmann et al., 1982). An environment that minimizes security concerns through the use of alarms and surveillance systems can reduce nursing home residents' anxiety, and increase their peace of mind and mobility.

The relationship of the entryway and the street raises many questions about security for residents. Research suggests that residents want an entrance that is clearly visible from a reception desk and that provides quick, secure entry from the street (Hartman et al., 1987). Regarding the issue of open space and security, Cranz (1987) found an overwhelming preference among elderly residents of public housing for a view of the street so they could watch people walk by. However, there was a difference among residents who feared the surrounding neighborhood. Those residents who felt their neighborhood was deteriorating tended to want the open outdoor space closed off so no one could look in, while residents who felt comfortable in a neighborhood preferred well-defined, but not opaque, boundaries separating the site from the street.

Technological innovations that increase the security of residents can help the elderly feel more safe and secure. These include motion-activated lights, surveillance systems, burglar alarms, cordless telephones, and security and emergency response systems that are activated by a button, pull cord, or a loud noise (Cluff, 1996). Minimal levels of night lighting contribute to the perception of safety (Butterfield and Weidemann, 1987). Higher levels of night lighting allow residents to see each other and provide an informal monitoring system.

Designing for increased *accessibility* can increase mobility, independence, and socialization. Illnesses can affect the physical reserve, endurance, stamina, and strength of older people, all of which affect their competence in the environment. A common characteristic of nursing home residents is functional impairment. A "prosthetic environment" can offer support, allowing residents to function at a higher level in spite of disabilities.

Figure 8-12 The area nearest the entrance of a nursing home is often the most popular area, where residents are most likely to congregate. Street scenes, parking lots, and pedestrian routes are views that might traditionally be screened, but that offer active scenes of daily living for those who have little mobility. Ideally a variety of types of views should be available to residents. (Eden Home, New Braunfels, TX.)

Minimum accessibility standards (ADA standards) may not be adequate for elderly adults who have multiple physical and psychological impairments. Therefore, additional accommodations may be necessary to provide accessibility to outdoor spaces for nursing home residents. Older wheelchair users may have greater difficulty using ramps than other wheelchair users because of the decreased upper extremity strength of many older people (Hiatt, 1979). Hasselkus (1974) has recommended higher and wider based steps for the elderly. Koncelik (1996) found that grip strength in the palm could decrease from 95 lb in youth to as little as 5 lb in the elderly and that the loss of pinching or tip prehension strength in the fingers could decrease from 30 lb to 0 for some.

Residents may be reluctant to use aids that project a less than completely independent image. The look of some products may negatively influence the acceptance of those devices among individuals whose self-esteem is dependent on their autonomy. Design sensitivity to the appearance of devices to improve accessibility can increase their acceptability among nursing home residents. Interventions such as fences and handrails should be unobtrusive as possible, while promoting independence.

TYPOLOGY

A variety of types of outdoor spaces can be observed in nursing homes today:

- Entry Gardens
- Grounds Not Associated With Entry
- Courtyards
- Solaria
- Viewing Gardens

Entry Gardens

An entry garden is that part of the landscaped grounds one sees upon approaching and entering the main door of the nursing home. It is a planted space similar in function to the front yard of a private residence. These spaces often function as marketing devices for the home, to sell the facility to the family and visitors of residents. They provide prestige value to the home, making residents feel better about being associated with the facility and letting family members feel better about placing someone in the home. This image making function of the entry garden is more than simply cosmetic, as the quality of the design of the entry garden can have a significant impact on how people view residents and how residents view themselves. A typical entrance garden in a suburban setting consists of a lawn setback with an automobile turnaround or parking area close to the entry door of the nursing home. Generally a small planted area containing one or more benches where residents can sit protected by an overhang is located in front of or adjacent to the entrance. A small sign identifying the home with a bed of colorful flowers planted underneath is often located near the entrance.

Many Americans do not want to be confronted with evidence of death and dependency in their neighborhoods, resulting frequently in a "NIMBY" (not in my backyard) attitude toward nursing homes. In response, some homes attempt to achieve an invisibility in their entrance design through the use of small, unobtrusive signs and benches for the residents placed back from the road.

Security is of particular concern in entry garden design. Although security devices such as gated entrances, fences, and guard houses can reduce anxiety and contribute to residents' peace of mind, they can also project a less than independent image, which could negatively affect the self-esteem of residents. Properly designed, these security devices can project a friendly, welcoming, private image without sacrificing a sense of security.

ADVANTAGES

- Can create a positive image for the institution, helping it to integrate into the neighborhood.
- Separates the home from the road, shielding the home from the sight of traffic, reducing street sounds, and increasing privacy from pedestrians.

Figure 8-13   The entry at Manor Care Health Services Home in Potomac, Maryland is typical of many that were built during the 1980s and 1990s. A small planted area immediately in front of the entrance contains several benches protected by a large overhang. A small sign identifying the home or an American flag with a bed of colorful flowers planted underneath is often located near the entrance to a nursing home.

- Often provides benches and an overhanging roof for the use of residents entering or leaving the home.
- Frequently the most popular area of the home, where residents congregate to sit together and watch the activity at the entrance to the home.

DISADVANTAGES

- Increases the travel distance from the home to the road.
- Residents sitting near the entrance can interfere with traffic into and out of the home.

Entry of the Manor Care Health Services Home in Potomac, Maryland

Manor Care Health Services is a large chain of for-profit homes, operating over 180 nursing centers nationwide. This facility is located on an 8-acre wooded site in Potomac, Maryland and is comprised of two buildings, one primarily for residents requiring skilled nursing care and the other for persons with Alzheimer's disease. The outward appearance of the buildings is a colonial Williamsburg style. A large portico overhang and semicircular roadway clearly marks the entrance of the main building (see Figure 8-13), but the overhang and a prominently sited American flag create a very institutional appearance. The lack of seating at the entrance, insufficient planting, and the lack of large trees make the space unpleasant to be in. Sitting in wheelchairs under the overhang, residents are not close enough to the road to see the street activity. A small patio to the right of the entrance provides shade in the afternoon and comfortable padded chairs. In good weather it could have been an excellent place for visitors to bring residents, but it is underused because it does not provide a view of the activity at the entrance of the building. The entry garden to the smaller building housing residents with Alzheimer's disease is sparsely planted with annuals and poorly maintained, giving the building an uncared for look. This entry garden does not address the need for usable outdoor space. In addition, no significant gardens or plantings are visible by residents from inside the building. Attention to seating/viewing needs would have made the entry space at this home more successful.

Grounds Not Associated with an Entry

Grounds refer to the extensive parklike area that may serve as the setting for a nursing home. In the past, nursing homes were often separated from the surrounding community by extensive lawns and low maintenance vegetation. The landscaped

Figure 8-14 This long, curving board-walk leads through some woods and over wetlands to local community gardens. It is universally accessible and is a very popular feature at this facility. (Doncaster Life Care Center, Bloomfield, Connecticut, photo by Felice Frankel Photography.)

grounds of contemporary nursing homes show considerable variation in both function and design. Although they are not always accessible to the majority of residents because of topography, security problems, or inaccessible design elements such as stairs, the grounds may be used for walking and sitting by the more mobile residents, visitors, and staff, and for passive viewing by other residents.

Modern nursing homes are often part of continuing care retirement communities. Unattached buildings are grouped in a quasi-campus arrangement in order to provide different levels of care on the same site, segregate residents with different levels of competence, and maintain a small-scale residential quality. The grounds at these facilities tie the buildings together visually as well as functionally. Often the nursing care buildings are placed to the rear of the site so that the residents of other buildings, who might be more mobile and likely to leave the home, have easy access to the street.

ADVANTAGES

- Creates a unified image to an institution that may contain many different elements.
- Provides a buffer separation between the street and the home.
- May support wildlife and provide for bird watching.

DISADVANTAGES

- Requires a large initial investment.
- Maintenance may be costly because of the size of the site.
- If poorly maintained, can create an unkempt, uncared for appearance, which adversely affects the image of the facility.
- Supervision of residents, if necessary, can be difficult.
- The lack of amenities and detailing can be frustrating for those residents who wish to use these areas.

Grounds of the Eden Home in New Braunfels, Texas

The Eden Home in New Braunfels, Texas was one of five nursing homes chosen to initiate the "Eden Alternative" program in Texas. The one-story Eden Home is part of a 15-acre continuing care complex that houses an assisted living facility and an independent living apartment building. It is an innovative project that used a number of simple alterations, collectively known as the "Eden Alternative," to renovate a traditional medical style building. The renovations are intended to deal with the loneliness, helplessness, and boredom that often afflict nursing home residents. The Eden Alternative emphasizes contact with nature to promote a vibrant, diverse, and harmonious environment. An abundance of living things, including animals, plants, and children in the home, community involvement with the home, and staff empowerment in the care of residents characterize Eden Homes.

The grounds of the Eden Home have many interesting features. It is set on a beautiful wooded site with numerous mature oak trees. The trees connect the building to the regional environment and the surrounding community. It has an extensive lawn, circular drive, and large trees around the building. A play structure, where children from a local day care center come to play, is prominently located. The children provide life and activity to the home environment. The home is closely tied to the local neighborhood since the landscaping is maintained by four gardeners who live nearby and who have brought plant material from their yards to the home. A handicapped accessible wooden gazebo located among the oaks in front of the building is very popular with family members seeking a private visit with residents.

Figure 8-15 Existing vegetation, particularly mature trees, is very valuable in providing a sense of maturity and stability to a home. The Eden Home in New Braunfels, Texas has a beautiful wooded site with numerous mature oak trees.

Courtyards

Outdoor spaces incorporated within the building footprint include courtyards, which provide residents with easy access to spaces that are designed for use and that are close by. These areas may be primarily planted or paved, open on one side or enclosed, visible from the interior of the home or screened from sight. Many have central visual features such as fountains, sculptures, or large trees. A cafe may be a part of the space, providing a place for residents to sit outside and eat, or a barbecue area may provide for cooking and eating outdoors. A range of seating arrangements, from individual chairs to group benches, are often provided in these areas.

A courtyard may be the most accessible outdoor space in a nursing home because of its central location. Often a glassed in hallway or solarium may be located on one side of the space, so that residents can sit inside while enjoying a view to the outside. Courtyards provide an internal focus to the building that is different from many other outdoor spaces. They bring light into the center of the building and, because they are generally smaller than other outdoor spaces, provide a more intimate and human scaled experience.

Specially designed courtyards may permit confused residents to leave the home environment, while allowing supervision and a reassuring sense of security. Traditionally units for confused residents were placed on the upper stories of a nursing home; however, the increasing recognition of the importance of outdoor space for these residents has led to a general relocation of these units to the ground floor to provide access to a specially designed outdoor space. Bartlett (1993), however, observed that common areas become less popular when use is shared with disoriented residents. Areas where confused residents are allowed may be viewed by other residents as being unavailable, resulting in residents' staying in their rooms. A management decision is needed to decide whether confused residents should be housed separately or mainstreamed with other residents. Some homes contain several different courtyards serving different populations such as those suffering from dementia, psychosis and the physically challenged (see Chemainus case study, in Chapter 9).

ADVANTAGES

- Can be secured, providing increased autonomy and peace of mind to residents and staff.
- Because of its generally central location, can be easily accessed and viewed by residents in adjacent buildings.
- Buildings may provide shade and wind protection for those outside while bringing sunlight into the center of the building.

Figure 8-16 Encouraging residents to explore the outdoors means taking into consideration their reduced mobility, increased sensitivity to temperature changes, and vision impairments. Making the spaces near the home attractive to those indoors and reducing the physical and psychological transitions between the interior and exterior will help encourage residents to use these spaces. (Jewish Home for the Aged, San Francisco, California.)

DISADVANTAGES

- Because residents can be generally observed while outside, may provide a "fishbowl" experience.

- Depending on its size and location, it may be permanently shaded by the adjacent buildings, creating a dark, unpleasant environment.

- Its proximity to the windows of adjacent buildings can create problems of privacy for those inside if the benches are placed too close to the windows or there are no buffer plantings.

Courtyard of the Jewish Home for the Aged in San Francisco, California

This large private nursing home located in a residential section of San Francisco houses over 450 residents. One of the most striking features of a large central courtyard in this facility is the creation of semiprivate spaces in a communal area through the use of landscape structures, such as seat-walls, benches, paving, and lawn. The courtyard is made up of several different areas. On one side, located near a cafe so that residents and their visitors can come outside to eat and talk, is a small patio approximately 30 × 30 feet, furnished with metal tables and chairs and adjustable umbrellas. A larger area located at the north end of the courtyard contains two long curved cement benches and a number of movable padded chairs where several groups of residents congregate daily to sit and socialize under the shade of the large pine trees. Large automatic doors enable access from the interior of the home. At the south end of the courtyard is a large lawn and fountain that is accessible only visually to residents because it lacks pathways and seating. It provides a wildlife habitat, attracting many species of birds to the bird feeders, which the residents enjoy watching. Large pine trees, some over 60 feet tall, provide shade during the part of the afternoon. In the center of the courtyard on a small mound is a large modern statute of a reclining woman and child over a pool of water. The slight and sound of water splashing over the base of the statute into the pool and the birds playing in the pool creates a stimulating and lively ambience.

The presence of a glassed-in corridor between two buildings gives the adjacent courtyard additional utility. The walkway is 15 feet wide and over 100 feet long and provides a sheltered space where residents can sit with friends, enjoy the sunlight, look into the courtyard, and watch birds coming to the bird feeders. This courtyard demonstrates that a simple configuration that is well designed can create spaces that are rich in vari-

Figure 8-17 This corridor provides a view to a courtyard for residents who preferred to remain in the building. Other large windows in the dining room and common room allow residents to remain inside while giving them a view of a landscaped area. (Jewish Home for the Aged, San Francisco, CA.)

ety and liveliness, and which can be enjoyed from inside as well as by those who can venture outdoors.

Solaria

Solaria are rooms or walkways that are enclosed by glass where residents can experience a sense of being "outdoors" while in a sheltered environment. These are quite commonly provided in contemporary nursing homes, with chairs facing the east, in order to maximize morning sunlight. In many nursing homes a solarium is the only common area available to residents, becoming a multipurpose room that is used for a variety of activities including religious services, watching TV and movies, playing bingo, participating in craft activities, and happy hour. However, a space used for multiple purposes may be confusing to some residents.

Glare is the most common age-related vision problem and is most frustrating to the elderly (Pastalan et al., 1976). The reduction of glare through the control and balance of daylight is important, especially during the transition between outside daylight and low interior lighting. According to the Center of Design for an Aging Society, the most common error designers make is placing a window or door with glazing at the end of a corridor, mistakenly believing that they are providing a view. The extreme contrast in light levels between the window and the corridor can create a glare problem that is extremely painful to the eyes of older adults (Noell, 1995). Window treatments and floor coverings should be carefully chosen, as glare can be a problem in these types of areas if dazzling sunlight from the window falls on to highly polished surfaces. In multipurpose rooms, which require room darkening ability, for the showing of movies, for example, as well as controlling the sunlight while preserving views, the window treatments can become quite complex.

ADVANTAGES

- Sitting in sunlight can be both pleasurable and medically important.
- Available to residents who have the greatest difficulty with mobility.
- Protects residents from the outside environment.

DISADVANTAGES

- When designed as a large space it does not promote a residential feel, and can reduce socialization because residents feel that others are watching them.
- If created as a multipurpose space, it can be confusing to residents.

- Can be frustrating to residents who want to go outside, if no outdoor access is available.
- Glare from large windows can be difficult for residents to tolerate.
- For some residents, sun should be avoided.

Solarium, Charlestown Senior Campus Living Community, Cantonsville, Maryland

The solarium at Charlestown Senior Campus Care Center is an extension of a small cafeteria where residents come in the morning to socialize. Groups of tables with padded chairs and adjustable umbrellas are available in the solarium and the courtyard so that residents can bring their meals outside when the weather is nice, or eat inside when it is cold. The exterior courtyard was designed to look like a Victorian garden with wrought iron benches and tables, herbaceous borders, and small flowering trees. There are many plants with seasonal interest including cherry trees, daffodils, and tulips. A selection of deciduous trees shelter the space during the summer. During the winter, shrubs containing berries attract birds and small animals. Access to the outdoor space from the solarium is through an automatic door. The psychological transition from the interior to the exterior is eased by extending the roof line of the solarium beyond the cafeteria wall, creating the sense of being outside while remaining in a climate controlled area. Although a short distance from the care center, the solarium and cafeteria provide an attractive destination for residents to walk to.

Figure 8-18   Solaria ease the transition between indoors and outdoors. Often the only common areas available to residents, they may also be used as a multipurpose room for watching TV and movies, playing bingo, participating in craft activities, enjoying happy hour, and so on. This solarium at the Charlestown Senior Campus in Cantonsville, Maryland is located on the southeast side of a building near a small cafe where residents come in the morning to socialize.

Viewing Gardens

Viewing gardens are spaces that can be viewed, but not entered. They are accessed visually from windows, solaria, porches, or patios. As the number of residents with ambulatory difficulties in nursing homes increases, viewing gardens will become more important. Care should be taken that the view can be enjoyed from a seated position. When viewed by a person who is seated, higher windows can cause neck soreness as a result of the head being bent back for a long time. Bartlett (1993) found, in her survey of five nursing homes in England, that half of her informants said the grounds of the home gave them considerable pleasure, even those who could no longer enter them. So in some ways many types of outdoor spaces become, in effect, viewing gardens.

A variation on the viewing garden is the viewing/walk-in garden, a small space that is designed predominately to be looked at, but that can seat a small number of people. Small viewing/walk-in gardens can provide a sense of security and privacy to residents.

ADVANTAGES

- Allows green space within a small area.
- Relatively inexpensive to maintain due to small size.
- Ease of supervision because of proximity and small size.

DISADVANTAGES

- Viewing gardens cannot be experienced directly, which may frustrate some patients because residents cannot walk or sit outside.
- May be rather dark because of small size and proximity to building.

CASE STUDIES

Five nursing home facilities have been selected here to illustrate the variety of outdoor space design for the elderly. These include nursing homes in the very different climatic settings of New Mexico and Alberta, Canada; the nursing care component of a continuing care retirement community in Maryland; and the extended nursing/care facilities in two medical centers, in southern California and British Columbia.

Charlestown Senior Campus Living Community Care Center, Cantonsville, Maryland

The Nursing Care Center is part of the Charlestown Senior Campus Living Community (see Figure 8-20), a continuous care retirement community that opened in 1983 in a suburb of Baltimore, Maryland. This 110-acre community was built on the former site of the St. Charles College and Seminary. A variety of interesting spaces where residents can socialize, and trails and paths for strolling through the woods near Herbert's Run Creek have been created. Throughout the campus, large windows provide views of the outdoors for those who are too frail to leave the facility. An artificial pond with an observation deck provides habitat for ducks and geese, and gives residents a tangible goal to encourage walking. It is used by residents as well as by staff, visitors, and volunteers.

Figure 8-19   This trail seems to be away from everything, though in fact the buildings are quite close. Although not suited for wheelchair use, it provides a sense of getting away to the more ambulatory residents, as well as to the staff. (Charlestown Senior Campus Living Community Care Center, Cantonsville, MD.)

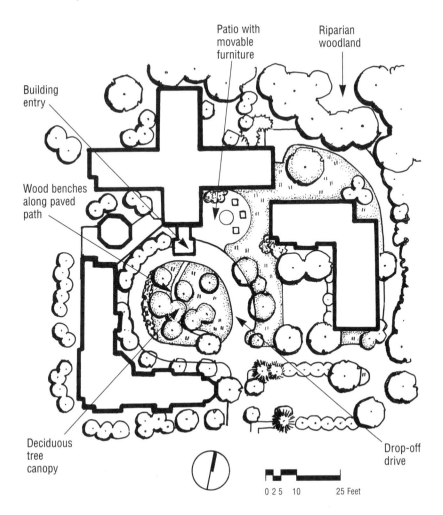

Patio with movable furniture

Riparian woodland

Building entry

Wood benches along paved path

Deciduous tree canopy

Drop-off drive

0 2 5 10   25 Feet

Figure 8-20   Site plan of the Charlestown Senior Campus Living Community Care Center, Cantonsville, MD.

Figure 8-21 Frail residents are easily deterred from leaving a nursing home building. Curbs are one of the most common obstacles. This seating area across from the entrance to the Care Center at the Charlestown Senior Campus uses painted detailing and a curb cut to make the level change clearly visible.

The descriptive brochure emphasizes the grounds: "Stroll the secluded Nature Trail ... take in the panorama from the skyline walking path. ... At Charlestown, you'll enjoy endless ways to bask in the campus's natural beauty and to exercise in the invigorating fresh air of the great outdoors." Photographs in the brochure show residents using the landscaped grounds, bicycling, feeding ducks, walking or sitting with friends. Charlestown is able to provide such grounds because of its rural location.

The nursing home care unit outdoor space is designed to serve a population who have a variety of physical and mental impairments. A small grove of tall oak trees with benches is located directly across from the entrance. Residents can sit in relative privacy, watch the shuttle bus come and go, and still be visible from the reception desk. This attractive, easily accessible space invites residents to leave the care unit, and is the most popular outdoor area.

A small patio is located to the east of the main entrance of the care unit. This space is designed to look like a suburban garden with traditional ornamental details such as a curved stone wall, high-quality wrought iron chairs and tables, and a round central planting bed with a statue in the middle. The design creates an image of family life and domestic security. The plantings of liriope, bulbs, and mondo grass were chosen to provide interest throughout the year, and yet be robust and low maintenance. The curved lines, low maintenance materials, and evergreen plantings recapture a sense of the 1950s. This patio provides an easily accessible spaces that avoids the appearance of being created for people with mobility impairments. The staff reports that even in the winter, residents can be seen outside bundled up in coats sitting at the tables in the courtyard talking and smoking. The tables and chairs are also used by staff, who eat lunch and smoke here.

To the west of the entrance a small lawn leads to a foundation planting of perennial coreopsis and day lilies, which are viewable by residents from their rooms. A variety of other spaces within walking distance of the care unit, including a rose garden dedicated to St. Joseph, provide an escape from the interior of the care unit and a destination for residents who have minimal stamina. A small courtyard at the rear of the building is protected from the sun and wind by the building. This courtyard incorporates a trellised area with wooden benches around the perimeter, creating a variety of seating areas both in the sun and in the shade. Although the rear courtyard is potentially easily accessible because of wide, automatically opening doors that exit from the reception area, reentering the building requires

Figure 8-22   Features of interest adjacent to a home, such as this small rose garden dedicated to St. Joseph at the Care Center at the Charlestown Senior Campus, provide areas of interest and pleasure that may encourage residents to leave the building. Roses are one of the most popular and frequently requested plants in nursing home gardens.

ringing the receptionist. This procedure, which is unfortunately all too common at outdoor spaces at nursing homes, discourages residents from using the space, which was only observed being used by residents who were accompanied by family members. As at many nursing homes, the outdoor space is used primarily during family visits. Staff members report that family members take residents outside because of the lack of private areas within the care unit. However, during the spring and summer up to a dozen residents at a time gather in the outdoor spaces in front of the care unit beginning at 9:00 A.M. to enjoy the morning light.

Villa Guadalupe, Little Sisters of the Poor, Gallup, New Mexico

The Villa Guadalupe is a complex of three one-story buildings set in a residential neighborhood of single family homes in Gallup, New Mexico. The strong influence of the sponsoring organization, the Little Sisters of the Poor, is evident in the religious and vernacular elements of the design. The Little Sisters is a Roman Catholic charity that came to the diocese of Gallup, New Mexico in 1983 to provide nursing home care to Native Americans and other underserved populations in the area. A temporary home for the elderly was established in 1984 in an old church building. The Sisters opened the Villa Guadalupe in 1989. It houses 42 residents, all over 60 years old, who are cared for by seven Little Sisters who live in the convent portion of the home.

The villa is located on a hilltop with a panoramic view of the surrounding city and the hills in the distance. The landscaped

Figure 8-23 Religion can be an important element in the lives of many nursing home residents. Collaboration between the home and sponsoring organization resulted in many religious garden ornaments at the Villa Guadalupe in Gallup, New Mexico. Located adjacent to the main entrance, this space is dedicated to the Virgin Mary.

Figure 8-24 Along the walk from the home to the parking lot at the Villa Guadalupe in Gallup, New Mexico are a number of benches where residents can wait to be picked up, or just sit and watch people coming and going.

front area of the villa is approximately 120 × 180 feet, with about one half of it composed of landscaped areas and the other half used for parking. This area consists of four distinct subareas. They include a patio with a hogan shaped roof, a shrine to Our Lady of Guadalupe, a 50-foot long covered walkway leading from the parking lot to the lobby, and a small garden beside the entrance containing a statue of the Virgin Mary. In addition to the planted areas in front of the building a large patio area beside the dayroom, a volleyball court, and a path leading up to a scenic overlook are located on the sides and rear of the site. Two cottages are also located on the site to provide housing for visiting family members. In the interior of the main building, a solarium is located to the east of the sunlit lobby looking out onto the front landscaped area.

On the north side of the building, benches along the covered walkway provide a shaded place for residents to sit and watch the activity of people entering and leaving the building. During the warm months, from April to October, between 6 and 12 residents use these benches to sit alone or sit and talk with family members. Residents sit outside even in July, which is the hottest month when the temperature can be over 100 degrees Fahrenheit. The staff believes that the heat does not bother many residents because they are acclimated to it. During the cooler months most residents prefer to stay inside.

The architecture has a neo-Spanish feeling with the street facade resembling a small ranch rather than a home for the elderly. The ranch concept promotes a unique relationship with nature by mimicking a working ranch in terms of style, organization, and materials. Elements relating to the history of the site, including a wooden wagon, are located on the grounds

Figure 8-25   Historical artifacts, like this wooden wagon at the Villa Guadalupe, can add interest and pleasure to nursing home landscapes.

near the front of the home where they are visible from residents' rooms and the street.

The plantings, plants, and climate sensitivity of local missions and ranches have inspired the landscaping at Villa Guadalupe, which includes native plants in addition to those brought to the area by settlers. Irises, pear trees, plum trees, as well as honeysuckle, lantana, and poplars surround the Villa, while cacti, agave, lantana, and other drought tolerant plants associated with the area are planted in a bed of river rocks that separates the facility from the road. A sensitivity toward the local landscape resulted in views of the surrounding hills being maximized and local materials being used to soften the transition between the building and the environment.

A 20 × 30 foot covered patio is located at the front of the site with a wooden roof resembling a traditional hogan—the residence of local Native American Navajos. The view from this open patio is of distant hills covered with native vegetation. It is a popular destination when family members visit and desire to take residents outside of the home in order to get some privacy.

Residents are required to be able to walk in order to be admitted into the home. Therefore many more residents are able to use the outdoor space than is typical. Staff members report that getting outside of the home and feeling the breezes and sunshine are important to residents, and lunch or snacks are sometimes served outdside. Other outdoor programs are also provided, such as cookouts, birthday parties, and ice cream socials.

The outdoor space at the Villa Guadalupe serves many purposes. The staff use a small side area near a fire exit to smoke, feeling, perhaps, that smoking in the public areas would be unacceptable. A volleyball court on the east side of the villa is well-used by staff and family members. The walls, plantings, and shelters throughout the site contribute wind breaks and sun screens to modify the heat of the New Mexico summer climate.

Villa Guadalupe emphasizes the homelike qualities of the environment and the quality of life of residents rather than medical care. The significance of the historical and cultural traditions of the area are an important part of the respect for the emotional needs of the residents. The gardens are meaningful in providing residents and their families with a sense of well-being and caring.

Jerry L. Pettis Veterans Memorial Medical Center Nursing Home Care Unit in Loma Linda, California

Responding to the need to house patients after the 1974 earthquake destroyed an earlier Veterans Administration hospital, the Jerry L. Pettis Veterans Memorial Medical Center was opened in 1977. The Nursing Home Care Unit was added in

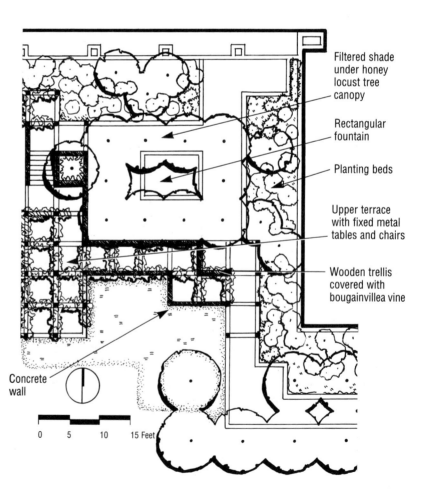

Figure 8-26 Site plan of the patio at the Jerry L. Pettis Veterans Memorial Medical Center Nursing Home Care Unit, Loma Linda, California.

Filtered shade under honey locust tree canopy

Rectangular fountain

Planting beds

Upper terrace with fixed metal tables and chairs

Wooden trellis covered with bougainvillea vine

Concrete wall

0   5   10   15 Feet

1988. Approximately 120 residents live in the Care Unit, which is a one-story wing on the south end of a large four-story-high facility that also houses an urgent care center and an alcohol and drug treatment unit.

Designed by the architecture firm Stone, Marraccini, and Patterson, and landscaped by Arutunian/Kinney Associates of Palo Alto, California, the Medical Center is located on a 28-acre site in a residential setting. There are four large interior courtyards on the second floor of the Medical Center and three small interior courtyard spaces and a patio within the Nursing Care Unit.

The Medical Center is set in extensive grounds with lawns, several courtyards, large shrubbery, and trees scattered around the edge of the building. A stream encircling almost the entire Medical Center provides interest and movement to the site. A path with bridges crosses the stream in a number of places. A pond with a fountain and several waterfalls are focal points along the way. Throughout the complex, the building has many large windows and balconies that look out onto these open spaces.

The patio adjacent to the Nursing Care Center is just over 115 feet wide and 54 feet long. It is bounded by four large rectilinear planters filled with a variety of plants including photinia, grape, mock orange, azalea, and periwinkle. Eleven honey locust trees are planted around a central fountain. The walls of the planters and fountain function as informal seating, while the chairs and tables are permanent assemblies firmly anchored to the ground. The tables are high enough to allow wheelchairs to be pulled up under them. The entrance to the patio is through several automatic doors, which make the space easily accessible.

Figure 8-27   Watercourses and ponds at the Jerry L. Pettis Veterans Memorial Medical Center Nursing Home Care Unit not only provide areas of visual interest, but attract wildlife, particularly birds, which residents enjoy watching.

Figure 8-28   Fountains can offer visual, auditory, kinesthetic, and tactile stimulation. They also serve as focal points that can help with orientation and way-finding.

During the month of July the outside temperature sometimes rises to over 100 degrees Fahrenheit in the Loma Linda area, but the patio remains cool because most of it is shaded by a wooden trellis covered with bougainvillea vines. The sense of being enclosed in a lush landscape filled with cooling plants makes the space feel like an oasis in an otherwise modern facility. Residents using the patio describe it as very beautiful and peaceful.

Those visitors who come to the patio are typically residents of the Care Unit who come to drink coffee or smoke, or to talk with friends or visitors. Many of the staff come to the outdoor space for lunch. Between 11:00 A.M. and 1:00 P.M., the space is crowded every day, except when it is rainy or very cold. Programmed activities such as employee appreciation day, barbecues, and birthday parties, are held there. The space is so popular that more chairs and tables need to be added to accommodate all those who want to eat lunch there.

The landscaping at this facility is a good example of how outdoor spaces can contribute to the lives of nursing home residents. It is well designed with a variety of amenities that bring enjoyment to residents. Its lush plantings, excellent maintenance, and thoughtful design provide a positive experience for many people.

Graham Garden, Saanich Peninsula Hospital, Victoria, British Columbia, Canada

By Deborah LeFrank, landscape architect

Description of the Facility and Its History

Saanich Peninsula Hospital is located in Saanichton, a small rural community north of Victoria. The hospital opened in 1973 with one extended care unit. In 1978, the acute care unit was added. In 1982 the second extended care wing was built. The facility now accommodates 64 acute care patients and 150 extended care residents for a total of 214 beds. The building is one story, which provides the ground-level rooms with views out toward adjacent fields or expanses of lawn.

This hospital is truly a community facility. People come here to have children, they return to get minor and major treatments, and at later stages in life they come for extended care. Farmers and business people on the hospital boards enthusiastically share their various expertise.

The garden for the hospital was desired for quite some time before the actual design and construction began. A significant initial donation from the Graham family in early 1996 allowed for the project to get started. All funding for the garden came from private donations obtained through a fund-raising campaign organized by the hospital foundation. The total project cost was $200,000 Canadian dollars. The official garden opening was held in October 1997.

Prior to building the garden, limited facilities existed around the hospital for outdoor walking or gathering. The existing patios and walkways caused accessibility and comfort difficulties for the physically frail and elderly. Some of the problems included rough surfaces of exposed aggregate with no edges to retain wandering wheelchairs, very limited shade opportunities and bright gray concrete with significant glare problems. In addition, there were very few areas where families and patients could have private time together.

The Graham Garden is located between the two extended care wings of the hospital. The majority of the garden's users are long term residents, however acute care patients, families, and staff also visit the space. Approximately 90 percent of the extended care residents use wheelchairs and about half of the population has some form of dementia, such as Alzheimer's.

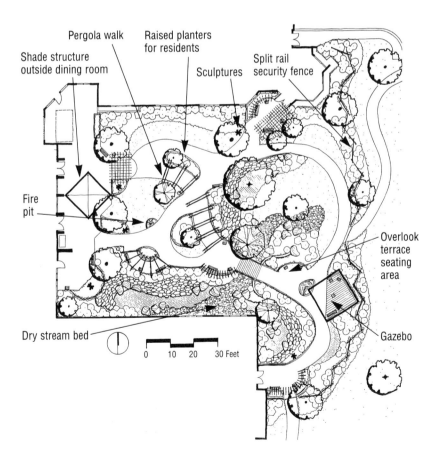

Figure 8-29   Site plan of the Graham Garden, Saanich Peninsula Hospital, Victoria, B.C., Canada.

Figure 8-30   Curving paths of colored concrete keep focus on destinations and their tinted color reduces glare. (Photo by D. LeFrank.)

Design Philosophy

The main design philosophy was to create a welcoming environment where people could get exercise and fresh air, have opportunities to grow their favorite plants, get away from the hospital routine, and have private time with visiting family and friends. The garden was designed to be interesting throughout the seasons, but it was recognized that the majority of use would be in the spring, summer, and fall seasons. The rural environment was used as a theme element in the structures and plant selections. Safety, motivation, and comfort concerns were incorporated into all elements of the garden including seating, paving, plant selection, and structures.

Description of Outdoor Space

The garden has an eastern exposure and opens out to views of fields, a small wild pond, and distant mountains. The hospital is set back from the main road and all hospital traffic arrives on the opposite side of the building. Only a fire lane passes nearby. An adjacent field is used by a local daffodil grower and in spring the fields are ablaze with yellow trumpets.

At 20,500 square feet, this garden is fairly generous in size. It can be accessed from three points in the building in addition to two exterior gates. The south gate connects with a path that comes from the acute care wings of the hospital. A split rail fence borders the garden on the open side. This fence creates a barrier without being solid and it reflects the rural character of the community. The U-shaped nature of the building form allows for a variety of viewing and supervision opportunities.

Resident rooms line two sides of the garden, and many bird feeders hang outside bedroom windows.

The east orientation keeps the garden fairly sheltered from the prevailing southwesterly winds. The majority of the garden receives good light, which, together with excellent agricultural soil, provides for an environment conducive to plant growth. Shade needed to be created in seating areas, however, to keep residents and patients comfortable. Two existing trees (Austrian pine and pin oak) provide some maturity to the garden and encourage bird life.

One of the garden features is a dry stream complete with a wooden bridge. There was a desire to have a significant water feature; however maintenance of such a feature was deemed to be prohibitive. The dry stream environment gives visual depth to a garden that needs to be level for easy access.

Other garden features include:

- A fire pit whose wooden lid can also serve as a small platform
- Raised mortared rock planters with wooden ledges that give comfort to leaning arms and provide knee space for wheelchair users
- Sculptures that reinforce way-finding for confused or disoriented residents
- Seating that incorporates a small table between two chairs
- Gazebo that resembles a local corn grower's market stall
- A pergola walk defines the center spine of the garden and provides shade for residents working on their planting beds, as well as creating a strong way-finding element

Figure 8-31 View across garden with dry stream in foreground. The gazebo is visible on left and bridge on right. (Photo by D. LeFrank.)

How the Garden Is Used

The garden is primarily used in the late morning and again in the afternoon when the temperature has warmed up. Most frequent use is informal in nature, people out for a tour around to see what plants are coming up. There is a small group of residents who have formed a gardening club and it is possible that the horticultural therapy program will be reintroduced.

Activation Staff encourage residents to use the garden by hosting barbecues and seasonal activities. The garden provides a focus for many visits and seasonal celebrations. At Halloween residents are brought outside to sit by the fire pit and enjoy the carved pumpkins and fireworks display. An evergreen tree and other garden structures are decorated for the Christmas season.

The main garden access is from the dining room, a room that is also used for many daily activities. An automatic door opener allows for ease of access. The large patio area is used for many outdoor programs, including games.

Near the garden entrance is a large shade structure that provides a stopping point for residents. This allows their eyes to adjust to the different light as well as to get inspired to venture further into the garden. A UV shade canopy will be seasonally erected in this area to provide additional cover. A garden entrance located at one end of the large patio is used for outdoor dining, cafe style. A decorative railing and small water fountain give ambience to this shady corner.

Numerous pathways allow residents to make choices about where they want to go. This can be viewed as being both positive and negative. Alert patients can make choices and have the feeling of wandering through a park. For some confused resi-

Figure 8-32 Pergola walk (decorated for Christmas) leads people into garden toward the bridge and gazebo. Raised planters line the walk, which is lightly shaded for resident comfort. (Photo by D. LeFrank.)

dents, however, the need to make a choice can cause frustration and disorientation. The garden has been designed with these different residents' needs in mind. The pathways have been created using gentle curves and guiding handrails. There are no corners to get stuck in. The paved surface is tinted concrete, which reduces glare.

Around the garden are private rest areas with seating and scented vines climbing the nearby shade structures. A large shade structure immediately outside the dementia care unit creates an immediate destination for staff and residents. Wayfinding elements, which guide residents through the garden and back to the doors, have also been incorporated. The strong axial structure of the pergola walk also provides shade, which is necessary for those using medications that cause light sensitivity or for those with aging eyes.

ADVANTAGES

- The garden was desperately needed and is now a much loved focus.
- Provides a level "walking" surface for the those in wheelchairs.
- Shade structures located near most doors provide a transition to lighter environment.
- Raised planters with wheelchair toe access allows residents to putter in the soil.
- Fruiting and flowering plants encourage people to get outside.

Figure 8-33 Shade structure outside north wing gives private area to the more confused patients. (Photo by D. LeFrank.)

DISADVANTAGES

- Even minimal slopes on some paving can still be significant for the very frail.
- Some physical plant staff view the garden as another maintenance problem.

Lynwood Continuing Care Center, Edmonton, Alberta, Canada

By Clare Cooper Marcus

In areas with long winters, the provision of an indoor garden creates a green setting for patients and staff to enjoy year-round. The Lynnwood Continuing Care Center in the suburbs of Edmonton provides a fine example of such a space.

Description

The care center is housed in a four-story building that encloses a glass-roofed garden atrium. This diamond-shaped space is surrounded by four stories of nursing care wards with adjacent balconies where residents can sit "outside" and look down on the greenery below. At ground level, the garden is an intricate, but negotiable, arrangement of concrete-edged, lushly planted beds, concrete pathways, and small and larger seating areas. The largest of these, like a mini-plaza in the garden, has five tables, twenty-four movable chairs, and a prominent aquarium.

The profusion of greenery, which ranges from creeping ground covers to 20-foot ficus trees, creates semiprivacy in the different seating areas, and gives the impression of a place that is larger than it actually is as paths angle in and around the planters. The outdoor feel of this lush and attractive space is further enhanced by a number of features: ample daylight flooding in through the glass roof and amplified by hanging fluorescent lights; street lamps; movable garden furniture with floral upholstery; two wooden arbors; and birds in cages. A maintenance company comes in once a week to water and tend the plants.

Use

Even those who cannot physically move around in the garden can look out and down on the greenery from the dining balconies of different wards, which jut out into the space. The small mini-plaza with movable furniture is often used for music and dance performances, easily viewed and heard from the balconies above.

The pathways—some with slight grades—which interlace the lushly planted beds, are highly used by residents, staff, and visitors. Seating clusters in small niches permit four or five staff colleagues on a break, or family visiting a resident, to gather for a snack or a chat in relative privacy. The staff of different departments tend to use the same tables each day, many preferring to bring their food here from the cafeteria, which is quite small and noisy when busy. The walking routes are sensitively designed to be easily accessible to residents, with paths wide enough for two wheelchairs to pass, and with attractive wooden handrails. Bordering the garden at ground level are a hair salon, recreation room, vending machine area, chapel, and the main foyer. Consequently the garden is the focus of ground-level circulation and is animated at all times.

ADVANTAGES

- Garden area usable in all seasons.
- Temperatures are kept stable.
- Space is secure.
- Garden is animated by use all day.
- Garden is visible to those unable to come down into it.
- Details of arbors, seating, lighting, and so on, all add to the garden image.

DISADVANTAGES

- A slightly "industrial" image is created by the supporting steel columns, and roof trusses.
- Concrete floor tends to be easily stained and difficult to keep clean.

DESIGN GUIDELINES

The following recommendations detail design approaches using research findings cited in the literature and established by observations of nursing homes. Nine groups of guidelines are described: (1) provide a homelike environment; (2) provide places for privacy; (3) provide sensory stimulation to increase mental alertness; (4) provide opportunities for socializing; (5) provide places to be with family; (6) provide space for outdoor activities; (7) provide a comfortable place; (8) provide a sense of security; and (9) provide accessibility.

1. Provide a Homelike Environment

- Designers will need to research the sociocultural background of residents in order to discover their image of a homelike outdoor environment.
- Avoid creating an institutional image by utilizing scale, type of amenities, materials, and design features which convey a residential image.
- Use traditional vegetation and mature plants.
- Use detailing and edge definition to create subareas that offer a sense of intimacy.
- Design entry porches as centers of activity where residents can safely gather with some sense of containment.

2. Provide Places for Privacy

- Provide seating areas where individuals can be alone or have a private conversation. Create seating arrangements that avoid uncomfortable visual and auditory closeness.
- Use landscape elements to limit visual access into spaces where residents sit and reflect.
- Provide both large, open outdoor spaces and small, individual enclosed spaces.
- Provide private areas where residents can interact with nature, such as personal garden plots, personal bird feeders, and private patios and balconies where residents can grow plants.

3. Provide Sensory Stimulation to Increase Mental Alertness

- Create a variety of different types of places for residents to experience nature such as formal gardens, raised terraces, nature trails, viewing gardens, and wildlife areas.
- Provide natural areas that are easy to view from indoors, as well as others that are further away from the building. Frame window views with plant materials. Make sure handrailings and window ledges do not obstruct the view to the outdoors for those who are seated.
- Use colorful plant materials and amenities to attract wildlife which can be seen from indoor lounge areas. Incorporate some warm, highly saturated hues—red, yellow, and orange—because they are easier for the elderly to see than are blue, purple, or green.

- Design for activity and movement in the landscape with water features, kinetic sculptures, and so on, which are viewable from both inside and outside the home.
- Use different leaf textures, forms, smells, and perhaps tastes, to stimulate the senses and memory.

4. Provide Opportunities for Socializing

- Outdoor areas at nursing homes should provide several kinds of outdoor spaces including those which allow residents to watch the street activity, sit alone, sit in the sun and or shade, look at greenery, listen to water, and sit in various sized groups to socialize.
- Locate a variety of spaces near centers of activity such as building and site entries and mailboxes to create opportunities for impromptu conversations.
- Provide adequate furniture, such as reasonably lightweight movable chairs and tables, to allow for the creation of small spaces for socializing and intimacy.
- Place seating at frequent intervals along main paths.
- Provide chairs and tables with umbrellas near areas where meals are served and where residents may wait before or after mealtimes. If there is a party room, provide a patio that can be used for group activities.
- Create both large and small spaces in order to encourage socialization as well as privacy and intimacy.

5. Provide Places to be with Family

- Create outdoor spaces to support social and educational programs activities, such as summer barbecues to encourage involvement of family, friends, and the community with residents.
- Provide outdoor play space to support the activities of young children who are visiting residents.
- Allow easy wheelchair access to nearby public recreation facilities and parks.

6. Provide Space for Outdoor Activities

- Different lengths and difficulty of walking routes will provide choice to residents with different needs. A covered arcade will allow residents to exercise outside during poor weather.

- Areas placed near recreation areas for sitting and watching can provide a interest for those residents whose ability to use outdoor activity areas is limited due to health or mobility problems.
- Prosthetic elements, such as handrails, will encourage less able residents to participate in outside activities.
- Create an outdoor physical therapy area, which might include a variety of different types of stairs and ramps, and a path with handrails similar to parallel bars.
- Consider the users' activity preferences prior to entering the home to accommodate the continuation of those activities.

7. Provide a Comfortable Place

- Transitional spaces between indoor and outdoor spaces, such as screened-in porches or overhangs, can provide protection from the climate, allow adjustment to bright outdoor light, increase the sense of safety, and provide a place to sit and watch the activities without being involved in them.
- Very stable pedestal tables allow accessibility by wheelchair users. Wheelchair accessibility requires 29 inches clearance under the tabletop.
- Toilets and functional items need to be clearly marked. Signs should not be placed higher than 54 inches above the floor. Door signs should be mounted on the wall on the side which opens. Although the size of the lettering is dependent on the lettering system used, large (a minimum of 5/8 inch in height) lettering on a contrasting background (light letters on a dark background are best) will help people with acuity problems. However, those with a loss of peripheral vision may have problems with lettering that is too big.
- The intensity and angle of sunlight fluctuates throughout the day. Therefore the design of exterior spaces needs to accommodate the intensity to the noon-day sun and the glare potential of the afternoon sun.
- Sun screens, trellises, fences, walls, baffles, and plant materials need to be used to ameliorate the sun and wind in outdoor spaces at nursing homes.
- Carefully place and select trees with dense canopies to reduce glare and control light penetration.

- Light bouncing off water, glass, metal, plastic, and shiny paint can cause glare problems. Utilize roof overhangs, arbors, or awnings to diffuse direct sunlight.
- Provide seating in sun for use during winter, in shade for use in the summer.
- Provide a clear organizational pattern with well identified paths, a clear hierarchy of spaces and features or focal points to help orient residents. Enclosed areas and looped paths can provide confused residents with outdoor spaces where they can walk unsupervised.

8. Provide a Sense of Security

- Design outdoor spaces that are visible from indoor spaces frequently used by staff and residents.
- Clearly define the boundary between space for residents only, and space for joint use with the community or neighborhood where such a juxtaposition occurs.
- Use lighting, ground cover, low shrubs, and high branching trees to help surveillance and safety.
- Use night lighting to provide a sense of safety and maximize the use of the outdoors in hot climates.

9. Accessibility

- Pathways should contrast in color with planting areas to help define the boundary between path and plantings for residents with reduced depth perception. The color of chairs and tables should contrast with the floor covering so they are distinguishable by people with sight impairments
- Using lever door openers instead of round knobs is one example of universal design that increases accessibility to outdoor spaces for people with arthritis, decreased strength, or other physical disabilities.
- Ramps for older wheelchair users should have a maximum pitch of 1:20 instead of the accessibility standard of 1:12. Doors should have a width of 32 inches, have a window, and be easy to open.
- A 4-inch-high step for older adults is recommended.
- Windows should be as large as possible and positioned so that a bedridden person can see both the ground and the sky. Combinations of shades, blinds, sheer curtains, mylar film, and drapes can control the sunlight.

- Ambulating aids such as handrails and seating should be placed on both sides of a walkway since residents may have use of only one side as a result of neurological damage due to strokes or illness.
- The most commonly mentioned discouragement to going outdoors is the difficulty of using the door, particularly getting over a raised threshold strip, which causes problems for residents whether they are walking or using a wheelchair. Automatic door openers with a net opening force of less than eight pounds can be used to increase accessibility.

CONCLUSION

The design process requires that designers keep struggling to answer the question, "What should we be designing for?" as a way of identifying how design can best meet the needs of the frail elderly. Well designed grounds, with views and accessible outdoor spaces, are important factors in the design of nursing homes and reflect an increasing awareness of the benefits of access to natural amenities on human welfare. New building arrangements have created new opportunities for outdoor spaces, making them seem more homelike and less institutional. New directions in garden designs create spaces that empower the individual, appeal to the senses, are task-oriented, and promote physical and emotional well-being.

The importance of improving the design of nursing homes cannot be overstated. An article in *The New York Times* reported a survey that found 30 percent of seriously ill people in hospitals would rather die than live permanently in a nursing home (Gilbert, 1997). This study of 3,262 patients in five hospitals in the United States was not the first to document the aversion that many older people have to nursing homes (Mattimore et al., 1997). Researchers in the field of long-term care are well aware of the dread and despair that nursing homes inspire in the elderly (Cohen, 1988; Vladeck, 1980). And yet, for many people, a nursing home will be their last abode. No other environment is so feared and despised by the people it is designed to serve. Well designed outdoor spaces can help to ensure that gardens and outdoor spaces remain lifelong pleasures, that nursing homes do not become prisons, and that the extra years added to our lifespans are worth living.

REFERENCES

American Hospital Association (1991). "The Quest for the Perfect Patient Unit Design." AHA Technical Document 055301, September.

American Association of Homes and Services for the Aging (1991). *Fact Sheet. Nursing Homes.* Washington. DC: AAHSA.

American Association of Retired People (AARP) (1997). Telephone conversation with Librarian at Research Information Center, Washington, DC.

American Institute of Architects (1992). *Design for Aging: 1992 Review.* Washington, DC: The American Institute of Architects.

American Occupational Therapy Association (1983). *Architectural Barriers/OT's Consulting to Architects.* Rockville, MD: AOTA.

Barney, J. L. (1974). "Community Presence's as a Key to Quality of Life in Nursing Homes." *American Journal of Public Health,* Vol. 64, March, pp. 265–268.

Bartlett, H. (1993). *Nursing Homes for Elderly People: Questions of Quality and Policy.* Langhorne, PA: Harwood Academic Publishers.

Binstock, R. H., L. W. Cluff, and O. Von Mering (Eds.) (1996). *The Future of Long-Term Care: Social and Policy Issues.* Baltimore: Johns Hopkins University Press.

Blankenship, L. M., V. Molinari, and M. Kunik (1996). "The Effect of a Life Review Group on the Reminiscence Functions of Geropsychiatric Inpatients." *Clinical Gerontologist,* Vol. 16, No. 4, pp. 3–18.

Bowersox, J. (1979). "Architectural and Interior Design." In L. J. Wasser, *Long Term Care of the Aging: A Socially Responsible Approach.* Washington, DC: American Association of Homes for the Aging.

Brody, E. M. (1977). "Environmental Factors in Dependency." In A. N. Exton-Smith and J. Grimley Evans (Eds.), *Care of the Elderly: Meeting the Challenge of Dependency.* New York: Grune and Stratton, pp. 84 ff.

Butler, R. (1983). "The Life-Review: and Interpretations of Reminiscence in the Aged Psychiatry." *Journal of the Study of Interpersonal Processes,* Vol. 26, pp. 65–76.

Butterfield, D. and S. Weidemann (1987). "Housing Satisfaction of the Elderly." In V. Regnier and J. Pynoos (Eds.), *Housing the Aged.* New York: Elsevier Science.

Carpman, J. R. and M. A. Grant (1993). *Design that Cares: Planning Health Facilities for Patients and Visitors.* Chicago: American Hospital Publishing.

Carstens, D. (1985). *Site Planning and Design for the Elderly: Issues, Guidelines and Alternatives.* New York: Van Nostrand Reinhold.

Christenson, M. A. (1990). *Aging in the Designed Environment.* New York: Haworth Press.

Cluff, L. E. (1996). "The Role of Technology in Long-Term Care." in R. H. Binstock, L. E. Cluff, and O. Von Mering (Eds.), *The Future of Long-Term Care: Social and Policy Issues*. Baltimore: Johns Hopkins University Press.

Cohen, E. S. (1988). "The Elderly Mystique: Constraints on the Autonomy of Elderly with Disabilities." *Gerontologist*, Vol. 28 (Supplement, June), pp. 24–31.

Cooper Marcus, C. (1978). "Remembrance of Landscapes Past." *Landscape*, Vol. 22, No. 3, pp. 34–43.

—— (1995). *House as Mirror of Self: Exploring the Deeper Meaning of Home*. Berkeley, CA: Conari Press.

Cooper Marcus, C. and M. Barnes (1995). *Gardens in Healthcare Facilities: Uses, Therapeutic Benefits, and Design Recommendations*. Martinez, CA: The Center for Health Design.

Cranz, G. (1987). "Evaluating Design Innovations in an Extended Care Facility." In V. Regnier and J. Pynoos (Eds.), *Housing the Aged*. New York: Elsevier Science.

Dovey, K. (1978). "Home: An Ordering Principle in Space." *Landscape*, Vol. 22, pp. 27–30.

—— (1985). "Home and Homelessness." In I. Altman and C. Werner (Eds.) *Home Environments*. New York: Plenum Press.

Finlay, O. W., T. B. Bayles, C. Rosen, and J. Milling (1983). "Effects of Chair Design, Age and Cognitive Status on Mobility." *Age and Aging*, Vol. 12, pp. 329–335.

Firestone, I. J., C. M. Lichtman, and J. R. Evans (1980). "Privacy and Solidarity: Effects of Nursing Home Accommodations on Environmental Perceptions and Social Preferences." *International Journal of Aging and Human Development*, Vol. 11, No. 3, pp. 229–238.

Gilbert, S. (1997). "A Nursing Home? Or Death?" *New York Times*, August 6.

Gowans, A. (1986). *The Comfortable House: North American Suburban Architecture 1890–1930*. Cambridge, MA: MIT Press.

Greene, V. L. and D. J. Monihan (1981). "Structural and Operational Factors Affecting Quality of Patient Care in Nursing Homes." *Public Policy*, Vol. 29, No. 4, pp. 571–583.

Hartigan, J. (1982). "The Dangerous Wheelchair." *Journal of the American Geriatric Society*, Vol. 30, No. 9, pp. 572–573.

Hartman, C. J. Horovitz, and R. Herman (1987). "Involving Older Persons in Designing Housing for the Elderly." In V. Regnier and J. Pynoos (Eds.), *Housing the Aged*. New York: Elsevier Science.

Harrington, C. (1991). "The Nursing Home Industry: A Structural Analysis." In M. Minkler and C. L. Estes (Eds.), *Critical Perspectives on Aging: The Political and Moral Economy of Growing Old*. Amityville, NY: Baywood Publishing.

Hasselkus, B. (1974). "Aging and the Human Nervous System." *American Journal of Occupational Therapy* Vol. 28, No. 1, pp. 16–21.

Hatton, J. (1977). "Aging and the Glare Problem." *Journal of Gerontological Nursing*, Vol. 3, pp. 38–44.

Henderson, J. N. (1994). "Bed, Body and Soul: The Job of the Nursing Home Aide." *Generations*, Vol. 18, pp. 20–22.

Hendy, H. M. (1987). "Effects of Pet and/or People Visits on Nursing Home Residents." *International Journal of Aging and Human Development*, Vol. 25, No. 4, pp. 279–291.

Hiatt, L. G. (1979). "Architecture for the Aged: Design for Living." *Inland Architect*, November and December, pp. 6–18, 41–42.

———. (1980). "Care and Design: Moving Outside and Making It a Meaningful Experience". *Nursing Homes*, Vol. 29, No. 3, pp. 34–39.

Hill, M. B. (1995). *Grandmother's Garden: The Old-Fashioned American Garden 1865–1915*. New York: Harry N. Abrams.

Horgan, J. (1997). "Seeking a Better Way to Die." *Scientific American*, May, pp. 100–105.

Howell, S. C. (1985). "Home: A Source of Meaning in Elders' Lives." *Generations*, Vol. 9, No 3, pp. 58–60.

Kane, R. A. (1995). "Autonomy and Regulation in Long-Term Care: An Odd Couple, An Ambiguous Relationship." In L. M. Gamroth, J. Semradek, and E. M. Tornquist (Eds.), *Enhancing Autonomy in Long-Term Care: Concepts and Strategies*. New York: Springer Publishing.

Kane, R. L. and R. A. Kane (1980). "Alternatives to Institutional Care of the Elderly: Beyond the Dichotomy." *Generations*, Vol. 14 (Supplement), pp. 86–89.

Kiernat, J. (1985). "Environmental Aspects Affecting Health." In *Care of the Elderly: A Health Team Approach*. Boston: Little, Brown & Co.

Koncelik, J. A. (1976). *Designing the Open Nursing Home*. Stroudsburg, PA: Dowden, Hutchinson and Ross.

——— (1996). "Characteristics of Aging." In R. L. Null and K. F. Cherry. *Universal Design: Creative Solutions for ADA Compliance*. Belmont, CA: Professional Publications.

Lemke, S. and R. Moos (1986). "Quality of Residential Settings for the Elderly." *Journal of Gerontology*, Vol. 41, pp. 268–276.

Mattimore, T., N. Wenger, N. Desbiens, J. Teno, M. Hamel, H. Liu, R. Califf, A. Connors, J. Lynn, and R. Oye (1997). "Surrogate and Physician Understanding of Patients' Preferences for Living Permanently in a Nursing Home." *Journal of American Geriatrics Society*, Vol. 45, pp. 818–824.

McClure, E. (1968). *More Than a Roof: The Development of Minnesota Poor Farms and Homes for the Aged*. St. Paul: Minnesota Historical Society.

Miller, P. H. and C. S. Smith (1981). "Personal Belongings—A Positive Effect?" *The Gerontologist*, Vol. 21, No. 1, pp. 85–90.

Moos, R. and S. Lemke (1980). "Assessing the Physical and Architectural Features of Sheltered Care Settings." *Journal of Gerontology*, Vol. 35, No. 4, pp. 571–583.

Najman, J. and L. Levine (1981). "Evaluating the Impact of Medical Care and Technologies on the Quality of Life: A Review and Critique." *Social Science and Medicine,* Vol. 15 (F), pp. 107–115.

Noell, E. (1995). "The Environment: a Silent Partner in Care Giving." Paper presented at the Symposium; Blueprint for Aging of the School of Public Health and Academic Geriatric Resource Program, University of California at Berkeley., Oakland, CA.

Null, R. L. and K. F. Cherry (1996). *Universal Design: Creative Solutions for ADA Compliance.* Belmont, CA: Professional Publications.

"Nursing Homes: When a Loved One Needs Care" (1995). *Consumer Reports,* August, pp. 518–528.

Office of the State Architect (1989). Excerpts from *California State Accessibility Standards: Interpretive Manual,* 3rd ed. Sacramento: State of California.

Osterburg, A. E. (1987). "Evaluating Design Innovations in an Extended Care Facility." In V. Regnier and J. Pynoos (Eds.), *Housing the Aged.* New York: Elsevier Science.

Ott, R. L. (1993). "Enhancing Validation Through Milestoning with Sensory Reminiscence." *Journal of Gerontological Social Work,* Vol. 20, Nos. 1/2, pp. 147–159.

Panero, J. and M. Zelnik (1979). *Human Dimension and Interior Space.* New York: Whitney Library of Design, Watson-Guptill Publications.

Pastalan, L., V. Cohen, E. Steinfeld, G. Weisman, and P. Windley (1976). *Age Related Vision and Hearing Changes: An Empathic Approach.* Ann Arbor, MI: Michigan Institute of Gerontology, University of Michigan.

Powers, B. (1988). "Social Networks, Social Support, and the Elderly Institutionalized People." *Advances in Nursing Science,* Vol. 10, No. 2, pp. 40–58.

Pregill, P. and N. Volkman (1993). *Landscapes in History: Design and Planning in the Western Tradition.* New York: Van Nostrand Reinhold.

Raschko, B. (1982). *Housing Interiors for the Disabled and Elderly.* New York: Van Nostrand Reinhold.

Regnier, V. (1985.) *Behavioral and Environmental Aspects of Outdoor Space Use in Housing for the Elderly.* Los Angeles: School of Architecture, Andrus Gerontology Center, University of Southern California.

———— (1995a). *Assisted Living For the Aged and Frail: Innovations in Design, Management and Financing.* New York: Columbia University Press.

———— (1995b). "Designing for Competency." Proceedings of the Symposium; Blueprint for Aging of the School of Public Health and Academic Geriatric Resource Program, University of California at Berkeley, Oakland, CA.

Regnier, V. and J. Pynoos (1987). *Housing the Aged.* New York: Elsevier Science.

Reznikoff, S. C. (1979). *Specifications for Commercial Interiors*. New York: Whitney Library of Design, Watson-Guptill Publications.

Richman, L. (1969). "Sensory Training for Geriatric Patients." *American Journal of Occupational Therapy*, Vol. 23, pp. 254–257.

Rowles, G. D. (1987). "A Place to Call Home." In L. L. Carstensen and B. A. Edelstein (Eds.), *Handbook of Clinical Gerontology*. New York: Pergamon Press.

Rubinstein, R. L. (1989). "The Home Environments of Older People: A Description of the Psychosocial Processes Linking Person to Place." *Journal of Gerontology, Social Sciences*, Vol. 44, No. 2, pp. 545–553.

Schultz, D. P. (1965). *Sensory Restriction: Effects on Behavior*. New York: Academic Press.

Schwarz, B. (1996). *Nursing Home Design: Consequences of Employing the Medical Model*. New York. Garland Publishing.

Sommer, R. (1970). "Small Group Ecology in Institutions for the Elderly." In L. A. Pastalan and D. H. Carson (Eds.), *Spatial Behavior in Older People*. Ann Arbor, MI: University of Michigan.

Spivack, M. (1973). "Archetypal Places." In W. F. E. Presier (ed), *Environmental Design Research, Vol. 1*. Community Development Series, Fourth International EDRA Conference, Stroudsburg, PA: Dowden, Hutchinson and Ross. pp. 33–46.

——— (1984). *Institutional Settings: An Environmental Design Approach*. New York: Human Science Press.

Stoneham, J. and P. Thoday (1996). *Landscape Design for Elderly and Disabled People*. Garden Art Press: Woodbridge, Suffolk, U.K.

Taylor, J. (1991). *Hospital and Asylum Architecture in England 1840–1914*. London: Mansell Publishing.

Thomas, W. H. (1996). *Life Worth Living: How Someone You Love Can Still Enjoy Life in a Nursing Home*. Acton, MA: VanderWky & Burnham.

Timko, C. and R. Moos (1990). "Determinants of Interpersonal Support and Self Direction in Group Residential Facilities." *Journal of Gerontology*, Vol. 45, No. 5, pp. 5184–5192.

US Department of Health and Human Services, National Center for Health Statistics (1985). *National Nursing Home Survey*. Washington, DC: Inter-University Consortium for Political and Social Research, Ann Arbor, MI.

US Department of Health, Education, and Welfare, Public Health Service, Office of Nursing Home Affairs (1975). *Long-Term Care Facility Improvement Study, Introductory Report*. Washington, DC: Government Printing Office.

Vladeck, B. (1980). *Unloving Care: The Nursing Home Tragedy*. New York: Basic Books.

Weidmann, S., J. R. Anderson, D. I. Butterfield, and P. M. O'Donnell (1982). "Resident's Perceptions of Satisfaction and Safety." *Environment and Behaviors*, Vol. 14, No. 6, November, pp. 695–724.

Wheeler, R. (1982) "Housing and the Elderly." In C. Philipson and A. Walker (Eds.), *Aging and Social Policy*. Aldershot, Hants, UK: Gower Publishing.

Willcocks, D., S. Peace, and L. Kellaher, (1987). *Private Lives in Public Places*. New York: Tavistock Publications.

Wolanin, M. O., and L. R. Fralich Phillips (1981). *Confusion, Prevention and Care*. St. Louis: C. V. Mosby Co.

Zedlewski, S. R., R. O. Barnes, M. R. Burt, T. D. McBride, and J. A. Meyer (1990). *The Needs of the Elderly in the Twenty-First Century, Urban Institute Report, 90–95*, Washington, DC: Urban Institute Press.

CHAPTER

9

Alzheimer's Treatment Gardens

John Zeisel and Martha M. Tyson

Alzheimer's disease is a progressive, degenerative disease that attacks the brain and results in impaired memory, thinking, and behavior. It is the most common form of dementing illness. A person with Alzheimer's disease may experience confusion, personality and behavior changes, impaired judgment, and difficulty finding words, finishing thoughts, or following directions. Impairments to the brains of people with Alzheimer's disease can limit their ability to comprehend present time, understand place, remember recent past experiences, and complete normal daily tasks such as dressing and bathing. From the first signs of impairment, the duration of the disease can last anywhere from three to twenty years with an average progression over twelve years (Alzheimer's Association, 1997, p. 1). Gardens in Alzheimer's facilities need to be carefully designed and constructed with a focus on the special needs of people with this progressive disease.

HISTORY

The number of older Americans suffering from Alzheimer's disease or a related disorder is estimated at four million, and continues to grow (Alzheimer's Association, 1997). By the year

437

2050, the United States will have 67.5 million people over the age of 65, over two and a half times the 25.5 million there were in 1990 *(ibid.)*. According to the statistics supported by the Alzheimer's Association, if a cure or significant means of prevention is not found soon, an estimated 12 to 14 million Americans will be affected by the year 2040. Today approximately 10 percent of those over 65 have Alzheimer's disease with the percentage nearly five times that (47.2 percent) among the group over 85.

The disease was discovered in 1907 when Alois Alzheimer, a German neuropathologist studying the brains of nonelderly adults who had had severe memory loss before their deaths, found a common set of conditions: neurofibulary brain plaques and tangles. Seventy-five years later, a team of researchers at New York University Medical Center developed a clear description of the predominant pattern of progressive functional loss associated with the disease (Reisberg et al., 1987).

Old age is not a disease. While occasional forgetfulness and confusion are normal occurrences, dementia is a medical condition. Dementia has many causes, the major one being dementia of the Alzheimer's type. While increased age is associated with increased incidence of Alzheimer's disease, normal aging and the development of Alzheimer's disease and related dementias are different processes.

Commonly used terms, like senile and feeble minded, when used to refer to older people with memory impairment, contribute to the myth that mental decline and old age are the same. The word "senile" is derived from the Latin root "senescere," which simply means to grow old (US Department of Health and Human Services, 1984) and the word "dementia" is derived from the root "dementare," meaning "deprived of mind." The earliest reference to dementia can be traced back to Greece in approximately 500 BC. From the time of Roman civilization, dementia associated with old age was feared and looked upon as a form of mental illness. During the sixteenth, seventeenth, and eighteenth centuries, medical practitioners began to use descriptions like forgetfulness, dulled senses, and a return to a childlike state to explain the symptoms of dementia in old age (Fox, 1986).

IMPORTANCE OF THE ENVIRONMENT

Presently, there is no cure for Alzheimer's disease. However, well-designed environments, good planning, and medical and social management can be used to reduce symptoms and ease the burdens on family members (Zeisel et al., 1999). While environment generally affects our state of mind and well-being, this is especially true for the elderly because of changes in our bodies and minds as we age. Decreases in visual and hearing ability that affect balance and orientation make older people particularly sensitive to the physical environment. To compensate for such losses older people need a higher level of sensory input to process information than younger people do, but they also are more sensitive to external conditions. For example, people need a higher level and intensity of light as they age, while at the same time they have a more intense reaction to glare and reflection. "To expect the aged to function somewhat 'normally' under the burden of the levels of sensory involvement we are accustomed to may be a little like expecting a computer to function on the power of a flashlight battery" (De Long, 1970, p. 80). Walking as well may not always be as easy when someone is over eighty. Each step takes special care; gait and movement require more level surfaces, wider pathways and defined edges to prevent falling, or to ease the fear of falling (Carstens, 1985, 1990). Biomechanics and aging studies show that older people move more slowly and take smaller steps to accommodate physical changes.

Figure 9-1   Elderly people often like to spend time near the front entrance of a residential facility. Man feeding birds near the main entry to The Lodge at Broadmead, Victoria, B.C., Canada. (Photo by Clare Cooper Marcus.)

RESEARCH REVIEW

Environmental design research is playing an increasingly central role in creating quality living environments for older people with dementia (Calkins, 1988, 1989; Cohen and Weisman, 1991; Coons, 1988, 1991; Zeisel et al., 1994; Zeisel et al., 1999). Current research shows that residents exhibit fewer dementia symptoms in more familiar homelike environments than in larger institutional nursing homes (Calkins, 1988; Cohen and Weisman, 1991; Coons, 1991; Zeisel et al., 1994; Zeisel et al., 1999). Designs planned in response to such research are now often modeled after small villages or country homes, emphasizing elements like the old front porch, individual gardens and family living (Carstens, 1998; Hoglund, 1985). A familiar, homelike atmosphere, in addition to being therapeutic for older residents, may also reduce anxiety for their families and the staff who care for them (e.g., Calkins, 1988; Cohen and Weisman, 1991; Coons, 1991).

Cohen and Weisman (1991) link behavior and design research with practical general principles for designing environments for people with dementia. They propose design and programming recommendations to meet specific therapeutic goals. Outdoor spaces are discussed as an important part of any complete therapeutic environment.

Margaret Calkins' pioneering *Design for Dementia* (1988) is the earliest architectural guide for administrators and architects to facilitate renovation of existing facilities as well as to design new units for people with dementia. Calkins clearly organizes empirical experience and research into a set of behavior-based design guidelines for older people with dementia. She provides general objectives for design and practical solutions for implementation under such environment-behavior headings as way-finding, orientation, privacy and socialization, personalization, safety, and security. Later research by Calkins focuses on specific design solutions, showing how environmental adaptations like eliminating full views of exit doors can decrease the number of exit seekers and change the patterns of wanderers (Calkins, 1989).

Importance of Gardens

One successful environmental element in treating Alzheimer's disease is a garden. People with Alzheimer's disease face problems of way-finding, as well as object and place identification, whether inside or outside, so that the design of gardens for this group takes special effort and design research knowledge. Bite and Lovering (1984, 1985) were among the first to address the issue of outdoor spaces in nursing home settings and the factors that affect their use by patients. An important question these authors ask is: "Why *don't* people go outside?" They found that outdoor space use depends on resident motivation, comfortable seating, protection from the elements, and staff initiated use. Residents did not use spaces that were isolated, preferring areas of activity. Carstens' *Site Planning and Design for the Elderly* (1985) is an excellent and complete resource for design professionals on guidelines for the normal aging population. Directed toward designers, administrators and students, this book is a general research-based guide for designing housing for the elderly. Specific issues related to site planning, circulation, and spatial and social needs of the elderly are addressed and practical design solutions are clearly identified and illustrated. In his early research publication, *Behavioral and Environmental Aspects of Outdoor Space Use in Housing for the Elderly* (1985), Regnier evaluated building characteristics, outdoor spaces, resident profiles, and actual use of outdoor spaces in several existing elderly housing complexes. His study defines patterns of use in detail, based on daily observation of residents, including times of day courtyards were most popular, sun conditions related to use, and places used to sit and visit. He assessed rea-

"I think a garden glorifies a house. When I walk out of my house, I feel young, lovely, and anxious to see beautiful flowers and green grass. Generally, it lightens my spirit. I feel like dancing. When I was a kid, they always gave me a spot in the garden. We had a big lawn surrounded by bushes of roses. If I had a house, I would have a garden."

(RESIDENT)

Figure 9-2   A courtyard garden for residents with Alzheimer's disease. Note the lush planting, pool and waterfall, seating for a single person or a couple, and hand rails for those unsteady on their feet. (The Lodge at Broadmead, Victoria, B.C., Canada, photo by Clare Cooper Marcus.)

sons for use or low use taking into account environmental factors such as sun and shade, wind currents, furnishings, parking and security as well as management issues such as rules and policies that may inhibit use. Carstens' more recent *Housing and Outdoor Spaces for the Elderly* (1998) offers designers information related to independent elderly people. This work employs case studies of existing facilities, and describes in detail the site, outdoor spaces as well as major uses and users; and identifies successful features and unsuccessful features in the form of a design review checklist. Carstens' and Regnier's research helped identify characteristics of outdoor space that influence resident preferences and frequency of use: location, proximity to other activities, relationship to indoor space, sun exposure, and the role of management.

When people with dementia live in a group setting all day, every day of the year except when they visit or take trips with their families or caregivers, it is not surprising that they too want to walk outside on their own sometimes. While research that addresses outdoor space design for the elderly is readily available (e.g., Bite and Lovering, 1984, 1985; Carstens, 1985, 1998; Regnier, 1985), findings addressing the specific needs of the elderly with Alzheimer's disease are limited (e.g., Cohen and Weisman, 1991; Lovering, 1990; Tyson, 1992; Gilson, 1994). A safe and secure garden attached to a residence enables residents to go outdoors easily, especially if it is available to residents most of the time and if residents can use it freely.

Tyson, in the *Journal of Therapeutic Horticulture* (1987), raised garden design issues for discussion and defined the rela-

"I like to garden; flower gardens best. My father always took care of the vegetable garden while my mother and I took care of the flower garden."

(RESIDENT)

tionship between design and recreational programming for gardens (Tyson and Maghakian, 1989). She applied these principles in a built garden and conducted follow-up research to explore the therapeutic potential of the outdoor environment in the care of older people with Alzheimer's disease (Tyson, 1989, 1990). Another study employing behavioral observations, resident and staff interviews, staff questionnaires, and application of therapeutic principles specific to the elderly with dementia, was conducted at the Champaign County Nursing Home in Urbana, Illinois (Tyson, 1992).

Research and clinical experience to date indicate that appropriate and therapeutic outdoor spaces for people with dementia need to be both accessible and supportive (Zeisel et al., 1994). Gardens need to be accessible to residents physically, visually and socially. They need to be designed to support physical needs as well as interaction with the natural environment and participation in social life. Personally involving residents in a garden's stewardship adds a dimension of home that helps transfer feelings of ownership away from the facility and designer, to the people who live there and their families.

Wandering and Walking

Among the most frequent activities that take place in gardens designed for people with dementia are walking and wandering. A great deal of environmental design and social behavior research addresses these issues (Calkins, 1989; Hiatt, 1978; White, 1990; Coons, 1988, 1991). This research suggests that the environment can either increase residents' confusion, causing aimless "wandering" behavior, or support the behavior of "walking" by providing adequate space, safety, circulation patterns, and destinations (Coons, 1988, Zeisel et al., 1994). Protecting residents from getting lost may limit their freedom, but at the same time it allows them to maintain independence and self-esteem and keeps them from harm. There are numerous explanations for wandering behavior. These include: reactions to crowds or noise, searching for someone, boredom, disorientation, searching for something to handle, or a need for exercise. The need for wandering is more than a physical need to move from place to place; safe walking paths that provide opportunities for interesting experiences appear effective in helping to reduce wandering behavior (Coons, 1988).

Leopold Liss, director of the Cognitive Disorders Clinic at Ohio State University's College of Medicine, has found that design can accommodate and neutralize disruptive behaviors in nursing homes for demented residents. He finds that fenced-in grounds made safe for wandering is one effective design

Figure 9-3 "Wandering" behavior is common among Alzheimer's patients. This linear garden is part of a looped route for people to walk outside and inside the building. (The Stroll, Chemainus Health Care Centre, Chemainus, B.C., Canada, photo by Clare Cooper Marcus.)

response. When patients' clothing is adequate, there is no reason why a wandering individual should not have the freedom to walk outdoors in all weather. Wandering can be ameliorated by supervised walks, which in turn lead to better general health, increased appetite, and better sleep patterns (Liss, 1986, p. 5).

One research study is particularly applicable to designing outdoor spaces for those with dementia. Kevin Lynch, in *Image of the City* (1960), studied how people organize complex spaces in their minds to more easily find their way. He identified five elements that people use for orientation and way-finding. As applied to garden spaces, these are:

- **Paths:** The channels along which people move; the predominant element in their image of their environment as they move through it
- **Edges:** Boundaries between two areas, either impenetrable barriers or seams that join parts of a garden together.
- **Districts:** Sections of a garden that are recognizable as having a unique identifying character.
- **Nodes:** Spots in a garden that are foci to and from which people travel. Nodes can be junctions, or places of intense activity.
- **Landmarks:** Reference points singled out from a field of elements in a setting, such as gazebos, fountains, trees, doorways.

Because of changes to the brains of people with Alzheimer's disease, remembering places and connections between them, is extremely difficult. Lynch's five categories are particularly useful because, when applied to garden design, they relieve the user from having to organize a mental cognitive map. Gardens designed with the principles make people with Alzheimer's disease more competent in their use of the garden.

GARDENING AND CAREGIVING

The use of the outdoor environment also benefits caregivers (Cohen and Weisman, 1991). A comfortable outdoor area provides a place that is different from the indoors. When working with residents who become agitated, staff or family can use outdoor spaces to involve residents in activities such as walking, potting plants, sweeping the patio, or hanging laundry.

Research in environmental psychology and horticulture demonstrates that the act of gardening has a positive psychological and therapeutic affect on people generally (Kaplan and

"Gardens and flowers offer a certain covert joy: they aren't missed if they are not there, but, when they are, they are recognized. They bring cheer and a sense of well-being that you can see on the residents' faces."

(ALZHEIMER'S FACILITY NURSE)

Kaplan, 1989; Stoneham, 1990). While digging and planting are two ways for older people to gain therapeutic value from a garden, merely observing can be therapeutic as well. "It is important to appreciate that, while some elderly people enjoy the opportunity to continue gardening, many will simply wish to sit out in the fresh air, or enjoy ... activities such as picking flowers and foliage for indoor hobbies" (Stoneham, 1990, p. 18). Older people with Alzheimer's disease are likely to benefit even more from sensory interaction with plants because of their heightened sensitivity to mood, emotion, and senses. Experiencing the familiar smell and sight of lilacs or roses, tasting a fresh tomato from the vine, touching the smooth leaves of an oak tree, or working the soil warmed from the sun prompt recall of memories of home and days of the past without requiring complex cognitive functioning (Healy, 1991).

When working with elderly people suffering from dementia, simple gardening provides opportunities for familiar activities that can be presented in easy stages. Environments that provide more information and cues than usual about time, place and purpose are especially therapeutic. A richly planted garden area can provide material for reality orientation, providing the therapist with opportunities for verbal cues "such as 'Look at the beautiful yellow daffodils,' 'What a lovely spring day' and for the use of actual objects in activities such as picking the fruit and then being able to eat it" (Hagedorn, 1990, p. 21). Little things can make a big difference. A successful garden will enable even demented residents to engage in simple tasks, such as watering a window box or re-potting a geranium.

Familiar Daily Life Activities

Daily life activities like setting a picnic table, feeding birds, watering plants, sitting in the sun, listening to music, preparing a meal, or simply watching out of a window are all ordinary everyday events for older people with and without dementia. Simple activities that can make the day worthwhile for many older people need to be seen as an integral part of design for their lives and health. Zgola (1987) points out that to accommodate such activities special consideration in design should be given to predictability, freedom from outside noise/distractions, ample space for activities, and clear traffic areas. After moving to a nursing home, assisted care residence or health care facility, older people often feel a loss of control over their surroundings. Taking part in ordinary daily life activities with which they are familiar, inside as well as in gardens, helps ease the transition and improve residents' well-being. With Alzheimer's disease, although short-term memory is affected, familiar daily life

Figure 9-4 Designing for patients with Alzheimer's disease needs to take account of people's desire to continue with normal daily activities such as gardening or putting seed in a bird feeder. (Oak Bay Kiwanis Pavilion, Victoria, B.C., Canada, photo by Clare Cooper Marcus.)

activities and living environments help to draw on deep memories of their earlier life (Calkins, 1988; Cohen and Weisman, 1991; Zgola, 1987). The most successful Alzheimer's programs systematically introduce tasks that reflect common activities from everyday life (Mace, 1993), and gardening can be among these. Beyersdorfer and Birkenhauer (1990) suggest that caring for dogs, cats and birds can be therapeutic for some residents. Lindenmuth and Moose (1990) and McArthur (1988) suggest that exercise can improve the physical and emotional health of older people, especially those with Alzheimer's disease.

GARDEN TYPOLOGY

Alzheimer's gardens have stringent requirements for:

- **Security:** Fences and locked gates.
- **Orientation and way-finding:** Paths with destinations and strong landmarks.
- **Places for programs:** Flat hard surfaces, patios and barbecue areas.
- **Paths for walking:** Pathways and shortcuts.
- **Locations for cultural memories:** Porches, hand pumps, clotheslines.
- **Adjacencies:** Connections between the dining room, etc. and the outdoors activity room.

Alzheimer's treatment gardens are essentially limited in type because they need to be totally secure, to cue way-finding and to be immediately adjacent to a residence or unit. Nevertheless there can be great variability in garden character and elements. Nine garden types to treat Alzheimer's disease are defined within these requirements, by juxtaposing two continuums: one, available spaces next to the residence that can be enclosed; and, two, a design emphasis placed on either a looping path or a central landmark.

Alzheimer's Treatment Garden Typology	
Available Adjacent Space	*Design Emphasis*
• Fenced on grade	• Pathway loop
• Atrium enclosed — with —	• Inside-outside stroll
• Rooftop	• Object focused

Every garden designed for Alzheimer's residents should have some sort of walking path. The way the path is planned defines the garden type.

- *Pathway loop gardens* have a central walking path that is entirely out of doors. Along the path there are familiar objects, plantings, and places for residents, families, and staff. There is generally a single doorway in and out, although there can be multiple doorways.
- *Inside-outside stroll gardens* include half a loop, while the remainder of the loop is inside the residence or special care unit. Located in narrow spaces adjacent to a residence, such gardens will generally have plantings and familiar objects, but no major landmarks. They are seen as places through which residents stroll.
- *Object focused gardens* have a central landmark as their defining feature. Arbors and cupolas to sit under are popular central features. Such gardens also have pathways, often circling the central object.

Each Alzheimer's garden can be located in any of three places next to an Alzheimer's residence or special care unit:

- *Fenced gardens* are defined at least on one side by a fence, with one or more sides usually defined by the building itself.
- *Enclosed atrium gardens* are interior courtyards defined on all four sides by the building itself.
- *Rooftop gardens* are located either on a partial roof balcony adjacent to an Alzheimer's unit or on the roof of the building in which the unit is located. These gardens generally are created when the unit itself is located on an upper floor.

DESIGN GUIDELINES

Much of the environmental design research discussed above relates the needs of older people and those with dementia to possible therapeutic garden design responses. None of this research delved into basic principles for organizing elements of outdoor space in ways that support orientation and a sense of well-being for this particular patient group. Having such princi-

Figure 9-5   Various looped pathways in this garden provide routes for "wandering" behavior without the fear of getting lost. (Oak Bay Kiwanis Pavilion, Victoria, B.C., Canada, photo by Clare Cooper Marcus.)

ples would make it easier to develop a system of garden design guidelines for people with dementia. The work of Kevin Lynch is useful in this regard (1960). Five elements by which people cognitively organize the city: paths, places, landmarks, nodes, and edges, are organizing cognitive principles that seem to hold for people with Alzheimer's as well. To Lynch's elements we have added four garden and dementia-specific categories—views, furnishings, plantings, and symbolic cues. In sum, the design guidelines presented here are organized in the following categories:

1. Paths
2. Places
3. Landmarks
4. Nodes
5. Edges
6. Views
7. Furnishings
8. Plantings
9. Symbolic cues

1. Paths

Paths are ways to get from one place to another and from there to the next place and back home again. Paths are the fundamental design element to orient and support walking outdoors for people with dementia. There are walking paths, shortcuts, and

A resident proudly announced to a visiting family member: "I walked around the path three times!"

"just passing through" paths. To orient people, all paths need a distinct beginning and end, with a series of goals and landmarks along the way.

Walking paths need to be wide enough for three people to walk side by side comfortably (5 to 6 feet minimum). This allows for an occasional wheelchair to pass but is not so wide that the path appears to be a small street. A walking path is the primary path in the garden for strolling, walking, and moving through and around the garden–a sort of garden promenade connecting places and people. For example in one of the case study sites, the Alois Alzheimer garden, the pathway brings residents full circle around the garden past interesting features along the way. At the Providence Centre case study site, the walking path leads to a large patio area and acts as a link between places. While the path in the Chemainus Stroll garden (see Figure 9-23) connects places and is a place in itself.

Shortcuts are smaller alternate pathways that provide a change of pace and a clear choice for residents. In this application, shortcuts imply slower movement so should be of a different material than the walking path, narrower, and with an end destination. Shortcuts placed at a 90 degree angle to walking paths present the greatest choice and least confusion. Shortcuts encourage people to walk, and provide easier routes for less mobile residents to return home. For example, in the Hearthstone Alzheimer Care case study site, a shortcut path divides the front and backyards while providing a slower path into the garden and the option of shorter walking distances for residents.

"Just passing through" paths pass through, around, or beside activity areas. Furnishings, plantings, surfaces, and activity areas planned next to such paths provide safe and interesting walking experiences for residents without being overprogrammed. These paths may move through patio areas, across lawns, alongside porches or beside seating alcoves.

2. Places

An Alzheimer's therapeutic garden designed with distinct and recognizable places within the enclosure of the garden will be the least confusing to residents. Places cue and encourage appropriate behaviors, increasing physical and social interaction with garden elements and people in the garden. Gathering places, away places, and symbolic places are three important types of places.

Gathering places can be porches, patios, and terraces—familiar residential places to get together. Planned parties, celebrations, and everyday use naturally occur when comfortable and accessible outdoor activity areas are located adjacent to indoor group activity areas such as lounges and activity rooms. Programmed table-based activities take place in flat gathering places outdoors. When paths pass through or by these places, opportunities for informal meetings are created, promoting lively outdoor life. For example, the arbor at the Alois Alzheimer Garden invites groups of residents and staff to spend time in this casual setting.

Away places are created by garden benches and seating alcoves separate from gathering places yet still along a path. They provide a clear choice for people who prefer a more remote place in the garden, to get away from activity and life indoors. Visible and accessible to staff or caregivers, an away place can be created by a combination of path layout, plantings and other partial screening materials. Away places provide necessary privacy and independence for residents and visitors. For example, at the Providence Centre an area under a large tree, covered by a simple tent canopy, provides a place in the garden that is far enough away to seem removed from the indoors, but close enough to stay connected. The three benches in the park area, some distance from the entrance in the Hearthstone garden, gives residents the opportunity to walk and arrive at a place off the main pathway.

Symbolic places have a distinct and familiar character reflecting culture, climate, geography, and context of the area where the facility is located. Such places are particularly important to evoke deep memories of those with memory impairment and cognitive loss. For example, a potting shed in the Chemainus Prairie Garden was designed to remind residents of the familiar backyard shed from their prairie homes.

Figure 9-6   *An example of a symbolic place, this potting shed is well used by residents. The design, which incorporates a simple shed, arbor, and patch of grass, evokes a typical backyard in the Prairie provinces, where most of the residents have spent their lives. (The Prairie Garden, Chemainus Health Care Center, Chemainus, B.C., Canada, photo by Clare Cooper Marcus.)*

3. Landmarks

Landmarks are visible reference points in the garden, providing cues for residents to find their way around the garden. Landmarks can serve as destinations. A series of landmarks along the main path organized in a definite hierarchy can naturally orient residents to the primary doorway back into the building.

Major landmarks are structural elements that can be seen from everywhere in the garden, giving it a visible unity. Recognizably distinct from smaller minor landmarks, such a major landmark might be an arbor or other large garden structure. For example, the gazebo in the Chemainus Garden gives residents a destination as well as a common orienting point within the gar-

Figure 9-7   *Landmarks in a garden assist Alzheimer's patients to find their way and provide interest for those who move slowly. Note the statuary, arbor, birdfeeder, benches, and seat wall. (The Lodge at Broadmead, Victoria, B.C., Canada, photo by Clare Cooper Marcus.)*

den. One major landmark that is particularly critical in all Alzheimer's gardens is the doorway back into the building, so that residents do not feel lost. Even when there are two doorways from the garden into the residence, one doorway should be more prominent than the other—especially if they are near each other.

Minor landmarks encourage movement and interest along garden pathways. They can be furnishings, plantings, significant landforms, benches, seating alcoves, or carefully selected and framed views that draw people through and into the garden. For example, at the Hearthstone Garden, a bench strategically located at the place where the shortcut meets the pathway provides a destination and cue for residents along the path, as do smaller ordinary garden features like animal sculptures and vegetable planting beds.

4. Nodes

Nodes are hubs of activity or natural gathering and stopping places along normal circulation routes. Nodes can be crossings of paths or planned destinations. A node is a place to say "Hello," or to have a short conversation like, "Fancy meeting you here" or "Beautiful day for a walk, isn't it?" For example, at the main entry to the garden at Hearthstone residents pass by one another coming and going for a stroll in the garden and encounter others engaged in activities on the back patio or the covered front porch.

Crossroads in a garden are like a crossing of country roads where people stop and gather. Paths that meet at right angles allows residents the option to choose a direction without a sense of disorientation. A bench or other element placed at a crossroads can support the node as well as present a temporary destination—a convenient place to stop and rest.

Destinations are strategically placed features that are natural places for stopping. There is no prescribed size or character for a destination, only that the feature be a place worth journeying to. Destinations provide a sense of purpose to the walking experience. For example, at Oak Bay Kiwanis the bridge and water feature create a place where people tend to stop and pause, a place that draws people out to the farthest point of the outdoor area.

5. Edges

Elements that enclose the garden provide security. Edges of paths and of places orient demented people by identifying and clarifying where these elements begin and end.

Enclosures such as a high fence or wall can be used if the building edge does not fully enclose the outdoor area. If an Alzheimer's facility has a frontyard, backyard, or garden area of any sort, the more secure it is, the more often the resident will be free to use it without being accompanied by a caregiver, allowing for spontaneous use and relieving staff of the constant concern for resident safety. Research has shown that caregivers restrict garden access to residents when enclosures do not present absolute security.

Surround the outdoor area with a high fence that is clearly too high to get over. An eight-foot fence (3.5 meters) usually achieves this. At Sedgewood Commons, which has several gardens (see case study, this chapter), enclosures range from a low picket fence to a solid screen fence to accommodate people at different stages of Alzheimer's disease. If a fence is not high enough to prevent all residents from climbing over, caregivers concerned about safety will keep the doors locked and will only permit residents outdoors with assistance. If it is possible to enclose the common garden without installing a gate—if fire regulations and maintenance issues do not dictate it—then do not install one. If a gate is necessary, make certain that it is either locked from the outside with an electronic device, or use a material of the same pattern and design as the fence to disguise the gate as part of the fence.

The *building edge* presents opportunities for the integration of life indoors and outdoors. Windows that allow views into—and doors that allow free access to—a garden encourage use. Outdoor areas that reflect adjacent indoor areas and activities— back patio near living room and raised vegetable planters near

Figure 9-8 A gate (open in this picture.) made from the same material and in the same design as a fence will be less noticeable as a gate, and evoke less agitation in those patients who want to "escape." Note light concrete in foreground, which caused glare problems. Garden beyond gate used tinted concrete. (Oak Bay Kiwanis Pavilion, Victoria, B.C., Canada, photo by Clare Cooper Marcus.)

kitchen—reinforce the indoor and outdoor connection. Transition zones such as patios, awnings, overhangs, and porches and stoops to extend the building edge into the garden, and ensure a gradual transition from indoor to outdoor levels of light, are essential for all older people. For example, the vine-covered trellis at the Alois Alzheimer's Center is a gathering place, while at the same time creating a shady transition to the outdoors.

Edges within the garden differentiate one place or path in the garden from another. Edges can be surface changes, walls, or hedge plantings. Plantings create a softened edge and transition between the dramatic height of a fence or building edge and the ground plane of the garden. Plantings used as a buffer between a fence and a path may reduce the frequency of residents trying to leave the garden. The lack of a clearly defined edge—such as a curb—between a path and a planting area may result in a person in a wheelchair mistakenly rolling into the plants or a person with poor eyesight stumbling off the path.

6. Views

Views into, within, and from the garden impact its use and the effect the garden has on residents. Views into the garden from interior rooms entice residents outdoors; if they are not aware of the garden, they will not use it. Views within the garden from one garden location to another encourage movement. Views out of the garden can be restful for some, yet may cause agitation to others who see the world beyond and want to escape. In these cases, views out of the garden should be blocked for residents' peace of mind and safety.

Window views from inside integrate life indoors with the outdoor life of the garden. What a person sees from the window is critical. Features like birdfeeders, other people, special activities, or seasonal displays of color attract residents once views out have made the connection. Views out also provide visibility for staff surveillance.

Distant views connect people with the surrounding landscape. In rural areas where the majority of residents have deeply rooted connections to the land, views of the fields may be an opportunity to help residents retain these connections. For example, the Alois Alzheimer garden provides views to the distant Ohio landscape. Care must be taken, however, to limit views through fences and other enclosures to parking lots, busy streets, and other places that might encourage elopement and increase anxiety. Such views should be blocked by solid fences. In the garden called the Stroll, at the Chemainus Health Care Center, a section of see-through fence had to be enclosed since views to an adjacent street caused problems for some residents. It seems that people and activity outside of a fence are the major source of problems in this regard.

7. Furnishings

Fixed benches, lighting, garden structures, and sculpture represent permanent furnishings. Other furnishings, intentionally kept movable, allow staff, residents, and visitors to adjust location and function to meet the needs of an activity they want to arrange. Nomadic furnishings like this range from lightweight (but sturdy) chairs to garden ornaments, potted plants, and other freestanding elements.

Structured fixed seating and lighting, gazebos, arbors, walls, and raised planters set the stage for social interaction and use of the garden. A meandering seating-height wall can provide an informal place to rest or visit; a sense of separation between places or enclosure for a place; and a shelf to set out potted plants along a path. Benches, arbors, and gateways fixed in strategic locations, create destinations, landmarks and circulation cues that encourage movement out into and through the garden. Fountains and other water features create natural sounds that may have more positive benefits than negative side effects.

For example, at Hearthstone a bench is set as a permanent fixture along the promenade path where it intersects the short-cut. Benches are also set in the park alcove at slight angles to provide opportunities for individuals or groups to sit together. A 2-foot-high stone seating-wall serves as a resting place and edge within the garden. (See Case Study p. 495.)

Figure 9-9 Wooden seats with backs and armrests allow older people to sit comfortably, and to lever themselves up from a seated position. Note additional light movable chairs, which permit someone to move to a more sunny or shady position, or to join a group. (Oak Bay Kiwanis Pavilion, Victoria, B.C., Canada, photo by Clare Cooper Marcus.)

Nomadic movable seating, small sculptures or garden art, tables, and container gardens allow residents, visitors, and staff to control and adjust the environment to best suit the needs of various activities without disrupting the overall structure and function of the garden. For example, a family member might move a chair under a tree for a visit, without feeling as though this interferes with the routine of the residence. Patterns of circulation and fixed furnishings can be complemented and augmented by the use of chairs, gliders, and tables when needed. Horticultural and other programs can be organized employing such movable furnishings as birdfeeders, birdbaths, garden art, and containers for flowers. For example, at the Chemainus Prairie Garden, a small worktable is moved around the garden. When people want to work in the shade it is moved under a tree. Otherwise it can be used in the morning sun.

8. Plantings

Plantings set gardens apart from all other forms of built environments. Plants change with the seasons, respond to soil and sun conditions, grow, and change in appearance, structure, and function. Consideration of the life cycle, growth rate, and structure of particular species is essential when selecting plants for this type of garden. Of particular importance is the issue of toxicity, since people with Alzheimer's disease may pick leaves, flowers, or fruits and eat them without being aware of potential effects on their health. The fruiting habits and leaf litter of trees, which may present hazards like slipping along pathways, should also be considered. Growth, maintenance, spatial needs, and characteristics that vary from plant to plant add to a garden's attractiveness and spiritual quality. The familiar fragrance of lilacs or sight of the first spring bulbs are significant to the lives of people who live in temperate climates, while the onset of winter rains and other seasonal plants may be significant to those from more tropical places. Plants create the *living* dimension of gardens far beyond any other elements.

Framework plantings such as trees, large shrubs, massed plantings, and perennial or annual gardens create the foundation of the garden. Just as structured seating provides the backbone for social places and circulation; framework plantings provide the structure and composition of the garden as a whole. For example, in the Oak Bay Kiwanis South Garden, cherry trees provide structure around the central patio, while preexisting large trees give a sense of familiarity to the garden at the Providence Centre. Each unique climate, culture, and setting encourages the use of a particular set of plant combinations.

"They look beautiful, they smell beautiful.... I love it, that's all."
(RESIDENT)

Evolving gardens within gardens that change over the years or are established anew with the changing seasons add to the ongoing life of a garden for residents, staff, and families. These include vegetable gardens, cutting gardens, herb gardens, and containers of annuals that encourage residents to garden themselves and enable structured therapy programs. Such evolving planting areas can be used to encourage family members to bring plantings from their own gardens. They create working gardens where residents, staff, and family can participate in the care of their garden.

Raised garden beds are provided or planned in all of the case study sites. At Chemainus, for example, the raised beds and potting shed in the Prairie Garden are popular places for working with plants.

9. Symbolic Cues

Every social and physical feature of a garden is enhanced when it evokes a symbolic or familiar purpose. For example, a bench set alongside a path where lilacs form a grove provides the opportunity to connect with springtime, with past memories of fragrances and with the momentary beauty of the blooms themselves. Orientation to time and place, and memory recall are essential functions of symbolic cues in the garden.

Orientation to time and place can be aided by plantings and garden features significant to particular times of the year. Seasonal holidays, significant religious celebrations, and ordinary and predictable changes in weather can be highlighted by the use of plantings and garden structures. Seasonal plantings like lilacs, spring bulbs, and autumn colors bring residents to a momentary awareness of the time of the year. Programming around these cues can be a highlight of garden activity.

Memory recall is aided by garden elements that reflect past culture and common activities, such as a clothesline, a barbecue, a compost pile, a hand pump. A rose blooming at the back door may bring back deep, otherwise forgotten memories. It is important for the designer to incorporate elements appropriate to the cultural background of the residents. For example, the Chemainus Prairie Garden incorporates a large outdoor thermometer on a potting shed, a familiar feature for residents, most of whom grew up in the prairies.

The old red Buick, bolted to the ground in the Oak Bay Kiwanis Garden, provides a strong visual and real-life connection to the past for the residents there. The staff reinforce memory recall by working with residents, washing the car, and reminiscing about the old days.

Figure 9-10   Raised beds for horticultural therapy enable those in wheelchairs to enjoy puttering in the garden. (Oak Bay Kiwanis Pavilion, Victoria, B.C., Canada, photo by Clare Cooper Marcus.)

Figure 9-11 A potting shed and raised beds for horticultural therapy. Note cut-away design of beds which facilitate use by a person in a wheelchair; and the small hanging basket for tools on the lip of the bed. Large thermometer is a familiar feature for many residents who grew up on the prairies. (Chemainus Garden, Chemainus Health Care Centre, Chemainus, B.C., Canada, photo by Clare Cooper Marcus.)

In conclusion, freedom to use a garden can best be achieved by providing an outdoor space surrounded by a secure enclosure, preventing residents from walking away; visible to caregivers located inside the residence; with clear pathways for residents; with plants and planting areas; and with clear choices of where to go and what to do outside.

If providing such an amenity is difficult, for example if the living area is on an upper floor, caregivers need to arrange alternative access to outdoor areas. An outdoor area could be located nearby at grade, or on an adjacent roof patio.

CASE STUDIES

Oak Bay Kiwanis Pavilion, Victoria, British Columbia, Canada

By Erna Jacobs, Director, and Twyla Rusnak, Landscape Architect

Description of Facility and Its History

The Oak Bay Kiwanis Pavilion is a 121-bed intermediate care facility located in the City of Victoria. The building is approximately 4,000 square meters in size and is located in a well established residential neighborhood. The facility is a forerunner in the care of residents suffering from dementia. It houses seventy-six residents with mild to severe dementia, as well as another forty-five residents who are cognitively well but physically frail.

The facility was built in 1982 by the Oak Bay Kiwanis Health Care Society. It was originally divided into three separate nursing areas with a central administration core. The main floor consisted of two forty-bed units for the physically frail with access to raised gardens and a cement patio. The upstairs housed forty residents with Alzheimer's or related dementias. The only access to the outdoors for this group was to come down the elevator and, under close supervision, walk in the raised flower garden and patio area.

In 1992–1993 the ever-increasing demand for dementia care units was recognized. The two main floor units were renovated and upgraded into two smaller units for residents with mild to moderate dementia and a forty-five-bed multilevel care unit was also built.

The garden project began in 1993, with the involvement of the Oak Bay Kiwanis Health Care Society's Board of Directors, staff, and families. The gardens were designed and built by Twyla Rusnak and Illarion Gallant. Funding for these gardens was achieved through an aggressive fund-raising campaign.

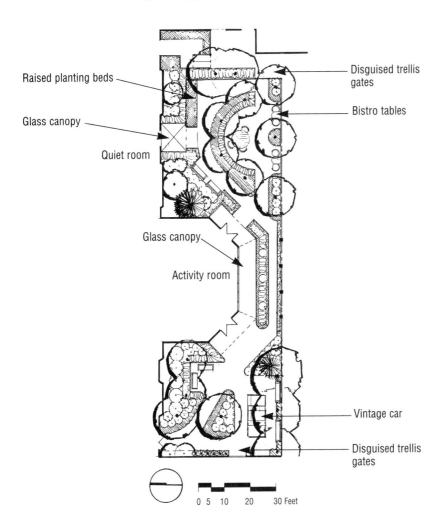

Figure 9-12   Site plan of the South garden, Oak Bay Kiwanis Pavilion, Victoria, B.C., Canada.

The primary purpose of the new gardens was to provide a secure and safe environment for the dementia care residents and their families to enjoy. The Oak Bay Kiwanis Pavilion has two Alzheimer's gardens, the South garden and the West garden. An additional garden is planned along the north side of the Pavilion.

Description of Outdoor Space

The South garden, running along the south wall of the building, is long and narrow with the activity room jutting out into its center. Points of entry into the garden are from either side of the activity room, from a quiet room at one end of the unit, and from a general unit exit at the other. The activity room and quiet room entrances have glass canopies to provide sheltered seating outside the doors and to cue the location of the entrance from the outside. In the garden, one follows level broom finish concrete walkways past the raised planting bed (constructed of mortared rock walls) filled with blooming annuals planted by staff and residents. A trellis fence holding grapevines leads the visitor to a shady seat at one of a couple of "bistro" tables under an arbor holding flowering climbers. For larger groups there is a picnic table with an umbrella in the central patio area. This patio is ringed by flowering Japanese cherry trees and a handrail for those who may totter in and out of their seats. A walk alongside the long narrow raised bed full of flowering annuals and climbers brings the visitor to the other end of the garden where there is an unusual feature sitting in the shade of Japanese maples: a 1962 Buick Skylark. This stationary vehicle was included to allow the residents to go through the motions of taking their spouse or friends "for a drive," and to awaken memories and stimulate conversation about past experiences. The space also becomes an activity center related to maintenance of the car. Two benches, a faucet, and a cupboard/closet holding chamois and buckets for washing the vehicle, provide the opportunity to participate in useful activities and conversation. Once through the car garden, one can walk back under the glass canopy of the activity room to one of the building entrances.

The West garden wraps around the south and west sides of the building. There are three building entrances into this garden: from the greenhouse and a general unit door on the south side of the building and from the activity room on the center of the west side of the building. A low dark trellis outside the activity room door was removed to allow more light into the building, and in the future a glass canopy will shelter and mark this entrance. The concrete paths throughout this garden area have

A resident reminisced:

"We had a family garden. I enjoyed picking the fresh vegetables. It made the yard look nice. I would enjoy sitting in the garden and watching the birds."

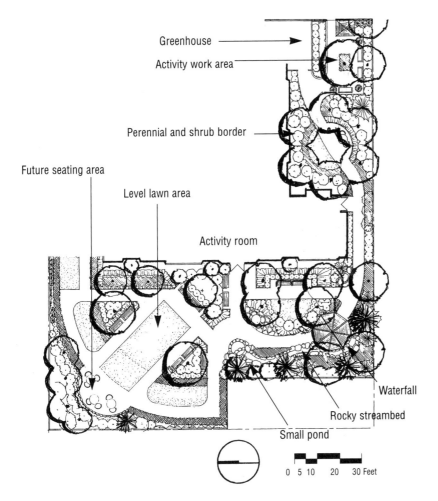

Greenhouse

Activity work area

Perennial and shrub border

Future seating area

Level lawn area

Activity room

Waterfall

Rocky streambed

Small pond

0 5 10   20   30 Feet

Figure 9-13   Site plan of the West garden, Oak Bay Kiwanis Pavilion, Victoria, B.C., Canada.

been colored to reduce glare. Entering the garden from the greenhouse, one sees an activity/work space, which is bordered by a raised planting bed, a toolshed, and a couple of garden benches in the shade of a trellis fence and Japanese maple trees. The path draws the visitor past a beautiful flowering perennial and shrub border next to a seating area for larger groups and then moves through a narrow space close to the building that leads into the west garden. The garden opens up as the path loops under a large open gazebo set into the slope of the site. The sound of a waterfall down the slope fills the space. A rocky stream bed feeds two small ponds holding fish and water plants. The slope behind the waterfall and stream is planted with trees, shrubs, and ground covers that bring the west coast woodland into the garden along with birds and butterflies. As one moves past the ponds there is a level lawn area surrounded by shade trees (still young) and garden benches. This area is large enough for outdoor events for residents and staff. Future development into the northwest corner of the site will extend the lawn out to a sitting area under existing large flowering trees. A walk around the lawn area along the flowering shrub borders brings the visitor to the activity room entrance and on to complete the loop back to the greenhouse.

An evaluation of the garden indicates that:

1. Safe and easy access in and out of the garden has been successful through level covered entrances/exits with broom finish concrete, glass canopies, nearby seating, and clear lines of sight into different garden areas. Residents have sure footing on level even surfaces (slopes do not exceed 2 percent). They see that they can have a seat right outside the door and at regular intervals along the path. They can see into the different garden areas, and know where they are, where they are going, and what to expect. Low voltage lighting was installed throughout the garden for security, safety, and aesthetics. It highlights the different garden areas and path system without strong lights glaring into the residents' windows or into the eyes of passersby.

2. Secure environment without the feeling of being trapped was successfully achieved with cedar trellis fences/gates and an overhanging trellis/arbor enclosing the garden. Trellis openings in the fence and gates are approximately 5 × 5 inches, allowing views into neighboring garden areas. The overhanging trellis/arbor prevents anyone from climbing over the fence. The garden gates look like part of the fence. They were designed for staff, maintenance crews, and to meet safety requirements—they are not recognized by the residents as "the way out." Magnetic security locks were put on the gates to allow coded entry by staff and to provide safety release in case of fire.

3. Continuous level looping pathways are successful in drawing residents through all parts of the garden while avoiding dead end situations that may cause dementia residents frustration. The broom finish concrete has no strong grade changes and no stairs. The coloring of the concrete in the west garden has been very successful in reducing glare.

4. Choice in the type of outdoor spaces are clear to the residents, staff, and families. Beyond a choice of sun or shade, the garden successfully gives the opportunity for large groups to gather in different areas for social activities/events. Also, individuals and small groups have the choice of sitting near the entrances, where they can watch activities going on around them, or finding a quiet corner for a more private/quiet visit. All

Figure 9-14 A classic red Buick in the South garden provides the opportunity for Alzheimer's patients to engage in familiar activities from earlier days, such as washing or polishing the car, or "going for a ride." (Photo by Hunter Photos, Victoria, B.C., Canada.)

garden seating and activity spaces are along the looping path system.

5. Items to stimulate memory, conversation, and activity were a major consideration for the garden and have been generally successful. Raised planting beds were provided for the staff and residents to plant with their own seasonal choices. The car was placed into one area of the garden as a conversation piece and center for activity. A woodland stream was developed along one edge of the garden with water plants, fish, and small waterfalls providing sights, sounds, and smells. As well, birds and butterflies are seen throughout the garden; even a lone blue heron was seen one spring by the ponds. A gazebo alongside the streambed provides a quiet shady place for refuge, visiting, or small group activities. A young family of swallows has nested in the gazebo. Birdhouses and birdbaths are to be added around the garden as funds are available. Two resident cats make all parts of the garden their home. An aviary which had been designed for the west garden area was cut in the final construction phase due to costs and maintenance concerns.

Figure 9-15   Patients enjoying a walk around a looped garden path in the West garden. Note seats with a table between for a cup of tea or a book. (Photo by Hunter Photos, Victoria, B.C., Canada.)

6. Safe planting designed to allow clear views through the garden allows visitors to look under the canopy of shade trees and over the tops of annuals, perennials, and flowering shrubs. All plants are nonpoisonous. Some plants were chosen as reminders of gardens of the residents' past, such as flowering Japanese cherry trees, lilac bushes, daisies, and annual plantings. A major consideration was the planting of additional shade trees; the existing landscape is very warm with south and west exposures and few existing shade trees. It will be a few years before the new trees provide adequate shade to make all the garden areas comfortable on hot summer days, but this is compensated for by the use of large colorful umbrellas.

7. Furnishings and amenities were chosen to give a comfortable "homey" feeling rather than an institutional finish. Cedar benches, tables with umbrellas, and seats with side tables are found around the garden; they were chosen for proper proportion and ease of getting in and out using armrests. Dark green powder coated aluminum handrails were installed in only a few areas as residents are able bodied, use walkers/canes, or have assistance from staff. The subtle color and simple design of the handrails avoids the "institutional" look while providing a low maintenance safety feature. If in the future additional handrails are necessary, they can be added easily as the concrete pathways were thickened at the edges to allow for this consideration.

Figure 9-16   Residents and staff gather along the pathway. Seating and layout of paths encourage socialization. (Photo by Hunter Photos, Victoria, B.C., Canada.)

ADVANTAGES

- Broom finish concrete paths increase traction.
- Paths in the West garden are tinted to reduce glare.
- Waterfall, stream, and ponds are attractive features and talking points.
- Lawn area large enough for social events.
- Pathway system is clear and forms level looping route.
- Plenty of choice of seating in sun or shade, in groups or alone.
- Gazebo provides a landmark and destination point.
- Items to stimulate memory—Buick Skylark, familiar seasonal flowers—have been successful.
- Trees and shrubs attract birds and butterflies.
- Security enhanced by views into all segments of garden and low voltage night lighting.
- Comfortable and attractive cedar benches in pairs with a table between.
- Range of fixed and movable seating, some with umbrellas for shade.
- Unobtrusive handrails in a few locations.
- Raised planter for staff and patients to plant annuals.

DISADVANTAGES

- Gray concrete in South garden causes glare problems.
- Stream was a hazard, but this has been rectified by screening with glass panels topped by wood at comfortable height to lean on.
- Concrete paths are not edged; slight drop from concrete to planting beds is a potential hazard.
- Some staff would prefer more color in the gardens: "The patients really respond to color!"
- Aviary in West garden had to be dropped for budgetary reasons; staff would like more special destinations to "lure" people outside.
- Three popular solaria looking onto gardens were originally fitted with automatic heat-sensitive blinds. The mechanism has broken and there is no budget to fix it. Staff have to make sure patients don't get overheated (as dementia progresses, internal "clock" that regulates heat, cold, and pain diminishes).

Providence Centre, Alzheimer Day Program Garden, Scarborough, Ontario, Canada

By Mary Jane Lovering, Vertechs Design, Toronto

Description of Facility and Its History

This garden is located on the grounds of Providence Centre in a suburb of Toronto, Ont. The 577-bed facility accommodates five distinct units for groups of individuals with special healthcare needs: the Home for the Aged, Continuing Care, Complex Medical/Palliative Care, Rehabilitation, and the Regional Geriatric Program.

The Alzheimer Day Program is a community based Day Program and part of the Home for the Aged. It provides individuals with Alzheimer's disease or a similar illness the opportunity for socialization, therapeutic recreation and relaxation in a homelike environment. Recreation therapists develop programs that are specifically designed for socialization and stimulation. The program is housed in a renovated portion of the hospital

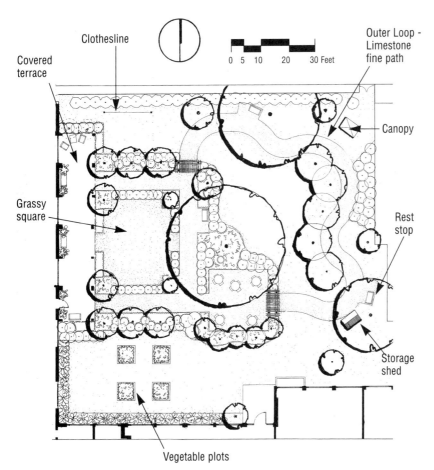

Figure 9-17   Site plan of the Providence Centre, Alzheimer Day Program Garden, Scarborough, Ont., Canada.

and presently operates five days a week and sees seventy seniors a month.

The garden was developed in concert with the renovation and is for the express use of these clients. It was anticipated that the location of this day program would be temporary and that it would be relocated to a new building housing the Home for the Aged. Accordingly, the budget was limited and decisions made about the choice of materials and landscape components were based on the "temporary" nature of the project. However, since completion of the planning stages for the new building, it was decided that the present location of the Day Care Program would be permanent.

The garden project began with the involvement of the director of the Day Program, the grounds maintenance staff, and the landscape architectural team. All stakeholders provided input regarding the program requirements of participants, safety concerns of staff, maintenance, and operational issues.

The primary purpose of the garden was to develop a space that would complement the ongoing interior programs, a place for clients to spend time in a purposeful way and to wander safely, offering choices and opportunities for activities that stimulate curiosity and are reminiscent of their daily routines at home.

Description of Outdoor Space

The garden was designed to motivate clients to go outdoors. Four microclimatic features necessary to facilitate comfortable use of the outdoor space in this region include: protection from glare, protection from sun, an absence of temperature extremes (heat traps), and an absence of wind. The goal was to provide a supportive environment for sitting and walking incorporating a range of sizes of spaces to accommodate large and small group gatherings and for a variety of activities.

Selection of nontoxic, thornless plant material including trees, shrubs, ground covers, and perennials introduces seasonal interest, change, and opportunities for sensory stimulation. The site had the advantage of an existing, covered concrete terrace immediately adjacent to the building exit doors, providing requisite shade for the clients. Three mature trees on the site not only possessed aesthetic appeal but also provided immediate shade, an asset with a restricted budget. The garden is enclosed on three sides by buildings, so new fencing and a gate were required only at the north end of the site. It was important that this gate for maintenance access remain unobtrusive; hence the pathway does not lead to it. The walkway system is a double loop, leading individuals from the terrace along an allée of flowering trees

Figure 9-18 Men's lawn bowling team at Providence Centre's Alzheimer's facility.

underplanted with perennials that bloom throughout the season. The main path leads to a large square patio, which provides an opportunity for groups to gather shaded by a mature Norway maple tree. The walkways link destination points or activity zones such as this throughout the garden.

The longer loop passes under an arbor covered with silver lace vine and proceeds past a rest stop and garden shed to follow a meandering route back to the terrace. All of the components within the garden provide landmarks or destination points to assist clients' orientation. The contrast between the green grass and crushed fines walkway provides a visual cue that leads people along the path to various destination points. It was originally intended that the path be constructed of concrete, which offers the ideal nonslip surface and minimum joints. However, there were considerable cost savings associated with the decision to use a crushed fines path instead of concrete, and the director of the program feels that this material is both less institutional and more residential in nature than concrete. Staff wanted as much grass as possible, not only for program use but also because it reflects most of the clients' home settings. The vegetable plot area provides designated spaces for clients to transplant seedlings, grow vegetables, weed the beds and harvest produce. Because the plots are not raised—as the budget did not allow for this at the time of construction—it is difficult for participants who have problems bending to work. Plans are underway to introduce some raised planters. The large grassy area along the meandering path is a place where small groups gather under a canopy providing needed shade. The scale and the decorative pattern of the canopy enhances the homelike ambience.

Figure 9-19 Women with Alzheimer's disease enjoy engaging in familiar activities from earlier days.

Figure 9-20 *The garden is a place for people to spend time in a purposeful way, involved in activities reminiscent of daily routines at home.*

An elderly male resident remarked:

"When I lived in Russia I had a garden. We could plant many things that were useful and necessary in daily life. My grandfather used to smoke tobacco so I learned from my neighbors how to grow and care for tobacco. It was very interesting. We also grew vegetables. We did big farming in my childhood. As grandkids, we learned how to grow tomatoes and cucumbers."

A clothesline has been provided at the northwest corner of the garden, close to the terrace, so that individuals can participate in familiar outdoor routines. Clothing and linens are washed indoors and hung on the line by the clients. The grassy square immediately adjacent to the terrace is used for games such as ball toss, bocce ball, croquet, and exercise groups. From time to time furniture is rearranged for lunches and tea parties in this space, which is close to the interior. The flexibility of the space allows staff to rearrange site furnishings to suit specific program requirements. Garden ornaments provide a residential ambience. Clay pots with annuals, an Adirondack chair, bird feeders, and garden sculpture provide interest for the clients and their families.

Use

The garden provides a milieu for socializing. On a typical day clients and staff can be seen engaged in an exercise program in the grassy square while two or three of the ladies are hanging linen on the line. A small group luxuriates in foot soaks under the maple tree while bird enthusiasts mix the seed for the feeders. The gardeners measure the height of the sunflowers, weed the tomato plants, and tie the beans to the obelisks within the garden beds. Clients use the garden independently to meander along the pathway or sit in one of the many spaces within the garden. Staff organize numerous special events, such as strawberry socials and ice cream parties. Families participate on a regular basis.

In the near future the day program will be extended to a continuous twenty-four hours. Plans are underway to incorporate raised beds within the vegetable plot area. A woodpile and wheelbarrows have been ordered to create opportunities for additional activities for some of the men in the program. There have been discussions about inclusion of a water feature incorporating fish and the possibility of a real car.

If this type of garden with its perennial plantings is contemplated, there must be a commitment at all levels, including administration and grounds maintenance, to ensure that the garden is cared for. It is not practical to assume that clients and nursing staff will be responsible for maintenance. Weeding or deadheading may be a program activity of short duration on any given day but attention spans are short and usually it is a one-on-one activity. Staff within this type of a program have too many responsibilities to be expected to maintain the garden. Staff have suggested in the future that plants be selected with which this age group is familiar: old favorites such as daisies, black-eyed susans, peonies, and hollyhocks initiate conversations about clients' own gardens from the past.

ADVANTAGES

- Covered porch creates shade and shelter from rain.
- Garden complements ongoing interior programs.
- Subareas offer choices and opportunities for numerous activities.
- Flexibility of space allows for simultaneous activities and change.
- Seasonal plantings introduce change.
- Mature trees provide immediate shade.
- Opportunities provide participants with daily routines of home.
- Designed to assist with way-finding and cueing.

DISADVANTAGES

- Lack of raised beds and paved access makes gardening difficult for some.
- Perennials require maintenance and this has presented problems.
- Lack of automatic watering system makes maintenance more difficult and inconvenient.

Figure 9-21   Clients work in the vegetable plot area, watering plants, transplanting seedlings, growing vegetables, weeding beds, and harvesting produce.

Chemainus Health Care Centre, Chemainus, British Columbia, Canada

Edward A. Stillinger, Landscape Architect[1]

Description of Facility and Its History

The small town of Chemainus is located on the east coast of Vancouver Island in British Columbia, Canada. The Chemainus Health Care Centre, built in 1898, is located on the site of the town's first hospital overlooking Horseshoe Bay. Over the intervening years the hospital has been transformed from an acute care hospital to primarily a long-term care facility providing residence for people with physical frailties and/or dementia. The provision of the new facility was in accordance with the Province of British Columbia Ministry of Health's program to provide community based long term care. The new facility would provide multilevel care from an emergency room with four beds and day surgery to full long-term care for seventy-four residents who could not be cared for in a home situation. The facility was to have a dedicated wing for residents with dementia related ill-

[1]The author would like to acknowledge the assistance of Clarice Guillon, Activation, Adult Daycare, and Volunteer Director, Chemainus Health Care Centre, in preparing the case study.

nesses (Alzheimer's being the most publicly recognized), with the balance of the facility to serve physically frail residents.

The Planning Process

Planning the outdoor spaces for this new facility began with a Garden Design Working Group consisting of a Ministry of Health representative, the facility administrator, a member of the Chemainus Auxiliary, a representative from the building architects, the Activation, Adult Daycare and Volunteer Director and the Landscape Architects. The group agreed on three significant goals for the garden:

1. To allow each resident to benefit to the maximum of his or her capabilities.
2. To be a significant aspect of the residents' daily life.
3. To be integral to the program of care provided at Chemainus Health Care Centre.

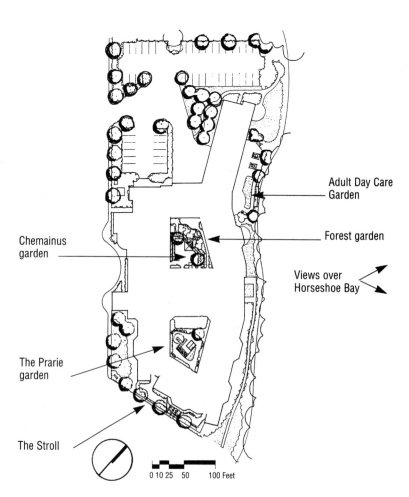

Figure 9-22 Site plan of Chemainus Health Care Centre, Chemainus, B.C., Canada.

Adult Day Care Garden

Forest garden

Chemainus garden

Views over Horseshoe Bay

The Prarie garden

The Stroll

0 10 25 50   100 Feet

These attitudes were felt to be important because, without commitment from the facility to fully utilize these spaces, they could too easily end up being ignored and become derelict. With the commitment to program the gardens for resident activities the designers had valuable input as to what might be appropriate in the garden design. At each step of the design process, all elements of the design were evaluated against the residents' abilities to utilize and benefit from them.

A significant inspiration for the Chemainus facility was the design model espoused by Dr. John Tooth at his dementia care facility in Tasmania, Australia. Tooth's model proposes creating an environment for the entire facility that resembles a normal residential home. The principals of this model are :

1. Create an environment familiar in appearance, which inspires a sense of home.
2. Provide residents with safe and secure places to wander, places that are calming and reassuring to residents.
3. Provide activities that residents are capable of undertaking and that are meaningful to them, promoting the highest level of functioning and self-esteem, and resulting in an improved quality of life.

In researching the backgrounds of residents for the sense of what is familiar to them, the Working Group discovered that the majority had lived the early part of their lives in one of the Prairie provinces. With this information, the group realized that the familiar environment to be recreated was the suburban/rural residential backyard found in many prairie towns and cities. This decision gave direction to plant material choices and suggested appropriate garden elements.

The Working Group also listed resident needs for outdoor environments:

1. Walking routes for wanderers, who need to "loop" back to starting points.
2. Shaded areas for passive and active pursuits.
3. Opportunity for solitary as well as group activities.
4. Need for moderate versus intense stimulation—sound, color, fragrance.
5. Nontoxic plant material.

The garden design development provided an opportunity for residents to participate directly and to exercise some control

A staff member spoke of the garden at the residence where she worked:

"A garden is a pleasant place where residents can get exercise while enjoying the benefits of sunshine, fresh air, and fond memories of their previous homes."

over their environment. In one instance a prototype of a proposed garden bench was supplied to the Healthcare Centre. It was placed in a resident common area and staff solicited comments from residents regarding the comfort of the bench. Comments were relayed to the manufacturer, and the bench design was altered. A second bench, incorporating the design changes, was provided for resident trial. Again comments were solicited and recommended changes sent to the manufacturer. It is this third version of the bench that is used at Chemainus. In another instance a consensus vote among residents determined the color scheme for the shed. Staff organized the discussion but offered no suggestions of their own and committed to accepting the residents' decision as final. In both these circumstances, residents were able to realize that their opinions about their "home" would be listened to and respected.

The program director's concerns included:

1. Walking surfaces that would be smooth, gently sloped, and provide good traction.
2. Flexible spaces to accommodate a variety of activities.
3. Activities other than gardening that residents enjoy, for example, basketball.
4. Access to drinking water in gardens.
5. Areas for residents to garden and worktable heights appropriate to residents' capabilities.
6. Watering system to be used by residents in gardening activities.
7. Night lighting to allow access to garden walkways twenty-four hours a day.
8. Storage for garden activity supplies.

Description of Outdoor Spaces

The outdoor areas consist of five distinct garden spaces: the Stroll, the Prairie Garden, Adult Day Care Garden, Chemainus Garden, and Forest Garden.

The garden known as the *Stroll* utilizes a narrow strip along the south side of the building, which—together with a parallel interior corridor—creates a continuous walking loop. Large canopy trees, a vine covered trellis, and the building orientation provide shade. Benches are arranged along the Stroll to take advantage of different shade opportunities and to provide places for solitary pursuits. A water tap that residents can operate independently is placed beside the route. An active zone was established at the west end of the Stroll that includes a basketball hoop and a clothesline. This active area is well used for bas-

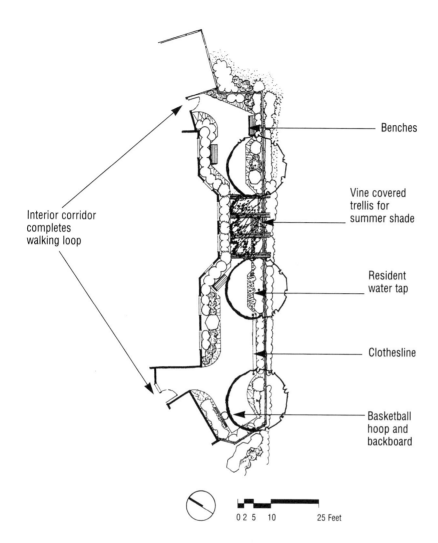

Benches

Vine covered
trellis for
summer shade

Interior corridor
completes
walking loop

Resident
water tap

Clothesline

Basketball
hoop and
backboard

0 2 5   10   25 Feet

*Figure 9-23   Site plan of the Stroll,
Chemainus Health Care Centre,
Chemainus, B.C., Canada.*

ketball games, either on an independent basis or as part of organized programs that include residents and staff. One notable
result has been the regular games of "hoops" between a grandfather and his thirteen-year-old grandson. The game allows the
grandson to relate to his grandfather in a nonthreatening environment. He does not have to face a "hospital" setting and does
not have to directly confront the decline in his grandfather's
health. The game has allowed the two to relate to each other
comfortably. The grandson might not visit as often or as long
without this activity to share. The clothesline also is used regularly. All manner of items are hung to dry—stuffed animals,
dish towels, shoes. Residents comment when something on the
line strikes them as funny. The benches along the outside portion of the Stroll are utilized for small group activities, such as

reading or reminiscing with family members. Mental aerobics classes are held out here as well.

The indoor/outdoor aspect of the loop works well for residents who need to wander. In fact, chairs have been added to the indoor corridor, in a similar fashion to the outdoor benches, for residents to use as rest points along their walk. Initial concerns that the limited available outdoor space would be insufficient have proven to be unfounded. The hybrid indoor-outdoor wandering loop has turned out to be successful. Staff speculate that some wanderers would not use the Stroll if it were not for the number of benches, as they enable residents to walk short distances before resting.

The basketball hoop and clothesline are used regularly and enable those who might not otherwise engage in any activity to get physical exercise. The clothesline provides an opportunity for some residents to engage in a familiar activity that provides a sense of accomplishment and contributes to their self-worth. Residents do not use the tap provided for them but having water available is valuable as staff do not have to leave an agitated resident in order to get water from inside the building. Dehydration is a significant concern for residents with dementia.

At one end of the Stroll the fence is chain-link. In 1997, one resident in particular was found clinging to this fence staring out in a highly agitated state. Remedial measures are proposed to provide a more solid fence, comparable to the other fences in the Stroll.

The Prairie Garden can be seen from the main dining area and residents who do not live in the dementia wing of the facility regularly observe activities that go on in the garden. For residents in the dementia wing it has become a center of their daily life. A toolshed serves the multiple purposes of familiar reference, garden supplies, storage, and inclement weather garden work area. Residents prepare potting soil mixtures and organize the pots and garden tools inside the shed. It has been designed to allow through passage to minimize agitation by wanderers. Resident activities in the shed can be observed by staff from any point in the garden, allowing residents to feel they are working on their own while staff can monitor for safety or socialization concerns. Only tools that are a safety concern, for example, pruning shears, are kept locked away.

Outside the shed residents pump water from an old-fashioned hand pump into watering cans for their regular garden watering rounds. A hand pump is a familiar image to prairie residents. One resident enjoys pumping water whether there are watering cans to fill or not. Other residents, working more independently, use the water taps in each raised planter. In the

Figure 9-24 A washing line (left) and basketball hoop are well-used by residents at Chemainus Health Care Centre. Clarice Guillon (Activation Director) and Edward Stillinger (Landscape Architect) discuss how the garden is used. (Photo by Clare Cooper Marcus.)

evenings residents who are restless wander through the garden alone or with assistance along the lighted paths.

The opportunity to "do for others" is important to residents' sense of self-worth, and the garden suggests activities that meet this need. Herbs from the garden are dried and packaged. Residents can sell these or offer them as presents. Over the winter residents construct birdhouses that hang in the garden. Another indoor project stimulated by the garden has been the stenciling and painting of planter pots that are displayed at the main entry and on decks outside resident lounges. The plants to in the pots are also selected by residents as a planned group activity.

The walkway system in this garden loops in three routes back to a starting point and has seating arranged to allow solitary experiences or observation of group activities. A movable worktable can be placed in the shady part of the garden under the vine covered trellis according to the time of day and season of the year. It can also be moved out of the way to allow for other group activities within the garden. Raised planters in the areas for active gardening involve residents to the greatest degree possible in gardening activities. Each planter has a tap that residents can operate to water the particular part of the garden they are working on that day.

Residents use this garden to enjoy activities with their families such as reading, visiting, playing games, and picking strawberries. Staff organize picnics and barbecues for residents and their families. They also organize activity programs specifically for the residents. The worktable is moved to the side and ring toss, bean bag throws, and bubble ball games are enjoyed in the central patio area. A reading group might use the space one afternoon a week. Residents plant, tend, and water raised garden beds with assistance from volunteers and staff. After sessions with residents to determine their preferences, herbs have been added to the garden for aromatherapy. The Prairie Garden is separated from the dining patio by a landscape buffer intended to represent the border planting between two traditional prairie homes. Plants with toxic qualities had been eliminated from the potential selections. Further to that point, plants with edible fruit (apple, strawberry, grape) have been incorporated into the garden. Residents are encouraged to pick the fruit when it is ripe.

Observations on design details include the need for more shaded area for project work. Residents cannot stay in the direct summer sun for long periods of time. Also, the shade devices designed must work in the short term. In this garden the trellis will work well when the vines cover it. Until then a bamboo screen has been placed over the trellis to provide the necessary shade over the project working table.

A staff member who encouraged residents to become involved in the garden remarked:

"Flowers and plants give residents responsibilities if they are used to gardening. They like to water them, look after them ..."

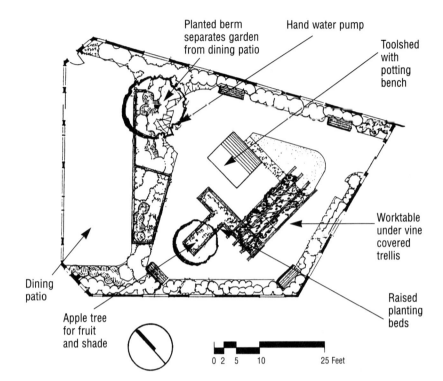

Figure 9-25 Site plan of the Prairie Garden, Chemainus Health Care Centre, Chemainus, B.C., Canada.

Planted berm separates garden from dining patio

Hand water pump

Toolshed with potting bench

Worktable under vine covered trellis

Raised planting beds

Dining patio

Apple tree for fruit and shade

0 2 5   10   25 Feet

Figure 9-26 Resident and volunteer preparing soil in the potting shed of the Prairie Garden.

Residents engage in gardening activities according to the limit of their individual capabilities and to the degree the garden design and gardening tools make it possible. For example, hand tools with oversized grips work best and encourage use. Watering cans need to be sized to respect the limited strength of the residents. The watering taps at the raised beds must be easily operable and at the right height as residents' strength and flexibility are limited. The raised planters and the worktables must be at heights that allow the residents to work without bending over. Residents who are not completely stable on their feet fall over if required to bend too far to garden or work on a project.

This garden has provided opportunity for solitary and independent activity, which has directly benefited several residents. One individual, formerly a regular "eloper," now wanders into the garden and becomes caught up in exploring the garden and no longer seeks to escape from the residence. Another, who had previously acted out anger and frustration by forceably removing anything that was hung on the walls in the dementia wing is now regularly active in the garden using the hand pump. The previous destructive activity has stopped. This is particularly significant as many other attempts to redirect resident's destructive behavior had proved unsuccessful. Another resident regularly goes into the garden to pick a flower to present to his wife when she comes to visit. For this person the garden has provided an opportunity to reinforce a significant relationship.

The Adult Daycare Garden also intended for use by people with dementia, is located on the east edge of the site in an area between the building and a steep bank down to the ocean. For safety reasons a combination of raised planter, deep garden beds, and chain-link fencing were employed to create a border along the bank edge. The garden has extensive raised planters (with water taps similar to the Prairie Garden), an open paved area, and a looped walkway system to accommodate the participants in the day care programs. In this garden plants that would normally be found in the Chemainus area have been selected since these would be familiar to the more highly functioning people in the day care program. Plants were reviewed for their potential toxic properties and edible plants (apple, strawberry, blueberry) were incorporated into the planting design and are appreciated by the clients.

All the activities described in the Prairie Garden can and do take place in this garden as well. The participants here are not residents but members of the local community who come for group activities once a week. The clients have personalized their garden adding a wishing well built by a local craftsman, birdhouses built by day care participants, and a large Canadian flag. Picnics for up to fifty people—families, friends, and staff—have been held in this garden.

The raised planters in this garden have provided two insights. First, the soil must be easy to work. The soil needed to be amended twice to make it sufficiently light for day care participants. Second, day care participants did not comprehend that the square planters were meant to have annuals planted around the edges. Instead the clients consistently tried to plant in rows. As a result, the planting plans for the square planters have been adjusted to conform the participants' preconceptions. These insights illustrate three important aspects of garden design for people with dementia. First, residents should not be challenged beyond their capabilities, Second, the garden must be designed to the users' perceptions. Third, if the design is not fully utilized by its users, or doesn't meet their needs, it must be changed as the users cannot be expected to adapt to it.

The Chemainus Garden is a courtyard garden that accommodates the grade change from the main floor to the lower floor level; approximately 10.3 feet. The upper portion of the garden—named the Chemainus Garden—was intended for cognitively well residents who are physically frail. Its design aims to provide gardening opportunities for people in wheelchairs. A raised planter designed to allow a person in a wheel-

A male resident reminisced:

"I like gardening. I had several of them at the house. I took four years of agriculture in school. I know how to raise chickens, too."

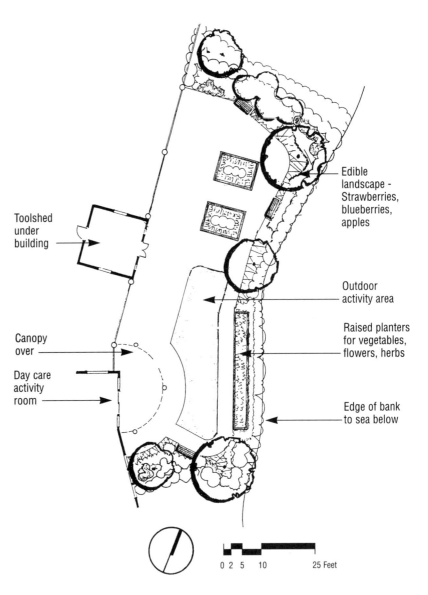

Toolshed
under
building

*Figure 9-27   Site Plan of the Adult
Day Care Garden.*

Canopy
over

Day care
activity
room

Edible
landscape -
Strawberries,
blueberries,
apples

Outdoor
activity area

Raised planters
for vegetables,
flowers, herbs

Edge of bank
to sea below

0 2 5   10   25 Feet

chair easy access to a planting bed runs along much of the garden perimeter. The particular design of the planter edge is significant. The edge timber is consistent in dimension for all
planters and worktables. Designed to hang off this edge is a
portable metal tool basket, which allows residents to organize
their gardening activities and undertake them with a high level
of independence. These are tool baskets which can be moved to
any planter edge or worktable to support a wide variety of garden activities, for example, they can hold a cup of coffee or a
book just as well as a trowel. A movable worktable and a fold-
down table have been included in this space to provide an even
greater setup area for gardening projects.

The central gazebo structure in the garden provides needed shade. The garden has a large open paved area to support a variety of group activities, or for use by residents in a gerry chair or bed. In this garden residents can be seen tending their garden plots daily. Groups gather around the worktable in the shade of the gazebo, mixing soil and preparing hanging baskets or planter pots. The patio area can be filled with extra tables and chairs for picnics or family dinners. This garden is open twenty-four hours a day and residents can be seen strolling through at all hours. Having a planting garden has also generated indoor activities. Plant selection for spring seeding has become an art collage project, as pictures from seed packets have been enthusiastically arranged by residents into a poster which can be hung on the activity room wall.

The planter edge designed for residents in wheelchairs has been successful. One resident confined to a motorized wheelchair previously had no outdoor activity that was within his abilities. After this garden was built, his family presented him with a gift of gardening tools and he now works daily on his garden. The movable tool baskets that allow residents to garden with a greater degree of independence have greatly assisted in the success of this garden. As in the other gardens, the gardening program has supported additional activities. Residents decorate the pots, choose the plants, assemble the pots, and then tend them over the growing season. Birdhouses and birdfeeders have been added as well. The gazebo provides the immediate

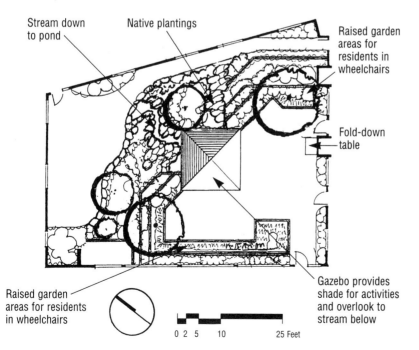

Figure 9-28 Site plan of the Forest and Chemainus Gardens, Chemainus Health Care Centre, Chemainus, B.C., Canada.

Figure 9-29   A side by side bench is excellent for visiting. Middle armrest greatly assists residents in getting up and sitting down. It's also a place for a cup of tea or a book. Two earlier versions of this bench design were tested out in the facility, and resident opinions solicited. The manufacturer altered the design until an acceptable bench was created.

Not all residents want to actively garden:

"I think gardens are beautiful. I myself do not garden. I don't like the hot sun or getting dirt under my fingernails. It's nice, though, when someone brings me fresh vegetables or beautiful flowers from the garden."

shade required for outdoor projects, allowing movable tables to be placed in the side for resident project sessions or moved out if the desire is to set up seating for a picnic, barbecue, or family meal. The fold-down table has proved remarkably helpful. It serves a variety of purposes such as a staff preparation area, watering wand holding spot, or resident worktable. The fact that it folds down out of the way is very useful in keeping the maximum space available for group gatherings like a barbecue.

Storage of gardening tools and supplies must always be considered. In the limited space in this garden, a full sized toolshed was not possible and items such as hoses and water wands can get left out, becoming a hazard to residents wandering through the garden.

The gazebo and raised planter creates the edge between this garden and the lower-level *Forest Garden*, which is not accessible to residents and which has a small patio area for staff. A small stream course starts at the base of the gazebo and travels down to a pond in the Forest Garden. Plants in this garden are native to the east coast of Vancouver Island. These two gardens are the only outside view for those resident rooms that face into this courtyard. Residents in these rooms are cognitively well and for that reason it was judged appropriate that the gardens they look upon be representative of the beauty in the gardens of their town and the surrounding natural environment.

Conclusions

Although only one year old at the time of this report, the gardens at Chemainus Health Care Centre have proved to be a highly positive contribution to the life of the residents and day care participants. Observations of positive benefits include reduction of aggression, signifcant elimination of "elopements," greater physical fitness, enhancement of self-esteem, and personal satisfaction.

That the garden design was as successful as it has been was in large part due to two factors in the design process:

1. Chemainus Health Care Centre had committed to fully utilize the therapeutic gardens as part of the complete program of care provided for long-term residents and day care participants.
2. The design process was a collaboration between designers, healthcare providers, and residents to create gardens that responded to the needs, desires, and capabilities of the residents and day care participants—a "user first" design policy.

The Centre's commitment was demonstrated through the invaluable input provided to the designers regarding the manifestations of dementia diseases and the physical and mental capabilities of residents and their known interests and activities. Currently fourteen staff have taken horticultural therapy training so that whoever is on duty can assist residents in gardening activities.

Lessons learned that bear repeating are :

1. The garden must be designed to the users' capabilities.
2. The users will not adapt to the garden design; it must be adapted to the users.
3. Attention to detail is very important. Proper paving treatments, bench designs, shade devices, planter heights, watering systems, gardening tools, and potting soil make an incalculable difference in how well the users can use and benefit from the gardens.
4. Gardens can generate additional year-round activities.
5. Design references and cues for long-term memory seem to be effective and should be considered when developing concept designs.

Suggestions that developed from this project are:

1. Post-occupancy evaluations and appropriate redesign are a particularly significant part of the design process since these particular users cannot easily adapt.
2. Inclusion of the garden design group from the outset of the facility design assists in creating garden spaces of sufficient size to accommodate desired programs appropriate to user needs while providing adequate privacy for resident rooms facing onto garden spaces.
3. Consideration of long-term maintenance of the gardens needs to be part of the facility planning/design process. Residents do not maintain gardens reliably, so staff will still be required to undertake regular maintenance.

Advantages

- Commitment of Chemainus Health Care staff to incorporate gardens into daily life of residents and day care participants has led to a "user first" approach to all garden design decisions.
- Care providers are educated in horticultural therapy.
- Resident participation in design has increased satisfaction—testing the bench design, choosing shed colors, adding birdfeeders and birdhouses.

Figure 9-30   Looking down the Stroll, showing benches in shade and sun for people to rest while "wandering."

- Gardens stimulate indoor activities.
- Elements in gardens referencing long-term memory are effective—hand pump, toolshed, clothesline.
- Raised planters with watering taps are well used.
- Garden planters designed for residents in wheelchairs very popular.
- The gazebo is a shady spot and is a center of group activities.
- Movable outdoor worktables have proved very useful.
- Indoor/outdoor wandering loop is well used.
- Open areas for group activities.
- There are lots of places to sit.
- Toolsheds incorporated into the garden eases the burden of maintenance and allows clients to participate.
- Tool baskets provide significant support for independent garden activity.
- Pathway lighting supports evening use of resident gardens.

DISADVANTAGES
- Need for additional shade until canopy trees and covering vines grow in.
- Transparent fences have caused distress in some residents.
- The planting plan for the square raised planters did not conform to residents' expectations.
- Soil in raised planters needed to be easier to work.
- Some of the gardens are not large enough for a toolshed.
- Not all garden spaces are of an adequate size to accommodate desired activities and provide privacy.
- Landscape buffer between Prairie Garden and dining patio had to be supplemented with fence to control wandering.

Sedgewood Commons, Falmouth, Maine
by Robert Hoover, Landscape Architect

Description of the Facility
Sedgewood Commons is located in Falmouth, Maine. It is modeled after the traditional one-story single-family home familiar to the majority of residents. Residential scale is achieved by breaking the facility into three wings, each a separate special care unit, with each unit further subdivided into two houses. The three wings, named after the New England poets Hawthorne, Longfellow, and Millay, provide a complete continuum of care for

all stages of Alzheimer's disease. The Hawthorne wing is home to those residents with mild conditions of Alzheimer's disease. The Longfellow wing is the nursing care unit for those in the moderate stages of the disease, and the Millay wing is the advanced nursing care unit for those in the moderately severe to severe stages of the disease. Directly associated with these three wings are three distinct therapeutic gardens. Inside each unit wandering paths and window views have been coordinated to reinforce the connection between the interior environment and the exterior landscape.

History
Sedgewood Commons, owned and developed by the Sandy River Group of Portland, ME, was opened in January 1994. The architectural firm, S.M.R.T., and the landscape architect, Robert Hoover, Studio L.A., worked in collaboration to produce the 95-bed, 46,000 square foot facility.

Description of Outdoor Space
The gardens at Sedgewood Commons were designed based on Hoover's theoretical design model called "Remembrance Therapy" (Hoover, 1995). Simply stated, Remembrance Therapy puts forth the concept that each stage of Alzheimer's disease—early, moderate, and severe—is associated with a corresponding regression through the stages of normal human development—late, mid, and early. Always respecting chronological age and individual dignity, the gardens are thus designed to respond to the emotional needs of each corresponding opposite stage of normal human development. Grounded in research, Remembrance Therapy takes root in Barry Reisberg's "progressive degenerative disease model" and "corresponding developmental studies" (Reisberg et al., 1982; Reisberg, 1986), in Eric Erikson's "stages of human development" (Erikson, 1982), in the "emotions" work of Elisabeth Kübler-Ross (Kübler-Ross, 1982), in the "landscape archetypal" studies of Julie Messervy (Messervy, 1990), and in the "design guidelines" of Mary Jane Lovering (Lovering, 1990) and Uriel Cohen and Gerald Weisman (Cohen and Weisman, 1991).

In addition to Remembrance Therapy, conceptual design guidelines were also incorporated into the design process. They were: (1) supporting individual autonomy and risk taking; (2) satisfying the fundamental need for emotional and physical safety; (3) providing for way-finding and orientation; (4) incorporating appropriate use of non-toxic plantings; and (5) providing for sensory stimulation without stress. By using Remembrance Therapy as a model against which to evaluate the above-referenced design guidelines, a flexible and thus individualized design response was achieved.

A resident recalled her life before moving to an Alzheimer's facility:

"I was president of the garden club. I enjoy seeing gardens grow and like growing vegetables."

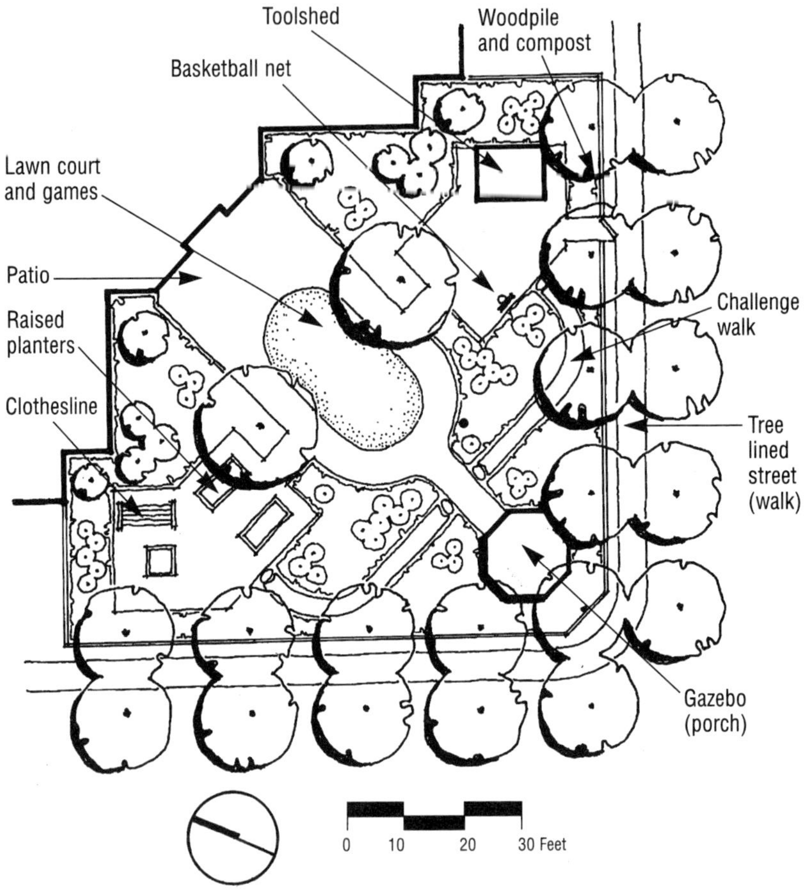

Figure 9-31 Site plan of the Hawthorne Garden, Sedgewood Commons, Falmouth, ME.

The Hawthorne Garden is designed for those in the early stage of the disease (Cohen and Weisman, 1991). Remembrance Therapy holds that this stage of the disease corresponds to those characteristics displayed in adult (late) normal human development (Reisberg et al., 1982; Reisberg, 1986). Accordingly, normal adult human development suggests the notion of independence, risk taking, and autonomy (Erickson, 1982). In response, the archetypal landscape selected conceptually implies a more traditional New England style home consistent with the cultural heritage of those residents who live there (Messervy, 1990). Elements consistent with a traditional New England home are reflected through the use of a white picket fence bordering a tree-lined street, which has been abstracted to a walking path. A woodpile, compost heap, and toolshed serve as activity areas and provide appropriate levels of stimulation. A basketball net, play court, and place for a putting green are also included. A laundry yard with a clothesline and gardens with wheelchair accessible raised planters as well as ground level planting beds are provided to support horticultural therapy and general gardening, in addition to more passive uses. A house with a screened-in porch, in this case abstracted into a gazebo, is also included. Two types of foot paths are provided. One foot path paved with a loose, crushed stone is often fondly referred to as "the challenge walk." It is the intent of this walk to support the notion of autonomy and risk taking. At the same time the primary brick paved strolling path includes both larger, more public, and smaller, more intimate, spaces, allowing for additional options of choice and self-determination.

Finally, plantings address bold colors and pleasant familiar fragrances. For users at this stage of the disease, plant toxicity is not considered an issue. Therefore, rhododendrons and azaleas are included along with lilacs, honeysuckle, and roses, all of which provide colors and smells that bring clients back in time and hopefully evoke memories.

The Longfellow Garden serves those in the moderate stage of the disease (Cohen and Wiseman, 1991) and is based on the resident needs associated with early to mid stages of normal human development (Reisberg et al., 1982; Reisberg, 1986; Erickson, 1982). The landscape archetype chosen for this garden was the cloister garden (Messervy, 1990). The cloister garden was then abstracted into a New England theme consistent with residents' cultural heritage

Figure 9-32 Hawthorne Garden , a traditional New England garden with multipurpose lawn panel reflective of home. (Photo by Jim Daniels.)

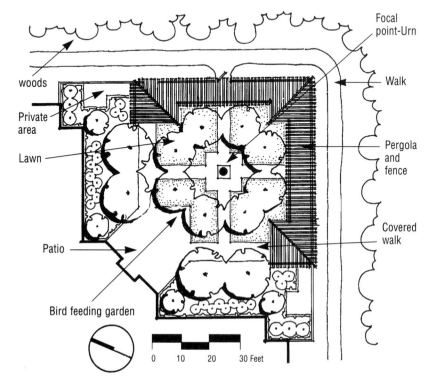

Figure 9-33 Site plan of the Longfellow Garden, Sedgewood Commons, Falmouth, ME.

Asked about the garden, a resident replied:

"It gives you a place to go, gives you sunshine and air. ... Yeah, the garden is important."

Figure 9-35 A quiet sitting spot in the Millay garden is consistent with the needs of late stage Alzheimer's disease. (Photo by Jim Daniels.)

through the use of a traditional, wooden pergola. It is the intent of the central open space of this garden to represent the notion of ongoing process, evolution, and development. This design is thought of as being consistent with characteristics associated with mid-stages of normal human development (Erickson, 1982). The exterior of the garden, the pergola, represents protection and security versus risk and decision making. A strolling loop for walking with ordered options and views back to the front door are provided to minimize disorientation, while a Grecian urn serving as a focal point is found in the middle of this garden and further serves as a place of reference. As a result, residents are allowed to express autonomy through choice in movement, yet at the same time can feel secure that all decisions ultimately lead back to the beginning. In addition there are several bird feeding stations and two raised planters designed for wheelchair use. Carefully placed plantings (toxicity can be an issue) of rhododendrons and azaleas, in addition to lilacs, honeysuckle, and roses, are included. This garden was designed to evolve and develop over time as residents and administrative needs change and are further defined and then again redefined.

The Millay Garden is designed for residents in the moderately severe to severe stage of the disease (Cohen and Weisman, 1991). Accordingly, this stage of the disease corresponds to early, normal human development (Reisberg et al., 1982; Reisberg, 1986). In this case the Japanese garden is abstracted into a traditional New England meadow stream, again consistent with the residents' cultural heritage, is employed as the archetypal landscape to meet the needs associated with early, normal human development (Messervy, 1990). This archetype represents, at its very core, peacefulness, safety, and security (Erickson, 1982). Within the garden the major focal points, acting as unifying elements, are a meadow, one large old tree, and a small winding brook. As the facility was not able to afford the costs associated with an active water feature, the brook was abstracted into a dry stream bed. It is this tree, meadow, flowers, and dry stream bed that provide the feeling of peacefulness and harmony consistent with the fundamental emotional needs of early, normal human development; yet at the same time they represent a dignified response appropriate for an adult. Another important design element for this stage of the disease is enclosure. Here a custom-designed fence with a horizontal overhang responds to the basic need for emotional safety. This gesture attempts to evoke a feeling of calm and what might be thought of as "embracing arms." Physical safety is further provided through the vertical design of the fence, which avoids potential "toe holds" that might be used for exiting. In addition, the overall size of the garden is carefully scaled to provide for several intimate settings, further reinforc-

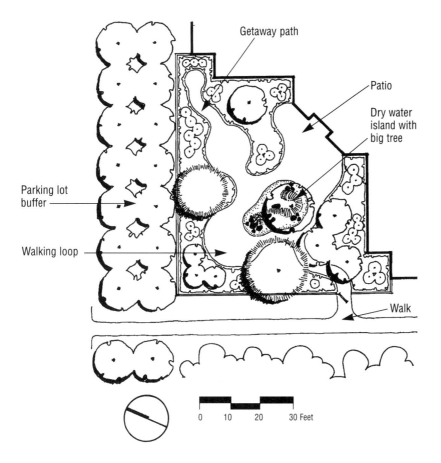

Figure 9-34   Site plan of the Millay Garden, Sedgewood Commons, Falmouth, ME.

ing the feeling of safety and security. A gently winding, self-contained strolling loop allows for ease of use, clarity of direction, and a return to the beginning. The use of exposed aggregate paving with hidden expansion joints further unifies the surface area and avoids potentially confusing paving patterns. "Old time," nontoxic plantings, such as lilacs, honeysuckle, and roses provides wonderfully fragrant smells evoking memories of the past, and birdfeeders for small birds further reinforce intimacy, providing another appropriate level of stimulation without stress for this stage of Alzheimer's disease.

Use and Evaluation

No formal post-occupancy evaluation study of these gardens has been conducted. The following anecdotes are illustrative of activities in the Hawthorne Garden.

One of the architects tells of an experience he had with his mother, who was a resident in the Hawthorne House. One morning at breakfast a fellow resident, who was agitated, hit her. After that experience she couldn't stop talking about "the bad, bad man," nor could she seem to relax. She was distressed

A female resident remarked to a staff member:

"I love gardening—when somebody else does it."

and nothing her son did helped. Fortunately, that same day an outdoor concert and cookout were scheduled. When the architect took his mother outside into the garden to join the concert and cookout, she immediately calmed down. Her fears "seemed to disappear," and all she could talk about was "Oh, what a wonderful day." Her previous agitation did not reappear. In the Hawthorne Garden every day at mid-morning one woman brings out her laundry in a laundry basket and hangs up her clothes on the line while she chats with a friend.

On one occasion, the landscape architect was catching a basketball for a resident in the Hawthorne Garden. At first there was only silence. After a short time, however, this gentle resident started to talk of his high school days and a playoff game he lost when he missed a free throw. This man was reliving his life with the help of the garden.

ADVANTAGES AND DISADVANTAGES

Hawthorne Garden

1. Remembrance Therapy appears to provide an environment that is used and appreciated by early-stage Alzheimer's patients.
2. The basketball hoop, clothesline, and raised planters are actively used.
3. The central lawn panel functions as intended. In addition to referencing a traditional frontyard, it is also used as a ball court and as a site for cookouts, concerts, and other social events.
4. The 4-foot high white picket fence located in the Hawthorne Garden did not meet the need for contain-

Figure 9-36 Traditional home activities in The Hawthorne Garden. (Photo by Jim Daniels.)

ment. Several residents attempted to exit the garden by climbing over the fence. As a result the fence was replaced with a 6-foot fence.

5. With the change to the 6-foot high fence, the intended visual connection to the natural environment beyond the garden was dramatically altered.

6. A key design issue here is what *is* an appropriate design for a fence that must contain approximately 2 percent of residents who try to leave, while also providing a sense of openness for the 98 percent who don't.

Longfellow Garden

1. With the deletion of the proposed central bosk in order to save money, the Longfellow Garden continues to appear rather empty and lacks adequate shade. This raises the important issue of establishing and committing to the entire landscape budget prior to completion of the design process.

2. According to staff, this garden does not have enough active space in it. Some residents appear content, however, just being able to get outside and to keep moving.

3. The strong shadowing created by the pergola does not appear to have any negative impact on resident use.

4. More immediate shade at the building entry/exit is desired.

5. The elaborate nature of the pergola is a potential maintenance issue.

Millay Garden

1. Remembrance Therapy appears to provide an environment that is used and appreciated by patients in the more advanced stages of Alzheimer's.

2. The fence design for the Millay Garden, providing views to the parking lot and outside environment, appears not to have resulted in any problems and brings into question the notion that all views to the outside must be screened.

3. The selection of a continuous, exposed aggregate concrete pavement without joints for the Millay Garden appears to be successful. There have been no signs of disruption to resident circulation due to ground plane pattern changes. However, one resident did describe the exposed aggregate as feeling like "going over railroad tracks." The result of this ambiguity has led to the deletion of exposed aggregate in further designs, using only colored concrete and minimizing joints.

4. More immediate shade at the building entry/exit is desired.

5. The staff has expressed a desire for additional "passive" activities.

Figure 9-37 Millay Garden, an "emotionally secured" New England mountain stream and wildflowers. (Photo by Jim Daniels.)

6. Bold flower colors appear to generate the greatest resident interaction. One resident who was confined to her bed placed bright red, wooden tulips in her window. Often she would comment on the beautiful flowers outdoors and she would ask if those outdoors could see her flowers on the window sill.

Conclusions of Landscape Architect

One garden is not enough to meet the needs of all stages of Alzheimer's disease. A minimum of two gardens is required, one "passive" and one more "active." However, both garden types, if provided with enough physical separation, could reside within the same garden perimeter.

If a garden is not perceived by the administration as a safe environment for residents, it will only be used in a limited fashion, if at all. Visual surveillance created through proper window placement and avoiding any hidden areas screened from view, as well as appropriate security fencing are key, fundamental issues.

The highest and best use of a garden is dependent upon its relationship with the interior circulation of the building and with the administrative policies. To best respond to the interior of the building the garden design requires collaboration between the architect and the landscape architect at the start of the design process.

Commitment to an agreed-upon landscape budget is essential. The deletion of elements during construction "to save money" may radically alter the appearance and usefulness of the garden.

An ongoing dialog between the design team and the administration must continue after completion of a project, so that needed modifications in the garden can be made. At Sedgewood Commons, several changes in administrative staff interrupted the hoped-for dialogue. Consequently, the gardens have not been further developed.

In order to address long-term issues, quality maintenance must be provided. Relying on volunteers may not provide the continuous link over time that is required.

Alois Alzheimer Center, Courtyard Garden, Cincinnati, Ohio

By Margarette E Beckwith, Landscape Architect, and SusanD. Gilster, Director

Description of Facility

The setting for this case study is the Alois Alzheimer Center, in Cincinnati. The center opened May 1, 1987, as the first freestanding dedicated Alzheimer residential facility in the United States. Situated on an 8-acre site that fronts on a quiet residential street, the property backs into Winton Woods, a major regional natural reserve of mature deciduous trees. Additional outdoor amenities include a 3-acre open area that accommodates a vegetable garden; a forest trail with benches; and a raised bed cutting garden that residents are able to use under staff supervision.

The Alois Alzheimer Center is divided into four units, with a total of 102 residents; the average age is 78. Individuals are assigned to a unit based upon their cognitive, social, emotional, and physical needs and abilities, which often correspond to the (early, middle, and late) stages of the disease. The interior environments must be different to accommodate the needs of individuals along the disease process, and so must the outdoor environments be similarly designed. A garden was designed for each unit addressing the needs and abilities of the individuals residing there and allowing immediate access to the exterior space. This case study involves the Courtyard Garden, which is associated with the assisted living wing and those individuals experiencing mild to moderate dementia.

History

The building that houses the Alois Alzheimer Center was originally an elementary school. Sensitively adapted to its new use as a home for individuals with Alzheimer's disease, large windows take in views of the courtyard and surrounding wooded site, providing the opportunity for natural surveillance, and allowing natural light to penetrate into the building. In 1994 a 15,000 square foot residential living assisted care wing was added to the 29,000 square foot existing facility. The expansion provided the opportunity to review the entire site and building. A master landscape plan for the total facility was executed, of which three gardens were key elements. The Courtyard Garden was the first of the three exterior spaces to be built.

Wings of the one story school building enclosed the garden on three sides. The new residential living assisted care building provided further enclosure of the courtyard. A wise decision was made early in the design process not to allow the new wing to completely enclose the courtyard but to preserve the view to the attractive, mature tree canopy of Winton Woods. In addition to protecting the view to the landscape, it also eliminated a connecting corridor to another unit, which prevents excessive through traffic, in a sense creating a "cul-de-sac" rather than a "through street." This promotes a sense of freedom versus a sense of confinement.

Staff are enthusiastic about the value of gardens:

"Gardens are important ... to give [the residents] something to participate in and something to take care of."

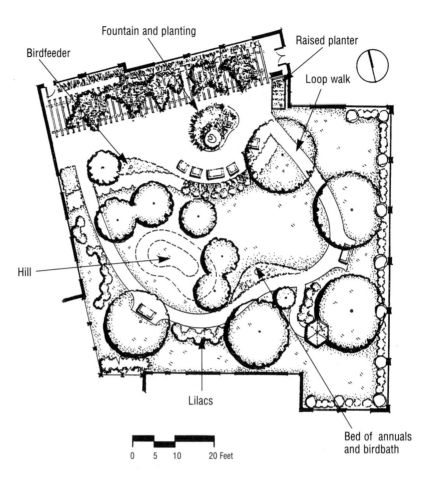

Birdfeeder
Fountain and planting
Raised planter
Loop walk
Hill
Lilacs
Bed of annuals and birdbath

0   5   10   20 Feet

Figure 9-38   Site plan of the Courtyard Garden, Alois Alzheimer Center, Cincinnati, OH.

Design Philosophy

Researchers have confirmed the therapeutic benefit of nature (Kaplan and Kaplan, 1989; Ulrich, 1984, 1991). Whether viewing a landscape from an interior space or walking in a natural setting, the experience of nature refreshes the mind and body. Does severe cognitive impairment diminish the value of this experience? Is the benefit dependent upon cognitive processing or encoding? Social psychologist R. B. Zajonc asserts that "Affective reactions can occur without extensive perceptual and cognitive encoding, are made with greater confidence than cognitive judgments, and can be made sooner. Experimental evidence is presented demonstrating that reliable affective discriminations (like-dislike ratings) can be made in the total absence of recognition memory (old-new judgments)" (Zajonc, 1980). People appear to have precognitive, affective responses to spaces such as landscapes and gardens. Even when individuals experience severe cognitive impairment, we can assume that the therapeutic value of nature remains. Those with the earliest symptoms of Alzheimer's derive pleasure from natural spaces based on cognitive functions that still might include reflection and remembering past experiences. Individuals in the later stages of the disease process, exhibiting little cognitive ability, are able to sense the peace, tranquillity, and beauty of a garden on a precognitive, affective basis. Further substantiating the precognitive theory, E. O. Wilson et al. in the *Biophilia Hypothesis* (1993) suggest that genetic "memories" of water, food, shade, and escape from predators form the basis of our survival instincts. These "natural reactions" appear to be housed, not in our cognitive processes, but in our intuitive or genetic reactions. With these assertions as a point of departure, researchers and designers were faced with the task of determining the landscape elements that were most highly preferred. Researcher Ervin Zube and others have carried out numerous studies of preferences for landscape types (Zube, 1975). Ranking high are: calm bodies of water, savannas, refuges, tree canopies, and prospects.

The Courtyard Garden at the Alois Alzheimer Center is centrally located in the building plan, allowing a view of the space from residents' rooms, the hallway, and some offices. It measures about 90 feet on a side. The space is not entirely enclosed by the wings of the building; an attractive 6-foot residential fence completes the enclosure, allowing views into the distant landscape. Access to the courtyard occurs through two doors on the south facing elevation, which open onto a patio. The curvilinear form of planting beds and paving seems to be "natural," comforting, forgiving, and provides a calming effect. The character of the path provides the opportunity for multiple views and orientations as one perambulates the serpentine walkway. Finally, the design of the space exhibits clarity in order and hierarchy; large spaces/small spaces; beginning/middle/end. Markers including the trellis, benches, birdbath, plantings, and fountain. all help to identify subspaces; they assist in what is called "way-finding." Features in the garden include a wooden trellis with trumpet vine, deciduous and evergreen trees, flowering shrubs, a planter with flowering perennials and a fountain, benches, umbrella tables, grill for outdoor cooking, patio space, a lawn, and a future gazebo. The patio is located against the south elevation where the doors provide access to the courtyard. A trellis, planted with vines, along this side of the building, creates a shaded transition from indoor to outdoors and provides a sense of psychological containment and enclosure. Exposed aggregate paving with dark pebbles further supports a comfortable transition from the dark interior to the sunny exterior. A small pool with fountain, surrounded with flowering

A staff member reflected on the emotions evoked by the garden at the facility where she works:

"Joy, peace, tranquillity, satisfaction—and rage when bugs and woodchucks destroy everything!"

Figure 9-39 A variety of features draw residents into the garden and assist in wayfinding – a looped path, birdbath, wind chimes, seating. (Photo by J. Hodgson.)

A resident reflected on what the garden means to her:

"It's soothing. You just want to sit down at certain times of the day. It's interesting to see how nature grows."

perennials and ornamental grasses, provides a focus for the patio space. The sound of the water adds further pleasure on a hot day. Umbrella tables offer seating and additional shade, creating a space for easy conversation and relaxation with residents, staff, and visitors.

The curvilinear patio space is gently contained by a boxwood hedge and yellow Stella D'Oro daylilies that delineate the edge of the lawn beyond, establishing clearly identifiable spaces. An exposed aggregate path begins at the west side of the garden and winds through the lawn. There are two bench spaces along the path wide enough to accommodate bench seating as well as a wheelchair. In the first one can rest facing an elliptical space contained by flowering crab apples with purple foliage. Future plans call for the addition of berm in the center, subtle enough not to cause difficulty for either an off-path walker or for a lawn mower. A birdbath set in a perennial flower bed marks the halfway point in the looped path. A small gazebo is planned to provide the opportunity to take refuge off the main path. The garden offers what Shepard describes as "The rhythm of being with and being apart from, coming and going and separation...a dynamic recognition of the livingness of nature" (Shepard, 1967, p. 35). The semimature silver maples on the southeast side of the courtyard shade the path and the second bench offers a view into the second subspace of the lawn. A large brick barbecue, from an earlier era and vital to facility cookouts, becomes the final marker before arriving at the east end of the patio and a planting of 6-foot high maiden grass that softens the edges of the building and rustles with the breeze. Planting along the paths is composed of shrubs and perennials selected for seasonal flowers and foliage and free from toxic or injurious properties.

Use

The Courtyard Garden is designed for individuals in the early to moderate stages of Alzheimer's disease and dementia; this group is for the most part ambulatory. Some individuals are physically and intellectually active and enjoy the opportunity for healthful exercise. They derive pleasure from contact with the plants, animals, and the change of season that the garden offers. This group also includes individuals who require the use of a wheelchair and who exhibit cognitive impairment. For these people, a protected environment is of considerable importance: the fence offers security, plants are selected for their nontoxic, noninjurious characteristics, and the paving is even, low glare and slip-resistant. The space is continually reviewed for potential hazards.

The courtyard space is freely accessible during the day. However, during inclement weather and at night, the access doors are secured. The gardens are used in two ways: Passive viewing from inside the building, a vicarious experiencing of landscape; and active use by going out into the space. Seeing an afternoon winter storm, the wind tussling the foliage, storm clouds, birds feeding, and the first blossoms of early spring are experiences that speak of the seasons and the diurnal clock, establishing a temporal, geographic, and climatic context for the residents.

As in any group of individuals, there are some people who enjoy physical activity and others who do not. For the residents who actively use the space and for those who enjoy passive use of the space, it is a valuable amenity. For many, it is an essential oasis offering a degree of normalcy in their lives.

Although spring begins the most intense use of the garden, the winter months in southwest Ohio are also periods of activity in the courtyard. Snow falling on a winter evening engages the viewer, and it is not uncommon for the residents to bundle up and take a stroll through the garden in the cooler months of the year when the frost has laid dormant the colorful perennials and other plants. Unless the weather is particularly warm in winter, the use of the space is limited to walking the path or sitting for limited period of time.

When spring arrives activity in the courtyard increases. The Stella D'Oro lilies get a head start along the south wall of the patio, and burst forth with golden color, beckoning residents to use the space. Most evident of the unstructured activities is sitting quietly and visiting with other residents or staff. The

Figure 9-40 A trellis over the south-facing patio softens the transition from inside to outside. (Photo by J. Hodgson.)

A resident reminisced about her childhood garden:

"We planted grapes and berries. We had a pear tree. I liked helping in the garden. I would like a garden with flowers and fruits."

umbrella tables on the patio offer shaded places to sit and talk. For more active individuals, walking the loop path ranges from counting repeated laps for a real exercise regimen, to a solitary stroll. This activity becomes more social when several friends join and walk together. Plants selected to provide interest throughout the growing season offer a continually changing focus of interest. Residents are encouraged to participate in maintaining, watering, and planting flowers. Vegetable gardening, under staff supervision, takes place in a garden established outside the courtyard.

Many residents actively participate in the garden through programmed events. Cookouts, picnics, carnivals—with fortune tellers and games—plus a modified version of the "Olympic" games have been some of the past activities scheduled to provide socialization and fun for the residents. For residents the garden poses an opportunity to make choices: to stay in or go out. It is an opportunity to exercise some control in their life, when the chances to do so are becoming fewer and fewer.

Interviews with members of the staff indicate that the courtyard is of significant value in the quality of life for the residents: "Residents go outside more without scheduled events, just for the enjoyment." The accessible outdoor space "decreases anxiety and agitation" on the part of residents; they are "more awake, aware, happier, contented, relaxed"; when they "eat lunch in the garden, they eat better."

More and more healthcare providers—from the newest staff member to the highest corporate executive—are beginning to understand the value that accessible, well designed outdoor spaces offer in healthcare facilities. Families of patients are reaching the same conclusions For the individual with Alzheimer's disease, these outdoor spaces seem to play a special role. Circumventing the cognitive process, the individual in the later stages of the disease is still able to appreciate and benefit from the experience of nature. For them, as for all individuals, the pleasures of the original landscape are basic: water; filtered sunlight; a gentle breeze. We have known these elements from the origins of our existence on the planet. They have allowed us to survive and have provided us with stimulation, pleasure, and a sense of our place in the universe.

ADVANTAGES:

- Clear views and access to the courtyard from the interior corridors invite residents to use the space.
- Different environments: trellis enclosure; tree canopy; umbrella tables, and open space offer a variety of spaces.

- Numerous places to sit, in various settings and with different views, are provided.
- A variety of plants selected for fragrance, color, and seasonal interest are used.
- The path provides the opportunity for a "journey," or a "lap" for exercise.
- Views to the park in the distance are uninhibited by solid wall or opaque fence and have not created problems of attempted elopement.
- Sound and visual activity of moving water enliven the space.
- Semimature trees provide a substantial canopy of shade.
- Birds and other animals are attracted by water or plants to the courtyard .
- The outdoor space offers a sense of control and mastery, nonconfining in appearance but secure.
- The garden provides a setting for cookouts and other programmed events.

DISADVANTAGES
- New planting, especially vines on trellis, need greater maturity to be effective.

Hearthstone at New Horizons, Marlborough, Massachusetts

By Martha Tyson, Landscape Architect,
and John Zeisel, President

Hearthstone at New Horizons, located in Marlborough, is one of several assisted living treatment residences operated by Hearthstone Alzheimer Care in the Greater Boston and New York City areas. This wing of a larger assisted living community comprises two upper residential floors housing nineteen and twenty-three people, respectively, a common ground floor with dining rooms, hearth, and living room, and the treatment garden. The design and programming of all Hearthstone treatment residences are based on the environmental design and medical outcomes research carried out by Hearthstone's research division.

A resident recalled a garden in his past:

"I had a garden when living in the Bronx and enjoyed it. I did a lot of gardening in my younger years."

Organizing Principles for the Garden
The Hearthstone concept of care is based on the understanding that the hearth—traditionally a place that combines food, warmth and sociability—is a primary element that defines "home." Each Hearthstone design incorporates what Erving Goffman (1960) defines as the two basic residential zones:

"front stage" including foyer, living room, and public areas, and "back stage," including hearth, kitchen, and more private living areas. Hearthstone's gardens reflect the same zone arrangement as does the indoor design of the residence. The principles of front stage and back stage are represented by patios and back yards and by front porches and front yards. The other primary organizing design principle incorporates paths, districts, land-marks, edges, and nodes—the five constructs Kevin Lynch (1960) identifies in his work on cognitive mapping employed by users of cities to find their way.

The principal organizing interior elements of the Hearthstone residential model are mirrored in the garden. Similar places inside and outside are located adjacent to one another to reinforce the image and life of a home: planting beds outside the kitchen window; activity patio outside the living room door; front porch outside the foyer window. Five primary places define the garden: front porch, frontyard, back patio, backyard, and park. The garden has two enclosing features: the

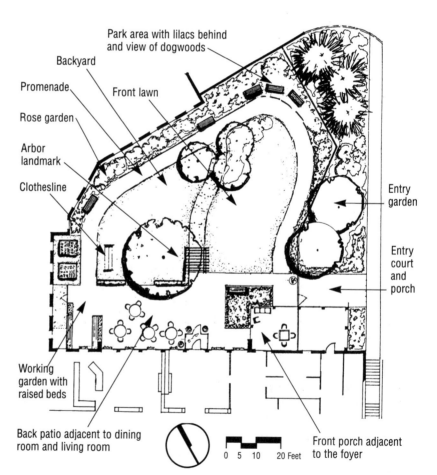

Figure 9-41   Site plan of Hearthstone at New Horizons, Marlborough, MA.

building edge and the perimeter fence. Three different types of paths with various degrees of hierarchy connect the places in the garden: the promenade passes around the garden, a short-cut halfway along the promenade links back to the patio, and a "just-passing-through" path is located at the edge of the patio area. Natural gathering places—an alcove in the park and a garden seat—are strategically placed along the paths to visually anchor the garden and to serve as destinations. The primary landmark is an entry arbor that reinforces the sense of arrival into and from the garden and is lined up with the "front door" of the residence. The "front door," made visually prominent in the garden by being located in an entryway that extends out from the building, acts with the arbor as a visual and symbolic cue to indicate "the way home."

Plantings and Ambience

The structured garden plan described above sets the stage for plants, flowers and lively activities. The front and back yards have extensive well kept lawns, giving the illusion of larger expanses. As you enter the main path, to the right of the entry in front of the picket fence, you pass a whimsical ceramic bird-bath. Continuing counter clockwise, you pass a series of gardens within gardens. The first is planted with annuals that family members have brought from resident's homes when they moved to Hearthstone. After passing the park area on the right with benches surrounded by forsythia that burst forth in yellow sprays in the spring, you come to a red rose garden on a berm separating "the park" from the building wall at that point. Residents like to touch the smooth blossoms when the roses first bloom and pick up the petals when they fall to the ground later in the summer.

The right angle intersection of the concrete main path and the crushed fines shortcut is signaled by a single bench on the right and flowering trees on both sides of the shortcut to the left. Every spring residents and staff plant flowering annuals at the base of the trees. Every fall, when the weather gets chilly, the annuals are replaced with brilliant yellow, orange, and purple mums.

Continuing along the main path, residents pass a trim hedge near the edge of the path, and come to two 24" high raised planters set in the crushed fines. One spring, residents planted vegetable seedlings there, provided by the local garden club. Tomatoes, zucchini squash, beans and other vegetables grew all summer. Another spring, residents and garden club members planted annuals that were nice to touch and hid small constructions among the leaves—a little birdhouse and a windmill. You

A resident was asked about the garden at her residence:

"I think gardening is wonderful. I admire other people's work. I can recognize a weed. I think men are better gardeners."

never know what you will find in the planters because there is no predetermined plan. Each year the raised planter gardens surprise and delight family members and visitors. Crossing the back patio from the end of the path, there is a 36" high planter separating the patio from the working garden shelves. Although several summers ago one resident took this planter over as a tomato garden, for the last few years it has become the seedling staging area managed by family members. Small flowering plants are set in soil early in the spring and transplanted throughout the garden by families and residents later when they are hardy. Finally, all summer long, pots of flowering gardenias and trailing vines are hung from the extended beams of the arbor at the start of the shortcut. Small concrete animals— a turtle, squirrel, dove, and raccoon—are hidden among the plants to enrich the stroll experience of those on the main path.

Every day, no matter what the weather, residents freely walk around the paths, look at or touch the plants, sit on the park benches, and even stroke the animal sculptures. In good weather staff organize a structured group event every morning and every afternoon on the back patio. These include activities that might otherwise take place indoors like throwing a ball around or listening to stories. Garden related activities like planting seeds and transplanting seedlings are also organized. When it is not too windy or hot, lunch is served on the patio tables, and at least once a week in summer dinner is a backyard barbecue. All summer, parties which family members attend— like the 4th of July celebration—are held in the garden.

Interviews

The design of the garden employed empirical research from similar garden settings, interview data from family members, direct involvement of staff, and direct conversations and informal interviews with residents. Resident interviews were structured as informal gatherings between the designers and residents and consisted of a directed conversation about gardens and familiar outdoor activities. Employing key phrases like "back porch," "outdoor work," "Saturday chores," "front porch," and "family picnics," residents were asked about past experiences. To our pleasant surprise, when given a small-scale model of the garden to look at, several residents were able to translate and discuss the model in terms of the future built garden. Comments from residents that were addressed in the design include: "storing plants, pots along the edge" (stone wall for setting pots); "a place to sit in light rain" (covered front porch); "raking leaves with father" (backyard with trees); "fresh lilacs in the spring" (lilac grove in park area); "throw seeds for birds on the snow" (year-round access from door in living

A resident commented:

"[It is] a pleasure to watch the plants come alive. I am peaceful."

Figure 9-42 A "node" at the meeting of the promenade, and a shortcut.

room); "vegetable garden—we will enjoy eating them" (raised garden beds); "a worktable with watering source" (worktable-bench); "a place to get dirt on your hands...and no one cares" (potting area-workbench).

Other comments residents made that may be addressed in future design revisions include: "a garden swing, lighted pathways, trees, and victory gardens." As a layout and in concept, the garden appears to be successful at bringing residents outdoors without any staff encouragement; however, details of plantings, furnishings, and maintenance need to be addressed more carefully in follow-up designs.

Use

Two anecdotes illustrate the story of the garden. Early in the first summer of the garden, Amy, a resident and enthusiastic gardener, asked for a pruning tool we were using. It was handed over. Before long, and to our surprise, the lilacs in the park were not more than 12 inches high and shrinking rapidly. Later a staff member told us that Amy was "an enthusiastic pruner." A critical question became clear to us: Do you take away the tool, do you give residents the opportunity to work at what they enjoy, or do you introduce other similar safe activities that "protect the plants" yet still allow residents to become more involved in gardening? Is replacing plants periodically more worthwhile to the overall quality of life for this resident than preventing her from engaging in her work?

The answers to such questions—in fact the discussion itself—becomes an integral part of Amy's treatment plan. For each person, the answer is different, taking into account the individual's needs and those of other residents and their families. Of course, there is no simple answer.

Figure 9-43 View from back patio to a lawn, arbor landmark, promenade, and enclosure fence.

During that same summer, Paul, another resident, planted and cared for a dozen thriving tomato plants. The plants grew large and leafy yet the fruit remained green with only a hint of red despite their large size. One day we visited only to find that Paul had denuded all the plants—the leaves were all cut off leaving several dozen large and ungainly green tomatoes on the vines. A bit shocked, we asked Paul why he did this. "This late in the season," Paul explained, "if the tomatoes are still green, you want to make sure they sun hits them directly. Removing the leaves prevents the tomatoes from growing too large and cracking before they get red." He remembered how to care for his plants, even if he forgot he had a garden when he went inside. Experts need to remember that residents, staff, and families are also experts—each in his or her own way.

People need to work, enjoy, and maintain themselves. To fully contribute to a home environment, a garden's design needs to incorporate opportunities for residents, family members, and staff to engage in the normal social life of the garden. It also needs to include elements that act as catalysts for activities such as eating, gardening, and repairing that are also part of a person's daily life whether inside or outside.

With the balance of a good theoretical foundation based on environment-behavior research, and practical knowledge of the physical environment and landscape design, the Hearthstone at New Horizons garden serves as the model for other Hearthstone.

ADVANTAGES

- Residents go outdoors unassisted.
- Front porch and park alcove are comfortable.
- Garden bench at end of shortcut is a clear destination and is well used.
- The pathway layout functions as intended; residents find their way easily.
- Residents take ownership of the garden through pruning and planting.
- Garden is a place for informal visiting with families and staff.
- Perimeter plantings along the fence act as a buffer.

DISADVANTAGES

- There is not enough visual distinction between frontyard and backyard.
- Soil needs improvement.
- Raised vegetable gardens are located in shaded area.
- Raised boxes are heavy in appearance.

- Plantings are not thriving; they need fertilizing and pruning.
- More variety in plant selection would provide continuous seasonal blooms.
- Maintenance needs more attention.
- Worktable receives low use.

CONCLUSION

In sum, gardens for people with Alzheimer's disease present designers, researchers, and staff with an intriguing set of opportunities and challenges.

- To provide a prosthetic environment that is also spiritual and uplifting.
- To create a safe place that supports independence while remaining interesting and challenging.
- To respond to a complex set of needs and requirements while being easy to understand without instructions.
- To accommodate groups of residents as well as enable individuals to identify with the garden and flourish.
- To enliven gardens with events while promoting places for people to relax alone and be in touch with themselves.
- To provide healing opportunities for residents while participating in garden life or observing its use.

A woman reflected on the garden at the residence where she lives:

"I enjoy the flowers and the vegetables. I like gardening, but only God can make a tree."

By thoughtfully creating and using Alzheimer's gardens, residents and their families, as well as staff, designers, and researchers will all benefit. We will learn to create better gardens. We will enjoy them more. We will contribute to each other's knowledge and well being. And we will help each other maintain our orientation to the world around us through nature.

REFERENCES

Alexander, C. (1979). *The Timeless Way of Building.* New York: Oxford University Press.

Alexander, C., S. Ishikawa, and M. Silverstein (1977). *A Pattern Language.* New York: Oxford University Press.

Alzheimer's Association (1997). Information on Research and Medical Issues. Chicago: The Alzheimer's Association.

Anderson, T. (1990). "Provision for the Elderly Mentally Ill." *Landscape Design,* No. 189, April, pp. 23–24.

Beyersdorfer, P. S. and D. M. Birkenhauer (1990). "The Therapeutic Use of Pets on an Alzheimer's Unit." *The American Journal of Alzheimer's Care and Related Disorders and Research*, Vol. 5, No. 1, January/February, pp. 13–16.

Bite, I. and M. J. Lovering (1984). "Design Opens Doors for the Elderly." *Landscape Architecture*, November/December, pp. 79–81.

——— (1985). "Design for the Elderly." *Landscape Architectural Review*, Vol. 4, No. 3, pp. 9–14.

Calkins, M. (1988). *Design for Dementia: Planning Environments for the Elderly and Confused*. Owings Mills, MD: Williams and Wilkins.

——— (1989). "Designing Cues for Wanderers." *Architecture*, October, pp. 117–118.

Carstens, D. Y. (1985). *Site Planning and Design for the Elderly: Issues, Guidelines and Alternatives*. New York: Van Nostrand Reinhold.

——— (1998). "Housing and Outdoor Spaces for the Elderly." In Cooper Marcus, C. and C. Francis (Eds.) (2nd edition), *People Places*. New York: Wiley.

Cohen, U. and G. Weisman (1991). *Holding Onto Home*. Baltimore, MD: Johns Hopkins University Press.

——— (Ed.) 1991. *Specialized Dementia Care Units*. Baltimore, MD: Johns Hopkins University Press.

Coons, D. (1988). "Wandering." *The American Journal of Alzheimer's Care and Related Disorders and Research*, Vol. 3, no. 1, pp. 31–36.

Cooper Marcus, C. and C. Francis (Eds.) (1998). *People Places*, 2nd ed. New York: Wiley.

DeLong, A. J. (1970). "The Micro-Spatial Structure of the Older Person: Some Implications of Planning the Social and Spatial Environment." In Pastalan, L. and D. Carson (Eds.) *Spatial Behavior of Older People*. Ann Arbor, MI: University of Michigan Press.

Erikson, E. (1982). *The Life Cycle Completed*. New York: W. W. Norton and Company.

Fox, P. (1986). "Alzheimer's Disease: An Historical Overview." *The American Journal of Alzheimer's Care*, Fall.

Gilson, K. K. (1994). *Design Criteria for Outdoor Space and Human Behavior: A Better Fit for Alzheimer's Disease Patients*. Masters Thesis. Department of Landscape Architecture: University of Texas at Arlington.

Hagedorn, R. (1990). "Occupational Therapy and Environmental Consciousness." *Landscape Design*, No. 189, April, pp. 21–22.

Healy, V. (1991). Personal interview concerning the use of plantings in hospice and health care settings. University of Illinois at Urbana-Champaign. April 26.

Hoglund, D. (1985). *Housing for the Elderly: Privacy and Independence in Environments for the Aging*. New York: Van Nostrand Reinhold.

Hoover, R. (1995). "Healing Gardens and Alzheimer's Disease". *The American Journal of Alzheimer's Care and Related Disorders and Research*, March/April, pp. 1–9.

Kaplan, R. and S. Kaplan (1989). "Nearby Nature." In *The Experience of Nature, A Psychological Perspective*. Cambridge: Cambridge University Press. pp. 150–176.

Kübler-Ross, E. (1982). *Working It Through*. New York: Macmillan.

Lindenmuth, G. F. and B. Moose (1990). "Improving Cognitive Abilities of Elderly Alzheimer's Patients with Intense Exercise Therapy." *The American Journal of Alzheimer's Care and Related Disorders and Research*, Vol. 5, No. 1, pp. 31–33.

Liss, L. (1986). "Letter to the Editor." *The American Journal of Alzheimer's Care*, Vol. 1, No. 4, p. 5.

Lovering, M. J. (1990). "Alzheimer's Disease and Outdoor Space." *The American Journal of Alzheimer's Care and Related Disorders and Research*, May/June, pp. 33–40.

Lynch, K. (1960). *The Image of the City*. Cambridge, MA: MIT Press.

Mace, N. L. (1993). "Observations of Dementia Specific Care Around the World." *American Journal of Alzheimer's Care and Related Disorders and Research*, Vol. 8, No. 3, pp. 36–39.

McArthur, M. G. (1988). "Exercise as Therapy for the Alzheimer's Patient and Caregiver: Aggressive Action in the Face of an Aggressive Disease." *American Journal of Alzheimer's Care and Related Disorders Research*, Vol. 3, No. 6, pp. 36–39.

Messervy, J. (1990). *Contemplative Gardens*. Charlottesville, VA: Howell Press.

Mooney, P. and P. L. Nicell (1992). "The Importance of Exterior Environment for Risk Management." *Healthcare Management Forum*, Vol. 5, No. 2, pp. 23–29.

Pastalan, L. and D. Carson (Eds.) (1970). *Spatial Behavior of Older People*. Ann Arbor: University of Michigan Press. pp. 68–86.

Randall, P. (1989). "Exterior Space for Alzheimer's Disease Patients." Proceedings of the Environmental Design Research Association Conference, Urbana, IL.

Regnier, V. A. (1985). *Behavioral and Environmental Aspects of Outdoor Space Use in Housing for the Elderly*. Los Angeles: University of Southern California, Andrus Gerontology Center.

——— (1994). *Assisted Living Housing for the Elderly: Design Innovations from the United States and Europe*. New York: Van Nostrand Reinhold.

Reisberg, B. (1986). "Dementia: A Systematic Approach to Identifying Reversible Causes." *Geriatrics*, Vol. 41, pp. 30–46.

Reisberg, B., S. H. Ferris, M. J. Leon, and T. Crook (1982). "The Global Deterioration Scale for Assessment of Primary, Degenerative Dementia." *American Journal of Psychiatry*, Vol. 139, pp. 1136–1139.

Rothert, G. (1994). *The Enabling Garden*. Dallas, TX: Taylor.

Shepard, Paul (1967). *Man in the Landscape, A Historic View of the Esthetics of Nature*. New York: Alfred A. Knopf.

Stoneham, J. (1990). "Sheltered Landscapes." *Landscape Design*, No. 189, April, pp. 17–20.

Stoneham, J. and P. Thoday (1996). *Landscape Design for Elderly and Disabled People*. Woodbridge, Suffolk, UK: Garden Art Press, a division of Antique Collectors Club Ltd.

Tyson, M. M. (1987). "Memories of Grandma's Backyard." *Journal of Therapeutic Horticulture*, Vol. 2, November, pp. 26–35.

———— (1989). "Pieces to the Puzzle: Environments for Alzheimer's Patients." Unpublished paper. University of Illinois at Urbana-Champaign.

———— (1990). "Tracing the Wanderer's Path." Unpublished paper. University of Illinois at Urbana-Champaign.

———— (1992). "The Role of the Outdoor Environment in the Care of Older People with Alzheimer's Disease." MLA Thesis, University of Illinois at Urbana-Champaign.

———— (1998). *The Healing Landscape: Therapeutic Outdoor Environments*. New York: McGraw-Hill.

Tyson, M. M. and S. Maghakian (1989). "Gardening as Therapy." *Minnesota Horticulturist*, October/November, pp. 24–29.

Ulrich, R. S. (1984). "View Through a Window May Influence Recovery from Surgery." *Science*, Vol. 224, pp. 420–421.

———— (1990). "Aesthetic and Affective Response to Natural Environment." In I. Altman and J. F. Wohlwill (Eds.), *Human Behavior and the Environment*, Vol. 6. New York: Plenum. pp. 85–125.

———— (1992). "How Design Impacts Wellness." *Healthcare Forum Journal*, September/October, pp. 20–25.

Ulrich, R. S., R. F. Simons, B. D. Losito, and E. Fiorito (1991). "Stress Recovery During Exposure to Natural and Urban Environments." *Journal of Environmental Psychology*, Vol. 11, pp. 201–230.

US Department of Health and Human Services, National Institutes of Health. (1983). "Medicine for the Layman: Brain in Aging and Dementia." Bethesda, MD. NIH Publication No. 83–2625.

———— (1984). "Report of the Secretary's Task Force on Alzheimer's Disease." Bethesda, MD: DHHS Publication No. (ADM) 84–1323, September.

White, B. J. (1990). "Physical Features for Wayfinding and Orientation in Specialized Dementia Units." Unpublished Paper. Department of Housing, University of Kansas, Manhattan, KS.

Zeisel, J., J. Hyde, and S. Lefkoff (1994). "Best Practices: An Environment-Behavior (E-B) Model for Alzheimer's Special Care Units." *American Journal of Alzheimer's Care and Related Disorders and Research*, Vol. 9, No. 2, March/April, pp. 4–21.

Zeisel, J., N. Silverstein, J. Hyde, L. Shi, M. Lawton, S. Levkoff, and D. Holmes (1999). "Design Contributors to Health Outcomes in Special Care Alzheimer's Units." Working paper. Hearthstone Alzheimer Care, Lexington, MA.

Zeisel, J. and M. M. Tyson (1997). "Hearthstone Alzheimer Care Garden System Research." Post-Occupancy Evaluation Working Paper. Hearthstone Alzheimer Care, Lexington, MA.

Zgola, J. M. (1987). *Doing Things: A Guide to Programming Activities for Persons With Alzheimer's Disease and Related Disorders*. Baltimore, MD: The Johns Hopkins University Press.

Zube, E. H., D. G. Pitt, and T. W. Anderson (1975). "Perception and Prediction of Scenic Resource Values of the Northeast." In Zube, E. H., R. O. Brush, and J. G. Fos (Eds.), *Landscape Assessments: Values, Perceptions and Resources*. Stroudsburg, PA: Dowden, Hutchinson & Ross. pp. 151–167.

CHAPTER

10

Hospice Gardens

Clare Cooper Marcus

Many Western societies have an ambivalent attitude toward death and dying. In earlier centuries, death was omnipresent as famine and illness took their toll from young and old alike. With better food, sanitation and medical care, the industrialized West witnessed a significant shift in mortality figures during the twentieth century. As hospitals improved and utilization increased, death—like birth—moved away from home into a medical setting.

From the 1930s to the 1960s, this trend accelerated as more and more people died in hospitals because caring for a dying relative could not be accommodated in small apartments, attended by family members who were all working, or who lived at great distances from each other. "With the hospitalization of the dying, most families became less acquainted with death and less able to cope with it when it occurred" (Lindheim, 1981, p. 18).

With increased use of medical technology, death in the hospital became more and more depersonalized. An increasing number of people within and outside the medical profession began to question whether the hospital offered the most appropriate services and philosophy of care for the terminally ill (Lindheim, 1981, pp. 18–19). The stage was set for the emergence of the modern hospice movement—embracing both a philosophy and a place, with an emphasis on pain control and relief of symptoms, rather than cure. Hospice care in the home brings a multiprofessional team of hospice workers to the bedside in a person's familiar environment. Hospice care in a hospi-

A young couple, given the news that their baby, after a long illness, was finally within just hours of its death, asked that the elaborate paraphernalia of life-support machinery be removed so that they could hold their child in their arms as its life passed away.

...They decided to carry the baby into the garden, where they settled themselves in a quiet corner, waiting for death to come. The day was so beautiful... the death very peaceful.

(HOWETT, 1990, P. 257)

505

Figure 10-1 Founded in 1891, Trinity Hospice has occupied these buildings overlooking Clapham Common in a residential neighborhood of south London since 1900.

tal ward, or in a facility separate from a hospital provides the same care in a specially designed environment. In both cases the aim is to care for the whole family and for the dying patient, in terms of their emotional, physical, social and spiritual needs. Hopefully, this may become a model for all hospital care, which currently often neglects the whole person, the whole family.

The hospice movement has grown rapidly in the last two decades, and today it can be said that death in North America has come "out of the closet." Compared to a decade ago, there are many more books available to the general public on death and dying. Just as Birth Centers sprang into existence when the "Baby Boomer" generation demanded more humane and home-like birth environments, perhaps the same things will happen as regards hospices as this generation approaches death ("All Things Considered," National Public Radio, No. 3, 1997).

HISTORY OF HOSPICE MOVEMENT

The word "hospice" is believed to have derived from the Latin word "hospes," meaning both "host" and "guest." The root word also evolved into the English terms "hostel," "hospital," and "hotel" (Stoddard, 1978).

> Once Christianity was legalized in 313 A.D., the Eastern Church sponsored nursing homes for the sick ("nosocemeia"), and for travelers ("xenodocia"), and for many others stricken by need. On a pilgrimage to Palestine, the wealthy Roman matron Fabiola was inspired by the care of the sick she witnessed in Eastern monasteries, and brought the concept back to Italy" (Kerr, 1993, p. 13).

Figure 10-2 Opened in 1994, Joseph Weld Hospice in Dorchester, UK was built in traditional red brick, in harmony with the residential neighborhood nearby.

In the medieval period, many monasteries in Western Europe provided physical and spiritual comfort to pilgrims, the homeless, the sick and dying. With the decline of monasticism, hospice settings declined in number, but did not disappear; examples appeared in seventeenth century France and eighteenth century Germany and Ireland (Movahed, 1995, p. 17).

"Over time, a distinction was drawn between the hospice — a house for permanent occupation by the poor, the orphaned, the insane and the incurable; and the hospital — a place where the sick were accommodated temporarily for medical treatment." (Kerr, 1993, p. 13). Pilgrims were often cared for in both, and some hospices later evolved into hospitals. The care of the dying was only one aspect of early hospice care, and it did not become its sole function (at least in the English-speaking world) until the founding of Our Lady's Hospice for the Dying by the Irish Sisters of Charity in 1879. This hospice, which inspired many others, was itself inspired by the selfless life work among the poor and dying of Mother Mary Aikenhead, foundress of the Irish Sisters of Charity (Kerr, 1993).

In 1906, the English Sisters of Charity established St. Joseph's Hospice in London, and it was here that Dr. Cicely Saunders, in the 1950s and 1960s, developed her work in pain control and counseling of dying patients and their families. A dream fostered by Dr. Saunders and some of her patients had its fruition with the founding of St. Christopher's Hospice — the first *modern* hospice — in London in 1967.

The recent burgeoning hospice movement had its beginnings with St. Christopher's, which combined the traditional concepts of hospitality and compassion with the modern skills

Figure 10-3 Patient rooms with semi-private patios look out over a familiar, domestic landscape of lawns and trees at San Diego Hospice.

of symptom control, pain relief, and bereavement support. A speech by Dr. Saunders in New Haven, Connecticut, sparked the establishment of the first modern hospice in the United States in the early 1970s. Hospice, Inc., or New Haven Hospice as it is now called, was developed with an emphasis on home care. The first free-standing hospice building, Hillhaven Hospice, opened in Tucson, Arizona, in 1977. The following year, the New Haven Hospice opened an inpatient facility to supplement its home care (Movahed, 1995, p. 18).

The birth of the modern hospice movement in the United States, together with the pioneering work of Swiss-born Dr. Elisabeth Kübler-Ross on the psychological processes of dying and training of death-and-dying counselors, have revolutionized the care of the terminally ill.[1]

> Harking back to the medieval monastic model of palliative care, the modern hospice movement is based on the premise that the dying need compassionate rather than clinical or bio-medical care. The inpatient hospice facility is a small part of the overall movement to care for the dying in their preferred environment, the home (Carey, 1986, p. 18).

A primary design focus in such facilities is to create a noninstitutional, homelike environment where—in most cases—a garden, or the surrounding natural landscape forms an intrinsic part of the overall environment of care and repose.

THE INPATIENT HOSPICE FACILITY

The range of purpose built or remodeled inpatient facilities are described by Carey in one of the few studies of hospice design based on empirical research. She categorized the architecturally distinct and autonomous or semiautonomous hospice inpatient facilities as falling into four groups:

1. Large, purpose built facilities for the terminally ill, such as Calvary Hospital in the Bronx and Rosary Hill Home in Hawthorne, New York.
2. Medium-sized, purpose built hospice facilities not associated with an affiliated hospital, such as the Connecticut Hospice, San Diego Hospice, and a facility presented as a case study later in this chapter, Joseph Weld House in Dorchester, UK.

Figure 10-4 *Sculpture of a boy playing a flute in the grounds of San Diego Hospice.*

[1]Vince Healy, who has worked closely with Kübler-Ross, reports that she is deeply aware of the profound benefit gardens can have on the healing process and maintenance of the psyche. (Correspondence, 1998.)

3. Medium-sized hospice facilities not affiliated with a hospital that are in remodeled freestanding buildings. Examples include Hospice of Cincinnati, Hospice of Northern Virginia in Arlington, and two facilities presented as case studies, Hospice House in Portland, Oregon, and Trinity Hospice in Clapham, London, England.

4. Medium and small hospice units within large hospital facilities which consist of wards or segments of the hospital that have been remodeled to form more homelike, palliative care settings. This is the most common form of hospice provision in the United States (in terms of the proportion of total beds). The hospice ward at Laguna Honda Hospital in San Francisco is presented in one of this chapter's case studies.

HOSPICE GARDENS

The need for a garden or access to the natural landscape is so clear and essential in a freestanding hospice environment that it is doubtful that many have been developed without such an amenity. Why is this? Perhaps the fact that hospice buildings are designed to be as homelike as possible presupposes a garden—the freestanding house and garden representing the American Dream. Thus, the hospice is unique among quasi-medical settings in that the need for access to nature is virtually taken for granted. The restorative power of nature at times of extreme stress surrounding death and dying is so obvious that "proof" of its importance is not needed.

Hospice gardens should be designed to serve a number of functions:

1. As a green, homelike setting for the building.
2. As a buffer between the building and the outside world.
3. As a restorative environment to look out onto.
4. As a place where staff and family members can go to walk or sit for purposes of stress reduction.
5. As a place where the children of visitors or of staff may go to run off steam.
6. As a place where family members or staff can take patients.
7. As a setting in which patients may choose to die.
8. As a place where family members and staff may spend time in the process of bereavement.
9. As a setting for memorial gatherings.
10. As a setting for annual fund-raising events.

Figure 10-5 The problem of how to display the names of donors is handled in a pleasing way with a pattern of small inscribed leaves on a garden wall. (San Diego Hospice, California.)

Typology of Hospice Gardens

Gardens associated with freestanding hospice buildings and hospice wards vary by size, location, and relationship to the building. The following are among the most frequently found:

1. Extensive landscaped grounds. Example: Hospice of Northern Virginia, Arlington, Virginia.
2. Walled or fenced back garden/yard. Examples: Trinity Hospice, London; Zen Hospice, San Francisco, California.
3. Back garden/yard with extensive views out (embracing the notion of "borrowed landscape"). Example: Joseph Weld House, Dorchester, UK.
4. Front garden/yard, designed so as to create a private setting. Example: Hospice House, Portland, Oregon.
5. Walking route around building through natural or designed landscape. Examples: San Diego Hospice, San Diego, California; Central Coast Hospice, Monterey, California.
6. Courtyard enclosed by buildings. Examples: Laguna Honda Hospital, Hospice Ward, San Francisco, California; Calvary Hospice, Bronx, New York; St. Mary's Hospice, Tucson, Arizona; Nathan Adelson Hospice, Las Vegas, Nevada; Princess Alice Hospice, Esher, Surrey, UK.
7. Roof garden. Examples: Cabrini Hospice at Cabrini Hospital, New York, New York; Joel Schapner Memorial Garden, Cardinal Cooke Hospital, New York, New York.
8. Terrace or deck with planters. Examples: Connecticut Hospice, Branford, Connecticut; Coming Home Hospice, San Francisco, California.
9. Individual patios or gardens adjacent to private patient rooms. Examples: San Diego Hospice, San Diego, California; Central Coast Hospice, Monterey, California; Kaiser Permanente Hospice, Norwalk, California.

CASE STUDIES

Trinity Hospice, Clapham, London

Brief Description of the Facility and Its History

Trinity Hospice provides care for the terminally ill in a tradition that goes back to its founding in 1891, and is the oldest organization of its kind in England. Since 1900 it has been located in a residential neighborhood at 30 Clapham Common North Side,

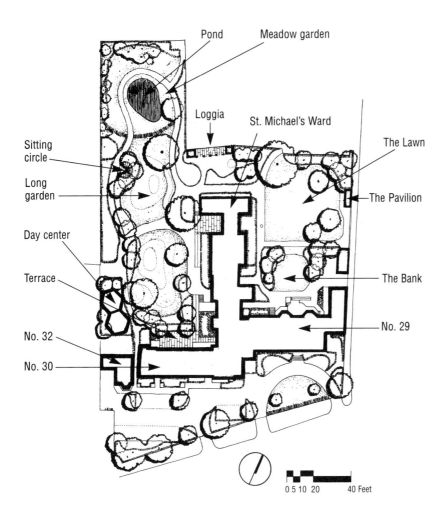

Pond
Meadow garden
Loggia
St. Michael's Ward
The Lawn
Sitting circle
Long garden
The Pavilion
Day center
The Bank
Terrace
No. 29
No. 32
No. 30

0 5 10 20   40 Feet

in a handsome Georgian building. Set behind ornate iron gates, this building was at one time the home of Sir Charles Barry, architect of the Houses of Parliament and Trafalgar Square; it looks out over Clapham Common, an extensive area of public open space. After World War II, the hospice expanded to include two adjacent houses and gardens, and a nurses' residence with private garden around the corner. Originally run by the Sisters of the Order of St. Margaret, since 1977 it has been staffed by medical and lay personnel under the auspices of a Lay Council, and offers free care to the terminally ill of several south and central London boroughs. One-third of its income comes from statutory resources (local health authorities), the remainder from gifts, donations, and fund-raising. Many hundreds of people are cared for each year as inpatients at the Hospice, as outpatients visiting the Day Center at the Hospice, and at home through a Palliative Care Team.

St. Michael's Ward, a new one-story wing opened in 1953, extends at a right angle from the older buildings, into the garden area at the back. In the early 1980s, all the buildings were renovated and the outdoor areas became quite derelict with builders' rubbish. A major restoration of the garden was undertaken in 1983. Design proposals were sought from Lanning Roper, an American who had made England his home as a garden writer and designer since the late 1940s. Due to illness, he was unable to contribute more than an outline of verbal suggestions. After his death in 1983, the garden was designed by John Medhurst (of London Landscape Consortium) with David Foreman.

The Outdoor Space

The almost 2 acres of gardens at Trinity Hospice comprise three main segments: a long rectangular area behind Nos. 30 and 32 Clapham Common North, consisting of the Long Garden, the Meadow Garden, the Pond, and the Sitting Circle; a square space behind No. 29 consisting of the Bank, the Lawn, and the Pavilion; and a narrow connection between the two comprising a Loggia and small Loggia Garden. Enclosed on all sides by brick walls covered by the rambling roses favored by Lanning Roper, the garden's original strength was in the variety of existing mature trees providing height and shade at strategic points.

The garden designers were especially inspired by the work of Gertrude Jekyll and by the use of planting color. The planting round the lawn of No. 29, with its sitting pavilion placed to catch the setting sun, is appropriately full of golden hues (gold-leafed fuchsias, roses, and false acacia), with light touches

Figure 10-7   Subtly mounded lawns of the Long Garden at Trinity Hospice, London, UK.

of silver and purple. Brick paths in the Long Garden are bordered with shrubs, and the soft colors of lavender, artemisia, heuchera, and white roses. A sense of certainty and continuity is provided by seasonal changes in the garden, from the first spring bulbs, emerging seedlings, cherry blossoms, summer perennials, autumn colors, attractive seed pods, and so on.

The present gardener, Anne Wood, who has cared for the facility since 1983, maintains the original planting plan with an emphasis on seasonal color, plants and shrubs that are familiar to patients and their families (roses, lilies-of-the-valley, etc.), plus some species which are less common and that often evoke curiosity ("What is that plant with the large white flowers?"). The extent of the garden is large and varied enough to permit massings of plants and shrubs, allowing patients who can't actually get out into the garden to be able to appreciate the broad brush of its design from their windows above. "It is intended as a garden, first and foremost, not a 'Garden for the Disabled.' We didn't want an excess of handrails though most paths are wide and solid. We wanted it to be practical without rubbing it in that this is a place for the infirm" (Anne Wood).

While the garden is first and foremost a visual experience, the other senses have not been forgotten. Lavender, nicotiana, roses, and other sweet-smelling plants are used liberally in the garden. A small raised bed outside the Day Center is planted with plants to eat—marrows (summer squashes) and tomatoes. A wind chime hangs in a tree near the lily pond; a crow has made its nest in a tall plane tree; a waterfall designed by William Pye directs a sheet of water down over a textured bronze incline into a small pond. The sounds of this gentle water feature are heard by outpatients sitting on the Day Center patio (and there has never been an incident of these sounds inducing anyone to urinate, as some had feared).

One of the most attractive features of the garden's design is the fact that it is subtly subdivided into a number of outdoor "rooms"—the Long Garden, the Meadow Garden, the Loggia Garden, the Sitting Circle, and so on. This is a tradition of English garden design and is especially suited to a hospice setting where people may want to sit in semiseclusion, may enjoy the sense of mystery and surprise as one comes upon an unknown corner, and may appreciate the sense of being far away from the buildings even though the actual distance is not far.

The Long Garden comprises peripheral brick-paved paths bordered with shrubs and perennials, curving gently beside a long lawn. Another path bisects the area but the subtle mounding of the lawn renders this path all but invisible from the main

Figure 10-8 A meandering brick path leads through a beech hedge to the Meadow Garden.

terrace and from the hospice buildings: the Long Garden appears to be one long sweeping expanse of grass. A small seating circle bordered with lavender, roses, and cistus is situated just to the side of the west perimeter path.

A curved beech hedge divides the Long Garden from the Meadow Garden at the far end of the site. Here the garden completely changes character. Central to this more remote garden is a serene, oval lily pond bordered by a meadow of wild flowers and grasses, ablaze with bulbs in the spring. The Meadow Garden is bounded by cherry trees and a black mulberry, underplanted with shade-loving plants. In the middle of the pond is a subtly moving, brushed stainless steel kinetic sculpture by the American artist, George Rickey, entitled "Four Open Squares Horizontal Tapered," commissioned for the garden. The horizontal, window frame–like forms swivel in the breeze on their corner pivots, making new configurations as they overlap, and creating quivering reflections in the pond. The Head Gardener, Anne Wood, reports that those who come into the Meadow Garden are split about half and half between those who love to watch the almost hypnotic, subtle movements of this sculpture and those who find it "too modern."

The Long and Meadow Gardens are connected to the garden behind No. 29 by a brick path through the Loggia Garden. The Loggia, with seating against a brick wall and under a glass roof, looks out onto a small lawn backed by an intimate border of nepeta, hemerocallis, hardy geraniums, and roses.

The windows and patio of No. 29 look out over The Bank, The Lawn, and The Pavilion. The Bank, at a higher level, comprises a path bordering a small lawn backed by shrubs and low trees. Beyond and below it, the larger expanse of The Lawn is bordered by a few very large trees, the flat expanse of grass proving an ideal location for a large tent erected for fund-raising events. Although providing a pleasing green view from hospice rooms in No. 29 and St. Michael's Ward, The Lawn is not usable by infirm patients and those in wheelchairs as the paths are all of deep gravel. These will eventually be changed to brick, and the decaying structure of The Pavilion replaced.

Places to sit in the gardens at Trinity Hospice are many and varied: movable iron garden furniture outside the Day Center; stone benches in a brick-paved Sitting Circle; wooden benches with backs and arms tucked around the trunks of a large horse chestnut and an old plane tree; south-facing wooden park benches off the brick path that loops around the lily pond; more wooden benches in the glass-roofed loggia, with views to a herbaceous border and the lawns beyond. Moving around the garden, one's view is constantly changing—rounding a bend and coming upon the Sitting Circle; passing through a narrow gap in a beech hedge and seeing the moving shapes of the mobile sculpture reflected in the lily pond; turning a corner and finding a narrow path leading to the secluded seating Loggia. It is clearly an environment that was designed by professionals who understood the subtleties of what a garden can be.

There has only been one major alteration to the garden since its original construction. A small corner known as the Wild Dell had to be sacrificed for the construction of two octagon-shaped pavilions for a Day Center (with offices of the Home Stay staff underneath). Palliative care patients who are living at home can come here once a week to see a doctor, or the chiropodist, have their hair done, or take part in an arts and crafts program, which uses flowers, leaves, and vegetable matter from the garden for art and paper making.

Figure 10-9   A bench by a lily pond provides a place of contemplation.

Users

The most consistent users of the garden throughout the year are the relatives of inpatients who need time away from the bedside to recoup. "Sometimes I meet family members in the garden quite early in the morning after they have sat up all night at the bedside of a dying relative. When the sun comes up, and the day-shift of nurses comes on duty, they want a break" (Anne Wood).

The next most frequent users are the staff, particularly in the summer, but some of them make use of the garden throughout the year. In good weather, staff meetings are sometimes held in the Loggia. "A few staff have told me they took the job because of the garden! They came for an interview, saw the garden, and said to themselves—'This is a place where I could work!'" (Anne Wood). For the staff, the garden offers a quiet respite from the stress on the wards; a chance to escape from or meet colleagues, a place to eat lunch and relax.

Patients come out by themselves or with family members, mostly in summer. "By the time they're admitted, they're beginning to lose weight and feel the cold—so it has to be really good weather for them to feel comfortable outdoors. But sometimes —even in winter—I see a patient bundled up in blankets being wheeled around the grounds by a friend" (Anne Woods). The variety of seating and its location in private clusters permits families and patients to engage in intimate conversations, meditation, or prayer. The high boundary walls create a feeling of seclusion from neighbors and the outside world.

For the hospice organization, the garden is a very attractive asset to show prospective donors, and the large flat expanse of The Lawn provides a venue for fund-raising events.

Figure 10-10 The loggia is a popular place for staff and family member to take a break.

ADVANTAGES

- High walls enclose the garden and provide a sense of seclusion and privacy.
- The gardens cover a large area with many different sub-spaces, offering ample opportunity to "get away."
- Meandering paths and contoured lawns give the park–like terrain its interest and flow.
- Appeals to many of the senses — reflective water, falling water, wind chimes, fragrant plants, textual and color variations, and so on.
- Near to seating areas in particular, subtle contrasts in color, form, and texture of planting offer visual, tactile, and olfactory interest.
- Planting offers a range from familiar species to those that are unfamiliar and that may stimulate curiosity and conversation.
- For a patient viewing the garden from inside the hospice buildings, bold plant massing provides an interesting aesthetic appearance from a distance.
- Great variety of places to sit, differing by design and materials; views from a seated position; sense of enclosure/openness; distance from the buildings, and so on.
- Places for people to sit alone, or with others, and be quite private.
- Places to sit where the pond and sculpture or a herbaceous border could provide a focus for conversation.

- For a patient viewing the garden from a moving wheelchair, the planting and meandering paths offer many changing views.
- Very large mature trees provide a sense of timelessness.
- Very well maintained; a serene atmosphere.
- Patients and staff in rooms looking in the opposite direction from the garden have the benefit of expansive views over the grass and trees of 220 acres of Clapham Common, a complement to the hospice garden. (See Figure 10-1.)

DISADVANTAGES

- The building with the most expansive views of garden from its windows (No. 30) is a listed (i.e., historic) building that could not be altered for inpatient use, and therefore houses offices, a small coffee shop, and spaces for support staff.
- Buildings used by inpatients (No. 29 and St. Michael's Ward) look over segments of the garden (the Lawn and the Bank) with gravel paths that cannot be used by wheelchairs or by those who are sometimes infirm. However, there is access through the adjacent building (No. 30) into the larger expanse of the garden which *is* accessible. The gravel paths will be reconstructed in brick.
- One attractive group of benches under a horse chestnut tree in the Long Garden is constantly spattered with bird droppings, though to move the benches would be a shame since the prospect-refuge effect of sitting in this location is especially pleasing.
- Patients in the Day Center prefer to do arts and crafts outdoors on warm days rather than in the designated indoor space. The wrought iron garden furniture on the patio is awkward to use for this activity; wooden or glass tables would have been more workable.

Figure 10-11 *Patients in wheelchairs have access to most parts of the garden on smooth-surfaced paths.*

Joseph Weld Hospice, Dorchester, UK

Brief History of the Facility

Joseph Weld Hospice is located on the edge of Dorchester, a medium-sized market town in southern England and the county seat of Dorset. It is a fourteen-bed facility with a day center, and it was funded entirely by charitable contributions. Over £4 million was raised in just three years to build the hospice. It provides free services to its patients; the operating budget comes from charitable donations and charity shops. Opened in 1994, Joseph Weld

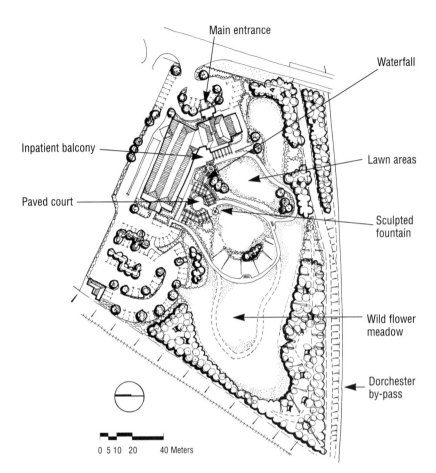

Main entrance

Waterfall

Inpatient balcony

Lawn areas

Paved court

Sculpted
fountain

Wild flower
meadow

Dorchester
by-pass

0 5 10 20   40 Meters

*Figure 10-12   Site plan of the Joseph
Weld Hospice, Dorchester, UK.*

Hospice was designed by Dorchester architect Stephen Hebb in
a traditional red brick style in harmony with the
nineteenth–twentieth century residential neighborhood nearby
(and no doubt with a "nod" to the Prince of Wales who owns
much of the land on which Dorchester stands and who is a firm
proponent of traditional architectural styles). On approaching
the main entrance off Herringston Road, one could be forgiven
for assuming this was an "old" rather than a new building, so
much does it draw on traditional styles and materials. (See
Figure 10-2.) It is domestic in scale and image, and its front hall
with flowers, wall hangings appliquéd with local Wessex scenes,
and comfortable chairs in floral fabrics, has the feel of a small
hotel. Servicing and most parking spaces are discreetly located
west of the building, neither marring the domestic scale front
entrance nor intruding on the attractive hospice gardens.

The Outdoor Space
Plantings at the front of the hospice provide a soft, welcoming
image and buffer the building from an adjacent road. The gar-

dens at the back of the hospice cover approximately two-thirds of the 4.5 acre site and were seen from the start as an integral part of the hospice environment. With a reasonable budget earmarked for development and installation, the gardens were finished before the first patients moved in. The landscape architect was Michael Oldham, of Environs Partnership, Dorchester.

The steeply sloped site was cut and filled in equal proportions to avoid the cost of removing anything from the site.

> Through careful articulation of the landform, the gardens of this attractive hospice have already begun to fit snugly into the gently rolling, west Dorset landscape. The landscape treatment owes as much to the influence of location [context] as it does to the functional brief [program] of the hospice (Fieldhouse, 1995).

The site slopes south approximately 25 feet from the building. It was necessary to design vehicular access to the rear of the site, to avoid conflict with the gardens and views to the south, as well as to design for access for people in wheelchairs to all parts of the building and gardens. The garden is subtly designed on four levels, each with a different character. A small lawn bounded by trees and shrubs forms the upper level, on the east of the site. Direct access from the building occurs on the middle two levels. The higher of these is a brick-paved terrace under a pergola outside the Orangery, looking out over a manicured lawn to the surrounding countryside. Patients and visitors can easily move out onto this terrace from the sun-catching

Figure 10-13 Patient rooms on the upper floor at Joseph Weld Hospice look out over the garden and surrounding countryside.

Orangery, or from a balcony running around the building and serving patient rooms.

At a level below this balcony are the kitchen, laundry, offices, and so on, as well as the Day Center (for patients living at home who may come in once a week). From this lower level, patients, staff and visitors can walk out onto brick-paved paths that form two half-moons under wooden pergolas. A central paved and brick court leads to a small formal fountain of sculpted leaves and frogs. This part of the garden is illuminated at night. The pergola supports a number of species of clematis, of different colors and flowering at different times. Fragrant plants near the seats include evergreen daphne, myrtle, lavender, and honeysuckle. To maintain interest in the winter months, the planting around the courtyard also includes species of hebe, jasmine, euonymus, and rose that flower or display berries in early winter or early spring. Completing this more formal, sheltered, close-to-the-building section of the garden is a large naturalistic waterfall of rough blocks of local Purbeck stone. The water runs from a pool at the upper level, down two waterfalls to a channel at the lower level, and the sound of rushing water envelops all of the seating areas close to the hospice.

The more naturalistic segment of the garden slopes slightly downhill from the formal brick paths and arbors. The surface of pathways changes to buff aggregate; they become narrower in width and meandering in character. Walking—or being wheeled—on these paths provides a quite different experience with views out to the Dorset countryside and views of the garden itself appearing and disappearing as the path loops around low planted mounds and through a wild flower meadow mown only twice a year.

Several kinds of paving material are used throughout the site. The main parking areas are tarmac with a red bull-nose brick as edging between the hardscape and turf. This brick is used throughout the scheme as edging material to give visual continuity to both walls and paved surfaces. The brick is also used as a paving material adjacent to the main entrance; on the terrace outside the Orangery, and in the lower courtyard. The main paving material used throughout the scheme is a lightly textured buff-colored paving slab. Where extensive paths loop round the less formal lower levels of the garden, a buff aggregate in a clear bitumen binder was used to achieve a smooth surface, important for wheelchairs, while still providing a gravel–like appearance, more sympathetic to a garden setting. Retaining walls in the garden are constructed of the same brick used for facing the building, to provide a harmonious link between the hospice and its gardens.

Figure 10-14   Seating along the arbor is backed by fragrant plants.

Figure 10-15 Soothing sounds in the garden from a waterfall, a fountain and moving pampas grass.

The serenity of this garden is remarkable considering its relative "youthfulness" (installed in 1992–1993), and the fact that the site is bounded on one side by Herringston Road; on another by a railway line on an embankment; and on the third side by the Dorchester bypass in a shallow cutting. Material excavated during road construction was banked up to further screen the motorway. This mounding combined with the sounds of the waterfall and fountain, completely mask any traffic sounds. The grassy railway embankment is no eyesore and a view of passing trains from a bench in The Meadow may be a pleasing distraction for patients.

Quite dense woodland plantings of a typical mix of species for this region (field maple, aspen, oak, ash, hazel, hawthorne, blackthorn, and rowan) will eventually screen part of the railway and create a more enclosed feeling to the lower segment of the garden, while still allowing views out to the more distant Dorset downland. Since the garden is not overlooked by any buildings (except the hospice itself), and since feelings for the countryside run deep in the British psyche, the strong visual connection to the surrounding landscape is especially appropriate and pleasing. The design, which decreases in formality with greater distance from the hospice buildings, successfully blends the site into its context and—on a more symbolic level—permits hospice patients to feel themselves not "set apart" from the community, and yet to be in a peaceful setting that offers privacy and seclusion.

Uses of the Garden

The most regular users of the garden, in terms of both daily and seasonal use, are the relatives of patients in the hospice. Being able to walk in a private, peaceful setting, or to sit and look at the distant Dorset landscape, provides some solace and respite from the very emotional experience of sitting by a loved one's bedside.

In the spring and summer months, patients are taken around the garden, often in wheelchairs, by relatives or members of the nursing team. The balcony area off the wards provides a space where patients, if well enough, can sit outside and look over the whole garden and the countryside beyond. On occasions, patients have asked to be wheeled in their beds onto this balcony to die outside.

Day Centre patients are those who are largely cared for at home, but who come once a week to a hospice to give family members a respite. In good weather these patients sit out in the lower courtyard, directly accessible from the Day Centre, enjoying the garden or engaged in various activities with the staff.

Another important use of the gardens is by the staff who go outside for lunchtime breaks, and for periods of quiet reflection to balance stressful experiences in their work. A less significant, but still important use of the garden is by children visiting a patient, for distraction and release of energy and tension.

Finally, the large lower meadow is used once a year for a fete attended by more than 2,000 people. This is a major fund-raising event for the hospice, and it is critical that there is space on which to erect a large tent and accommodate a huge influx of visitors.

ADVANTAGES
- Garden blends functionally and aesthetically with hospice building.
- Different levels permit users to find places of seclusion and privacy.
- Looped pathways provide a user who is walking, or being pushed in a wheelchair, changing views of formal gardens, less formal meadows, and the natural landscape beyond.
- Building and garden design capitalize on views to the surrounding countryside, allowing hospice users to feel some temporal and spatial continuity with life around them.
- Many benches are placed with sensitive consideration for multisensory experience (sounds, smells, views).
- Grading, planting, and the sounds of a waterfall and fountain subtly combine to mask the sight and sounds of a busy traffic bypass adjacent to the site.
- The design of the gardens—from more formal adjacent to the building to informal at the southern boundary—reflect on a small scale the context of Dorchester in its country setting.

Figure 10-16 A meandering pathway leads down to a less formal part of the garden with a wildflower meadow and views to the Dorset countryside.

- The use of local materials, such as Purbeck stone and brick, together with familiar native trees and popular perennials, create an environment to which patients, visitors, and staff alike can relate and find comforting and familiar.

Laguna Honda Hospice Memorial Garden, San Francisco, California

Laguna Honda Hospital is located on a hilly, 64-acre site in San Francisco. It was originally founded in 1866 as an almshouse for the city's indigent population, and after the 1906 earthquake was rebuilt as a shelter for the indigent homeless. The present 1,147-bed hospital was built in 1926, and is the nation's largest municipally owned and operated long-term care facility.

Description of the Garden

The garden is located in a narrow courtyard between the ward-wings of this old pavilion-style hospital. The garden is shaped like a flag on a pole. The larger, square portion is approximately 40 × 40 feet; the narrow extension is a wide pathway lined with shrubs and two smaller gardens leading out to an access road. Five-story, buff-stucco buildings surround the garden on three of its four sides.

Stepping out of the ground level hospice ward into the garden, one finds oneself in a quiet, green oasislike space with pigeons cooing from the top of one large tree, and the sounds of trickling water from two small Japanese-style water features. Even in this small space, there are six different subspaces where an individual or a family group can find some privacy. Immediately outside the entry door is a small concrete patio, bounded by a low railing on two sides, and furnished with a table, chairs, and a barbecue. A few steps away, but out of earshot, an umbrella-table and chairs is located next to a simple water feature where the water falls from a bamboo pipe onto rocks, and a miniature Japanese maple casts shadows on the water. A large paved patio forms the end of the garden, against the building, furnished with tables, chairs, potted plants displayed on an étagère, and plants in large cement pots and wooden tubs. A small area with a different, zenlike character consists of a wooden garden bench set into gravel, bounded by bamboo and looking onto an "island" rock and bonsai tree, low planting, and a small Japanese water feature.

An important feature of the Hospice garden is the subspace outside the window of a "Quiet Room," where imminently dying patients are brought for intensive caring, and where relatives may stay overnight in privacy. In the window box is a jas-

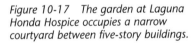
Figure 10-17 The garden at Laguna Honda Hospice occupies a narrow courtyard between five-story buildings.

mine bush, which emits its fragrance into the room as a form of aromatherapy. Outside the window is a massive Thai urn containing a globe-shaped water fountain, which transmits the soft sound of water falling into water. Along with the sound of wind chimes, the rustle of the breeze through the bamboo, and the view of swaying greenery, the Quiet Room admits the healing presence of nature. Instead of a frantic and mechanized experience, it is hoped that those who attend a death will perhaps subliminally experience dying as something natural.

As one walks down the wide pathway lined with San Francisco cobblestones, which leads from the main part of the garden to an access road, three more small garden spaces come into view. The first is a half-moon shaped stucco bench set under three large cottoneasters. The second is a Children's Garden with a backdrop of a mural painted on the wall of the hospital depicting a Beatrix Potter-like scene of a child's day from dawn to dusk. "The idea was to create a garden for the child in all of us; a place to look back on one's own childhood, to review one's life" (Derek Kerr, Attending Physician). A looped path of yellow brick, recalling the Wizard of Oz, leads through this small garden from one simple wooden arbor gate to another—the two gates donated in memory of a husband and wife who both died in the hospice and who were themselves childless. Elements in the mural—a pond, rose quartz crystals, a row of carrots—are repeated in the garden itself. Just before this long narrow outdoor space terminates in an access road, another small garden appears—this one an area of ivy with a classical fountain.

The Hospice garden was designed to appeal to all five senses because patients often have sensory impairments. Hence, there are visually pleasing architectural elements; varying shades of green; the sound of wind chimes and water; fragrant herbs and flowers; textured plants at wheelchair level; and tasty herbs, tomatoes, and strawberries in summer. Virtually any hospice patient, no matter how impaired, can experience nature in the garden if they want to.

Use of the Garden

The garden is highly used, particularly in the warmer months, by patients, staff, family members, and volunteers. Patients are sometimes served their meals outside at the round garden tables. Family members bring a patient outside in a wheelchair or sit in a private space to consult with a physician. Staff go outside for coffee or lunch breaks, or to hold meetings.

One measure of the success of, and need for, this small, low-budget garden is the fact that families visiting patients in other wards of the hospital bring them down to the Memorial Garden on weekends (having seen it from upper windows), and two doctors from other departments regularly come to sit by the Japanese bamboo fountain for "stress reduction." Despite the huge area encompassed by the Laguna Honda Hospital, with spacious lawns and grounds, the hospital was built with little concern for easy access to the outdoors, and there is no other quiet, reflective garden space like this one next to the Hospice.

Since Laguna Honda is a county hospital providing care for the indigent, and since it is housed in a very old facility, there is

Figure 10-18 Options of where to sit provide semi-private settings for patients and their visitors.

little that can be done to improve the interior environment of the hospice ward. The transformation of a bleak courtyard into a garden was one way that staff and volunteers could enhance the environment, creating a space where terminal patients in a twenty-eight-bed open ward could find some privacy and spiritual nourishment. For family members, it provides a setting in which to grieve, and in which they can leave a living memorial when a loved one dies. For the staff and volunteers who designed and built it, and continue to maintain and add to it, the garden has become the energizing heart of their hospice work.

> Inside the ward, no one really sees the good work we do, tending dying patients—one hundred and twenty last year. The garden is kind of a symbol of how much we care. People see the garden—alive and flourishing and cared for—and they think—'These are good people here; I will be cared for…" (Derek Kerr, Attending Physician).

ADVANTAGES
- The garden is visible and easily accessible from the ward.
- The garden is "domestic" in scale.
- It is totally wheelchair-accessible.
- Plant materials, water features, wind chimes, birds, and so on, create a soothing, multisensory experience.
- The area is sheltered from the wind and is private.
- A selection of semiprivate subspaces in sun or shade provide choices.
- Use of the gardens is supported by staff and programmed activities.
- Designed and implemented by staff and volunteers, the garden is a source of pride and is well-maintained.

DISADVANTAGES
- Shade created by the narrow site and tall buildings reduces the use of the garden on cool days.
- Plaques on planters, benches, and so on, indicating a gift in memory of someone who has died may—in time—create a "graveyard" image.
- Although the garden is secluded, there are other wards above, and sometimes cries from a patient disturb the tranquillity of the garden.

Hospice House, Portland, Oregon

By Arezu Movahed (Portland State University)

Brief Description of the Facility and Its Setting

This facility is one of the few freestanding hospice facilities in North America. Located in Hillsdale, Oregon, one of Portland's west-side neighborhoods, Hospice House offers inpatient care for the terminally ill in a homelike atmosphere with specially trained nursing staff. Providing care to the person close to death, controlling pain and other symptoms, fostering communication and spiritual growth, and giving the dying person's family the support they require is the mission of Hospice House. The hospice philosophy recognizes that once curative treatment is not appropriate, the focus of the ill member and family turns to the quality of their remaining time together. The distress that comes with terminal illness is alleviated at Hospice House by offering a peaceful, homelike atmosphere to patients and their families, where people have opportunities to be together and talk, walk through the gardens, and play with the dog. The setting of natural beauty, careful landscaping, and comfortably furnished rooms contributes immeasurably to the atmosphere of warmth and comfort.

Very close to the city center, on the outskirts of the community of Hillsdale, Hospice House is set in 3.5 wooded acres, giving the visitor a feeling of being out in the forest. It is a peaceful place for individuals and families facing one of life's most difficult and challenging experiences.

Interviews with the founder, the architect, and the interior designer all revealed the main intentions in the design of the facility to be creating a connection to the outdoors, enhancing the quality of life by creating simple yet pleasant spaces to care for patients and their families, using homelike features as much as possible, and creating defined spaces to break up the continuity often seen in institutional settings.

Brief History of the Facility

In 1980, a group of compassionate healthcare providers, social service professionals, and other individuals determined that existing services for the terminally ill and their families in Portland, Oregon needed to be improved. Three areas of need were identified: bereavement care for those who have suffered a loss through death; practical help for those who are caring for a terminally ill person at home; and a facility, not affiliated with a hospital, where patients could go for respite or final care.

Figure 10-19 Patient care wing at Hospice House, Portland, Oregon.

Hospice House was incorporated in 1980 as a nonprofit, nonsectarian corporation. It provided information, referral, community education, and trained volunteers to work with patients from local hospice home care and hospital programs. In 1982, the Arigo Counseling program was organized to provide professionally trained counselors for those suffering a loss through death. Throughout the years, the main goal of building a freestanding facility remained. After a three-year search for a site, a 3.5 acre forested property that included a 1926 vintage mansion (Henningsen House) was donated to Hospice House at its present location at 6171 SW Capitol Highway, a 10-minute drive from downtown Portland. Staff and existing programs moved into the house, which was used for administrative and counseling offices. The next two years were spent continuing to train and place hospice volunteers in patients' homes and nursing homes, offering the Arigo counseling program, raising funds for planning and building the inpatient wing, and developing the inpatient program. In 1986, Hospice House began construction of their new patient care facility, created as a wing on the side of the existing mansion. The first patient was admitted in September 1987, and Hospice House became Oregon's first and only freestanding inpatient hospice. Patients and their families were served by the staff and volunteers of Hospice House until December 1990, when the operations were suspended because of financial difficulties. A few months later, in August 1991, Hospice House merged with the Ecumenical Ministries of Oregon, and the house reopened in November of 1991, as Hopewell House. Since most of the information for this study was collected when the facility was called Hospice House, that name is used throughout.

Description of Outdoor Space

Landscape Architect Carol Reed of Meyer & Reed, Portland) designed a great variety of outdoor spaces, in terms of size, image, accessibility, and location. On approaching the hospice building, one is immediately aware of its calm, green setting—formal gardens in front, a wooded ravine behind, totally screening the hospice from a nearby traffic thoroughfare and a small shopping center. The hospice building housing administrative offices and patients care rooms is surrounded on two sides by the forested ravine. On the other two sides of the building, closer to the front entrance, are the more formal garden areas. Changes in elevation across the property allow for several segregated garden areas. . All of the garden areas are well-maintained, with seasonal flowers, vegetables, and perennials always

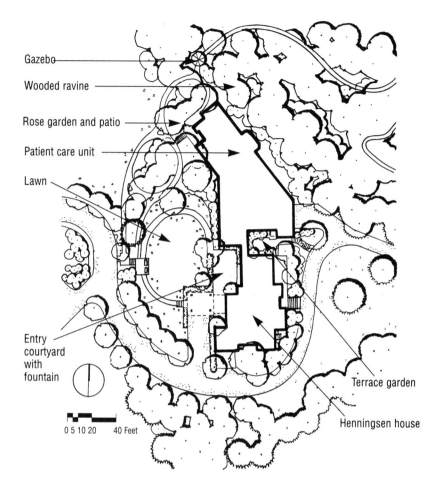

Gazebo

Wooded ravine

Rose garden and patio

Patient care unit

Lawn

Entry
courtyard
with
fountain

0 5 10 20   40 Feet

Terrace garden

Henningsen house

Figure 10-20   Site plan of Hospice House, Portland, Oregon.

in bloom from spring to fall. There are expansive areas of lawn, and brick walkways lead to a rose garden and a large gazebo with a swing, just above the patient care unit, on the north side of the property. Garden accents such as trellises with climbing flowers, birdfeeders, birdbaths, and brick paths with a simple black metal fence along the edge are used throughout. On the north and northeast sides of the patient care unit, a wooded area provides nature views from all patient rooms.

Use of Outdoor Spaces[3]

Throughout the interviews that were conducted, the grounds of the facility were mentioned by everyone as an outstanding feature of the facility. Staff unanimously reported that the grounds

---

[3]A Ph.D. dissertation on Hospice House by the author is the source of particularly detailed information on how the outdoor spaces are perceived and used (Movahed, 1995).

were the most beautiful part of the facility, the parklike setting creating a sense of "home." One staff person remarked that when she first went to Hospice House for a job interview, she thought it was a country club, and that she was at the wrong address. A volunteer stated: "One of the things that impressed me was the old estate feeling of Hospice House ... the beautiful grounds, and all the work that went into making it lovely. ..." Volunteers felt that outdoor space was essential to a hospice program.

Some family members reported that they felt reluctant to visit Hospice House the first time, but that the beauty of the grounds and well-maintained gardens was the first thing that positively affected their feelings toward the idea of "hospice." A family member of a patient explained: "The setting was very soothing and healing with the trees and the woods around it; and then the gardens on top of that made it more beautiful." Another family member, referring to her husband who was a patient, reported: "I think he was very impressed with the outdoors. It was in the fall, and the grounds were just beautiful."

A brick-paved courtyard with fountain and movable garden furniture on the west side of the building and close to the front entrance is one of the areas most heavily used by staff, volunteers, patients, and their families. Staff and volunteers go there to eat lunch or take a break; patients and family members sit outside to relax, and visiting children take off their shoes and socks and play in the fountain. Patients who cannot walk on their own are carried out there in wheelchairs or on gurneys.

Figure 10-21 A courtyard near the main entrance, with moveable furniture and a fountain, is a favorite spot for staff, patients, and visitors to sit outside.

One of the extremely valuable features of the courtyard is the cement-and-brick water fountain, its sound and the feel of the water. Plants grow up on the pillars of this area, many flower pots are set about the Courtyard, and a topiary rabbit sitting on a chair at the front entrance greets people as they approach. A volunteer reported that there was one patient "who just loved to go out there and sit by the fountain; he would sit there for hours. In fact, evenings he would sit there until it was time to go to bed." A staff member referred to another patient who spent twenty-two out of every twenty-four hours outdoors. She had always wanted to go camping as a child but had not been allowed to. So now, in her last few months of life, she was doing it. The staff supported her, brought out her meals, tucked her into her wheelchair with blankets, and left her under the entry where she sat at the portico reading, dozing, and looking at the garden.

Another well-used area very accessible from the building is a sunken patio at the end of the patient care area. Patients who are ambulatory enjoy moving about the facility, especially to this patio, one of their favorite places to sit. A round table with umbrella and chairs encourages patients and visitors to have their meals out there. A volunteer remarked that it was especially attractive because it is "...a very private area, down below the hill, snugly warm."

West of the courtyard and main entrance is a semiformal garden of lawns, perennials, flowering shrubs, and winding brick pathways. This garden wraps around the north end of the building as a terraced rose garden and gazebo. Unfortunately, because of the slope of the land, it is difficult for patients to maneuver themselves or be pushed by volunteers or family members into these parts of the grounds. However, since the land slopes up from the building, these gardens provide attractive garden views for those seated in the fountain courtyard or sunken patio. Staff encourage visitors to pick flowers for the patient rooms. Family members needing a break from visiting a bedridden patient especially like the rose garden and gazebo as a place to "get away." It is a place too where counseling of relatives takes place.

At the angle where the old mansion of Henningsen House meets the new patient care wing is a small Terrace Garden, a favorite with family members because of its proximity to the patient rooms. A staff member remarked how everyone commented on its attractiveness. "It is just delightful...a miniature garden, very comforting because of its size and because it is protected on three sides."

The wife of a hospice resident recalled:

"Towards the last three or four days my husband could no longer speak, and he was agitated becuse he had gone off the medication, so I thought it might be pleasant for him before he lapsed into a coma that maybe I could take him outside... So, we put him in a wheelchair and bundled him up with blankets, and I took him outside, and pushed him all around the yard. He was so touched... I started singing to him every song I could think of, we stopped and looked at each one of the flower bushes. He was not able to speak, but I wheeled him around for one hour, and when we came back to come down into the building, I had to go in front of him to take him down the pathway, because it was a bit steep. I looked at him, and he had tears rolling down his face. I think he was so profoundly touched by the beauty, the incredible beauty."

Figure 10-22   The hospice faces onto a garden, and is backed by a forested ravine.

The wooded ravine surrounding the hospice on its north and east sides was viewed very positively by staff and volunteers. A staff member explains:

The woods are a symbolic foundation for a great deal of mythic thought. Having access to the big Douglas firs and a wooded walk with animals and a creek—quiet in the midst of all the fury—is the best feature of the facility.

Since the dirt trails are not wheelchair-accessible, patients cannot be taken into this beautiful area. Occasionally, the area is used by a visitor to get away: "People can still see the building and they know that a staff member could call them back from one of the patient room windows if necessary."

In one significant way, patients *do* have access to this forested area, and that is by viewing it from their rooms, all of which were designed to have this restorative outlook. There is at least one birdfeeder outside the window of each of the patient rooms, a small but significant feature that was appreciated by everyone. A volunteer explained: "Patients and their families really appreciate having that kind of life outside their rooms. Squirrels and chipmunks and birds eat at the feeders and most people have a sensitivity to those things at that point in their life." A woman, referring to her husband, remarked "When he first got to Hospice House, he was very pleased that he had a window that looked out into the trees. He thought that was really, really beautiful; and that there was a birdfeeder outside, he was thrilled by that." Many family members mentioned that the wildlife was a very positive feature both to them and to the patients, and that the birdfeeders were a nice diversion to take their minds off their grief.

ADVANTAGES

- Sited in a natural setting, where users have easy and direct access to the outdoors.
- Centrally located in the metropolitan area.
- Offers a variety of beautiful garden areas.
- Provides for a variety of outdoor activities—sitting, walking, enjoyment of nature, and so on.
- Access to a wooded area and trails for walking.
- All patient rooms have views of a wooded area and wildlife.
- Every patient room has a birdfeeder outside the window.
- Facility and furnishings are homelike, flexible, and comfortable.
- Grounds provide opportunities to get away, but still be within proximity of the patient care unit.
- Natural elements are brought indoors (natural light, house plants, etc.).
- Covered canopy at front entrance creates a sheltered place to sit outside in rainy weather.

Figure 10-23   Patients appreciate the views to a forested landscape from their rooms.

DISADVANTAGES

- Insufficient level areas outdoors to maneuver patients who are in wheelchairs.
- Reflected heat from the cement paving of the courtyard and the white paint of the building make it uncomfortable to sit out on hot days.
- Some staff worry that the fountain in the courtyard is not safe for children to play in.
- Some walkways are too steep for wheelchairs.
- Forest trails are not wheelchair-accessible.
- A level pathway that went completely around the building would have been appreciated by family members taking patients in wheelchairs out for a change of view.

DESIGN GUIDELINES

Familiar Landscape

At the first annual American Conference on Hospice Care in Boston in 1985, a speaker asked the audience where they would prefer to die. When he posed the option "in a hospital," no one raised a hand; four or five responded that they would prefer to die in a hospice; the majority (a hundred or so) responded enthusiastically to the option of dying at home (Healy, 1986, p. 18). "Thus the hospice patient and visitor are likely to feel more at ease when the facility building and grounds retain as much reference as possible to domestic scale, layout, and ambiance. Elizabeth Kübler-Ross put it succinctly, 'Keep it homey!'" *(ibid)*.

In times of stress, people are comforted by what is familiar and understandable. This is particularly true for family members and patients in hospice environments. The interior design of hospice settings often emphasize homelike materials, textures, colors, lighting, furnishings, and so on. Similarly, it is very important that outdoor areas be designed and detailed so that they appear as much as possible like a home-based garden. This will require that the designer appreciate the essential elements of a residential garden in the region in which the hospice is located.

A Transcendent Image

In a study leading to recommendations for a hospice in Houston, Texas, Verderber proposed the concept of "Hospice as Waystation"—"a midpoint between the everyday existence-home-community milieu and the spiritual milieu of the here-after" (Verderber, 1982, p. 15). Whatever a patient's or family member's beliefs about life after death, there is no doubt that the process of dying and death represents a major event, and that needs to be honored in the design of the hospice environment. "It should transcend the common realities of everyday

Figure 10-24 A landscape that is familiar and reassuring is welcomed by hospice patients. (Trinity Hospice, London, UK.)

life while embracing all that is associated with home and the familiar. It should be a meaningful synthesis of the ordinary and the unique... it must simultaneously look outward, inward, and upward..." (*ibid*, p. 15). Translating these qualities into a garden design is probably one of the most challenging assignments that any designer will ever face.

Cultural Appropriateness

When a hospice is located in a setting where there is cultural and ethnic diversity in the population being served, it is critical that the design of outdoor elements incorporate plants, design elements, art, and symbolic features that communicate comfort, familiarity, and emotional sustenance to people of different cultural, language, and religious backgrounds. This may prove to be difficult in melding the landscape preferences of different groups, for example, native Hispanics and newcomer Anglos in the American southwest. In a situation like this, two or more distinct subareas could be provided, or the cultures could be interwoven as they are in the surrounding community.

Design to modify contrast between light quality indoors and outdoors. Older people and those suffering from several terminal illnesses have difficulty adjusting to the glare that may trouble them as they leave a building and move into a brightly lit, sunny garden. Doorways and patios outside rooms should have arbors, overhangs, tree-shade, or other devices to help ameliorate the transition.

Similarly, while outdoors, patients may have difficulty adjusting their eyes to extreme contrasts of light and dark in different areas of the garden. "Reducing contrast between the garden's sunny and shady areas can compensate for the patient's difficulties. Lawn, pavements of darker color value, pergolas, summer houses, and other shade structures all help reduce the glare in the garden's sunny areas. Pavements and ground covers of lighter color hue and value, trees and shrubs with translucent and/or variegated foliage will also aid in brightening shady areas" (Healy, 1986, p. 21).

Consider the provision of soothing natural sounds in the garden. Hearing is often the last of the senses to leave the dying patient. As a disease progresses, however, loud sounds tend to be painful and soft sounds inaudible. Sounds at the mid-range are desirable and—fortuitously—those are the levels of many sounds experienced in nature: leaves rustling, water

Figure 10-25 Many hospice patients have difficulty adjusting to extreme contrasts of light and dark. An arbor or trellis transition at building exits is appreciated. (San Diego Hospice.)

Figure 10-26 The sounds from a near-by motorway are masked by this water-fall, which adds a soothing tone to the garden. (Joseph Weld Hospice, Dorchester, UK.)

falling, birds singing, and so on (Healy, 1986, p. 20). The garden should be designed so that it provides a symphony of natural sounds: consider the differing sound quality of the breeze moving through various kinds of trees and shrubs; birdbaths, bird-feeders, and berry bushes that may attract songbirds; water features that can be heard from specific seats; wind chimes that magnify the sound of a breeze. The details of a garden planted outside the window of the Quiet Room at Laguna Honda Hospice, San Francisco, California, where patients are taken when death is imminent, have been sensitively selected to provide a variety of natural sounds.

Care should also be taken to keep air conditioning equipment, recycling pumps, and other noise-producing machines away from the garden; if that is not possible, they should be adequately muffled. The hospice grounds at Joseph Weld House (Dorchester, UK) were designed so that an embankment and waterfall screen out sounds from an adjacent motorway, thus enhancing the experience of being in the garden.

Design to avoid extremes of temperature and humidity. Just as extremes of sound and light level are difficult to adjust to, so are extremes of temperature and humidity. A hospice garden needs to be sensitively designed and furnished so that microclimates are created that are warm in winter or at cool times of the day, and cool in summer; that are protected against the wind or invite cooling breezes in hot climates; that incorporate water features to humidify the garden in dry and desert climates. The same features that mitigate glare can also be useful in keeping the microclimate comfortable (Healy, 1986, p. 22). In areas with extended periods of hot or cold weather, a glassed-over atrium, solarium, or conservatory may be very much appreciated.

Design a meandering walking path. Walking outside with changing views and sensory input can provide an important stress-reducing experience, particularly important for family members and staff in a hospice setting. The route of a pathway needs to be sensitively planned so that those walking, or patients being pushed in a wheelchair, experience a sense of "getting away" from the hospice, with a variety of subspaces providing distracting distant views or views focused on nearby garden details.

Select appropriate paving. Paving needs to accommodate the easy movement of wheelchairs; provide a surface that does not produce problems of glare; and that is made of a material that is not easily fractured or up-lifted by nearby tree roots. While brick is a warm and pleasing material to many, high standards of initial laying and further maintenance are essential so that it does not become a serious hazard.[4]

Design a covered walkway. Where the grounds are large enough and the weather is often rainy, the provision of covered walkways, perhaps terminating in a gazebo or greenhouse, should be considered. Volunteers at a hospice in Portland, Oregon remarked that such walkways would have enabled them to take patients outdoors in wheelchairs in the rainy season (Movahed, 1995, p. 78).

Provide places to sit and contemplate. Some benches need to be located so that a person can sit alone in a protected, private semi-enclosed setting in order to pray, meditate, or grieve, near to but away from, the hospice environment. While a chapel might provide for such an experience inside the hospice building, the religious function of this space may render it unacceptable to some people. A refuge-space for meditation in nature—which may or may not be specifically designated as such—can allow for very meaningful experiences.

Provide an overhead canopy. Those people who sit outdoors in a hospice garden are likely to be particularly stressed and anxious. For this reason, the positioning of a bench and design of its immediate surroundings should be approached with especial care and sensitivity. Humans feel secure when their back is protected; an overhang or canopy creates a sense of protective "roof." Hence some benches need to be located against a tree, hedge, or wall, and with the protection of tree branches, a pergola or trellis overhead. At Trinity Hospice, London, a particularly popular seating place comprises a garden loggia with glass roof, back wall of brick, movable garden chairs, and views to a lawn and herbaceous border (see Figure 10-10).

Provide places to socialize and talk. A combination of appropriately designed benches and movable garden chairs need to be located so that a patient and family member, or two members of staff, or relatives of a recently deceased patient, can sit and talk quietly in a completely private, secluded setting.

Figure 10-27 A meandering pathway provides changing views for someone who is walking slowly, or is being pushed in a wheelchair. (Trinity Hospice, London, UK.)

---

[4]Vince Healy points out that the craft of laying brick remains at a higher calibre in Europe than is true in North America (Correspondence, 1998).

Figure 10-28 A gazebo in the garden provides a destination point and a setting for private conversation. (Hospice House, Portland, Oregon.)

Sitting in a garden, particularly at a time of bereavement, surrounded by trees, plants, and wildlife, seemingly indifferent to the cycles of life and death, can provide some sense of solace—that life goes on.

Design for touch. The affirmation of touching and being touched is incredibly important to the dying patient (Healy, 1986, p. 20). Plants can play a role in that those that are soft or furry to the touch, and those that release a pleasant fragrance when rubbed, can be pleasing and bring back memories. However, it is important to remember that many hospice patients suffer from ansomnia (inability to smell), so fragrance in the garden may be more important for visitors and staff.

It is also important to avoid plants that are thorny or might cause itchiness, flowers that attract insects whose bites or stings could bring on serious allergic reactions, or whose pollen could cause adverse reactions.

Water as a palliative agent. It is important that the spiritual and symbolic aspects of water be incorporated into the design of a hospice garden. Still reflective water can provide a setting for meditation or prayer, while the sound and view of moving water is undeniably soothing and restorative.

Princess Alice Hospice in Esher, Surrey, UK, located in the flood plain of the River Mole, incorporates a holding reservoir that laps right up to the building. A cantilevered boardwalk overhangs the edge of the lake and a rich variety of natural life passes by the windows of the hospice (Fieldhouse, 1995, p. 39). At Trinity Hospice in London, a large lily pond provides a locale of calm and reflection. At Joseph Weld House in Dorchester, UK, a naturalistic, man-made waterfall masks the sound of nearby traffic and creates an atmosphere of repose in a small courtyard at its base. A two-story interior waterfall inside San Diego Hospice is less successful in that the dark rocks and filtered light introduce a somber component to the potential restorative benefits of this water feature.

The sound and location of a moving water feature need to be carefully discussed with hospice staff. Some consider such a feature problematic because it may trigger the desire to urinate in some patients. Others discount this as a problem.

Provide features in the garden that would engage a child's attention. Family members often have to—or want to—bring young children to a hospice to visit a dying relative. For the child there can be a range of feelings from fear to boredom. Spending time in the garden permits a child more freedom and relieves adults of stress. San Diego Hospice, for example, includes a simple play-equipment area in their garden, visible from—but not too near to—a number of patient rooms. Another approach would be to include items equally engaging to a child and a sick adult: hummingbirds at a feeder, goldfish swimming in a pool, a stream of water bouncing over rocks. "The beauty in this kind of situation lies in the fact that the patients have the freedom and discretion of watching the chil-

"I flew across the country with my five year old daughter to be with my father while he slowly died in a large extended care ward. The ward scared my daughter with its strange noises and odd smells. It became our habit to wrap my father in blankets and wheel him out of the building into the garden. While my father and I chatted my daughter chased squirrels and played with sticks. She could relate to my father in the garden and he to her—with a dignity that was denied him in the ward. The garden was not scary. The garden normalized their last moments together."

(L. T. H.) Victoria, B.C., Canada

Figure 10-29   A playground for visiting children at San Diego Hospice.

dren observe the garden elements or sharing observations with the child" (Healy, 1986, p. 34).

Provide a view from the window. In a hospice, more than in many other medical facilities, a view out to nature for the bed-bound patient is critical. The sense of serenity, connectedness, and spirituality that nature embodies for many people is particularly important during the confusing, and often painful, period leading to death. The view from the window might be thought of as a kind of painting or diorama. The architect, interior designer, and landscape architect need to work closely together from the start to ensure that the view from every bed encompasses elements that provide a variety of sensory input: a tree with spring bloom and fall color; a birdfeeder to attract the movement and sounds of wildlife; the sound of water; the view to a section of sky providing a vista of escape may be an ideal combination. In a study of a hospice in Oregon (Hospice House, Portland), patients were particularly thankful for views out to a forest with individual birdfeeders placed outside each window.

The furniture in a patient's room needs to be arranged so that both the patient (in a bed or chair), and a visitor (sitting or standing) can look out at the view. When there are awkward pauses in the conversation, when the patient is dozing, or if a visitor experiences a stressful sense of entrapment, either one can subtly turn their attention to the view outside and effect a graceful cognitive escape (Healy, 1986, p. 33).

Provide views from a horizontal position. Some hospice designs make allowance for patient beds being rolled out onto a patio or balcony. When this is the case it is essential that care be taken to consider a view to greenery and sky, interesting roof features, and so on, from a horizontal position.

Where appropriate provide panoramic viewpoint. Contemplation of a panoramic view is often sought by people experiencing extremes of stress, grief, or confusion (Francis and Cooper Marcus, 1992). Perceiving an expanse of sky and landscape, ocean, or cityscape seems to facilitate a mood-shift, enabling the viewer to "get things into perspective." The need for this kind of experience is especially salient in a hospice environment. At Joseph Weld House (Dorchester, UK), patient rooms, an outdoor terrace and extensive gardens all look out to views over the agriculture downland of Dorset. At San Diego Hospice (Sand Diego, California), its location atop an escarpment

Figure 10-30   A panoramic view of the cityscape from a seat in the garden helps a visitor to "get things into perspective." (San Diego Hospice.)

ensures views over a distant freeway and extensive urban landscape from the dining room and from strategically placed benches in the narrow garden space that encircles the building. Bailey House, the first US residence for homeless persons with AIDS, is located in an old hotel looking over the Hudson River in New York. A journalist recalled the names of particular residents who had recently died and "...all the dead who once gazed out the windows of this place by the river, watching the gulls soar as they are soaring now and the tugs passing upstream and the water alive with light" (Brown, 1992, p. 55). Being able to view life-going-on may be especially important for hospice patients and their families.

Where possible, provide a private garden retreat for staff.
The success of a hospice depends on the facility having qualified staff, and on retaining them. Unfortunately, there is a high potential for burn-out in hospice work, resulting in the need to constantly train new personnel (Healy, 1986, p. 34). Therefore anything that can be done to alleviate staff stress is critically important. One environmental solution is to provide a comfortable staff lounge with an adjacent private garden or patio where staff members can seek privacy for dealing with their own sense of loss as patients die.

If the hospice garden is moderately large, it may be enough to provide many semiprivate retreats outdoors so that a staff person can find a place away from the building and from patients and visitors. The extensive garden at Trinity Hospice works well in this regard; in fact, it has been a positive recruit-

"A garden which appears to be in a 'poetic state of disrepair' (rather than unkempt) when slightly fallow, reminds us that it is forgivable to have elements in our lives that seem out of place—and which may be quite in place according to some concept of order we do not as yet understand."

VINCE HEALY

ing asset as staff considering an appointment see the garden and recognize its value in their daily mental health needs.

At the twenty-eight-bed hospice ward at Laguna Honda Hospital, staff caring for the indigent terminally ill have very few private indoor places, and use the small garden they themselves created and help maintain as a welcome retreat from the stress of their work.

Provide a small private garden next to the viewing room or chapel. If the hospice has its own chapel and/or a room where family members can spend time quietly with a loved one after his or her death, an adjacent garden will be much appreciated. This should be screened for privacy, have seating and, ideally, incorporate a water feature so that the sound of water complements the sound of tears (Healy, 1986, p. 34).

Include a garden room or conservatory. A temperature-controlled space with plants, garden furniture, water, perhaps an aviary, can be beneficial to many patients who are vulnerable to even slight variations in temperature. Where possible, this should face onto an outside garden with trees and "real" weather.

Design with materials that improve, rather than wear out, with age (Healy, 1986, p. 35). There is something timeless and reassuring about a garden that looks like it has been there, and will be there, for a very long time. Materials that develop an attractive patina or that encourage the growth of moss; plants that take care of themselves and live a long time; fast-growing vines that cover a trellis or wall—all these will add to the sense of a garden's rootedness and longevity, and perhaps provide a metaphor for the continuance of life.

Educate the staff, visitors, and patients in the use of the garden. It is important that nursing staff understand how the garden was designed to function, which areas are sheltered from the wind, catch the morning sun, provide a view to the world beyond the hospice, and so on. As the body deteriorates, patients have to adjust to new handicaps and the worsening of existing handicaps. They also proceed through different psychological stages of dealing with death. The staff can assist in patients' and visitors' use of the outdoors if they can guide them to which garden areas may or may not meet their needs (Healy, 1986, p. 21). It would be desirable if the designer produced a

Figure 10-31 Staff need a place to get away from the stress of working in the hospice environment. (Laguna Honda Hospice, San Francisco.)

simplified garden plan, annotated with subspaces for different experiences, and reproduced this in a pamphlet handed to patients, visitors, and new members of staff. (For example see p. 295.)

REFERENCES

"AIDS Hospice" (1990). *Interior Design*, Vol. 61, No. 5, March, pp. 204–205.

"A Place of Passage: Coming Home Hospice" (1988). *Architectural Record*, Vol. 176, No. 13, pp. 104–105.

Brown, C. (1992). "A Last Good Place to Live: Inside a Residence for the Homeless with AIDS," *Harper's Magazine,* February.

Carey, D. A. (1986). *Hospice Inpatient Environments: Compendium and Guidelines.* New York: Van Nostrand Reinhold.

Chan, L.-Y. (1976). "Hospice: A new building type to comfort the dying," *American Institute of Architects Journal,* December 1976, pp. 42–45.

Fieldhouse, K. (1995). "A Healing Art," *Landscape Design,* April.

Francis, C. and C. Cooper Marcus (1992). "Restorative Environments," *Proceedings of the Environmental Design Research Association Conference,* Boulder, CO.

Healy, V. (1986). "The Hospice Garden: Addressing the Patients' Needs Through Landscape," in *The American Journal of Hospice Care,* Vol. 3, No. 5, pp. 18–23 and Vol. 3, No. 6, pp. 32–36

Howett, Catherine (1990). "Gardens are good places for dying," in M. Francis and R. T. Hester, Jr. (Eds.), *The Meaning of Gardens.* Cambridge, MA: MIT Press.

Infield, D. L., A. K. Gordon, and B. C. Harper (Eds.) (1995). *Hospice Care and Cultural Diversity.* New York: The Haworth Press.

Kerr, D. (1993). "Mother Mary Aikenhead, the Irish Sisters of Charity and Our Lady's Hospice for the Dying." *The American Journal of Hospice and Palliative Care,* May–June, pp. 13–20.

Koff, T. H. (1980). *Hospice: A Caring Community.* Cambridge, MA: Winthrop Publishers.

Lindheim, R. (1981). "Birthing Centers and Hospices: Reclaiming Birth and Death," *American Review of Public Health,* Vol. 2, pp. 1–19.

Movahed, A. (1995). *Physical and Environmental Features that Contribute to Satisfaction with Hospice Facilities.* Ph.D. dissertation in Urban Studies, Portland State University, Portland, OR.

Stoddard, S. (1978). *The Hospice Movement: A Better Way of Caring for the Dying.* Briarcliff Manor, NY: Stein and Day.

Verderber, S. (1982). *Environment-Behavior Design Factors and the Architecture of the Hospice.* Houston, TX: College of Architecture Pamphlet.

CHAPTER

11

Getting It Done

Marni Barnes and
Clare Cooper Marcus

The primary aim of this book is to provide design practitioners with relevant information to facilitate the creation of
therapeutic environments. The research covered in
Chapter 2 draws correlations between patient access to nature
and improved medical outcomes; the significance of nature in
stress reduction for staff and visitors is also reviewed. These
facts make a good case for the dedication of funds toward the
installation and maintenance of therapeutic outdoor spaces.
However, at the present time the process of creating a healing
space on the grounds of a medical facility, especially an existing
one, often seems an insurmountable task.

The case histories presented in this chapter focus on the
how-to-get-it-done aspect of the creation of exterior healing
spaces. The situations presented here cover a variety of circumstances. At San Francisco General Hospital in California, for
example, two gardeners began by transforming a leftover space
into a simple flower garden. As the improved space was noticed
by the medical staff, it began to be used, was recognized as
being a healing space, and was subsequently named "The
Comfort Garden." A second example of a grassroots effort is the
North Derbyshire Royal Hospital in Chesterfield, UK, where the
initial idea, the design, and energy to follow through with creating a horticultural therapy garden all came from the medical

545

practitioners in a mental health unit. This same institution subsequently created a second garden for passive use, again through the fund-raising and energy provided by the nursing staff. A bereavement support group at San Diego Children's Hospital in California was the starting point for the Leichtag Family Healing Garden, initially conceived of as a meditation garden. The idea was supported by the administration and blossomed into a fund-raising campaign and the creation of a space very different from the initial vision. At the prompting of the Medical Director, who walked the grounds for exercise, West Park Hospital in Toronto, Ontario, Canada took advantage of its extensive underutilized site by making it accessible to patients when the institution was converted from an old TB sanitorium into a Rehabilitation Facility. Good Samaritan Medical Center in Phoenix, Arizona had an established Healing Committee and it was this committee's recommendation to remodel an underused rooftop courtyard into a healing garden.

Some of these gardens were created by "nondesigners," others were crafted by professional landscape architects or architects. Each story has twists and turns that provide valuable insight into the process and pitfalls of creating a therapeutic outdoor space.

CASE HISTORIES

Comfort Garden, San Francisco General Hospital, San Francisco, California

Background

The Comfort Garden at San Francisco General Hospital is a place of respite created by the gardeners for the enjoyment of staff, patients, and visitors. It is part of the extensive campus of a County Hospital, which has been on this site in San Francisco since the early 1900s. In 1920, the hospital employed thirteen gardeners and had its own nursery. By 1980, there were only five, and by the late 1990s, only two full-time and two part-time workers. The current full-time gardeners—Joan Varney and Alain Kinet—were hired in 1982 and 1984, respectively. These two were taken on as the first employees dedicated exclusively to gardening at the hospital in a long while, as in the years prior to this, the exterior maintenance was considered to be part of the janitorial services.

When Joan and Alain were hired they were faced with tackling the sprawling 23-acre site that was at that time a complex of buildings interspersed with expanses of lawn, parking lots, and access roads. Alain recalls that "We had one power mower, one lawn trimmer, no budget for plants—and a room in a basement." Their first move was to divide the grounds into separate areas of responsibility, which they in turn assigned themselves. They made improvements, a little bit at a time, literally chipping away at the lawns, adding entry beds, focal points, and shrubbery screening. Their pride in their work and a playful competitiveness between them spurred them on to excel and the appearance of the hospital grounds began to improve dramatically.

Financing

Changes in management were reflected in varying degrees of financial support for the landscaping improvements. However, Alain notes, as the physical surroundings improved the emotional environment improved as well, and the medical staff began to comment on the landscaping. These positive comments prompted increasing support from a new boss, himself a home gardener, and the funding situation improved.

Throughout their years on the job, Alain and Joan have done what they like to do best: put salvaged items to good use. They have been resourceful in seeking donations from nurseries as well as collecting cuttings from all over the city, primarily on their own time. They have gathered and placed rocks and driftwood salvaged from the hospital site as well as from the beaches across town.

They have also been on the look out for help with labor. Through the volunteer department of the hospital, an independent arrangement was made with a nonprofit agency called Project Opportunity. Project Opportunity is an independent organization that places and supervises young adults who are developmentally disabled. These helpers often tend to come and go, but one man has been with the hospital for many years now. Sometimes it seems that the energy needed to provide guidance to these volunteers nearly cancels out their labor contributions, but when appropriate jobs are prepared, these helpers can be put to good use doing simple tasks. They respond well to jobs that show immediate gratification, so the gardeners line up tasks, such as turning compost, wheelbarrowing mulch, and other straightforward and visually "big jobs," that enable these young adult volunteers to happily provide real help.

Planning and Creation of the Comfort Garden

Prior to 1985, the site of the Comfort Garden was a neglected area of the grounds. Shady and crisscrossed by the roots of several large pine trees, it was a problematic area where even grass

Figure 11-1 The gardeners who created the Comfort Garden used materials found elsewhere, such as donated plants, boulders, and log rounds for stepping stones and bed edging. (San Francisco General Hospital, San Francisco, CA.)

Figure 11-2   An eclectic collection of plants and fire-burned tree stumps from the 1906 earthquake help to create an eye-catching herbaceous border in the Comfort Garden.

didn't grow. Joan and Alain had been using it as a place to pile their clippings and it had developed into a composting site. As the compost kept growing—"The one advantage of all that lawn is lots of clippings for the compost heap!"notes Alain—the soil in the area was enhanced by the amendment. The gardeners decided to take their fresh clippings elsewhere and use this new rich soil to create a mixed flower border.

Salvaged plants from other areas of the hospital grounds where new construction was going up, boulders that had been exposed by the extension of a new parking area, and gnarled roots that had been burned by the fire after the 1906 earthquake became the "bones" for this truly organic garden. When told to take down a climbing structure after a child had fallen from it, the gardeners sawed the timber up and reused the pieces as an edging to a flower bed. Rescuing laurel bushes thrown out by the city nursery at Golden Gate Park, the gardeners created a hedge to stop people from cutting across the lawn and protect the beds. The success of this venture prompted Alain and Joan to approach other nurseries for castoffs, which were then nursed back to health and incorporated in the garden.

As the garden developed Joan and Alain began to notice new plants appearing, clearly planted by someone else. It became apparent that the flowers that were appearing were not only potted plants from patients' bedsides, but that relatives of patients and staff who had died were transplanting special plants from gardens at home, because they knew that the transplants would receive good care from the gardeners there.

As the garden grew, people began to come out to have lunch near, and soon, *in* the garden. People would step over and around plants to find a seat on a log, or a rock where they could be close to the fragrances in the garden. Taking their cue from the footprints, Joan and Alan modified the garden, putting in more seating and creating paths that meander into and through the plantings. "People started to say 'Hello' to us. We were pleased! We got acknowledgment from the garden's users long before we did from our bosses. We're self-starters. We wanted to create a place we could be proud of" (Alain Kinet). The result is a lovely garden that invites the curious and provides a peaceful respite from the stresses of a medical facility.

Dedication and Ownership

In 1990 the Comfort Garden was dedicated to the memory of hospital staff who had recently died. A plaque was designed; Alain wove a rose arbor from ash tree trimmings—"We needed a door so they could cut a ribbon"—and the garden was named in a dedication ceremony. The garden now hosts an annual

Figure 11-3   An art grant in the early 1990s resulted in an addition of these granite features, by artist Peter Richards, to the Comfort Garden.

memorial service for patients and staff who have died in the previous year. Participants are encouraged to place the names of loved ones on small stakes and "plant" them temporarily in the garden.

In the early 1990s, the retrofitting of a hospital power plant resulted in $16,000 for art being assigned to the grounds. A local artist, Peter Richards, selected by the City Arts Commission, installed some simple granite features, which created a modern design that contrasted with the "cottagey" feel of the Comfort Garden. Joan remarked, "It didn't really fit in well, but then, an elderly Italian couple donated their rose bushes and we planted them near the granite blocks...." Plants continued to be donated. A man dying of AIDS met with the gardeners and told them which plants he wanted them to have from his garden. An ex-patient who moved to Chicago donated roses he'd been growing in tubs. "Eventually we had too many. Now we ask for money instead of memorial plants. Everybody wanted a tree" (Alain Kinet).

By the mid-1990s, the administration began to see the grounds and garden as a marketing tool. "They wanted the corporate look: weed-free lawns and straight rows of trees. They wanted us to use chemical pesticides. But we protested, citing our own health, the health of patients and a publication— 'Designer Poisons' by Marion Moses. We really went to bat— and we won!" (Moses, 1995).

In 1994, the Comfort Garden won an award from San Francisco Beautiful, a nonprofit organization that promotes the aesthetics of city environments. The garden began to be used for formal events—for example, for a press conference when the owner of the San Francisco Giants announced that a dollar from every ticket sold would be donated to AIDS research. One of the interesting facets of this garden is that seemingly everyone who uses it feels that it is there especially for them. Despite its plaque to the memory of staff, the patients of the adjacent HIV clinic refer to it as the AIDS Comfort Garden. The methadone clinic in the nearby building has group meetings on the lawn adjacent to the flower border and they affectionately refer to it as "their" garden as well. Individuals come here to scatter ashes of loved ones, and to plant commemorative plants. Although it is hard to say why this particular garden engenders so many claims to ownership, perhaps part of the reason lies in its unassuming yet lush appearance and the loving attention that it receives daily from the gardeners. Thus with minimal budget, but much hard work and ingenuity, a forgotten corner of the hospital grounds was transformed from a compost pile to a much-loved place with a name, a history, and grateful users who all consider it to be "their" garden. (For a fuller account of the design and use of this garden, see the case study on pp. 176–181.)

The Courtyard at the Acute Day Therapy Service, Hartington Wing, Chesterfield and North Derbyshire Royal Hospital, Chesterfield, United Kingdom

By Helen Tilley, Occupational Therapist

Background

The Acute Day Therapy Service is a day hospital for adults who have acute mental health problems. It is situated on the ground floor of the Mental Health Unit, known as the Hartington Wing. The Day Hospital takes up to thirty patients a day, and also provides a service to ward patients. It serves the population of Chesterfield and other smaller towns in North Derbyshire, UK. The patients receive a wide range of therapeutic interventions, from individual counseling and specialized therapy groups— for example, psychodrama, assertiveness training and relaxation training—to more practical sessions in cookery, pottery, art, gardening, and woodwork.

Prior to 1994 the courtyard at the Day Hospital was in a state of neglect. It was an unattractive and underused rectangular area. Although it housed a greenhouse and a flower bed, it was hard to motivate patients in the gardening group to do simple gardening tasks when a complete makeover was necessary.

The gardening group is made up of one member of staff and approximately six to eight patients. It runs for 1½ hours on the same day each week. In spring and summer the group meets twice a week. The aims of gardening as a therapeutic activity are for the patients to:

- Improve cognitive functioning, for example, concentration and ability to follow instructions
- Develop self-esteem through seeing plants grow
- Be encouraged to do some light physical exercise
- Work together and cooperate as a group
- Learn gardening skills that can be transferred from the hospital to the home environment
- Develop an interest in gardening as a recreational pastime

Due to the courtyard's neglected state the gardening group was underutilized, and the benefits of gardening as a therapeutic activity were not being fully realized.

The author, and a staff member who has a City and Guilds qualification and has worked as a landscape assistant, decided to try to transform this courtyard area. Although there was no money to fund the project, it had the full support of the Manager of the Acute Day Therapy Service.

The Funding
A Patient's Committee for the Day Hospital had been established in 1993 and it was decided to involve the members in this scheme. The Committee were very enthusiastic and, with staff support, raised funds by holding a successful Autumn Fayre. In addition to the financial success there were important therapeutic gains for

Figure 11-4 Careful thought was given to the location of planting beds and benches in this small horticultural therapy garden at the Hartington Wing, Chesterfield, North Derbyshire Royal Hospital, Chesterfield, UK. The use of curved forms and climbing vines serve to "soften" the space.

the patients who were involved, with increased levels of confidence and self-esteem arising from their achievements.

Another fund-raising project was a Christmas Barn Dance with supper and a live band. A staff member's husband plays in a folk band and offered his band for the dance. This was very welcome, as it meant that the money raised did not need to go towards paying costs. This social event was well supported and helped toward the total needed. Other monies came from numerous raffles and a contribution from the Trust Funds.

The fund-raising, in addition to being time consuming, also raised some political issues. Some staff felt that the National Health Service should provide the money for this project as it was a patient therapy area, and therefore they did not involve themselves in the fund-raising. However, all staff were supportive of the courtyard being transformed.

The Planning

The two staff who spearheaded the renovation consulted with patients and other staff, and a consensus was reached that the following changes would be made to the area:

- Paving stones would be laid to replace the thin gravel (through which weeds were growing).
- The shape of the existing flower bed would be changed, and raised.
- Another smaller flower bed would be added, and a small herb garden would be planted in the corner of the courtyard.
- Trellising would cover some of the courtyard walls and screen off part of the greenhouse.
- Numerous planters would be situated around the area.
- A small shed and workbench would be situated at one end of the courtyard for a working area.
- Two attractive wooden benches were donated and completed the courtyard, providing space for patients to relax and enjoy the garden.

The planning was somewhat haphazard. The hospital Works and Estates Departments were contacted but there was no one available to draw out an accurate plan to scale and cost out the materials required. Small quantities of paving stones, bricks, and coping stones, were ordered as needed, rather than ordering everything at once. No one was sure of the quantities required, and there was nowhere to store building materials at the Day Hospital.

The Manager suggested that the Probation Service could be contacted to ask if their service could carry out the building work. The Probation Service was known to have helped with other projects in healthcare settings in North Derbyshire. After some preliminary meetings the Probation Service agreed to provide the necessary labor.

The Work in Progress

Young offenders doing Community Service as part of their probationary period did the construction work under supervision. Progress was slow as they were only able to work one day a week, and when the Supervisor was off sick or on vacation the work was delayed.

There were also other issues to be considered:

Figure 11-5 The greenhouse, often an awkward element to incorporate into a courtyard, is nicely set off by the adjacent planting bed.

- **Security:** Sharp tools had to be locked away after each session as some of the patients deliberately self-harm. Certain entrances and exits had to be kept locked during construction.
- **Privacy:** Young offenders had to be kept away from the patients, due to confidentiality issues and to limit any disruption in patient care.
- **Coordination:** Building materials had to be delivered on the day of the work to ensure that piles of bricks and paving stones could be moved from the busy car park through to the courtyard. This had to be negotiated with the building suppliers. The author sometimes used the trunk of her own car to transport materials.

At one point, due to money running out, another raffle was organized and plans changed slightly to buy cheaper paving stones to be set around the greenhouse.

Toward Completion

Once all the building work was finished and the flower beds filled with soil, garden centers were asked for donations of small shrubs and plants. Only two of the centers responded, but more plants were bought from the Day Hospital budget.

The courtyard was finished toward the end of 1994. It was officially opened by the Chairman of Chesterfield and North Derbyshire Royal Hospital N. H. S. Trust, who planted a Bay Tree at the Day Hospital Open Day in October 1995. There is also a plaque on the wall of the courtyard to make a record of the project, for staff, patients, and visitors who are new to the Acute Day Therapy Service.

Conclusion

The responsibility for the project, all of the planning, organizing, communication and shopping for building materials were in addition to the author's existing clinical caseload as an occupational therapist and primary worker in a busy Day Hospital. It was difficult; however, the satisfaction of transforming the courtyard far outweighed the feelings of stress and frustration.

The courtyard is now much better utilized than before the makeover. There is generally an increased attendance of patients in the gardening groups. Staff and patients take more pride in this environment and the courtyard is used now more recreationally, to sit in during meal breaks, for example; visitors also remark positively about the area.

The transformation of the courtyard, the therapeutic gains of the patients involved, the improvement of the therapeutic area, and the personal experience gained made the whole project worthwhile, and inspired the subsequent redesign of another courtyard in this facility.

The Leightag Family Healing Garden, Children's Hospital, San Diego, California

By Mary Jane Ensberg, Director, Patient and Family Services

The story of the Leichtag Family Healing Garden at Children's Hospital and Health Center in San Diego, California begins in the late 1980s with the hospital's Bereavement Committee. That group, comprised of nurses, social workers, and child life specialists, had come together around the desire to assist grieving families whose children had died at the hospital. The Bereavement Committee envisioned a garden as a therapeutic place for parents to meditate or pray; to retreat from the hospital environment. They also wanted a place to hold the Celebration of Life Ceremony, held every two months at the hospital to commemorate the children who have died in that time period.

Although the vision was there, the critical mass of energy necessary to plan, fund, and build the garden did not materialize until the idea was proposed to the Healing Environment Committee in late 1994. Blair Sadler, President of Children's Hospital, had charged Mary Jane Ensberg with developing a comprehensive healing environment program, based on the belief that healing is a result of the body, mind, and spirit working together. For Children's that means that optimal well-being is achieved not only through the highest quality medical care, but also through the physical and relational environment surrounding families and staff.

To guide the development of the comprehensive healing environment, a Healing Environment Steering Committee consisting of clinicians, managers, and parents, was formed in 1994. A performing arts program was developed and a significant amount of work was accomplished in the physical environment; family lounges and waiting areas were transformed into spaces specially designed to create calm and diversion. In 1995, the committee took on the task of developing the Healing Garden.

Planning

The planning and design process used was key to the success of the project. The significant principles of the design process were involvement, intent, and evaluation. Involvement meant including stakeholders throughout the design and implementation process. Intent meant stating well-developed goals at the beginning of the process. Evaluation meant evaluating the results or outcomes of the process, and comparing them with the original intent.

The first step in the design process was establishing a design team that would include the stakeholders for the garden working in partnership with the designers. The Children's Hospital art consultant, Annette Ridenour, suggested we contact a landscape architect, Topher Delaney, of Delaney, Cochrane and Castillo, to guide us in the development of the vision and goals for the Garden. It was Ensberg's responsibility to pull together the stakeholders and plan a design workshop. Stakeholders included several nurses, a social worker, a child life specialist, and the hospital chaplain. Most of these people were part of the Bereavement Committee, and so had a significant interest in seeing the garden come to fruition. Paul Hagen, the Vice President for Facilities, was an essential stakeholder as he represented the hospital administration and it later became his responsibility to oversee construction of the garden. Other key stakeholders were two parents: one mother who had lost a child to leukemia, and another parent, Deborah Burt, whose son Sam had multiple long term problems caused by a genetic accident. Both parents became key players in molding our thinking about the garden. The President of our Hospital Auxiliary was also involved and was able to represent the views of a significant donor and support base for Children's.

The design workshop for the healing garden was a six-hour affair. We began by having each member of the group describe his/her image of a healing garden. The images were all of traditional gardens ranging from an English garden to Southwestern

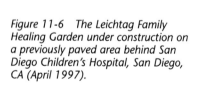

Figure 11-6 The Leichtag Family Healing Garden under construction on a previously paved area behind San Diego Children's Hospital, San Diego, CA (April 1997).

to Japanese. All envisioned a garden that was rather small, secluded, and intended for adults. Ms. Delaney led the group through a process of imaging and brainstorming. In the final stages of the session we entered a lively discussion of what we wanted the Children's Hospital healing garden to mean for families and staff. It was then that the most creative and nontraditional thinking emerged. The parents in the room were key players in transforming the vision of the garden from one of rather somber seclusion intended primarily for adults into one of a garden that would provide diversion from the hospital environment as well. The parents urged us to create a place symbolizing hope and celebrating life. Other key ideas were that the garden would engage all senses and appeal to all cultures. The group also concluded that the garden would be a place for children and adults alike.

The goals were that visitors to the garden would be able to:

- Experience a diminishing of the emotions and symptoms of stress and report increased feelings of calm and peacefulness.
- Report renewal of energy levels, increased feelings of hope, and increased coping ability.
- Report responses of joy and wonder resulting in feelings of being more relaxed.

Following the design workshop, Ms. Delaney submitted the initial plans for the garden. Responses were mixed. Indeed, this was not a traditional garden of grass, trees, and flowers. It abounded with the symbols of life created by sculpture as well as nature. The design group discussed the concept with the designer. The most important factor in keeping the group focused were the original vision and goals. Without this vital document, the group would have been hopelessly divided and consensus would not have been reached. A second key factor was the inclusion of the parents and the auxiliary members in the process. It was the parents who were able to bring the discussion back to the intent for the garden. The involvement of the Auxiliary members at the table was crucial in their buy-in to the design.

Funding

As the design work progressed through various iterations, the work of fundraising started. This hospital, like others in a market completely penetrated by managed care, had been making significant changes in operations in order to reduce costs. It was felt that it would be inappropriate to spend scarce operating monies for the garden. It was at this time that the principle of involving stakeholders in the project again proved to be a turning point. Deborah Burt, one of the parents on the design team, and Darlyn Davenport, president-elect of the Auxiliary, became champions for the project in the community. The large design team was dissolved and a small group consisting of Mrs. Burt and Mrs. Davenport, Paul Hagen, Facilities Vice President, Karen Hendrix, for the Children's Hospital Foundation, Sue Cox, R.N., representing the Bereavement Committee and the clinical staff, and Ensberg formed a small Task Force whose job it would be to shepherd the project to completion.

The Task Force formulated a strategy for funding the garden that included soliciting cash donations as well as donations in kind. Significant time was spent costing out elements of the garden and forming a detailed plan for donations. The plan outlined which elements of the garden would be appropriate for donations-in-kind and what companies might be approached to make these donations, as well as which elements would be appropriate for cash donations.

Mrs. Burt, a floral designer, began making endless telephone calls to the people in the growing and landscape business, many of whom she knew as professional colleagues. The passion she brought to the phone conversations about the benefit of the garden for families at Children's, not to mention her first-hand experience as a parent, undoubtedly sold the project to almost everyone with whom she spoke. Deborah's husband, Buck, was responsible for telling the story of the garden to Lee Leichtag, who became the largest single donor for the garden

Figure 11-7   The Healing Garden after completion and dedication (summer 1997). View from upper floors of hospital.

and for whom it is named. Darlyn Davenport, as Auxiliary President, sponsored a major fund-raiser, and encouraged other Auxiliary monies to be used for the garden. Darlyn and her husband Chuck also gave a major gift. It was Darlyn's involvement from the beginning of the project that enabled her to enthusiastically champion the cause.

Implementation

Paul Hagen took over the next phase of the development of the garden. Paul, too, spent significant amounts of time contacting contractors and convincing them to contribute time and materials. He used a federally funded job corps group to build the walls surrounding the garden. He and a staff architect, Tony Figueras, continued to work with Ms. Delaney on the design details and supervised the construction.

Throughout the final design and the construction phase of the garden, the Task Force continued to meet to review design changes and fund-raising progress and to solve problems as a team. The President of Children's, Blair Sadler, continued to support the garden at every opportunity, motivating us to stay on task when energy levels lagged. The dedication of the Leichtag Family Healing Garden, in July 1997, proved to be a very moving occasion and an opportunity to celebrate the work that had been accomplished by the efforts of many on the hospital staff and in the community.

Work on the Leichtag Family Healing Garden did not end with its formal opening. Children's Hospital has made a commitment to evaluate all aspects of the Healing Environment

Program and to engage in research regarding the effects of the various components of the environment on the physiological and psychological states of patients, families, and staff. Evaluations include post-occupancy evaluation and evaluation of the effects of the Healing Environment Program on customer satisfaction.

A post-occupancy evaluation of the garden was conducted in the summer of 1998, after allowing time for the garden plants to begin to mature and usage patterns to be established. Trained observers were posted in the garden to determine who was using it, what parts were used most, at what times of the day, and for what purposes. Interviews were conducted with garden users to solicit their feedback. Nonusers of the garden were also interviewed. Questions regarding the garden were also added to the written patient satisfaction survey. The purpose of this evaluation was to improve the garden and learn about possible mistakes that should be avoided in future projects. (A summary of the results of this evaluation appear in the case study on pp. 362–369.)

In summary, what were the lessons learned about designing and building a healing garden? First, determine who the stakeholders are and involve them throughout the design and building process. This approach creates "buy-in" and creates champions of the project. Secondly, articulate the intent of the garden through a vision statement and well-defined goals. This will keep the design true to its original intent and allow later evaluation of its effectiveness. Third, evaluation needs to be a part of the plan from the beginning since it is only through evaluation that the value of such projects as a healing garden can be demonstrated to management, funding sources, and the community.

Figure 11-8 *A father and his two sons explore the garden on a fall afternoon.*

West Park Hospital Landscaping Project, Fund-Raising Plan, Toronto, Ontario, Canada

By Sandra Fawcett, Manager, Public Relations; and Mary Jane Lovering, Landscape Architect

Background

Founded in 1904 as a treatment center for the indigent with tuberculosis, West Park Hospital is now metropolitan Toronto's western region rehabilitation center and continuing care facility, treating respiratory, neurological, amputee, and geriatric medicine clients. The hospital is sited on 27 acres of ravine property in a residential neighborhood adjacent to the Humber River. Before 1987 the therapeutic value of the extensive grounds was limited, as much of the property was inaccessible to the hospital's population, many of whom used walkers, canes, wheelchairs, electric scooters, or needed oxygen tanks. These individuals found it very difficult, if not impossible, to make their way over grass paths between the five buildings on the hospital campus.

In 1986 Allan Johnson, the medical director of the hospital and a keen naturalist, and newly appointed hospital president Barry Monaghan, who often took walks together on the grounds, agreed that something needed to be done to improve the property to enable clients to benefit from their surroundings. This seemed an ideal project on which to focus the energies of the fledgling West Park Hospital Foundation.

Planning

A Landscaping Committee was formed in mid-1986 to explore options. The committee was comprised of the hospital's planner, a nursing unit manager, a program director, the medical director, facilities and maintenance staff, clients, and the hospital's landscape architect, Mary Jane Lovering of Vertechs Design Inc., Toronto, Ontario, Canada. Within six months, after circulating a survey to clients (i.e., patients), family members, and staff to determine what they felt was needed in a landscape plan, a "wish list" of proposed enhancements had been developed and a master plan for the site created.

The estimated cost for all of the changes was $675,350, an amount that far exceeded the hospital's means. The items were therefore arranged by priority need, in consultation with the clients and staff. The consultation took a number of forms. In addition to the client representatives on the Landscape Committee itself, clients and family members attending the hospital's Residents' Council also had an opportunity to review the "wish list" of items to indicate their priorities. Family members of the Special Care unit for individuals with Alzheimer's disease and other dementias, for example, decided that while they would very much like to have a fountain within an enclosed garden, that it was more important to have a shady place to sit; a gazebo was therefore placed higher on their list of needs than the fountain. These considerations were factored into the master plan, to ensure that where possible, infrastructure such as plumbing lines for the fountain would be roughed in if the item was not a top priority, to ensure that there would be minimal disturbance to the landscape during implementation of successive phases of the master plan.

Description and Implementation

A phased-in approach to implementation and fund-raising was then undertaken, with the Foundation's Board of Directors

Figure 11-9 Flowering dogwood, low native plants, and a donated bench in a courtyard outside the Recreation Therapy department at West Park Hospital, Toronto, Ont., Canada.

making a commitment to fund what could not be raised by public subscription.

In the period 1987–1997, the following projects were implemented:

PHASE I: THE KINGSLEY AND HAZEL FOX COURTYARD

Total cost: $256,482; Amount raised: $94,053

Project start date: early spring, 1987; Completion date: June, 1987

The Landscaping Committee identified as a priority the need for a central gathering place to welcome the community, as well as a place for clients to get away from the hospital for some safe solitude or to meet in small groups. The Kingsley and Hazel Fox Courtyard was created and consists of an 8- to 12-foot wide concrete, tree-lined walkway from the main building to a large (60 × 70 foot) central courtyard with a 15 × 15 foot gazebo, and beyond to an allée of flowering crab apple trees leading to a private enclave featuring a sundial that had been on the property when the hospital was founded in 1904. The tree-shaded courtyard provides space for large and small social gatherings, and also affords intimate meeting spots for clients, their friends, and family members. Benches and groups of plantings (flowering crab apple trees, pines and spruces) create a parklike setting, and the variety of plant material offers visual interest as the seasons change. The gazebo provides a stage for band concerts and other entertainers and its slatted roof, covered in vines, provides shade for clients who are intolerant to heat and glare. The gazebo is raised two feet above ground and is reached by either a short

Figure 11-10   The Kingsley and Hazel Fox Courtyard was partially funded by donations and added a much needed gathering place on this medical campus for social and fund-raising events, and for small groups of rehabilitation patients to get away from the hospital.

flight of steps with hand rails or by a gently sloping ramp (5 percent gradient), which accommodates two-way traffic with frequent rest stops along its length. The walk leads on beyond the courtyard to the ruins of a farmhouse (in which the hospital was originally established), which forms a challenging destination for clients using wheelchairs. (See Figure 1-14.)

A late addition to the plan was the installation of underground sprinklers on a computerized timer system to irrigate the plantings. Without such a system, clients would have been prevented from using the patio area in the summer months due to the maze of hoses needed to water the plants. Irrigation was built into each successive phase of the project.

PHASE II: RECREATION PATIO AND RAISED GARDEN BEDS

Total cost: $228,000; Amount raised: $79,216

Completion date: August, 1988

This project consisted of a patio area outside the lower level of the Recreation Therapy department and raised gardens on an upper level. Both areas were designed not only for the use of organized recreation/rehabilitation activities but also for the leisure-time enjoyment of individual clients.

On the lower level there is a tree-shaded plaza and a pergola; the central space is designed to accommodate fifteen to twenty people, with smaller groups being accommodated within the pergola and enclaves on the perimeter of the space. Seat-height dry stone walls along the patio edge enable those unable to bend to appreciate the perennial plantings.

The upper and lower levels are connected by an access ramp with a 5 to 6 percent gradient. The ramp provides for two-way traffic and frequent rest stops. Bordering the ramp are fragrant plantings, herb gardens and shrub roses, which provide olfactory stimulation, an important consideration for the elderly and those who have some visual impairment.

On the upper level are both ground level and raised garden beds. The raised beds vary in height. Ground level beds may be used by individuals able to stand independently or those working on rehabilitation activities to improve balance, standing tolerance and spatial coordination. Gardening beds at lower than wheelchair height allow those with limited standing tolerance to sit on the side of the beds. Wheelchair height beds are easily accessed by those in wheelchairs or electric scooters. There is room for access from all sides and room to allow those in wheelchairs/scooters to pass. A garden toolshed has a gentle ramp for accessibility.

Figure 11-11   Gardening beds at varying heights are used in the horticultural therapy program at West Park Hospital.

PHASE III: SPECIAL CARE GARDEN

Total cost: $182,348; Amount raised: $217,835

Completion date: May, 1992

Phase III addressed the need for an enclosed, secure garden for clients with dementias who are resident in our Special Care unit. Designed in cooperation with the Alzheimer Society of Canada, the garden permits clients to wander safely outdoors. Surrounded by 10-foot residential design fence, the space includes a picnic area, secluded areas for private meetings with friends and family, a place to sit in the sun, a shady gazebo, and raised garden beds planted with nontoxic plants. The variety of plant material creates seasonal interest and attractive views from clients' windows year-round.

The Fund-Raising Plan

West Park Hospital was very committed to the implementation of landscaping changes. Barry Monaghan, the hospital president and CEO, Kingsley Fox, the chair of the hospital's Board of Governors in the 1980s, and the Landscaping Committee all believed that it would be possible to raise funds in the community for such a project, but that it might take time to do so. The members believed strongly, however, that once people could see tangible evidence of the project that they would be more inclined to contribute. Consequently, the hospital's Board of Governors asked the West Park Hospital Foundation to fund the Phase I courtyard construction with a grant to enable the landscaping project to begin. The Foundation was then to undertake a fund-raising appeal to recoup these costs.

The Foundation seized this opportunity to develop a donor cultivation and recognition program. A brochure was developed that described the Central Court project, or Phase I of the Landscaping Plan, and that broke the component parts of the plan into named gift opportunities with assigned gift values, for example, $6,000 for the Boulevard walkway, $26,732 for the gazebo and ramp, $720 for park benches. For a donation of the specified value, a contributor would be recognized publicly.

A direct mail package that included the brochure and a letter from the chair of the Residents' Council was sent to 728 major donors and corporations and to 37 service clubs. The letter described from a client's perspective what it would be like to enjoy the outdoors.

A Lasting Tribute program of living memorials for donors was also created. Naming opportunities were identified for the installation of additional trees, benches, and archways. Internal audiences were also solicited for support. Raffle tickets were sold to raise funds for the Phase I project. Appeals also were made to hospital staff, family members of clients, and individuals in the community. In total 201 donors responded with a total of $94,053 toward the total cost.

But as the community responded, it quickly became evident that putting dedication plaques on every available surface would not be desirable. The Foundation staff chose to create a single dedication acknowledgment board for large gifts, following the Foundation's donor recognition policy levels. The dedication board, located beside the major walkway into the Hazel and Kingsley Fox Courtyard, includes:

- An outline of the philosophy of the development of the Landscaping Project
- A brief biography of Kingsley Fox, the chair of the hospital's Board of Governors, to whom, along with his wife Hazel, the courtyard was dedicated after his untimely death
- A listing of the major donors linked to a schematic drawing of the project

Dedication plaques were put on benches and trees only for Phase I of the Landscape Project.

Gifts to the general fund were acknowledged through the Foundation's Donor Recognition Rainbow Program, which saw donors' names entered into a Book of Honour that was displayed in the hospital's main lobby, and registered on a recognition wall as their cumulative gifts reached specific threshold levels.

Similar strategies were used with the second and third phases of the Landscaping Project. In Phase II a local nursery pledged support by providing much of the plant material. By Phase III, the objective of the fund-raising plan had evolved not only to raise funds for the Special Care Unit Garden, but also to increase public awareness for the hospital in the community. Contributions to the Landscaping Project continue to be made to this day.

In March 1989, the hospital received the Ontario Premier's Award for Accessibility for Phases I and II of the project. In 1994, the City of York's "Beautiful York Perennial Award" was awarded to West Park Hospital in recognition of its consistently high standards in landscape design and maintenance displayed by the grounds.

But the plans don't stop here. A Phase IV project, which will see the creation of a "Triumph Walkway," leading to the current Hazel and Kingsley Fox Courtyard, will provide additional naming opportunities. Visitors to the garden will be able to view the names of donors/honorees engraved in 800 bricks to be embedded along the length of the existing walkway.

TIPS

- Be sure to get support internally for the ongoing operating costs of maintaining your project. Plant materials need to be replaced from time to time, trees need to be pruned, and so on. These costs can be significant.

- If you seek donations of plant materials, be sure that the nurseries understand that substitutions are not allowed and why. In one case, in the Special Care Garden a clematis was substituted for another vine; the clematis was poisonous and a hazard to dementia clients who were likely to put plant material in their mouths. In another case, a specific plant had been chosen for its drying properties to support a recreational therapy program; the nursery chose to substitute a plant that had similar growing needs but that did not meet the therapeutic program's needs for dried plant material.

- Develop very specific lists of items you wish to have donated. Include photographs or illustrations, model numbers, color specifications, and places to purchase the items. This will ensure that you don't get "gifts" that you can't use or that are inappropriate for the design. Better yet, ask for the cash contribution and insist on buying items yourself.

- If your client population changes, you may need to review your landscape plan to determine whether it still meets client needs. West Park Hospital conducted such an evaluation in August 1997 and will be making necessary adjustments.

- Determine in what manner you will acknowledge donors before you solicit for funds. This will enable you to control your recognition costs.

- Establish a convention for the wording of memorial plaques. A sea of "In Memory Of" dedications will create a funereal atmosphere for clients who are supposed to be able to enjoy this environment.

- Be sure to build in the costs of your recognition when setting your naming opportunities. A good rule of thumb is plan to spend 1 percent on recognition from every gift. If, for example, it costs $150 to create a cast aluminum plaque with a pole to set into the ground with a tree, and the tree price is only $90, you'll lose money with every tree you dedicate if you haven't factored in the recognition expenses.

Good Samaritan Regional Medical Center Healing Garden Phoenix, Arizona

By Barbara Crisp, Architect

Figure 11-12 Tiered planting beds constructed in a formerly bleak rooftop courtyard became the core of the Healing Garden at Good Samaritan Medical Center, Phoenix, AZ.

Good Samaritan Regional Medical Center holds a high rise presence in downtown Phoenix, typical of a medical center campus in an urban setting. Like other medical centers, Good Samaritan offered no refuge from its sterile, functional, technological environment. People were forced to find a quiet place where ever they could. The one place that was provided outside was an existing concrete courtyard used by smokers. However, in 1994, a choice was made to begin the transformation of that courtyard, a 20,000 square foot over-structure space, into a garden environment that would assist in the healing process. Designed as a place of relaxation, reflection, and renewal for the entire hospital community—patients and their families, employees, physicians, volunteers, and visitors—Good Samaritan's Healing Garden is unusual within a healthcare setting. The addition of the garden has set this hospital apart in both the local and national healthcare communities.

The idea for the Healing Garden was a direct result of patient and staff satisfaction surveys. The complexities of the healthcare market, the influence of managed care, and the dictates of insurance companies were taking their toll on both patients and staff. For patients, the desire to have their emotional and spiritual needs, as well as those of their families, recognized and honored was of critical concern. For staff, the stress of job and equipment cutbacks, and the potential of a corporate merger created low morale and considerable unrest. Out of this issue of employee and patient satisfaction, an in-house Healing Environment Committee was formed, which consisted of doctors, nurses, administrators, and staff. The intent of the Committee was to examine broader issues of healing and be Good Samaritan's link to the Samaritan system-wide adoption of the Planetree philosophy, a patient-centered approach to care. The founding of this Committee coincided with the initiation of the Healing Garden project.

The Design Process

The principal designer (Barbara Crisp, Project Architect for Orcutt/Winslow Partnership, Phoenix) began working with the Healing Environment Committee soon after the initial meeting, and shortly thereafter, became an invited member, enabling her to be privy to current hospital thought on the integrative aspects of medical care and healing. The committee was open to learning about issues that would affect the design of the garden, such as the critical connection between design and sensory experience. They willingly participated in hands-on presentations about perception and sensory experience in which they were subtly challenged to reconnect with their own senses. When recommended, they read *A Natural History of the Senses*, by Diane Ackerman (1995), which broadened their knowledge base, reacquainted them with the potential of each sense, and fueled their interest. With this knowledge and insight, the committee gained a new understanding of the design potential for the project, ultimately enabling them to support it completely throughout the entire design process. Their new knowledge and support was critical because, as design work began and evolved, and existing constraints began to surface, the budget grew from $60,000 to $750,000.

Funding

Cost was a looming issue, at a time when the organization was experiencing cutbacks and considering alternatives for addressing patient and staff needs throughout the entire hospital campus. There were undercurrents of resentment from staff who did not fully understand the potential for the garden and how it would affect their life and work in a positive and sustaining way. An education campaign, with its focus on the entire staff, was

Figure 11-13 A quiet corner of the garden focuses on a pool—The Return—which marks the end of a watercourse that meanders through the garden.

initiated to ease uncertainty and to assure them that the garden was not taking money or opportunity away from them, but actually would be giving back tenfold. This process was ongoing and took place in the form of articles in the hospital newsletter, presentations by the design team, fact sheets about various aspects of the garden, and an interactive ceremonial "groundbreaking".

The hospital Auxiliary, comprised of volunteer members of the hospital community, were struggling internally about their support of the garden project as well. As the design concept was developed, they became divided in their support. Longtime members of the Auxiliary, who were used to giving money for the purchases of new equipment, items that support medical care, were not convinced by the garden or its potential at Good Samaritan. It took eighteen months for this segment to shift their support and truly understand the value of a garden in a healthcare setting. Many were not completely convinced until they observed the garden in use and saw how people responded to this nurturing outdoor environment.

Ultimately, due to the support and donations from the medical staff, the Good Samaritan Auxiliary, and the Samaritan Foundation, no operating capital funds were used to see the project through to completion. Especially important was the Auxiliary's annual Candlelight Capers holiday ball. For three years, the event theme centered around aspects of healing: it experienced tremendous growth and success, with all proceeds being donated to the Healing Garden project and the hospital's healing environment efforts.

The Process

The Healing Environment Committee set the tone for success early on. Working with them enabled Crisp to lay the groundwork for conceptual thinking to begin about the garden and to introduce bigger issues of design that would be critical later on. In addition, a collaborative design team was developed, which included the architect Crisp, representing the firm for which she was working, a tile artist (Joan Baron), and a landscape architect (Christy Ten Eyck). All shared a common vision for what the project could be, and all were deeply committed to its ultimate success at Good Samaritan. Even though Crisp was the designated lead by contract, all design decisions were filtered through this collaborative team, which worked quite closely throughout the design process.

The design team was extremely committed to creating an environment that addressed the needs of all of its users, mentally, physically, and spiritually. The creation of interactive opportunities based on sight, sound, smell, taste, touch, body movement, and perception were critical to achieving the sense of healing within the garden. The concept for the project reflects the cycles of life, offering a symbolic sense of hope to those who experience it. The cyclical theme ensures that the experience of the garden will differ with each visit, depending on time of day and season of year. The key elements of the project that embody the design concept and its intention to fully engage the senses, body movement, and perception were the use of water, the selection of plant materials, the terracing of planting beds, the integration of art, and the full accessibility of the site for all users.

Implementation

Except for the sky above, the garden site is surrounded on all sides, as well as below, by functioning hospital facilities. This created a design challenge as well a staging and access challenge during the construction phase. The use of water as a key element of the design required that the existing deck be demolished down to the roof slab and resealed to protect it from potential water penetration to the functioning hospital space below. All construction was staged through a 12-foot wide by 12-foot high tunnel and materials were transported by Bobcat or wheelbarrow, and concrete was pumped. Construction issues arose because patient rooms were located on two sides of the construction site, and the Pharmacy was situated below. At one point, for a short period of time, two patient pods were shut down to accommodate construction needs. Scheduling was a critical issue in successfully dealing with increased noise levels,

Figure 11-14 Colorful ceramic "wisdom circles," hand-made by artist Joan Baron and fixed to one of nine, formerly unattractive columns, can be donated by members of the public.

unpleasant odors, and inconvenient disruptions that occurred throughout the process. The team made every effort to notify hospital personnel of weekly activities, so arrangements could be made well in advance and any problems that might arise could be circumvented.

The Healing Garden evolved over twenty-seven months, from its inception to the opening celebration, with many people dedicating time and energy to truly understanding what the potential for the project could be within the medical environment. The garden has become Good Samaritan's "signature" and represents the facility's commitment to broader issues of healing and care for the entire Good Samaritan community. (For a fuller account of the design and use of this garden, see case study in Chapter 5.)

CONCLUSION

These inspiring case stories present an array of methods and means used for the incorporation of exterior spaces into the overall therapeutic milieu of medical facilities. One consistent feature throughout these stories is that each garden needed a devoted individual or group, willing to push to get the job done. While we are thankful that these individuals exist, it is the hope of the editors of this book that, as the therapeutic benefits of gardens are increasingly recognized, it will become a matter of course to design *all* exterior areas in medical facilities as healing spaces, and that it will no longer be such an uphill battle of persuasion and extensive fund-raising from private sources.

REFERENCES

Ackerman, D. (1995). *A Natural History of the Senses*. New York: Vintage Books.

Moses, M. (1995). *Design Poisons: How to Protect Your Health and Home from Toxins*. San Franciso, CA: Pesticide Education Center.

12

Conclusions and Prospects

Terry Hartig, Marni Barnes, and Clare Cooper Marcus

The exploration in this book of the design of healing gardens has been motivated by recognition of the many values they may hold for people joined in inherently challenging situations. We see tremendous potential for helping patients, their families and friends, and their professional caregivers better deal with illness and pain, confusion, depression, the suffering and loss of loved ones, and heavy professional demands.

Exploration of the healing garden idea is timely. In the United States, converging contemporary trends are opening up new possibilities for establishing gardens in diverse health care facilities. Among those trends are

- Changes in the American health care system and the attendant increase in competition among health care providers.

- A growing interest in shaping all possible aspects of facilities to most effectively aid healing in the given users, exemplified by the activities of the Center for Health Design (e.g., Rubin and Owens, 1996).

571

- An increasing demand for long-term care facilities designed with sensitivity to the specific physical and psychological limitations of particular users, such as the elderly (see Chapters 8 and 9).
- A strengthening orientation to promote behaviours, relationships, and environments that increase *resistance* to health threats, as a complement to the long-standing efforts to control pathogens, toxic exposures, stressors, and other risk factors (Antonovsky, 1979; Schmid et al., 1995; Stokols, 1994; Syme, 1992).

"When dealing with our brightest minds, we develop an academic setting that is conducive for learning. When we want to create a company that promotes loyalty and trust and lets employees know we care, we create a corporate campus that offers a setting for growth of the mind. But in the life-and-death situations to cure the mind and body we have dropped all emphasis on the environment and digressed dramatically."

JIM BURNETT

Another trend, one we want to emphasize, is the increasing willingness within the conventional medical care establishment to consider possible values of complementary and alternative forms of medicine. A clear expression of this trend in the United States is the formation of the Office of Alternative Medicine (OAM) within the National Institutes of Health (NIH). Authorized by Congress in 1992, the OAM facilitates research on the effectiveness of alternative medical practices and disseminates information about alternative medicine to the public. As a World Health Organization Collaborating Center in Traditional Medicine, the OAM also acts within an international network of governmental and academic institutions concerned with traditional, alternative, and complementary medicine.

Paralleling the increasing willingness of the health care establishment to evaluate alternative medical modalities, and perhaps contributing to it, is the increasing acceptance of complementary and alternative modalities by the populace of the industrialised Western world. Practitioners are establishing clinics, insurance companies are increasingly willing to cover a percentage of charges from some of them, and beneficial results are being reported by many patients. The case of acupuncture is exemplary (see National Institutes of Health, in press). Non-conventional practices are being regarded as possible adjuncts to conventional medical practices and not necessarily in opposition to them. Although not meant to imply endorsement, the OAM's use of the term "complementary and alternative therapies" to describe non-conventional practices does make explicit their openness to the coexistence of some such practices with the currently conventional approaches. That openness reflects the public's openness.

Healing gardens can be seen as a part of this movement. The "gentler" treatment afforded by gardens is being accessed by many people on a frequent, albeit informal, basis. As a self-administered form of environmental therapy, episodes in gardens are being used to wind down, to revive flagging spirits, to stave off burnout, to provide time for reflection and acceptance, to join with supportive others, and for diverse other reasons connected to personal health. In light of these individual proclivities, we see numerous possibilities for more deliberate use of gardens within more formal efforts to help people heal. Gardens might be incorporated within treatment regimens or called on to serve preventive functions.

While we see exciting prospects for gardens in health care facilities, we also see a need to bear in mind some precautions as we try to make the best of the emerging possibilities. To begin, we would do well to acknowledge the limitations of the existing research on healing gardens. This is not to discount the many rich anecdotal accounts of benefits that gardens have provided to patients, staff, and visitors in health care settings. Nor is it to set aside circumstantial evidence from well-designed empirical studies of mild exercise, passive viewing of natural scenery, and other behaviors that may occur within gardens. It is simply to point out that at present there is little data from well-structured studies bearing directly on the kinds of questions that might be expected from administrators, doctors, and others who may influence key decisions about having a garden placed at a given facility. Those are, for example, questions about whether gardens in health care facilities are reliably therapeutic, and questions about whether there is enough to the claimed healing effects to recommend gardens over other available measures for improving service to patients.

Until the results of more focused research are available, we must use evidence from related areas of research to inform efforts to establish gardens in healthcare facilities. As demonstrated by Ulrich (Chapter 2), existing empirical research on aspects of nature experience can be drawn from diverse bodies

Figure 12-1   Images of nature in the hospital: Art must suffice when access to real nature is limited. Photo of a tree in a corridor at St. George's Hospital, London, UK.

of literature and organised to point out ways that gardens can be beneficial for patients, visitors, and staff in health care settings. Coordinated with the emotionally evocative, sometimes poignant anecdotal literature, such circumstantial evidence is quite compelling.

We anticipate that more focused research will make for an even more nuanced, more definitive set of arguments for gardens in healthcare facilities. As the chapters in this volume have shown, the particular needs for gardens and other outdoor spaces, the kinds of benefits potentially enjoyed, and the explanations for those benefits can be as varied as the patient groups served. While there may be some general principles that cut across patient groups, we expect that more focused research will reveal subtleties that may be as important for designing gardens as for understanding their effects.

Congruent with a sensitivity to nuances, we encourage a stance of enthusiasm with restraint. We are not promoting a view of the garden as a panacea. Gardens in healthcare facilities may not be therapeutic for all users in the same way, or even for particular individuals at all times. We would do well to keep an open mind about the therapeutic value of gardens relative to other environmental measures that could be used to meet user needs.

This openness to nuances also has its place in the design process. Current healing garden designs are hypotheses of a sort; there are implicit and explicit "messages" from the designer about ways in which aspects of the physical environment may facilitate behaviours such as aesthetic appreciation, socialising, and contemplation while at the same time reducing the likelihood of other behaviours, such as confused wandering and falling. There is not necessarily one right way; different designs may facilitate the same set of desired outcomes. Whether grounded in previous research or in intuition, design measures are put to the test when the garden is used. Structured observations attending the introduction of the new garden and well-conceived post-occupancy evaluations may or may not confirm the design assumptions, and may point out new lessons. When recorded and communicated, such evaluations can guide subsequent efforts. So informed, future designs—future hypotheses—are refined. The chapters in this volume have in one way or another exemplified stages in this process, including the citation of post-occupancy studies, statements about the applicability of particular design approaches, discussion of anticipated and unanticipated effects, and proposals for design guidelines. Clearly, there is a substantial body of accumulated experience for designers to draw on. Yet it is safe to assume that refinements can be made.

Figure 12-2 Images of nature in the hospital: Landscape paintings in a corridor at Glendale Adventist Medical Center, CA.

Prime concern for the users' needs is implicit. In the case of gardens in health care settings, perhaps more so than in any other instance of garden design, divergence of user and designer conceptions of what is aesthetically pleasing can have immediate, unpleasant, and significant consequences. This is well-illustrated in Ulrich's discussion (Chapter 2) of the Bird Garden at the Duke University Hospital. Perhaps more accurately described as a sculptural installation, it ultimately had to be removed because it was emotionally aggravating for a large enough number of patients. In short, an implicit aspect of the design philosophy espoused in this volume is that the designer also incorporates to some extent the role of researcher or associates with researchers in a direct way. This means taking on some responsibility for interpreting the available research relevant to a project, and subsequently collecting and communicating information on responses to the garden that is established (see also Chapter 3).

Consistent with the explicit emphasis of this book on the value of research-based design, and with the view of designers as both producers and consumers of research, in this, the concluding chapter, we frame the existing research and offer some thoughts on future research that is needed. More specifically, we want to frame the existing research in terms that are meaningful to designers and healthcare professionals. We also call attention to the limitations of the research and put those limitations into perspective in ways that should encourage continued effort. We then go on to outline some of the research needed to more convincingly substantiate the healing effects of gardens in healthcare settings. Subsequent to the discussion of needed research, we will point out some next steps that members of the design community can take to encourage and develop possibilities for healing gardens. Before any of this, however, we will revisit some fundamental issues of definition.

THE MANY MEANINGS OF HEALTH AND HEALING

To refer to a healing garden is to refer to a place, a process, and their intertwining. The chapters in this volume give numerous examples of places that can be described as healing, places that vary along physical and perceptual dimensions such as size and openness, but that have the presence of vegetation, water, and other natural features as a common denominator. Preserving the conventional contemporary meaning of the word "garden," it is this presence of natural features that we see as a first necessary characteristic of any place for which the description "healing garden" might be claimed.

The chapters in this volume have also indicated a wide variety of healing processes that might be supported by gardens, from ameliorating stress to achieving perspective on a life about to end. Getting a fix on how the term "healing" should be understood in this context presents a challenge for those who are seeking to build a research base that is credible to health professionals, the public, and others who might help to establish gardens in health care settings. "Healing" is a word rich with implications. It implies some conception of health. It implies past departure from some more or less stable condition of health. It implies a possibility for improvement of health or for achieving some new condition of health.

How we should conceive of health is a multi-faceted and controversial issue, and treating it in depth is far beyond the scope of this chapter (for a brief overview, see Noack, 1991). We simply want to point out that because the conception of health is a matter of debate, the credibility and utility accorded the healing garden concept will vary from one person to another. Some medical professionals committed to a conception of health as the absence of disease may be reluctant to consider a garden as an aid to healing. As we have been talking about placing gardens in settings where medical practitioners may exercise some control over the allocation of resources, there is some possibility of resistance to providing support for a healing garden. As can be seen in several of the vignettes presented in Chapter 11, this is not only an issue for facility administrators; the facility staff also have opinions about the prioritisation and allocation of scarce resources. One who will talk about healing

Figure 12-3   Images of nature in the hospital: Sian Tucker's "Falling Leaves", a seventy-five foot high mobile in an atrium at the Chelsea and Westminister Hospital, London, UK.

gardens or advocate for them should be prepared to articulate the underlying conception of health, and to recognise that it may not be shared.

In recent decades the prevailing conception of health in the United States has been changing, the previous overriding emphasis on individual physical soundness and absence of disease becoming softer. Over the past 50 years a broader conception of health has been promulgated by the most comprehensive of international public health organisations, the World Health Organization. The WHO defines health as "…a state of complete physical, mental, and social well-being and not merely the absence of disease or infirmity" (1996). A well-known critic of the emphasis on health as the absence of disease, Aaron Antonovsky (1979), commends the good intentions of those who developed the WHO conception, appreciates the recognition it gives to mental and social aspects of health, but also finds grounds to criticise that conception. His preference is to conceive of health as lying in a "health ease/dis-ease continuum," to distinguish it from overall well-being, to which health is but one contributor, and to ask questions about the generalised resources that help movement toward the more salutary end of the continuum.

A conception that recognises a diversity of physiological, personal, interpersonal, and social continua along which one can move between greater and lesser degrees of health is a conception that can encompass the multiplicity of forms of healing referred to in this volume. It does not place sole emphasis on improvement of the patient's physical health status. It allows for those situations in which, although there may be unavoidable deterioration along some dimensions relevant to health, there is positive change along others, change which is of significance for the patient and his or her caregivers, indeed, change which may not be confined to the patient alone. It allows for the possibility that a person can gain in psychological or spiritual health while dying. Amelioration of stress as a valued outcome in an of itself and as a general mechanism potentially important for a variety of accepted medical outcomes (see Ulrich, Chapter 2) can be accommodated by such a conception. So also can outcomes that might not be foremost from a conventional medical perspective, such as resolution of intra-family conflict by a terminally ill patient and his relatives. Stress coping as facilitated by the garden may aid such a conflict-resolution process, but may not be the only relevant agent of the healing afforded by the garden in such an instance. In short, a broad conception of health allows us to talk of "healing gardens" while acknowledging that different groups of patients have different clusters of

Figure 12-4 Nature in the hospital: Sub-tropical vegetation in a barrel-vaulted atrium at the Royal Alexandra Hospital, Edmonton, Alberta, Canada.

emotional, cognitive, and physical problems, some of which involve irreversible declines; that the experience of caregivers and their relations with the patient deserve consideration; and that a variety of mechanisms can work in the healing process.

How garden as place intertwines with healing as process is the root question for both the design of and research on healing gardens. When there is agreement on the kinds of places that can be called healing gardens and the forms of healing that they may support, then there is potential agreement on aspects of the physical design and on indices of healing that should be included in studies of garden effects. This is an iterative process; research can modify a previously agreed upon conception of how a healing garden should be shaped, opening the way for design refinements, and, in turn, further research.

EXISTING RESEARCH IN A LARGER CONTEXT

Compelling arguments for gardens in healthcare facilities require evidence showing that they are beneficial for patients, staff, and visitors. Because there are significant gaps in the research, it is instructive to consider other examples of health innovations that have been—or are—characterized by significant knowledge gaps. In doing this we mean to reinforce the point that the current need for a measure of restraint regarding claims of gardens' healing values does not mean that efforts to establish gardens in health care facilities should not go forward.

The approach to evaluating evidence that we sketch out here has been developed within epidemiology. In studying the distribution and determinants of disease frequency in populations, epidemiologists provide guidance for the activities of public health and medical professionals (Hennekens and Buring, 1987). Epidemiologists seek a high degree of confidence when trying to determine whether there is a causal association between some health outcome and an environmental factor that can be targeted by public health and preventive medical interventions. They know that actions indicated by their research can significantly affect the health of large numbers of people, for the better but possibly also for the worse. The judgment of a causal association typically must be based on a body of research comprised of different kinds of studies of widely varying quality, and epidemiologists typically refer to a set of criteria that help them establish the level of confidence warranted by the given set of studies. Among other things, they are interested in experimental evidence, the strength of the documented associations, the presence of a dose-response relation-

Figure 12-5   Nature in the hospital: A plant-filled solarium with views to the garden at Lambeth Community Care Centre, London, UK.

ship, consistency across studies, and the plausibility of the hypothesized relationship. We will take each of these in turn.

Historically, public health measures have been directed at the environments of groups of people thought to be at risk, so that their risk would be reduced. Some public health measures have aimed to reduce risk by removing possibilities for exposure to particular risk factors. For example, policies constraining smoking in public places are meant to eliminate exposures to second-hand smoke. Alternatively, public health and social medicine practitioners might *introduce* something into the environment in an attempt to improve people's resistance to certain undesirable outcomes so that they are less likely to occur. Infectious illness vaccination programs and fluoridation of water to reduce the incidence of dental caries are just two examples of such primary prevention at a community level. In contrast to such primary prevention interventions, secondary or therapeutic interventions are usually targeted at individuals with the aim of diminishing symptoms of a given disease, preventing its recurrence, or decreasing the risk of dying from it (Hennekens and Buring, 1987, p. 179). The healing garden is in the spirit of therapeutic intervention.

Ideally, tests of the value of therapeutic interventions are true experiments. Random assignment to study conditions and controlled exposure to treatment are two strategies for fortifying the validity of conclusions that investigators can subsequently make about whether it is actually the treatment that is responsible for the outcomes observed. Such randomized trials thus permit relatively strong statements about the presence of an association between a treatment and specified outcomes.

Figure 12-6 Nature in the hospital: The Healing Garden in a courtyard at the Oncology Department of Marin General Hospital (California) can be entered, and can be viewed from the waiting room.

Although there are no randomized clinical trials to be found in the literature on healing gardens, there are some approximations, in the form of laboratory and field experiments that have looked at aspects of restoration as aided by natural versus built settings. These focus on some of the most basic experiences that gardens can provide; that is, physiological and psychological recovery while viewing natural scenery or strolling in a natural setting. The laboratory experiments so far completed have found more positive change in emotions (Ulrich, 1979; Hartig et al., 1996) and faster and more complete psychophysiological stress recovery (Ulrich et al., 1991) in non-patient subjects who had passive visual experiences of natural versus urban settings. In Ulrich et al.'s study, change in physiology was monitored while subjects were seated in a laboratory watching 10-minute videotapes of the assigned settings. Its blood pressure findings have since been replicated in a field experiment, with stressed subjects who had either a view of trees or no window view at all (Hartig et al., submitted; see also Hartig, 1993a). After the initial 10-minute period of sitting—with or without a view of trees—the subjects in the field experiment also walked in a nature reserve or an area of medium-density urban development. Blood pressure readings obtained from them at regular intervals during the walk also speak to a stronger stress dampening effect of the contact with nature. An earlier field experiment (Hartig et al., 1991) found that subjects who walked in a regional wilderness park after completing forty minutes of fast-paced, attentionally demanding tasks experienced more positive emotions and made fewer errors on a proofreading task than subjects who walked in an urban area or sat in a windowless laboratory reading magazines and listening to music (cf. Tennessen and Cimprich, 1995). The proofreading results are important because they point to another aspect of restoration—recovery of a capacity to focus attention—that may underlie other possible outcomes of healing processes, such as a change in perspective on one's life situation (Kaplan and Kaplan, 1989; S. Kaplan, 1983; Kaplan and Peterson, 1993; Kaplan and Talbot, 1983).

Because there is still little such experimental evidence with direct relevance to healing properties of gardens, claims of therapeutic effects must also rely on data from studies in which the research design may not allow as much confidence in the conclusions. The results of these nonexperimental studies should be evaluated using criteria that, if satisfied, can bolster confidence. One of those criteria is *strength of association.* If patients who make use of a garden in a healthcare facility manifest some specified sign of healing more frequently than patients who do not use the garden, then one can point to an association between use of the garden and healing in the specified sense, assuming that other potentially important variables, such as the severity of the patients' illness, have been taken into consideration. Importantly, the stronger the association between exposure and outcome, the less likely it is that uncontrolled chance factors or bias are responsible. Possibly the best known of studies in the literature on healing values of nature in the healthcare context, Ulrich's (1984) retrospective observational study of patients recovering from gall bladder surgery, is important in part because it documented an association between views of nature, and significant medical outcomes (intake of potent pain killers; time in the hospital postoperation). The observed effects are not likely to be due to differences between the patients on potentially important variables such as gender and smoking behaviour because patients were matched on those variables. The fact that the effects were statistically significant despite the small number of matched pairs of patients suggests that those effects were fairly substantial.

An attribution of a causal association between an environmental factor and a health outcome as based on non-experimental data would also be supported by evidence of a *dose-response relationship*. For example, if it were observed that elderly people who regularly spent *four* hours a day in the garden at a residential care facility were less depressed than those who spent only *two* hours every other day, who were in turn less depressed than those who did not spend *any* time at all in the garden, then the argument that the garden worked to reduce depression would be stronger. However, there is a risk that the relationship between amount of time in the garden (the "dose") and degree of depression ("response") could be explained by some third, confounding factor. For example, variation in amount of time spent in the garden might have been due to variations in mobility limitations, which might of themselves explain the variation in depression, independently of time in the garden. Thus with nonexperimental data the presence of a dose-response relationship is not sufficient evidence for causality. As it stands, to our knowledge, no such dose-response relationships have been reported in literature specifically concerned with gardens in healthcare facilities. There has, however, been discussion of the extent to which it is necessary to have abundant plant life in such gardens, a discussion which *implies* that dose-response relationships might be uncovered (Thompson, 1998); that is, given indicators might show progressively better health effects with increasing vegetation and decreasing hardscape. This is a question for coordinated design and research activities to consider.

Figure 12-7 Water features in the hospital: A rock wall and waterfall at San Diego Hospice.

Another relevant criterion for evaluating the evidence is *consistency* across investigations carried out by independent researchers. A recurrent pattern of findings, obtained under varying conditions, with associations that are similar in form (positive or negative) and magnitude, lends greater credence to an association, even if individual studies suffer from one or more methodological limitations. Application of the consistency criterion to the healing gardens literature is difficult, because for most of the many health outcomes that might be of interest, there are few or no reported associations based on observations structured and analysed in such a way that biases can be ruled out. There is, however, considerable consistency among the small number of experimental studies of restoration in natural versus built environments. Applying the consistency criterion loosely, one can also emphasize the agreement found across survey and anecdotal accounts attesting to therapeutic values of gardens, both outside (Barnes, 1994; R. Kaplan, 1983; Francis and Cooper Marcus, 1992) and inside health care settings (Cooper Marcus and Barnes, 1995). The extensive literature on benefits of recreation in various outdoor natural settings (see Knopf, 1987; The President's Commission on Americans Outdoors, 1986) and numerous historical analyses of themes in human-nature relations (e.g., Nash, 1982; Schama, 1996; Schmidt, 1990; Thomas, 1983) may not include direct evidence that gardens in health care settings improve particular health outcomes, but do help us understand the use of such gardens as being among a broad range of personally beneficial forms of nature experience with deep biological and cultural roots (Hartig, 1993b). This global aspect of consistency also deserves consideration (cf. Lindheim & Syme, 1983).

A final criterion to mention here is *plausibility of the hypothesis*. The plausibility of a hypothesis about the effect of an environmental exposure is judged with regard to knowledge of a mechanism that can produce the effect. Epidemiology mainly has been concerned with biological plausibility. A hypothesized causal association is more plausible if it fits with biological knowledge. For example, the hypothesis that drinking water from a particular source is behind an epidemic is more plausible if it is known that the disease is caused by water-borne bacteria. Discussions in this book suggest that in addition to biological factors, a variety of psychological, social, and cultural factors also operate in healing processes promoted by gardens. Healing processes incorporating such factors are, for example, assumed in Ulrich's discussion (Chapter 2) of the ways in which gardens promote healing to the extent that they stimulate supportive social relationships, improve

Figure 12-8 Water features in the hospital: Decorative fountains at the main entry to Stanford University Medical Center.

possibilities for the exercise of control, and otherwise aid stress coping and recovery. Because the hypotheses he proposes are grounded in findings from research on social support, control, exercise, and views of nature, they have greater plausibility. Other plausible hypotheses might be drawn from other bodies of research.

Because the plausibility criterion rests on current knowledge, it sometimes cannot be fully satisfied. Hennekens and Buring (1987) refer to historical cases in which there was sturdy evidence of a causal association between an environmental exposure and a health outcome, yet biological knowledge had not yet advanced to the point that a plausible mechanism could be identified. A classic case is set in London during the 1850s. By studying the death rates from cholera in areas served by one or the other or both of two water suppliers, a physician named John Snow arrived at the hypothesis that a cholera epidemic was being caused by water that was being taken by the Southwark and Vauxhall company from the Thames River near a sewage outfall. Although Snow ultimately was able to confirm his hypothesis, it wasn't known until some time later that the diarrhea, dehydration, and death could be attributed to infection of the small intestine by the *Vibrio cholerae* bacteria that had been carried in the water.

The example of cholera in London illustrates a critical point for us to bear in mind: Although there may be gaps in available knowledge, the available knowledge may nonetheless provide a sufficient basis for action. Clearly, there are gaps in the available knowledge about the power of garden experiences to foster positive health outcomes. Yet in our estimation, the evidence that we *do* have is sufficient to warrant further efforts to estab-

Figure 12-9 Water features in the hospital: Fountain and goldfish pond in a courtyard at Middlesex Hospital, London, UK.

lish gardens in healthcare facilities so that users might benefit and researchers might have better possibilities for observing their use and assessing the benefits of use.

The case of acupuncture raises some additional points for us to consider as we reflect on the current state of research on gardens in healthcare facilities. Millions of Americans have received some form of acupuncture treatment, and acupuncture is gradually being incorporated into the American healthcare system. In 1997 the Office of Alternative Medicine and the Office of Medical Applications of Research of the National Institutes of Health (NIH) convened a conference "to evaluate the scientific and medical data on the uses, risks, and benefits of acupuncture procedures for a variety of conditions" (NIH, in press, p. 3). Among those presenting were experts in the fields of "acupuncture, pain, psychology, psychiatry, physical medicine and rehabilitation, drug abuse, family practice, internal medicine, health policy, epidemiology, statistics, physiology, [and] biophysics" (*ibid.*, p. 1). With a view to developing a consensus statement, to be made available for comment to the audience of 1,200, the experts had been asked to address the following five questions:

- What is the efficacy of acupuncture, compared with placebo or sham acupuncture, in the health/medical conditions for which sufficient data are available to evaluate?
- What is the place of acupuncture in the treatment of various conditions for which sufficient data are available, in comparison with or in combination with other interventions (including no intervention)?
- What is known about the biological effects of acupuncture that helps us understand how it works?
- What issues need to be addressed so that acupuncture may be appropriately incorporated into today's health care system?
- What are the directions for future research (*ibid.*, p. 3)?

Answers to the question of the formal efficacy of acupuncture (i.e., the first question) were sought from experimental studies that fulfilled a number of criteria for rigor. Despite "the paucity of high-quality research assessing efficacy of acupuncture compared with placebo or sham acupuncture," it was possible to conclude, for example, that needle acupuncture "is efficacious for adult postoperative and chemotherapy nausea and vomiting" but "does not demonstrate efficacy for cessation of smoking" (NIH, in press, pp. 3, 4). Here, then, is a simple but interesting parallel with the research on gardens in health care settings. As with the research on acupuncture, there is a lack of experimental studies on the formal efficacy of gardens in health care settings. Yet, just as the available experimental data on acupuncture allow a few rather focused statements about effects on postoperative nausea and other specific conditions, the available experimental data relevant to healing gardens as discussed above permit some focused statements about restorative effects of viewing and walking in natural settings.

Some of the most direct evidence for therapeutic effects of gardens consists of observations like those used to support the clinical worth of acupuncture. Again, the question was, "What is the place of acupuncture in the treatment of various conditions for which sufficient data are available, in comparison with or in combination with other interventions (including no intervention)?" (NIH, in press, p. 3) The larger part of the consensus response is as follows:

> Assessing the usefulness of a medical intervention in practice differs from assessing formal efficacy. In conventional practice, clinicians make decisions based on the characteristics of the patient, clinical experience, potential for harm, and information from colleagues and the medical literature. In addition, when more than one treatment is possible, the clinician may make the choice taking into account the patient's preferences. While it is often thought that there is substantial research evidence to support conventional medical practices, this is frequently not the case. This does not mean that these treatments are ineffective. The data in support of acupuncture are as strong as those for many accepted Western medical therapies.

> One of the advantages of acupuncture is that the incidence of adverse effects is substantially lower than that of many drugs or other accepted medical procedures used for the same conditions. As an example, musculoskeletal conditions, such as fibromyalgia, myofascial pain, and "tennis elbow," or epicondylitis, are conditions for which acupuncture may be beneficial. These painful conditions are often treated with, among other things, anti-inflammatory medications (aspirin, ibuprofen, etc.) or with steroid injections. Both medical interventions have a potential for deleterious side effects, but are still widely used, and are considered acceptable treatments. The evidence supporting these therapies is no better than that for acupuncture (NIH, in press, pp. 4–5).[1]

---

[1]Note that the consensus statement on acupuncture "is an independent report of the consensus panel and is not a policy statement of the NIH or the Federal Government" (NIH, in press, p. 1).

Figure 12-10   Hospital garden environments: Intimate waiting area with flowers near the outpatient psychiatric department. (Kaiser Permanente Medical Center, Oakland, CA.)

We will not go farther with the example of acupuncture here, although the remaining questions posed above also also have their parallels in discussions around gardens in healthcare facilities. Although the example of acupuncture involves a non-conventional therapeutic intervention that is more focused than gardens in healthcare facilities, the parallels we have pointed out are nonetheless instructive. The example as it stands enables us to make the point that at present and in practice, the body of research we have to go on has some of the same insufficiencies as much better known and widely used conventional and nonconventional therapeutic approaches with accepted clinical value.

Our use of the example in this way is not meant to imply that gardens should be substituted for clinical procedures. Nor is it meant to downplay the need for research that is more rigorous than the anecdotal observations of the kind that also support the use of acupuncture and other clinical interventions. Well-designed experimental and nonexperimental studies will help to better establish and elaborate our understanding of the ways in which gardens can and do promote healing. Such studies, it is to be hoped, will also be used to guide design. We turn now to outline some of the research that is needed.

RESEARCH NEEDS

Research that will more convincingly substantiate the therapeutic values of gardens in healthcare settings can be organized around three basic questions:

1. Is a garden in a healthcare facility more therapeutic than other settings in the facility which are available for use for similar purposes?
2. What are the underlying therapeutic processes which come into play in the experience of the garden?
3. Do variations in garden characteristics produce variations in health outcomes?

We won't attempt to sharpen these questions here, but instead talk at a similar level of generality about the kinds of studies needed to address them and the possibilities for implementing such studies. The design of individual studies would focus on research questions stated more precisely with respect to comparison settings, the people under study, the activities those people are engaged in, the therapeutic process of interest, the garden features to be varied, and so forth. Our primary interest here is in providing designers with some basic conceptual tools that they might use in promoting research on the gardens they are designing.

We have referred to the need for experimental studies, and all of the above questions are amenable to experimental inquiry. Experiments need not be carried out in laboratories, though there are some advantages to working within settings in which the researcher can exercise a high degree of control over environmental variations. In the laboratory it may be easier to monitor subtle processes that would be difficult to detect against background "noise" from uncontrolled factors operating in field settings. For example, along the lines of the previously mentioned experiments on restorative effects of passive and active experiences of natural environments, it may be possible to work in the laboratory with members of various patient groups in studying psychophysiological and cognitive processes that contribute to restoration in the course of a brief nature experience.

Similarly, in laboratory studies one can simulate different design alternatives to get a sense of the effects each might have on given outcomes. For example, if the concern is for what patients see through the window from their hospital room, then it is possible to simulate the window view, varying view contents along one or more dimensions of interest, such as the dominance of natural features. Such a simulation study would yield an estimate of the relative efficacy of the different design alternatives for supporting restoration and other outcomes of interest (cf. Orland, 1993; Stokols, 1993; Zube and Simcox, 1993). Studies of this type can also shed light on whether there is a graded relationship between the amount of vegetation and the magnitude of response (i.e., a dose-response relationship).

Figure 12-11   Hospital garden environments. A garden that welcomes exploration, at Lambeth Community Care Centre, London, UK.

Figure 12-12 Hospital garden environments: An open garden for play and exercise at Kaiser Permanente Medical Center, Walnut Creek, CA.

However, laboratory studies have their limitations. The amount of time that a person can spend in the laboratory will be limited, and it may not be appropriate to work with members of particular patient groups in laboratory settings. To some in the environment-behavior field, research that has been carried out in the actual settings is much more satisfying, and some have rejected laboratory experimentation because it introduces structure into the person-environment exchange that might not be found in the everyday settings of human behavior (e.g., Barker, 1990). While laboratory experiments do offer some advantages, there are good possibilities for experiments in the health care facilities themselves. The challenge is to arrive at a study design that allows confident conclusions about the garden as a causal agent; that is, a design that allows one to rule out the possibility that other environmental variations are responsible for the observed effects.

The installation of a garden or other reconfiguration of outdoor space can be viewed as an experimental manipulation around which measurements can be structured to test hypotheses. Within such a natural experiment the assessment of effects due to introduction of the garden would require measures from the same people - patients, staff, and/or visitors - before, perhaps during, and then after the garden was put in place. A problem arises, however, if there is no comparison group, as change that may take place from the first to the last measure, or the absence of change across those measures, could owe to other changes in the environment—the passing of the seasons, expenditures on other aspects of the facility, and so on. Without one or more comparison groups, it would be difficult to interpret the results. A comparison group should be composed of comparable individuals who would have access to a space *without* natural features, in which they could engage in social exchange, passive recreation, exercise, or other behavior that might otherwise take place in the garden.

In some cases it may be possible to achieve the equivalent of the random assignment procedure that imparts so much strength to true experimental designs. The best chances for implementing random assignment would be in short-term care facilties which have a high patient turnover. For example, a study might involve random assignment of incoming patients to rooms that vary in the contents of their window view but are alike in all other important respects. It may be desirable to screen potential study participants according to some set of criteria before assigning them to a room (e.g., have not been hospitalized there before, the condition is not one that renders them unconscious to the surroundings).

Published studies can provide useful templates for further naturalistic research. Ulrich's (1984) retrospective observational study illustrates how the use of records from matched pairs of former patients might be used to detect an association between more positive health outcomes and access or exposure to a given environmental feature. An example relevant to more active involvements with gardens is provided by Cimprich's (1993) prospective study of postoperative breast cancer patients who engaged in self-chosen, often nature-based, activities to aid in the recovery process.

We have available a great number and diversity of research tools for investigating the therapeutic effects of gardens in healthcare facilities. Here we have mentioned only a few of the strongest and most fundamental, relating them both to basic research issues and to the possibilities for carrying out the research in the healthcare settings themselves. (For a thorough discussion of problems that arise in field research, see Cook and Campbell, 1979). We have assumed in the foregoing that all necessary and appropriate measures would have been taken to ensure ethical treatment of human subjects.

The questions that we have so far set out and discussed have to do with the basic issues of whether gardens in healthcare facilities can actually provide benefits that may be claimed for them. There are, of course, other research qestions that can be posed and research needs to be fulfilled, some of which follow from the research discussed above. At this stage in the development of healing gardens, it would be helpful to have some estimates of the cost of gardens relative to the benefits actually engendered, paired with consideration of whether similar benefits could have been achieved through other measures that might have been taken with the resources dedicated. Although cost/benefit analyses might involve problems with assigning values to benefits that flow from garden experiences, they are consistent with a stance that gardens are but one potential means to improve results.

We realize that relatively few designers have the resources and training needed to carry out the kinds of research we have discussed. Our assumption in this discussion has been that if designers are informed about the research needed and ways in which it might be carried out, they would be better prepared to *promote* research on the gardens they are designing. Against this background, we would like to suggest some specific things that designers might do to facilitate progress in research in the course of their ongoing professional activities.

In contracting for the design and construction of a garden, the landscape architect might propose to the client that the

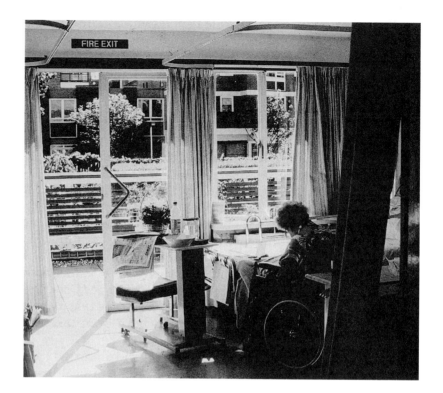

Figure 12-13   The view through the window: View from a patient room onto the garden at Lambeth Community Care Centre, London, UK.

introduction of a garden is a natural experiment that could be turned to some advantage. Funds would have to be set aside for the work to be carried out. As the operations of some healthcare facilities are closely integrated with the ongoing activities of research institutions, there may be both an openness to the idea of investigating effects of the change and staff capable of carrying out such a study (for example, see Center for Child Health Outcomes, 1998). Also, many healthcare facilities are now parts of chains that may want to use the information so obtained to guide decisions about gardens at other facilities. If a client is unable to guarantee the requisite resources, then the designer might seek contacts with researchers at a local university or other institution. For example, architecture and landscape architecture programs often require that students complete a design research project in partial satisfaction of the requirements for a graduate degree. The possibility to carry out a study along lines suggested above might be welcomed by the university.

If a natural experiment can be carried out, then the landscape architect might be alert to the possibility of staggering the integration of different design features, allowing an appropriate period for data collection before proceeding with the next phase of construction, after which another round of data collection could take place, and so forth. Of course, whether this is possible will depend on the client's requirements, other jobs in which the designer is involved, and so forth. We mention the possibility here nonetheless, anticipating that in some cases a client may want to take a garden addition or a renovation in increments. Staggered implementation may be valuable from a research perspective because it opens up possibilities for representing different questions in an experimental design. Communication between designer and researchers will then be necessary to coordinate construction and data collection activities.

SOME NEXT STEPS

The foregoing are ways in which the designer can facilitate experimental research focused on the therapeutic efficacy of gardens, the underlying therapeutic processes, and the features of gardens that may influence outcomes. Such studies can ultimately be a source of specific guidelines. However, there are other things that designers can do now to help develop relatively "hard" data regarding the specifics of therapeutic garden settings. One simple action that landscape architects might take is to annotate their garden designs, commenting on their expectations of the ways in which users might behave in and benefit from a space configured in a particular way. As discussed earlier in this chapter, every design represents the designer's expectations about the way in which given design measures will affect the experience and behavior of users. The authors of Chapters 4 through 10 have worked from "best practice" standards in suggesting design guidelines, standards that typically reflect substantial amounts of accumulated experience. We have tremendous respect for the sensitivity and power of observation that these and other designers have brought to their work, and we are pleased that so much of their experience has been captured in a form that can be communicated, put to the test, and refined if necessary. We also lament the fact that the fruits of a designer's experience may be lost when no record is made of expectations about the influence some design feature will have on a person entering the space. Not only would annotated designs be of value to future students and other designers, they can also aid communication among researchers and potential clients. Those studying the therapeutic values of gardens in health care facilities could be aided by design source material for different facilities, allowing consideration of the way in which different design measures were employed toward similar ends, or similar measures were used toward different ends.

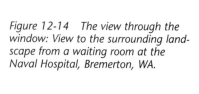

Figure 12-14   The view through the window: View to the surrounding landscape from a waiting room at the Naval Hospital, Bremerton, WA.

Annotating plans with the presumed health implications of various components of the design is just one way to improve the breadth of the knowledge-base that landscape architects can draw upon to guide their designs for gardens in healthcare facilities. Other helpful activities include disseminating available information regarding design measures that appear to be successful and those that fall short, and becoming conversant with studies from scientific and clinical disciplines regarding patients' needs for control, exercise, social support, aids to wayfinding, natural and aesthetic features, and other resources. User needs assessments and post-occupancy evaluations are of vital importance. They provide valuable data on the features that patients, staff, and visitors want in these settings, and on the behaviors of the users. Such studies can contribute much to the body of professional knowledge. Participatory design is another approach to consider. Although working directly with hospital patients and staff may be more difficult than working with other populations (e.g., neighborhood residents), it can be done. For example, Perkins and Barnhart have had some useful results in working with the staff and patients at Homewood Health Centre in Guelph, Ontario (see case study on pp. 293–304).

Another important role for the landscape architecture profession is to help medical practitioners and administrators see outdoor space as something more than a cosmetic extra or a marketing feature. Maintenance guidelines provided when a garden is installed can be expanded to include a section on the intended use and function so that the potential healing aspects of the design can be recognized and understood by those who are to take over the responsibility for the garden. The results of post-occupancy evaluations can be disseminated to medical staff and hospital administrators so that they will recognize the potential in such settings. In relation to the relatively low cost of a garden, the potential they offer for ameliorating stress, staff burnout, and turnover is worth serious consideration. It would also be an important and encouraging development if the significance of the physical healthcare environment for patient well-being were treated in the education of medical and nursing staff. Design professionals can and should take an active role in educating healthcare professionals along these lines whenever the opportunity presents itself.

We see a number of other steps that can be taken within the landscape architecture profession. They include encouraging team work and partnership between architect and landscape architect, so that the exterior becomes an integral part of the concept of the therapeutic environment from the outset; introducing healing gardens as a specialty area in landscape architecture education, via lectures and studio projects; and training students how to access relevant research and keep abreast of research developments. A significant and self-reinforcing step could be taken by establishing prestigious national and international awards for research-based hospital gardens. The design world in general needs to take note of this work, better understand it, make it known to hospital clients, and incorporate it into healthcare design.

SUMMARY

This volume has viewed healing gardens in medical facilities from several perspectives. The historical and cultural roots of gardens in healthcare facilities, combined with the presentation of rigorous research on aspects of garden experience, have provided the foundation for the consideration of gardens as healing spaces. An analysis of present-day approaches to healing garden design has documented and critiqued various ways in which landscape architects have set about creating therapeutic spaces in medical settings. A path for the future has been presented, linking current research on health factors and the natural environment to the design process. Subsequent chapters have explained through analysis and example the constituent principles and procedures of "best practice" today. This work has been discussed at a level of detail appropriate to the design of therapeutic outdoor spaces for targeted patient groups. The

"The comforting sound of falling water and the borders of ferns and blooming pink and white azaleas which led up to the main entrance of the hospital made what was possibly the most difficult decision I have made in my lifetime only slightly less agonizing. Having admitted my son aged nineteen to the locked psychiatric ward of a hospital, I felt upon leaving that I had left a part of me. Over the next five days of visits I was consoled by the blossoming flowers and waterfalls which led me in and out of the building, reminding me that life in its many forms has cycles of dying and rebirth, beauty and pain.

(C. M.) CALISTOGA, CA

specifics of "how to get it done" have been presented through five case histories, for funding remains an uphill battle. In this chapter we have provided perspectives on the possibilities for healing gardens, on the underlying concepts and the present research base, on research needs, and on future directions for landscape architects. This volume has collected and presented the best available information to date. It is hoped that it will be used well and augmented with additional work as this field continues its rapid expansion.

REFERENCES

Antonovsky, A. (1979). *Health, Stress, and Coping.* San Francisco: Jossey-Bass.

Barker, R. G. (1990). "Settings of a Professional Lifetime." In I. Altman and K. Christensen (Eds.), *Environment and Behavior Studies: Emergence of Intellectual Traditions.* New York: Plenum Press.

Barnes, M. A. (1994). *A Study of the Process of Emotional Healing in Outdoor Spaces and the Concomitant Landscape Design Implications.* Unpublished master's thesis, University of California, Berkeley.

Cimprich, B. (1993). "Development of an Intervention to Restore Attention in Cancer Patients." *Cancer Nursing,* Vol. 16, pp. 83–92.

Cook, T. D. and Campbell, D. T. (1979). *Quasi-Experimentation: Design and Analysis for Field Settings.* Boston: Houghton Mifflin Company.

Cooper Marcus, C. amd M. Barnes (1995). *Gardens in Healthcare Facilities: Uses, Therapeutic Benefits, and Design Recommendations.* Martinez, CA: The Center for Health Design.

Francis, C. and C. Cooper Marcus (1992). "Restorative Places: Environment and Emotional Well-Being." In *Proceedings of the 23rd Annual Conference of the Environmental Design Research Association.* Oklahoma City, OK: EDRA.

Hartig, T. (1993a). *Testing Restorative Environments Theory.* Unpublished doctoral dissertation, University of California, Irvine.

——— (1993b). "Nature Experience in Transactional Perspective." *Landscape and Urban Planning,* Vol. 25, pp. 17–36.

Hartig, T., M. Mang, and G. W. Evans (1991). "Restorative Effects of Natural Environment Experiences." *Environment and Behavior,* Vol. 23, pp. 3–36.

Hartig, T., A. Böök, J. Garvill, T. Olsson, and T. Gärling (1996). "Environmental Influences on Psychological Restoration." *Scandinavian Journal of Psychology,* Vol. 37, pp. 378–393.

Hartig, T., G. W. Evans, L. D. Jamner, D. S. Davis, and T. Gärling (submitted). "Stress Recovery Enhanced by Natural Environment Experiences."

Hennekens, C. H. and J. E. Buring (1987). *Epidemiology in Medicine.* Boston: Little, Brown & Company.

Kaplan, R. (1983). "The Role of Nature in the Urban Context." In I. Altman and J. F. Wohlwill (Eds.), *Behavior and the Natural Environment.* New York: Plenum Press.

Kaplan, R. and S. Kaplan (1989). *The Experience of Nature: A Psychological Perspective.* Cambridge: Cambridge University Press.

Kaplan, S. (1983). "A Model of Person-Environment Compatibility." *Environment and Behavior,* Vol. 15, pp. 311–332.

Kaplan, S. and C. Peterson (1993). "Health and Environment: A Psychological Analysis." *Landscape and Urban Planning,* Vol. 26, pp. 17–23.

Kaplan, S. and J. F. Talbot (1983). "Psychological benefits of Wilderness Experience." In I. Altman and J. F. Wohlwill (Eds.), *Behavior and the Natural Environment.* New York: Plenum Press.

Knopf, R. C. (1987). "Human Behavior, Cognition, and Affect in the Natural Environment." In D. Stokols and I. Altman (Eds.), *Handbook of Environmental Psychology: Vol. 1.* New York: Wiley.

Lindheim, R. and S. L. Syme (1983). "Environments, People, and Health." *Annual Review of Public Health,* Vol. 4, pp. 335–359.

Nash, R. (1982). *Wilderness and the American Mind,* 3rd ed. New Haven: Yale University Press.

National Institutes of Health (in press). *Acupuncture,* NIH Consensus Development Statement 107, November 3–5, 1997; version from February 4, 1998, as accessed online.

Noack, H. (1991). "Conceptualizing and Measuring Health." In B. Badura and I. Kickbusch (Eds.), *Health Promotion Research: Towards a New Social Epidemiology* (WHO Regional Publications European Series No. 37). Copenhagen: World Health Organization.

Orland, B. (1993). "Synthetic Landscapes: A Review of Video-Imaging Applications in Environmental Perception Research, Planning, and Design." In R. W. Marans and D. Stokols (Eds.), *Environmental Simulation: Research and Policy Issues.* New York: Plenum Press.

Rubin, H. R. and A. J. Owens (1996). *Progress Report: An Investigation to Determine Whether the Built Environment Affects the Patients' Medical Outcome.* Martinez, CA: The Center for Health Design.

Schama, S. (1996). *Landscape and Memory.* New York: Vintage Books.

Schmid, T. L., M. Pratt, and E. Howze (1995). "Policy as Intervention: Environmental and Policy Approaches to the Prevention of Cardiovascular Disease." *American Journal of Public Health,* Vol. 85, pp. 1207–1211.

Schmidt, P. J. (1990). *Back to Nature: The Arcadian Myth in Urban America.* Baltimore: The Johns Hopkins University Press.

Stokols, D. (1993). "Strategies of Environmental Simulation: Theoretical, Methodological, and Policy Issues." In R. W. Marans and D. Stokols (Eds.), *Environmental Simulation: Research and Policy Issues.* New York: Plenum Press.

————— (1994). "Translating Social Ecological Theory into Guidelines for Community Health Promotion." *American Journal of Health Promotion,* Vol. 10, pp. 282–298.

Syme, S. L. (1992). "Social Determinants of Disease." In J. M. Last, R. B. Wallace (Eds.), *Public Health and Preventive Medicine,* 13th ed. Norwalk, CT: Appleton & Lange.

Tennessen, C. M. and B. Cimprich (1995). "Views to Nature: Effects on Attention." *Journal of Environmental Psychology,* Vol. 15, pp. 77–85.

The President's Commission on Americans Outdoors (1986). *A Literature Review.* Washington, DC: United States Government Printing Office. See also: *The Report of the President's Commission—Americans Outdoors: The Legacy, the Challenge.* Covelo, CA: Island Press, 1987.

Thomas, K. (1983). *Man and the Natural World: A History of the Modern Sensibility.* New York: Pantheon Books.

Thompson, J. W. (1998). "A Question of Healing." *Landscape Architecture,* Vol. 88, pp. 68–92.

Ulrich, R. S. (1979). "Visual Landscapes and Psychological Well-Being." *Landscape Research,* Vol. 4, No. 1, pp. 17–23.

—— (1984). "View Through a Window May Influence Recovery from Surgery." *Science,* Vol. 224, pp. 420–421.

Ulrich, R. S., R. F. Simons, B. D. Losito, E. Fiorito, M. A. Miles, and M. Zelson, (1991). "Stress Recovery During Exposure to Natural and Urban Environments." *Journal of Environmental Psychology,* Vol. 11, pp. 201–230.

World Health Organization (1996). "Constitution and Bylaws." In *WHO Basic Documents,* 41st ed. Geneva: Office of Publications, WHO.

Zube, E. H. and D. E. Simcox (1993). "Landscape Simulation: Review and Potential." In R. W. Marans and D. Stokols (Eds.), *Environmental Simulation: Research and Policy Issues.* New York: Plenum Press.

Index